OTHER IEEE PRESS BOOKS

Advanced Microprocessors, II, *Edited by A. Gupta*
Adaptive Signal Processing, *Edited by L. H. Sibul*
System Design for Human Interaction, *Edited by A. P. Sage*
Microcomputer Control of Power Electronics and Drives, *Edited by B. K. Bose*
Advances in Local Area Networks, *Edited by K. Kümmerle, J. O. Limb, and F. A. Tobagi*
Load Management, *Edited by S. Talukdar and C. W. Gellings*
Computers and Manufacturing Productivity, *Edited by R. K. Jurgen*
Being the Boss, *By L. K. Lineback*
Effective Meetings for Busy People, *By W. T. Carnes*
VLSI Signal Processing, II, *Edited by S. Y. Kung, R. E. Owen, and J. G. Nash*
Modern Acoustical Imaging, *Edited by H. Lee and G. Wade*
Low-Temperature Electronics, *Edited by R. K. Kirschman*
Undersea Lightwave Communications, *Edited by P. K. Runge and P. R. Trischitta*
Multidimensional Digital Signal Processing, *Edited by the IEEE Multidimensional Signal Processing Committee*
Adaptive Methods for Control System Design, *Edited by M. M. Gupta*
Residue Number System Arithmetic, *Edited by M. A. Soderstrand, W. K. Jenkins, G. A. Jullien, and F. J. Taylor*
Singular Perturbations in Systems and Control, *Edited by P. V. Kokotovic and H. K. Khalil*
Getting the Picture, *By S. B. Weinstein*
Space Science and Applications, *Edited by J. H. McElroy*
Medical Applications of Microwave Imaging, *Edited by L. Larsen and J. H. Jacobi*
Modern Spectrum Analysis, *Edited by S. B. Kesler*
The Calculus Tutoring Book, *By C. Ash and R. Ash*
Imaging Technology, *Edited by H. Lee and G. Wade*
Phase-Locked Loops, *Edited by W. C. Lindsey and C. M. Chie*
VLSI Circuit Layout: Theory and Design, *Edited by T. C. Hu and E. S. Kuh*
Monolithic Microwave Integrated Circuits, *Edited by R. A. Pucel*
Next-Generation Computers, *Edited by E. A. Torrero*
Kalman Filtering: Theory and Application, *Edited by H. W. Sorenson*
Spectrum Management and Engineering, *Edited by F. Matos*
Digital VLSI Systems, *Edited by M. I. Elmasry*
Introduction to Magnetic Recording, *Edited by R. M. White*
Insights into Personal Computers, *Edited by A. Gupta and H. D. Toong*
Television Technology Today, *Edited by T. S. Rzeszewski*
The Space Station: An Idea Whose Time Has Come, *Edited by T. R. Simpson*
Marketing Technical Ideas and Products Successfully! *Edited by L. K. Moore and D. L. Plung*
The Making of a Profession: A Century of Electrical Engineering in America, *By A. M. McMahon*
Power Transistors: Device Design and Applications, *Edited by B. J. Baliga and D. Y. Chen*
VLSI: Technology and Design, *Edited by O. G. Folberth and W. D. Grobman*
General and Industrial Management, *By H. Fayol; revised by I. Gray*
A Century of Honors, *An IEEE Centennial Directory*
MOS Switched-Capacitor Filters: Analysis and Design, *Edited by G. S. Moschytz*
Distributed Computing: Concepts and Implementations, *Edited by P. L. McEntire, J. G. O'Reilly, and R. E. Larson*
Engineers and Electrons, *By J. D. Ryder and D. G. Fink*
Land-Mobile Communications Engineering, *Edited by D. Bodson, G. F. McClure, and S. R. McConoughey*
Frequency Stability: Fundamentals and Measurement, *Edited by V. F. Kroupa*
Electronic Displays, *Edited by H. I. Refioglu*
Spread-Spectrum Communications, *Edited by C. E. Cook, F. W. Ellersick, L. B. Milstein, and D. L. Schilling*
Color Television, *Edited by T. Rzeszewski*
Advanced Microprocessors, *Edited by A. Gupta and H. D. Toong*
Biological Effects of Electromagnetic Radiation, *Edited by J. M. Osepchuk*
Engineering Contributions to Biophysical Electrocardiography, *Edited by T. C. Pilkington and R. Plonsey*
The World of Large Scale Systems, *Edited by J. D. Palmer and R. Saeks*
Electronic Switching: Central Office Systems of the World, *Edited by A. E. Joel, Jr.*
A Guide for Writing Better Technical Papers, *Edited by C. Harkins and D. L. Plung*
Low-Noise Microwave Transistors and Amplifiers, *Edited by H. Fukui*
Digital MOS Integrated Circuits, *Edited by M. I. Elmasry*
Geometric Theory of Diffraction, *Edited by R. C. Hansen*

Multi-Microprocessors

Edited by
Amar Gupta
Sloan School of Management
Massachusetts Institute of Technology

A volume in the IEEE PRESS Selected Reprint Series, prepared under the sponsorship of the IEEE Computer Society.

The Institute of Electrical and Electronics Engineers, Inc., New York

PRINTED IN THE UNITED STATES OF AMERICA

IEEE Order Number: PC0216-2

Library of Congress Cataloging-in-Publication Data

Multi-microprocessors.

(IEEE Press selected reprint series)
Includes indexes.
1. Microprocessors. 2. Multiprocessors.
I. Gupta, Amar.
QA76.5.M7934 1987 004.16 87-3565

ISBN 0-87942-230-0

Contents

Preface vii

Part I: Overview 1

Multiple Microprocessor Systems: What, Why, and When, *E. T. Fathi and M. Krieger* (*IEEE Computer*, March 1983) 4

Computers That Are 'Never' Down, *G. Zorpette* (*IEEE Spectrum*, April 1985) 14

Part II: Alternative Interconnection Topologies 23

A Survey of Interconnection Networks, *T-Y. Feng* (*IEEE Computer*, December 1981) 24

Communication Structures for Large Networks of Microcomputers, *L. D. Wittie* (*IEEE Transactions on Computers*, April 1981) 40

Fault-Tolerance Considerations in Large, Multiple-Processor Systems, *J. G. Kuhl and S. M. Reddy* (*IEEE Computer*, March 1986) 50

Increasing Throughput of Multiprocessor Systems, *A. Gupta and H-M. D. Toong* (*IEEE Transactions on Industrial Electronics*, August 1985) 62

Part III: Busing Standards and Practices 71

Computer Buses—A Tutorial, *D. B. Gustavson* (*IEEE Micro*, August 1984) 72

MicroStandards Special Feature: A Comparison of 32-Bit Buses, *P. L. Borrill* (*IEEE Micro*, December 1985) 88

Part IV: Software Issues 97

Software Opens the Way to True Concurrency for Multiprocessing, *C. Patton* (*Electronic Design*, August 8, 1985) 98

Issues in the Design of a Distributed Operating System for Ada, *D. A. Fisher and R. M. Weatherly* (*IEEE Computer*, May 1986) 105

Operating Systems for the Micronet Network Computer, *A. M. van Tilborg and L. D. Wittie* (*IEEE Micro*, April 1983) 115

An Executive for Task-Driven Multimicrocomputer Systems, *E. T. Fathi and M. Krieger* (*IEEE Micro*, October 1983) 125

Events and Interrupts in Tightly Coupled Multiprocessors, *H. Kirrmann* (*IEEE Micro*, February 1985) 135

Multiple-Microprocessor Programming Techniques: MML, a New Set of Tools, *M. Boari, S. Crespi-Reghizzi, A. Daprá, F. Maderna, and A. Natali* (*IEEE Computer*, January 1984) 149

A Security Kernel for a Multiprocessor Microcomputer, *R. R. Schell* (*IEEE Computer*, July 1983) 161

Part V: Performance Evaluation 169

Microcomputers in Industrial Control Applications, *A. Gupta and H-M. D. Toong* (*IEEE Transactions on Industrial Electronics*, May 1984) 170

Evaluating the Performance of Multicomputer Configurations, *D. P. Agrawal, V. K. Janakiram, and G. C. Pathak* (*IEEE Computer*, May 1986) 181

A Closed-Form Solution for the Performance Analysis of Multiple-Bus Multiprocessor Systems, *K. B. Irani and I. H. Önyüksel* (*IEEE Transactions on Computers*, November 1984) 194

Part VI: System Examples 203

Fault-Tolerant Systems in Commercial Applications, *O. Serlin* (*IEEE Computer*, August 1984) 205

Fault Tolerance Achieved in VLSI, *R. Emmerson and M. J. McGowan* (*IEEE Micro*, December 1984) 217

The Modiac Multiprocessor—A 286-Based Design, *G. Neri and T. S. Cinotti* (*IEEE Micro*, February 1986) 227

The TX16: A Highly Programmable Multi-Microprocessor Architecture, *J-L. Gaudiot, M. Dubois, L-T. Lee, and N. G. Tohme* (*IEEE Micro*, October 1986) 236

A Microprocessor-Based Hypercube Supercomputer, *J. P. Hayes, T. Mudge, Q. F. Stout, S. Colley, and J. Palmer* (*IEEE Micro*, October 1986) 250

Author Index 261

Subject Index 263

Editor's Biography 267

Dedicated to
Shefali, Sonali, and Their Parents.

Preface

DESIGN and implementation of multi-microprocessor systems require knowledge of a number of different areas. The major areas are:

(1) *Microprocessor Characteristics*
The general characteristics and specifications of the current generation of microprocessors must be studied first.

(2) *Support for Multiprocessing*
The hardware and software features of these microprocessors must be analyzed to determine their merits and demerits in a concurrent processing environment.

(3) *Interconnection Alternatives*
There are many alternative strategies for connecting processing elements. Each topology offers a different level of overall throughput and system resilience.

(4) *Bus Protocols*
A number of bus protocols have become widely accepted in recent years. It is better to use a standard protocol, whenever possible, than to design a new one.

(5) *Performance Modeling and Simulation*
The use of more than one microprocessor is frequently motivated by performance considerations. A designer must be aware of various analytic modeling and simulation options.

(6) *Hardware Factors*
High-performance systems involve careful design of both processing and communication elements. This, in turn, requires use of sophisticated hardware techniques.

(7) *Software Issues*
In order to benefit from the multiple processing elements, it becomes necessary to adopt new software methodologies that turn traditionally sequential activities into parallel ones.

(8) *Security Aspects*
With multiple microprocessors executing in parallel, security issues become more complex than in a uniprocessor environment.

Many excellent papers are available on each of the topics mentioned here. The best of these papers have been brought together in this book to present a unified discussion of the whole domain of multi-microprocessors.

This book assumes familiarity with fundamental concepts of microprocessor technology. For an in-depth discussion of this subject, readers may wish to refer to *Advanced Microprocessors* (IEEE PRESS, 1983) and *Advanced Microprocessors, II* (IEEE PRESS, 1987).

AMAR GUPTA
Massachusetts Institute of Technology
Cambridge, Massachusetts

Part I
Overview

THE term "multi-microprocessors" includes all systems that use more than one microprocessor to perform a desired application. The spectrum of such systems ranges from low-cost personal computers which frequently utilize a second microprocessor for decoding the key depressed on the keyboard, to powerful supercomputers and array processors which contain hundreds of microprocessors working in parallel. Apart from general-purpose computer systems, the concept of multi-microprocessors is relevant in cases of special-purpose computers, automated industrial control, business data processing, and virtually all other application scenarios. Multi-microprocessors are used in areas requiring one or more of the following:

(a) very high computational bandwidths and/or short response times,
(b) high system resilience and fault-tolerance capabilities,
(c) ability to operate under adverse environmental conditions,
(d) geographically distributed computing with an associated need for effective communication between centers,
(e) storage and retrieval of large volumes of data within a relatively short time period,
(f) very close interactions between equipment and human beings.

Before delving into the field of multi-microprocessors it is appropriate to briefly summarize the major forces that have motivated the use of multi-microprocessors. We begin by studying the broad trends in the microprocessor industry. (Readers may wish to refer to *Advanced Microprocessors* and *Advanced Microprocessors, II* (IEEE PRESS, New York) for a more comprehensive discussion.)

Microprocessor Technology

A microprocessor is the central arithmetic and logic unit of a computer scaled down so that it fits on a single silicon chip (sometimes several chips) holding several thousand transistors, resistors, and similar circuit elements. A microcomputer contains the memory and peripheral control circuitry in addition to the central processing unit. If all these functions are implemented on a single chip, it is referred to as a single-chip microcomputer. Since a fraction of the chip area must be allocated for memory and peripheral support functions in single-chip microcomputers, these chips offer less processing power than single-chip microprocessors with the same number of devices implanted on the chip. The upper limit on the number of devices is a function of process technology and has risen from 2300 in 1971, the year marking the commencement of the microprocessor era, to about a million today. The increase in the number of devices, accompanied by bigger and more powerful instruction repertoires, has enabled the overall throughput provided by a single chip to increase by more than three orders of magnitude during the past 16 years.

Although the first "computer-on-a-chip" was fabricated by Intel in 1971, the term "microprocessor" was first used in 1972. Subsequently, single-chip microprocessors using 8-bit, 16-bit, and 32-bit word sizes were introduced in 1972, 1974, and 1981, respectively. Apart from the main microprocessor that performs the control and the data processing functions, additional chips are required to perform memory management and input–output functions. Sometimes, several identical chips are organized in parallel to implement systems that offer higher accuracy than is possible with a single chip. Using this technique, called *bit-sliced organization,* multiple 4-bit chips can be used to integrate systems with an effective word size of 8 bits, 12 bits, 16 bits, or even more. With the advent of advanced microprocessors with wider word sizes, the primary charm of using bit-sliced microprocessors for achieving higher accuracy has gradually eroded over the years. Instead, the objective of using multiple microprocessor chips has shifted toward higher throughput and superior resilience.

Multiprocessors

Long before the advent of microprocessor technology, designers had proposed the concept of multiprocessors as a mechanism to go beyond the upper bound of performance feasible with a single processor. In the ideal case, a system with n identical processors could offer n times the throughput available with a single processor. Alternatively, the additional processors could be used as backups, on an automatic basis, in case the primary processor malfunctioned. There is effort involved in controlling the operations of the different processors, and it becomes necessary to transfer information between the different processors. As such, the ideal case cannot be practically realized. However, it should be mentioned here that large multiprocessor system configurations have been used for defense, air traffic control, and a few commercial applications for the last 20 years.

The development of powerful mainframe computers in the sixties and the seventies served to discourage the multiprocessor approach. Grosch's Law hypothesized that processor performance was proportional to the square of its cost. As such, it became widely accepted that it was preferable to invest in a more powerful processor than to buy two smaller processors within the same budget.

The above situation was radically altered by the advent of microprocessor technology. Instead of large processors being more cost-effective, the balance became heavily tilted in favor of very low cost processors. In essence, an inverse Grosch Law became applicable. Over the past 16 years, microprocessors have become increasingly sophisticated and powerful. By virtue of their low cost and wide functionality, contemporary microprocessors are ideally suited for use as basic building blocks for complex systems.

Interconnection Issues

In a single-processor system shown in Fig. 1, the number of message paths is ${}^3C_2 = 3!/2! = 3$. When several of such monoprocessor systems are connected together, any element of the system (CPU, Memory, or I/O) should be capable of communicating with any other element of the system (CPU, Memory, or I/O), and a typical two-processor system, shown in Fig. 2, permits ${}^6C_2 = 15$ different message paths. It is obvious that, as the number of processors increases, the load on the interface increases sharply. If one provides a different bus for each path, the cost of such multiple-bus connections increases as the square of the number of processors. On the other hand, if only one bus is used, the contention problem between different messages may become critical.

Estimates of bus usage in several current systems show that a single processor and a single memory cause bus utilization to be around 60% on the average. With more processors/memories, the bus becomes a performance bottleneck. Most designers opt for multiple-bus solutions. The resulting network is named on the basis of its geometry as a star, a cube, a hypercube, a hypertree, a snowflake, a cluster, and by other similar self-explanatory names. In all of these cases, a few pairs of resources have direct links with each other, but other pairs must communicate via one or more intermediate nodes, thus introducing time delays and performance degradation. In the case of microprocessors, each additional bus mandates more pins on the chip (unless one resorts to multiplexing with its inherent performance limitation), and hence increased production costs. Often, additional buses will cause the number of pins needed by the microprocessor chip to exceed the limits of commercially feasible chip carriers. Thus, it is desirable to minimize the number of buses. A single central bus is the ideal solution provided it can handle the required communication load.

In order to reduce the load on the bus, it is now becoming common for individual processors to have cache memories. On the other hand, the intelligence of I/O control units is increasing, and the dividing line between processor and I/O elements is becoming blurred. We categorize devices into two major groups:

(a) *Primary Processing Modules (PPMs)*: These are elements with higher levels of intelligence; these elements *control* the operation of other elements. A traditional CPU is an example of a PPM. Another term for such modules is "masters."

(b) *Secondary Processing Modules (SPMs)*: These are elements that control no other elements. A typical example is a memory. The operation of a SPM is initiated and controlled by a PPM. Another term for such modules is "slaves."

In traditional single-processor systems, there is one and only one PPM, and typically more than one SPM. In multi-microprocessor systems, there are several PPMs each "controlling" the functions of a number of SPMs, in coordination

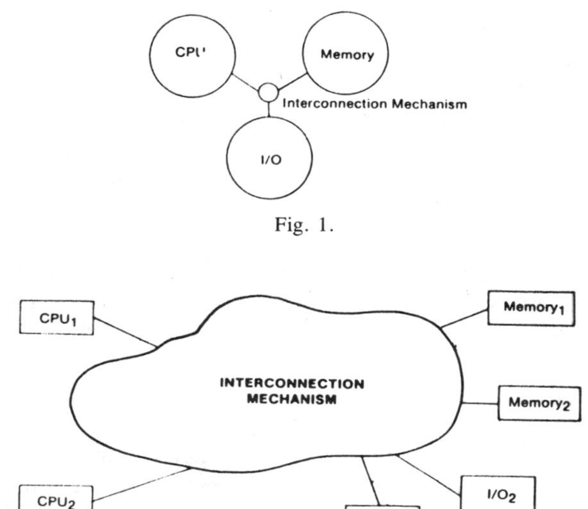

Fig. 1.

Fig. 2.

with other PPMs. The term processing module (PM) is used to designate an element which may be either a PPM or a SPM.

By choosing an appropriate interconnection scheme and by careful arrangement of PPMs and SPMs, one can reach the objective of arriving at a system configuration that meets a predefined level of performance and resilience.

It should be mentioned here that the interconnection aspect is important at several different levels. At the basic hardware level, there is a need to communicate (over very small distances, usually of less than 1 m) data and information between processors and memory, and between processors and fast peripheral units. Backplane buses (such as Multibus, S-100, and VME) are used for this purpose. At the next level, I/O buses (such as IEEE 488) are used to communicate between the processor and I/O units. Then, local area networks (LANs) are used to provide data communication capabilities in buildings and over a few square kilometers. The issue of different bus standards will be examined in depth in Part III of this book.

Organization

In the preceding paragraphs, three distinct aspects of multi-microprocessors were considered. These issues, and other related issues, are discussed in further detail in various papers in this book.

This book is organized into six parts as follows:

Part I: Overview

The field of multi-microprocessors is discussed in terms of its origin, different areas of progress, and current trends.

Part II: Alternative Interconnection Topologies

Various schemes for interconnecting processing elements are discussed. The relative advantages and disadvantages of each scheme are analyzed.

Part III: Busing Standards and Practices

Sustained efforts by various professional and international organizations have culminated in the establishment of a number of formal bus standards. These standards are described.

Part IV: Software Issues

In order to profit from the availability of multiple hardware resources, new software methodologies must be used to enable a maximum degree of parallelism. These software issues are discussed.

Part V: Performance Evaluation

In this part, various techniques for evaluating the performance of multiprocessor configurations are described.

Part VI: System Examples

Designs of a number of different multi-microprocessor systems are presented in the final part of this book.

There are two papers in Part I. First, Fathi and Krieger describe what multi-microprocessor systems are, why they are used, and when they are most useful. They also establish several dimensions for classifying multi-microprocessor systems. In the second paper, Zorpette emphasizes the use of multiple processors in order to increase fault tolerance and to enhance system resilience capabilities.

Multiple Microprocessor Systems: What, Why, and When

Eli T. Fathi and Moshe Krieger
University of Ottawa

Multiple microprocessor systems can provide an appropriate solution to the demand for additional computing power to meet new requirements and to support complex applications. To clarify the concept and its associated terminology, this article considers the "what," "why," and "when" of multiple microprocessor systems. Aspects that apply to all processors, regardless of size, are presented in general terms. However, since our main interest lies with microprocessor-based systems, aspects that depend on processor power and input/output flexibility are related specifically to microprocessors.

As the number of applications with more elaborate computational demands increases, we need to provide more processing power. This can be achieved at the processor level, by relying on technological improvements to push the microprocessor beyond its current maximum capabilities, or at the system level, by extending the capabilities of a single microprocessor through concurrent execution.

Microprocessor technological improvements are made exclusively by the manufacturers, and even though user feedback may influence developments, they are beyond the control of the average user. There are definite limits to the extent and type of improvements possible with existing technology. Thus, unless new technology is developed, all technological improvements can be regarded as evolutionary rather than revolutionary. As such, they concentrate on the following areas:

- Relatively simple applications. Provide more complex single-chip systems by adding memory and various I/O capabilities to the chip.
- Moderately complex applications. Increase microprocessor capability and/or throughput by providing longer words, more addressing capability, more extensive and powerful instruction sets, and higher operating speeds coupled with reduced power consumption.
- Complex applications. Facilitate modular increases to system performance by introducing additional control lines to implement multiple microprocessor architectures and by adding various software support functions to the chip.

The last point indicates a definite trend by the industry to move toward multiple microprocssor systems by providing the hardware and software support that facilitates their design.

At the system level, performance can be enhanced by exploiting the concept of concurrent execution. This requires segmenting the process into tasks and using a real-time multitasking executive to schedule, control, and synchronize the various tasks. The result can be either apparent concurrency using a single microprocessor in a timeshared mode or true concurrency using a multiple microprocessor system.

The first approach, useful only in small special-purpose systems, seeks maximum resource utilization from a single microprocessor. Because microprocessors are physically limited, this method is more appropriate for minicomputers or mainframes. The second method, however, attempts complete utilization of the system, not of individual microprocessors. In that context, a system is balanced whenever the work load can be evenly distributed among system elements. Distribution of the work load is referred to as load sharing and can be either dynamic (accomplished during system operation) or static (fixed during the design phase). With the addition of more processors for a multiple microprocessor system, the system can be regarded as being independent of the microprocessor's physical characteristics. Thus, theoretically, this method provides unlimited room for expansion and improvement.

The idea of using more than one processing element to improve system performance preceded the development of microprocessors, but that technology now permits the

Reprinted from *IEEE Computer*, pp. 23–32, Mar. 1983.

use of computing power in a wide range of applications that had been impractical because of the computer's cost and physical size. The use of multiple microprocessor systems extended the range and capabilities of single microprocessors to more complex areas previously in the domain of large computers and has led to other system enhancements—for example, improved reliability and ease of design.

What are multiple microprocessor systems?

Logical structure. To provide harmonious operation, the logical relations among the various elements of a multiple processor system must be well defined. Here, logical structure refers to the way the control responsibility is distributed among the sysem elements. The two most obvious relations are vertical and horizontal. In a vertical system, elements are hierarchically structured, implying a master-slave relation; in a horizontal system, the elements are logically equal, implying a master-master relation.

Vertical organization. In its simplest form, a vertical organization has a single master with multiple slaves and has the following main characteristics:

- Not all elements are logically equal.
- At any given time only one element can act as a master; however, several elements may have the potential of becoming a master.
- All interprocessor communications must go through the master or be initiated by the master.
- The slaves' hardware may be identical, with customizing to a special task done via the software.

In vertical organizations, number crunching is usually done by the master processor (generally the most powerful) and I/O processing by slave processors, thus achieving very high throughput.[1] Systems may also contain more than one level of master-slave arrangement, thus forming a pyramid configuration.

Horizontal organization. Horizontally organized systems require more sophisticated coordination. They have the following main characteristics:

- All elements are logically equal.
- Coordination can be done with or without a floating controller.
- Any element can communicate with any other element in the system.

In general, horizontal systems are more flexible than vertical systems and are capable of dynamic load sharing. However, they are not efficient for applications having many vastly different tasks.

Except in the case of the newest high-performance microprocessors, the large processing overhead required to coordinate horizontal systems precludes their effectiveness for multiple microprocessor systems. Vertical organizations are more appropriate.

Physical structure. The physical structure of a multiple processor system refers to the method of information exchange and is a function of the interprocessor communication arrangement and the interconnection topology.

Interprocessor communication arrangement. Data transfers between processors can be carried out either via a common memory structure or via a bus structure, often referred to as centralized and distributed structures, respectively.[2] In the common memory structure, all data transfers are via the common memory, and elements have no direct access to each other. In the system bus structure, a logical link established on the bus structure creates a communication path between elements; in the most general case, data transfers are initiated and performed in a distributed fashion.

In systems with frequent and/or large data transfers, the above extreme arrangements are not efficient due to increased contention for the shared resource. This problem is further aggravated in microprocessor systems because of the memory-processor bottleneck and limited I/O capability.

Interconnection topology. We must also consider the way in which the elements are connected, that is, the interconnection topology. Physically, there are many ways of interconnecting N elements in a system, but in establishing the interconnection scheme, reliability and expandability are important factors. A reliable interconnection scheme provides an alternate path in case a link, a direct path between two elements, fails. An expandable interconnection scheme facilitates the addition of more elements without affecting the existing structure. The four most basic interconnection schemes are common bus, star, ring, and fully connected (see Figure 1). Other topologies are basically combinations or variations of these schemes.

The data transfer mode and interconnection topology are the most basic elements of the intercommunication system. But in designing multiple processor systems, we must also decide on direct or indirect data transfer between elements, centralized or decentralized control, etc.[3]

Mode of interaction. The two most prominent taxonomies classify computer systems according to mode of interaction and mode of processing. Using mode of interaction as the basis, systems can be classified by the degree of coupling and the nature of the intercommunication between processors. Coupling refers to the ability of the various elements to share resources, with the two extremes being loosely coupled and tightly coupled systems.

Loosely coupled systems. Loosely coupled multiple processor organizations, also known as computer networks,[4] have the following characteristics:

- Autonomous computers. The system contains a number of independent computer systems that can be geographically dispersed.

- Communication interface. The various computers in the system are interconnected via a communication interface.
- Communication protocol. Intercomputer communication follows rigid communication protocol.
- Serial communication. The intercomputer communication links are generally high-speed serial lines.
- On-site computation. In general, the network is used only for communication. Actual computing is done at a single site.
- Computer accessibility. A user at any site can use the computing facilities at all other sites.

The best known and largest computer network is the Advanced Research Projects Agency Network, which connects over 50 major computing facilities across the United States.[5]

Currently, computer network organizations, with their rigid interprocessor communication requirements and extensive nodal computing requirements, are not directly applicable to microprocessor-based systems. However, with further increases in applications that require distributed computing and enhancements in microprocessor technology, it is likely that modified versions of computer network organizations will be used soon.

Tightly coupled systems. Also known as multiprocessor systems,[6] tightly coupled multiple processor systems have the following characteristics:

- Common memory. A primary memory can be accessed by all processors in the system. In addition, each processor may have a separate data memory.
- Common operating system. A single common operating system controls and coordinates all interactions between processors and processes.
- Shared resources. I/O facilities and other system resources are generally shared among the processors. However, some resources may be dedicated to specific processors.
- Equal processing power. General-purpose processors are symmetrically configured and exhibit similar capabilities.
- Dynamic load sharing. Dynamically distributing the load of an overloaded processor permits uniform load sharing across all processors.
- Processor autonomy. Each of the cooperating processors can execute significant computations individually.
- Synchronization. Synchronization between cooperating processors is needed.

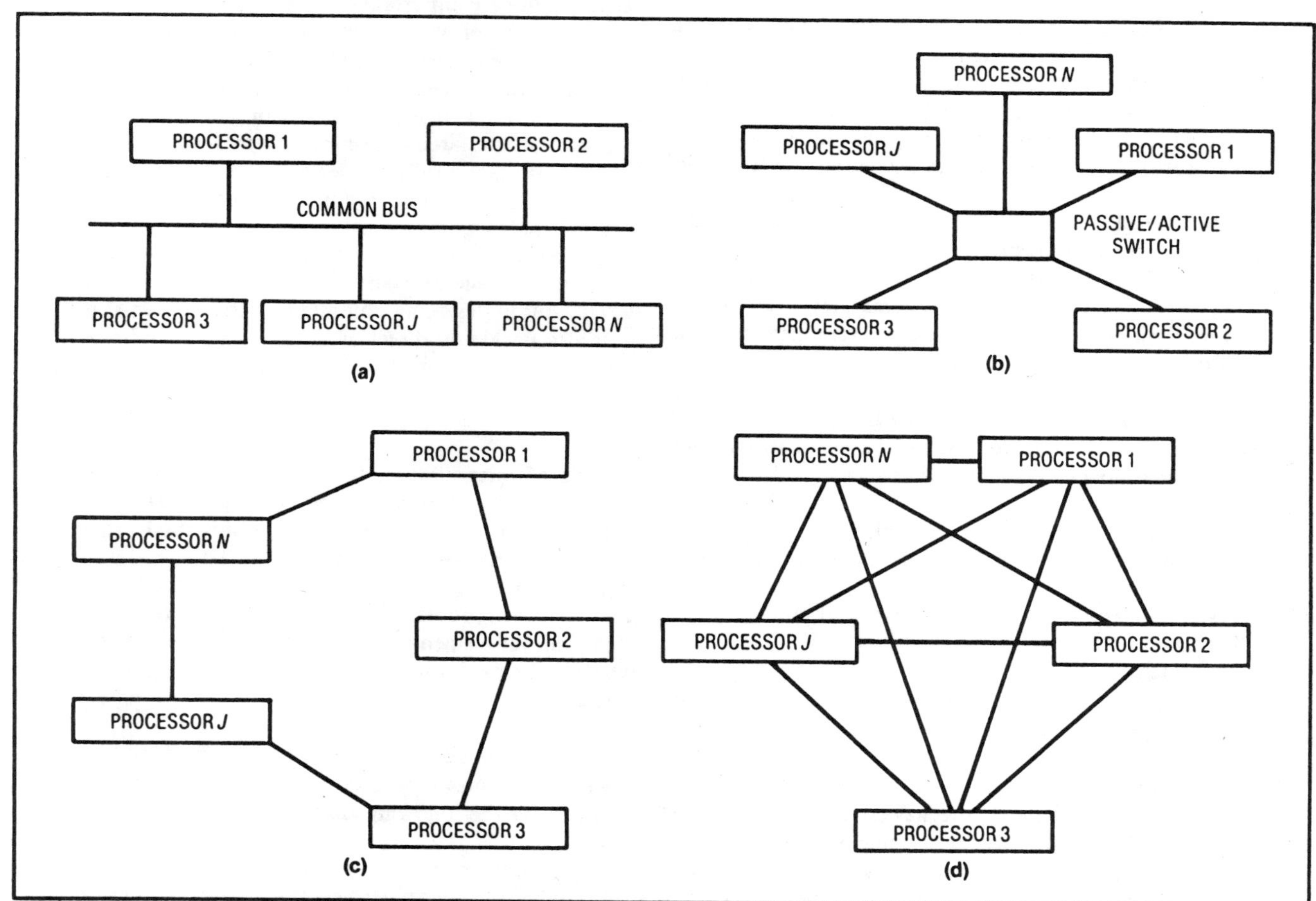

Figure 1. Interconnection topologies: (a) common bus, (b) star, (c) ring, and (d) fully connected.

The major limitation of a tightly coupled multiple processor organization is the possibility of primary memory access conflicts. This restriction tends to put an upper bound on the number of processors which can be effectively supported by a single operating system. Most processor-memory switching structures attempt to reduce the amount of main memory access conflicts. The three most fundamental processor-memory organizations are (1) the common bus, where all system elements are connected to a single bus; (2) the crossbar switch, where the elements are connected to a separate module, called the crossbar switch, which can provide several simultaneous connections between elements; and (3) the multiport memory, where each memory element has more than one access port and is connected to the other elements via a multibus system. (Further details can be found in Enslow.[7])

Basically a collection of low-speed processors performing the work of a single high-speed processor, the multiprocessor organization has been used in the implementation of various computer systems.[8] However, the memory-processor bottleneck—characteristic of microprocessors—limits its applicability to multiprocessor organizations. Multiprocessor systems using microprocessors can be implemented in special cases where a large number of similar, relatively independent processes exchange only small amounts of data; one example of a system that utilizes microprocessors is Stanford University's Minerva.[9]

Distributed microprocessor systems. Tightly coupled and loosely coupled structures are the two extremes of multiple processor organization. Other structures that combine the better qualities of each are more suitable for microprocessor-based systems. These moderately coupled microprocessor-based designs are known as multimicrocomputer systems[1] and are often called distributed intelligence microcomputer systems, or DIMSs.[10]

In a distributed microprocessor system, the general work load is partitioned into relatively independent tasks, which can then be assigned to various system elements. Such a system has the following main characteristics.

- Autonomous elements. Each individual element generally consists of a CPU, local program, and data memory, and may use or control additional peripherals.
- Processors dedicated to a task. Ideally, each element is dedicated to a specific task that determines its relative complexity.
- Processors with varied complexity. System configuration is not necessarily symmetrical since its elements vary in complexity.
- Software and hardware optimization. Each element's hardware and software is tailored to the specific task it performs.
- Data level communication. Interprocessor communication is generally at the data level. However, in certain situations data may contain commands or include responses to specific requests.
- Separate application and communication processors. In general, each element handles both I/O control and system communication. In the case of heavy communication activity, one of these functions may be delegated to another processor.[11]
- Static load sharing. Because the processors are dedicated, a minimal system cannot support dynamic load sharing; thus, proper load balancing must be done during the design phase. However, some load sharing can be introduced by including additional units.

Mode of processing. One of the earliest classifications of computer systems, introduced by M. J. Flynn when he was considering speed-up techniques, is based on instruction and data flow.[12] Flynn defined four classifications:

- Single-instruction single-data stream. An SISD machine is the classical von Neumann computer that executes instructions sequentially, one at a time.
- Multiple-instruction single-data stream. There is some argument as to the type of computer included in the MISD class.[13] One candidate is the variety of pipeline processor that segments computations into consecutive stations.
- Single-instruction multiple-data stream. Vector, array, and associative processors belong in the SIMD class. They generally have a single, central control unit that fetches and decodes the instructions and then broadcasts control to the processing elements.
- Multiple-instruction multiple-data stream. The MIMD class, the most general one, can have different processors—each with its own control unit.

Although Flynn's classification has been accepted as the most basic one, it considers execution only at the instruction level and is much too restrictive. To include more recent organizations, a number of modifications and extensions to Flynn's taxonomy have been suggested in the literature.[6,14,15] In its most general form, a multiple processor system capable of concurrently executing a number of tasks, each utilizing different sets of data, can be called a multiple-task multiple-data, or MTMD, system.[16]

In terms of multiple microprocessors, SISD machines correspond to multi-ALU systems or uniprocessors consisting of bit-sliced microprocessors; MISD and SIMD machines correspond to multiple microprocessor systems used to implement a single special-purpose CPU; and MIMD machines correspond to multiple microprocessor systems used to implement distributed processing systems. The latter are mostly MTMD systems in which each microprocessor also has local memory.

Since mode of processing and mode of interaction are closely related, the classifications based on those factors can be integrated as shown in Figure 2.

Why a multiple processor system?

To properly evaluate multiple processor systems, one must postulate a number of system performance measures related to processing capabilitiy, reliability, and design and development. Certain properties of these

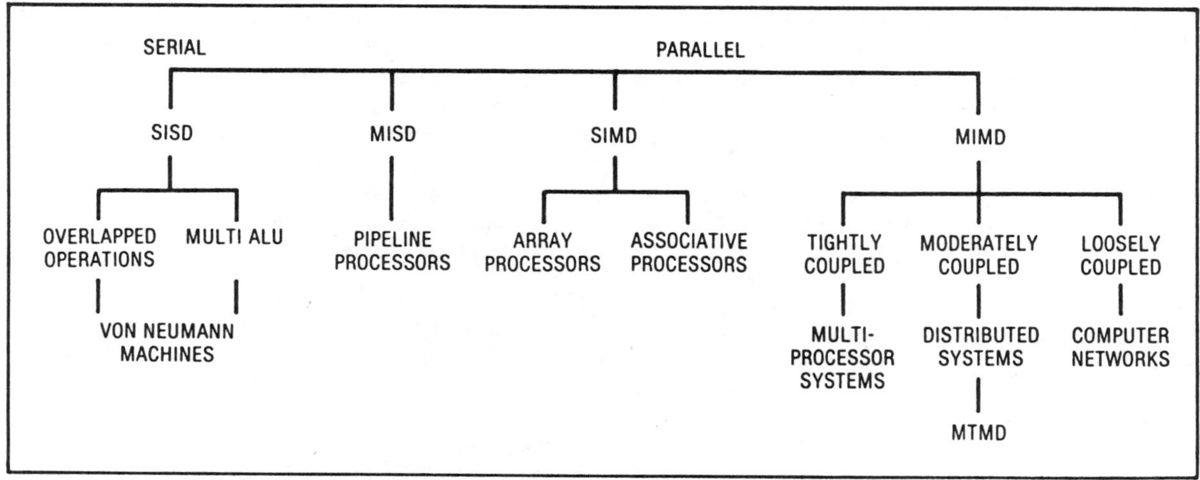

Figure 2. Classification tree of multiple processor organizations.

measures are strongly related and, although included in only one specific category below, one may influence others.

System processing capabilities. Measures related to system processing capabilities include cost-performance, throughput, and resource sharing.

Cost-performance. On a system level, it is generally accepted that processor performance increases with cost; the question is "how?" In a uniprocessor system, processor performance increases more rapidly than cost. At one time, Grosch's Law[17] suggested that processor performance was proportional to the square of its cost. Thus, using more than one processor solely to obtain more raw processing power was not economical. However, with advances in microprocessor technology, we are approaching the era of "no cost" processing power relative to the cost of other system parts and can now develop an incremental cost/performance curve that is more linear, as indicated in Figure 3. Thus, it is becoming economically attractive to use additional processors to increase system performance. Theoretically, the optimum performance of a multiple processor system equals the sum of the optimum performance of each processor. In practice, it will be less.

We should, of course, consider other costs associated with multiple processor systems. Even if we do not consider high software costs, it is obvious that the prices of many hardware elements—boards and connectors, for example—do not decrease as rapidly as those of microprocessors and memories. Therefore, the reduction in the incremental cost/performance ratio may be offset by other system costs.

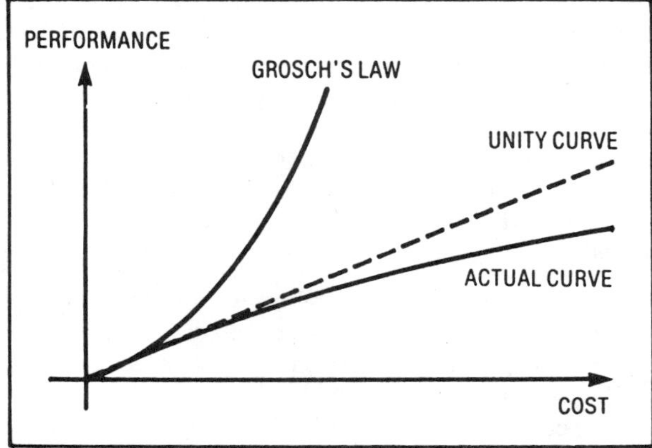

Figure 3. Performance of a system as a function of cost.

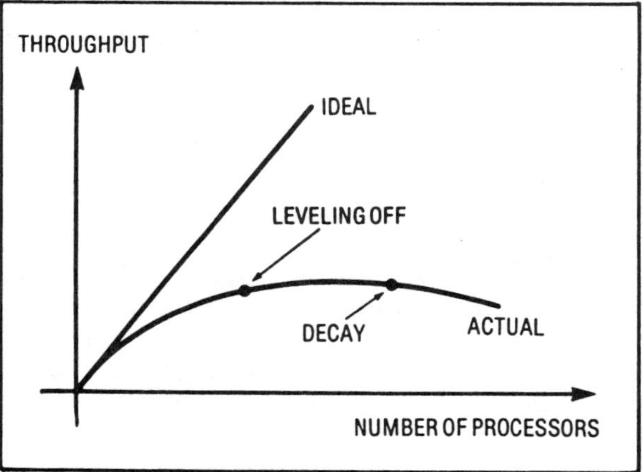

Figure 4. The saturation effect.

Throughput. System throughput, defined as the reciprocal of the time required to execute a given set of algorithms, is an appropriate indicator of system performance. It is measured in number of operations per unit time.

Ideally, throughput increases in proportion to the number of new processors added to a multiple processor system. In practice, due to the saturation effect, the relationship between throughput and the number of processors resembles the curve shown in Figure 4.

The saturation effect[18] is defined as the degradation in throughput for incremental increases in the number of computing elements. Initially, system throughput follows the ideal linear curve, but as more processors are added to the system, throughput levels off and finally decreases. This effect can be attributed to the fact that as the number of processors increases, so does the amount of contention on the shared resources. There is also an increase in the amount of overhead information required for proper interprocessor communciation.

The leveling off and decay points may be different for various multiple processor organizations. Ideally, we would like to operate on the linear portion of the curve, which can be extended by reducing the amount of contention and interprocessor communication activity. This can be achieved by partitioning the main job into smaller independent tasks that require little intercommunication.

Resource sharing. A general characteristic of most multiple processor systems, resource sharing is influenced mainly by financial considerations. In general, when the utilization factor of a given resource is low, it makes sense to timeshare the resource among the processing elements in the system.

Timesharing of resources must be done in an orderly manner to avoid resource overload and to maintain conflict-free systems. The types of resources that may be shared in a multiple processor system range from a dumb printer or memory module to a sophisticated high-speed arithmetic processor.

System reliability measures. The classical definition of reliability is the conditional probability that a system will survive interval $(0, \Delta t)$, given that it was operational at time $t = 0$. A measure of reliability is mean time before failure.

For multiple processor systems, where execution of a given job may require the cooperation of several processors, some of which may operate under different external conditions, the classical definition of reliability is too general. For these systems, reliability is more appropriately defined as the probability of executing a given task under a given condition for a specified time.[19]

For reliability analysis, most systems can be classified as redundant or nonredundant systems.[20] In nonredundant systems, each component must function properly for the system to work. In redundant systems, duplication of part, or all, of the system ensures at least limited operation in the event of a failure. To obtain the reliability model of a redundant system, both the reliability of each system module and the model of the fault-tolerant scheme that is used must be determined.

Since most multiple processor organizations are inherently redundant, they can be classified as redundant systems. In addition, their reliability can be improved by duplicating both physical elements and processor tasks.

Fault tolerance. A fault-tolerant system is capable of overcoming hardware malfunctions and/or software errors without human intervention, thus extending overall system MTBF beyond that of individual elements. To achieve this, the system may employ either massive or selective redundancy.[21]

Systems with massive redundancy use identical units operating simultaneously to protect against failures and/or errors. The effects of the faulty unit are logically masked out by the remaining, properly operating units.

Systems with selective redundancy employ real-time recovery procedures to automatically switch from a faulty unit to a standby unit. Successful initiation of the recovery procedures involves fault detection, fault containment, and fault diagnosis.[22]

Hardware faults and software errors must be detected as soon as possible. During the detection latency period (the time between fault occurrence and fault detection), the fault containment unit must prevent fault-damaged data from propagating through the system and contaminating it. After detection, diagnostic programs determine the extent of the failure and localize the faulty part. Subsequently, the part is logically isolated, and recovery procedures are initiated to restore overall system operation while maintaining data integrity.

In multiple processor systems, fault-tolerance is obtained by transferring job responsibilities. If the system design includes a limited number of standby elements, the functions of the faulty element will be assigned to one of them. Otherwise, the remaining, properly functioning elements will be asked to accept additional assignments. Fail-safe operation is obtained if transfer of responsibility does not affect system performance. On the other hand, if the system maintains only reduced-capacity operation because of partial transfer and/or general slowdown, it is in a fail-soft mode. In the fail-soft mode, some computing power is traded for continuous operation.

Multiple processor systems achieve flexibility mainly through software, but hardware must support it.

Flexibility. The ease of reconfiguring system topology and reallocating job responsibilities among other system elements comprises the flexibility measure. This characteristic is necessary to facilitate system recovery procedures in the case of element failure.

Providing uninterrupted operation at full or reduced capacity requires real time flexibility—that is, system reconfiguration in real-time under program control. Multiple processor systems achieve flexibility mainly through software, but the hardware must support it. The introduction of flexibility generally implies the use of more complex hardware and software, which—if done improperly—can reduce individual element reliability.

System flexibility can facilitate future system expansion and is closely related to the degree of system modularity.

Serviceability. Both maintainability and repairability are aspects of serviceability. Maintainability is concerned with preventive maintenance—for example, continuous running of diagnostic routines and periodic maintenance checks. Repairability is the ease of detecting and locating hardware failures and/or software errors once the system is down. A measure of maintainability is mean time to repair, defined as the sum of the expected mean time for periodic maintenance and the expected time for repair after failure.[23]

Since serviceability is concerned with repairability, it complements the fault-tolerance property. Both guard against total system failure—fault-tolerance while the system is up, and serviceability while it is either up or partially or completely down. Fault-tolerance is introduced during the design phase as a logical function to mask out the effects of a faulty unit. Serviceability, on the other hand, is mainly physical in nature; it is concerned with the physical repair of a faulty part and the prevention of future failures.

Multiple processor systems generally facilitate serviceability since total system complexity is broken down into simpler subsystems. The reduction in subsystem complexity implies that testing and repair will be easier and, occasionally, may be partially carried out while the system is operating. In some multiple processor systems, processing elements may have very similar or even identical hardwre, thus eliminating the need for large spare-part inventories and, since the faulty unit can be replaced by a spare, maintaining a low MTTR.

Availability. Availability is a figure of merit describing system availability to users, that is, the probability that the system will be operational at time t. It can be expressed as the percentage of time the system is up (available) and is given by

$$\text{Availability} = \frac{\text{MTBF}}{\text{MTBF} + \text{MTTR}}$$

Multiple processor systems offer good availability because of higher MTBF figures achieved by higher reliability and lower MTTR figures obtained by improved serviceability.

System design and development measures. In complex applications, it is desirable to partition the main job into smaller tasks to minimize interdependency between tasks. Ideally, each task would be assigned to a dedicated processor, thereby limiting interprocessor communication to the data level. A properly partitioned multiple processor system improves performance in terms of system deployment, modularity, and prolonged life cycle; it also facilitiates human engineering.

System deployment. A multiple processor system has a greater potential for use, even if it is only partially implemented, than a single processor system. Furthermore, the time required to become operational is less for a multiple processor system since the development, implementation, and installation phases can overlap. Once a functionally independent subsystem is developed, it can be implemented, installed, and used. Subsystems can be added to the existing section until the system is complete and operating at full capacity.

Modularity. System modularity can be defined in terms of the compactness and isolation of all its elements. Modular designs, which feature independent, less complex hardware and software modules, generally shorten development and debug time and facilitate serviceability.

Modular systems are also more responsive in that each subsystem's software and hardware can be optimized for a specific task. This permits a faster, more efficient response. For example, consider a subsystem that controls a process requiring rapid responses to interrupts. If one processor is not sufficient, more processors can be added to optimize response time.

System modularity can improve system versatility. The association of software functions with specific hardware modules, if done properly, enables controlling the software configuraton within the different end-user systems, thus making the system more versatile.

Prolonged life cycle. System modularity also facilitates system enhancement. Traditionally, systems designed around a single processor had to be replaced once optimal performance limits were reached. This implied a major financial investment, often beyond the means of an average user. However, a modular multiple-processor system can be upgraded to meet new requirements at minimal cost, thus prolonging system life.

Enhancement of an existing system may be desirable to eliminate a bottleneck, add more features, and/or improve performance in terms of speed and power. Also, modularity implemented with multiple processor architecture allows fine-tuning of system operation. One portion can be modified without affecting the rest of the system.

Human engineering. Many computer-controlled systems are being developed for applications involving nonprofessional users. Such systems are generally highly interactive to accommodate users who have relatively little or no experience in computer technology, and they use human engineering concepts to provide simple man/machine interfaces that can be easily understood. This requirement can be achieved most economically by using a local, dedicated processor for the interface.

When to use multiple microprocessor systems

The application of a multiple microprocessor system is closely related to the capabilities of the various processors used in the system. In general, a microprocessor has neither the computational power nor the communication flexibility of a larger computer, due to technological constraints and pin limitations, respectively. However, the microprocessor—a versatile, low-cost source of computing power—has made digital processing practical and financially attractive for many new applications.

Design considerations. Basic design considerations must be examined before we can define *when* to use multiple microprocessor systems. Whenever complex systems are considered, overall system operation must be decomposed into a number of relatively independent tasks; however, the problem of task partitioning in distributed data processing systems will not be considered here, since it is highly application oriented and has been extensively discussed in the literature.[24-26]

In multiple microprocessor systems, tasks are initiated asynchronously by external stimuli and/or internally within the system, and they are executed by a number of cooperating elements. This may introduce execution difficulties in terms of concurrency and conflict.[27] However, the problem of concurrency and conflict can be dealt with independently of physical structure by using task, event, and communication concepts as logical equivalents of physical structures.[28] To obtain harmonious operation, the system must be capable of the following control aspects: arbitration, allocation, and coordination.

Arbitration. Efficient task/resource allocation depends on the resolution of all potential contention through identification of events/requests and verification of the status of requested tasks/resources. The real-time demands for tasks/resources are physical entitites in the form of asynchronous requests/interrupts. These demands can be represented by events which are their logical equivalents. Thus, the system software can treat all demands the same, regardless of their physical characteristics.

Arbitration procedures can be carried out centrally by a single self-contained unit or in a decentralized fashion by small, dedicated units distributed among the various system elements.[29] The most commonly used arbitration control schemes are daisy chain, polling, and asynchronous requests/interrupts.

Task/resource allocation. Apart from the resolution of contention and subsequent arbitration, system resources must be properly allocated. A shared resource can be thought of as any system part, hardware or software, that could be used in more than one process, where a process is a logical entity related to the execution of any well-defined procedure. In multi-microcomputer systems, a process is the logical grouping of one or more tasks with their associated data, where each task represents the smallest independent entity of a procedure. As outlined previously, a multi-microcomputer system consists of a number of cooperating task execution units. In other words, process execution may involve assignment of a number of units. Thus, resource and task allocation are synonymous concepts in these systems. The allocation method can be either static or dynamic.[30]

Task/resource interaction and coordination. In a multiple microprocessor system, some sort of interaction and coordination among several concurrent tasks is necessary. Thus, we can talk about intertask/process communication procedures instead of communication between physical entities. This provides a uniform description of all system elements and eliminates concern with actual hardware characteristics. Also, providing the proper task/process communication procedures at a logical level (before implementation) permits a more efficient definiton of actual physical communication procedures. The coordination problems associated with concurrent processes can be stated in terms of determinancy, synchronization, deadlock, and mutual exclusion.[6]

System executive. All the above control aspects are in the domain of the system executive. The implementation of an effective multi-microcomputer system is greatly influenced, if not determined, by the proper design of its executive. The design of a multiple microprocessor executive is very complex[31,32] and beyond the scope of this article; however, ideas used in the design of real-time executives for uniprocessor system are applicable.[33-36]

Application characteristics. Multiple microprocessor system implementation should be considered for

- Elaborate process-control applications with diversified computational demands and real-time constraints. For most of these applications, the heavy processing requirements far exceed the capabilities of a single microprocessor-based system.
- Applications with extensive I/O processing. The need to interface with a large variety of I/O processes generally imposes unacceptable control overhead on a single microprocessor and causes severe degradation in system responsiveness.
- Applications that demand high reliability but, due to financial and/or space constraints, cannot support massive redundancy.

Avoid using multiple microprocessor systems if one or both of the following conditions exists:

- All that is needed is more raw processing power. In this case, it is advantageous to get a more powerful CPU or to add one or more dedicated, specialized processors.
- The global task to be executed cannot be partitioned into relative independent tasks with minimal intertask communication needs.

Distributed microprocessor system architecture—an example. Up to now, we have discussed multiple microprocessor systems in general terms. We now present a specific distributed architecture developed to exploit the advantages of concurrent processing while maintaining a simple, reliable system.

The task-driven multi-microcomputer system[37] consists of a hierarchical controller that supervises a number of heterogeneous processors, each having private program memory, read/write data memory, and some I/O capabilty. The system may also have global resources that include a global data memory used as a message center and for storage of common variables. The controller, called the task allocation and arbitration unit, accepts requests from internal and external sources and initiates the proper control actions. The required task synchronization and coordination are done via asynchronous handshaking signals through a control/handshake bus. A simplified block diagram of a task-driven multi-microcomputer system is shown in Figure 5.

The various tasks available to the system are permanently stored in the local program memories of the in-

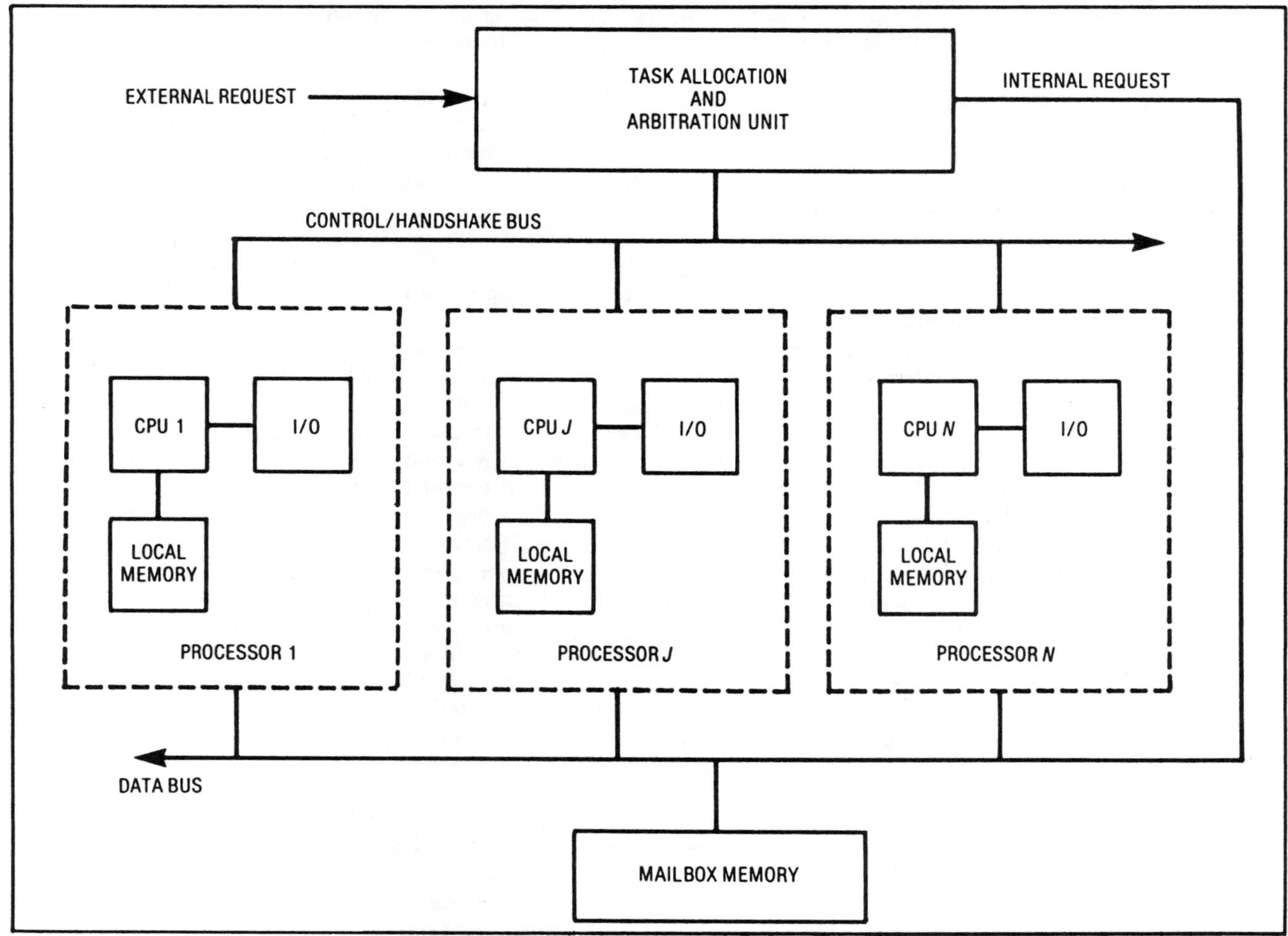

Figure 5. Simplified block diagram of a task-driven multi-microcomputer system.

dividual processors. When a task is to be executed, it is awakened by specifying its starting address, not downloaded from a central memory. For reliability and to maintain system performance at a specified level, each task is stored in two or more local program memories.

A dedicated controller "frees" the processors from performing anything but their assigned tasks. This reduces individual processor complexity, which in turn results in a modular, more reliable unit. By designing the controller to be a highly reliable unit, complete system reliability is enhanced. The design of a general-purpose executive for a task-driven system was outlined in another work.[38]

The trend toward distributed microprocesor systems described in this article is being recognized by microprocessor manufacturers. They are now producing chips that simplify interaction and coordination by providing additional control signals as well as real-time, multitasking operating system primitives. However, this is only a first step. To develop effective distributed microprocessor systems, additional work is needed in the areas of hardware architecture, system executives, and communication facilities. ■

References

1. P. M. Russo, "Interprocessor Communication for Multi-Microcomputer Systems," *Computer,* Vol. 10, No. 4, Apr. 1977, pp. 67-76.
2. C. V. Ramamoorthy et al., "Hardware Software Issues in Multimicroprocessor Computer Architectures," *Proc. First Annual Rocky Mountain Symp. Microcomputers: Systems, Software, Architecture*, Fort Collins, Colo., Aug./Sept. 1977, pp. 73-99.
3. G. A. Anderson and E. D. Jensen, "Computer Interconnection Structures: Taxonomy, Characteristics, and Examples," *Computing Surveys,* Vol. 7, No. 4, Dec. 1975, pp. 197-214.
4. S. H. Fuller et al., "Multi-Microprocessors: An Overview and Working Example," *Proc. IEEE,* Vol. 6, No. 2, Feb. 1978, pp. 216-218.
5. M. Schwartz, *Computer Communication Network Design and Analysis,* Prentice-Hall, Englewood Cliffs, N. J., 1977.
6. B. A. Bowen and R. J. A. Buhr, *The Logical Design of Multiple Microprocessor Systems,* Prentice-Hall, Englewood Cliffs, N. J., 1980.
7. P. H. Enslow, Jr., "Multiprocessor Organization—A Survey," *Computing Surveys,* Vol. 9, No. 1, Mar. 1977, pp. 103-129.

8. M. Satyanarayanan, "Commercial Multiprocessing Systems," *Computer,* Vol. 13, No. 5, May 1980, pp. 75-96.

9. L. C. Widdoes, Jr., "The Minerva Multi-Microprocessor," *Proc. Third Ann. Symp. Computer Architecture,* Clearwater, Fla., Jan. 1976, pp. 34-39.

10. L. H. Anderson, "The Microcomputer as Distributed Intelligence," *Proc. Int'l Symp. Circuits and Systems,* Boston, Mass., Apr. 1975, pp. 337-340.

11. W. L. Spetz, "Microprocessor Networks," *Computer,* Vol. 10, No. 7, July 1977, pp. 64-70.

12. M. J. Flynn, "Very High Speed Computing Systems," *Proc. IEEE,* Vol. 54, No. 12, Dec. 1966, pp. 1901-1909.

13. J. L. Baer, "Multiprocessing Systems," *IEEE Trans. Computers,* Vol. C-25, No. 12, Dec. 1976, pp. 1271-1277.

14. L. C. Higbie, "Super Computer Architecture," *Computer,* Vol. 6, No. 12, Dec. 1973, pp. 48-58.

15. D. Prener, "Large Multimicroprocessor Systems," *Microprocessors and Microsystems,* Vol. 3, No. 6, July/Aug. 1979, pp. 271-276.

16. M. Krieger and E. T. Fathi, "Design Aspects of a Simple Distributed Microprocessor System," *Int'l Conf. Communication, Circuits, and Systems,* Yadvapur University, Calcutta, Dec. 1981.

17. A. Baum and D. Senzig, "Hardware Considerations in a Microcomputer Multiprocessing System," *Digest of Papers Compcon Spring 75,* San Francisco, Calif., Feb. 1975, pp. 27-30.

18. C. J. Jenny, "Process Partitioning in Distributed Systems," *IEEE NTC Conf. Record,* 1977, Vol. 2, pp. 31:1-1 to 31:1-10.

19. C. G. Davis and C. R. Vick, "The Software Development System," *IEEE Trans. Software Engineering,* SE-3, No. 1, Jan. 1977, pp. 69-84.

20. D. P. Siewiorek, "Multiprocessors: Reliability, Modeling, and Graceful Degradation," *System Reliability and Integrity, State-of-the-Art Report,* Infotech, Ltd., Maidenhead, England.

21. C. Weitzman, *Distributed Micro/Minicomputer Systems, Structure, Implementation, and Applications,* Prentice-Hall, Englewood Cliffs, N. J., 1980.

22. D. A. Rennels et al., "Distributed Fault-Tolerant Computer Systems," *Computer,* Vol. 13, No. 3, Mar. 1980, pp. 55-65.

23. D. Popovic and D. Danziger, "Total Life Calculations With and Without Maintenance," *Microprocessors and Microsystems,* Vol. 3, No. 6, July/Aug. 1979, pp. 257-261.

24. B. P. Buckles and D. M. Hardin, "Partitioning and Allocation of Logical Resources in a Distributed Computing Environment," *Tutorial: Distributed System Design,* IEEE Computer Society, 1979, pp. 247-276.

25. J. T. Lawson and M. P. Mariani, "Distributed Data Processing System Design—A Look at the Partitioning Problem," *Proc. Compsac 78,* Chicago, Ill., pp. 358-363.

26. E. D. Jensen and W. E. Boebert, "Partitioning and Assignment of Distributed Processing Software," *Digest of Papers Compcon Fall 77,* pp. 348-352.

27. Y. P. Chien, "Multitasking Executive Simplifies Realtime Microprocessor System Design," *Computer Design,* Jan. 1979, pp. 109-117.

28. P. Brinch-Hansen, "A Keynote Address on Concurrent Programming," *Computer,* Vol. 12, No. 5, May 1979, pp. 50-56.

29. K. J. Thurber et al., "A Systematic Approach to the Design of Digital Bussing Structures," *AFIPS Conf. Proc.,* Vol. 41-II, 1972 FJCC, pp. 719-740.

30. B. C. Searle and D. E. Freberg, "Microprocessors," *Computer,* Vol. 8, No. 10, Oct. 1975, pp. 75-83.

31. E. T. Fathi, "Task-Driven Multi-Microcomputer System," master's thesis, University of Ottawa, 1981.

32. P. Brinch-Hansen, "Distributed Processes—A Concurrent Programming Concept," *Comm. ACM,* Vol. 21, No. 11, Nov. 1978, pp. 934-941.

33. K. C. Kahn, "A Small-Scale Operating System Foundation for Microprocessor Applications," *Proc. IEEE,* Vol. 66, No. 2, Feb. 1978, pp. 209-216.

34. D. A. Townsen, "A Task Scheduling Executive Program for Microcomputer Systems," *Computer Design,* Vol. 16, No. 6, June 1977, pp. 194-202.

35. F. V. D. Linden and I. Wilson, "Real-Time Executive for Microprocessors," *Microprocessors and Microsystems,* Vol. 4, No. 6, July/Aug. 1980, pp. 211-218.

36. C. J. Tavora, "A Basic Technique for Real-Time System Design," *Computer Design,* Vol. 19, No. 10, Oct. 1980, pp. 147-152.

37. M. Krieger, "Task-Driven Multi-Microprocessor System," *Proc. First Canadian Workshop Design and Development of Computer Systems,* May 1979, pp. 81-88.

38. E. T. Fathi and M. Krieger, "Executive for Task-Driven Multi-Microcomputer Systems," accepted for publication in *IEEE Micro.*

Computers that are 'never' down

Fault-tolerant systems based on multiple microprocessors trade off throughput for enhanced reliability

Fault-tolerant computers have caught up with the microprocessor revolution. A new approach to fault-tolerant computer design—systems based on multiple microprocessors—is winning followers and challenging the decade-old approach that relies on central processing units (CPUs) made up of medium- and large-scale integrated circuits. Like their predecessors, the multiple microprocessor systems trade throughput for reliability and are proving invaluable in financial transactions, telephony, and a number of other applications that demand high reliability.

One reason for the renewed interest in fault-tolerant computers is the increasing use of computers at the heart of businesses. For example, as networks of computer systems and workstations proliferate, reliability in the central, coordinating processor for such networks is assuming paramount importance. As one prominent technology watcher, Omri Serlin, put it: "Failures are more likely to get management's attention."

Also contributing to the increased activity has been the divestiture of the American Telephone & Telegraph Co., which has long used proprietary fault-tolerant electronic switching systems. Divestiture has led the company to offer for other applications the computer controller for its latest system. At the same time, competitors have moved into AT&T's communications territory with systems of their own.

The multiple microprocessor approach has been the route taken in virtually all of the recently introduced fault-tolerant systems, and even in a few non–fault-tolerant systems that use the multiple processors strictly to boost throughput. Yet only a few years ago this approach would not have been feasible. The chips were largely limited in performance, and those that were not were too expensive.

The battle is joined by IBM

But today, noted Keith Johnson, manager of corporate marketing at Stratus Computer Inc., "the economics are so obvious that for us to spend time designing a CPU is just not feasible." Stratus, based in Marlborough, Mass., makes a line of fault-tolerant computers that includes a model with 24 Motorola MC68010 microprocessors. In January the company signed an agreement giving IBM rights to sell products using the Stratus line.

Activity like this represents the first challenge to the design approach taken by Tandem Computers Inc., the oldest and most successful manufacturer of fault-tolerant computers. Its systems are based on CPUs made up of MSI and LSI circuits.

Tandem was founded in 1974, when microprocessors were too expensive and not powerful enough for typical fault-tolerant applications, so the company invested the time and money to design its own multichip TTL central processing units and to write the software for them. Rival companies say that Tandem is constrained by this investment to outmoded fault-tolerant systems, but Tandem sees it differently.

Glenn Zorpette Associate Editor

"A $100 million investment in venture capital over the last 10 years has not led to a fault-tolerant architecture that is an improvement over Tandem's," insisted Gerald D. Held, director of strategic planning at Tandem. He believes the company will continue to use its current architecture for at least the next 10 years.

Another Tandem employee, Bob Horst, asserted, "Microprocessor-based systems may be adequate at the low end of the performance range, but they cannot yet approach the transaction volumes required for large applications such as credit card verification, airline reservation systems, and on-line banking." According to Horst, who designed the CPUs for Tandem's Nonstop TXP computers, hardware tests have proved that the systems are linearly expandable to at least 32 processors, while studies predict that expansion should be possible up to the 224-processor limit of the system's fiber-optic bus extension. Regarding microprocessor-based systems, he said, "there is no evidence to date that shows that the upper limit is more than 10 or 20 microprocessors." At the root of the problem, Horst added, is the fact that the speed of a microprocessor "will always be limited by the number of pins, which limits the bandwidth to and from the chip."

Notwithstanding disputes over capabilities, makers of the microprocessor-based systems are after at least a portion of the 60-percent share of the fault-tolerant transaction-processing market enjoyed by Tandem. This market was estimated at $923 million by InfoCorp, a market research company in Cupertino, Calif. The market involves computers that handle mainly finan-

Defining terms

MSI- or LSI-component processor: a processing unit built around medium-scale and/or large-scale integrated circuits, as opposed to one built around a monolithic processor, such as a microprocessor.
Downtime: any period of time during which a system cannot be used as a result of a failure or routine maintenance, or for any other reason.
Fault: a failure of a hardware or software component in a system that may lead to a system failure or error or some other manifestation that can be detected by a user.
Redundancy: the basic strategy used in nearly all fault-tolerant systems. The most common form involves the use of multiple hardware and/or software components that can assume the tasks of one or more other subsystems if the need arises. In the case of processors, results are sometimes also checked by a second unit. With "time redundancy," a related concept, the same processor may check its own results by recomputing them.
Transaction processing: the largest single application for fault-tolerant computers, which involves repetitive, typically financial tasks in banking, stock trading, and the like.

Reprinted from *IEEE Spectrum*, pp. 46–54, Apr. 1985.

cial transactions—for example, in banking and stock trading. And the stakes are getting higher; InfoCorp estimates that this fault-tolerant market will grow to $2.3 billion by 1989.

Micros introduce new issues

As more of the new fault-tolerant computer systems use microprocessors, designers are confronting new issues. "If you use a microprocessor, you're betting that it will be popular, so you can get compatible software," noted Philip A. Bernstein, vice president for software at Sequoia Systems Inc., also in Marlborough, Mass. "It's interesting—now semiconductor manufacturers are setting the standards for CPU instruction sets."

For new fault-tolerant computers aimed at the on-line transaction-processing market, the most popular microprocessors are the Motorola MC68000 and its successor, the MC68010.

The popularity of the microprocessors in fault-tolerant systems is also of concern to users of the systems. "People ask what microprocessor you're using, and they want to hear that you're using the most popular one available," said Bernstein. "Components are now important subsystems."

Another issue is the choice of architecture. Basically there are two: loosely coupled and tightly coupled. According to the most commonly held definition, processors in loosely coupled systems are more or less independent of one another; each has its own memory and copy of the operating system. In tightly coupled systems, processors have a common clock and frequently a common memory and operating system as well. The new microprocessor-based systems, some of tightly coupled and some of loosely coupled design, have introduced variety to a field once dominated entirely by the loosely coupled Tandem systems.

"There is no one approach that can be clearly identified as superior," according to Serlin, who is president of Itom International Co., a research and consulting concern in Los Altos, Calif.

The advantages of the loosely coupled architectures include relative ease in implementing a high degree of fault isolation, the function designed to keep a faulty processor or incorrect memory segment from corrupting other system elements or data bases in the computer. With loosely coupled processors, a faulty processor and its associated memory can be isolated relatively quickly without affecting the other processor–memory pairs. A form of loose coupling is implemented in the microprocessor-based designs of Auragen Systems Corp. of Fair Lawn, N.J., and Tolerant Systems Inc. of San Jose, Calif., among others.

The chief disadvantage of loosely coupled systems is that they generally process less efficiently than tightly coupled systems, pointed out Herbert Hecht, president of SoHaR Inc., a Los Angeles, Calif., consulting and research company specializing in fault tolerance. The greater degree of independence between processors in loosely coupled systems, he noted, often leads to situations in which one processor must wait to use the results being computed in another processor. Also, loosely coupled systems require more extensive communications protocols between processors, which can further reduce efficiency.

Tightly coupled systems predominate

Most microprocessor-based fault-tolerant systems introduced recently have been tightly coupled, or they have used some form of tight coupling in their architectures. Such systems generally have better processing efficiencies, but there are drawbacks related to the common memory. For example, the memory hardware is typically nonredundant and is thus a potential single point of failure that could affect the whole system. "Hard" memory failures, in which a segment of memory ceases to respond to read or write commands, can also be more problematic; the failure may affect all of the processors if it occurs in a key piece of software, such as a compiler or the operating system.

In addition, the shared memory of tightly coupled systems may become a bottleneck if several of the processors need to use it simultaneously. To avoid this, most tightly coupled systems have a cache—or auxiliary memory—for each processor to hold small, often-used programs. The caches reduce the number of times the processors need to access the main memory.

Although a minimal amount of computer downtime can be tolerated in on-line transaction processing, the integrity of the data must be preserved at all times. If the computer is part of a bank's automated teller network, for instance, infrequent short periods of inactivity are less disastrous than the incorrect recording of many transactions. This calls for hardware and software in the fault-tolerant system that can accommodate multiple copies of data and preserve the data in the event of a failure. To accomplish this in tightly coupled systems, the activities of the processors, the cache memories, and the main memory must be carefully coordinated.

Tightly coupled fault-tolerant systems usually have duplexed main memories to reduce the possibility that a main memory failure will disable the entire system. The memories are usually "mirrored," which means that they store two copies of every page of data in memories accessed by independent buses and ports. The memories may be located on different printed-circuit boards. Thus if there is a problem with one copy of data, the chances are

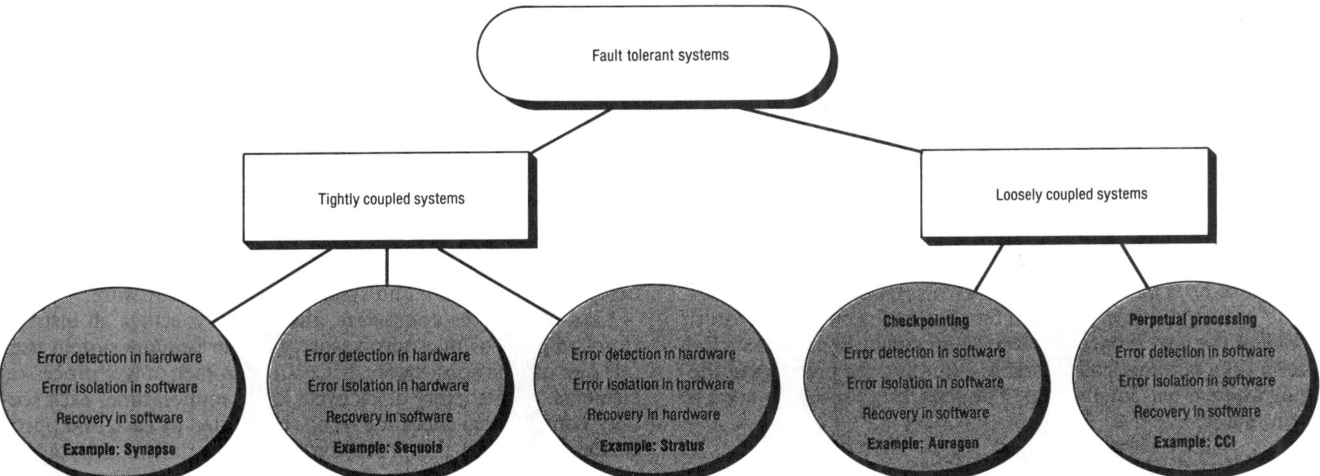

The recent wave of microprocessor-based fault-tolerant computers for transaction processing has resulted in a variety of approaches to the design of these systems. The two primary strategies are loose and tight coupling of the processors, but within these approaches designers are opting for either hardware or software implementations of the chief fault-tolerant functions: error detection and isolation and system recovery. As noted, loosely coupled systems rely primarily on software.

good that the other copy can be used.

A more difficult problem with tightly coupled systems is ensuring that corrupted data are never entered into the main memory, which is more likely to happen during a fault in the system. In a tightly coupled system the main memory is accessed by all of the system's microprocessors, so if data in the main memory are corrupted, the bad data can quickly spread to the other processors.

Hardware or software may be used in fault-tolerant computers to isolate system faults. Either hardware or software may also be used to carry out the other chief functions of the computers: error detection and system recovery. Three tightly coupled systems—by Synapse Computer Corp. of Milpitas, Calif., and Stratus and Sequoia—will serve as examples.

One solution: reliance on software

The Synapse designers opted for an approach primarily dependent on software in the company's N+1 system. Expandable from 2 to 28 processors, the N+1 system has a main memory capacity between 1 and 16 megabytes. The general-purpose processors are based on a single MC68000, and each has a 16-kilobyte cache.

The N+1 system uses a unique "bus ownership" protocol to ensure consistency among copies of data in its caches and main memory. Under this scheme, when a processor must access program code or read-only data, it issues a "public read request" for the data. The "owner" of the data, either a cache or the main memory, sends a copy of the data to the cache of the processor that issued the request. This copy, however, is a "read-only" one, which means that the processor may not modify it. Should a processor require a memory segment that needs modification, it would have to become the owner of the data. For this, it would issue a "private read request." Other processors monitor their common bus for such a request involving data elements in their caches; when it is detected, they invalidate their copy of the data.

Applications software for the N+1 system is written in small, indivisible "program units," each corresponding to a flexible number of instructions that make up a complete task or transaction. When the application is run, a component of the system software called the transaction-processing manager automatically places "checkpoints" at the end of each program unit. The checkpoints indicate states in the program where the amount of data to be recovered would be minimal if the system failed after that state. At each checkpoint the portion of these data necessary for recovery is automatically saved, so that only data entered or computed since the previous checkpoint need be reentered in the event of a system interruption. After the interruption, a component of the system software, the relational database management system, obviates the effects of all incomplete transactions and uses the stored data to restore those of completed ones.

Faults are detected by various hardware approaches, such as memory error-correcting codes and parity. If the fault is caused by hardware, the faulty system component is isolated, and a monitor program reconfigures the system to circumvent the failed unit. After this the operating software is reinitialized and the relational data-base management system restores the data base by recovering or rejecting transactions. The transaction processing manager is then reinitialized. This software keeps track of the data being displayed on each terminal at the time of the fault, as well as the next program unit to be executed. In most cases the system then automatically resumes executing the program at the point where it was interrupted. The restarting procedure takes a few minutes.

Putting the stress on hardware

For applications that cannot tolerate even a few minutes of downtime, Stratus has a tightly coupled system that depends primarily on hardware for its fault tolerance. The system uses pairs of MC68010 microprocessors that simultaneously execute all instructions in an application. Comparators check the results computed by the two microprocessors to make sure they are equal; if they are not, the system assumes that a fault has occurred in one of the processors. Even the duplicate microprocessors are duplicated again in the system. If the results disagree in one pair of microprocessors, that pair is automatically disconnected, and the system continues processing with the other pair without missing a clock cycle.

Stratus introduced its top-of-the-line XA 400 and XA 600 systems last year. The XA 400 has four general processors, each with two pairs of microprocessors. A mirrored main memory ranges from 2 to 8 megabytes, and no cache memories are used. A 16-megabyte-per-second data bus connects the general processors to the main memory.

The XA 600 has six general processors, up to 16 megabytes of duplexed main memory, and an 8-kilobyte cache and arithmetic coprocessor for each general processor. The 24 microprocessors and the logic needed to manage the flow of data between them and peripheral devices is on two three-level circuit boards. This logic was contained on about 70 ICs in the company's earlier FT 200 system, but now it is done by a single gate array in the XA 600, according to Keith Johnson, the company's marketing manager. Thus the company's engineers could fix six MC68010 microprocessors and management logic on one board.

By reducing the number of chips required, the gate array also reduced the number of connections to the printed-circuit board, which in turn increased reliability. Such connections are a significant source of failure, according to Johnson. Other reductions in board space and connections will be achieved when the company begins using 256-K random-access memory chips, possibly later this year, he said.

The XA systems maintain a single copy of the virtual operating system in the main memory. Tasks are divided among the general processors by the use of processes—virtual memory set aside when a user logs on that holds the user's programs and a copy of the virtual operating system. Processes are handled by the system's general processors in an order according to their priority, which is set up in two stages. First, the user selects a priority based on a range set by the system's local administrator. Second, a software utility in the operating system called the scheduler may vary the priority based on such factors as whether the process is interactive and how much CPU time it requires.

The Stratus systems, with their four microprocessors for each general processor, employ more hardware per processing capability than the Synapse system does, but this has not been translated into higher costs. On the contrary, the base model, two-processor Synapse N+1 system costs $364 000, while the Stratus XA600, with six general processors, is listed at $274 000. However, the costs for the Synapse system reflect the fact that it can be expanded into a tightly coupled system of 28 processors. The Stratus system can be expanded beyond the six-processor system, but only in a loose coupling of XA systems.

A hardware-software compromise

A third tightly coupled system, designed by Sequoia, is something of a compromise between the primarily software approach of the Synapse system and the primarily hardware approach of the Stratus computers. The Sequoia system implements fault detection in hardware and system recovery in software.

Like the Stratus computers, the system executes all instructions on pairs of microprocessors, but the Sequoia system uses one pair of microprocessors, MC68010s, in each of its "processor elements." With every clock cycle, or 10 million times each second, comparators check the results computed by each microprocessor. A fault in the processor element is indicated by a discrepancy when the results are compared. The discrepancy causes the comparators to disconnect the processor element's interface to the bus, isolating the fault from the rest of the system.

Once the hardware has detected and isolated a processor fault, the operating system initiates recovery, transferring the program that had been running on the failed processor to the queue of

AT&T Bell Laboratories (photos)

A long-standing application for fault-tolerant computers is in telephone switching. The 3B20D computer controller for AT&T's most recent telephone-switching system, the No. 5 Electronic Switching System, averages about 6 minutes of downtime per year and is expected eventually to average only 2. The computers are built at AT&T's Oklahoma City Works in Oklahoma. Left, a system undergoes testing at the Works. The first No. 5 ESS was installed in Seneca, Ill., in January 1982 (below).

tasks in main memory awaiting execution. Here the program is picked up by another processor, typically within a few tenths of a second, so that the total delay caused by the fault is limited to a few seconds.

"Our argument is that faults happen so infrequently that a couple of seconds for software recovery isn't a problem," said Bernstein, the company's software chief.

The Sequoia computer uses a minimum of one and a maximum of 64 processor elements, which are served by a main memory of from 4 to 256 megabytes. Besides the two MC68010 microprocessors, processor elements have two comparators and an unusually large cache memory of 128 kilobytes. The large caches ensure that 99 percent of all main-memory references can be handled by the caches, according to the company.

The Sequoia system maintains data consistency between the caches and the main memory with a double "flush" mechanism. Updated pages of main memory are mirrored. When the operating system asks a processor to flush its cache—that is, transfer its updated cache entries to main memory—it actually flushes twice, first to overwrite the primary copy of the pages and again to create a backup copy on a different module in the mirrored memory. The double flush is implemented in hardware and generally takes only a few hundred microseconds.

If the cache is being flushed when a fault occurs, either the primary or the backup copy of the data sent from the cache may not be correct, since the cache flush of the failed processors was interrupted by the fault. In this case, the incorrect copy is refreshed from the correct one, and the program is in a state from which it can resume normal execution on another processor. The cache is flushed on every input or output operation, so data are not lost when a processor fails.

After a module fails and is disconnected from the bus, it executes an internal diagnosis to determine whether the fault was transient. If it was, the element is reconnected to the system and brought back on line. If it was not, the element remains unconnected and a telephone call may be placed automatically by the system to a service center.

Loosely coupled systems lean on software

Whereas tightly coupled systems reveal a variety of approaches ranging from primarily software to primarily hardware, in most loosely coupled fault-tolerant systems the emphasis is on software. In particular, several loosely coupled systems rely for their fault tolerance on a strategy pioneered by Tandem in 1976 that is known as checkpointing.

With checkpointing, each applications program is assigned to two CPUs. In one the program is a primary process; in the other it is a backup process. The program is executed only on the primary processor, and it remains in a "wait state" on the backup, except when the backup is receiving checkpoint information from the primary processor. This information consists of all necessary data modifications to keep the backup process current with the primary process. If the primary processor fails, the backup takes over execution as of the last checkpoint.

This basic idea has been implemented on two loosely coupled microprocessor-based systems—one designed by the Auragen Systems Corp. of Fair Lawn, N.J., and the other by Tolerant Systems Inc. of San Jose, Calif. Auragen is using a combination of loose and tight coupling in its System 4000 fault-tolerant computer. Moreover, because the company received preshipment samples of Motorola's new microprocessor, the MC68020, its fault-tolerant system is the first to use this chip.

The main processing element in the System 4000 is called a cluster, and the system may use from one to 32 of them. Inside the cluster is an MC68010 executive processor and as many as four MC68020 applications processors, according to Eli Lisnyansky, Auragen's chief hardware engineer. Up to 8 megabytes of memory are dedicated to each cluster. The executive and applications processors are tightly coupled within the cluster, but up to 32 clusters in a System 4000 are loosely coupled.

The executive processor handles task scheduling and other supervisory chores within the cluster, while the applications processors execute the user's programs and control virtual memory. Users logging onto the system are automatically assigned two clusters, and all data entered by the user are read by both clusters. However, only one cluster executes the user's programs; the other acts as a backup.

Periodically the processor executing the programs updates its backup with the results of calculations. The updates are received by the backup cluster's executive processor, so the execution of the program on the backup cluster is not affected. The updates are sent at intervals set by the operating system, so the user is not aware of them.

If the backup fails to receive an update within a prespecified time, it transmits an inquiry to the processor. If there is no response, the backup cluster transfers the user program to itself. The backup also finds another backup cluster for itself, bringing it up to synchronization with the program it has transferred.

The fault-tolerant computer by Tolerant Systems has not been formally introduced yet, but the company says its design is based on what it calls system building blocks. Each block has a real-time processing unit based on a National Semiconductor NS32016 microprocessor, which runs an operating system that handles real-time tasks. A user processing unit, also based on the NS32016, runs a variation of the UNIX operating system and handles the user's programs. A third NS32016-based unit, the communications-interface processor, handles communications with terminal devices and the like. All of the processing units, with the possible exception of the communications processor, will be upgraded with the NS32032 microprocessor when this component is available in quantity, according to Shirley Henry, Tolerant's marketing director.

The system building blocks are connected to one another by a system-interconnection bus. In each block the real-time processing unit communicates with this bus for the rest of the block. The system maintains a running copy of each applications program on one system building block and a "quiescent" copy on one or more others. As in the Tandem and Auragen systems, the quiescent copies are periodically updated by the primary program, and the backup processors each execute primary programs of their own. In the event of a failure of the primary system building block, this system disconnects itself from the system interconnection bus and the quiescent copies are activated in the other system building blocks.

The system uses up to 12 system building blocks. Each block has as much as 14 megabytes of memory, and in addition one-half megabyte is set aside for the real-time processing unit in each block.

A third loosely coupled system, made by Computer Consoles Inc. of Rochester, N.Y., does not use checkpointing. Its fault-tolerant computer, the Power 5/55, is a microprocessor-based system that may use as many as eight application processors and is

Landing jetliners by computer in 50-meter visibility

Boeing Commercial Aircraft Co.

Ultrareliable computer-based automatic landing systems are helping airliners land when the visibility is as low as 50 meters and the ceiling is virtually at ground level. Such conditions are classified by the International Civil Aviation Organization as Category IIIb.

The use of electronics for landing aircraft dates to the late 1940s, when radar procedures were developed in the military to enable ground personnel to "talk" a pilot through a difficult landing. In the mid-1960s, landings of airliners in Category II meteorological conditions (30-meter ceiling, 350-meter visibility) were achieved.

The pilots followed their instruments down to the 100-foot level and, if visual contact with the runway was established, completed the landing as they usually did.

Even though an average of 95 percent of all scheduled flights can be completed in Category II conditions or better, some major airports have a much higher incidence of limited visibility. Here automatic landing systems rated for Category IIIb are particularly useful. The new Boeing 757 and 767 twin jets were the first to introduce systems certified for such landings.

An operational scenario

To describe the operation of the digital automatic landing system, these typical initial conditions are assumed to exist:

• The aircraft is approximately 10 minutes from landing.
• The autopilot is engaged and controlling the aircraft's altitude and heading.
• The autothrottle is engaged and automatically adjusting required thrust settings.

The captain presses the APP (approach) pushbutton on the automatic flight-control panel in the glareshield, just below the plane's windshield. The pushbutton command is processed simultaneously by two independent microprocessors within the mode-control panel and conveyed by independent buses to the major components of the automatic landing system—three identical flight-control computers—which illuminate the bottom half of the button, advising the captain that the computers have received his command.

The flight computers then initiate a comprehensive self-testing routine to determine their own operational status and that of the associated sensor subsystems. The status assessment is shared via high-speed cross-channel data buses between the three computers. If the system is fully operational, an automatic landing status annunciator in front of each pilot displays LAND 3, indicating that the system is now armed and waiting only for the ILS (instrument landing system) radio receivers to detect the glideslope and localizer directional beams being transmitted from the runway.

When the airplane flies into the path of either of the ILS beams (the localizer providing lateral position information relative to the runway and the glideslope the vertical information), the approach mode is activated. The airplane automatically banks to follow the localizer and to line up with the runway. As the glideslope beam is intercepted, the pilot extends the aircraft's flaps to the landing position and drops the landing gear. This is his last manual action prior to landing.

As the airplane descends on the final leg of the approach, a thrust-management computer readjusts the engine throttles so the airplane will fly at an airspeed 30 percent above stalling speed. The pitch and roll attitude of the airplane is controlled to guide it to within a touchdown area that is smaller than 1500 ft long by 150 ft wide. To be qualified for use in commercial service, the system must demonstrate conclusively that it will not land the plane outside this area more than once in 1 million times regardless of wind or weather conditions.

By design the landing system guides a 767 jetliner across the end of the runway at an altitude of 50 ft and an airspeed of approximately 130 knots. The flight-control computers begin the flare maneuver, guiding the 767 along an exponential path that intersects the runway surface at a vertical speed of approximately 2 feet per second. At 30 ft above the runway, the thrust-control computer begins retarding the throttles so the airplane will gradually lose flying speed and settle onto the runway. Within seconds of touchdown, several automatic actions occur.

Ground spoilers (airbrakes on the upper surface of the wings) deploy, the wheel brakes are applied according to a pilot-selected deceleration profile, the autothrottle control disengages, and the flight computers lower the nose until the nose gear is solidly on the ground. The flight computers then control the rudder and nose gear to maintain the airplane on the centerline of the runway until the airplane comes to a complete stop or the pilot takes over to turn off onto a taxiway.

Protecting the flight path

The first automatic landing system certified in the United States was installed on a Boeing 727 and was a "fail passive" design. With this type of design, before a fault in the system can disturb the aircraft's flight path, the fault is detected and the system is

to be modified soon to accommodate 32. All of these processors are based on a Motorola MC68010 or MC68012 microprocessor, and each has as much as 8 megabytes of memory.

An identical architecture is used on a new fault-tolerant computer, the Power 6/55, which CCI expects to deliver in late 1985. The processors in the 6/55, however, use eight 4-bit Advanced Micro Devices microprocessors in a bit-slice configuration. The configuration and the use of Schottky technology boost throughput to the range of 4 to 7 million instructions per second.

In addition to the application processors, the Computer Consoles systems have a synchronization processor, a Motorola MC68000, that monitors traffic on the bus connecting the application processors. The primary function of this processor is coordinating the communications between application processors and data bases, but they also play a key role in the system's fault-tolerant mechanisms.

Applications software for the systems is written as a series of transactions that are indivisible and may stand alone—a single application processor need not process all of the transactions in the application. This independence of transactions from particular processors facilitates recovery if an application processor fails between transactions, because the next transactions that a failed processor would have handled may be rerouted to another application processor (this routing is done by the synchronization processor). If an application processor fails during a transaction, however, recovery is harder and in most cases will depend on the type of transaction being executed at the time of the failure.

For example, if the application processor is about to write data into one of the data bases, it first notifies the synchronization processor, specifying the intended data base. After receiving permission from the synchronization processor, the other processor writes to the data base and notifies the synchronization processor afterward that it did so successfully. If the application processor fails during the writing of the data, it either notifies the synchronization processor that it did not write the data and indicates the type of error that prevented it from doing so, or it gives no acknowledgement whatsoever. In either case, the synchronization processor notifies all other application processors of the failure.

automatically disengaged, allowing the pilot to take over. This type of design was adequate for use in Category II conditions, but operation in the more severe Category IIIb required a "fail operational" design.

The fundamental design requirement for a fail-operational system is that it prevent a single failure from adversely affecting the operation of the system. Also, the system must be shown to be safe in the presence of any failure or combination of failures that are not determined to be extremely improbable (the definition of extremely improbable is generally taken to be an occurrence of less than 1 in 100 million events). The system must detect that a failure has occurred and automatically reconfigure itself in such a way as to continue operation without any discernible effect on the airplane's flight path.

The digital automatic landing system, a basic feature of the 757 and 767 airliners, is a fail-operational system based on triplex redundancy architecture, and it has 13 minicomputer- or microprocessor-based subsystems. Each channel of the system can be broken down into three major components: sensor subsystems, flight-control computers, and electrohydraulic servo subsystems.

The three flight-control computers are internally structured with an autonomous I/O controller and cross-channel data bus. This organization allows each flight computer to share its incoming sensor data with the two other computers. Redundancy management is essentially based on "voting planes" at strategic points within the system [see figure]. At each plane, three independently derived input values are compared and a median value is selected. Forward equalization provides an effective weighting process to determine a stable median value that is compensated for tolerance differences and short-term stochastic perturbations of the input values. Therefore the output of each voting plane is a weighted median used in common by the downstream functions.

The system can sustain any single failure, detect the failed component by measuring deviance from the median, and prevent the further processing of the failed component output. The overall system can survive several dissimilar failures without impairment of operation.

The voting presupposes that there are no latent or hidden failures within the system that could compromise the accuracy of the final product. Consequently extensive internal monitoring and self-testing must be provided for each major component in the automatic landing system.

Approximately half of the lines of code embedded in each flight-control computer are dedicated to internal and intrasystem testing and surveillance, as well as to recording detected faults for display to a line-maintenance crew. All of the digital subsystem operating programs are structured into a foreground-background organization. The foreground includes the basic functional requirements of the subsystem; the background is dedicated to such tasks as recursive testing of the CPU and surveillance and testing of the I/O. In addition, nonrecursive tasks, such as power-up testing and operating-mode prerequisite tests, are also included in the background.

—James H. Boone
Flight Management Systems
Boeing Commercial Aircraft Co.
Renton, Wash.

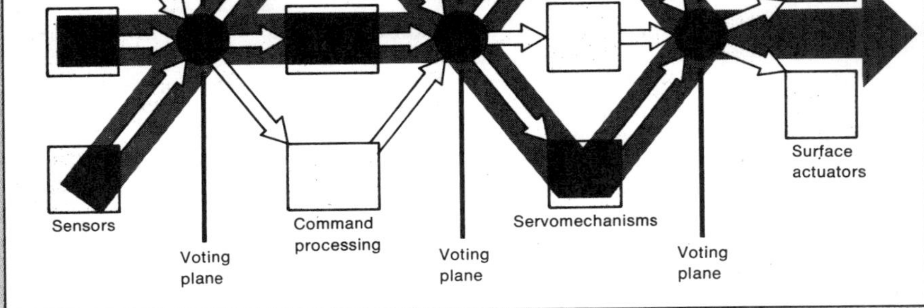

A computer system that lands Boeing's 757 and 767 airliners when visibility is less than 50 meters relies on triple redundancy to ensure reliability. At strategically positioned "voting planes," three independently derived signal values (I) are compared, and a median (M) is computed. The median is used by the next system in the command chain (above).

Fault tolerance for space applications

Unlike earthbound applications, in which an occasional error or infrequent periods of downtime can be tolerated, space applications require continuous availability and absolute data integrity. The space shuttle, for example, is virtually a fly-by-wire craft during critical phases of each mission, such as liftoff and landing. At these times, the shuttle's computers essentially fly the vehicle, while the crew primarily monitor the vehicle's progress. The computers take over control of the ship 25 seconds before launching, enacting the final countdown, initiating the firing of the shuttle's rockets, and setting the ship's course. The computers also jettison the fuel tank and stop the engines at the right time.

Coordinating and controlling these activities is a 120-pound, five-computer complex built by IBM's Federal Systems Division in Owego, N.Y. During the ascent of the vehicle, four of the computers perform all operations for quadruple redundancy, while the fifth is in a standby mode, ready to take over for the others at the command of the crew in the event of failure.

"NASA doesn't want computers turning off computers," said Joseph Militano, IBM communications specialist for the space shuttle programs.

In the redundant mode, the computers use synchronization points for error detection. These points, processed at a rate of 200 a second, are placed in the IBM flight-control operating system; a copy is in each of the four computers. During processing the first computer to reach a synchronization point issues a message on an interprocessor bus notifying the other computers that it has done so. It waits 4 milliseconds for the three other computers to acknowledge that they have reached the same point. If one computer does not reach the point within the 4 milliseconds, it is overruled by the three others and processing continues. The crew is notified of the incident.

Only a relatively severe problem would prompt the crew to switch to the single fifth computer, noted B.J. Thomas, IBM's space shuttle manager for hardware engineering. Such a problem might be a "two-on-two split," in which two computers reached a synchronization point within the 4-ms period while two did not, although this has never happened, according to Thomas.

The only significant disruption that has occurred so far took place shortly before the first launching in April 1981. Twenty minutes before the liftoff the fifth computer began monitoring the input and output to and from the four other computers, reprocessing instructions executed by the computers, a standard procedure that ensures that all of the results are logically consistent. The fifth

NASA

computer has an operating system written by Rockwell International, and it performs the same functions as the operating system on the four other computers, even though it was written independently. Two or more programs written independently for the same purpose are called redundant software. The premise is that the probability is very low that a "bug" or error in one program will also occur in the other.

Such was the case with the shuttle's software, when in the 1981 preflight check the fifth computer detected a logical inconsistency in the data computed by the four other computers. The problem was caused by an error in a high-level program that caused an interruption in processing lasting one half of a clock cycle. "There was one chance in 60 that it would have happened," Thomas said.

Once it is in orbit, the shuttle's computers split up to handle different tasks. Two of them control guidance and navigation, although on a long trip only one may be used for these tasks, to conserve energy. Another computer is assigned to system management—regulation of the atmosphere and so forth—and also payload deployment. A fourth computer stores a reentry configuration for the spacecraft's position, which would be used if an emergency forced a sudden return to the earth. The remaining one or two computers store the normal reentry configuration.

IBM is evaluating a new shuttle computer, which will also be a five-processor complex and will use the same software as the current model. The new system would occupy about one half the space of the current system and would be about half as heavy, but it would have a processing rate of about 1 million instructions per second, and twice the memory of the present model, which averages about 400 000 instructions a second.

Fault tolerance aboard Voyager probes

On board the Voyager 1 and 2 space probes are six computers: two computer-command subsystems (CCSs), responsible for overall supervision and control of the craft; two flight-data subsystems (FDSs), to control the probe's scientific instruments and format all telemetry data; and two attitude- and articulation-control subsystems (AACSs), which orient the platform on the spacecraft that holds the remote sensing instruments, such as cameras and telescopes, in space. The AACSs also control the spacecraft's attitude and maneuvers.

Each subsystem has two completely redundant sets of hardware. In the FDS and AACS subsystem pairs, one subsystem is

The divestiture of AT&T adds yet another candidate for fault-tolerant computing: the company's 3B20D computers, formerly used solely for communication applications. Divestiture has also led some makers of fault-tolerant computers for transaction processing to seek new markets in communications. But adapting computers from one market to the other is not so simple, noted Richard Watters, head of peripheral development at AT&T Bell Laboratories in Naperville, Ill.

Whereas data integrity is the overriding concern in on-line transaction processing, high availability is the crucial characteristic of computers used to control telephone switching. In this application an error in the data base that might lead to an incorrectly dialed call can be tolerated, but even short periods of downtime may inconvenience thousands of people.

Early on, AT&T set a goal of no more than 2 hours of downtime in 40 years for its fault-tolerant switching systems. The 2 hours were in turn broken down so that one third of the time, or 1 minute a year, was applied to the switching part of the system and the remainder, or 2 minutes a year, was applied to the computer controller. The goal has been achieved with the early generations of Electronic Switching Systems (ESS), Watters said.

The computer controller for AT&T's current telephone switching system averages just under 6 minutes of downtime a year, Watters said, but it is expected to achieve the company's goal of 2 minutes a year. There are about 500 of the switches, known as No. 5 ESS switches, in service. The fault-tolerant computer used, the 3B20D, also controls the 800 area-code toll-free network, and it can be used as an auxiliary processor on the No. 4 ESS switches.

The computer has two multichip, 32-bit processors, each with two arithmetic-and-logic units. The processors are tightly coupled but only one is active at a time; the other is in a standby mode but active enough to check the operation of the other processor on every clock cycle. Diagnostic software runs periodically to make sure that the standby processor and parity and error-detection hardware on both processors are functioning properly.

Like several other fault-tolerant systems, the 3B20D uses a ver-

designated the primary and the other the secondary. During normal operation, the primary executes all functions while the secondary remains in an inactive state, ready to take over for the primary if the need arises.

The two CCS units, however, are typically used in parallel, executing different instruction sets. Each of the CCS subsystems has 4000 18-bit words of memory, of which 3000 are devoted to failure protection. The remaining 1000 are used to store instructions related to spacecraft tasks; in each of the CCS computers, these 1000 words are devoted to different tasks, which effectively doubles the memory available to the CCS.

Commands critical to the spacecraft's well-being are stored redundantly in each CCS memory to provide fault tolerance, according to Michael Urban, leader of the advanced software development group for the Voyager project at the Jet Propulsion Laboratory in Pasadena, Calif. This is so because the CCS issues critical commands to the two other subsystems in either of two fault-tolerant modes. In the parallel command mode, a command is issued redundantly from each of the two computer command subsystems, and the receipt of either command by the intended subsystem suffices. In the tandem command mode, one subsystem is designated the "master" and the other the "slave." Again, the command is issued from both subsystems, but prior to this the master subsystem checks the command from the slave for agreement in both data and timing. If both are not identical, the command is not issued and an abort routine is initiated.

A tandem command, for example, would start a maneuver that would temporarily take the craft's antenna off "earth point," thus interrupting radio contact. Such a command must be issued flawlessly to minimize the possibility that contact is not lost for good. On the other hand, a command to point the antenna back at the earth would be issued in parallel, in order to maximize the possibility that the command is received at all.

The applications software run by the computer command systems is divided into alternating "time" and "event" words. The complete set of time and event words required to execute a task is called a time-event region. The event word normally includes a command from the subsystem, while the time word is usually a delay or pause before the next event. As an additional measure of reliability, this scheme allows the insertion of checkpoints at the beginning of a time-event region in which critical commands are to be executed. At these checkpoints the computer-control subsystem may check that a flag has been set, indicating that the craft's critical subsystems are in good working order. If the flag is not set, the time-event region is disabled. "If the gyroscope had failed, you wouldn't want to initiate a maneuver," Urban said.

Regarding the FDS and AACS computers, since each of the pairs in these subsystems is redundant, the craft can continue to function with no impairment in performance if one subsystem in a pair fails. For example, the memory in one of the flight data subsystems on the Voyager 1 spacecraft has failed, but by selecting the working subsystem memory the spacecraft continues to operate normally. If one of the CCS units were to fail, the amount of memory available for storing instructions would be halved, thus impairing performance and fault tolerance but not necessarily ending the mission. —G.Z.

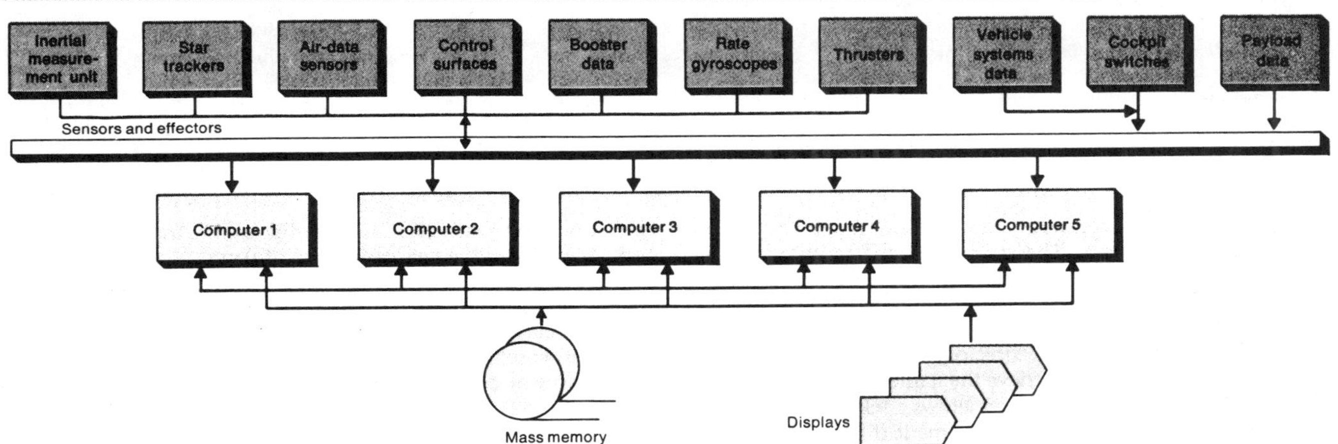

During liftoff, the space shuttle is virtually a "fly-by-wire" craft that is controlled by a five-computer complex built by IBM. During critical phases of the flight, such as liftoff, four of the computers process all instructions for quadruple redundancy, with the fifth unit ready to take over if the others suffer a large enough failure—for example, if two or more of the systems fail simultaneously.

sion of the UNIX operating system modified to support multiple processors and memories as well as communication between processors. Called UNIX RTR (for real-time reliable), the operating system begins running an analysis program after an error is detected, to try to determine the source of the error. The program may take the ailing unit out of service and activate its backup, depending on its findings. Besides the processors, the memory, data buses, peripherals, and power supply are also duplicated.

The error-analysis program then activates a diagnostic program that determines whether the fault is transient. If it is, or if the program cannot find the source of the trouble, it makes the primary unit available again, either as an active or a standby system. If the fault occurs again, the recovery process is repeated. For each hardware system, there is an error threshold—a number of times an error can occur before a higher level of recovery, such as swapping a larger system element, is attempted. The computer is equipped with remote alarms to keep maintenance personnel aware of actions taken, but only in relatively rare cases is human intervention required in the recovery process.

AT&T's proprietary 32-bit microprocessor, the WE32100, may find its way into a future fault-tolerant system, but the decision is still open. "We've done a lot of preliminary development, but as far as what we're going to do in marketing, I can't say," Watters remarked. In the meantime the company has been offering the $340 000 3B20D in the transaction-processing market since March 1984.

Meanwhile, among the fault-tolerant–system manufacturers looking for new opportunities in the telecommunications market is Tandem, which created a strategic sales and marketing group dedicated to the market in March 1984. Tandem has sold its fault-tolerant NonStop systems to five Bell operating companies, where they are typically used in bill collection and other transaction applications.

Computer Consoles Inc. of Rochester, N.Y., has also moved quickly to address the market, having secured over 60 percent of the operator-services segment of the U.S. telephone industry

The Intel 432: fault tolerance in a micro

With the growing use of microprocessors in fault-tolerant systems, it was only a matter of time before microprocessors themselves began to reflect the trend. The first to include logic on the chip for use in fault-tolerant systems is the Intel iAPX 432, a 32-bit microprocessor considered by some to be an advanced unit for its time.

In addition to the fault-tolerant logic, the chip has hardware for floating-point arithmetic, memory management, a cache memory, and registers. In a fault-tolerant system, two of the microprocessors can be used if self-checking processors are needed, or four can be used if instantaneous recovery is also needed as in the Stratus system.

Comparators on the chip are connected to the output data lines. If a single chip is used, the comparators are disabled. If two pairs of chips are used in a self-checking central processing unit, both execute all instructions in a program, but only one—the "primary"—releases information on the data bus, while the other—the "shadow"—uses its comparator to check the results against its own. If an error is detected, a signal sent from the comparator disables the data lines before the erroneous data reach the data bus.

As a further reliability measure, logic on the microprocessors causes the two pairs in a self-checking CPU to alternate the primary and shadow roles with each clock cycle, thus ensuring that all of the microprocessors are always up to date and that both modes are working on the chips. Special memory chips have also been developed for the 432, and they, too, alternate between primary and shadow modes if implemented in pairs. These memories have 40-bit word lengths—32 bits for data, 7 bits for error-correction codes, and a single bit that can be used in the event of the "hard" failure of any of the other bits.

Most fault-tolerant systems take advantage of their multiprocessor architectures to increase throughput under nonfault conditions. How efficiently the systems match processing tasks to processors depends on the load-balancing scheme used.

With the 432, load balancing is implemented in the form of a work queue, an integral part of the operating system written for the microprocessor. All tasks awaiting execution are entered into this queue, which a microprocessor turns to any time it is idle, such as when its current program is suspended for data input or output. To enhance the efficiency of the match of the tasks to the processors, the operating system may restrict the processors that may execute certain tasks, based on the size of the task or the processors' other activities.

Despite these attractive features, the 432 has not been used in commercial fault-tolerant computers, and its status as a product is apparently uncertain at this point. "The technology has been very well received, but it has not been a commercial success," acknowledged an Intel engineer.

The primary problem, according to the engineer, was that insufficient software was available for the 432 when it was introduced. For example, the operating system for the chip was not entirely complete when the chip was made available, forcing users in some cases to attempt to complete it on their own. Also, the only high-level language available for the chip was Ada, which was not very popular at the time of the chip's introduction in 1980.

Another problem cited was the 432's complex instruction set, with more operating system primitives, or low-level instructions, than the standard instruction sets used by ordinary microprocessors. "Potential customers sometimes find the architecture too far in the future," the engineer said.

Regardless of the future of the machine, the engineer noted, "we're working to correct the problems that are keeping it from being a commercial success, but without losing the important technologies. You'll see the technologies developed in the 432 propagate into other VLSI devices. But the 432 will not be another 8086." —G.Z.

with its fault-tolerant computer-based system for storing names and telephone numbers. The system is used by directory-assistance operators. The company has developed other fault-tolerant systems for the market, according to Richard Moore, the telephony systems product-marketing director. One system permits an operator to search the directory-assistance data base using a telephone number to retrieve the name and address associated with that number. The system allows a telephone company to tell a customer to whom a call was made if the customer disputes having made the call. Several Bell operating companies are also offering the service to individuals and companies for a fee.

The future of fault tolerance

The use of fault-tolerant computers in crucial applications, such as landing aircraft, is also spurring new research [see "Landing jetliners by computer in 50-meter visibility," p. 18]. Some of the research is challenging the basic tenets behind today's designs.

"The assumption that two faults won't happen at once in a system has been the cornerstone of fault-tolerance work, but it needs to be challenged today," said SoHaR's Hecht, whose firm specializes in fault-tolerant systems for aeronautical applications.

One computer being developed for flight control is Sift, developed at SRI International in Menlo Park, Calif. Capable of handling multiple faults, the computer has a processor redundancy ratio of 6 to 1. It is undergoing evaluation at the NASA Langley Research Center in Hampton, Va.

According to Jack Goldberg, the Sift project leader at SRI, verifying the computer's reliability began before any components were assembled. Formal mathematical models were used to specify system behavior, and some critical parts of the design were subjected to mathematical proof of correctness. Goldberg believes that for complex fault conditions, the use of such methods, together with a new generation of formal verification tools, may be a much more efficient way to establish the feasibility of a design than conventional simulation.

Other current research on fault tolerance is stressing redundant software, an approach taken with the U.S. space shuttle's five-processor complex [see "Fault tolerance for space applications," p. 20]. In addition, fault tolerance in highly parallel, non-Von Neumann computers is receiving attention, according to Dr. Goldberg. He suggested that it might be possible to implement fault tolerance in these machines with less hardware than in Von Neumann computers, because of the greater use of similar processing elements. Further, the highly parallel machines offer more inherent flexibility in connectivity between processing elements.

Through the use of architectures and techniques such as these, researchers are already designing systems with probabilities of failure as low as 10^{-10} in 1 hour. With such a number, the computer for all practical purposes simply does not break down.

To probe further

The August 1984 issue of *Computer*, the magazine of the IEEE Computer Society, was devoted entirely to the topic of fault-tolerant computing. For a copy, contact the IEEE Service Center, 445 Hoes Lane, Piscataway, N.J. 08854. An excellent article published in the March 1984 issue of *ACM Computing Surveys* may also be helpful; see Won Kim's "Highly Available Systems for Database Applications." The surveys are published by the Association for Computing Machinery in New York City. Finally, a well-known textbook on the subject is *The Theory and Practice of Reliable System Design* by Daniel Siewiorek and Robert Swarz, published by the Digital Equipment Corp.'s Digital Press (Bedford, Mass.) in 1982. ◆

Part II
Alternative Interconnection Topologies

THE overall performance of multi-microprocessor configurations is affected by the number and the type of processors, the communication mechanism between the computing resources, the characteristics of the computational workload, and the control program. Whereas the major constraint in uniprocessor systems is the speed of the processor, the critical factor in multiprocessor systems is the speed of the interconnection mechanism. Given its pivotal role in the success (or failure) of the overall system, it is appropriate to begin the discussion with the subject of alternative interconnection topologies.

Consider a simplistic world in which each computer consists of the processor alone. That is, no separate memory or I/O facility is required. If there are two such processors, there must be one pathway to connect these two computing resources. What happens if this pathway becomes inoperational? Then, the two processors cannot talk to each other. One way to mitigate this problem is to make two distinct pathways between the two processors. Now, there is a higher probability that at least one of these pathways will continue to be operational. However, there is still a finite chance that both links may be inoperational at some point in time.

If a third processor is added, then the number of pathways must be increased. Also, the memory and the I/O units must be considered. If each computing element is to be connected with all other computing elements, then the number of message paths comes to ${}^{n}C_2$ where n is the total number of computing elements. Except for very small configurations, it is impractical to design systems with such a large number of links due to considerations of cost and maintainability.

Once the number of pathways is reduced, there is increased load on the remaining pathways. Also, only a subset of the computing resources now have direct links with others. This implies that some pairs of computing resources are obliged to communicate via one or more intermediate nodes, causing time delays and performance degradation. A number of theoretical and experimental studies have evaluated various interconnection topologies and have concluded that some topologies offer higher bandwidths, others offer higher fault tolerance, and still others offer the benefit of lower costs.

In the first paper of this part, Feng describes the different interconnection alternatives. His discussion covers a broad spectrum of links ranging from simple linear arrays to the completely connected situation, with all other configurations falling in between. Dynamic network topologies are also considered.

In the second paper, Wittie looks at the issue of connecting thousands of microcomputers together. Although there is some overlap with the paper by Feng, the main attraction of Wittie's paper is Table 1 which summarizes the major performance parameters for all popular network topologies.

In the third paper, Kuhl and Reddy focus on the fault-tolerance aspect of multiprocessor systems. They emphasize that the choice of an appropriate interconnection medium is a key issue in the design of any system with multiple processing resources.

Cases in which it becomes necessary to use complicated network topologies are relatively rare. Even though a particular topology may appear to offer high performance based on theoretical considerations, the practical aspect of implementing a complex structure should not be underestimated. When dealing with off-the-shelf microprocessors, it is desirable to minimize the number of buses, whenever possible. Also, it is preferable that the topology be modular enough to permit an additional processor to be added into the system at a later stage. Both these desirable goals are fulfilled by a single global bus. In the fourth paper of this part, a modified version of this bus, incorporating a split-transaction protocol, is described. This bus offers superior performance, by an order of magnitude, over traditional global buses. This enables an increased number of processors to be attached to a single split-transaction, demand-based, time-shared global bus.

Having decided on the interconnection topology, it is necessary to think in terms of physical implementation of the selected topology. Busing standards and practices are discussed in Part III of this book.

A Survey of Interconnection Networks

Tse-yun Feng
The Ohio State University

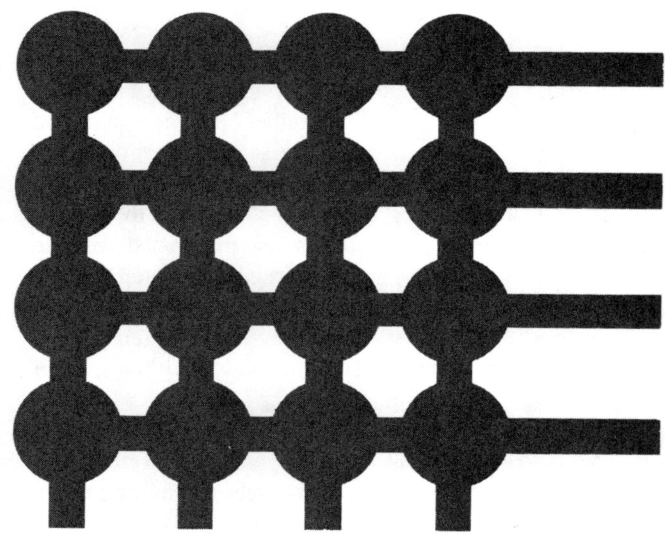

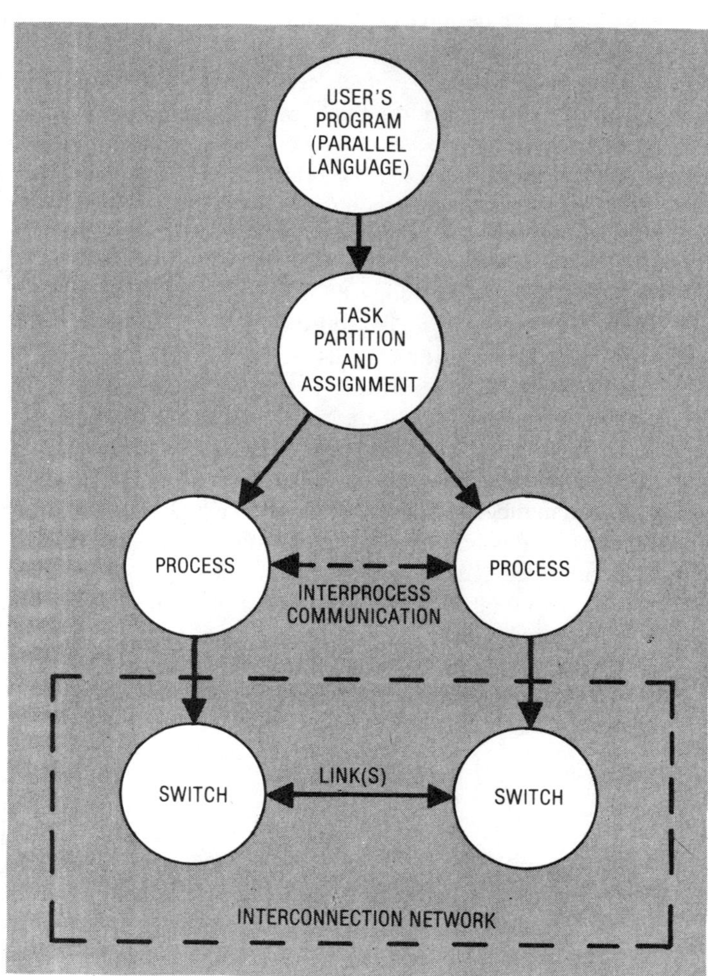

Figure 1. An overview of concurrent processing systems.

Concurrent processing of data items is considered a proper approach for significantly increasing processing speed.[1] In many real-time applications—such as image processing and weather computation, which need an instruction execution rate of more than one billion floating-point instructions per second—concurrent processing is unavoidable. And now, with the advent of LSI technology, it is economically feasible to construct a concurrent processing system by interconnecting hundreds—even thousands—of off-the-shelf processors and memory modules.

A basic concurrent processing system is shown in Figure 1. Processes, generated by compiling and partitioning a user's program, are assigned to individual processors, and an interconnection network implements interprocess communication. A general model of the hardware system is shown in Figure 2. The interconnection network facilitates communication not only among the n processors and the m memory modules but also between the processors and memory modules.

Many interconnection networks have been reviewed in other surveys.[2-9] In this article we consider interconnection networks from a practical design viewpoint. We examine design decisions that are essential in choosing a cost-effective communication network, survey the various topologies and communication protocols, and discuss connection issues related to concurrent processing.

Design decisions

In selecting the architecture of an interconnection network, four design decisions can be identified.[10] They concern operation mode, control strategy, switching method, and network topology.

Reprinted from *IEEE Computer*, pp. 12–27, Dec. 1981.

Operation mode. Two types of communication can be identified: synchronous and asynchronous. Synchronous communication is needed for processing in which communication paths are established synchronously for either a data manipulating function[11] or a data/instruction broadcast. Asynchronous communication is needed for multiprocessing in which connection requests are issued dynamically. A system may also be designed to facilitate both synchronous and asynchronous processing. Therefore, typical operation modes of interconnection networks can be classified into three categories: synchronous, asnychronous, and combined.

Control strategy. A typical interconnection network consists of a number of switching elements and interconnecting links. Interconnection functions are realized by properly setting control of the switching elements. The control-setting function can be managed by a centralized controller or by the individual switching element. The latter strategy is called distributed control; the first strategy is called centralized control.

Switching methodology. The two major switching methodologies are circuit switching and packet switching. In circuit switching, a physical path is actually established between a source and a destination. In packet switching, data is put in a packet and routed through the interconnection network without establishing a physical connection path. In general, circuit switching is much more suitable for bulk data transmission, and packet switching is more efficient for short data messages. Another option, integrated switching, includes capabilities of both circuit switching and packet switching. Therefore, three switching methodologies can be identified: circuit switching, packet switching, and integrated switching.

Network topology. A network can be depicted by a graph in which nodes represent switching points and edges represent communication links. The topologies tend to be regular and can be grouped into two categories: static and dynamic. In a static topology, links between two processors are passive and dedicated buses cannot be reconfigured for direct connections to other processors. On the other hand, links in the dynamic category can be reconfigured by setting the network's active switching elements.

The cross product of the set of categories in each design decision—{operation mode} × {control strategy} × {switching methodology} × {network topology}—represents a space of interconnection networks. Obviously, the cross product contains some uninteresting cases, but a network designer can obtain a meaningful subspace by exercising a practical view of engineering technology.

Topologies

Network topology is a key factor in determining a suitable architectural structure, and many topologies have been considered for telephone switching connections.[12] Here, we review those proposed or used for connections in tightly coupled multiple-processor systems (see Figure 3).

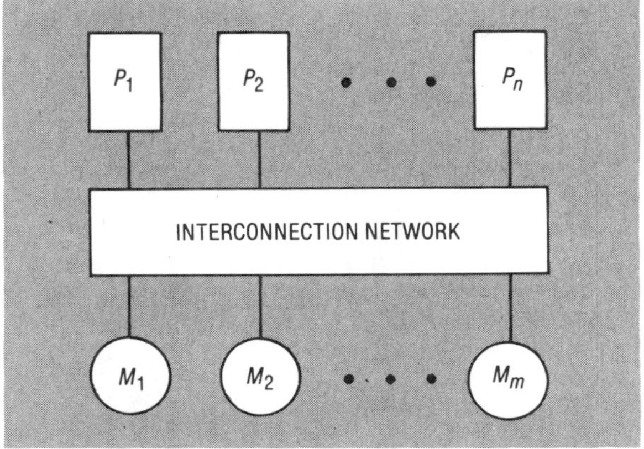

Figure 2. Hardware model of concurrent processing systems.

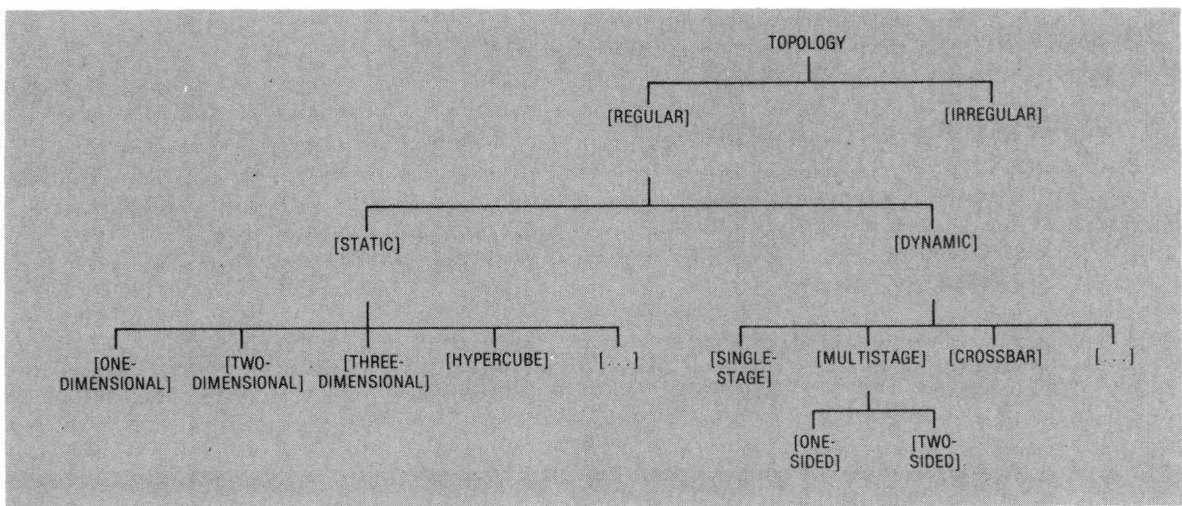

Figure 3. Topologies of interconnection networks.

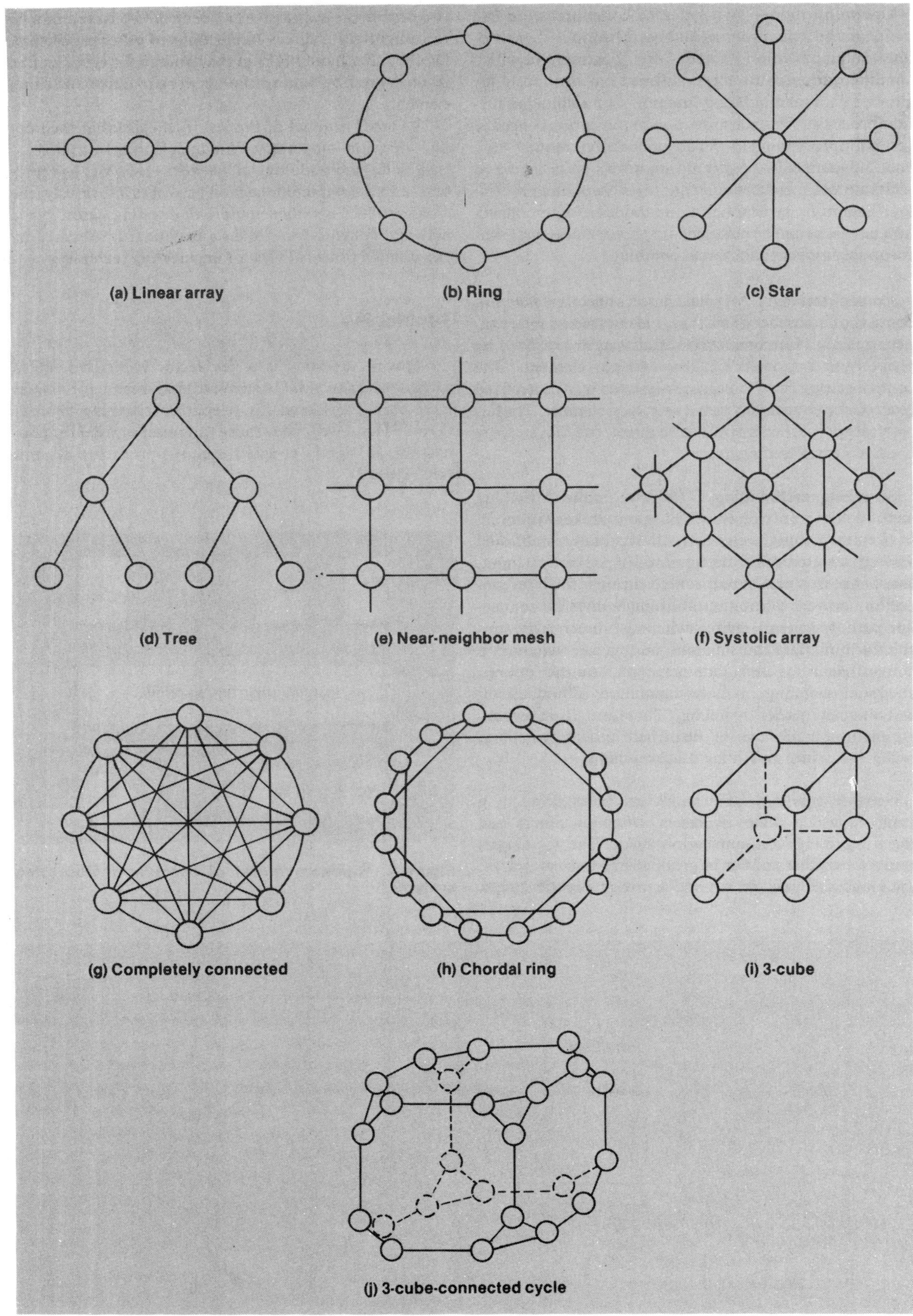

Figure 4. Examples of static network toplogies: (a) one dimensional; (b-f) two dimensional; and (g-j) three dimensional.

Static. Topologies in the static category can be classified according to dimensions required for layout —specifically, one-dimensional, two-dimensional, three-dimensional, and hypercube as shown in Figure 3. Examples of one-dimensional topologies include the linear array used for some pipeline architectures (Figure 4a).[13] Two-dimensional topologies include the ring,[14,15] star,[16] tree,[17] near-neighbor mesh,[18] and systolic array.[13] Examples are shown in Figure 4b-f. Three-dimensional topologies include the completely connected,[19] chordal ring,[20] 3-cube,[21] and 3-cube-connected-cycle[22] networks depicted in Figure 4g-j. A *D*-dimensional, *W*-wide hypercube contains *W* nodes in each dimension, and there is a connection to a node in each dimension. The near-neighbor mesh and the 3-cube are actually two- and three-dimensional hypercubes, respectively. The cube-connected-cycle is a deviation of the hypercube. For example, the 3-cube-connected-cycle shown in Figure 4j is obtained by replacing each node of the 3-cube by a 3-node cycle. Each node in the cycle is connected to the corresponding node in another cycle.

Dynamic. There are three topological classes in the dynamic category: single-stage, multistage, and crossbar (see Figure 5).

Single-stage. A single-stage network is composed of a stage of switching elements cascaded to a link connection pattern. The shuffle-exchange network[23] is a single-stage network based on a perfect-shuffle connection cascaded to a stage of switching elements as shown in Figure 5a. The single-stage network is also called a recirculating network because data items may have to recirculate through the single stage several times before reaching their final destination.

Multistage. A multistage network consists of more than one stage of switching elements and is usually capa-

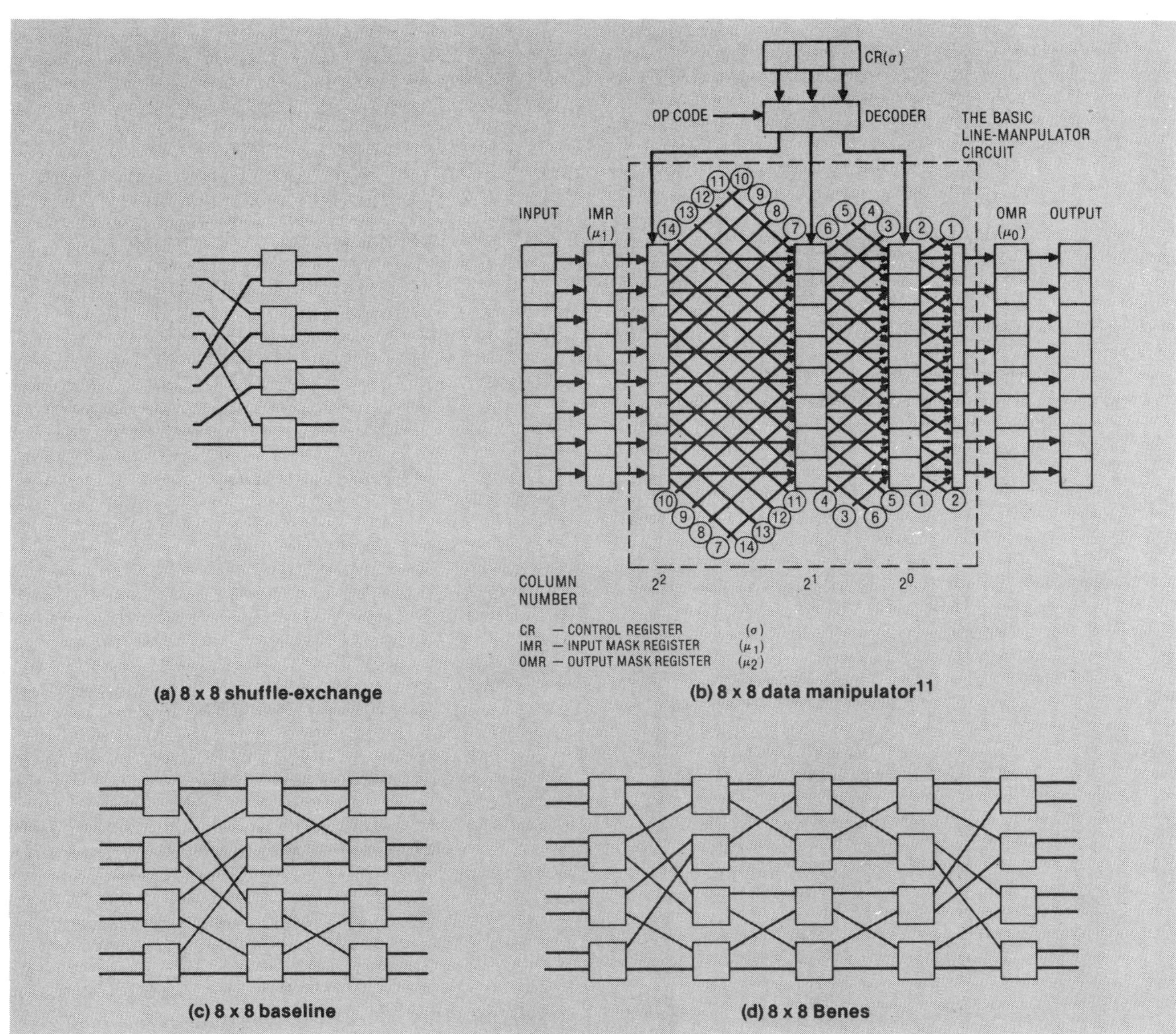

Figure 5. Examples of dynamic network topologies: (a) single stage; (b-i) multistage; and (j) crossbar. (Cont'd on p. 28.)

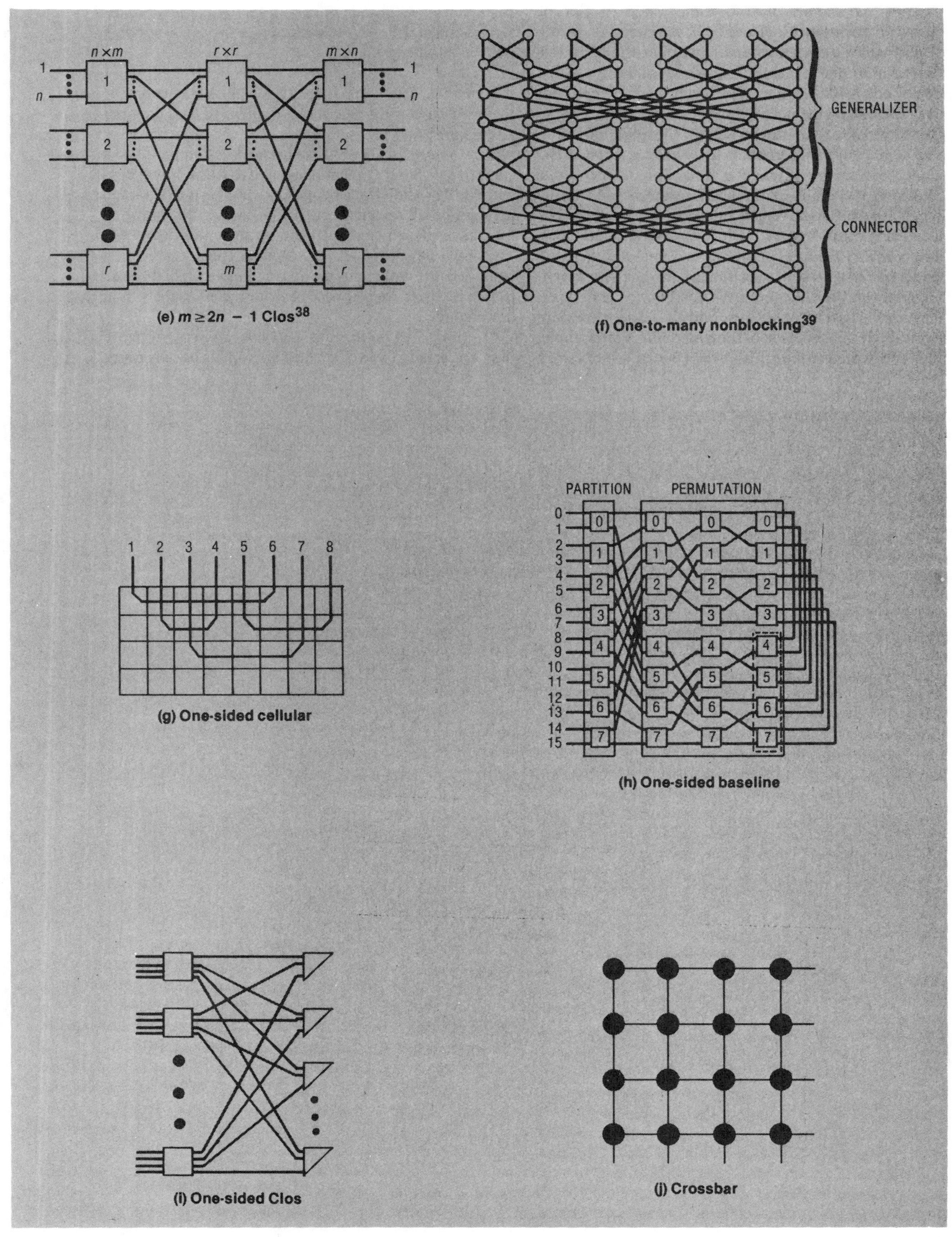

(e) $m \geq 2n - 1$ Clos[38]

(f) One-to-many nonblocking[39]

(g) One-sided cellular

(h) One-sided baseline

(i) One-sided Clos

(j) Crossbar

Figure 5 (cont'd from p.27). Examples of multistage and crossbar (j) dynamic network topologies.

ble of connecting an arbitrary input terminal to an arbitrary output terminal. Multistage networks can be one-sided or two-sided. The one-sided networks, sometimes called full switches, have input-output ports on the same side. The two-sided multistage networks, which usually have an input side and an output side, can be divided into three classes: blocking, rearrangeable, and nonblocking.

In blocking networks, simultaneous connections of more than one terminal pair may result in conflicts in the use of network communication links. Examples of this type of network, which has been extensively investigated, include data manipulator,[24] baseline,[25,26] SW banyan,[27] omega,[28] flip,[29] indirect binary *n*-cube,[30] and delta.[31] A topological equivalence relationship has been established for this class of networks in terms of the baseline network.[25,26] A data manipulator and a baseline network are shown in Figure 5b and 5c.

A network is called a rearrangeable nonblocking network if it can perform all possible connections between inputs and outputs by rearranging its existing connections so that a connection path for a new input-output pair can always be established. A well-defined network, the Benes network[12] shown in Figure 5d, belongs to this class. The Benes rearrangeable network topology has been extensively studied for use in synchronous data permutation[32-35] and asynchronous interprocessor communication.[36,37]

A network which can handle all possible connections without blocking is called a nonblocking network. Two cases have been considered in the literature. In the first case, the Clos network[38] shown in Figure 5e, a one-to-one connection is made between an input and an output. The other case considers one-to-many connections.[39] Here, a generalized-connection network topology is generated to pass any of the N^N mapping of inputs onto outputs where N is the number of inputs or outputs (see Figure 5f). In a one-sided network (or full switch), one-to-one connection is possible between all pairs of terminals.[40,41] A cellular implementation, a base-line topology construction, and a Clos construction are shown in Figure 5g-i.

Crossbar. In a crossbar switch every input port can be connected to a free output port without blocking. Figure 5j shows a schematic which is similar to one used in C.mmp.[42] A crossbar switch called a versatile line manipulator has also been designed and implemented.[43,44]

Communication protocols

The switching methodology and the control strategy are implemented in switching elements (or switching points) according to required communication protocols. The communication protocols can be viewed on two levels. The first level concerns switching control algorithms which generate necessary control settings on switching elements to ensure reliable data routings from source to destination. The first-level protocols are referred to as routing techniques here. The second level is concerned with the link control procedure that provides the handshaking process among switching points. The handshaking process is a basic function implemented by switching elements.

Routing techniques. The routing techniques depend on the network topology and the operation mode used. More or less, each multiple-processor system needs a routing algorithm. Here, we use several well-defined routing algorithms for examples.

Near-neighbor mesh. Bitonic sort has been adapted by several authors[45-47] for the routing of an $n \times n$ mesh-connected, single instruction-multiple data stream system. The procedure developed by Nassimi[47] is as follows:

Procedure SORT (n,n)
1) K ← S ← 1
2) **While** K < n **do**
   a) consider the n × n processor array as composed of many adjacent K × 2K subarrays
   b) **do** in parallel for each K × 2K array HORIZONTAL_MERGE(K, 2K)
   c) S ← S + 1
   d) Consider the n × n processor array as composed of many adjacent 2K × 2K subarrays
   e) **do** in parallel for each 2K × 2K subarray VERTICAL_MERGE(2K, 2K)
   f) S ← S + 1; K ← 2 • K
end
end SORT

The HORIZONTAL_MERGE sorts a bitonic sequence arranged in two arrays with the increasing sequence on the left array and the decreasing sequence on the right array, or vice versa. Similarly, the VERTICAL_MERGE sorts a bitonic sequence arranged in two arrays with the increasing sequence on the upper array and the decreasing sequence on the lower array, or vice versa. A complete example of sorting a 4 × 4 array is shown in Figure 6. The order into which a subarray gets sorted is determined by the SIGN function, "+" and "−", used during a comparison-interchange where "+" is for nondecreasing order and "−" is for nonincreasing order. In Figure 6, the initial values given go through an HM sort on two 1 × 1 arrays, a VM sort on two 1 × 2 arrays, an HM sort on two 2 × 2 arrays, and finally a VM sort on two 2 × 4 arrays.

Shuffle-exchange network. Both centralized and distributed routings have been worked out for the shuffle-exchange network. It has been shown that the shuffle-exchange network can realize an arbitrary permutation in $3(\log_2 N) - 1$ passes where N is the network size.[48] An example is shown in Figure 7 for the following permutation:

$$p = \begin{pmatrix} 0 & 1 & 2 & 3 & 4 & 5 & 6 & 7 & 8 & 9 & 10 & 11 & 12 & 13 & 14 & 15 \\ 14 & 12 & 5 & 7 & 15 & 8 & 9 & 13 & 4 & 3 & 10 & 6 & 1 & 0 & 2 & 11 \end{pmatrix}$$

The control setting developed consists of three matrices, $\overline{F}$, $\overline{S}$, and $\overline{T}$. Among these three control matrices, $\overline{S}$ is independent of the permutation and $\overline{F}$ and $\overline{T}$ are modified matrices obtained by performing some prescribed operations on the control matrix for the Benes binary network. The detailed transformation is shown in Wu and Feng.[48] The shuffle-exchange network can also be constructed to adapt to a distributed control scheme. The construction

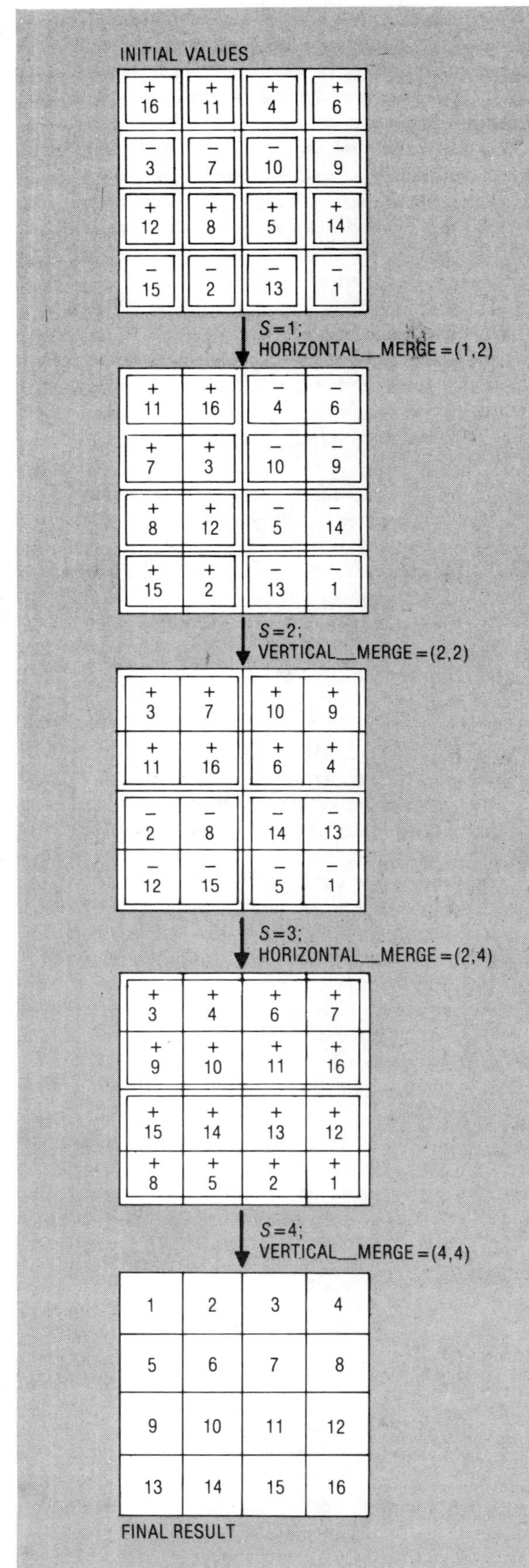

Figure 6. A complete example of sorting a 4 x 4 array.

can be considered as a sorting network, and the binary codes of the destination names are used as the values to be sorted.[23,49] Figure 8 illustrates an example for 2^n elements where $n = 4$. Each of the n^2 steps in this scheme consists of a perfect-shuffle followed by simultaneous operations performed on 2^{n-1} pairs of adjacent elements. Each of the latter operations is either "0" (no operation, straight connection), "+" (comparator module which sends the larger value to the lower link), or "−" (a reverse comparator module). The sorting proceeds in n stages of n steps each: during stage s, for $s \leq n$, we do $n-s$ steps in which all operations are "0", followed by s steps in which the operations consist alternately of 2^t "+" followed by 2^t "−" for $t = 1, 2, \ldots, s$. During the last stage, all operations are "+".

Data manipulator. A centralized control scheme is designed for implementing data manipulating functions such as permuting, replicating, spacing, masking, and complementing.[11] To implement a data manipulating function, proper control lines of the six groups (U_1^{2i}, U_2^{2i}, H_1^{2i}, H_2^{2i}, D_1^{2i}, D_2^{2i}) in each column must be properly set through the use of the control register and the associated decoder. A "duplicate spaced substrings down" operation is illustrated in Figure 9. The two substrings to be duplicated are *AB* and *EF*. For this operation the control line groups D_1^{2i} and H_1^{2i} or H_1^{2i} and H_2^{2i} are activated, depending on whether the control bit is 1 or 0 as determined by substring length. In this example, the substring is 2; thus, only the control bit for column 2^1 has a value of 1, all others are 0's. Thus, in columns 2^2 and 2^0, H_1^{2i} and H_2^{2i} are activated, and in column 2^1, D_1^{2i} and H_1^{2i} are activated. With this control pattern, the substrings can be generated at the output register.

A distributed control scheme has also been developed by McMillen and Siegel.[50] It uses a routing tag which contains $2n$ bits and is of the form $F = (f_{2n-1} \cdots f_{n+1} f_n f_{n-1} \cdots f_1 f_0)$. The n low-order bits represent the magnitudes of the route, and the n high-order bits represent the sign corresponding to the magnitudes. In stage i, a given switching element examines bits i and $n+i$ of the routing tag. If $f_i = 0$, the straight link is used, regardless of the value of f_{n+i}. If $f_i = 1$, bit $n+i$ is examined. If $f_{n+i} = 0$, the $+2^i$ link is used; if $f_{n+i} = 1$, the -2^i link is used. The source processor generates its own routing tag. For example, in a data manipulator of $N = 2^4$, if the source is 13 and the destination is 6, one possible value for F is 00000111. The path traversed is straight, $+2^2$, $+2^1$, $+2^0$. Multiple paths exist between a source-destination pair. For example, an alternative routing tag from source 13 to destination 6 is (0001 1001). The example is shown in Figure 10. A general rule to calculate the routing tag is shown as

$$D = S + (-1)^{f_{2n-1}} (f_n 2^{n-1}) + (-1)^{f_{2n-2}} (f_{n-1} 2^{n-2}) + \ldots (-1)^{f_n} (f_0 2^0)$$

where S and D are the addresses of the source and the destination, respectively.

Baseline network. Routing techniques for baseline networks described here are also useful for other topological-

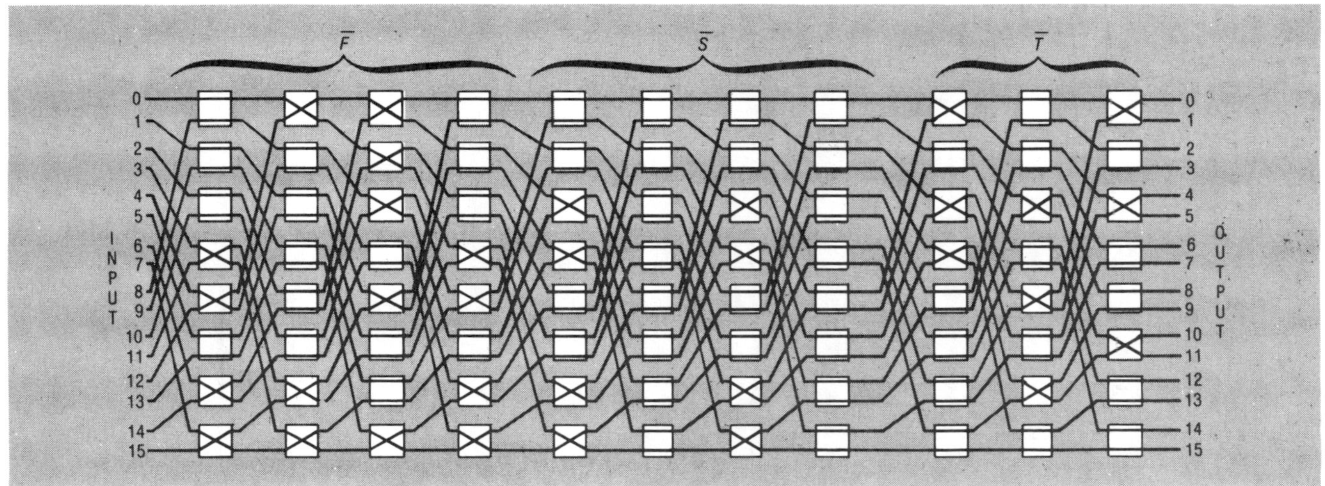

Figure 7. An example for universal realization of permutations.[48]

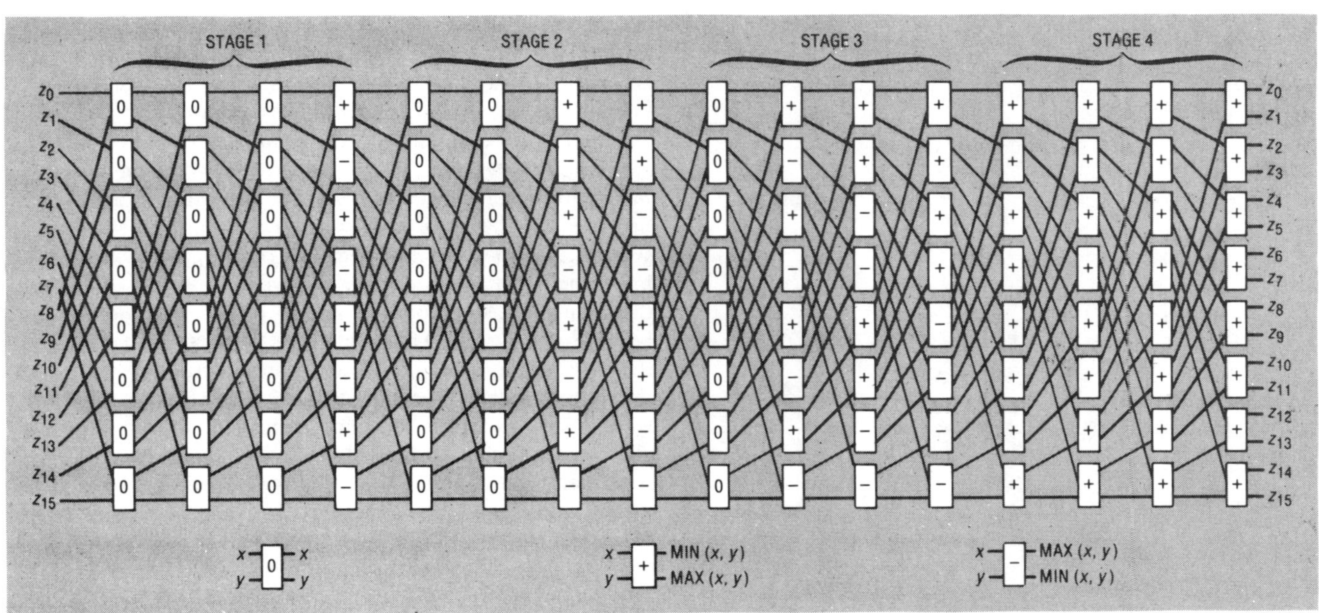

Figure 8. Sorting with shuffle-exchange. (Adapted from *The Art of Computer Programming, Vol. 3: Sorting and Searching* by D. E. Knuth; Addison-Wesley, Reading, Mass., © 1973.)

ly equivalent blocking multistage networks.[25] Basically, two types of routing are available: recursive routing and destination tag routing.[25,28,51] The recursive routing algorithm determines the control pattern according to permutation names. For some permutation, useful in parallel processing, the control pattern can be calculated recursively on the fly as the data pass through the network. Six categories of such permutations have been identified. For our purpose, we describe one here and show the recursive routing algorithm. The flip permutation function[29] is described as follows:

$$F_k^{(n)}\ (0 \le k < 2^n):\ p(X^r \oplus k) = X \text{ and } p(X \oplus k) = X^r$$

where X^r is the number whose binary representation is the reverse of X. Let $k = 2k^1 + k_0$ and $[L;R]$ denote the cascaded matrix whose left part and right part are L and R, respectively. Also let $V^{(n-1)}(b)$ be the 2^{n-1} bit vector whose components are all equal to b. The control pattern $K^{(n)}$ of the flip function can then be expressed in terms of the following recursive formula:

$$K^{(n)}(F_k^{(n)}) = [V^{(n-1)}(k_0); K^{(n-1)}(F_{k'}^{(n)})],$$

where

$$K^{(1)}(F_k^{(n)}) = [V^{(n-1)}(k)].$$

For example, assuming

$$p = \begin{pmatrix} 0 & 1 & 2 & 3 & 4 & 5 & 6 & 7 \\ 1 & 5 & 3 & 7 & 0 & 4 & 2 & 6 \end{pmatrix}$$

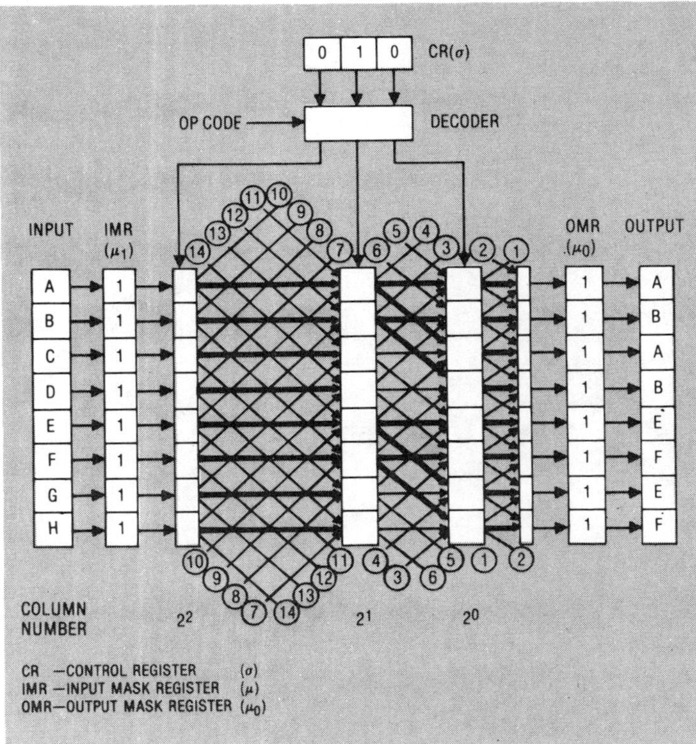

Figure 9. Duplicate spaced substring down on data manipulator.[11]

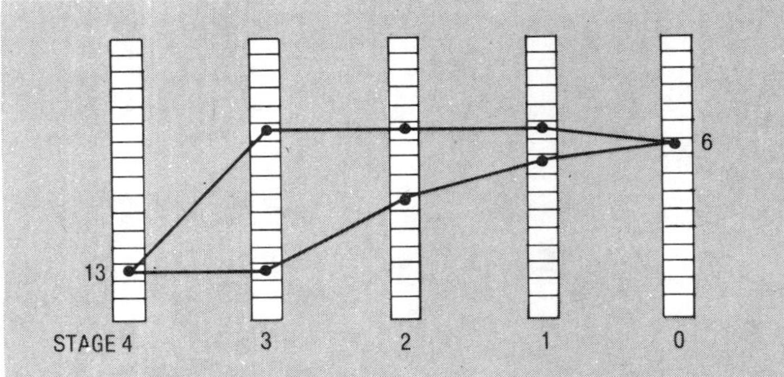

Figure 10. Distributed routing on the data manipulator.

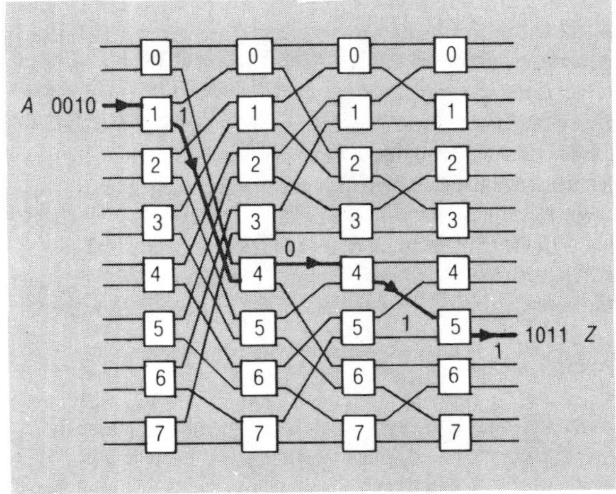

Figure 11. Distributed routing on a baseline network.

p can be described by

$$F_4^{(3)}: p(X^r \oplus 4) = X.$$

Accordingly, we have

$$K^{(3)}(F_4^{(3)}) = [V^2(0);\ V^{(2)}(0);\ V^{(2)}(1)].$$

Hence

$$K^{(3)}(p) = \begin{bmatrix} 0 & 0 & 1 \\ 0 & 0 & 1 \\ 0 & 0 & 1 \\ 0 & 0 & 1 \end{bmatrix}$$

The destination tag routing uses the binary representation of the destination as a routing tag. Let the source terminal link and destination terminal link be A and Z, respectively. Also, let the binary representation of Z be $z_{n-1}z_{n-2} \ldots z_0$. Starting at A, the first node to which A is connected is set to switch A to the upper link if $z_{n-1} = 0$ or the lower link if $z_{n-1} = 1$. The second node in the path is again set to switch A to the upper link if $z_{n-2} = 0$ or the lower link if $z_{n-2} = 1$. This scheme is continued until we get the proper destination. For example, in Figure 11, $A = 2$ and $Z = 11$ (i.e., $z_3z_2z_1z_0 = 1011$). Switching element 1 of the left-most stage switches A to the lower link because $z_3 = 1$. At the next stage, switching element 4 switches A to the upper link because $z_2 = 0$. Again, switching element 4 in the third stage and switching element 5 in the right-most stage both switch A to the lower links because $z_1 = z_0 = 1$. If we consider Z as the source and A as the destination, using the binary representation of A as the routing tag and repeating the same routing procedure will lead us to choose the same path. This routing tag algorithm will connect the only path available between a source and a destination and is extremely suitable for a distributed control scheme. A conflict resolution scheme[25] has also been developed for implementing destination tag routing in terms of centralized control.

Benes network. Sequential routing algorithms[34,52] need $O(N \log N)$ steps where N is the network size. Many researchers have worked toward improving this time complexity in terms of parallel processing technique,[53] heuristic method,[37] or recursive formula.[35] Here, we demonstrate the very basic routing algorithm, called the looping algorithm. The basic principle, in terms of the permutation to be realized by the Benes binary network shown in Figure 5d, is

$$p = \begin{pmatrix} 0 & 1 & 2 & 3 & 4 & 5 & 6 & 7 \\ 3 & 7 & 4 & 0 & 2 & 6 & 1 & 5 \end{pmatrix}$$

The loop algorithm starts recording the permutation, p, as shown in Figure 12. The two output numbers of a switching element in the output stage are shown in the same column, and the two input numbers of a switching element in the input stage are shown in the same row. We then choose an arbitrary entry in the chart as a starting point. For example, electing to start at row 23 and column

01, we then look for a same-row or column entry to form a loop and, in Figure 12, choose row 23 and column 45. The process continues until we obtain a loop by re-entering row 23 and column 01. The loop's member entries are then assigned "*a*" and "*b*" alternately. The second loop can be formed in the same way. Then, we assign input and output lines named "*a*" to subnetwork *a* and those named "*b*" to subnetwork *b*. The control of the input and output switching elements must be set as depicted in Figure 13. This looping algorithm can be applied recursively to the two subnetworks.

Construction of interconnection networks. Interconnection networks are usually designed so they can be constructed of a single type of modular building block called a switching element. The switching element realizes communication protocols which specify the control strategy and the switching methodology.

The logic design of switching elements has been explored in many projects,[54-56] including recent LSI implementations.[10,57] Here, we describe in more detail three designs that have been implemented and are operational.

Flip network 2 × 2 switching element. The flip network uses centralized control and circuit switching.[29] The 2 × 2 switching element can be set by a control line into a direct-connection or crossed-connection state. Assume that I_0, I_1, O_0, O_1, and C represent the two inputs, the two outputs, and the switching element control. The switching element's output function can be expressed as follows:

$$O_0 = \overline{C}I_0 + C \cdot I_1, \text{and}$$

$$O_1 = \overline{C}I_1 + C \cdot I_0$$

where $C=0$ means straight connection and $C=1$ crossed connection (see Figure 14).

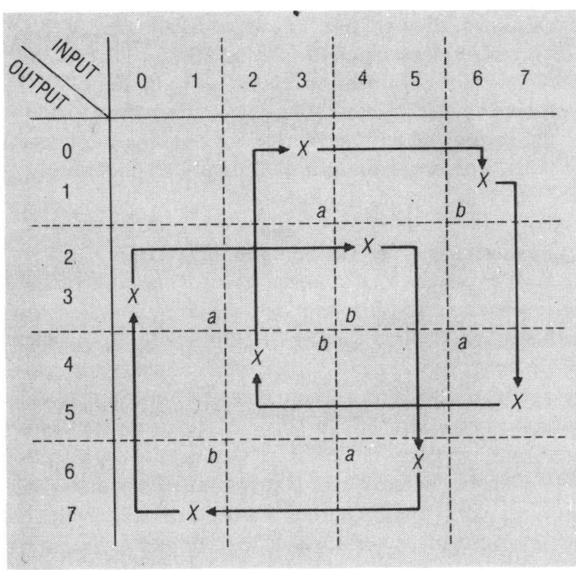

Figure 12. An example of the looping algorithm.

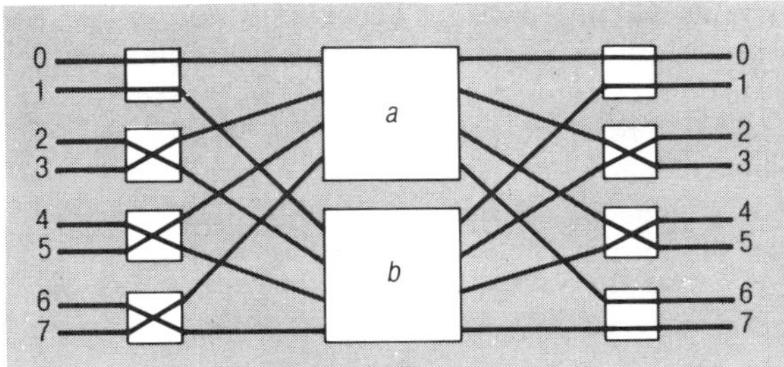

Figure 13. Control setting result from the first iteration of the looping algorithm.

Dimond 2 × 2 switching element. A switching element with two input and output ports, called Dimond for dual interconnection modular network device,[58] allows modular construction of interconnection networks. A packet of messages (containing routing information) arriving at a Dimond is switched to a designated output port, where it is stored in a register. Figure 15 shows an implementation of Dimond which requires one control clock for all interconnected switching elements. The central clock has two phases. In the first clock phase, it is determined which inputs have to be copied into which registers. The copy allowances so determined are stored in four flip-flops: C_{00}, C_{01}, C_{10}, and C_{11} (C_{01} is the allowance for copying in_0 into reg_1). In addition, output signals of copy acknowledgments ($cack_0$ and $cack_1$), internal control signals ($cross_0$, $fill_0$, and $fill_1$) are generated. More precisely, we have the following:

$$C_{00} = creq_0 \cdot \overline{des_0} \cdot \overline{stat_0} \cdot (\overline{creq_1} + des_1 +, \overline{prio}) \;;$$

$$C_{01} = creq_0 \cdot des_0 \cdot \overline{stat_1} \cdot (\overline{creq_1} + \overline{des_1} + \overline{prio}) \;;$$

$$C_{10} = creq_1 \cdot \overline{des_1} \cdot \overline{stat_0} \cdot (\overline{creq_0} + des_0 + prio) \;;$$

$$C_{11} = creq_1 \cdot des_1 \cdot \overline{stat_1} \cdot (\overline{creq_0} + \overline{des_0} + prio) \;;$$

$$Cack_0 = C_{00} + C_{01} \;;$$

$$Cack_1 = C_{10} + C_{11} \;;$$

$$Cross = C_{00} + C_{11} \;;$$

$$Fill_0 = C_{00} + C_{10} \;;$$

$$Fill_1 = C_{01} + C_{11} \;;$$

where *prio* is the priority line indicating the index (0,1) of the input served first in the event of conflict, and des_0 and des_1 are destination lines for in_0 and in_1. In the second clock phase, two actions are performed concurrently. Inputs are copied into the output register, if required, and

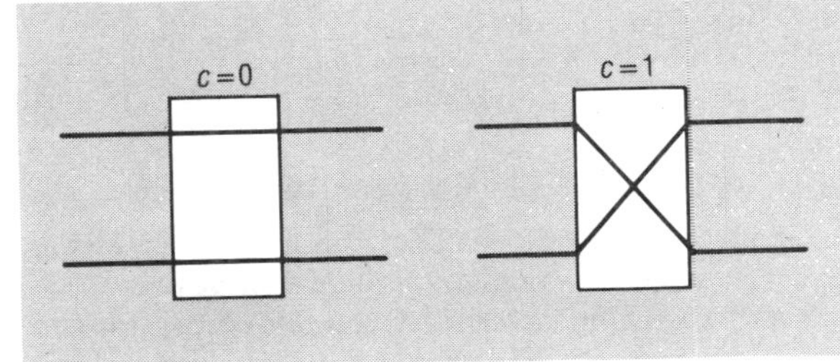

Figure 14. A 2 x 2 switching element.

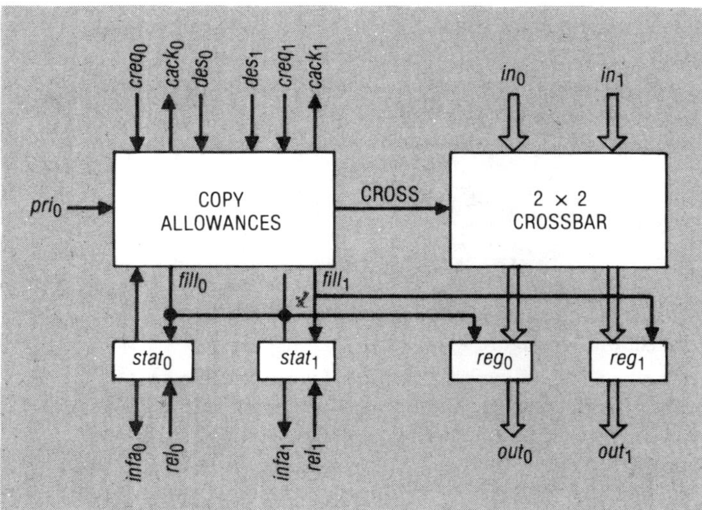

Figure 15. A 2 x 2 dual interconnecting modular network device—Dimond[58]—for packet switching.

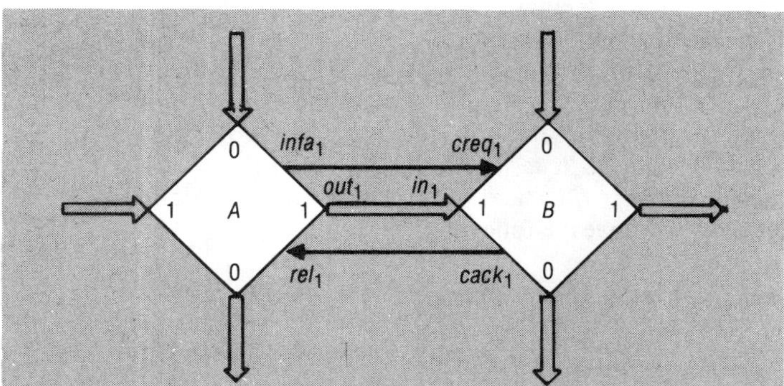

Figure 16. Connecting two Dimonds.[58]

the status flip-flops, $stat_0$ and $stat_1$ (status of reg_0 and reg_1, respectively) are adapted. Precisely, we have the following:

$$Fill_0 \rightarrow reg_0 = cross \cdot in_0 + \overline{cross} \cdot in_1 \quad ;$$

$$Fill_1 \rightarrow reg_1 = \overline{cross} \cdot in_0 + cross \cdot in_1 \quad ;$$

$$Fill_0 \cdot rel_0 \rightarrow stat_0 = 1 \quad ;$$
$$rel_0 \rightarrow stat_0 = 0 \quad ;$$

$$Fill_1 \cdot \overline{rel_1} \rightarrow stat_1 = 1 \quad ;$$
$$rel_1 \rightarrow stat_1 = 0 \quad .$$

The information-available lines are connected to the status flip-flops:

$$infa_0 = stat_0 \quad ;$$
$$infa_1 = stat_1 \quad .$$

The interconnection of two Dimonds is shown in Figure 16, which depicts the relation of handshaking lines.

64 × 64 switching element. A centralized-control and circuit-switching 64 × 64 versatile data manipulator[11] (see Figure 17) is operating in conjunction with the Staran computer at the Rome Air Development Center.[44] The data manipulator operates under the control of the Staran computer's parallel input-output unit. The contents of the input and output masks, of the address control register, and of the input and output control registers, as well as the data to be manipulated, are entered via the 256-bit wide PIO buffer interface. The manipulated data leave the data manipulator via the same interface. The data manipulator's instruction repertoire allows one to load the various address registers and masks and to start and stop data manipulation. Self-test is performed by loading address and input-data registers, allowing verification of correct operation without assistance from the Staran computer. There are 64 × 64 cells in the basic crossbar circuit. The output gate of cell (i,j) is controlled by the ith address control register through a decoder. The decoder has 64 outputs to control the 64 output gates in a basic-crossbar-circuit row.

Connection issues for concurrent processing

Two approaches—array processing and multiprocessing—have been tried to provide processing concurrency. Since array processors, which consist of multiple processing elements and parallel memory modules under one control unit, can handle single instructions and multiple data streams, they are also known as SIMD computers. Existing examples include Illiac IV and Staran. An overall SIMD machine organization[59] is shown in Figure 18. The N processing elements, or PEs, are connected by two interconnection networks to the M parallel memory modules. The control unit in the center provides control over PEs and memory modules.

Array processors allow explicit expression of parallelism in user programs. The compiler detects the parallelism and generates object code suitable for execution in the multiple processing elements and the control unit. Program segments which cannot be converted into parallel executable forms are executed in the control unit; program segments which can be converted into parallel executable forms are sent to the PEs and executed synchronously on data fetched from parallel memory modules under the control of the control unit. To enable synchronous manipulation in the PEs, the data are permuted and arranged in vector form. Thus, to run a program more efficiently on an array processor, one must develop a technique for vectorizing the program (or algorithm). The interconnection network plays a major role in vectorization.

The second approach for concurrent processing uses multiprocessing. The multiprocessor can handle multiple instructions and multiple data streams and hence is called an MIMD processor. Examples of the MIMD architecture include HEP,[60] data flow processor,[61] and flow model processor.[62] A configuration of MIMD architecture[62] is shown in Figure 19. The N processing elements are connected to the M memory modules by an interconnection network. The activities are coordinated by the coordinator. Unlike the control unit in an array processor, the coordinator does not execute object code; it only implements the synchronization of processes and

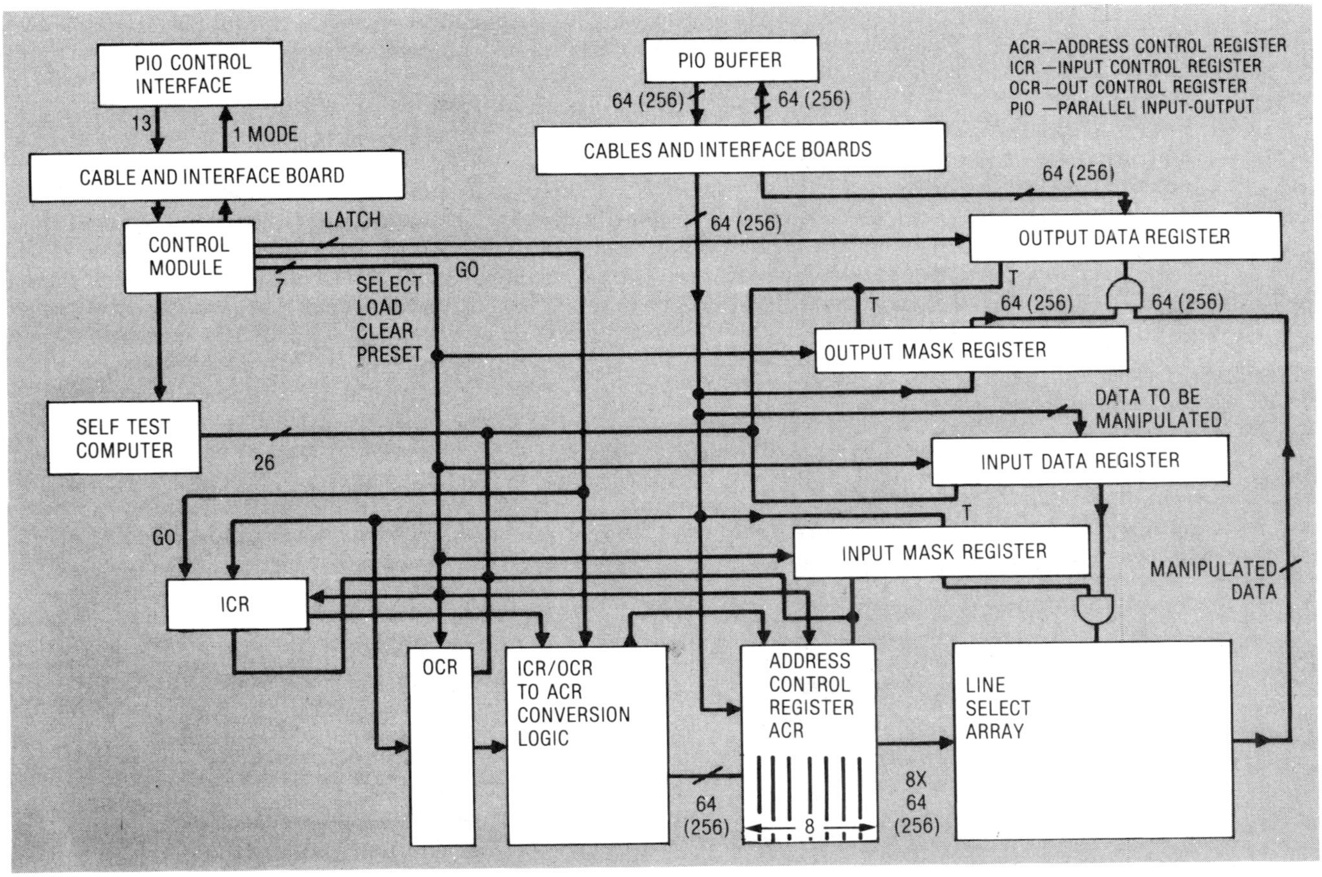

Figure 17. Block diagram of a versatile data manipulator.

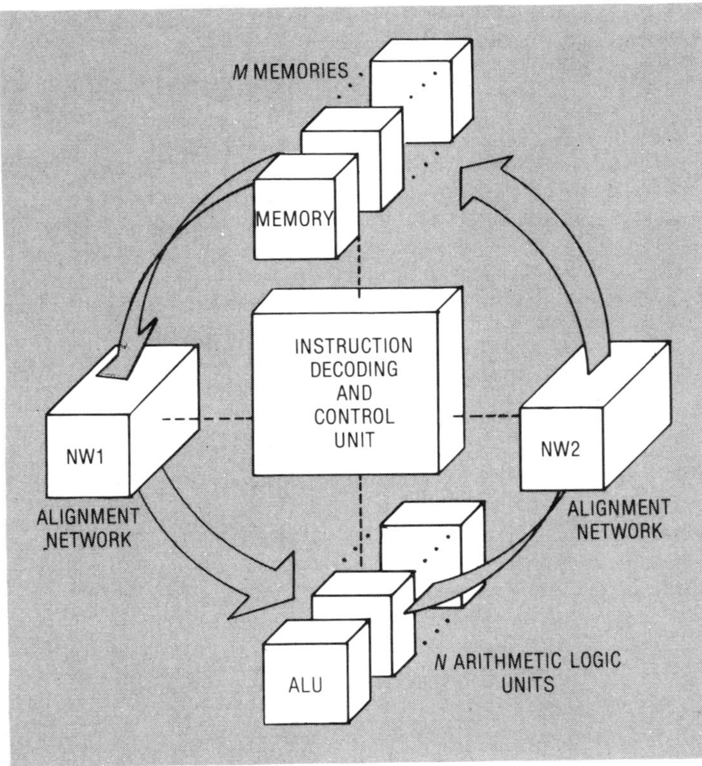

Figure 18. SIMD model.[59]

smooths out the execution sequence. Again, the compiler must be designed to partition a computation task and assign each piece to individual processing elements. Effective partitioning and assignment are essential for efficient multiprocessing. The criterion is to match memory bandwidth with the processor processing load, and the interconnection network is a critical factor in this matching.

Below, we address some problems and results regarding the role of the interconnection network in concurrent processing.

Combinatorial capability. In array processing, data are often stored in parallel memory modules in skewed forms that allow a vector of data to be fetched without conflict.[63-65] However, the fetched data must be realigned in prescribed order before they can be sent to individual PEs for processing. This alignment is implemented by permutation functions of the interconnection network, which also realigns data generated by individual PEs into skewed form for storage in the memory modules.

In the computer architecture project, one should question whether the interconnection network chosen can efficiently perform the alignment. The rearrangeable network and the nonblocking network can realize every permutation function, but using these networks for alignment requires considerable effort to calculate control settings. A recursive routing mechanism has been provided for a few families of permutations needed for parallel processing[35]; however, the problem remains for the realization

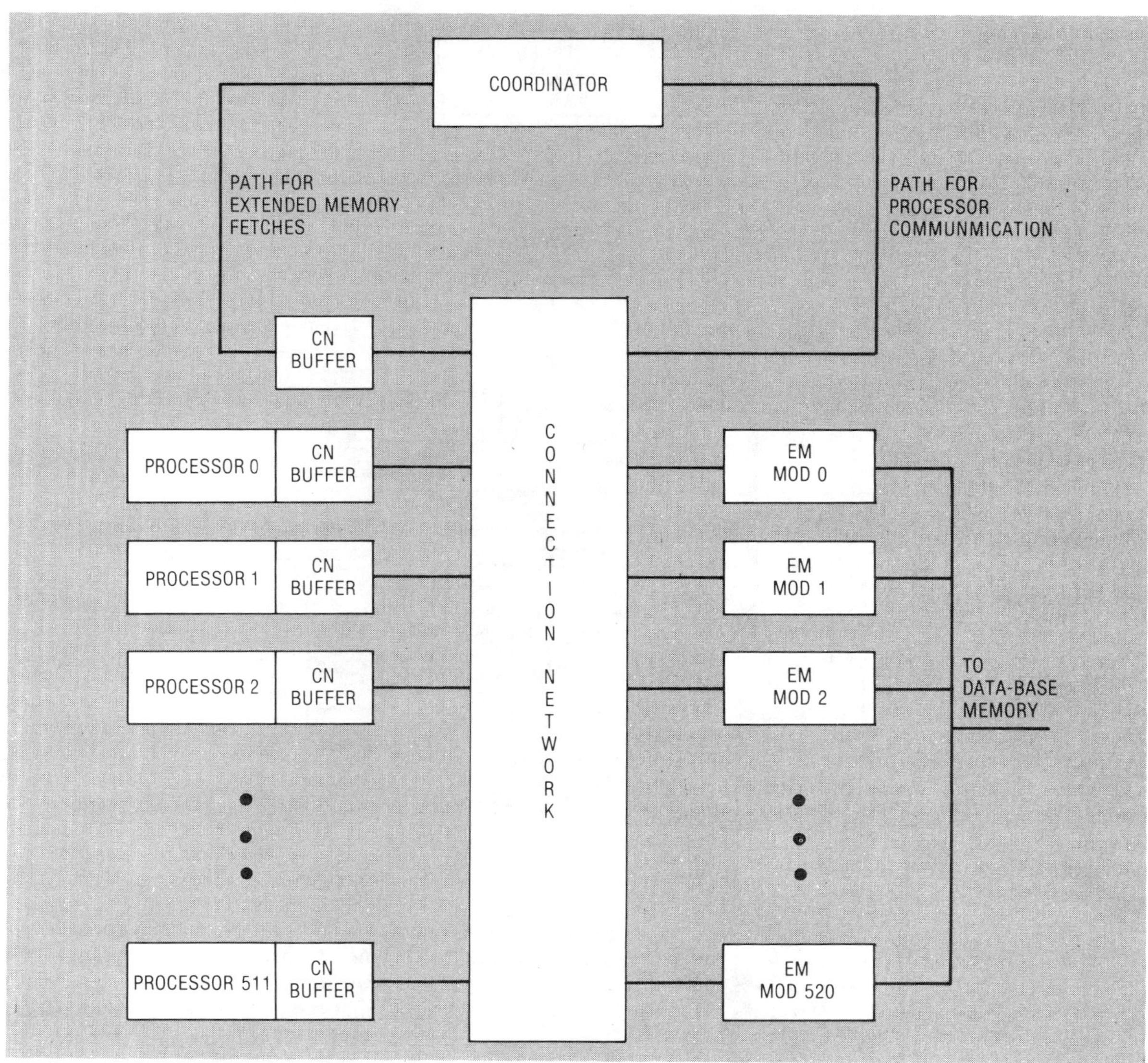

Figure 19. MIMD model.

of general permutations. Many articles[45,51,66,67] concentrating on the permutation capabilities of single-stage networks and blocking multistage networks have shown that these networks cannot realize arbitrary permutations in a single pass. Recent results show that the baseline network can realize arbitrary permutations in just two passes[51] while other blocking multistage networks, such as the omega network, need at least three passes.[66] As mentioned previously, the shuffle-exchange network can realize arbitrary permutations in $3(\log_2 N) - 1$ passes where N is the network size.[48]

Task assignments and reconfiguration. Consider a parallel program segment using M memory modules and N processing elements. During execution, data is usually transferred from memory modules to processing elements or vice versa. It is also necessary to transfer data among processing elements for data sharing and synchronization. Simultaneous data transfers through the interconnection network, which implements the transfers, may result in contention for communication links and switching elements. In case of conflict, some of the data transfers must be deferred; consequently, throughput decreases because the processing elements which need the deferred data cannot proceed as originally expected. To minimize delays caused by communication conflicts, program codes must be assigned to proper processing elements and data assigned to proper memory modules. The assignment of data to memory modules, called mapping,[68] has recently been extended to include assignment of program modules to processing elements.[69]

A configuration concept has been proposed to better use the interconnection network.[51] Under this concept, a network is just a configuration of another one in the same, topologically equivalent class.[25] To configure a permutation function as an interconnection network, we can assign input/output link names in a way that realizes the permutation function in one conflict-free pass. The problem of assigning logical names that realize various permutation functions without conflicts is called a reconfiguration problem. It has been shown that, through the reconfiguration process, the baseline network can realize every permutation in one pass without conflicts.[69] This implies that concurrent processing throughput could be enhanced by proper assignment of tasks to processing elements and data to memory modules.

Partitioning. In partitioning—that is, dividing the network into independent subnetworks of different sizes—each subnetwork must have all the interconnection capabilities of a complete network of the same type and size. Hence, with a partitionable network, a system can support multiple SIMD machines. By dynamically reconfiguring the system into independent SIMD machines and properly assigning tasks to each partition, we can use resources more efficiently.

Several authors have noted the importance of partitioning.[30] One recent study[70] shows that single-stage networks, such as the shuffle-exchange and Illiac networks, cannot be partitioned into independent subnetworks, but blocking multistage networks, such as the baseline and data manipulator, can be partitioned.

Bandwidth of interconnection networks. The bandwidth can be defined as the expected number of requests accepted per unit time. Since the bus system cannot provide sufficient bandwidth for a large-scale multiprocessor system and the crossbar switch is too expensive, it is particularly interesting to know what kind of bandwidth various interconnection networks can provide.

The analytic method has been used to estimate bandwidth.[31,71,72] However, one cannot obtain a closed-form solution, and the analytic model is sometimes too simplified. Just for example, one result showed that for a blocking multistage interconnection network of size 256×256, the bandwidth is 77 requests (per memory cycle) and for a crossbar switch of the same size, the bandwidth is 162. However, the crossbar costs about 20 times as much as the multistage network, and with buffering (packet switching), the performance of the multistage network is quite comparable to the crossbar switch.[71]

Numerical simulation, also used to estimate the bandwidth,[71] can simulate actual PE connection requests by analyzing the program to be executed. The access conflicts in the network and memory modules can be detected as shown by Wu and Feng.[25] Using the simulation method, Barnes[73] concluded that the baseline network is more than adequate to support connection needs of a proposed MIMD system which can execute one billion floating-point instructions per second.

Reliability. Reliable operation of interconnection networks is important to overall system performance. The reliability issue can be thought of as two problems: fault diagnosis and fault tolerance. The fault-diagnosis problem has been studied for a class of multistage interconnection networks constructed of switching elements with two valid states.[74] The problem is approached by generating suitable fault-detection and fault-location test sets for every fault in the assumed fault model. The test sets are then trimmed to a mimimal or nearly minimal set. Detecting a single fault (link fault or switching-element fault) requires only four tests, which are independent of network size. The number of tests for locating single faults and detecting multiple faults are also workable.

The second reliability problem mainly concerns the degree of fault tolerance.[75] It is important to design a network that combines full connection capability with graceful degradation—in spite of the existence of faults. ■

Acknowledgment

The author wishes to acknowledge the original contribution of Dr. C. Wu in preparing this article.

References

1. T. Feng, editor's introduction, special issue on parallel processors and processing, *Computing Surveys,* Vol. 9, No. 1, Mar. 1977, pp. 1-2.
2. C. V. Ramamoorthy, T. Krishnarao, and P. Jahanian, "Hardware Software Issues in Multi-Microprocessor Computer Architecture," *Proc. First Annual Rocky Mountain Symp. Microcomputers,* 1977, pp. 235-261.
3. K. J. Thurber, "Interconnection Networks—A Survey and Assessment," *AFIPS Conf. Proc.,* Vol. 43, 1974 NCC, pp. 909-919.
4. K. J. Thurber, "Circuit Switching Technology: A State-of-the-Art Survey," *Proc. Compcon Fall 1978,* Sept. 1978, pp. 116-124.
5. K. J. Thurber and G. M. Masson, *Distributed-Processor Communication Architecture,* Lexington Books, Lexington, Mass., 1979, 252 pp.
6. H. J. Siegel, "Interconnection Networks for SIMD Machines," *Computer,* Vol. 12, No. 6, June 1979, pp. 57-66.
7. H. J. Siegel, R. J. McMillen, and P. T. Mueller, Jr., "A Survey of Interconnection Methods for Reconfigurable Parallel Processing Systems," *AFIPS Conf. Proc.,* Vol. 48, 1979 NCC, pp. 387-400.
8. G. M. Masson, G. C. Gingher, and Shinji Nakamura, "A Sampler of Circuit Switching Networks," *Computer,* Vol. 12, No. 6, June 1979, pp. 32-48.
9. T. Feng and C. Wu, *Interconnection Networks in Multiple-Processor Systems,* Rome Air Development Center report, RADC-TR-79-304, Dec. 1979, 244 pp.
10. C. Wu and T. Feng, "A VLSI Interconnection Network for Multiprocessor Systems," *Digest Compcon Spring 1981,* pp. 294-298.
11. T. Feng, "Data Manipulating Functions in Parallel Processors and Their Implementations," *IEEE Trans. Computers,* Vol. C-23, No. 3, Mar. 1974, pp. 309-318.
12. V. Benes, *Mathematical Theory of Connecting Networks,* Academic Press, N.Y., 1965.
13. H. T. Kung, "The Structure of Parallel Algorithms," in *Advances in Computers,* Vol. 19, M. C. Yovits, ed., Academic Press, N.Y., 1980.
14. D. J. Farber and K. C. Larson, "The System Architecture of the Distributed Computer System—the Communica-

tions System," *Proc. Symp. Computer Comm. Networks and Teletraffic,* Brooklyn Polytechnic Press, Apr. 1972, pp. 21-27.

15. C. C. Reames and M. T. Liu, "A Loop Network for Simultaneous Transmission of Variable Length Messages," *Proc. Second Symp. Computer Architecture,* Jan. 1975, pp. 7-12.

16. S. I. Saffer et al., "NODAS—The Net Oriented Data Acquisition System for the Medical Environment," *AFIPS Conf. Proc.,* Vol. 46, 1977 NCC, pp. 295-300.

17. J. A. Harris and D. R. Smith, "Hierarchical Multiprocessor Organization," *Proc. Fourth Symp. Computer Architecture,* Mar. 1977, pp. 41-48.

18. G. H. Barnes et al., "The Illiac IV Computer," *IEEE Trans. Computers,* Vol. C-17, No. 8, Aug. 1968, pp. 746-757.

19. E. M. Aupperle, "MERIT Computer Network: Hardware Considerations," in *Computer Networks,* R. Rustin, ed., Prentice-Hall, Englewood Cliffs, N.J., 1972, pp. 49-63.

20. B. W. Arden and H. Lee, "Analysis of Chordal Ring Network," *IEEE Trans. Computers,* Vol. C-30, No. 4, April 1981, pp. 291-295.

21. H. Sullivan, T. R. Bashkow, and K. Klappholz, "A Large Scale Homogeneous, Fully Distributed Parallel Machine," *Proc. Fourth Symp. Computer Architecture,* Nov. 1977, pp. 105-125.

22. F. P. Preparata and J. Vuillemin, "The Cube-Connected Cycles: A Versatile Network for Parallel Computation," *Comm. ACM,* Vol. 24, No. 5, May 1981, pp. 300-309.

23. H. S. Stone, "Parallel Processing with the Perfect Shuffle," *IEEE Trans. Computers,* Vol. C-20, No. 2, Feb. 1971, pp. 153-161.

24. T. Feng, *Parallel Processing Characteristics and Implementation of Data Manipulating Functions,* Rome Air Development Center report, RADC-TR-73-189, July 1973.

25. C. Wu and T. Feng, "On a Class of Multistage Interconnection Networks," *IEEE Trans. Computers,* Vol. C-29, No. 8, Aug. 1980, pp. 694-702.

26. C. Wu and T. Feng, "On a Distributed-Processor Communication Architecture," *Proc. Compcon Fall 1980,* pp. 599-605.

27. L. R. Goke and G. J. Lipovski, "Banyan Networks for Partitioning Multiprocessing Systems," *Proc. First Annual Computer Architecture Conf.,* Dec. 1973, pp. 21-28.

28. D. H. Lawrie, "Access and Alignment of Data in an Array Processor," *IEEE Trans. Computers,* Vol. C-24, No. 12, Dec. 1975, pp. 1145-1155.

29. K. E. Batcher, "The Flip Network in STARAN," *Proc. 1976 Int'l Conf. Parallel Processing,* Aug. 1976, pp. 65-71.

30. M. C. Pease, "The Indirect Binary n-Cube Microprocessor Array," *IEEE Trans. Computers,* Vol. C-26, No. 5, May 1977, pp. 548-573.

31. J. H. Patel, "Processor-Memory Interconnections for Multiprocessors," *Proc. Sixth Annual Symp. Computer Architecture,* Apr. 1979, pp. 168-177.

32. A. Waksman, "A Permutation Network," *J. ACM,* Vol. 9, No. 1, Jan. 1968, pp. 159-163.

33. A. E. Joel, Jr., "On Permutation Switching Networks," *B.S.T.J.,* Vol. 67, 1968, pp. 813-822.

34. D. C. Opferman and N. T. Tsao-Wu, "On a Class of Rearrangeable Switching Networks—Part I: Control Algorithm; Part II: Enumeration Studies of Fault Diagnosis," *B.S.T.J.,* 1971, pp. 1579-1618.

35. J. Lenfant, "Parallel Permutations of Data: A Benes Network Control Algorithm for Frequently Used Permutations," *IEEE Trans. Computers,* Vol. C-27, No. 7, July 1978, pp. 637-647.

36. T. Feng, C. Wu, and D. P. Agrawal, "A Microprocessor-Controlled Asynchronous Circuit Switching Network," *Proc. Sixth Annual Symp. Computer Architecture,* 1979, pp. 202-215.

37. Y-C. Chow, R. D. Dixon, T. Feng, and C. Wu, "Routing Techniques for Rearrangeable Interconnection Networks," *Proc. Workshop on Interconnection Networks,* Apr. 1980, pp. 64-69.

38. C. Clos, "A Study of Nonblocking Switching Networks," *Bell System Tech. J.,* Vol. 32, 1953, pp. 406-424.

39. C. D. Thompson, "Generalized Connection Networks for Parallel Processor Intercommunication," *IEEE Trans. Computers,* C-27, No. 12, Dec. 1978, pp. 1119-1125.

40. J. Gecsei, "Interconnection Networks from Three-State Cells," *IEEE Trans. Computers,* Vol. C-26, No. 8, Aug. 1977, pp. 705-711.

41. Y-C. Chow, R. D. Dixon, and T. Feng, "An Interconnection Network for Processor Communication with Optimized Local Connections," *Proc. 1980 Int'l Conf. Parallel Processing,* Aug. 1980, pp. 65-74.

42. W. A. Wulf and C. G. Bell, "C.mmp—A Multimicroprocessor," *AFIPS Conf. Proc.,* Vol. 41, 1972 FJCC, pp. 765-777.

43. T. Feng, *The Design of a Versatile Line Manipulator,* Rome Air Development Center report, RADC-TR-73-292, Sept. 1973.

44. W. W. Gaertner, *Design, Construction, and Installation of Data Manipulator,* Rome Air Development Center report, RADC-TR-77-166, May 1977, 80 pp.

45. S. E. Orcutt, "Implementation of Permutations Functions in an Illiac IV-Type Computer," *IEEE Trans. Computers,* Vol. C-25, No. 9, Sept. 1976, pp. 929-936.

46. C. D. Thompson and H. T. Kung, "Sorting on a Mesh-Connected Parallel Computer," *Comm. ACM,* Vol.20, No. 4, Apr. 1977, pp. 263-271.

47. D. Nassimi and S. Sahni, "Bitonic Sort on a Mesh-Connected Parallel Computer," *IEEE Trans. Computers,* Vol. C-28, No. 1, Jan. 1979, pp. 2-7.

48. C. Wu and T. Feng, "Universality of the Shuffle-Exchange Network," *IEEE Trans. Computers,* Vol. C-30, No. 5, May 1981.

49. D. E. Knuth, *The Art of Computer Programming, Vol. 3: Sorting and Searching,* Addison-Wesley, Reading, Mass., 1973.

50. R. J. McMillen and H. J. Siegel, "MIMD Machine Communication Using the Augmented Data Manipulator Network," *Proc. Seventh Symp. Computer Architecture,* June 1980, pp. 51-58.

51. C. Wu and T. Feng, "The Reverse-Exchange Interconnection Network," *IEEE Trans. Computers,* Vol. C-29, No. 9, Sept. 1980, pp. 801-811; also *Proc. 1979 Int'l Conf. Parallel Processing,* pp. 160-174.

52. S. Anderson, "The Looping Algorithm Extended to Base 2^t Rearrangeable Switching Networks," *IEEE Trans. Comm.,* Vol. COM-25, No. 10, Oct. 1977, pp. 1057-1063.

53. G. Lev, N. Pippenger, and L. G. Valiant, "A Fast Parallel Algorithm for Routing in Permutation Networks," *IEEE Trans. Computers,* Vol. C-30, No. 2, Feb. 1981, pp. 93-100.

54. D. H. Lawrie, *Memory-Processor Conneciton Networks,* UIUCDCS-R-73-557, University of Ilinois, Urbana, Feb. 1973.

55. *Numerical Aerodynamic Simulation Facility Feasibility Study,* Burroughs Corporation, Mar. 1979.

56. U. V. Premkuma, R. Kapur, M. Malek, G. J. Lipovski, and P. Horne, "Design and Implementation of the Banyan Interconnection Network in TRAC," *AFIPS Conf. Proc.,* Vol. 49, 1980 NCC, pp. 643-653.

57. M. A. Franklin, "VLSI Performance Comparison of Banyan and Crossbar Communication Networks," *IEEE Trans. Computers,* Vol. C-30, No. 4, Apr. 1981, pp. 283-290.

58. P. G. Jansen and J. L. W. Kessels, "The DIMOND: A Component for the Modular Construction of Switching Networks," *IEEE Trans. Computers,* Vol. C-29, No. 10, Oct. 1980, pp. 884-889.

59. D. J. Kuck, "A Survey of Parallel Machine Organization and Programming," *Computing Surveys,* Vol. 9, No. 1, Mar. 1977, pp. 29-59. Also in *Proc. 1975 Sagamore Computer Conf. Parallel Processing,* pp. 15-39.

60. B. J. Smith, "A Pipelined, Shared Resource MIMD Computer," *Proc. 1978 Int'l Conf. Parallel Processing,* pp. 6-8.

61. J. B. Dennis, "Data Flow Supercomputers," *Computer,* Vol. 13, No. 11, Nov. 1980, pp. 48-56.

62. S. F. Lundstrom and G. Barnes, "A Controllable MIMD Architecture," *Proc. 1980 Int'l Conf. Parallel Processing,* pp. 19-27.

63. D. J. Kuck, "ILLIAC IV Software and Application Programming," *IEEE Trans. on Computers,* Vol. C-17, No. 8, Aug. 1968, pp. 758-770.

64. K. E. Batcher, "The Multi-Dimensional Access Memory in STARAN," *IEEE Trans. Computers,* Vol. C-26, No. 2, Feb. 1977, pp. 174-177.

65. D. H. Lawrie and C. Vora, "The Prime Memory System for Array Access," *Proc. 1980 Int'l Conf. Parallel Processing,* pp. 81-87.

66. A. Shimer and S. Ruhman, "Toward a Generalization of Two- and Three-Pass Multistage, Blocking Interconnection Networks," *Proc. 1980 Int'l Conf. Parallel Processing,* pp. 337-346.

67. T. Lang and H. S. Stone, "A Shuffle-Exchange Network with Simplified Control," *IEEE Trans. Computers,* Vol. C-25, No. 6, Jan. 1976, pp. 55-65.

68. H. T. Kung and D. Stevenson, "A Software Technique for Reducing the Routing Time on a Parallel Computer with a Fixed Interconnection Network," in *High Speed Computer and Algorithm Organization,* Academic Press, N.Y., 1977, pp. 423-433.

69. C. Wu and T. Feng, "A Software Technique for Enhancing Performance of a Distributed Computer System," *Proc. Compsac 80,* Oct. 1980, pp. 274-280.

70. H. J. Siegel, "The Theory Underlying the Partitioning of Permutation Networks," *IEEE Trans. Computers,* Vol. C-29, No. 9, Sept. 1980, pp. 791-801.

71. D. M. Dias and J. R. Jump, "Analysis and Simulation of Buffered Delta Networks," *IEEE Trans. Computers,* Vol. C-30, No. 4, Apr. 1981, pp. 273-282.

72. D. A. Padua, D. J. Kuck, and D. H. Lawrie, "High-Speed Multiprocessors and Compilation Techniques," *IEEE Trans. Computers,* Vol. C-29, No. 9, Sept. 1980, pp. 763-776.

73. G. H. Barnes, "Design and Validation of a Connection Network for Many-Processor Multiprocessing Systems," *Proc. 1980 Int'l Conf. Parallel Processing,* pp. 79-80.

74. C. Wu and T. Feng, "Fault Diagnosis for a Class of Multistage Interconnection Networks," *Proc. 1979 Int'l Conf. Parallel Processing,* pp. 269-278.

75. J. P. Shen and J. P. Hayes, "Fault Tolerance of a Class of Connecting Networks," *Proc. Seventh Symp. Computer Architecture,* 1980, pp. 61-71.

Communication Structures for Large Networks of Microcomputers

LARRY D. WITTIE, MEMBER, IEEE

***Abstract*—This paper compares nine network interconnection schemes and introduces "dual-bus hypercubes," a cost-effective method of connecting thousands of dual-port single-chip microcomputers into a room-sized information processing system, a "network computer." Each network node is a chip containing memory and a pair of processors for tasks and input/output. Nodes are linked by shared communication buses, each conceptually spanning a D-dimensional, W-wide hypercube of $N = W^D$ nodes. Each node shares two buses. Each bus is shared by up to W nodes. The number of bus connections per node is fixed to satisfy chip pin limitations.**

Dual-bus hypercubes can be extended to vast numbers of computers. As network size increases, connection costs increase only linearly with N, the number of nodes in the network. Average path lengths and total delays for nonlocal messages increase only as the logarithm of N. Of the connection methods for large networks, dual-bus hypercubes and cube-connected-cycles have identical order-of-magnitude cost-effectiveness ratings. They are much less costly than other interconnection schemes. Average message path lengths are slightly shorter in dual-bus hypercubes than in cube-connected-cycles.

***Index Terms*— Bus topologies, communication structures, cube-connected-cycles, distributed computers, dual-bus hypercubes, extensible interconnections, hypercube spanning buses, microcomputer architectures, network computers, parallel computers.**

Manuscript received June 4, 1980; revised October 20, 1980. This work was supported by the National Science Foundation under Grant MCS7803166.

The author is with the Department of Computer Science, State University of New York at Buffalo, Amherst, NY 14226.

INTRODUCTION

THE advent of very large scale integrated (VLSI) circuit technology promises single chips of millions of gate equivalents within this decade. Effective architectures for individual chips of this complexity and for information processing systems built as ensembles of these chips need to be devised. The primary intent of this paper is to compare several network interconnection schemes and to introduce "dual-bus

Reprinted from *IEEE Trans. Comput.*, vol. C-30, no. 4, pp. 264–273, Apr. 1981.

hypercubes" as a cost-effective method for connecting large numbers of single-chip computers to form information processing networks. Although the chips could be spatially dispersed, the method is meant to produce a "network computer," an MIMD (multiple-instruction-stream multiple-data-stream) parallel computer housed in a single instrument cabinet.

An adequate functional organization for each network node is sketched in Fig. 1. Each is a complete microcomputer with two ports onto high-speed shared buses for network communications and one port for direct memory access by peripherals and other processors. Its two 32-bit processors share 256 kbits of error-correcting memory used for arithmetic tasks, input/output (I/O) protocols, and data buffers. The I/O processor can handle network communication functions, such as message packet relaying, without significantly degrading local task performance.

The computer proposed in Fig. 1 requires about 3 500 000 gate equivalents: 2 900 000 for memory and 600 000 for logic. Allowing three years for device densities to quadruple, it should be realizable as a single chip by about 1988 [1]. This proposed chip is also comparable to Patterson's detailed projection for 1985 [2]: a 32-bit computer chip of about 1 000 000 gates, including 200 000–300 000 for logic and microinstructions and the rest for read-write memory. The chip is intended to be a universal VLSI building block for both logic and memory systems with enough versatility to offset its design costs through volume production. Much of the architecture for this chip has already been realized in the MICRONET project [3], using 16-bit Digital Equipment Corporation (DEC) LSI-11 components along with custom-designed high-speed packet-switching interfaces.

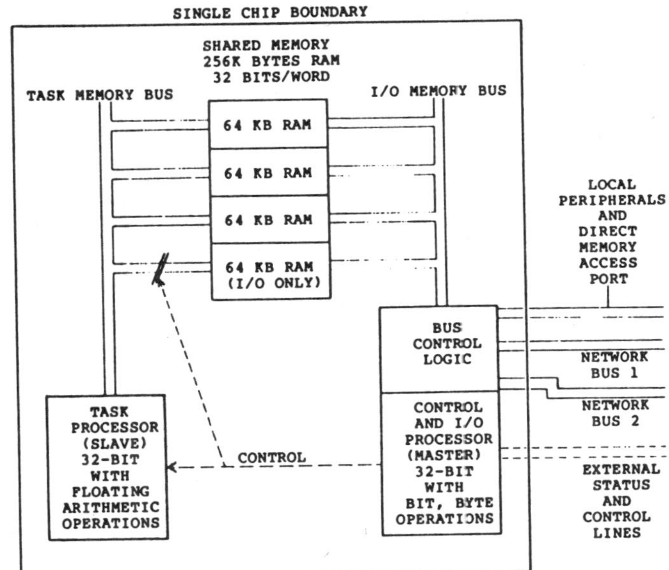

Fig. 1. Functional organization of a single chip microcomputer proposed as a node for large network systems. Each node has separate task and I/O processors, a total of 256 kbits of 32-bit memory, a direct memory access bus, and two network communication buses.

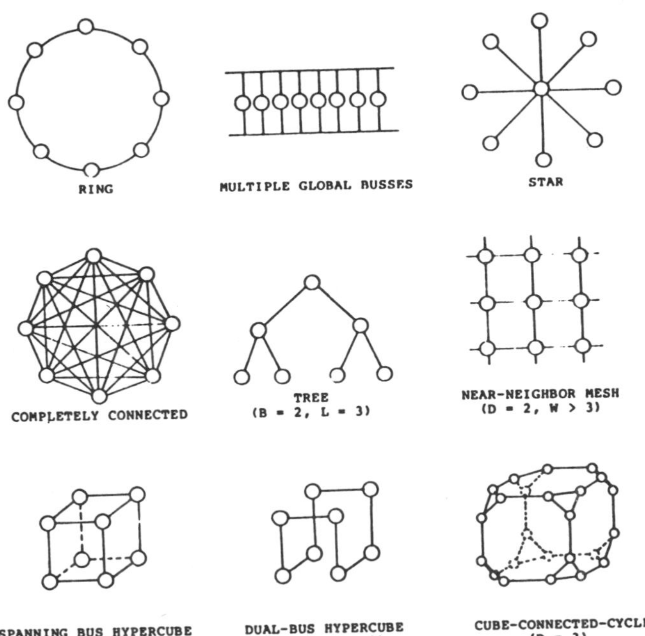

Fig. 2. Examples of connection topologies for multicomputer networks. Each node is a computer with its own memory and peripherals. Links are communication lines between computers.

Microcomputer Network Interconnections

There are many connection methods, or topologies, for linking networks of computers. Each topology shown in Fig. 2 and covered in the text consists of active computing nodes connected by passive communication links. All active switching occurs at the nodes. This paper concentrates on methods suitable for inexpensively interconnecting vast numbers of standard computer modules to form networks of thousands, or even millions, of nodes.

This paper does not consider reconfigurable multistage switching networks, such as the Banyan [4], Omega [5], shuffle-exchange [6], and indirect binary N-cube [7] networks. These methods have most often been suggested for data routing in SIMD (single-instruction-stream multiple-data-stream) machines, although some could be used to interconnect MIMD nodes. There is a rich literature comparing these reconfigurable interconnection methods [8]–[12].

In this paper the strengths and weaknesses of several passive-link methods for connecting large numbers of nodes are discussed briefly. Each will be characterized by determining the rates of increase of several key factors as N, the total number of nodes in the network, increases. These factors include average message delay, message traffic density, total connection costs, and the number of connections per node. Additional factors in comparing topologies include ease of routing messages between nodes and reliability in recovering from single point failures. Together these factors indicate the suitability of each topology for linking very large MIMD networks. Essentially the same factors, although by different names such as "modularity," "fault-tolerance," and "bottlenecks," have been discussed elsewhere [13], especially for small MIMD networks. The ease of laying each network onto a two-dimensional plane for a VLSI chip implementation [14] is not considered here because each computer node is assumed to be complex enough to fill an entire chip.

The analyses of message delay and message traffic density assume a uniform distribution of messages across the network:

TABLE I
EVALUATION OF DIFFERENT NETWORK CONNECTION STRUCTURES WITH RESPECT TO RELIABILITY AND TO ORDER OF MAGNITUDE CHANGES IN AVERAGE MESSAGE DELAYS, MESSAGE TRAFFIC DENSITIES, TOTAL NETWORK CONNECTION COSTS, AND CONNECTIONS PER NODE AS THE NUMBER OF NODES IN THE NETWORK INCREASES TO VERY LARGE VALUES OF N. THE TWO MESSAGE CRITERIA ASSUME THAT MESSAGES ARE DISTRIBUTED UNIFORMLY THROUGHOUT THE NETWORK

		DEPENDENCE OF CRITERIA UPON N ORDER OF DEPENDENCE : VALUE				RELI- ABILITY	
NETWORK STRUCTURE	NOTES ABOUT STRUCTURE	AVERAGE MESSAGE DELAY IN PATH USE TIMES	MESSAGE DENSITY IN MESSAGES PER LINK PER TIME UNIT	TOTAL CONNECTION COSTS PER NETWORK	CONNECTIONS PER NODE	WORST LOSS IF ONE POINT FAILS	TOTAL VALUE FOR LARGE NET SIZES N
One-Way Ring		N/2 N :0	N/2 N :0	2N N :6	2 Fixed :6	Paths Extra:2	14
Global Bus	(if N slots/bus)	N/2 N :0	N N :0	N N :6	1 Fixed :6	Busses Extra:2	14
Star	(1 hub) (N-1 arms)	2 Fixed :6	in hub N on arm 2 >N :1	2(N-1) N :6	at hub N-1 at arm 1 >N :1	Fail at hub Total:0	14
Completely Connected		1 Fixed:6	2/N Fixed:6	$(N^2-N)/2$ N^2 :0	N N :0	None :6	18
Tree (Fix Branch) (Vary Level)	(1 root) (B^{L-1} leaves) $N=(B^L-1)/(B-1)$	2(L-1) log N:4	root N leaf 2 >2N :1	2(N-1) N :6	B+1 Fixed :6	Fail at root Extra:2	19
Nearest Neighbor Mesh	($N=W^D$) (if D = fixed) (if W = fixed)	DW/4 $N^{1/D}$:2 log N:4	W/4 $N^{1/D}$:2 Fixed :6	2DN N :6 N log N :4	2D Fixed :6 log N :2	None :6 :6	22 22
Spanning Bus ($N=W^D$) Hypercube	(W slots in bus) (if D - fixed) (if W - fixed)	DW/2 $N^{1/D}$:2 log N:4	W $N^{1/D}$:2 Fixed :6	DN N :6 N log N :4	D Fixed :6 log N :2	None :6 :6	22 22
Dual-Bus Hypercube ($N=W^D$)	(if W slots/bus) (if low-use bus) (width W-fixed)	DW 2D log N:4	DW DW log N:4	2N 2N N :6	2 2 Fixed :6	None :6	26
Cube Connected Cycle	($N=D*2^D$) (dimension D)	7D/4 log N:4	5D/4 log N:4	3N N :6	3 Fixed :6	None :6	26
Best		Fixed :6	Fixed :6	N :6	Fixed :6	None :6	30
Good		log N :4	log N :4	N log N :4	... :4	Local:4	20
Fair		Root N:2	Root N:2	... :2	log N :2	Extra:2	10
Poor		N :0	N :0	N^2 :0	N :0	Total:0	0

the average rate at which node A sends messages to node B is the same for all nodes A and B, where $A \neq B$. To normalize for comparison of message traffic density factors, the average rate at which each node originates messages is assumed to be fixed at one message per time unit regardless of network size N. No limit is imposed upon the rate at which nodes relay messages sent from elsewhere. Together the message rate and distribution assumptions imply that each node will also terminate one message per time unit.

To simplify the analysis of message traffic densities on shared buses, most buses are assumed to be time-division-multiplexed with one message slot per node sharing the bus. For slotted buses, total message delay is proportional to the number of nodes sharing each bus multiplied by the number of buses per path. Alternately, buses with low rates of use may be assumed to have message traffic densities well below half saturation (below the queueing knee). For low contention buses, message delays vary only as the number of buses per path.

In counting connections, dedicated links between two nodes are assumed to allow bidirectional flow of data, although sharing by even two sources of data implies some access control logic. Using one-way, dedicated links for two-way flow would nearly double connection costs per node.

For each of the network topologies that are analyzed in the next sections, Table I summarizes the dependence of network message and connection criteria upon network size N, the reliability of the network as measured by the worst possible effect of a single component failure, and a general evaluation of the suitability of the connection method for large networks. Only the order of magnitude of the dependence upon N is significant in the evaluations.

The most suitable, highest valued topologies are listed last in Table I, followed by the weights assigned to three or four representative values for each of the five evaluation criteria. The criterion of network reliability after a single component failure is divided roughly into four levels: "None" if only the failed component is disabled; "Local" if only nearby nodes may be eliminated from the network; "Extra" if the entire network may stop functioning unless redundant components have been added; and "Total" if a single failure may disrupt the entire network. The highest valued topologies are the dual-bus hypercube and the cube-connected-cycle, which are discussed in more detail later.

The analysis of each topology includes the Anderson and Jensen [13] classification for the structure in parentheses, where the first three letters tell whether messages are transferred: along single (Direct) or multiple (Indirect) links, with no (·), centralized (C), or decentralized (D) control of routing, and on dedicated (D) or shared (S) links. The fourth letter in each classification usually abbreviates the common name for the structure.

SIMPLE CONNECTION STRUCTURES

There are a number of simple connection structures that have been used or proposed for computer networks with small numbers of nodes. With the exception of the complete connection structure and structures with more than two global busses, these structures can easily be arranged in a two-dimensional plane. Each of these structures is regular enough that it can be analyzed in one of the short sections of text that follow.

Ring

A ring (D.DLoop or ICDLoop) [15] relays messages from node to node one-way around a loop. The ring is limited to small numbers of computers because average message delay and message traffic density increase linearly with N, the number of nodes on the ring. Because of the message traffic assumptions, during one time unit each node starts a message that passes about halfway around the ring (an average delay of $N/2$ links) before it is accepted. The average message density in each of the N links is $N/2$ messages per time unit. Unless redundant or overlapping ring paths are used, rings are unreliable because failure of a single node or path in the ring stops most communication.

Global Bus System

A global bus system (D.SBus) [16] similarly is limited to small numbers of nodes because message density increases linearly with N. In addition, N must be small because electrical factors restrict the number of nodes sharing the same bus. The figure for message delay in Table I assumes that the global bus has N slots, one for messages from each node. On the average, a node will have to delay for $N/2$ slot times to access the bus, but there is no relaying of messages. Since each of N nodes sends one bus message per time unit, bus message traffic density increases as N. If there is only one global bus and it fails, all message flow will cease. Multiple global buses [17] can help reduce message traffic density and bus failure problems, but link and switch costs increase with N^2 if there are N busses for N nodes.

Star

Star networks (ICDStar) [18] are quite common, primarily because control of the network from the central computer is relatively simple for small N. If uniformly distributed, most messages pass along two arm links each. Table I ignores the potentially huge queueing delay at the hub. For each of $N-1$ arm nodes to send and to receive one message, each arm link is used twice and $N-1$ messages pass through the hub, severely limiting network size N. For bidirectional links, each arm node needs one connection but the hub needs $N-1$, another limit on N. A single failure at the hub can disable the whole network. It is not practical to have redundant hub nodes, since the hub is by far the most expensive node in the network. However, line and connection costs are low, growing only linearly with network size N.

Completely Connected Networks

Completely connected networks (D.DComplete) [19] have a dedicated link between each pair of nodes. They are rarely used for $N > 5$ since line and connection costs grow as N^2. For fixed message sending rates at each node, bidirectional message traffic density in a complete network wastefully decreases as N increases, since there are more links than nodes.

Trees

Tree networks (IDDRegular) [20] are similar to stars in being limited by message traffic density through single nodes (at or near the root) and by the fatal consequences of a failure in a critical node. In both cases, line and connection costs grow inexpensively, only linearly with network size N.

In a tree with B branches below all nodes except the leaves and with L node levels from root to leaves, each node can be a standard module with connections for $B+1$ bidirectional links. Each of the $N-1$ nodes below the root has one upper link. In each subtree of j levels, the number of nodes is

$$M(j) = 1 + B + \cdots + B^{j-1} = (B^j - 1)/(B-1).$$

To calculate message traffic density on a link above a k-level node, consider a time of $N-1$ units during which each node on average will have sent a message to each of the others. The link above each k-level node must be used for any message which enters or exits its k-level through L-level subtree. In $N-1$ time units, each node inside the subtree should pass one pair of messages between itself and each node outside. The message traffic density above each k-level node is

$$D(k) = 2 * M(L-k+1) * [N - M(L-k+1)]/(N-1).$$

For $k = 1$, density $D(1) = 0$; there is no traffic above the root. Just above each leaf the traffic density is $D(L) = 2$, as would be expected for each leaf to send and receive one message. For $k = 2$, the traffic density on each of the B links just below the root reduces to

$$\begin{aligned} D(2) &= 2 * B^{L-2} \\ &= 2 * [(N-1) * (B-1)/B + 1]/B \approx 2 * N/B, \quad \text{for } B \gg 2. \end{aligned}$$

Hence, B^{L-1} ($\approx N$) messages per time unit pass through the root. The activity on each link just below the second level nodes simplifies to

$$D(3) = 2 * B^{L-2} * [1 + (B^{L-2} - B)/(B^{L-1} - 1)].$$

The total number of messages passing through each second level node is

$$\begin{aligned} D(2) + B * D(3) &= B^{L-2} * [2 + (B^{L-2} - B)/(B^{L-1} - 1)] \\ &\approx B^{L-2} * [2 + 1/B]. \end{aligned}$$

For binary trees ($B = 2$), the message traffic density is highest in the second level nodes, which pass messages from both above and below. For all other trees ($B > 2$), traffic is densest ($=B^{L-1}$) at the root.

The average path length for each message can be calculated from the total number of link utilizations in the entire network as $N * (N-1)$ messages are sent. Since there are B^{k-1} k-level nodes in a tree, the total number of k-level utilizations in $N-1$ time units is

$$U(k) = B^{k-1} * D(k) * (N-1).$$

The average path length for uniformly distributed messages is

$$P = [U(2) + \cdots + U(L)]/[N * (N-1)]$$

which simplifies to

$$P = 2 * [L - 1 - 2/(B-1) + 2 * L/(B^L - 1)] * B^{L-1}/(B^{L-1} - 1)$$

which (for $B \gg 1$) yields an approximate average path length of

$$P \approx 2 * (L-1) \approx 2 * \log_B M(L) = 2 * \log_B N.$$

If uniformly distributed, almost all messages in a nonbinary tree pass along some path connecting two leaves via the root. For binary trees, the average path length is approximately 2 $* (L-3)$, reflecting the higher activity just below the root.

Ignoring queueing delays near the root, average message delay in a tree for even the highly nonlocal uniform distribution grows slowly as the logarithm of network size N. Unfortunately, if messages are distributed nonlocally, tree size must be limited to avoid severe traffic bottlenecks in the nodes at and near the root. One way to lessen the congestion near the root and reduce the consequences of a failure in one node or link is to provide extra links connecting nodes at the same level in the tree. Such a hybrid tree structure has been proposed for the X-Tree [21] project and has been analyzed extensively [22].

Hypercube Connection Structures

There are several connection structures that join large numbers of computer nodes as if they lie on or near the $N = W^D$ lattice points within a W-wide, D-dimensional hypercube. Each node can be specified by the D place, base W number giving its coordinates in the W^D hyperspace. As will be seen, even though connections costs are well-controlled, these structures can allow message delays to increase as slowly as log N (i.e., D) so that huge numbers of computers may efficiently communicate with each other.

Nearest Neighbor Meshes

The regular nearest-neighbor array (IDDRegular), or W-wide D-dimensional mesh ($N = W^D$), architecture is well known. It is used for the slave processing element connections on the SIMD Illiac IV [23]. Papers on parallel machines and algorithms frequently feature two-dimensional meshes, with W varying as needed to increase $N = W^2$. One proposed machine CHoPP [24] instead keeps W fixed at 2 and increases D as needed to form a binary hypercube ($N = 2^D$). Message routing in regularly structured meshes is easy. Component failures require exceptional paths around local irregularities.

In a W^D mesh with end-around connections, uniformly distributed messages flow identically in each dimension and from each of the W positions along each axis. For bidirectional flow, the maximum distance in each dimension is $W/2$. The average of W distances is

$$\sum_{i=0}^{W-1} \min(i, W-i)/W = W/4 \quad \text{if } W \text{ is even and}$$
$$= W/4 - 1/(4W) \quad \text{if } W \text{ is odd.}$$

Ignoring the $1/(4W)$ term, the average message path length in a W^D hypercube is

$$P \text{ mesh} = D * (W/4) * [N/(N-1)] \approx D * W/4.$$

The ignored $N/(N-1)$ factor occurs since a node does not pass messages to itself.

Since each mesh node connects to its two neighbors in each of the D dimensions, there need to be $2D$ connections per node, yielding $2D * N$ link connections and $D * N$ links for the whole network.

Since the average message path involves $D * W/4$ links and in total there are $D * N$ links serving the N nodes issuing messages, the average message traffic density for each link in a mesh is

$$T \text{ mesh} = D * W/4 * N/(D * N) = W/4.$$

There are two extreme ways in which network size $N = W^D$ may increase:

1) dimension D may be fixed and width W may grow as $N^{1/D}$ or

2) width W may be fixed and D may increase as log N.

Each extreme has its good and bad points.

If W grows as $N^{1/D}$, the number of connections per node is constant. The same module can be used regardless of network size. However, both message delay and traffic density increase relatively rapidly, as the Dth root of N.

If W is fixed as N increases, (i.e., the binary hypercube), average message delay and traffic density increase only slowly as log N ($= D$), but connection costs grow as N log N and, in particular, the number of connections ($= 2D$) per node grows as log N. Slow (log N) growth in message delay and traffic density is very desirable. With log N growth in message overhead, allocation of tasks to nodes is easier since the nearness of communicating nodes is not a critical performance factor even in very large networks.

However, a log N increase in connections per node means that fixed width, expanding dimension hypercube meshes cannot be arbitrarily extended if standard modules are used for each node. A standard node would have to include the $2D$ local ports for the largest possible dimension D. After D is reached, N can be increased only by changing W and causing a matching increase in message traffic density and message delays.

Spanning Bus Hypercubes

The D-dimensional, W-wide hypercube with spanning busses (IDSRegular) is a connection structure similar to the mesh. Every node is connected to D busses, each spanning a different dimension in the hypercube address space. Nodes sharing a bus spanning the hypercube in the ith dimension (an "i-bus") have identical coordinates except in the ith position. The ith coordinate varies from node to node along an i-bus.

Spanning busses require half as many ports per node (D) as do bidirectional links ($2D$) used in a mesh. Moreover, the average number of relays along spanning buses is less than that along mesh links by a factor of $W/4$. In each dimension of its path, a message in a W^D hypercube needs one spanning bus or an average of $W/4$ nearest neighbor links.

However, if each bus is partitioned into W time slots, one for messages from each node sharing the bus, the average wait for access to each bus is $W/2$ bus-use-time slots. The average message path delay is

$$P\,\text{span} = D * (W - 1)/W * W/2 = D * (W - 1)/2.$$

The $(W - 1)/W$ factor reflects the fact that there are only W choices $(0 \cdots W - 1)$ for each coordinate value. On the average, in $1/W$ of all cases, the ith coordinate for the source and destination nodes will be the same and no i-bus will be used. For each i, there is a probability $(W - 1)/W$ that an i-bus will be needed to relay a given message.

Since W nodes share each bus, there are ND/W spanning buses in all. Including $D * (W - 1)/W$ relays per message, the traffic density for each bus is

$$T\,\text{span} = N * [D * (W - 1)/W]/[N * D/W] = (W - 1).$$

Like meshes, spanning bus hypercubes built of standard modules should not expand by increasing the dimension D, since the number of ports per node $(=D)$ would have to increase. The width W of nodes sharing each bus is limited by bus bandwidth and by driver/receiver characteristics. All in all, regular spanning bus hypercubes are harder to extend than meshes. The next sections show how to limit spanning bus connections to only two bus connections per node to form an improved structure.

Bus Routing in Hypercubes

Fig. 3 shows two varieties of three-dimensional spanning bus hypercubes. The fully regular hypercube has three $(=D)$ bus connections at every node. For any D, the dual-bus hypercube (IDSIrregular) has only two bus connections per node. Dual-bus hypercubes can be expanded without increasing the number of ports per bus. As is shown below, message paths in dual-bus hypercubes are only twice as long as those in regular spanning bus networks. Message delays and traffic densities for dual-bus hypercubes increase slowly only as $\log N$ $(=2D)$ as N $(=W^D)$ increases.

Both regular and dual-bus hypercubes have simple message routing algorithms. For regular hypercubes of width W and dimension D, an algorithm for sending a message from node A to node B is as follows:

Express the indices of A and B as coordinates in a W^D lattice. Each index is a base W, length D integer. In turn, compare each ith one of the D coordinates for the source node containing the message (initially A) to the ith coordinate for the destination node (always B). If the source and destination differ in the ith coordinate, route the message along the ith dimension bus from its present source to the node which has its ith coordinate equal to that of the destination (B) and all other coordinates equal to those of the present source. The new node becomes the present source and the routing algorithm repeats for the next i until the message reaches B.

The algorithm terminates because each bus relay of the message brings it closer to B along one of the D dimensions. For regular hypercubes, at most D bus relays are needed for any message path. The order in which the D coordinates are checked is not specified in the algorithm since, without loss of generality, it may be varied to eliminate unneeded routing steps.

Dual-Bus Hypercubes

To permit a similar routing algorithm for dual-bus hypercubes, every node has a spanning bus passing through it in the same direction, arbitrarily called the 0th dimension and shown as the vertical direction in Fig. 3. In each $(D - 1)$-dimensional plane perpendicular to the vertical direction in the D-dimensional hypercube, all nodes have their second connection to buses spanning the same dimension. The second bus direction differs from plane to plane, but may repeat if $W > D - 1$. In the right half of Fig. 3, nodes in two planes have bus connections in the in–out direction. Nodes in the other two planes have left–right bus connections. All nodes connect to vertical busses.

The message routing algorithm for dual-bus hypercubes is identical except that the elimination of a difference between the present source and the final destination in the ith coordinate position usually requires two bus relays instead of one. The first relay uses a 0th dimension bus (0-bus) to reach a node connected to an i-bus. The second uses the i-bus to move closer to the destination in the ith dimension. The message routing algorithm for dual-bus hypercubes has been analyzed [25], although the analysis is presented in terms of a hierarchy of buses overlapping in two dimensions.

For nodes A and B with coordinates differing in all D dimensions, the dimensions of the buses used to relay a message from A to B for the fully regular spanning bus hypercube are

$$(D - 1), (D - 2), \cdots 2, 1, 0: \qquad D \text{ relays.}$$

For dual-bus hypercubes, the longest path needs

$$0, (D - 1), 0, (D - 2), \cdots 0, 2, 0, 1, 0: \qquad (2D - 1) \text{ relays.}$$

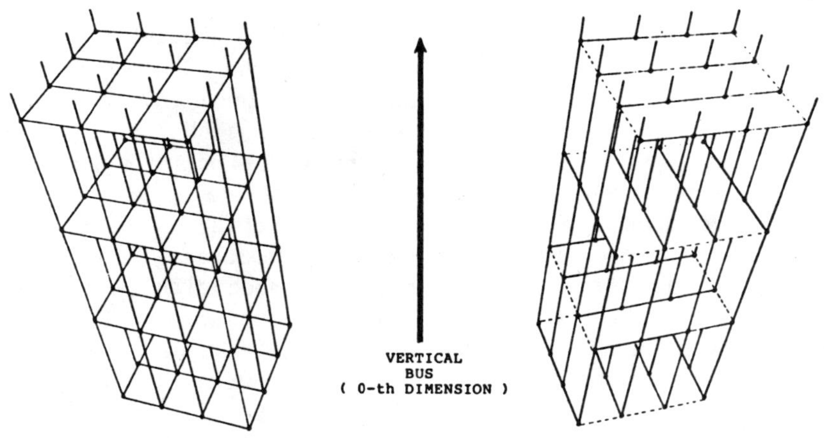

Three bus connections ( ) at every node.
Fully regular spanning bus hypercube.

Two bus connections (or) per node.
Dual-bus hypercube.

Fig. 3. Regular and limited spanning bus hypercubes of width $W = 4$ (nodes per bus) and dimension $D = 3$ (bus directions). Each node in the regular hypercube has connections to buses in all D (= 3) dimensions. Each node in the dual-bus hypercube has only two bus connections, always with one to a vertical bus.

Message paths and bus delays in dual-bus hypercubes are about twice as long as those in similarly shaped, regular hypercubes.

By an analysis similar to that for the fully regular hypercubes, if uniformly distributed messages are relayed on shared busses partitioned into W time slots, the average message path delay in dual-bus hypercubes is

$$\begin{aligned} P\text{ slot} &= [2 * D * (W-1)/W - 1] * W/2 \\ &= D * (W-1) - W/2. \end{aligned}$$

However, as will be seen, dual-bus networks may be expanded with only a log N increase in message traffic density. It is feasible to design a system with enough bus bandwidth to keep message traffic density below the queueing knee near half saturation. There need not be fixed partitions of a low-use bus, since queued access requests can be serviced in essentially constant time, about equal to one message transmission time. For low-use buses, the average message delay is

$$\begin{aligned} P\text{ queue} &= 2 * D * (W-1)/W - 1 \\ &\approx 2 * D - 1, && \text{for } W \gg D \text{ and} \\ &\approx 2 * (D-1) - 1 \\ &= 2 * D - 3, && \text{for } W = D \text{ or } W = D - 1. \end{aligned}$$

There are two spanning buses per node for dual-bus hypercubes versus D for regular hypercubes, so network connections cost slightly less. However, since there are $D/2$ times fewer busses for just as many messages and each message uses nearly twice as many busses, the average message traffic density for dual-bus hypercubes is D times that for regular spanning bus hypercubes

$$T\text{ aver} \approx D * T\text{ span} = D * (W-1).$$

Since dual-bus hypercubes are not completely regular, care must be taken in allocating buses to the $D - 1$ nonvertical dimensions so that traffic density is the same for all dimensions. Ignoring the $(W-1)/W$ factors in the equations for P slot and P queue, the average message path involves D uses of the vertical buses and one use of a bus in each of the other $D - 1$ dimensions.

If the W other connections along each vertical bus are evenly divided among the other $D - 1$ dimensions, there will be W vertical buses for every set of W/D or $(W/D + 1)$ buses in each of the other dimensions. For even allocation, the number of buses for each dimension very closely matches the D to 1 to 1 $\cdots$ to 1 distribution of traffic over the buses. Traffic density in each spanning bus closely approximates

$$T\text{ even} \approx T\text{ aver} \approx D * W.$$

Since routing in dual-bus hypercubes requires that every vertical bus have a direct relay to some bus in each of the $D - 1$ other dimensions, $W \geq D - 1$. As a dual-bus hypercube expands by increasing D, W must also slowly increase, as approximately $(\log N)/\log \log N$. The maximum number of nodes in a network with buses of width W is $N = W^{W+1}$. For $W = 4$, $N = 1024$; for $W = 5$, $N = 15\,625$; for $W = 8$, $N \approx 130\,000\,000$–a vast number of computers. For even the $W = 8$, $D = 9$ case, the maximum message path among 130 000 000 nodes requires only 17 bus uses and the average for uniformly distributed messages requires slightly fewer than 15 buses.

Ten or more nodes ($W = 10$, $N = 10^{11}$) can easily share a bus for most wired-OR driver/receiver combinations. If bus bandwidth is great enough for the message traffic density from 10 nodes to be below the queueing knee, queueing delays will not significantly increase for W increasing to 10. Effectively, dual-bus hypercubes can be expanded by increasing W and D as log N, causing connection costs to increase only linearly as N, message traffic densities as $\log^2 N$, and message delays only slowly as $D = \log N$.

Cube-Connected-Cycle

The cube-connected-cycle (IDDRegular) is a newly developed hypercube topology suitable for very large networks. This topology has been shown to be very time-efficient for a large number of distributed algorithms and to have an area-efficient VLSI layout [26]. As will be shown in this section and as is summarized in the last two entries in Table I, a cube-connected-cycle (CCC) has exactly the same evaluation as a dual-bus hypercube for each of the five order-of-magnitude criteria used in this paper. However, for networks larger than 100 nodes, dual-bus hypercubes have shorter average message delays than do CCC's of similar sizes. For networks with thousands of nodes, average message delays in dual-bus hypercubes are about one-half as great as delays in CCCs.

A CCC for dimension $D = 3$ is shown in the lower right corner of Fig. 2. A CCC of dimension D contains $D * 2^D$ nodes arranged as a cycle of D nodes around each of the 2^D vertices of a binary ($W = 2$) hypercube of D dimensions. Each node is connected to exactly three others by dedicated bidirectional links: two links to neighbors on the same cycle and one link crossing the hypercube in one of the D dimensions to the corresponding node in another cycle.

An efficient routing algorithm for CCC's is similar to that for other hypercube topologies. To facilitate routing, the node with a cross-link in the ith dimension should be in the ith position in each cycle. To send a message from node A to node B in a CCC of dimension D:

Express the indices of A and B each as a cycle position followed by a coordinate in a 2^D lattice: $P\, C_0\, C_1 \cdots C_{D-1}$, where $0 \le P \le (D-1)$ and all $C_i = 0$ or 1. For each source node (initially A) containing the message, compare binary coordinate C_i of the source to that of the destination (always B), where $i = P$, the cycle position of the source node. If the coordinates differ, use the ith dimension cross-link to relay the message to a new node with the same index as the source except in the C_i coordinate. If the ith coordinates are equal, but the message has not yet reached the cycle of the final destination (B) (i.e., not all the binary coordinates match), use a cycle-link to move to the node in the next position within the same cycle (i.e., to the node with index: $[(P+1) \text{ modulo } D]\, C_0 \cdots C_{D-1}$). If the message has reached the final cycle, determine whether the destination node (B) is closer in the forward ($P+1$) or the backward ($P-1$) direction along the cycle and use a cycle-link to move one position closer to the final destination (B). Repeat the comparison and use of a cross-link or a cycle-link, until the message reaches destination node B.

The node indices of A and B differ in at most D binary coordinates and at most $|P_A - P_B|$ cycle positions. Every comparison and link-use step either:

1) moves the message closer to B by changing only one of the coordinates or cycle-positions, or

2) moves it closer to a node with a cross-link in the next dimension in which the coordinates differ.

There are at most $(D-1)$ extra cycle-link steps mingled with at most D cross-links to reach the cycle of the final destination (B). There are at most $D/2$ additional steps along the final cycle to reach B. In total, the maximum path length to route a message in a CCC of dimension D is

$$P\,\text{max} = D + D - 1 + D/2 = D * 5/2 - 1.$$

However, on the average for uniformly distributed messages, the coordinates of A and B will differ in only $D/2$ of the D coordinates since each has only 2 possible values. Using the CCC routing algorithm given above and noting that $1/2^k$ is the probability that k cycle-uses are not needed because the indices of A and B are identical in the last k binary coordinates; the average message path delay in a CCC of dimension D is

$$\begin{aligned} P\,\text{ccc} &= D/2 + D - 1 - \sum_{k=1}^{D-1} k/2^k + D/4 \\ &= D/2 + D - 1 - 2 + (D+1)/2^{D-1} + D/4 \\ &= D/2 \text{ cross-uses} \\ &\quad + [D * 5/4 - 3 + (D+1)/2^{D-1}] \text{ cycle-uses} \\ &= D * 7/4 - 3 + (D+1)/2^{D-1} \text{ link-uses} \\ &\approx D * 7/4 - 3 \text{ link-uses.} \end{aligned}$$

For any large CCC ($D \gg 1$), the $(D+1)/2^{D-1}$ fraction is negligible. In a CCC there are $D * 2^D$ cycle-links and $D * 2^{D-1}$ cross-links in all. Since the average message path uses $D/2$ cross-links and $(D * 5/4 - 3)$ cycle-links, the average message traffic density for a CCC with all $D * 2^D$ nodes sending uniformly distributed messages is

$$T\,\text{ccc} = D/2 * D * 2^D/(D * 2^{D-1}) = D, \text{ for cross-links}$$

and

$$= (D * 5/4 - 3) * D * 2^D/(D * 2^D) = D * 5/4 - 3, \text{ for cycle-links.}$$

Comparison of Dual-Bus Hypercubes to Cube-Connected-Cycles

Similar to dual-bus hypercubes, cube-connected-cycles have average delays and traffic density factors for nonlocal messages which are proportional to dimension D, roughly equal to the logarithm of N, the number of nodes in the network. Each topology has a fixed number of ports per node (2 for dual-bus hypercubes and 3 for CCC's) regardless of the size of the network.

The major advantage of CCC's over dual-bus hypercubes is that CCC's use more simply controlled dedicated links, whereas dual-bus hypercubes use shared busses to connect nodes. The average traffic density on each bus is slightly greater than that on each link for CCC's and hypercubes with roughly the same number of elements. However, because the dimension D for a CCC is much greater than that for a hypercube with the same number of elements, the traffic density factor for highly nonlocal uniformly distributed messages is less than three times greater for all hypercubes with fewer than 10^{14} nodes, i.e., for all practical networks.

The main advantage of dual-bus hypercubes over cube-connected-cycles is that average message delays for highly nonlocal distributions are shorter in large hypercubes than in CCC's of similar sizes. The main reason is that CCC's are based on binary ($W = 2$) hypercubes and have much higher dimensions D for similar large numbers of nodes than do dual-bus hypercubes with greater widths.

In a CCC of dimension Dc, the number of nodes is

$$N = Dc * 2^{Dc}.$$

Dc can be determined from N by solving the recurrence equation

$$Dc_{n+1} = \log_2 N - \log_2 Dc_n.$$

Especially for large values of N, the approximate value of Dc is

$$Dc \approx \log_2 N - \log_2 \log_2 N.$$

Similarly, in a dual-bus hypercube of dimension Dh and width $W = (Dh - 1)$, the number of nodes is

$$N = (Dh - 1)^{Dh}.$$

Using $Dh_{n+1} = \log_2 N/\log_2 (Dh_n - 1)$, Dh is approximately

$$Dh \approx \log_2 N/\log_2 (\log_2 N - 1).$$

Thus, for the same number of nodes N, the dimension Dc of a CCC is about ($\log_2 \log_2 N$) times larger than the dimension Dh of a dual-bus hypercube. The formulas for average message path delay are

$Ph_{\text{aver}} = Dh * 8/4 - 3$ for dual-bus hypercubes

and

$Pc_{\text{aver}} = Dc * 7/4 - 3$ for cube-connected-cycles.

The average delay formula for the hypercube has a slightly larger coefficient. However, for similar sizes of N ($N > 100$ nodes), Dc is sufficiently greater than Dh that average message delays are larger in CCC's than in hypercubes. Moreover, the maximum path lengths in all dual-bus hypercubes are shorter than those in CCC's of similar size because the formulas are

$Ph_{\max} = Dh * 4/2 - 1$ for dual-bus hypercubes

and

$Pc_{\max} = Dc * 5/2 - 1$ for cube-connected-cycles.

The advantage of dual-bus hypercubes over CCC's can be seen by comparing average message delays in a few pairs of networks. For networks of around a 1000 nodes, say $Dc = 7$ for 896 nodes in the CCC and $Dh = 5$ for 1024 nodes in the hypercube, the average delay factors are 9.3 for the CCC, but only 7 for the slightly larger hypercube. Similarly, for networks of about 250 000 nodes, say $Dc = 14$ for 229 376 CCC nodes and $Dh = 7$ for 279 936 hypercube nodes, the delays are 21.5 for the CCC and only 11 for the hypercube. For $Dc = 18$ (4.5 million CCC nodes) and $Dh = 8$ (5.8 million hypercube nodes), the delays are 28.5 for the CCC and only 13 for the larger hypercube. Thus for networks of any practical size, messages are passed about two times faster in dual-bus hypercubes than in cube-connected-cycles with similar numbers of nodes.

Conclusions

By using microcomputer chips with two communication bus ports each, large numbers of microcomputers can be connected into networks for parallel information processing. The logic to control a shared bus is distributed equally over all nodes accessing it. Buses connecting nodes are only inexpensive passive conductors.

Nodes can be connected to shared buses to form a dual-bus hypercube. This bus connection scheme has several advantages:

1) the network can easily be extended to vast numbers of nodes by adding buses with new nodes on them and by slightly increasing the number of nodes on existing buses;

2) connection costs increase linearly with network size N since there are two buses for every W nodes;

3) the number of pin connections needed for each node is independent of the size of the network so that a standard VLSI chip may be used;

4) all network bus logic is distributed over all nodes connected to a shared bus, so there are no extra costs for bus arbiters;

5) message delays increase as only the logarithm of network size N, so that strong localization of communicating tasks is not needed to avoid long message delays even in networks of thousands of nodes;

6) the dual spanning bus connection pattern is regular enough that a simple, locally calculated message routing algorithm may be used, except for local irregularities around missing or failed nodes; and

7) the connection pattern is highly redundant so that alternate routes can be used to bypass failed components.

At first glance, networks of many thousands of computers may not seem justified. However, difficult perceptual and coordination problems such as visual processing, speech analysis, speech generation, and complex system control and simulation will probably be solved using large parallel networks of inexpensive computer components. Practical parallel machines will enable increasingly larger numbers of people to interact directly with computer systems by using speech and pictures.

References

[1] D. Queyssac, "Projecting VLSI's impact on microprocessors," *IEEE Spectrum*, vol. 16, pp. 38–41, May 1979.

[2] D. A. Patterson and C. H. Sequin, "Design considerations for single-chip computers of the future," *IEEE Trans. Comput.*, vol. C-29, pp. 108–115, Feb. 1980.

[3] L. D. Wittie, "MICRONET: A reconfigurable microcomputer network for distributed systems research," *Simulation*, vol. 31, pp. 145–153, Nov. 1978.

[4] L. R. Goke and G. J. Lipovski, "Banyan networks for partitioning multiprocessor systems," in *Proc. 1st Annu. Symp. on Comput. Arch.*, Dec. 1973, pp. 21–28.

[5] D. Lawrie, "Access and alignment of data in an array processor," *IEEE Trans. Comput.*, vol. C-24, pp. 1145–1155, Dec. 1975.

[6] T. Lang and H. S. Stone, "A shuffle-exchange network with simplified control," *IEEE Trans. Comput.*, vol. C-25, pp. 55–66, Jan. 1976.

[7] M. C. Pease, "The indirect binary N-cube microprocessor array," *IEEE Trans. Comput.*, vol. C-26, pp. 458–473, May 1977.

[8] K. J. Thurber, "Interconnection networks—A survey and assessment," in *AFIPS Conf. Proc., vol. 43, NCC 1974*, pp. 909–919.

[9] H. J. Siegel, "Analysis techniques for SIMD machine interconnection networks and the effects of processor address masks," *IEEE Trans. Comput.*, vol. C-26, pp. 153–161, Feb. 1977.

[10] C. D. Thompson, "Generalized connection networks for parallel processor intercommunication," *IEEE Trans. Comput.*, vol. C-27, pp. 1119–1125, Dec. 1978.

[11] H. J. Siegel, "A model of SIMD machines and a comparison of various interconnection networks," *IEEE Trans. Comput.*, vol. C-28, pp. 907–917, Dec. 1979.

[12] D. S. Parker, Jr., "Notes on shuffle/exchange-type switching networks," *IEEE Trans. Comput.*, vol. C-29, pp. 213–222, Mar. 1980.

[13] G. A. Anderson and E. D. Jensen, "Computer interconnection structures: Taxonomy, characteristics and examples," *ACM Comput. Surveys*, vol. 7, pp. 197–213, Dec. 1975.

[14] C. D. Thompson, "Area-time complexity for VLSI," in *Proc. 11th Annu. ACM Symp. on Theory of Comput.*, May 1979, pp. 81–88.

[15] D. J. Farber and K. C. Larson, "The system architecture of the distributed computer system—The communications system," in *Proc. Symp. on Comput. Commun. Networks and Teletraffic*, Brooklyn Polytechnic Press, Apr. 1972, pp. 21-27.

[16] R. M. Metcalfe and D. R. Boggs, "Ethernet: Distributed packet-switching for local computer networks," *Commun. Ass. Comput. Mach.*, vol. 19, pp. 395-403, July 1976.

[17] M. Maekawa *et al.*, "Experimental polyprocessor system (EPOS)—Operating system," in *Proc. 6th Symp. on Comput. Arch.*, Apr. 1979, pp. 188-195.

[18] S. I. Saffer *et al.*, "NODAS—The net oriented data acquisition system for the medical environment," in *AFIPS Conf. Proc.*, vol. 46, NCC 1977, pp. 295-300.

[19] E. M. Aupperle, "MERIT computer network: Hardware considerations," in *Computer Networks*, R. Rustin, Ed. Englewood Cliffs, NJ: Prentice-Hall, 1972, pp. 49-63.

[20] J. A. Harris and D. R. Smith, "Hierarchical multiprocessor organizations," in *Proc. 4th Symp. on Comput. Arch.*, Mar. 1977, pp. 41-48.

[21] A. M. Despain and D. A. Patterson, "X-Tree: A tree structured multiprocessor computer architecture," in *Proc. 5th Symp. on Comput. Arch.*, Apr. 1978, pp. 144-151.

[22] J. R. Goodman and C. H. Sequin, "Hypertree, A multiprocessor interconnection topology," Dep. Elec. Eng. and Comput. Sci., Univ. of California, Berkeley, 1979, 27 pp., submitted for publication.

[23] G. H. Barnes *et al.*, "The ILLIAC IV computer," *IEEE Trans. Comput.*, vol. C-17, pp. 746-757, Aug. 1968.

[24] H. Sullivan and T. R. Bashkow, "A large scale homogeneous, fully distributed parallel machine, I," in *Proc. 4th Symp. on Comput. Arch.*, Mar. 1977, pp. 105-117.

[25] L. D. Wittie, "Efficient message routing in mega-microcomputer networks," in *Proc. 3rd Symp. on Comput. Arch.*, Jan. 1976, pp. 136-140.

[26] F. P. Preparata and J. Vuillemin, "The Cube-Connected-Cycle: A versatile network for parallel computation," in *Proc. 20th Symp. on Found. of Comput. Sci.*, 1979, pp. 140-147.

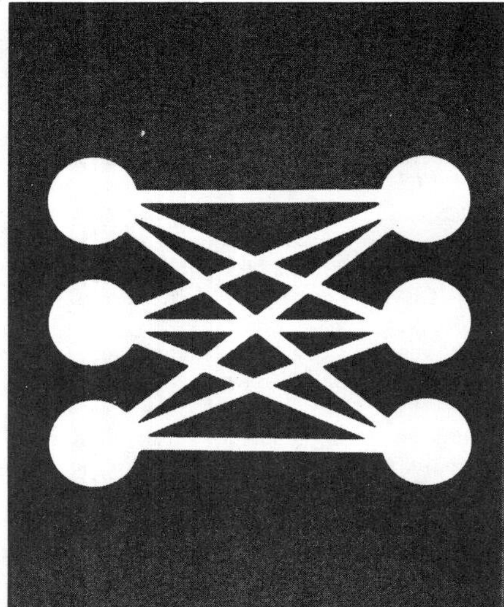

Fault-Tolerance Considerations in Large, Multiple-Processor Systems

Jon G. Kuhl and Sudhakar M. Reddy
University of Iowa

The size and complexity of large multicomputers dictates the need to consider reliability and fault-tolerance as basic system design issues.

Researchers have long conjectured upon the possibility of constructing large, massively-parallel computing engines by interconnecting many conventional processing elements to form an integrated supersystem.[1-3] The rapid expansion in very large scale integration, or VLSI, circuit technology during the past decade has accelerated research in this direction. As advances in VLSI push basic component or chip functionalities to the processor level and beyond, it becomes natural to view complex processing elements as the basic components of much larger systems. Several names for such systems have been proposed, including network computers, multicomputers, and distributed multiprocessors. We use the term multicomputer here.

Despite the naming differences, these systems have the following salient features:

(1) A large number of basically autonomous processing elements interconnected by a structure that allows high-bandwidth communication between them. At the system level, these processing elements and interconnection facilities are viewed as the basic components of the system. Each processing node has its own local memory and there is no sharing of memory between nodes.

(2) A high degree of distribution of control or operating system functions among the processing elements.

(3) Highly parallel computation performed by constructing applications as collections of several or many distinct *tasks*. These tasks may execute concurrently on different processors, with necessary intertask communication carried out over the communication facilities linking the nodes. The collection of cooperating tasks comprising an application is sometimes referred to as a *task force*.[4]

The trend toward constructing computing systems incorporating several or many processing elements has resulted in a two-sided relationship involving reliability and fault-tolerance considerations. On the one hand, it is argued that the multiplicity of processing resources can be exploited to enhance system reliability. This argument is based on the notion that if processing elements and other system components are non-scarce resources in the system, then it may be possible to gracefully tolerate the failure of one or several of them, in a manner that does not severely affect the performance of the system.

On the other hand, as the number of active elements in a computing system increases, the probability of a failure existing somewhere in the system at any time also

Reprinted from *IEEE Computer*, pp. 56–67, Mar. 1986.

increases. It has been estimated[5] that a system containing two thousand VLSI chips would suffer from transient failures at a rate on the order of one every fifty hours and permanent hardware failures at a rate of one every 500 hours of operation. At these failure rates, clearly efforts must be made to provide for a system-level reliability level greater than the probability of all hardware behaving in a fault-free fashion. However, the complexity and distributed nature of very large multicomputer systems requires a new approach to the problems of dealing with hardware malfunctions among the constituent system components. These problems have motivated a large body of recent research activity. A number of new problem areas within the field of fault-tolerant computing have been identified as a result of this work.

We survey here the methods and techniques for achieving hardware fault tolerance in large multicomputer systems, focusing on those systems that employ distributed control, since such systems represent the most general case, and highlighting the most interesting problems.

General framework for fault tolerance in distributed multicomputers

The general principles of fault tolerance and their application in the design of current computer systems were recently surveyed in several excellent articles[6-8] and we refer the reader to these sources for a broad perspective on fault-tolerant computing. However, interest in large multicomputers, and distributed computation in general, has resulted in a new perspective on fault-tolerance issues and spawned several new areas of active research. In this section we briefly focus on the system-level fault-tolerance paradigms relevant to large multicomputer systems. These then form the framework for the discussions that follow.

We begin by pointing out several aspects of large multicomputer systems that pose unique problems with respect to fault-tolerance issues:

(1) Since the components of these systems are very complex (i.e., processing elements and communication facilities), the realm of possible failure modes may be large and varied. Thus simple fault models may not suffice. In fact, much recent work has been performed under the assumption that faulty processing nodes may act in an anomalous fashion. This often results in correspondingly complex mechanisms for dealing with the effects of failures.

(2) The highly distributed nature of these systems, and the absence of any central facilities or external entities for coordinating fault-tolerance activities, implies that distributed methodologies for achieving fault tolerance must be employed, probably as an integral part of the architecture and software of the system nodes. Making these facilities robust without incurring prohibitively high overheads in use of system resources is a difficult problem.

(3) Since fault tolerance is likely to be a basic requirement for any large multicomputer, the design of the facilities for implementing it becomes an integral part of the system design process itself. This implies that the costs and overheads associated with these facilities must also be factored into any proposed multicomputer design, in contrast to more conventional systems wherein the costs of adding fault tolerance are weighed against the specific reliability requirements of a particular application.

The tolerance of hardware faults in a computer system can be achieved in one of two ways:

(1) through the masking or hiding of the effects of faults or
(2) by identification of sources of failure, followed by undertaking actions to appropriately compensate for the effects of identified failures.

In the former case, some sort of hardware redundancy must be employed to mask failures. The redundancy often takes the form of *replication and voting*, where multiple copies of an entity are utilized, with outputs decided by majority vote. This approach is formally referred to as *n-modular redundancy*. If n copies are employed, failures in $(n-1)/2$ of the copies can be tolerated. This sort of redundancy can be employed at various levels of granularity, ranging from the circuit level to the processor level and beyond. In the context of multicomputer systems, the appropriate level to consider replication is the level of processors or nodes and communication paths in the interconnection structure. Such replication can be achieved in several distinct ways. In one view, system nodes are constructed in n-modular redundant form. That is to say, failures are masked at the boundaries of individual nodes and no faulty information produced by a faulty processor is ever seen outside of the node to which that processor belongs (so long as more than half of the processors comprising the node produce correct outputs). The potential for failures in the interconnection structure of the system may also need to be considered and perhaps replicated.

A less restrictive notion of failure masking in multicomputer systems involves replication of applications or processes being executed at several different nodes in the system. While this approach allows more flexibility in tailoring the fault-tolerance requirements of individual applications, it introduces a new facet to the voting problem: Processes must now vote on inputs produced as outputs of other replicated processes. This notion has in itself spawned an active area of research.

The cost of hardware replication for masking failures is clearly quite high. To tolerate m failures requires at least a $(2m+1)$ replication of hardware in the case of node-level masking and, as we shall see, as much as a $(3m+1)$ replication in some cases. While this cost may be justified in situations where extreme reliability is required, such as control of dynamically unstable aircraft,[9] it may represent an inefficient use of resources under less stringent circumstances. Even though processors might be plentiful in a large multicomputer, maximizing performance and justifying cost dictates that they should be used as efficiently as possible within the reliability constraints of the system.

In contrast to masking failures, a second potential approach to fault tolerance in multicomputer systems involves attempts to force failures to exhibit themselves. Once the failures are identified, explicit mechanisms for dealing with their effects are invoked. Formally, the process can be categorized into[10]:

(1) fault detection,
(2) fault diagnosis (location),
(3) system repair or reconfiguration, and
(4) system recovery.

The first two steps concern the detection and location of a source of failure to the

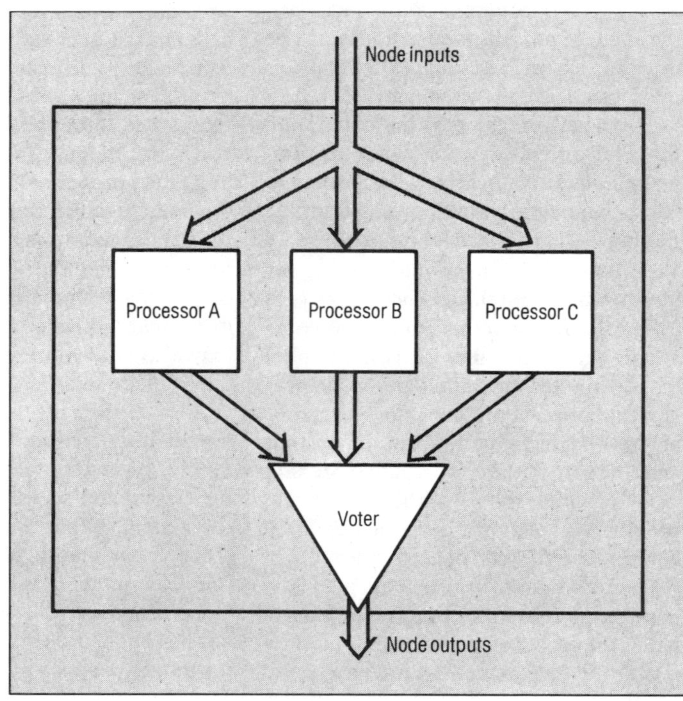

Figure 1. A triple-modular redundant processing node.

appropriate level of granularity (typically the node level in a multicomputer system). The third step involves logical or physical removal of the failed component from the system, along with rearrangement of the remaining system elements to compensate for the loss of the failed component. This may involve a physical reconfiguration of system components or, more likely, a logical reallocation of the workload of the faulty processor among the other processors in the system. Reconfiguration of the interprocessor communication facilities may also be required. The final step in the process, recovery of the system state, is perhaps the most challenging problem for large multicomputer systems. This step involves restoring data and computations in the system to a consistent state (a state equivalent to that prior to the occurrence of failure). This may involve rolling back computations to a pre-failure state and then restarting them.

Fault tolerance through replication and masking

A straightforward, if expensive, way to achieve fault tolerance in any system is through the use of *n*-modular redundancy techniques.[6] In a multicomputer system, the appropriate level at which to employ this replication would be the processor or node level. Figure 1 shows a triple modular-redundant implementation of a node. If a multicomputer were constructed as an interconnection of such nodes, then all single failures of processors in the system would be masked at the node level and all internode interactions would be correct.

There is, however, a problem with the application of modular redundancy in this fashion to large multicomputer systems. If the use of redundant nodes is the only fault-tolerance mechanism employed, then the failure of this mechanism at any node (due to multiple processor failures within the node or failure of the voter) could allow faulty information to propagate in the system—tantamount to the failure(s) within the node having escaped the firewalls meant to contain them within the node. This may result in a system failure since the integrity of internode traffic in the network can no longer be insured. In conventional systems, the level of redundancy employed is chosen to achieve an acceptably low probability that the ability of the system to mask faults will be exceeded. However, for a multinode system, where the nodes employ a given level of modular redundancy, the probability that some node will exceed its fault-masking ability increases as the number of nodes increases. Thus, somewhat paradoxically, as the size of a multicomputer grows, the level of redundancy used at each node may have to increase just to maintain a constant level of system reliability.

Apart from the theoretical aspects discussed above, node-level redundancy represents a somewhat inflexible approach to multicomputer fault tolerance. An alternative to the static redundancy of this approach takes advantage of the multiplicity of processing resources in a large system in order to tailor fault-tolerance facilities for specific applications.

Two possible advantages favor the notion of pushing fault-tolerance responsibilities to the application level. First, the implementation of these mechanisms with respect to the needs and requirements of a specific application may result in more efficient use of the available processing resources. Second, if each application has its own independent fault-tolerance mechanisms, then the failure of a particular application does not directly affect the integrity of other applications executing in the system. Thus, it is possible to separate the notions of application failure and system failure.

In order to discuss the details of application-level fault masking, we must first expound briefly on the structure of applications. As mentioned earlier, applications are usually constructed as task forces. A task force is a collection of interacting, or communicating, tasks. Each task executes on a particular processor and the collection of tasks comprising a task force may be distributed over several or many processors. All communication between tasks executing on different processors takes place through the interprocessor communication facilities of the system. A high degree of parallelism can be obtained through the potential for simultaneous execution of tasks on different processors.

For the sake of simplicity, we will focus on a small portion of an example task force. Figure 2a shows two tasks, called Task *A* and Task *B*. The arrow from Task *A* to Task *B* is meant to indicate that Task *A* sends information to Task *B*. Again for simplicity we will look only at this communication and ignore any other inputs that Task *B* may receive from other tasks in the task force, or any communication that Task *B* may perform with Task *A* or other tasks. Figure 2b shows a fault-tolerant implementation of the task-force portion in Figure 2a. Here, single-fault tolerance is achieved by replicating both Task *A* and Task *B*. Note that each copy of Task *B* receives inputs from all three copies of Task *A*. Thus, each copy of Task *B* can vote upon the inputs from Task *A* and hence is protected from any single failure affecting the integrity of one of the copies of Task *A*. Likewise, the replicated nature of Task *B* renders the task force immune to failure of any single copy of Task *B*. In fact, it is easily seen that a task force constructed in this fashion would be capable of tolerating up to one failure affecting each of the tasks in the task force.

This example illustrates the simple utilization of modular redundancy by application software, with replication employed at the task level. Note that there is no direct analogy to the hardcore voter of the replicated node structure discussed above. Rather, each task votes independently upon multiple copies of all incoming messages. The price paid for this, however, is a dramatic increase in the amount of intertask communication. In the example, the number of messages sent to copies of Task *B* by copies of Task *A* in the configuration of Figure 2b is nine times the number of messages which would be sent in the nonreplicated case. In general, for a replication factor of n, the message traffic generated by the copies of a task must grow as the square of n. This translates into a considerable load on the internode communication facilities.

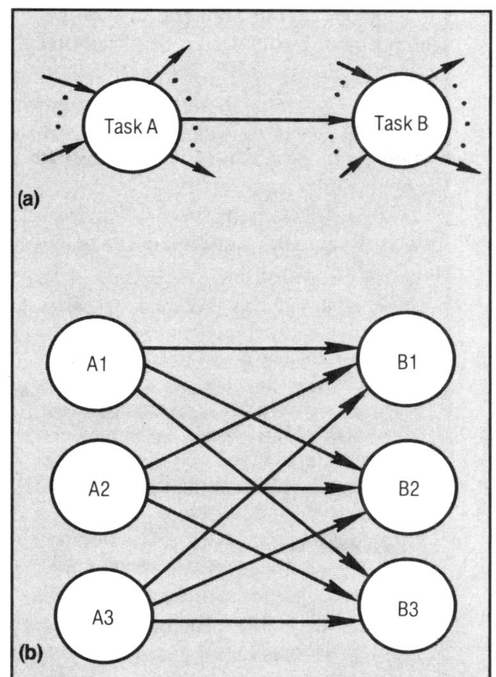

Figure 2. Example of two communicating tasks: (a) non-replicated and (b) replicated for fault tolerance.

The problems of software voting in failure-prone environments are generally complex. A considerable body of research has addressed itself to this matter.[11,12] To get an idea of the difficulties, consider the situation shown in Figure 3. Here, the enti-

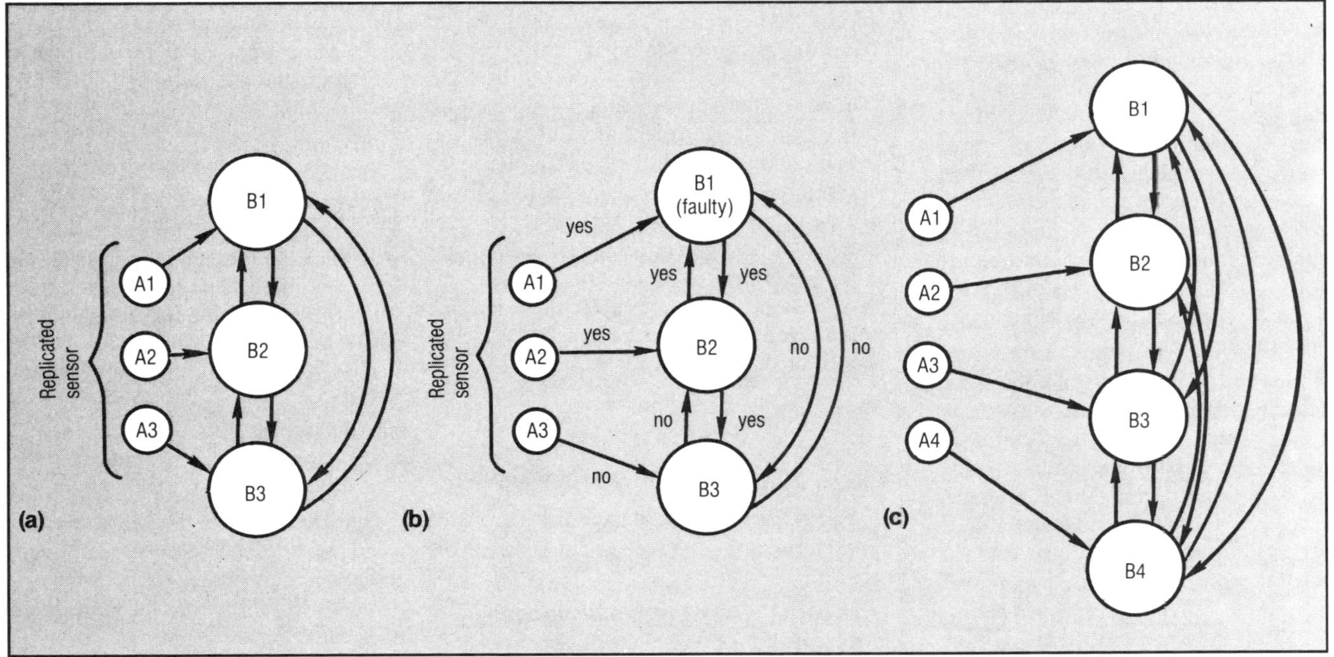

Figure 3. Example of Byzantine agreement problem: reading a replicated sensor. (a) Configuration for which Byzantine agreement cannot be assured. (b) Example of inability to reach agreement. (c) A configuration for which Byzantine agreement can be guaranteed.

Byzantine agreement is necessary with respect to the dissemination of each node's local sensor value to the other nodes.

ty *A* represents not a task, but rather a sensor monitoring some external event, such as in a real-time control system. The sensor is replicated to allow tolerance of sensor failure. Each copy of Task *B* reads one of the sensors. The sensor readings may differ perhaps due to slight differences in their calibration or placement, or because the processes read their respective sensors at slightly different times (or, of course, because of failure of one of the sensors). Now, the copies of Task *B* must agree upon a common value to use for the sensor data, in order that the copies compute identical outputs to be voted by other tasks. Intuitively, this may seem a simple matter of information exchange between the copies of Task *B*, with each copy voting upon its own local value and the values obtained from the other two copies. Somewhat surprisingly, however, this is not the case. In fact, it can be shown that if one of the copies of Task *B* can fail in an arbitrary manner, no algorithm can assure that the remaining two copies of the task will reach consensus on an identical version of the input data.

To see this, consider Figure 3b. Here, we assume that the sensor reading is a simple binary value, denoted "yes" or "no." Sensors *A1* and *A2* produce value "yes," while *A3* produces "no." In this example, task copy *B1* is faulty and disseminates erroneous information, as shown. On the basis of the information exchange, *B2* will choose value "yes," while *B3* will choose "no." The reader can verify that any more complex protocol for reaching a consensus among copies of Task *B* is also doomed to failure under pathological circumstances.

The above example illustrates an important problem in the design of distributed fault-tolerant systems: *interactive consistency* or, more popularly, *Byzantine agreement*. The term *Byzantine agreement* comes from the abstract formulation of the problem by Lamport et al.[11] As it applies to distributed processing environments, Byzantine agreement basically states the following:

> Consider an interconnection of processors. Allow that up to *m* processors may fail, with faulty processors allowed to act in any arbitrarily malicious manner. Suppose that one processor wishes to send a message to each of the other $(n-1)$ processors. Byzantine agreement is achieved if and only if all fault-free processors can agree on the same version of the message, and if the version of the message agreed upon is the correct one (provided that the originator is fault free).

In the example, Byzantine agreement is necessary with respect to the dissemination of each node's local sensor value to the other nodes, in order to insure that all fault-free nodes will reach the same consensus. Lamport et al. were able to show that Byzantine agreement can be guaranteed if and only if more than two thirds of the processors are fault free (i.e., $n > m$). Thus, in the example of Figure 3, an algorithm to allow copies of Task *B* to reach consensus on sensor readings in the presence of one fault could be derived if four copies of Task *B* were employed instead of three. Such a configuration is shown in Figure 3c.

The somewhat counter-intuitive results to the Byzantine agreement problem have sparked considerable interest. A number of variations of the problem have been investigated, together with a variety of applications of the agreement algorithms to the design of fault-tolerant distributed systems. (Lamport et al. were able to show algorithms for achieving agreement when the necessary conditions are satisfied.)

Fault tolerance through diagnosis, repair, and recovery

Although the high overheads and complexities of the active replication schemes described above may be justified by the reliability requirements of many applications, less costly techniques may suffice for others. The use of active redundancy can be characterized as a methodology that expends a large amount of resources during fault-free situations, in order to assure minimal disruption of operations in the event of a failure. If real-time system response and total confinement of errors are required, as in critical control applications, this approach may be appropriate or even necessary. However, if some temporary disruptions of service can be tolerated, as in the execution of large computationally-intensive jobs without real-time constraints, then the use of more passive forms of fault tolerance may be prudent.

In particular, it is clearly desirable to minimize the amount of resources dedicated to fault-tolerance-related activities to that level necessary to provide an acceptable degree of performance in the event of failure. In a general-purpose computational environment, it may be acceptable to absorb a relatively large overhead following the relatively rare occurrence of failure in order to restore the integrity of computations. If this is the case, it may be possible to reduce the resources devoted to fault tolerance and hence increase the resources available for normal computing. As discussed earlier, one way to achieve this is to replace fault masking with mechanisms for the detection and diagnosis of faults. Following the diagnosis of a fault, procedures can be invoked to isolate the faulty component from the system. Then, the state of computations that may have been damaged by the failure must be restored and normal system operation can be resumed. Although the cost of diagnosis, reconfiguration, and recovery may be relatively large, it is only incurred following failures, so the impact on the system may not be unduly large. The costs associated with detection of failures should be kept low enough to make this approach attractive from the standpoint of system throughput.

While the process just outlined may sound straightforward, its application to large distributed systems poses nontrivial problems at each step. We will now briefly discuss each of the four aspects—fault detection, diagnosis, reconfiguration, and recovery—in the context of large multicomputer systems.

Fault detection. As stated earlier, the appropriate level of granularity for fault detection in large multicomputers is generally the processor level. The detection of failures at this level can be distinguished in two ways: *external detection* and *internal detection*. External detection implies that responsibilities for detection of failure of a node are given to facilities external to the node. In large distributed systems these external facilities are generally other nodes of the system. Given the complex nature of a node, its failure could be manifested by a wide range of anomalous behavior. In order for the failure of the node to be detectable with zero latency (i.e., at the time when it first manifests itself outside of the boundary of the node), the other nodes interacting with this node must be capable of detecting any deviation of the node from expected behavior. This is not a realistic assumption in most cases.

Alternatively, the nodes charged with the responsiblity for detecting failures in another node may perform some sort of testing activities upon that node at appropriate intervals. This testing is an attempt to exercise the node in a manner that will force failures to exhibit themselves. Of course, we must question the ability of a processor to thoroughly test another processor for several reasons. First, processing elements are complex entities, with a large number of internal states and many points of potential internal failure. Any test set would necessarily be very large and its application complex and time-consuming. Second, the only access to the processor under test by the testing node is through the internode communication media. This does not provide the tester with a large degree of direct control or observation of the node under test.

The alternative approach, internal testing, places the failure detection mechanisms for a node within that node. Several techniques are possible, including designing the node to check itself,[7] using concurrent error detection schemes,[13] or employing simple replication and matching. (Only two copies are required for single-error detection, since it is only necessary to detect a mismatch between outputs from the copies.) In any of these methods, once a failure has been detected internally, the environment external to the node must be made aware of the failure. Furthermore, the mechanism for performing this external notification may have to be hardcore in nature, since at least part of it must lie outside the domain of

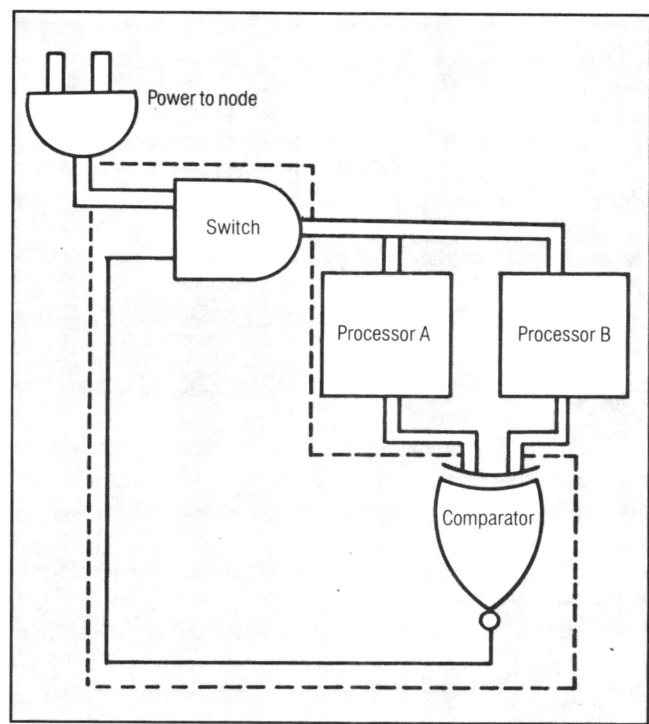

Figure 4. Simple example of a node employing internal fault detection (portion inside dashed line represents system hardcore).

the built-in detection facilities of the node. For instance, consider a node employing simple replication as shown in Figure 4. Any mismatch between the outputs of the replicated processors results in the node powering itself down. This serves as the external notification mechanism, assuming that other nodes can detect the complete loss of the node. Note, however, that the circuitry within the replicated node for performing power-down following detection of a failure must operate reliably or a faulty node could be left undetected in the system.

In fact, we can easily argue that any scheme that relies entirely on internal fault detection with external notification must contain some point or points of hardcore which must be assumed entirely reliable to assure that faulty nodes are not allowed to remain undetected in the system. Although the amount of this hardcore can be made arbitrarily small by utilizing appropriate redundant design techniques, the costs may become unacceptably high.

A workable approach to fault detection might employ a combination of internal and external detection. In such a scheme, we could rely on internal mechanisms for detection of failures within the node. However, external validation by other nodes would be employed to test circuitry associated with signaling of fault conditions. Though much additional research is needed into the details of this type of approach, it appears to provide a reasonable solution to the testing problem.

A proposed variation on this idea combines the notions of duplication and matching with external validation.[14] In this scheme, designated pairs of nodes execute identical software modules and exchange information in order to compare results. Note that this differs from the sort of internal comparison discussed earlier, in that each of the nodes maintains its autonomy and a reported comparison mismatch represents only a piece of data to be used in a subsequent diagnostic process. (No unilateral action is taken in response to a mismatch.) On the negative side, this approach requires strong assumptions regarding the degree to which normal processing activities force the exhibition of faulty behavior in a node.

Diagnosis of faults. Diagnosis refers to the process of determining the location of a fault or faults in the system. Correct diagnosis of faults is necessary to allow proper reconfiguration and recovery actions to be carried out. The complexity of

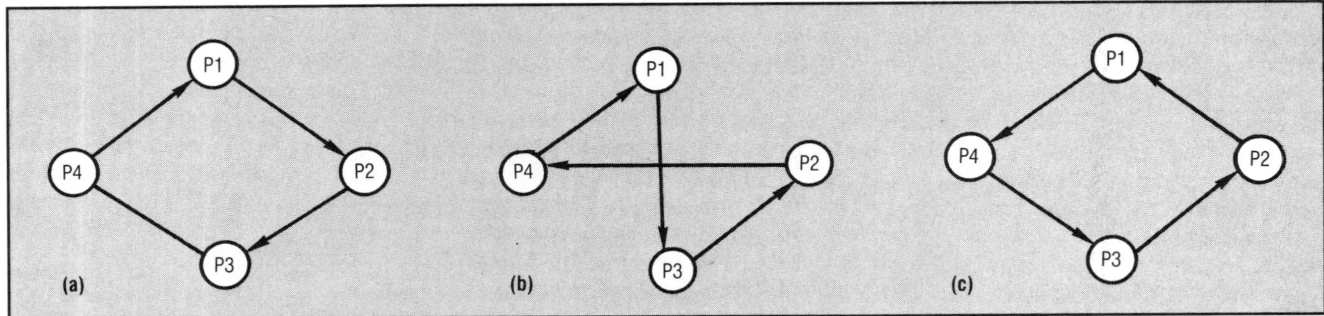

Figure 5. Example of distributed fault diagnosis: (a) testing structure (node at tail of arc tests node at head); (b) dissemination of diagnostic information—a scheme that does not work; (c) dissemination of diagnostic information in a manner that allows all single faults to be diagnosed.

the diagnosis problem for large distributed systems is governed by two factors:

(1) the nature of the fault model assumed, and
(2) the extent of the diagnosis required (Who needs to know what?).

In the most general and difficult formulation of the problem, the answers to these questions are that a faulty node is assumed capable of any arbitrary or even malicious behavior, and that every fault-free node is required to diagnose the condition of all other facilities in the system. We have studied the problem under these assumptions.[15] Our work utilizes a graph model of a distributed computing system. Nodes of the graph represent processing elements and edges connect nodes that have the ability to communicate directly with one another. (Such nodes are called neighbors.) Nodes are assumed capable of testing certain of their neighbors. Each node in turn may test some or all of its neighbors. The model used for testing assumes that a fault-free node always carries out its testing duties correctly, i.e., a fault-free unit testing another node will always correctly identify the node under test as faulty or fault free. However, a faulty node may reach incorrect conclusions regarding the tests that it performs. This model is essentially the same as that used in traditional system-level fault-diagnosis.[16]

Unlike conventional system-level fault diagnosis, which utilizes the results of testing to compute a single, centralized diagnosis for the system, our model assumes that each fault-free node in the system must independently produce its own diagnosis, utilizing the results of its own tests and the testing information received from other nodes through the system communication facilities. In line with the general fault model, a faulty node may alter or destroy any testing information passing through it. We were able to find several algorithms for performing this distributed diagnosis and to prove conditions under which the algorithms are guaranteed to work correctly for a given maximum number of faults present in the system. In addition, we showed that the ability of a system to achieve a given level of diagnosability can be tied to certain properties of the interconnection structure and the testing structure of the system, independent of any algorithm.

A very simple example serves to illustrate problems of distributed diagnosis. Figure 5a shows the testing structure of a four-node system. The directed arcs indicate that the node at the tail of the arc tests the node at the head of the arc. Let us suppose that node *P2* is faulty. Now, *P1* is the only node that can directly diagnose the failure of *P2*, since it is the only node that tests *P2*. Other nodes must rely upon the dissemination of testing information in order to make their diagnosis. Suppose that following testing, nodes transmit testing information along the path shown in Figure 5b. Note that any information reaching node *P4* concerning the results of tests performed upon *P2* or *P3*, must pass through *P2*. Hence, the information is subject to loss or corruption. If *P2* incorrectly indicates that *P3* has failed rather than itself, or that no failures have occurred, then *P4* will reach an incorrect diagnosis. On the other hand, if the dissemination of testing information occurs as shown in Figure 5c, then it is easily verified that all fault-free nodes can correctly diagnose the failure of a single node. For example, in the case of *P2* being faulty, the test of *P2* by *P1* would fail. *P1* would pass the indication that *P2* is faulty to *P4*. Since *P4* has tested *P1*, it knows it can trust this information. Hence, *P4* will correctly diagnose *P2* as faulty. In a similar fashion, *P4* can pass the information on to *P3*, allowing it to also diagnose *P2* as faulty.

These results have been extended to consider diagnosis of failures affecting the internode communication facilities,[15] systems containing nodes with limited or no ability to perform testing,[17] and to allow dynamic repair and return to service of formerly faulty facilities.[18] Holt and Smith[19] have proposed an alternative model for distributed fault diagnosis. Their approach differs from the one discussed above in two respects. First, they assume that a complete test of a system facility may require the cooperation of several other distinct facilities, the failure of any of which could invalidate the test. Second, rather than requiring that all system nodes diagnose failures, they assume that the system contains special facilities called analyzers and controllers. Test result information is routed to analyzers, which diagnose failures. The diagnosis produced by analyzers is then utilized by controllers to carry out corrective actions.

Reconfiguration and recovery. We discuss these last two steps together. In a very large system, where processing elements are non-scarce resources, it is unlikely that much effort would be expended toward on-line hardware reconfiguration. There are two reasons for this. First, the rationale for physically reconfiguring the hardware resources of a system following a failure is primarily to compensate for the loss of a critical resource, without which the system could not function adequately in its previous configuration. In a large multicomputer this does not apply. So long as the interconnection structure is sufficiently rich and robust, the loss of a modest number of facilities due to failure should not significantly affect the ability of the system to function.

A second factor mitigating against hardware reconfiguration in large systems relates to cost and reliability. Since any facilities to switch-in spare nodes, redirect communication paths, etc. would have to be distributed throughout the system, the cost of such facilities would rise at least in proportion to the size of the system. This would make hardware reconfiguration an expensive proposition for very large systems. In addition, there is the obvious concern about the robustness of the reconfiguration facilities, since failure of any of them to operate correctly could have system-wide consequences.

As an alternative to hardware reconfiguration in large systems, a *logical* reconfiguration of the system can be undertaken following diagnosis of faults. Assuming that the fault or faults in a system have been correctly diagnosed, each fault-free processing node can reorient its view of the system to avoid interaction with diagnosed faulty facilities. In this way failed nodes and communication links can be effectively isolated from the system without physical removal.

At the application level, however, task forces affected, or potentially affected, by a diagnosed fault must be recovered to a guaranteed error-free state. This requires that tasks executing on the faulty node must be logically removed from the task force and replaced with alternate versions. If active replication is not employed, it is necessary to somehow bring the alternative task up in a state consistent with that of the original task prior to its failure. In fact, it may be necessary to roll back the state of all communicating tasks in the task force, including those executing on fault-free nodes, to a common point before allowing the computation to continue, in order to achieve global consistency between the tasks. This procedure, commonly known as *backward error recovery*, has been widely studied in the context of systems of communicating processes. Only a portion of this work, however, has dealt with the problem under the assumption of

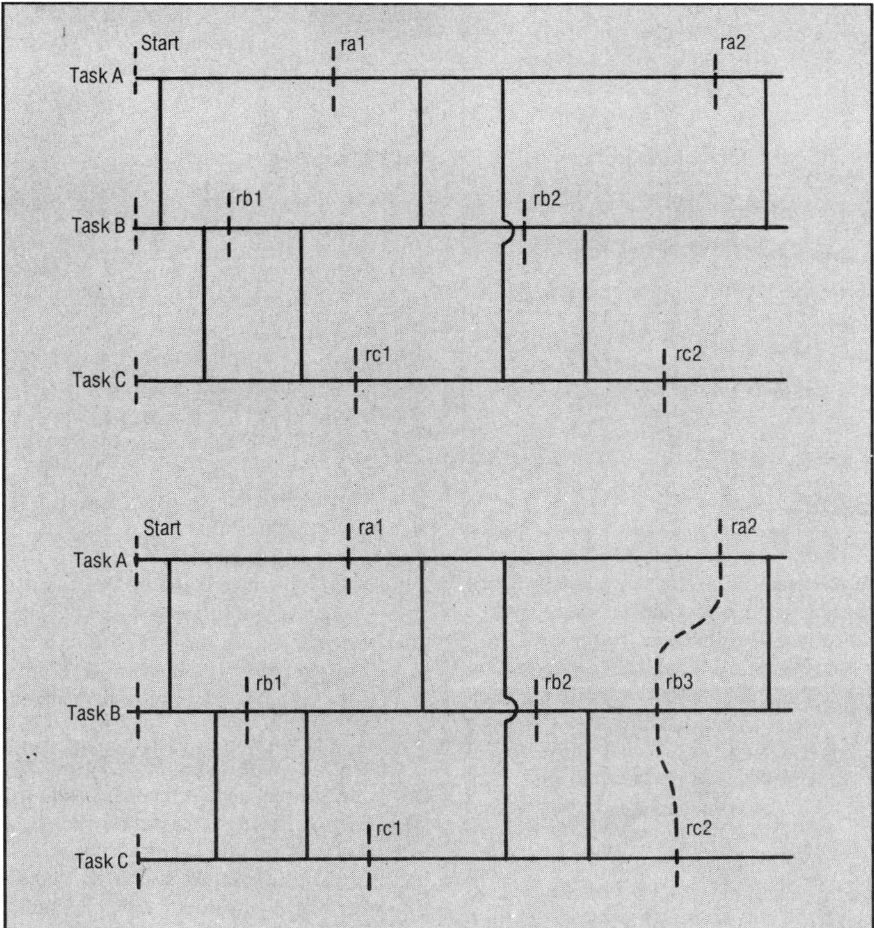

Figure 6. Illustration of backward error-error recovery problem for three communicating tasks: (a) a situation that can lead to domino effect; (b) establishment of a recovery line.

a fully distributed system structure.[10,20,21] It is widely recognized that error recovery problems become difficult in a distributed environment, and it is clear that much additional work is needed to fully understand and solve these problems. We will not attempt to discuss the entire range of issues involved in distributed error recovery here. Instead, we limit our discussion to a brief introduction of the techniques involved and one of the inherently difficult problems encountered. We direct the reader to the references cited above for a more detailed treatment of these issues.

A point in its computation history to which a task can be rolled back in the event of failure is called a recovery point. Establishing a recovery point for a task involves saving a copy of all necessary information about the current state of the task. The necessary state information is that which will allow the task to be restarted at the point of the setting of the recovery point, and in the same state (i.e., values of all data objects, registers, etc., the same) that it was in at that point. The place where the recovery point is saved depends on the system under consideration and the strategy employed. In a large multicomputer without facilities for hardware reconfiguration or sharing of devices (such as disk drives) between nodes, a recovery point would probably be transmitted to one or more neighboring nodes for storage. Note that setting a recovery point is not as difficult or complex as it may appear. In fact, it is exactly analogous to what many conventional operating systems supporting multiprogramming must do when they swap processes in and out of memory.

While setting a recovery point for an individual task may be relatively simple, coordinating the establishment of a set of recovery points for a task force may be very difficult. The source of this difficulty is a phenomenon known as the *domino effect*. To understand this effect, consider the example of three communicating tasks, shown in Figure 6a. The solid lines between tasks indicate points of communication (or access to common data objects) between tasks. (The direction of

The choice of an appropriate interconnection medium and structure is a key issue in the design of any multicomputer.

communication is not important here.) The dashed lines represent recovery points established for the tasks.

Now, suppose that the processor on which Task *A* is executing suffers a fault subsequent to establishment of recovery point *ra2*. Then Task *A* can be restarted on another processor from point *ra2*. But since Task *A* communicated with Task *B* subsequent to establishing *ra2*, Task *B* must be rolled back to maintain proper synchronization with Task *A*. But rolling back Task *B* to point *rb2* results in the need to roll Task *C* back to point *rc1*, which requires Task *A* to roll back to *ra1*, etc., until eventually all three tasks are rolled back to their starting points. This admittedly contrived example illustrates the fact that if the setting of recovery points for the tasks in a task force is not done in a coordinated fashion, the need to roll a task back can trigger a cascade of roll-back activity among the tasks of the task force. This is a serious problem not only in that it results in the need to redo a potentially large amount of work, but also because recovery points may need to be saved for an arbitrarily long time to allow for the possibility of a domino-effect roll-back. Since recovery points may entail a substantial amount of information, it may not be practical to maintain a large number of them for a task.

In the example of Figure 6a, if a recovery point for Task *B* had been established following its communication with Task *C*, as shown in Figure 6b, then it could be assured that no failure would cause a backup of the task force beyond points *ra2*, *rb3*, and *rc2*. Thus, all earlier recovery points could be discarded. In this case the set of recovery points {*ra2, rb3, rc2*} are said to constitute a *recovery line* for the task force. In a distributed environment, the dynamic (automatic) maintenance of recovery lines for large task forces that exhibit a high degree of intertask communication requires complex protocols and a potentially large amount of overhead.[22,5] Alternatively, the responsibility for establishing recovery lines can be placed within the applications themselves, by requiring the tasks of a task force to explicitly interact in the setting of recovery points. Between these two extremes lies the notion of restricting the programming model available to the application designer, in a manner that allows easy management of the recovery line by the system.[23] Whichever method is utilized, the problem is compounded by the fact that the procedures for establishing and maintaining recovery lines must themselves be made robust with respect to failure.

Several recent works have dealt specifically with the problem of error recovery in large fully-distributed systems. Hosseini et al.[22] have considered the problem of integrating fault diagnosis and error detection in such systems under a general fault model that allows arbitrary faulty behavior. Although the model of computation used in this work is somewhat restrictive, the results clearly indicate the complexity inherent in the error recovery process. A recent work by Tamir and Sequin[5] deals with the establishment of global recovery points in a large multicomputer. The work assumes that nodes are designed in a self-checking fashion that causes them to immediately notify neighbors when they fail. The authors describe a scheme for establishing coordinated system-wide recovery points at periodic intervals. These recovery points represent a snapshot of the system at a logical point in time and hence represent a recovery line for the entire system. Although the overhead of the proposed scheme is large, it is thought suitable for systems executing large noninteractive computations that can absorb the periodic suspension of progress for recovery point establishment and the relatively large degree of roll back in the event of failure.

Another recent work of interest is that of Strom and Yemini.[24] These authors propose a scheme called optimistic recovery, which seeks to avoid the need for maintaining a consistent recovery line at all times. More work may be aimed in this direction, given the apparent complexities of the problem.

Fault-tolerance considerations for communication facilities

The system-level fault-tolerance methodologies that we have discussed here are based upon the exchange of information between the processing nodes of a multicomputer. In describing these notions, we assumed the ability of the underlying communication facilities of the system to carry out the required information transfers. Now we will briefly focus on the architecture of the internode communication facilities of a multicomputer system with respect to reliability and fault-tolerance issues.

Communication facilities for multicomputer systems can be classified into three major categories:

(1) link-based,
(2) bus-oriented, and
(3) connection-network based.

In link-based systems, nodes are connected by discrete communication links. Generally, a node is incident upon several links that connect the node to several neighboring nodes in the system. To communicate with nodes to which it does not have a direct link, a node must rely upon messages routed to the remote node over several links, hence through several intermediate nodes. A bus-oriented architecture places several or many processing nodes on a common shared bus. In addition, several buses may be interconnected to form a larger system. The use of a connection network as an internode communication facility allows a large number of node pairs to establish direct communication paths simultaneously, by use of a switching circuit, such as a crossbar or a multistage connection network.[25] Hybrids of these or others of this type of communication architecture are also possible.

The choice of an appropriate interconnection medium and structure is a key issue in the design of any multicomputer, as it is central to many system level issues, such as performance, throughput, and reliability. From the standpoint of system fault-tolerance and reliability, there are two important features required of the communication facilities:

(1) robustness, and
(2) reconfigurability.

By ***robustness***, we refer to the inherent redundancy of communication paths provided by the interconnection structure. This redundancy is a measure of the ability of the system to maintain reliable communication between processors in the presence of failures of nodes, links, buses, or switches. *Reconfigurability* is a related notion that refers to the degree to which the redundancy of the interconnection structure can be practically exploited. In a large system the movement of information between nodes by routing it through multiple links, buses, or switches may involve complex algorithms to control the routing process. At the same time, however, the overhead associated with routing must be kept low, since the volume of information moved in the system is very large. Thus, interconnection structures are usually designed to allow message routing to be performed in a simple, well-structured fashion. The reconfigurability attribute of a communication architecture is concerned with the degree to which these properties can be preserved in the presence of failures.

Graph models have often been used to analyze and design communication facilities. Classical graph theory is most directly applicable to the modeling of link based systems. In such systems, a node of a graph represents a processor and an edge represents a communication link. Both directed graphs, or digraphs, and undirected graphs are used to model communication facilities. In a similar fashion, graphs can be used to model distributed computations, with nodes representing tasks and edges representing required paths for intertask communication. In a sense, such a model represents the computational requirements of an application. The ability of a multicomputer to execute the application could be equated to the ability to match the application's computation graph to a portion of the graph representing the multicomputer system. This type of model has been employed to study the potential for fault tolerance of a particular application executing upon a system with a given number of processors and interconnection structures.[26]

However, the most common use of graph theoretic models of communication structures is to analyze the general suitability of various topologies for use in networks or multicomputer systems. A number of parameters may come into play in such an analysis. Some of these relate directly to performance issues, while others relate to reliability and fault tolerance. At the abstract level, one of the most widely studied problems is that of designing graphs with a maximum number of nodes for a given *degree* and *diameter*, where degree is the maximum number of edges incident on any node and diameter is the maximum number of edges in the shortest path between any two nodes. In a practical sense, this corresponds to the largest system that could be constructed such that the number of communication links supported by any processor does not exceed some bound and any two processors are connected by a path of at most a given length. In its graph theoretic formulation, this problem is known as the $N(d,k)$ problem.[27] For a given d and k, what is the largest graph that can be constructed with degree less than or equal to d and diameter not greater than k? Despite considerable research efforts, no general methods are known to design graphs with the maximum number of nodes, or even a good upper bound. For digraphs, however, solutions to the $N(d,k)$ problem have met with much better success.[28]

Several other parameters of interest are also used to ascertain the *figure of merit* or the usefulness of a graph in the design of multicomputer systems. The *average distance* of a graph is the internode distance averaged over all the node pairs. Average distance clearly is a measure of the average delay. More importantly, it also gives a measure of the maximum throughput as suggested by the following simple argument:

> Distance between a node pair also gives the number of links used in communicating from one node to the other. Hence, average distance is a measure of the average number of links used in transmitting and receiving information. If one were to assume that every node is equally likely to communicate with any other node, then the average distance is a measure of the average number of information packets spawned by an average packet initiated by a node. Therefore if d_{AV} is the average distance of a multiprocessor network and N is the total number of information packets that can be supported on the network in a unit of time, the effective capacity of the network is less than or equal to N/d_{AV} packets per unit time.

The primary factor relating directly to the robustness of a graph-modeled interconnection structure is its *connectivity*. The *node* or *link* connectivity of a graph is the minimum number of nodes or links that must be deleted to break the graph into two or more disjoint parts. This can be viewed as a measure of the ability of the corresponding communication structure to continue to function in the presence of failures of processing nodes and links. Clearly, the connectivity of a graph is less than or equal to the degree of the graph. Currently, direct methods to design graphs with desired connectivity, degree, and diameter are not available. Fortunately, most known graphs with a good diameter also have maximum connectivity.

Apart from their direct relationship to the robustness of an interconnection structure, connectivity and sometimes certain other graph-theoretic properties are important factors in many of the fault-tolerance methodologies and algorithms discussed earlier. For instance, the diagnosability level achievable by the distributed fault-diagnosis algorithms discussed previously are a direct function of the connectivity of the testing structure of the system.[15] Certain forms of Byzantine agreement are also directly related to the connectivity of the internode communication facilities.

Given the desire for a graph with a particular number of nodes and a given diameter, degree, and connectivity, it may be useful to try to minimize the number of edges or links required to achieve these objectives. This would translate into the need for less communication links in the corresponding interconnection structure. The number of edges or links in a graph is called the *size* of the graph. Graphs designed with minimal size as the primary criterion are usually irregular (i.e., the degree of nodes is not a constant), unlike the $N(d,k)$ graphs. A class of graphs called binomial graphs whose size is approximately equal to the number of nodes N, with diameter $\log_2 N$ and maximum degree $\log_2 N$ is known.[29] The interesting property of these graphs is that their node connectivity is two, the same as that of a ring or loop, and the diameter is $\log_2 N$, compared to N for a loop, while the sizes of loops and binomial graphs are approximately the same.

While connectivity is an important measure of the robustness of a multicomputer interconnection structure, other parameters may also need to be considered. In particular, the effect of loss of nodes or links (i.e., faults) upon the diameter and average distance of the remaining structure, may be an important factor. Only a limited amount of work has addressed these factors. We feel that additional study is prudent in this area.

Many of the analytical studies related to the design and analysis of bus-oriented systems have only been done recently. The design of bus-oriented systems was shown to be equivalent to the design of bipartite graphs with desired properties.[30] Most current results, however, use the graphs constructed for link-oriented systems and then derive the bus-oriented systems in an indirect way. For example, given a graph, a link is regarded as a processor and a node as a bus to derive bus-oriented system architectures. Thus, each processor is connected to two buses and a bus may be connected to several processors in designs based on this proposal.

Another approach is to associate a processor with a node in a graph and then generalize the links in the graph to a bus that can be connected to several newly introduced nodes, thus augmenting the original graph.[31] Even though these indirect methods have yielded good architectures, it appears that direct methods to derive bus-oriented architectures could yield better designs, in which the design parameters can be addressed in a more direct manner. In the bus-oriented architecture, the design parameters of interest are degree of a bus (i.e., the number of processors incident on a bus), processor degree, number of gateways per bus (i.e., the number of processors or switches used for interbus communication), degree of gateways, maximum and average delays, and fault tolerance.

The design and analysis of interconnection networks has been a very popular area of research because of the applications in communication networks and, more recently, in multicomputer systems. The design of high-performance connection networks that can simultaneously connect arbitrary or large numbers of source/destination pairs has been the subject of extensive research. Several excellent survey articles on this area have appeared recently.[25] Several of the supercomputer projects currently being undertaken to study large-scale parallel computation use interconnection networks for communication between processors and memories.[32,33] The current emphasis in this area is the design of high performance, highly reliable interconnection networks.[34] These networks admit simple distributed and fault-tolerant routing and use the available hardware to increase throughput and hence reduce delay, as well as improve reliability.

In all three different types of communication structures discussed above the desired robustness property is related to the existence of multiple node/switch disjoint paths between processors. Ease of reconfiguration must be addressed through exhibiting fault-tolerant routing schemes. The fault-tolerant routing schemes have taken two forms. In one of these, the state (faulty or fault free) of a processor/switch or link/bus used in routing must be known to all users (i.e., processors/switches in the network). This requirement leads to static routing schemes and often to inefficient use of the available redundancy in the network. The other class of routing procedures require only that the state of a processor/switch or link/bus be known to processors/switches directly connected to them. These procedures lead to dynamic rerouting and hence are capable of utilizing the available redundancy both when faults occur and when (temporary) message congestion is noted. Exactly for this reason the recently proposed interconnection networks simultaneously achieve high performance and high reliability.[34]

Even though the issues of robustness and reconfiguration have received attention in the design of communication facilities for multiprocessor systems, the effect of failures on system performance (for example, throughput and delay) have not been adequately considered. Such analysis is especially desirable when considering competing designs, equal under other design considerations.

An area of increasing interest is the potential for VLSI/WSI (wafer scale integration) of multicomputer systems on a single chip or wafer.[35] This will likely accelerate research into robust interconnection structures that would allow an integrated multicomputer to function effectively despite fabrication flaws, or subsequent failures, in some of its processing elements or interconnection facilities.[36]

We have attempted to present, in an integrated fashion, a broad range of issues related to the achievement of fault tolerance in large multicomputer systems. In doing so, we have touched upon a number of important and highly active research areas. It would be impossible to adequately discuss or even cite all important work in these areas here, and we have not endeavored to do so. Rather, we hope that the presentation given here will serve as a springboard to induce interested readers to delve deeper into one or more of the specific problem-areas addressed. We would be happy to respond to requests for a more complete list of references in any specific area of interest.□

Acknowledgments

Our involvement in this research area has been supported in part by National Science Foundation Grant ECS-8205188, U.S. Army Research Office Contract No. DAAG29-86K6, and Semiconductor Research Corporation Contract No. SRC-83-01. We gratefully acknowledge this support.

We also acknowledge and appreciate the assistance of Ranganathan Ramanujan and Vijay Kumar in the preparation of this article.

References

1. A. Despain and D. Patterson, "X-tree: A Tree-Structured Multiprocessor Computer Architecture," *Proc 5th Ann. Symp. Computer Architecture*, Apr. 1978, pp. 144-151.
2. R. J. Swan. S. H. Fuller, and D. P. Siewiorek, "Cm*—A Modular Multiprocessor," *Proc. 1977 AFIPS Conf.*, Vol. 46, Mar. 1977, pp. 637-644.
3. L. Wittie, "MICRONET: A Reconfigurable Microcomputer Network for Distributed Systems Research," *Simulation*, Vol. 31, No. 11, Nov. 1978, pp. 145-153.
4. A. K. Jones et al., "StarOs, A Multiprocessor Operating System for the Support of Task Forces," *Proc. 7th Symp. Oper-*

ating System Principles, Dec. 1979, pp. 117-127.

5. Y. Tamir and C. H. Sequin, "Error Recovery in Multicomputers Using Global Checkpoints," *Proc. 1984 Int'l Conf. Parallel Processing*, Aug. 1984, pp. 32-41.
6. D. A. Rennels, "Fault-Tolerant Computing—Concepts and Examples," *IEEE Trans. Computing*, Vol. C-33, No. 12, Dec. 1984, pp. 1116-1129.
7. O. Serlin, "Fault-Tolerant Systems in Commercial Applications," *Computer*, Vol. 17, No. 8, Aug. 1984, pp. 19-30.
8. D. P. Siewiorek, "Architecture of Fault-Tolerant Computers," *Computer*, Vol. 17, No. 8, Aug. 1984, pp. 9-18.
9. J. H. Wensley et al., "SIFT—Design and Analysis of a Fault-Tolerant Computer for Aircraft Control," *Proc. IEEE*, Vol. 66, No. 10, Oct. 1978, pp. 1240-1255.
10. K. H. Kim, "Error Detection, Reconfiguration and Testing in Distributed Processing Systems," *Proc. 1st Int'l Conf. Distributed Computer Systems*, Oct. 1979, pp. 284-295.
11. L. Lamport, R. Shostak, and M. Pease, "The Byzantine Generals Problem," *ACM Trans. Programming Language Systems*, Vol. 4, No. 3, July 1982.
12. M. Pease, R. Shostak, and L. Lamport, "Reaching Agreement in the Presence of Faults," *JACM*, Vol. 27, No. 4, Apr. 1980, pp. 228-234.
13. T. Sridhar and S. M. Thatte, "Concurrent Checking of Program Flow in VLSI Processors," *1982 Int'l Test Conf.*, Nov. 1982, pp. 191-199.
14. M. Malek, "A Comparison Assignment for Diagnosis of Multiprocessor Systems," *Proc. 7th Int'l Symp. Computer Architecture*, May 1980, pp. 31-36.
15. J. G. Kuhl and S. M. Reddy, "Fault-Diagnosis in Fully Distributed Systems," *Proc. 11th Int'l Symp. Fault-Tolerant Computing*, June 1981.
16. A. D. Friedman and L. Simoncini, "System-Level Fault Diagnosis," *Computer*, Vol. 13, No. 3, Mar. 1980, pp. 47-53.
17. C. C. Liaw, Y. K. Maliya, and S. Y. H. Su, "Self-Diagnosis in Nonhomogeneous Distributed Systems," *Proc. 12th Int'l Symp. Fault-Tolerant Computing*, June 1982, pp. 349-352.
18. S. H. Hosseini, J. G. Kuhl, and S. M. Reddy, "A Diagnosis Algorithm for Distributed Computing Systems with Dynamic Failure and Repair," *IEEE Trans. Computers*, Vol. C-33, No. 3, Mar. 1984, pp. 223-233.
19. C. S. Holt and J. E. Smith, "Self-Diagnosis in Distributed Systems," *IEEE Trans. Computers*, Vol. C-34, No. 1, Jan. 1985, pp. 19-32.
20. P. M. Merlin and B. Randell, "State Restoration in Distributed Systems," *Proc. 8th Int'l Symp. Fault-Tolerant Computing*, June 1978, pp. 129-134.
21. W. G. Wood, "A Decentralized Recovery Control Protocol," *Proc. 11th Int'l Symp. Fault-Tolerant Computing*, June 1981, pp. 159-164.
22. S. H. Hosseini, J. G. Kuhl, and S. M. Reddy, "An Integrated Approach to Error Recovery in Distributed Computing Systems," *Proc. 13th Int'l Symp. Fault-Tolerant Computing*, June 1983, pp. 56-63.
23. T. Anderson and P. A. Lee, "Chapter 7: Error Recovery," *Fault Tolerance—Principles and Practice*, Prentice-Hall Int'l, London, 1981, pp. 173-230.
24. R. E. Strom and S. Yemini, "Optimistic Recovery: An Asynchronous Approach to Fault Tolerance in Distributed Systems," *Proc. 14th Int'l Symp. Fault-Tolerant Computing*, June 1984, pp. 374-379.
25. T-y. Feng, "A Survey of Interconnection Networks," *Computer*, Vol. 14, No. 12, Dec. 1981, pp. 12-27.
26. J. P. Hayes, "A Graph Model for Fault-Tolerant Computing Systems," *IEEE Trans. Computers*, Vol. C-25, No. 9, Sept. 1976, pp. 875-884.
27. B. Elspas, "Topological Constraints on Interconnection Limited Logic," *Switching Circuit Theory and Logical Design*, Oct. 1964, pp. 133-147.
28. S. M. Reddy et al., "On Digraphs with Minimum Diameter and Maximum Connectivity," *Proc. 20th Ann. Allerton Conf. Communication, Control, and Computing*, Univ. Illinois, Urbana-Champaign, Oct. 1982, pp. 1018-1026.
29. S. M. Reddy, P. Raghavan, and J. G. Kuhl, "A Class of Graphs for Processor Interconnection," *Proc. 1983 Int'l Conf. Parallel Processing*, Aug. 1983, pp. 154-157.
30. K. Doty, "Dense Bus Connection Networks," *Proc. 1983 Int'l Conf. Parallel Processing*, Aug. 1983, pp. 158-160.
31. M. Mickunas, "Using Projective Geometry to Design Bus Connection Networks," *Proc. Workshop on Interconnection Networks*, Apr. 1980, pp. 47-55.
32. D. Gajski et al., "Cedar—A Large-Scale Multiprocessor," *Proc. 1983 Int'l Conf. Parallel Processing*, Aug. 1983, pp. 524-529.
33. A. Gottlieb et al., "The NYU Ultracomputer—Designing an MIMD Shared Memory Parallel Machine," *IEEE Trans. Computers*, Vol. C-32, No. 2, Feb. 1983, pp. 175-189.
34. V. P. Kumar and S. M. Reddy, "Design and Analysis of Fault-Tolerant Multistage Interconnection Networks with Low Link Complexity," *12th Int'l Symp. Computer Architecture*, June 1985, pp. 376-386.
35. F. T. Leighton, *Complexity Issues in VLSI*, M.I.T. Press, Cambridge, Mass., 1983.
36. J. W. Greene and A. El Gamal, "Configuration of VLSI Arrays in the Presence of Defects," *JACM*, Vol. 31, No. 10, Oct. 1984, pp. 694-717.

Increasing Throughput of Multiprocessor Systems

AMAR GUPTA AND HOO-MIN D. TOONG, MEMBER, IEEE

Abstract—**Many industrial applications require the use of multiple computing elements. The overall performance of such multiprocessor systems is a strong function of the communication capacity of the interconnection bus. By increasing this capacity one can integrate more processors, memory units, and input-output devices together and obtain a higher overall system throughput. In this paper, an analytic model is used to analyze alternative bus architectures. Both the local memory and global memory cases are analyzed; the instance in which the global memory case can be simplified is identified. Finally, the overall impact of implementing queues to increase computational throughput is analyzed.**

I. INTRODUCTION

DATA collection, data communications, and data analysis are the three key facets of most industrial electronics applications. Each decentralized process control application can be characterized in terms of its own set of computing, communication, and fault-tolerance requirements. In recent years the advent of inexpensive minicomputers and microprocessors has increased the motivation of using multiprocessors to achieve higher computational throughput, better system reliability, fault-tolerance, and enhanced system modularity. In our previous paper [1], we had shown the importance of multiprocessors in increasing the productivity of machine-tool operations.

We consider here another application of interest to readers of this transactions. In many "hands-free" work situations, it would be advantageous to interact with control systems through the medium of speech. *Voice recognition* involves the use of speech to input information to the computer in the form of spoken, rather than typed commands and data. The complementary process of *speech synthesis* involves synthesizing or reproducing speech through a combination of voice primitives and patterns stored in the computer. The level of processing involved in several speech-recognition scenarios is summarized below [2]:

Scenario	Syntax	Vocabulary in words	Processing speed required in mega-instructions per s
a) Isolated words, speaker-dependent	Limited	200	1-10
b) Continuous speech, speaker-independent	Limited	1000	100
c) Isolated words, speaker-dependent	Unlimited	5000	300
d) Isolated words, speaker-independent	Unlimited	20 000	1000
e) Continuous speech, speaker-independent	Unlimited	20 000	100 000

In view of their lower requirements for computing speed and memory, speaker-dependent systems are more common. In such systems the user first defines the vocabulary of interest. Next, the user speaks each word several times to enable the computer to store alternative pronunciations. The system is now ready for use. The system "hears" words spoken by the user and compares them with words in its stored vocabulary database. If a match occurs, the reference word is identified; if not, the user makes a fresh attempt or inputs information into the computer using a more traditional mechanism. The size of the mass storage and its retrieval rate determines the maximum size of the vocabulary. The Texas

Manuscript received July 31, 1984; revised March 29, 1984.

The authors are with the Sloan School of Management, Massachusetts Institute of Technology, Cambridge, MA 02139.

Reprinted from *IEEE Trans. Ind. Electron.*, vol. IE-32, no. 3, pp. 260–267, Aug. 1985.

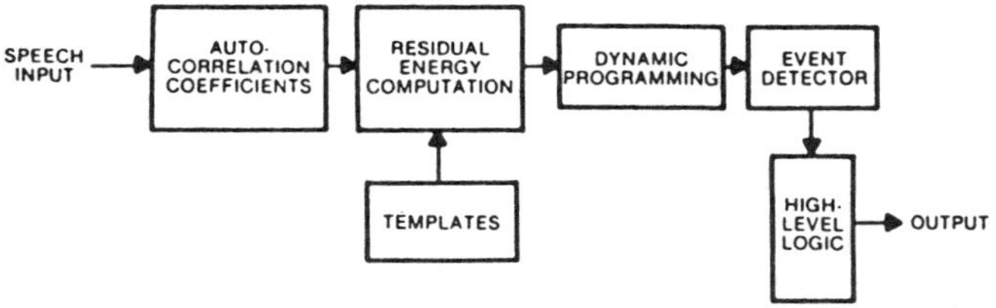

Fig. 1. Speech recognition algorithm flow.

TABLE I
BUS UTILIZATION IN CURRENT SYSTEMS

	8080*	8080**	6800	6502	9900	LSI-11
ADD8	82%	58%	92%	93%	55%	47%
SUB8	88%	58%	92%	93%	55%	47%
MULT8	71%	48%	66%	84%	39%	26%
DIV8	74%	50%	71%	80%	36%	20%
ADD16	82%	55%	92%	84%	55%	50%
SUB16	88%	58%	92%	84%	55%	50%
MULT16	74%	50%	75%	86%	39%	21%
DIV16	79%	53%	75%	83%	34%	20%
ADD32	81%	54%	92%	84%	48%	47%
SUB32	88%	58%	92%	84%	48%	47%
MULT32	87%	58%	82%	72%	37%	32%
DIV32	77%	52%	70%	77%	44%	37%
SORT8	77%	50%	57%	82%	45%	45%
SORT16	77%	52%	52%	80%	44%	44%
INTERRUPT	85%	57%	82%	60%	81%	46%

* 8080 uses bus during T1 (SYNCH) time.
** 8080 does not use bus during T1 (SYNCH) time.

Instruments (TI) Speech Command System is capable of recognizing vocabularies of up to 50 words each, with spoken words replacing up to 40 keystrokes [3]. Also, it allows for recognition of connected words without compelling the user to pause between words.

The sequence of steps involved in a typical speech recognition system is shown in Fig. 1. In the case of the Texas Instruments (TI) Speech Command module, eleven autocorrelation coefficients are calculated. The availability of multiple processors would enable these autocorrelation coefficients to be computed and other calculations to be performed in less time. Whereas today it is necessary to use speaker-dependent systems and hours must be spent training the system, the future will witness more efficient means of man–machine communications, made feasible in part by the advent of superior multiprocessing capabilities.

As compared to uniprocessors, multiprocessor configurations embody more complex interconnection mechanisms and control programs. By definition, the interconnection mechanism provides for transfer of instructions and data between the processing elements, the memory units, and the peripherals. A single processor and a single memory can cause bus utilization to exceed 80 percent as seen in Table I [4]. With more processors and memory units, the bus becomes a performance bottleneck. One option is to use more than one bus. Depending on its geometry, the resulting network is termed a tree [5], star [6], cube [7], hypercube [8], snowflake [9], cluster [10], and so on [11]. In all these cases, there are many pairs of system resources with no direct link between each other. Any transfer of information between such pairs involves multiple transfers using intermediate nodes. This increases the total effort, introduces time delays, and wastes computing resources. In the case of microprocessors and other single-chip elements (e.g., single-chip memories and I/O interface units), each

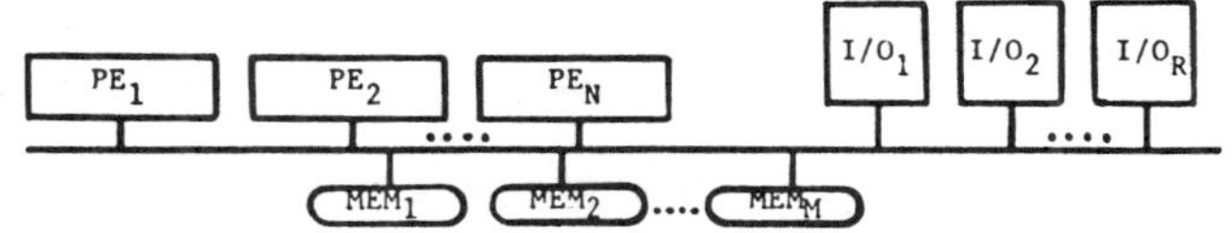

Fig. 2. Global bus system.

additional bus mandates more pins on the chip (unless one resorts to multiplexing with its inherent performance drawbacks), and hence increased costs (especially after 64 pins). It is, therefore, desirable to minimize the number of buses. Ideally, one should use only one bus to interconnect all computing resources. In this paper we describe one method that helps achieve this goal.

II. GLOBAL BUS SYSTEMS

Consider a system of N processing elements, M memory units, and R input/output devices, all attached to a single time-shared bus, as shown in Fig. 2. Each processor alternates between two states, Busy (B) and Waiting (W). The processor enters the W state when it issues a bus reference (for either memory or I/O service), and returns to the B state when the resulting bus cycle is complete. A bus cycle is a single use of the bus. Bus cycle time (T_{bc}), the time that the bus is busy per bus use, is determined by a number of factors, including bus protocol, processor selection time, processor memory, and I/O speeds. Available (or useful) bus bandwidth is the time between successive bus uses by the processor. The bus utilization (β), by any processor, is equal to T_{bc}/T_{pc}, where T_{pc} is the time between successive bus usages by the processor. For the case with no I/O devices, Reyling [15], has shown that the ratio of maximum throughput (with maximum contentions) to the minimum throughput is given by

$$\text{Ratio (max/min)} = \frac{1}{1+\beta(N-1)}.$$

This result has been expanded by Fung and Torng [16] to accommodate multiple buses. Ravindran and Thomas [14] analyzed the effective throughput neglecting the impact of I/O devices, and the theoretical possibility of all processors being simultaneously in W. We extend their analysis to include these aspects.

We first consider the case where no DMA transfers are permitted. Let us express time as a discrete variable, in bus cycle time (T_{bc}) units. Every T_{bc} seconds, one processor makes the transition from W to B, unless no processor is in W. Also, any processor may make the transition from B to W with a probability, $\beta = T_{bc}/T_{pc}$.

Suppose that at instant t_n, Y (of the N) processors are in the B state. At t_{n+1}, one processor would have made the transition from W to B, and up to Y processors would have moved from B to W. The probability that Z processors remain in B, is equal to the probability that $(Y - Z + 1)$ processors move from B to W, and is given by the binomial distribution

$$A(Y, Z) = \begin{bmatrix} Y \\ Y-Z+1 \end{bmatrix} \cdot \beta^{Y-Z+1} \cdot (1-\beta)^{Z-1},$$
$$0 \le Y < N,\ 0 < Z \le Y+1. \qquad (1)$$

TABLE II
EFFECTIVE THROUGHPUT AS A FUNCTION OF β FOR A 3-PROCESSOR CONFIGURATION

β	Probability of Processors Being Busy				Effective Throughput
	3 Processors Busy	2 Processors Busy	1 Processor Busy	Idle State	
0.1	.7315	.2447	.0230	.0007	2.7070
0.2	.5241	.3996	.0721	.0042	2.4436
0.3	.3665	.4915	.1321	.0099	2.2147
0.4	.2463	.5363	.2017	.0158	2.0131
0.5	.1538	.5385	.2885	.0192	1.8269
0.6	.0844	.4939	.4035	.0182	1.6445
0.7	.0369	.3985	.5520	.0126	1.4596
0.8	.0106	.2630	.7209	.0054	1.2788
0.9	.0012	.1190	.8789	.0009	1.1205

Note that Z must be greater than 0, because one processor will always enter B, irrespective of how many are left; also Z must be no greater than $Y + 1$ which is the case when no processor left B. An exception occurs when $Y = N$. In this case

$$A(N, Z)=\begin{bmatrix} N \\ N-Z \end{bmatrix} \cdot \beta^{N-Z}(1-\beta)^{Z}, \qquad 0 \le Z \le N. \quad (2)$$

At any point in time, the state of the system is given by the number of processors in the B state. The $A(i, j)$ are state transition probabilities, and can be used to compute the steady-state probability that Y processors are in the B state as

$$\begin{aligned} p_Y &= p_{Y-1} \cdot A(Y-1, Y) \\ &\quad + p_Y \cdot A(Y, Y) + p_{y-1} \cdot A(Y+1, Y) \\ &\quad + \cdots = \sum_{i=Y-1}^{N} p_i A(i, Y), \qquad 1 \le Y \le N,\ i>0 \end{aligned} \quad (3)$$

and the effective system throughput is

$$TP_{\text{effective}} = \sum_{j=1}^{N} j \sum_{i=j-1}^{N} p_i \cdot A(i, j), \qquad i>0. \quad (4)$$

For example, consider $N = 3$. The matrix of $A(i, j)$ is

$$A = \begin{bmatrix} 0 & 1 & 0 & 0 \\ 0 & \beta & 1-\beta & 0 \\ 0 & \beta^2 & 2\beta(1-\beta) & (1-\beta)^2 \\ \beta^3 & 3\beta^2(1-\beta) & 3\beta(1-\beta)^2 & (1-\beta)^3 \end{bmatrix}$$

Now let $\beta = 0.1$. Using the matrix (3), and the fact that $(p_0 + p_1 + p_2 + p_3) = 1$, we get

$$p_3=0.73,\ p_2=0.24,\ p_1=0.23, \text{ and } p_0=0.0007.$$

Hence, $TP_{\text{effective}} = 1(0.023) + 2(0.24) + 3(0.73) = 2.71$, or a 10-percent degradation in overall throughput. As β increases, the probability of processors being in the WAIT state increases, and the effective throughput reduces as summarized in Table II. For $\beta = 0.3$, the equivalent degradation as compared to TP (max) of three is almost 30 percent. Experimentally, using Intel 8080 Multibus [13], the effective throughput with two and three processors was 1.57 and 1.58, respectively. From Table I the value of β is about 0.58 and our theoretical model indicates a throughput within 5 percent of the experimental results. This deviation can be attributed mainly to the inaccuracy in the measurement of β.

The DMA transfers will increase the bus utilization further, and degrade the overall system performance; these transfers use the system bus on a cycle steal basis. Let the probability of such bus usage by the R I/O devices be $\alpha_1, \alpha_2, \cdots$, respectively, and let the overall sum of such probabilities be denoted by α. If TBW denotes the total bus bandwidth, the bus bandwidth for non-DMA operations, BW, is given by

$$\text{BW} = \text{Total Bus Bandwidth} - \text{Bandwidth used for DMA purposes} = \text{TBW}(1-\alpha). \quad (5)$$

We had previously used β to denote the probability of a processor using the bus over a given time period. Now the processor must fulfill its bus requirement during $(1 - \alpha)$ of the time period, and hence its probability of using the bus during this time period is given by

$$\beta^* = \beta/(1-\alpha). \quad (6)$$

Equations (1) and (2) are altered with β^* substituted in place of β to analyze this case. In general, $\alpha_1, \alpha_2, \cdots, \alpha_R$ depend on the effective throughput of the system (e.g., the number of accesses to a disk unit per unit time depends on the overall CPU speed). Equations (1)–(5) must be used iteratively to solve the system by trial and error. The algorithm converges very fast for small values of α.

The above analysis is independent of the value of M, N, R, and the probability of access to different units as only one memory or I/O unit can be used at one time. In the case of memory reference, the memory service time affects the value of T_{bc} as follows:

$$T_{bc} = T_{ij} + T_{\text{MEM}(j)} + T_{ji} \quad (7)$$

where

T_{ij} Bus Service Time to transmit Memory Read/Request or Memory Store Data from PE_i + MEM_j,

$T_{MEM}(j)$ Memory Service Time (Read/Write) of MEM_j,

T_{ji} Bus Service Time to transmit information from Mem_j to PE_i (in case of Read Operation) or the Bus Service Time to transmit WRITE ACKNOWLEGE.

In case the size of messages (instructions as well as data) on the bus is constant, then

$$T_{ij} = T_{ji} = T_{BUS}, \text{ a constant for } 1 \geq i \geq P \text{ and } 1 \geq j \geq M$$
$$\text{and } T_{bc} = 2 \times T_{BUS} + T_{MEM(j)}. \quad (8)$$

In general, T_{MEM} is one to two orders of magnitude larger than T_{BUS}. Thus in traditional bus architectures, if the bus is busy for a total time T_{bc}, it is used only for a very small fraction of time ($2 \times T_{BUS}$) and is forced to be idle for the remaining time ($= T_{MEM}$).

III. SPLIT-TRANSACTION BUS

This idle period is used for serving other bus requests in the case of the split-transaction bus architecture. As its name implies, the split-transaction protocol causes an operation that utilizes the bus to be decomposed into two or more operations in order to reduce bus idle time to the minimum. This efficient bus protocol, which has been implemented in commercial systems such as the Honeywell Level 6 and the HP 3000, has been further refined in recent years by equipping memory units with high-speed input and output buffers. This allows for the bus to be released immediately after the memory request is latched from the bus into the input buffer of the memory unit. The data is transferred from the memory to its output buffer; the bus is then used to transfer the data to the requesting processor. Using these refinements, the total bus usage for a memory-read operation is reduced to $2 \times T_{BUS}$, which is the absolute minimum time from theoretical considerations. Hence, the bus usage is fully optimized using the improved split-transaction protocol. However, since the memory must also now contend (with processors) for control of the bus, an additional wait state is generated. The actual throughput increase depends on the ratio of the memory service time to the bus service time, and the total duration of the two wait states. We develop an analytic model to estimate this increase.

The resource-contention problem has been examined previously by a number of researchers. Kurtzberg [18] has analyzed the memory interference problem for a two-processor system, but his quadratic programming technique cannot be extended. Baskett and Smith [12] analyze a multiple processor system, but they consider the effect of memory interference only, and neglect bus timings altogether. Bhandarkar [19] uses Markovian chains to analyze systems with processing times equal to or less than memory write times and Hoogendoorn [20] assumes processing times to be larger than memory write times; these models do not assume any queueing up of requests for service at the memory in case of conflict. Fung and Torng [16] analyze a general case but assume that the average number of instruction references made by a processor on a memory is independent of the bus and memory response time. In view of the assumptions, none of these models can be used to determine the overall throughput of a split-transaction bus.

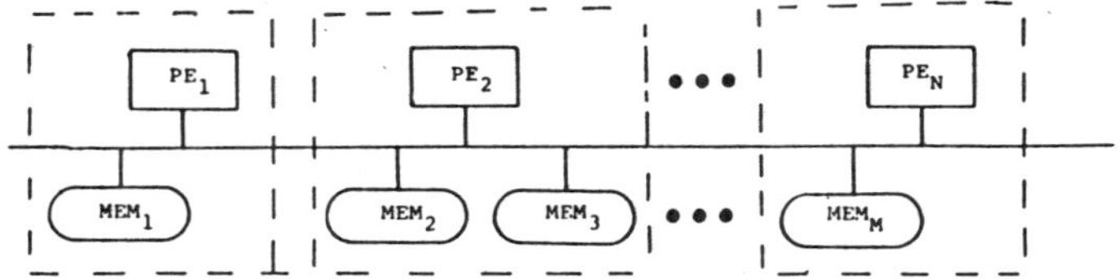

Fig. 3. Local "memory" type of multiprocessor configuration.

We distinguish between two distinct classes of multimemory systems—one in which each memory unit is preassigned to a particular processor unit, and the other in which any memory unit can be accessed by any processor unit. Both "local memory" and "global memory" systems, respectively, have their own advantages. We first model a local memory system with no I/O devices, as shown in Fig. 3. Note that each PE may reference several memory units, but only one memory at any instant of time. For analytic ease, assume that all memory units have identical service times.

At any instant, PE_j is either B or W. If PE_j is W, then Mem_j can be either in B (memory service) or in W. The last case indicates that information is either being transferred from PE_j to MEM_j (or vice versa) or is awaiting transfer. Suppose that at instant t_n, Y_p (of the N) PE's and Y_m (of the M) MEM's are in the B state ($Y_p + Y_m \leq N$). We have two alternative cases.

Case I: The present (or next busy) bus cycle involves a MEM to PE data transfer. In this case, one processor would have moved from W to B and up to Y_p processors would have moved from B to W. The probability that Z_p processors remain in B is equal to the probability that $(Y_p - Z_p + 1)$ processors moved from B to W, and is given by

$$A(Y_p, Z_p) = \begin{bmatrix} Y_p \\ Y_p - Z_p + 1 \end{bmatrix} \cdot \beta^{Y_p - Z_p + 1}(1-\beta)^{Z_p - 1},$$
$$0 \leq Y_p \leq N \text{ and } 0 \leq Z_p \leq 1. \quad (6)$$

(The case of $Y_p = N$ is not physically possible since an MEM to PE data transfer is occurring.)

Case II: The present (or next busy) bus cycle involves a PE to MEM transfer. Considering the number of busy MEM's (instead of PE's), we get

$$A(Y_m, Z_m) = \begin{bmatrix} Y_m \\ Y_m - Z_m + 1 \end{bmatrix} \cdot \alpha^{Y_m - Z_m + 1}(1-\alpha)^{Z_m - 1},$$
$$0 \leq Y_m < N \text{ and } 0 < Z_m \leq Y_m + 1 \quad (7)$$

where

$$\alpha = \frac{T_{bc}}{T_{mc}},$$

and T_{mc} = Time between successive bus usages by the memory.

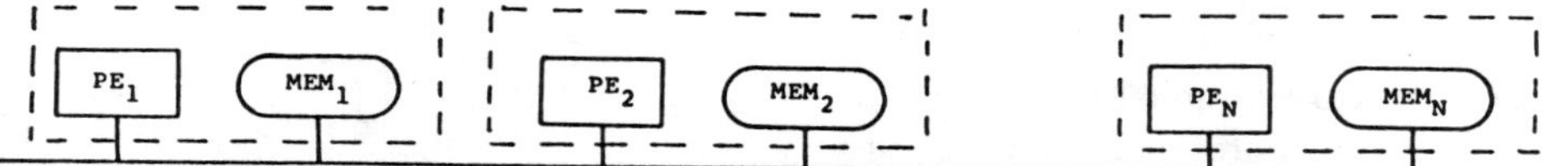

Fig. 4. Alternative equivalent local memory configuration.

TABLE III
IMPROVEMENT IN EFFECTIVE THROUGHPUT USING SPLIT-TRANSACTION PROTOCOLS IN 3-PROCESSOR CONFIGURATION

β	Effective System Throughput		
		Split-Transaction Bus Protocols	
	Traditional Bus Protocol	Bus Speeds = 10 Times Memory Speeds	Bus Speeds = 20 Times Memory Speeds
0.1	2.7070	2.9500	2.9727
0.2	2.4436	2.9003	2.9455
0.3	2.2147	2.8510	2.9184
0.5	1.8269	2.7542	2.8644
0.6	1.6445	2.7070	2.8376
0.7	1.4596	2.6607	2.8111
0.8	1.2788	2.6153	2.7847
0.9	1.1205	2.5709	2.7586

Depending on the computing environment, one can determine the relative probabilities of Case I and Case II occurrences. If the number of responses from MEM's is identical to the number and duration of requests from their respective PE's, then the two probabilities are equal, and the set of equations can be solved.

There is, however, a simpler solution to the above problem. Reconfigure the system shown in Fig. 3 to the one shown in Fig. 4 and consider an element j, denoted as E_j, to be in B if either PE_j or MEM_j is busy, and in W if both PE_j and MEM_j are in W. The probability of transition from B to W equals the probability of using the bus and is given by

$$\gamma = \frac{\text{Bus Time}}{T_{pc}} = \frac{2 \times T_{\text{BUS}}}{T_{pc}}. \tag{8}$$

The above system is identical in analysis to the non-split-transaction case considered at the beginning of this paper. Equations (1)–(5) can be used directly with γ substituted in place of β. The relation between γ and β can be determined from (8), and the fact that memory service times are 10–20 times larger than bus service times. For a ratio of 10, we have

$$T_{bc} = T_{\text{BUS}} + T_{\text{MEM}} + T_{\text{BUS}} = 12T_{\text{BUS}}$$

hence

$$\gamma \triangleq \frac{2T_{\text{BUS}}}{T_{bc}} \times \frac{T_{bc}}{T_{pc}} = \frac{2T_{\text{BUS}}}{12T_{\text{BUS}}} \times \frac{T_{bc}}{T_{pc}} = \frac{\beta}{6}$$

when $\beta = 0.1$, $\gamma = 0.0167$, and solving (1)–(4), we get

$$p_3 = 0.95 \quad p_2 = 0.48 \quad p_1 = 0.001 \quad p_0 = 0.000004,$$

Effective Throughput = 2.95.

When $\beta = 0.3$, $\gamma = 0.05$, we get a degradation of only 5 percent (as compared to the previous 30 percent) as seen from the theoretical results summarized in Table III. Using a split-transaction structure implemented with Intel-8080 chips, the effective throughput with two and three processors was measured to be 1.99 and 2.98, respectively. With $\beta = 0.58$, $\gamma \simeq 0.1$, and the overall throughput should have been 1.86 and 2.70, respectively. This experiment showed that the degradation is lower than calculated because the ratio of β to γ is more than six since bus speeds are usually more than 10 times higher than memory speeds. In our experiment, ECL interface circuitry gave much higher ratios.

IV. GLOBAL MEMORY CONFIGURATION

In this case, any PE can reference any of the secondary elements. The finite probability that the particular memory unit referenced is currently servicing a request from another PE complicates use of the methodology used in the previous examples. The bus is the "central server," and one could use the central server algorithms developed by Buzen [17]. The authors have developed an interactive design package, IMMPS [21], which uses this method. Unfortunately, this method assumes that the requests to the bus are at a fixed rate. In reality, the requests from the PE's are determined by bus response time and the memory response time. We, therefore, introduce a more realistic model here.

We assume that each memory has an equal probability ($= 1/M$) of being referenced. The memory service time ($= T_{\text{MEM}}$) is assumed equal and constant for all memories. If the memory is busy when another reference occurs, the new request is queued in the memory input buffer. A processor issues a new request after a fixed time, T_{PROC}, after receipt of previous information. As such, it is not possible for input data to be received at a busy processor. Also, assume that all bus usages are of identical duration and that the frequency and duration of data flow from Processor i to Memory j is equal and identical to the data flow from Memory j to Processor i. This is based on the assumption that each instruction can be fetched in one operation and that it involves one transfer in each direction between the processor and the memory.

Assume that in the steady state the total bus utilization (by all processors and memories) is η. Then, since each instruction requires two bus usages, $\eta/2$ instructions are processed in unit time, and hence knowing η, we know the overall system throughput. We now obtain a method to determine η.

The bus receives service requests from $(P + N)$ sources. Independent of the individual distributions, the overall arrival rate, $A = \eta/T_{BUS}$ and the bus response time $= T_{BUS}/1 - \eta$. Of the A_{BUS} arrivals to the bus, only $A_{BUS}/2$ are messages from the processors to memories. Thus a given memory has an overall arrival rate

$$A_{MEM}=\frac{1}{M}\times\frac{A_{BUS}}{2}=\frac{1}{M}\times\frac{\eta}{2T_{BUS}}=\eta/2MT_{BUS}. \tag{9}$$

The memory has an overall response time

$$R_{MEM}=\frac{T_{MEM}}{1-A_{MEM}\cdot T_{MEM}}$$
$$=\frac{T_{MEM}}{1-\dfrac{\eta T_{MEM}}{2M\cdot T_{BUS}}}=\frac{2MT_{MEM}\cdot T_{BUS}}{2MT_{BUS}-\eta T_{MEM}}. \tag{10}$$

The aggregate memory cycle time as seen by processor

T_{CT}= Bus Response Time + Memory Response Time + Bus Response Time

$$=\frac{T_{BUS}}{1-\eta}+\frac{2MT_{MEM}\cdot T_{BUS}}{2MT_{BUS}-\eta T_{MEM}}+\frac{T_{BUS}}{1-\eta}. \tag{11}$$

Lemma: For $T_{BUS}/\eta \gg T_{MEM}/2M$, the global memory case can be analyzed as a local memory system.

Proof: From (11)

$$T_{CT}=\frac{4MT_{BUS}{}^2+2T_{MEM}\cdot T_{BUS}[M-\eta-M\eta]}{(1-\eta)(2MT_{BUS}-\eta T_{MEM})}. \tag{12}$$

Now, $\eta < 1$ and $M > 1$, hence $M \gg \eta$ or η can be dropped in comparison to $M\eta$ from the second term in the numerator. Then

$$T_{CT}=\frac{2MT_{BUS}}{2MT_{BUS}-\eta T_{MEM}}\left[\frac{2T_{BUS}}{1-\eta}+T_{MEM}\right]$$

or

$$T_{CT}=A\left[\frac{2T_{BUS}}{1-\eta}+T_{MEM}\right]$$

where

$$A\triangleq\frac{2MT_{BUS}}{2MT_{BUS}-\eta T_{MEM}}=\text{time amplification factor}$$

$$\frac{2T_{BUS}}{1-\eta}=\text{bus time factor of } T_{CT}$$

and

$$T_{MEM}=\text{memory time factor of } T_{CT}.$$

Thus for $T_{BUS}/\eta \gg T_{MEM}/2M$

$$A\simeq 1,\text{ and } T_{CT}=\left[\frac{2T_{BUS}}{1-\eta}+T_{MEM}\right]$$

which indicates that the memory response time is the same as memory service time, or that there is no memory contention. This proves the lemma.

If $A \neq 1$, then we proceed as follows. From bus consideration, the time elapsed between two successive arrivals at a particular processor

$$=\frac{2PT_{BUS}}{\eta}. \tag{15}$$

Also, this time is the sum of the processor service time and the aggregate memory cycle time as seen by the processor; hence

$$T_{PROC}+T_{CT}=\frac{2PT_{BUS}}{\eta} \tag{16a}$$

i.e.,

$$T_{PROC}+\frac{2MT_{BUS}}{2MT_{BUS}-\eta T_{MEM}}\left[\frac{2T_{BUS}}{1-\eta}+T_{MEM}\right]=\frac{2PT_{BUS}}{\eta}. \tag{16b}$$

Cross multiplying, we have

$$\eta^3T_{MEM}\cdot T_{PROC}-\eta^2(T_{MEM}\cdot T_{PROC}+2MT_{BUS}\cdot T_{PROC}+2MT_{BUS}\cdot T_{MEM}+2PT_{BUS}\cdot T_{MEM})+\eta(2MT_{BUS}\cdot T_{PROC}+4MT_{BUS}{}^2+2MT_{BUS}\cdot T_{MEM}+2PT_{BUS}\cdot T_{MEM}+4M\cdot P\cdot T_{BUS}{}^2)-4MPT_{BUS}{}^2=0. \tag{17}$$

Equation (17) is too complex to be solved analytically. However, all variables, except η, are known beforehand, and the true root of η can usually be identified by physical considerations. Dividing throughput by $T_{PROC}\cdot T_{MEM}$, and neglecting terms containing $T_{BUS}{}^2/(T_{PROC}\cdot T_{MEM})$ in comparison to other terms containing η, we get

$$\eta^3-\eta^2\left[1+\frac{2T_{BUS}}{T_{PROC}}(M+P)+\frac{2T_{BUS}\cdot M}{T_{MEM}}\right]+2\eta T_{BUS}\left[\frac{M}{T_{MEM}}+\frac{1}{T_{PROC}}(M+P)\right]-4MP\frac{T_{BUS}{}^2}{T_{PROC}\cdot T_{MEM}}=0. \tag{18}$$

For $T_{MEM} = T_{PROC} = 20T_{BUS}$, and $M = P = 3$, we get $\eta^3 - 1.9\,\eta^2 + 0.9\,\eta - 0.09 = 0$.

One root of (18) is $\eta = 0.13$, the other two roots are imaginary and can be rejected.

Let us compare the effective throughput of this configuration with a single processor, single memory, and single bus system. In the latter case

$$\eta = \frac{\text{Total time bus is used in one cycle}}{\text{Total cycle time}}$$

$$= \frac{T_{BUS} + T_{BUS}}{T_{PROC} + T_{BUS} + T_{MEM} + T_{BUS}} = \frac{2T_{BUS}}{42T_{BUS}}$$

$$= 0.0476.$$

Since, in the split-transaction case, the effective throughput is directly proportional to the load on the bus, and hence bus utilization, the overall improvement in using three processors is

$$\text{Improvement factor} = \frac{\eta \text{ using 3 processors}}{\eta \text{ using 1 processor}}$$

$$= \frac{0.13}{0.0476} = 2.73.$$

Thus in our example, the degradation per processor is less than 10 percent.

V. Impact of Input–Output Devices

The impact of DMA transfers is analyzed by replacing γ by $\gamma^* = \gamma/(1 - \alpha)$ and $\eta^* = \eta/(1 - \alpha)$ in our equations where α represents the fraction of bus utilized by DMA transfers. The non-DMA type of I/O operations are considered by treating I/O devices along the same lines as memory devices. The analysis in either case is identical to the analysis of I/O activity in the non-split-transaction environment.

VI. Impact of the Job Mix

In the above analysis, it has been assumed that the probability of bus usage for transfer of information from memory to processor is equal to the probability of bus usage for transfer of information from processor to memory. This scenario is valid for the following cases:

(a) fetching of instructions by processor from memory;

(b) reading of data by processor from memory when the size of data retrieved equals the size of request on the bus for retrieval of data.

While (a) is generally valid, (b) may not always hold. Also, the scenario is not true for WRITE-ONLY environment.

Assume that the job mix contains only memory-read operations and no memory-write operations (e.g., reading a ROM). In such a case, the total number of requests to memory equals the total number of responses from memory, both as instructions and as data. Since in this environment the bus is available to other processors and memory units when a particular memory is being read, the full benefits of using a split-transaction protocol will be available, and the preceding mathematical analysis will hold without any change.

At the other extreme, assume that the job mix is comprised of write-only operations only. In this case, there would still be memory-read operations in order to fetch instructions. In a WRITE-ONLY environment, with split-transaction protocol the bus is released immediately after the data has been acknowledged as having been received by the memory. In most traditional (non-split) protocols, the bus is not released until after the data has actually been written into the memory. Thus even in a WRITE-ONLY environment, a split-transaction protocol results in lower bus utilization.

Since real situations fall in between the two extreme cases considered above, a split-transaction bus will always offer better performance than an equivalent non-split-transaction bus. Also, more devices can be integrated on a split-transaction bus in all computing environments.

VII. Impact of Pipelining

So far, the processor is assumed to wait for the memory to respond; hence there is zero pipelining.

It is feasible to enhance system performance by implementing both input and output queues at all modules. The advantage of output queue lies in higher bus utilization, and the ability of the processor/memory to continue with other work while a just-completed transaction is waiting for the bus. The advantage of input queue lies in higher utilization of system resources. The probability of queue overflow can be made as small as desired by increasing the queue capacity [21].

Consider two different scenarios, both implemented with split-transaction protocols. In the first case, assume that there are no queues, and a message must be retransmitted if the recipient module is busy. In the other case, assume that there are adequate queues available to guarantee acceptance of all information by the recipient module.

We take the same numbers as considered earlier immediately following (18). These numbers are: $T_{MEM} = T_{PROC} = 20T_{BUS}$, $M = P = 3$, giving $\eta = 0.13$. In this case (no queues)

Processor utilization

$$= \frac{T_{PROC}}{\text{Time elapsed between two successive arrivals at a particular processor}}$$

$$= T_{PROC} \div \frac{2PT_{BUS}}{\eta} \text{ (from (15))}$$

$$= 20T_{BUS} \times \frac{\eta}{2PT_{BUS}} = \frac{20 \times 0.13}{2 \times 3} = 0.433 = 43.3 \text{ percent.}$$

The utilization of other processors and memory units is also the same (as $T_{PROC} = T_{MEM}$ and $M = P$). Thus even with a split-transaction protocol, a zero-pipelined case results in suboptimal utilization of system resources; in fact, in this particular example, no resource is used more than half of the total time. Note that if processors share memory units, there is a 43 percent chance of the memory being busy, resulting in the processor being blocked up if queues were not implemented.

With queues and overlapped arbitration, it is possible to increase processor memory utilization to almost unity, enabling concurrent usage of all system resources. In such a case,

$$\text{bus utilization} = \frac{2PT_{BUS}}{20T_{BUS}} = \frac{2 \times 3}{20} = 0.3.$$

Since bus utilization is directly proportional to overall system throughput, the overall system throughput with queues is more than twice the system throughput without queues; similar positive factors are true for other configurations, too. As utilization of system resources increases, there is increased contention, and response times on individual transactions may increase because of increased wait times. Overall, a split-transaction protocol with queues represents a significant performance improvement in terms of throughput over a split-transaction protocol without queues, which in turn is better than non-split-transaction traditional architectures.

VIII. CONCLUSION

The split-transaction protocol, using queues and overlapped arbitration, gives performance improvements of almost an order of magnitude over conventional bus protocols. As interprocessor communication needs increase, this improved split-transaction protocol offers an effective mechanism of increasing useful system bandwidth at minimal cost.

The use of the split-transaction protocol along with inexpensive microprocessors offers the potential of implementing multimicroprocessor-based systems that offer both high computing power and the desired level of decentralized operation. Such systems have already become popular for fault-tolerant applications. Instead of having to use multiple buses to meet the desired communication loads, split-transaction protocols represent an innovative technique of meeting similar objectives at much lower costs.

REFERENCES

[1] A. Gupta and H-M. D. Toong, "Microcomputers in industrial control applications," *IEEE Trans. Ind. Electron.*, vol. IE-31, pp. 109–119, May 1984.

[2] R. Reddy and V. Zue, "Recognizing continuous speech remains an elusive goal," *IEEE Spectrum*, vol. 20, pp. 84–84, Nov. 1983.

[3] J. F. Bucy *et al.*, "Ease-of-use features in the Texas Instruments professional computer," *Proc. IEEE*, vol. 72, pp. 269–282, Mar. 1984.

[4] Ira A. Gerson, "Evaluation of microprocessor bus requirements for application to multiprocessor configurations," S. B. thesis, Dep. Electrical Eng. and Computer Science, M.I.T., Cambridge, MA, 1976.

[5] E. Horowitz and A. Zorat, "The binary tree as an interconnection network: Applications to multiprocessor systems and VLSI," *IEEE Trans. Comput.*, vol. C-30, pp. 247–253, Apr. 1981.

[6] H. D. Toong, "Micro-star—A microprocessor controlled distributed minicomputer network," in *IEEE COMPCON 77*, pp. 320–324, 1977.

[7] F. P. Preparata and J. Vuillemin, "The cube connected cycles: A versatile network for parallel computation," *Comm. Ass. Comput. Mach.*, vol. 24, no. 5, pp. 300–309, May 1981.

[8] L. D. Wittie, "Communication structures for large networks of microcomputers," *IEEE Trans. Comput.*, vol. C-30, pp. 264–273, Apr. 1981.

[9] R. A. Finkel and M. H. Solomon, "Processor interconnection strategies," *IEEE Trans. Comput.*, vol. C-29, pp. 360–371, May 1980.

[10] S. B. Wu and M. T. Liu, "A cluster structure as an interconnection network for large multimicrocomputer systems," *IEEE Trans. Comput.*, vol. C-30, no. 4, pp. 254–264, Apr. 1981.

[11] K. J. Thurber and G. M. Masson, *Distributed-Processor Communication Architecture.* Lexington, MA: Lexington Books, 1979.

[12] F. Baskett and A. J. Smith, "Interference in multiprocessor computer systems with interleaved memory," *Comm. Ass. Comput. Mach.*, vol. 19, no. 6, pp. 327–334, June 1976.

[13] *Intel Multibus Specification*, Manual Order Number 9800683-02, Intel Corporation, Santa Clara, CA, 1979 (IEEE 796 Bus Standard is based on Multibus).

[14] V. K. Ravindran and T. Thomas, "Characterization of multiple microprocessor networks," in *1973 Proc. IEEE Comput Soc. Int. Conf.*, pp. 133–137.

[15] G. Reyling, Jr., "Performance and control of multiple microprocessor systems," *Computer Design*, pp. 81–86, Mar. 1974.

[16] K. T. Fung and H. C. Torng, "On the analysis of memory conflicts and bus contentions in a multiple-microprocessor system," *IEEE Trans. Comput.*, vol. C-27, pp. 28–37, Jan. 1979.

[17] J. P. Buzen, "Fundamental operational laws of computer system performance," *Acta Informatica*, vol. 7, pp. 167–182, 1976.

[18] J. M. Kurtzberg, "On the memory conflict problem in multiprocessor systems," *IEEE Trans. Comput.*, vol. C-23, pp. 286–293, Mar. 1974.

[19] D. P. Bhandharkar, "Analysis of Memory Interference in Multiprocessors," *IEEE Trans. Comput.*, vol. C-24, pp. 897–908, Sept. 1975.

[20] C. H. Hoogendoorn, "A general model for memory interference in multiprocessors," *IEEE Trans. Comput.*, vol. C-26, pp. 998–1005, Oct. 1977.

[21] A. Gupta, *Design and Evaluation of Multimicroprocessor Systems*, S. M. thesis, M.I.T. Sloan School, Cambridge, MA, 1980.

Part III
Busing Standards and Practices

THE various parts of a multi-microprocessor system are connected together by buses. Most systems contain several different buses.

A ''bus'' denotes the mechanism of communication between more than two computing resources. For connections restricted to two devices, terms such as wires or traces are used instead. Also, in most cases, a bus implies a parallel structure with multiple bits being transferred simultaneously.

The concept of buses is the theme of the first paper of this part by Gustavson. He discusses how buses work, how signals are transmitted, how it is decided who will use the bus next, how to determine the reliability of the bus, and how to design software for efficient operation. The last part of his paper contains interesting personal anecdotes.

The above material is complemented by an informative paper by Borrill who compares and contrasts all of the popular 32-bit buses. Their major characteristics have been summarized in a single table. Vendors of microprocessors usually offer support for only one type of bus. Thus, the choice of the bus determines, to a large extent, the microprocessor to be used, and vice versa.

In Part IV, we will look at the software issues involved in the designing of high performance multi-microprocessor systems.

Computer Buses—A Tutorial

David B. Gustavson
Stanford Linear Accelerator Center

Computer buses are the communication paths between the various parts of a computer system. Most computers, even small ones, contain several different buses, each optimized for a particular kind of communication. Most buses are private, hidden within an integrated circuit or confined to a single circuit board. Other buses appear in accessible places and are described in the computer's documentation, allowing optional equipment or features to be easily added. Some buses are not only easily accessible but follow public standards; this allows easy communication among a variety of devices made by different manufacturers.

Though there are many different buses in common use, they merely represent different choices in the solution of a few basic design problems. We will not discuss any one bus design (or "architecture") in detail, but will rather describe the general problems which each bus must solve. For each of these problems, we will cite a few of the more commonly used solutions. This approach should provide the reader with a perspective for understanding the detailed documentation for any particular bus of interest. Since many readers have no background in electrical engineering, in this article we will review elementary principles as needed.

Work on this article was supported by the US Department of Energy under contract number DE-AC03-76SF00515.

The term "bus" implies the possibility of communication among more than two devices. (Connections limited to two devices are usually called wires, traces, or signals.) Furthermore, "bus" usually implies parallel related connections—several related signals traveling together along approximately the same route at approximately the same time. Parallel structures can also be simulated by a sequence of signals on a single connection, which is then called a serial bus. The focus of this tutorial is the parallel bus.

How buses work

Today's buses are made of electrical conductors, usually copper wires, copper line patterns etched on printed-circuit boards, or fine aluminum line patterns on integrated circuits. Optical communication is not yet economical for bus structures—optical signals are difficult to distribute to multiple destinations, and converting between electrical and optical signals is expensive.

Using Figure 1 as a reference, we can describe how one device on a bus communicates with another. For example, if M3 wishes to communicate with S5, M3 sends signals on the bus that cause S5 to respond. The signals that select S5—rather than some other device on the bus—are collectively called the *address*. If M3 sends data to S5, we say M3 *writes to* S5. On the other hand, if S5 sends data to M3, we say M3 *reads from* S5. M3 tells S5 whether

Reprinted from *IEEE Micro*, pp. 7-22, Aug. 1984.

this is a read or write communication by sending a control signal in addition to the address.

The device that initiates and controls the communication is called the *master* (hence the label M), and the responding device is called the *slave* (label S). Some devices (such as M4/S2) can act as either masters or slaves, but usually not at the same time.

What if another device (M6, for example) wishes to use the bus? If M6 starts to put signals on the bus while M3 is using it, confusion will result because bus lines can carry only one signal at a time. Therefore, any device that wants to use the bus must ensure that the bus is free before putting signals on it.

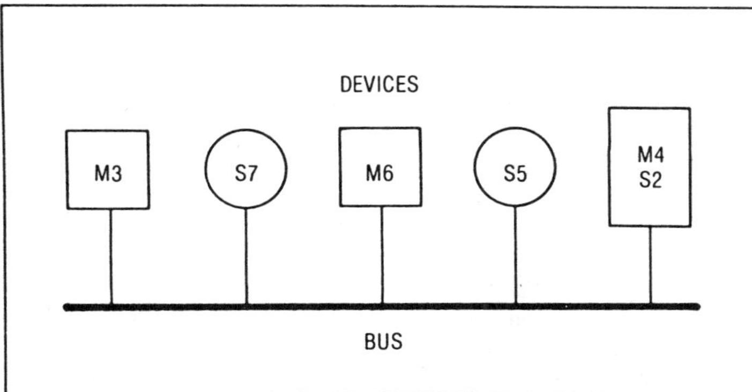

Figure 1. Several master and slave devices attached to a bus.

What if both M3 and M6 decide at the same time they want to use the bus? Each would detect that the bus was free and would interfere with the other in trying to send its signals. The bus mechanism that prevents this from happening is called *arbitration*. Arbitration can be handled in several good ways, one of the reasons buses can differ.

Other problems appear when we look at bus operation more carefully. For example, how are signals sent and received electrically? How does the receiver know when there is data to be received? In the example of Figure 1, how did S5 know to look for its address? How did S5 know what its address was? How are connections to the bus made?

To answer these and other questions, let us start at the beginning, with the mechanical aspects of a bus, and then examine bus operation in more detail.

Bus mechanics

Figure 2 shows a typical arrangement for a publicly accessible bus. The *motherboard,* or backplane, has copper printed-circuit traces in approximately parallel lines, with connectors located at convenient intervals. The bus devices are printed-circuit cards (sometimes called mod-

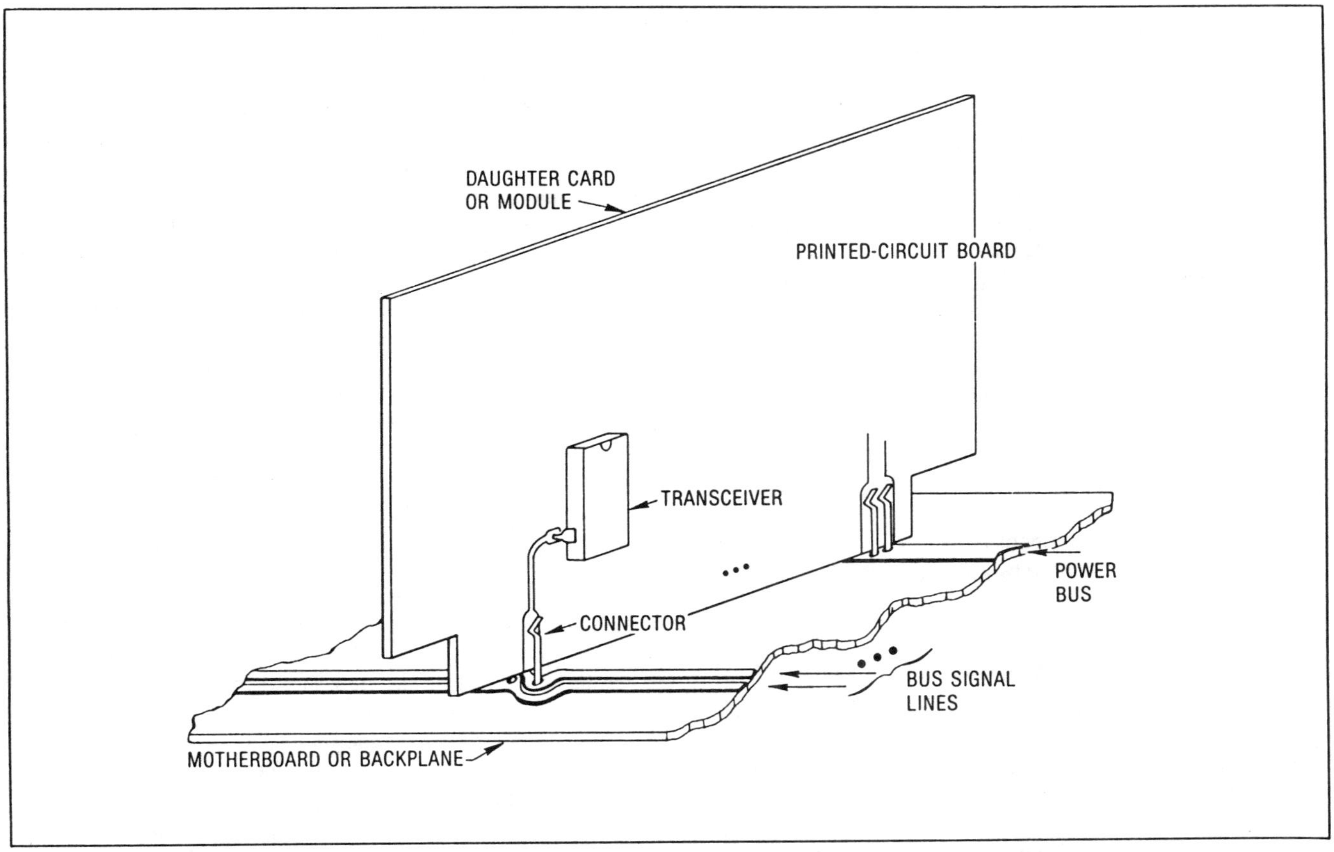

Figure 2. A typical motherboard, or backplane, and daughterboard. Springy contacts connect printed-circuit traces on the daughterboard to the bus lines, thereby connecting drivers and receivers to the bus and providing the daughterboard with electrical power and ground.

ules or daughterboards) which plug into the connectors to make contact with the backplane. In addition to signal lines, the backplane usually has heavy conductors providing the electrical power needed by the daughterboards. Several connector pins are also connected to an electrical common point, or *ground*—either a broad inner copper layer (ground plane) in the motherboard or a broad trace on the back of the motherboard.

The card-edge connector shown in Figure 2 is made by plating gold in a finger pattern on the edge of the daughterboard. Contact springs on the motherboard make a sliding contact as the daughterboard is inserted. These springs usually make separate connections to signal traces on both sides of the daughterboard and are protected by a plastic housing (not shown) which guides the daughterboard into proper alignment.

In two-piece connectors—now gaining in popularity—contact is achieved by means of machined contact pins in a plastic shell, which is attached to the daughterboard. A corresponding plastic shell with machined sockets is mounted at each access point on the motherboard. The many variations of this configuration use different contact and connector sizes, as well as reversed sockets and pins.

The primary problem in connector design is maintaining good and reliable contact (even after hundreds of uses or after years in dirty and mildly corrosive environments). This must be done without requiring large insertion and removal forces—even when the mating pieces are not perfectly aligned and the circuit boards are not perfectly flat.

Most systems require that the electrical power be turned off before inserting or removing daughterboards. In multiple-processor systems, this may result in significant delay due to the need to reload and reinitialize every processor. Therefore, some systems are designed to tolerate power-on insertion and removal—generally called "live insertion" capability. This feature preserves the state and contents of other boards but may still require bus activity to be temporarily stopped, since boards are likely to generate interference as they are powered on or off. A board that has been removed and replaced is no longer in its original state; it must be initialized, and programs communicating with it may need to be restarted. In some cases this may prove so complex that live insertion offers no advantage.

Bus specifications normally include the details of mechanical aspects such as board sizes, card guide size and location, cable connector locations, and the maximum allowable component height on the boards. A few also specify maximum power dissipation and provide for cooling air flow.

Bus signal transmission

Signal transmission is very simple. All devices using the bus are electrically connected to each signal line, and the signal lines act as electrical conductors. When the master puts a voltage on a signal line, the same voltage appears everywhere along the bus and can be sensed by all receivers. To send signals, the master simply changes the voltage from time to time.

Although this description is almost correct, it is not adequate for modern buses. We'll return to this subject after a short discussion of drivers and receivers.

Bus drivers. The circuit that changes the voltage on the signal line is called a bus driver. Any ordinary digital integrated circuit would almost do, since a digital output is always at one of two possible voltage levels. But since bus signal lines have to be shared (driven by different devices at various times), some method is required for disconnecting an ordinary digital output when it is not using the bus.

One solution is to use a three-state driver, which has the output states *high, low,* and *off.* A special input to the driver turns it off when it is not using the bus. The output voltage can then be determined by another driver without interference. Two devices must never try to drive a line at the same time; otherwise, they will fight each other, resulting in high-current spikes, indeterminate voltage levels on the bus, electrical noise, and possible premature component failures.

Another solution is to tie the signal line to a voltage source through a resistor, and use drivers that let the line float or else force it to a particular voltage level. If no driver is turned on, the line will float to the signal level set by the voltage source. If two drivers are turned on at once, each forces the line to the same level, so they share the load and there is no conflict. These drivers are called *open-collector* drivers in the TTL families of integrated circuits, or *open-drain* drivers in MOS circuits. All ECL circuits have this kind of output, called *open-emitter.* This scheme not only eliminates the possibility of electrical conflict on the bus but makes possible a very useful kind of logic, called *wire-OR* (or *wire-AND,* depending on the assignment of voltage levels to logic values). If any driver or combination of drivers is turned on, a signal appears which is the logical OR of all the driving signals. This is useful in solving the arbitration problem, as we shall see later. Most buses use wire-OR for at least a few lines; some allow its use on all signal lines.

Receivers and transceivers. Receivers are circuits that compare the signal voltage at their input with a standard value—usually set by internal circuitry—and then generate a logic-level output suitable for use on the rest of the daughterboard. Transceivers contain a receiver and a driver internally connected to a common pin.

We can now return to the description of signal propagation begun in the first paragraph of this section, this time taking into account the time it takes for a signal to travel. No signal can travel faster than the speed of light in empty space (about 300 mm/ns); on a typical bus made of practical materials the signal speed is a fraction of this.

A more complete description would thus begin with the bus line held at one signal voltage level by a resistor tied to a voltage source at the end of the line. When a driver turns on somewhere along the line, it pulls the line to the other signal level at the point where the driver is attached. The resulting voltage change travels in both directions away from the driver, moving a bit slower than the speed of light, until the whole line is at the new signal level.

Even this, however, does not completely explain what happens in real buses. Electrical charges are distributed along the signal line in proportion to the voltage. They repel one another, but are attracted to any nearby charges of opposite polarity. More voltage helps them crowd together, but the precise number and distribution of the charges depends on both the detailed shape of the line, and on the distribution of electrical charges in the neighborhood of the line (that is, on the dielectric constant of the circuit board and on the configuration of neighboring conductors). The charge present per voltage applied is the capacitance of the line, and the capacitance per unit length varies from point to point depending on the local shape and environment of the line.

When a driver turns on and changes the voltage, the charges move, making a current. The moving charges create a magnetic field which affects the motion of nearby charges. The net effect, called *inductance,* tries to keep the current from changing. The inductance depends on the precise shape of the signal line and nearby materials, and the inductance per unit length varies from point to point in a way different from the way the capacitance varies.

The ratio of the signal voltage to the resulting signal current, called the characteristic impedance (Z_0), depends on the inductance per unit length (L_0) and the capacitance per unit length (C_0):

$$Z_0 = \sqrt{L_0/C_0}$$

How much current flows when the driver turns on? This depends on the characteristic impedance and varies from point to point. The speed of the signal traveling along the bus depends mainly on the effective dielectric constant of the bus; the propagation delay per unit length is

$$T_{pd} = \sqrt{L_0 \cdot C_0}$$

Both answers are simple for an ideal signal line (transmission line) like the coaxial cable shown in Figure 3a. A real line, however, looks more like Figure 3b, with strange projections due to connectors, circuit traces, and components on connected daughterboards.

As the signal travels along a real line, it encounters regions with different propagation velocities and impedances. Wherever the impedance changes, the signal cannot proceed unchanged because the relationship of current and voltage required by the line no longer matches the signal. Part of the signal continues onward, but the rest is reflected in the direction from which it came; part of that portion of the signal may be subsequently re-reflected and so on, leading to a very complex signal on any real bus. When the signal reaches the end of the line, all of it reflects back unless absorbed by proper terminating resistors. If a resistor whose value is equal to the line impedance is placed at the end of the line, the signal is absorbed without reflection. These termination resistors, which must be located at each end of the line, determine how much current flows to the driver after the reflections have died out. Because real line impedances are never precisely known—and depend anyway on where each board is connected—the resistors never perfectly match the line, and some reflection always occurs. Further, the electric and magnetic fields produced by signals changing on any one signal line create signals in neighboring lines—that is, *crosstalk.*

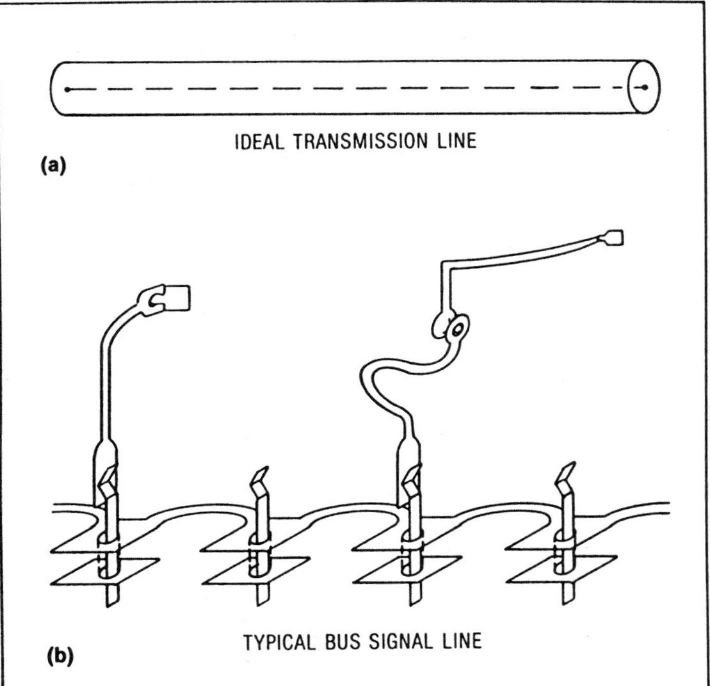

Figure 3. Transmission lines—a section of coaxial cable, an ideal shielded uniform line (a); a typical real bus line, with branches, neighbors, loads, and antennae (b).

All signal propagation problems become more manageable if the bus is designed to have a low impedance and a grounded conductive plane near all signal lines (usually a buried layer inside the motherboard). Due to imperfections in the lines, signal edges change shape as they propagate, implying that pulses change shape as well. Any bus has a minimum pulse width that can survive propagation from end to end. This puts an ultimate limit on the number of pulses per second—or bandwidth—the bus can support. Normally, other factors limit the bus throughput before the bandwidth limit is approached. A possible exception will be discussed later.

In effect, the driver sees two lines at once (one going in each direction), so it must supply twice the current needed by one line. The impedance seen by a driver on a practical bus is often less than 20 ohms, resulting in currents of 150 milliamperes for 3-volt signals. This output is well beyond the data sheet ratings for most bus drivers available today, but real devices happily exceed their rated output if shorter lifetime, lower reliability, and degraded signal levels can be tolerated.

Current does not flow only in the signal lines. Signal currents complete their circuit through the ground pin of the driver. When all the signal lines are active at once, this ground current can be very large. Unfortunately, this current is irregular and has very-high-frequency components because the drivers turn on and off rapidly. The resistance and inductance of the ground plane allow the ground pins of the circuits on the daughterboard to have different voltages from each other and from those of other boards. This, in turn, may cause receivers to evaluate signals incorrectly, and can cause a malfunction of logic circuitry on the boards. This ground noise is better avoided in the design than dealt with at a later time. In addition to good ground planes on the daughterboard and motherboard, the solution requires well-distributed connections between the motherboard and daughterboard ground systems.

High-speed buses should provide approximately one ground pin per four signal pins. Further, the daughterboard should be designed so that the ground current from a given driver flows to a connector pin near the corresponding signal pins. The motherboard ground is usually a buried copper layer in a multilayer printed circuit; clearance holes around the connector signal pins prevent short circuits to this ground. The size of these holes must be controlled: the grounds on each side of the connector must be connected in many places along its length, rather than separated by a row of merging holes. The connector should be wide enough to allow room on the daughterboard for the transceivers to be located near the connector, thus minimizing trace lengths, which disturb the bus.

Until recently, most bus designers have handled these problems rather poorly by (1) aiming at high-impedance lines on the motherboard because they seem easier to drive with available circuits, (2) ignoring the effects of connector pins and circuit traces on connected daughterboards, (3) neglecting ground planes, and (4) failing to provide the necessary distribution of ground pins across the connector.

If buses have been so poorly designed, why do they work so well? Generally, they are saved by being slowed down until they work. If the signals could be made to change slowly from one level to the other, the reflections would become small and the crosstalk insignificant. Unfortunately, most drivers are too fast for the buses they drive, so the resulting signals look terrible. These buses are usually saved by introducing delay in the system—often referred to as the *bus-settling time*—so that the signals become stable before they are used. Sometimes there is enough delay inherent in the kind of circuitry used, but explicit delays are often added for this purpose. Synchronous buses, which use a central clock to time every transition on the bus, can add delay easily by slowing the clock so that all signals are changed at one clock edge and not looked at until the other edge, providing enough delay for propagation and settling. Asynchronous buses must either solve these problems at their source or add artificial delays to nullify their effect.

Slowing the receiver circuits is also helpful in overcoming poor bus design. In some cases, low-pass filters are introduced to make the receivers insensitive to reflections and other high-frequency noise. The MITS Altair bus, for example, used high-power drivers and low-power receivers because the data sheet numbers implied an enormous fan-out (and therefore, the bus should have allowed a large number of boards to be plugged in). Because of the fast drivers and poor backplane design, the signals looked terrible, but the low-power receivers were slow enough to reject much of the "junk," and the bus usually worked—especially in short-length versions. Unfortunately, no complete specification existed for the bus (before IEEE 696 appeared), and many of the boards designed for it worked poorly—sometimes because they used receivers that were too fast.

As microprocessor speeds have increased, these slowed buses have become less and less acceptable. Buses must now be designed more carefully in order to solve these problems. Modern bus designs are pushing fundamental limits. Fast buses must (1) limit the length of traces on daughterboards, (2) reduce as much as possible the capacitance of transceivers and connectors, (3) provide good ground planes with plenty of ground pins, and (4) specify transceivers that can handle the real problems of imperfect transmission lines.

The TTL bus drivers and receivers used until now have not been very satisfactory. The Fastbus (IEEE Standard 960), a high-performance bus recently developed under the auspices of the US Department of Energy, changed from TTL to ECL to solve this problem. The IEEE P896 has specified a new transceiver that reduces capacitance, signal voltages, and edge speeds, and rejects noise in the receiver, while using TTL power supplies and signals on the daughterboard side. These transceivers and the bus driving problem are described in an article by R.V. Balakrishnan, also in this issue.

Bus arbitration

With our new understanding of how signals are sent, let us return to the arbitration problem. Any device that wants to use the bus must somehow get permission first, to avoid potential conflicts between two or more devices trying to talk at once.

What may be the simplest arbitration method uses special wiring on the backplane to form a *star* connection, as shown in the lower part of Figure 4. A bus request signal is connected from each device to a central arbiter. A second star connection carries a bus grant signal back to each device. Thus, each device has a private two-way connection with the arbiter. The arbiter may use any method it likes to decide who gets the bus. This versatile method allows any conceivable allocation scheme to be implemented and is very fast and efficient, but it has some serious disadvantages. For example, the special wiring on the backplane is expensive. Also, information about the arbitration is not present on the bus, so bus monitoring for diagnostic purposes is difficult. And it can be difficult to access the arbiter for initializing it via software—or for changing the algorithm—unless the arbiter is accessible from the bus. However, providing such access requires an expensive connection to a daughterboard.

A second arbitration method also uses special wiring—but a much cheaper kind called the *daisy chain* (shown in the central part of Figure 4). A daisy chain is a pair of pins in each connector, wired so that a signal enters the daughterboard on one pin and returns to the bus on the other. This allows a series connection of logic circuits from each daughterboard along the backplane. This connection is the basis for a very common kind of arbitration. It is used in conjunction with a wire-OR line, which is connected to one end of the daisy chain. When any device wants to use the bus, it drives the wire-OR bus request line and looks for a signal on its daisy-in pin. Each device passes the daisy-in signal to the daisy-out pin, unless it wishes to use the bus. Thus, the device nearest the end of the daisy chain connected to the bus request line has the highest priority, and always gets the daisy-in (bus grant) signal when it asserts a bus request. If the device does not want the bus, it passes the grant along (as does every other device in turn), until a requestor sees it and refuses to pass it further. More rules are needed to prevent a high-priority device from taking the bus away from a lower-priority device in midcycle—a problem that can be solved by synchronizing request assertions with other bus activity.

Although the daisy chain is very economical, it has several disadvantages: (1) it may be slow because signals have to travel through logic on each daughterboard; (2) it must have a daughterboard or a dummy board plugged in at every connector position, or the grant signal will be blocked and the system will fail; and (3) it provides very little information about arbitration, making diagnosis and monitoring difficult.

A new arbitration scheme that has gained much popularity in recent years was invented at Computing Devices of Canada (UK patent number 1,099,575, filed in 1966; the inventor's name was not listed) and rediscovered by Matthew Taub of IBM in 1975 (see Taub's article in this issue). It was rediscovered yet again by Leo Paffrath at SLAC for the Fastbus design project, and moved from there to IEEE 696 and IEEE P896; it now also appears in the TI NuBus and Intel's Multibus-II. Taub has recently developed an enhancement to this scheme for P896 which provides totally distributed control (requiring no central timer) and is independent of the speeds of the competing daughterboards. The other buses using this method all rely on timing generated by one particular device on the bus.

Taub's method uses only bussed signal lines, so all information about arbitration is present everywhere on the bus; it has no position dependence, requires no special backplane wiring, and is relatively efficient. Depending on the goals of the implementation, it uses two to four wire-OR signals for timing and control, and four to seven wire-OR lines for the actual arbitration bus. The basic idea is that every device that wants the bus tries to put its own priority number on the arbitration bus, removing its less significant bits if it sees a higher number present; after some delay, only the highest-priority number remains. The device that sees its own priority then controls the bus. After that device removes its number, the

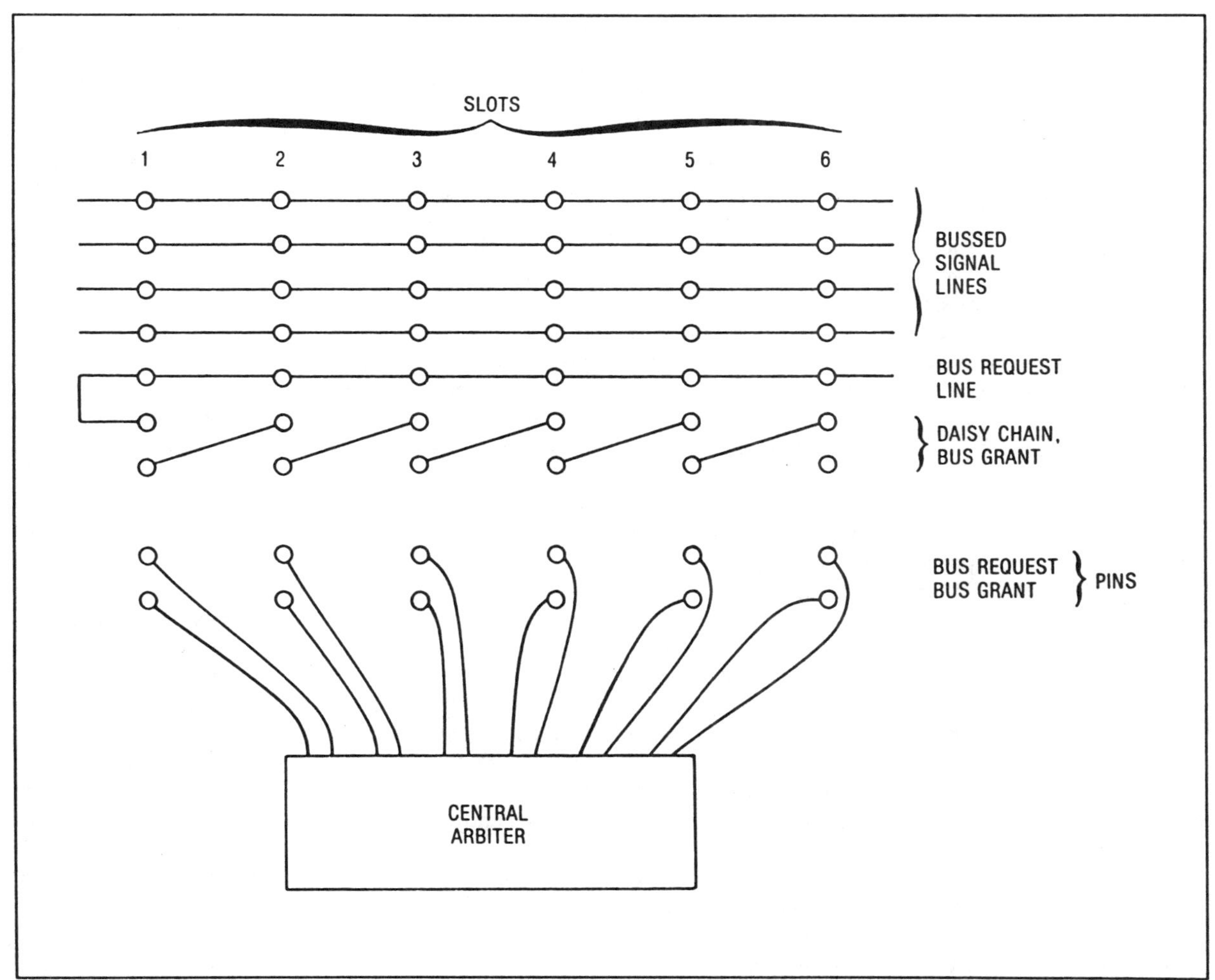

Figure 4. Typical bus features. The upper part shows simple bussed signal lines. The center part shows a daisy chain tied to a bussed grant line for arbitration purposes. The lower part shows unbussed connections to a central arbiter.

next-highest device wins, and so forth. Adding a simple rule (sometimes called "fairness") that prevents new requests while other requestors are competing produces a system that guarantees every applicant a turn, and prevents the highest-priority device from winning the bus all the time.

A degree of fault detection can also be added in this scheme simply by widening the priority number by one bit and assigning only odd-parity numbers (numbers with an odd number of bits asserted). The winning priority always appears with its own parity bit; simple logic can then check for valid parity. This improves the chances of detecting a failed driver or bad connector before it causes too much chaos in the system.

The real purpose of "priority" in modern multiprocessor backplane buses is to break ties between simultaneous requests for use of the bus. In a system with the "fairness" scheme just described, bus priority has little to do with determining which device gets the most access to the bus, and nothing to do with job or task priority. Confusion between bus priority (which is important for nanoseconds or microseconds) and task priority (which is important for milliseconds or seconds) has been common in bus design. In single-processor buses, however, the processor may be given the lowest priority so that it takes only the bus cycles remaining after the needs of disk transfers or other I/O have been satisfied.

Bus signal allocation

Now that we have an arbitration method to determine which of several devices may use the bus, we shall look more carefully at what happens while the bus is in use.

The first step the master takes is to assert an address on the bus, which selects one of the slave devices and establishes a connection between master and slave. The address usually contains additional information which specifies a particular part of the slave. For example, the more significant bits of the address may determine which of several memory boards is to respond, while the less significant bits determine which word in that board's memory is sought.

The bus may provide for more than one kind of address, with additional control signals to specify the address type. Frequently, the bus supports both a memory address and an I/O port address, similar to the scheme used in Intel's 8086 family of microprocessors. Processors that do not make this distinction can still use such a bus by adding hardware to translate a certain range of processor memory addresses into bus I/O addresses. Some buses have other kinds of addresses as well. Devices may have multiple address *ranges* as well as multiple *kinds* of addresses. The primary requirement is that addresses must be assigned uniquely, so that only one slave device responds to a given address of any kind.

Some systems extend this to allow for broadcast addresses (either special address values or special address kinds) which select multiple or all slave devices. Generally, this kind of addressing is used for broadcasting information from the master to all the slaves, but a few systems permit the corresponding read operation as well (sometimes called *broadcall*). Broadcall results in the bit-wise ORing of the information from all addressed slaves.

The maximum size of the address is determined by the number of signal lines allocated for this purpose, and is one of the most fundamental properties of any bus. The address size often limits the amount of memory that can be installed in a system, since each memory word usually requires a unique address in order to be useful. The address size is usually given as the number of bits or signal lines; these lines are often called the address bus.

The width of the data path, or data bus, is the next most important parameter of the bus. Most buses now use some multiple of eight lines (an integral number of bytes) for the data width. A data item that uses the full bus width is usually called a *word*, although in some cases the size of the word is defined by the architecture of a family of processors.

Most buses use addresses which specify a particular byte, so a series of transfers on a bus with multibyte width will have successive addresses incremented by the number of bytes in each transfer. Such buses usually provide a way to transfer information on a subset of the full bus width. This is especially useful for writes, where it may be convenient to change a particular byte in memory without affecting its neighbors.

Other buses address items of full bus width only, so each transferable item has one address. Any transfers of less width are taken care of by the master, which reads the whole word in, modifies the appropriate part, and then writes the whole word back to the slave.

When a bus transfers partial-width items, it may either leave them on the same signal lines they would have occupied if they were part of a full-width transfer (*unjustified*) or move them so that they occupy the least-significant signal lines (*justified*). Justified buses make it less expensive to start with a narrow subset of a wide bus. Extra justification hardware can be supplied for the wide boards when they are added later. The disadvantage of justified buses is that future systems with no narrow subset boards still need justification hardware on every board, though it no longer serves a useful purpose. A greater disadvantage is that a justified bus does not work well with all computer architectures, reducing its usefulness as a general-purpose interface. As an example, compare the specifications of the Multibus-II (justified) to those of the NuBus (unjustified).

Some buses include extra lines for error checking.One extra line for each byte of data allows byte parity checking along with simple partial-word transfers. A few more lines permit the use of an error detection and correction code, so that badly received data can be repaired by the receiver. This complicates partial-word transfers, however, because such a code becomes more efficient as it applies to more bits—and so would usually be applied to the full word rather than byte by byte. Error checking also requires a mechanism for telling the sender that the data arrived in bad condition, so it can be corrected by being sent again. Error checking may also be applied to addresses and other parts of the bus.

Address width and data width need not be related. Common address/data combinations are 16/8, 16/16, 20/8, 20/16, 24/16, 24/32, and 32/32.

The bus may have separate signal lines for address and data, or it may use the same lines at different times. The latter procedure, called *multiplexing*, slows a bus less than one might expect, because data are not useful until after addressing is complete. This is especially true for read operations, which require an additional wait for the access time of the slave. Multiplexing is especially attractive for wide buses because it saves so many lines, drivers, and receivers, thereby reducing system power consumption and noise and freeing circuit board space.

The bus also requires control signals. These specify whether a read or a write is to occur, how wide the transfer is to be and which bytes are to be valid, which type of address is being used, and, possibly, which protocol is to be used. Two to eight signals, sometimes called the control bus, are usually used for these purposes.

From one to four lines are often used to allow the slave to respond with error codes or status information, on a status bus.

The arbitration lines, described in the previous section, may add three to eleven more signals. Some buses include another set of lines for interrupts, which are signals from slave devices requesting service from a particular processor. Interrupts can be handled like arbitration, since the problem is one of deciding which of several interrupters should receive service first. Daisy chains and central arbitration circuits are common solutions. Buses that are designed to handle multiple processors, however, tend to eliminate special "single-processor" interrupt mechanisms from the bus; they usually require any device that requests service from another to write a request to it through the normal bus protocols. This simplifies the bus and eliminates the need for dedicated mechanisms to specify which processor is to handle the interrupt service.

Serial communication. It is becoming common practice to include one to four lines for connection to a serial local network. Because serial communication is necessarily slower than parallel bus communication, and networks can be implemented either way, disagreement has arisen about the usefulness of such a serial link in a fast parallel backplane. Some think it should serve as a full-function path providing redundancy in case of parallel bus failure. Others would assign it special functions such as interrupt handling or task priority sorting. Still others consider it an independent resource which might be used for communication with local-network peripheral devices. Some implementations limit the serial connection to the backplane, while others allow it to link multiple backplanes or even extend over kilometers. The Fastbus introduced the serial network because of a clear need for communication among diagnostic devices on different backplane bus segments. Communication with multiple segments is needed to diagnose problems in segment interconnect devices. Once a serial network is implemented, nothing prevents its use for other purposes.

Several buses now include four or five position-encoded pins on the connector so that each connector presents a unique code or slot number to the daughterboard. This code can be used for initializing each board with unique addresses or priority codes after a system power-on or reset.

The final group of lines, often the most important, requires the greatest care in bus design. These are the timing lines: strobes, syncs, and clocks. This group usually accounts for two to six lines, depending on the bus protocol.

When power supply pins and ground pins are added to the list, the need for big connectors becomes clear; it is barely possible to fit a 32-bit bus on a 64-pin connector. Some buses use connectors with hundreds of pins, including special-purpose sub-buses, free lines for private communication among parts of multiboard subsystems, many paralleled pins for passing heavy power-supply current, and so on. Table 1 summarizes connector pin allocation.

Table 1.
Typical allocations of pins to bus functions.

LINE NAMES	TYPICAL NUMBER OF PINS	
ADDRESS	16-32	MAY BE COMBINED IN
DATA	8-32	MULTIPLEXED BUSES
ARBITRATION	3-11	
CONTROL	2-8	
STATUS	1-4	
CLOCKS, STROBES	2-6	
SERIAL NETWORK	1-4	
POSITION CODE	4-5	
GROUND	2-20	
POWER	2-20	

Bus protocol

Although we have talked about addressing and transferring data, we have not really explained these operations. When a master puts an address on the bus, it is not likely that all the bits will arrive at the same time. Some may travel longer paths on the board; some may travel through mapping hardware that translates processor addresses to bus addresses. Some lines, drivers, and receivers are faster than others, which causes some bits to arrive before others, producing an effect called *skew*. All slave devices need to know when the address becomes valid, so that they can decide whether to respond.

The situation for data transfers is more complicated, because in most buses data can flow in both directions. In read operations, a delay occurs while the slave searches for the requested data; therefore the slave must signal when the data are valid. The system must allow for bus skew in data transfers as well.

The method chosen by the bus designer for signaling the validity of address, data, commands, and status is called the *bus protocol*. The addressing part of an operation is often called the *address cycle*, and each data transfer is called a *data cycle*.

There are two major classes of protocols, *synchronous* and *asynchronous*. Synchronous protocols time all signals relative to a system clock, while asynchronous protocols provide separate validity signals for each sub-bus. In actuality, every protocol includes some synchronous and some asynchronous aspects, but the styles of the two types are quite different.

Synchronous protocols often use fewer bus lines and are simpler to understand, implement, and test; however, they are less flexible than asynchronous protocols. Locked to a particular maximum clock rate—and thus tied to a particular level of technology—they cannot take advantage of advances in performance that occur after the design is frozen. Now that buses are approaching their ultimate physical speed limits, however, this disadvantage is becoming less serious.

Asynchronous protocols are self-timing—as a result, a mixture of fast and slow devices, using both old and new technology, can share a bus. Bus speed adapts automatically to the requirements of the devices communicating at the moment, providing naturally for the dynamic changes in timing requirements that are typical of shared memories or multiple-bus interconnects. Therefore, as technology improves, faster devices can be added to the system. It is not necessary to replace all the old devices to speed up the system, as it is with a synchronous system. The price for these advantages is some increase in complexity.

Although the trend in recent years has favored asynchronous buses, some of the latest high-performance designs are synchronous. With present technology, synchronous designs run a bit faster than asynchronous designs. Modern buses are now so near their ultimate speed limits that any speed increases resulting from future technology will make them only slightly faster than present synchronous designs.

Synchronous buses have a central clock oscillator which drives a bus signal line to distribute timing information throughout the system. Figure 5 shows a read operation using a simple synchronous protocol (essentially that of the TI NuBus). The rising edge of the clock is the time when bus signals make their changes. Signals are assumed to be valid—i.e., to have successfully propagated throughout the system—just before the next rising clock edge. Since NuBus uses an asymmetric clock, its falling edge serves as the time reference for valid signals—but this is a convenience rather than an essential feature. Other systems use delay from a clock edge instead.

A start signal marks the presence of the address and control information on the multiplexed bus lines. When the slave recognizes its address and finds the requested data, it puts the data and status on the bus and marks their presence with an acknowledge (ack) signal.

A write operation is similar, except that data are supplied by the master at the next clock cycle after the address, and remain on the bus until the acknowledge and status signals are sent by the slave.

In synchronous systems, the speed of signal travel does not appear explicitly in the protocol, but it must be considered in the bus design. The clock usually propagates along the bus at a normal signal speed, though it is possible (with some cost and effort) to deliver simultaneous clock signals at every bus connector. The clock frequency must be chosen to allow time for signals to flow from any starting point to every other point well before the end of the clock cycle, allowing for differences in clock arrival time as well. Thus, shorter buses can be designed to run faster. Simultaneous clock distribution allows higher speed than a centrally located clock source, which in turn is faster than a bus with a clock propagating from one end.

Note that all cycles have both read and write aspects, as well as a validity signal for each direction. Control and address always flow from master to slave, and status flows

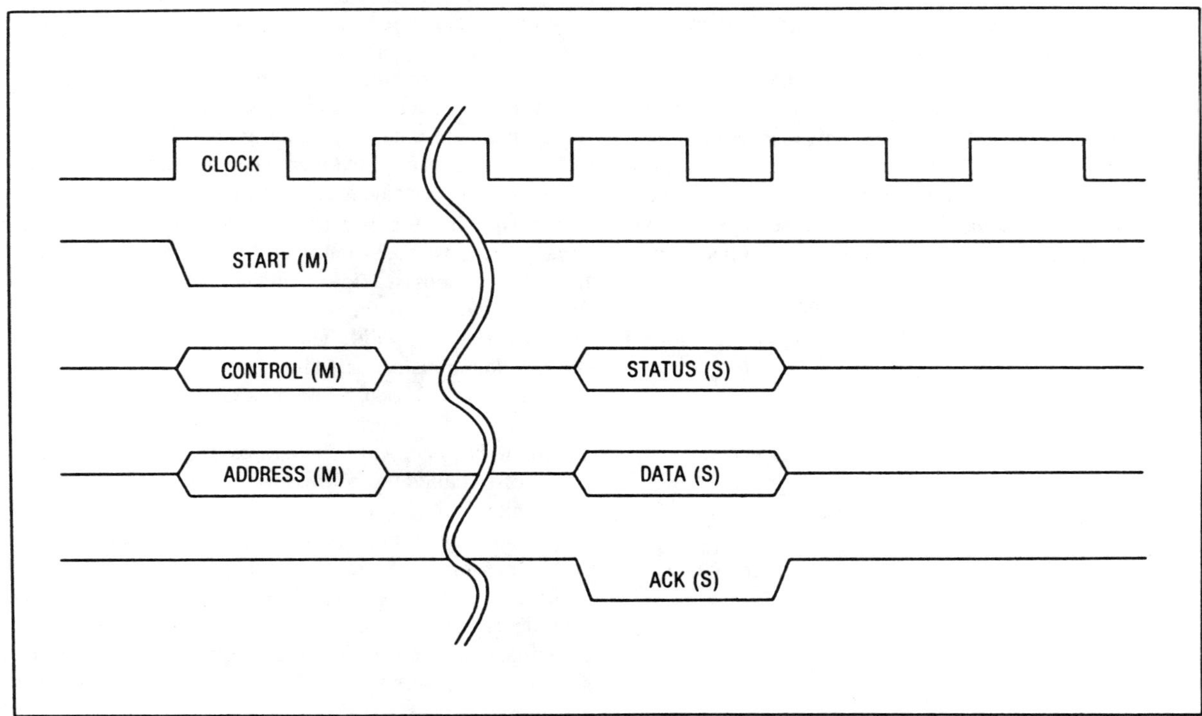

Figure 5. Synchronous bus read protocol. The clock marks off time for the whole system. The start signal shows when to look for an address and the ack signal marks the end of the transfer.

from slave to master. Data can flow either way.

In asynchronous protocols, every set of signals put on the bus is accompanied by a corresponding timing signal, called a *strobe* or *sync* signal. Timing signals generated by the slave are often called *handshakes* or *acknowledges*.

Figure 6 shows a read operation using an asynchronous protocol similar to that of the Fastbus or P896. The master asserts the address and control information on the bus, waits for a skew time, and then asserts the address sync to signal validity. The slaves look at the address and check whether to respond. The addressed slave then responds with a status signal, followed by an address acknowledge. When the master sees the address acknowledge, it knows that a connection has been established and it can check the status. The address is no longer needed on the bus, though the slave may have saved a copy of all or part of it.

The master then changes the control information, waits a skew time, and asserts the data sync. If this were a write cycle, the master would assert the data at the same time as the new control information. However, in the case shown, the control information tells the slave that this is a read cycle. The slave finds the data, puts them on the bus with new status information, and asserts the data acknowledge. When the master sees the data acknowledge, it reads the data from the bus and removes the data sync to indicate that it is finished with the data. In this simple example, the master also removes the address sync. In more complex examples, the address sync could remain in order to maintain the connection across several data cycles. When the slave sees the data sync removed, it removes all data and status information as well as the data acknowledge. The address acknowledge is also removed, in response to the removal of the address sync, restoring the bus to an idle condition.

The timing diagram of Figure 6 explicitly shows the effects of bus signal speed and device response speed, which are fundamental parts of an asynchronous system's operation. As in the synchronous case, every operation has both read and write aspects. In effect, control is always written and status is always read; data are timed and driven like control or status, as appropriate.

Part of the protocol must inform the arbitration circuitry when the bus is in use. In the synchronous example, the bus is busy from start to ack, and no special busy signal is needed. In the asynchronous example, assertion of either the address sync or the address acknowledge indicates that the bus is busy.

Note that the asynchronous system is fully handshaken; i.e., in every case both parties agree before any information is removed from the bus. Thus, although one device may be very fast and another very slow, they can still communicate successfully. This is one of the nice features of asynchronous systems, because it allows parts of a

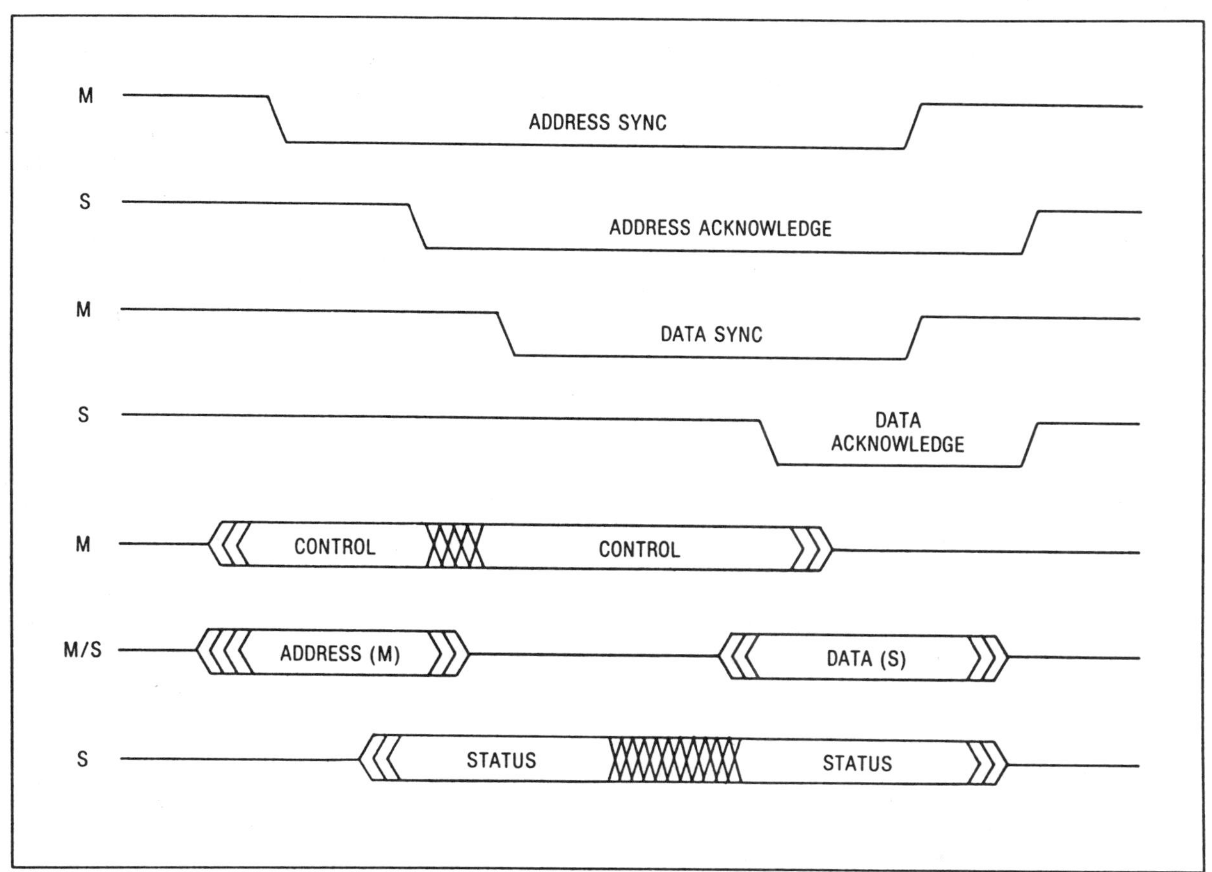

Figure 6. Asynchronous bus read protocol. Each direction of signal flow has its own timing signal: sync and acknowledge. Both edges of these signals are used. The actual duration of each signal depends on the distance between master and slave as well as on the observation point along the bus. These signals are shown at the master.

system to be gradually replaced with newer and faster circuits, with a resulting gradual improvement in performance.

The synchronous system is partially handshaken, in that the slave can take as many complete clock cycles as it needs to find the requested data before it responds with an acknowledge signal. On the other hand, there is an implicit requirement that the slave either finish with the address and control information in a fraction of a clock cycle, or quickly copy it before it disappears. Similarly, the master must be able to accept the read data within one clock, or the data will be lost. This can be a problem if the master is using dynamic memory and happens to be refreshing it when the data arrive. Extra buffer memories are normally used to handle problems of this sort. Notice also that if a synchronous slave is just a bit too slow to be able to respond in one clock cycle, the operation is lengthened by a full clock cycle. This can be a very significant disadvantage in comparison with asynchronous systems, which use only as much time as they need.

In fact, asynchronous systems are not really fully handshaken: in order to prevent the system from waiting forever for a response that will never come (due to programming error or hardware failure), time-outs are always provided to abort the operation after a reasonable wait with no response. This possibility introduces new problems—for example, what if the master times out just as the slave sends the acknowledge? Some circuit has to decide whether the acknowledge arrived in time and, if not, how to get the bus cleaned up again. Data cycle time-outs (which usually mean broken hardware) are rare, so the time-out can be set extremely long without hurting system performance. Address time-outs are more frequent. They occur when a program is initializing the system (and searching to see what devices are present, for example), and often occur when a program error results in a bad address. Therefore, the bus specification usually sets a fairly short time-out for addresses, requiring all slave address decoding to be fast enough to meet that fixed time. Thus, practical asynchronous systems have certain synchronous aspects as well.

Skew delay. Bus skew, which is the worst-case difference in propagation time between the fastest and the slowest signal line, has to be provided for in both kinds of systems. In synchronous systems, skew must be considered in order to determine the fastest safe clock rate, but it can be ignored elsewhere in the design. Asynchronous systems, however, must allow for skew in every handshake of every device. When the master asserts a sync signal, it waits a skew time after the data are on the bus, so that when the slave sees the sync it can assume that the data are good. The slave may also have internal data path skew; it can compensate by adding additional delay before using the sync signal it received. When the slave returns data to the master, it must wait a skew delay after asserting the data before it asserts the acknowledge.

Actually, the skew delay can be accounted for by either master or slave or a combination of the two, as long as enough delay is provided in total. The P896 bus provides for skew as described above, but the Fastbus puts all skew responsibility in the master: the slave asserts the acknowledge at the same time as the returned data, and the master waits a skew time before looking at the data. Skew delay is system-dependent, technology-dependent, and a property of the type and length of the physical bus implementation. The Fastbus expects to have various implementations, ranging from short backplanes to cable buses at least 10 meters long; since the Fastbus emphasizes data acquisition, there should be many more slaves than masters. By putting all skew responsibility in the master, the Fastbus reduces the number of devices that have to be adjusted when the bus properties change. Slaves are still responsible for taking care of their own internal skew problems. P896, however, is solely concerned with a standard backplane bus with known properties, and expects to have mostly master devices in a multiple-processor system. Thus, P896 uses a symmetric approach in which each sender of information accounts for the bus skew itself.

These simple protocol examples do not exhaust the possibilities, especially for multiplexed buses, which pay a time penalty for every address cycle. For example, it may be useful to have a read-modify-write operation to one address. The details of these more complex operations follow the same principles we have discussed, but vary from bus to bus.

Block transfers. Block transfer is a single address cycle followed by multiple data cycles (either read or write, but normally not intermixed). Usually the address is presumed to start from the given initial value and increment after each data cycle. Transfers to I/O devices or FIFOs (first-in, first-out queues), however, may not have any increment implied. The difference mainly affects slave internal design, but it also has implications for the master if error recovery is needed. For example, what address does the master use if it wants to repeat the transfer of the tenth word in a block because of a parity error? Both synchronous and asynchronous systems may implement block transfers. However, asynchronous systems can make yet another improvement.

The data transfer illustrated in Figure 6 shows that the final edges of the data sync and the data acknowledge are not really used for transferring data, but instead provide time to turn off drivers and let the signals disappear, thus cleaning up the bus. This is necessary for some operations, such as those which change the bus direction from read to write, but not for those sending a block of data in one direction. Therefore, some protocols allow block transfers to go at twice the rate of single transfers by using both the leading and the trailing edges of the data sync and data acknowledge for data transfer. The bus still has to be cleaned up at the end of the block, however, and this may require an extra cycle. The handshake is still complete, as either party can slow the transfer whenever necessary. Only the unneeded bus clean-ups have been removed.

Ultimate blinding speed. There is still another possibility for asynchronous systems. Observe that the time it takes to transfer a word includes both the time it takes the word to travel from sender to receiver and the time for the acknowledging handshake to return to the sender. In addition, there are internal delays in both master and slave, and there are extra handshake edges for bus clean-up. During a block transfer, it may be possible to avoid all these delays and run at the maximum throughput that the bus transmission line bandwidth and skew can support, by allowing the sender to proceed to the next data cycle without waiting for the handshake. Cycle-by-cycle error recovery is impossible, and the transfer rate must be carefully tailored to the needs of the particular transfer, but ultimate blinding speed is available. The bus becomes a pipeline carrying data in one direction and handshakes in the other. The only system we know of that provides this mode is the Fastbus; it is probably worth the trouble only in a system that permits long cable buses.

Metastable synchronizers. One more problem should be discussed here, since it affects both kinds of buses and all interfaces to the real world: the synchronization (or metastable-state) problem. Consider a microprocessor interfaced to a keyboard. From time to time, the micro reads a status register to see whether a key has been struck. The status register has to "decide" and return a one or a zero. What if the key is struck just as the status register is being read? Did it happen in time for this read, or not? It does not matter which way the decision goes; if the key is not sensed this time, it will be sensed a few milliseconds later when the micro checks again. The decision is usually made by a clocked register, a bistable flip-flop with a data input, a clock input, and a data output. When the clock occurs, the flip-flop decides whether the data input was a one or a zero, and remembers it at the data output until the next clock.

Any bus system has a limit on its capacity, or throughput, that depends on the bus width, speed, and protocol.

This trivial problem presents fundamental difficulties. The specification for any real flip-flop gives a time interval near the clock signal during which the input is not permitted to change. But if the data signal is not already synchronized to the clock because it comes from an independent source such as a keyboard, another microprocessor, or some other system, there is no way to prevent it from changing during the forbidden interval. When this happens, the flip-flop may go into a metastable state and simply refuse to decide for a while. Its output may be an ambiguous intermediate voltage level for an uncertain length of time before some random noise pushes it one way or the other. Meanwhile, other circuits (possibly internal to the package) have proceeded to take action based on their interpretation of the ambiguous output of the flip-flop. When the flip-flop finally decides, the interpretation may prove wrong, but it will be too late to undo the action. The system may end up in a logically inconsistent state, causing a serious error.

The problem is not just that the flip-flop is badly designed; it represents a fundamental property of nature like the uncertainty principle of quantum physics: the nearer the criterion, the slower the decision.

Although the problem cannot be solved in principle, careful design can reduce the probability of error during the lifetime of the system. The method is to use proper components, because some flip-flops do decide faster than others, and to allow more time for the decision. Applying a delayed clock to a second flip-flop that decides about the output of the first one can reduce the probability of error to insignificance. Unfortunately, many designers have ignored the problem and it has caused occasional errors.

Both asynchronous and synchronous systems will encounter this problem when they interface with the external world, or even with various subsystems. For example, a synchronous microprocessor may interface with a bus that uses a clock rate different from its own. Decision delays in such interfaces must be minimized to maintain high system speed.

Asynchronous systems do have another option, however: circuitry can be added to detect metastable states, and an asynchronous system can simply wait until a decision is made before proceeding.

Efficiency

Any bus system has a limit on its capacity, or throughput, that depends on the bus width, speed, and protocol. There may also be overheads such as arbitration (unless it takes place while the previous master is still making good use of the bus). Even a single fast microprocessor may be able to use up the entire capacity of a backplane bus—especially if it is fetching instructions as well as data, and not using block transfers.

For multiple-processor systems, therefore, it is a good idea to think of the backplane bus as a communication path between the various processors and a few I/O controllers, and to provide each processor with its own private memory for instructions and most of its data. This greatly reduces the load on the backplane bus. If the processors use the bus primarily for I/O and message passing, most of the traffic can use block transfers, resulting in an almost twofold increase in throughput. A message-passing system, however, begins to act more like a network than a simple I/O bus. Depending on the number of processors and the nature of the application, the bus may still become a bottleneck. In fact, if the bus is not idle a reasonable fraction of the time, processors will spend an unacceptable amount of time waiting for it.

One solution to the throughput problem is to use more buses with fewer processors on each. The Fastbus takes this approach, using a single address space shared by a number of separate buses, called segments. These operate independently, but link together automatically as required whenever a master on one segment addresses a slave on another. This automatic linking results in interference with traffic on all intermediate segments, however, so it must be used sparingly to avoid bottlenecks. If high-traffic paths are provided with their own shortcut cable segments, this problem can be controlled. The judicious use of store-and-forward nodes, along with a network message protocol, can further reduce congestion by smoothing the load and allowing the maximum number of segments linked at a time to be as low as two.

Reliability and fault tolerance

Fault tolerance—a feature that compensates for errors in bus operation—is a popular topic in bus design discussions. The hoped-for system will use error-correcting codes on the bus, so that any single component failure or temporary noise burst can be detected and the problem automatically corrected—a common practice in large memory systems.

Unfortunately, the problem is not that simple. Several sets of signals need independent protection (such as control, data, status, and arbitration signals). Error-correcting codes tend to be inefficient for small numbers of signals, so a heavy burden of extra correcting signals is required. Further, the time required to compute the checks and corrections slows the bus. Complexity may also reduce reliability, so the gain may be less than desired, and external interference may cause errors in many signals at once. A method for protecting timing signals in such schemes has not yet emerged. The resulting complexity, slowed performance, and additional hardware costs make other solutions more attractive.

Higher-level solutions—which check and correct whole blocks of data or whole actions of programs rather than individual cycles on the bus—are more practical. Redundant processors and buses can check one another; software can make intelligent changes to the system configuration when problems are detected and notify the operator when units need replacing. Even if the bus itself implements error correction, some level of higher intelligence is still needed for these functions to prevent a system from gradually deteriorating until the correction mechanisms can no longer compensate.

Certain common hardware implementations should be avoided in systems that are concerned with fault tolerance. If an error is detected, it should be possible to retransmit the data in order to correct it. This implies that the original transmission can have no irreversible side effects. For example, if reading data from a peripheral device erases the original data or clears status flags as a side effect, the read cannot be repeated successfully. FIFOs have similar problems, since bad data stored inside cannot be retrieved and corrected. Queues and buffers should instead be in addressable memory, and clears or resets should be explicit commands rather than side effects. FIFOs can be made to work if extra addressable buffers are added to hold data until successful transmission is complete.

Software aspects

Bus and bus interface design have significant software implications. Rather than attempting to analyze the possible solutions for specific software problems, we will raise some questions that should be kept in mind when evaluating any bus system. For example: How is a system to be initialized? How are addresses and arbitration priorities allocated to the various devices? Does the bus provide enough start-up support and programmable flexibility to allow automatic reconfiguration when new devices are added? If the bus supports live insertion or removal, how does the system reconfigure while running?

Existing processors do not automatically support the kind of block transfers offered by modern buses. How can the software interface cause block transfers to occur? How do processors interface to the bus interrupt mechanism, and how do devices find out where to address their interrupts? If the bus address types do not correspond directly to the processor address types, how does the software access them?

In many cases software requires exclusive access to certain system tables. In a multiple-processor system, the bus often provides a locking mechanism to prevent access by other processors until the table is again available. If the system has multiple-port memories, the lock mechanism on one bus port may need to affect access from the other port as well. Processors with multiple bus interfaces have similar problems.

How do processors of various kinds communicate on the bus? A mailbox facility may be necessary at a well-known address on the bus, with some agreed-on format for messages. The two common byte-addressing schemes (left-to-right vs. right-to-left within a word) often cause problems in this area.

It is becoming common practice to define certain special addresses as part of a bus specification. This makes it easy to locate registers needed for system initialization or housekeeping functions. Registers which set the arbitration priority or logical address of a device, contain its model and serial number, or contain control bits which reset or restart it are all more useful if they can be easily found by general system support software. The address space that contains these registers is often called control and status register (CSR) space.

CSR space is usually accessible via special addresses which depend on a device's physical position on the bus, information about which is provided by the position-encoding pins in the connector. This makes it possible to address devices by their position in order to initialize them, to assign logical addresses in the normal address space, and to assign arbitration priority codes. If sufficient information and control are provided, automatic configuration of systems becomes possible, eliminating troublesome mechanical switches.

We have made a brief examination of the main aspects of computer buses. The many choices inherent in bus design explain the existence of so many different buses. As modern designs approach physical limits, designing a successful bus becomes more difficult and therefore more expensive. The resulting high cost of a proven design may reduce the rate of creation of new buses. ■

Acknowledgments, and a bit of history

The problems of the MITS Altair bus got me interested in this subject. I bought serial number nine of that first

S-100 machine, and got actual blueprints in late 1974 so that I could start building interface boards and a useful memory in advance of hardware delivery in February 1975. The computer came with a 256-byte memory board, expandable to 1024 bytes! Still, it was a bargain at $495 (assembled and tested) at a time when the 8080 CPU chip was selling for $350 by itself. Len Shustek—then a graduate student at Stanford and now vice-president of Nestar Systems—had been helping me design a similar system when we learned about the Altair and abandoned our own design. He had built an earlier machine using the Intel 8008, with a graphics display, a three-voice music generator, and a lot of nice software. We noticed from the blueprints that there was no way to turn off the CPU's bus drivers—a limitation that eliminated the possibility of having multiple bus controllers for DMA or multiprocessor systems. MITS responded to my anguished call by adding driver-disabling signals on the bus, further delaying hardware shipment. Unfortunately, none of us recognized the problems which would be caused by the inverted write signal—when bus masters were changing and no one was driving it, it caused writes to memory—and we did not understand the need for better grounding.

Bob Stewart, now vice-president of the IEEE Computer Society, was annoyed by these problems in his Altair and had the audacity to suggest that the situation could be improved if the IEEE would get involved in standardizing the Altair bus—then called the S-100 because of its 100-pin connector. MITS got a good deal on those connectors and so used them even though they didn't know what to do with all the pins. Every other manufacturer thought of lots of different things to do with them, though—a situation which brought on incompatibility and chaos.

Bob Stewart's incredible energy and perseverence got the project rolling, and I joined up partly because I felt guilty for missing those bus problems which could have been fixed so easily in 1974. George Morrow (Thinker Toys), Howard Fullmer (Parasitic Engineering), Kells Elmquist (InterSystems), Tim Paterson (Seattle Computer, now of MS-DOS fame), Mark Garetz (CompuPro), Gary Feierbach (Inner Access), and numerous others made real contributions to that project, called IEEE P696. One offshoot from this project was P896, an effort to start fresh and do it right for 32-bit buses, in the hope of heading off another round of chaos in the industry. Now addicted to this punishment, I joined that project, too, and both the technical and sociological parts of the project were a real education for me. I benefited from the efforts of many contributors to that project, but I am particularly grateful to Paul Borrill, whose understanding of buses and many other things is both broad and deep, and to Matthew Taub, for his analysis of the performance of his arbitration scheme.

During the P696 work, I was invited to join the Fastbus design team. The Fastbus was an effort sponsored by the US Department of Energy and was intended to deliver the maximum performance possible (while remaining simple and inexpensive) to help handle the enormous data acquisition and computing needs of high-energy physics experiments. It had to be very flexible and general, because no one knew what its future requirements might be. Though reality always requires compromises, the Fastbus did a good job of meeting those goals, and I gained a lot from that design effort. My simultaneous work on the 696 and 896 projects proved to be synergistic, since I served as a conduit for ideas and experiences among the projects.

I am particularly glad that the US Department of Energy enabled Bob Downing, of the University of Illinois at Urbana/Champaign, to spend a year at SLAC working on the system design. Discussions with Bob and with Leo Paffrath at SLAC were very stimulating and productive, and I think that year had a lot to do with the coherence of the Fastbus. I do not mean to minimize the important contributions made by many other members of the design team, but good design requires more sustained interaction than is possible in committee. Ray Larson of SLAC was responsible for the design project and was very helpful and generous in his support. I recall with special pleasure many discussions with Ed Barsotti of Fermilab, John Biggerstaff of Oak Ridge, Ken Dawson (the Fastbus editor) of TRIUMF, and Don Machen of Los Alamos (now with Scientific Systems International).

Special mention is also due Louis Costrell of the National Bureau of Standards, chairman of the NIM committee. The NIM committee brought us the NIM module standard—which had no data bus at all but is still widely used—and collaborated with the European ESONE committee to bring us CAMAC (IEEE 583), which has a 24-bit data bus. The NIM committee then sponsored the Fastbus (IEEE 960) with support from the US Department of Energy, responding to pressure from the user community. Lou got things started and kept them moving, finding trouble spots and maneuvering around them, handling the sociological problems as well as participating in the mechanical and thermal design, and handling the distribution of information in this multilaboratory, multinational project.

The list of references and suggestions for further reading was greatly enhanced by Bob Dobinson of CERN (Geneva, Switzerland), presently at the University of Illinois at Urbana/Champaign, who recently taught a course on buses and who is a collaborator in the Fastbus project. Many useful comments were also provided by the IEEE Computer Society's reviewers and editors and by Bill Ash of SLAC.

For further reading

There is a great deal of useful information and many helpful references in the other articles in this special issue. Of particular relevance to the topics mentioned in this paper are

- "The Proposed IEEE 896 Futurebus—A Solution to the Bus Driving Problem," by R.V. Balakrishnan. Also see its references to related articles covering noise, crosstalk, and reflections.
- "Arbitration and Control Acquisition in the Proposed IEEE 896 Futurebus," by D.M. Taub. This article describes the arbitration mechanism for P896 in detail. See also Taub's early paper on the arbitration

scheme, "Contention-resolving Circuits for Computer Interrupt Systems," *Proceedings of the IEE,* Vol. 123, No. 9, Sept. 1976, pp. 845-850.

There is an excellent discussion of the synchronization problem in *Introduction to VLSI Systems,* by Carver Mead and Lynn Conway, Addison-Wesley, Reading, MA, 1980. See especially page 220 and pages 236-242. References to early work on the problem are also given.

The problems and features of the wire-OR bus connection are discussed more fully in "Wire-OR Logic on Transmission Lines," by D. B. Gustavson and John Theus, *IEEE Micro,* Vol. 3, No. 3, June 1983, pp. 51-55.

IEEE bus standards are especially relevant to our subject. They are available from the IEEE Service Center, 445 Hoes Lane, Piscataway, NJ 08854. See especially

- *IEEE Standard 696-1983, Interface Devices.* This is the S-100 bus, widened and improved. It is presently finding wide use as a 16-bit bus but will probably not be stretched to 32 bits.
- *IEEE Standard 796-1983, Microcomputer System Bus.* This is essentially the Multibus, improved.
- *IEEE Standard 488-1978, General-Purpose Interface Bus.*
- *IEEE Standard 728-1982, Code and Format Conventions for Use with ANSI/IEEE Std 488-1978.* This makes IEEE 488 more useful by defining the format of information to be transmitted.
- "A Standard Data Busing System for Use with NIM Modules," by Frederick A. Kirsten, *IEEE Transactions on Nuclear Science,* Vol. NS-31, No. 1, Feb. 1984, pp. 175-177. This paper describes the incorporation of IEEE 488 into an existing class of standard modules (the NIM standard) which dates back to 1964 but is still widely used.
- *Tutorial Description of the Hewlett-Packard Interface Bus,* Hewlett-Packard, Palo Alto, CA, Jan. 1983. The HPIB is Hewlett-Packard's implementation of IEEE 488.
- *CAMAC Instrumentation and Interface Standards,* IEEE, New York, 1982. This volume includes IEEE 583 and several related standards which form a family of standards called CAMAC (Computer Automated Measurement and Control). Additional standards relate to software and other aspects of CAMAC. This book (IEEE catalog number SHO8482) is available from the IEEE Service Center, 445 Hoes Lane, Piscataway, NJ 08854. CAMAC has a 24-bit data bus, and is optimized for use in single-processor data acquisition systems. It is the predecessor of the Fastbus, a faster and more symmetric 32-bit system. Though CAMAC's bus technology is fairly old (it dates from the early 1970's), the system is still very cost-effective. Many manufacturers supply catalogs full of useful modules containing the latest technology.
- "A CAMAC Primer," by P. Clout, Report LA-UR-82-2718, Los Alamos National Laboratory, Los Alamos, NM, 1982. This is a good introduction to CAMAC.

Another important bus standard is the Fastbus, recently approved by the IEEE (*IEEE Standard 960-1984, Fastbus—Modular High Speed Data Acquisition and Control System for High Energy Physics and Other Applications*). The Fastbus is just beginning to appear in manufacturers' catalogs. Prototype systems are operating now, and large systems are being built. Though it was designed for the needs of high-energy physics applications, it should be of use in many other applications once it becomes widely available. The Fastbus is of some theoretical interest as well, because of its support for independent bus segments which dynamically link together as needed, its automatic message routing mechanisms, its ideal solution to the wire-OR cable driving problem, and its extensible architecture. It has significantly influenced the development of other contemporary buses. Information about the current status and latest developments of the Fastbus (and also CAMAC) is available from Louis Costrell, Chairman, NIM Committee, c/o National Bureau of Standards, Gaithersburg, MD 20899. Pending publication of *IEEE Standard 960-1984,* Costrell will also provide copies of the current US NIM Committee Fastbus document (DOE/ER-0189).

A number of bus standards are currently being developed by working groups of the IEEE Computer Society. Available draft documents include

- *IEEE P896/D6.2, Backplane Bus.* The draft is available from Paul Borrill, Chairman, IEEE P896 Working Group, c/o University College London, Mullard Space Science Laboratory, Holmbury St. Mary, Dorking, Surrey RH5 6NT, England. This is the Futurebus project.
- *IEEE P961/D2, Proposed Standard for a Microprocessor System Bus Based on the STD Bus.* The draft is available from Matt Biewer, Chairman, IEEE P961 Working Group, c/o Pro-Log Corporation, 2411 Garden Road, Monterey, CA 93940. Also available is the *STD Bus Technical Manual and Product Catalog,* Pro-Log Corporation, Aug. 1982.
- *IEEE P1000/D3, STE Bus.* The draft is available from Bill Shields, Chairman, IEEE P1000 Working Group, c/o Seaport Computer Systems, Inc., 4901 Morena Blvd., Suite 804, San Diego, CA 92117. This bus is similar to the STD bus, but uses Eurocard packaging and has some other differences.
- *IEEE P970, Advanced Backplane Bus (Versabus).* The draft is available from John Black, Jr., Chairman, IEEE P970 Working Group, at 3407 East Hubbell, Phoenix, AZ 85008. This is a very wide bus, with large daughterboards.
- *IEEE P1014, Versatile Backplane Bus (VME).* The draft is available from Wayne Fischer, Chairman, IEEE P1014 Working Group, at 82 Shereen Place, Campbell, CA 95008.

Digital Equipment Corporation has developed a variety of buses which have become de facto standards. The following references may be of interest:

- *Computer Engineering: A DEC View of Hardware Systems Design,* by C. Gordon Bell, J. Craig Mudge, and John A. McNamara, Digital Press, Bedford, MA, 1978. Chapter 11, by John Levy, describes the general properties of DEC buses—the Unibus, the LSI-11 bus (Q-bus), the Massbuss, and the SBI bus.

- *The PDP-11 Bus Handbook,* Digital Press, Bedford, MA, 1979. This publication contains a full Unibus description, along with some information on the LSI-11 bus (Q-bus), Massbuss, and PCL-11 bus (an interesting network-like time-slotted bus).
- *The PDP-11 Architecture Handbook, 1983-84,* Digital Press, Bedford, MA, 1983.This contains a short description of the Unibus, a detailed up-to-date reference to the LSI-11 bus (Q-bus), and a technical specification (Appendix E).
- *The VAX Hardware Handbook,* Digital Press, Bedford, MA, 1983. This describes the VAX SBI bus, a high-speed synchronous design.

Other manufacturers have also specified buses, often offering them for standardization through the IEEE. Documents should be available from these manufacturers' local representatives. Also, every microprocessor defines its own local bus. Publications of particular interest are

- *Multibus-II Bus Architecture Specification Handbook,* Pub. No. 146077-B, Intel Corporation, Santa Clara, CA. Multibus-II is a 32-bit justified synchronous bus.
- *Intel Multichannel Bus Specification,* Pub. No. 142804—Rev. C, Intel Corporation, Santa Clara, CA.
- *Intel iLBX Bus Specification,* Pub. No. 145695—Rev. A, Intel Corporation, Santa Clara, CA.
- *NuBus Specification,* Pub. No. TI-2242825-0001, Texas Instruments Incorporated, Dallas, TX. The NuBus is a 32-bit unjustified synchronous bus.
- John W. Conway, "Approach to Unified Bus Architecture Sidesteps Inherent Drawbacks," *Computer Design,* Vol. 16, No. 1, Jan. 1977, pp. 71-76. This is a description of the Honeywell split-cycle bus, a nice example of a write-only system.

There are a number of bus-specific books available. Two useful ones are

- *Interfacing to S-100/IEEE 696,* by Sol Libes and Mark Garetz, Osborne/McGraw-Hill, Berkeley, CA, 1981.
- *Interfacing to the IBM Personal Computer,* by Lewis C. Eggebrecht, Howard W. Sams & Co., Inc., Indianapolis, IN, 1983. This is highly recommended.

General references

- K. J. Thurber et al., "A Systematic Approach to the Design of Digital Busing Structures," *AFIPS Conf. Proc.,* Vol. 41, Part II, 1972 FJCC, pp. 719-740. This is a classic article, although it does not use current nomenclature.
- Paul Borrill, "Backplane Bus Standards, Why We Need Them, What We Have Got, Who Makes Them," introductory article to a special issue of *Microprocessors and Microsystems,* Vol. 6, No. 9, 1982, pp. 450-454. This issue includes useful articles on the STD, S-100, and VME buses, and on the Versabus, Multibus, Eurobus, and P896 Futurebus.
- Paul Borrill, "Microprocessor Bus Structures and Standards," *IEEE Micro,* Vol. 1, No. 1, Feb. 1981, pp. 84-95.
- Harold S. Stone, *Microcomputer Interfacing,* Addison-Wesley, Reading, MA, 1982. Chapter 3 has a useful discussion of bus protocols and arbitration. Other chapters cover transmission lines, shielding, and use of specific integrated circuits in interfacing.

MicroStandards Special Feature: A Comparison of 32-Bit Buses

Paul L. Borrill
University College London
Mullard Space Science Laboratory

As promised in the October MicroStandards column, I am presenting a comparison of several well-known 32-bit buses in tabular form this month. Because of the danger of reading too much into this table, and the potential for misunderstanding, I will elaborate on many of the issues. If further clarifications are needed, contact me at Holmbury St-Mary, Dorking, Surrey RH5 6NT, England. It is intended that this subject could form an ongoing discussion in *IEEE Micro,* and user comments and experience are actively solicited to refine the understanding of the relative advantages and disadvantages of these buses, to benefit the readers of *IEEE Micro*.

While the October column concentrated on redressing the balance between the previous comments published in August by Hubert Kirrmann[1] concerning Multibus II and the Futurebus, this month I put considerable effort into producing a balanced overview of the features of more 32-bit buses. In particular, representative proponents of each of the buses were asked to comment and help refine this version. However, ultimate responsibility for any remaining errors lies with the author. The sequence of discussion in this text follows the sequence in the table.

Support. To avoid the inevitable numbers game each of the vendors tend to play when claiming multiple sources for compatible products, I present only the primary sponsor and supporters of each bus as an indication of its genealogy.

Bus bandwidth. The performance figures are calculated values taking into account realistic assumptions that are applied consistently to each bus as far as possible. Included in the calculations are bus driver and receiver propagation delays, transmission line driving delays (the bus-driving problem and signal propagation delays down the backplane), logic and backplane skews, setup and hold times for latches, and slave access times. Since a synchronous bus must have a clock period slow enough to cope with a fully loaded system, the calculations for the asynchronous buses also assume a fully loaded system, even though this may not always be true. An asynchronous bus may be faster with shorter backplanes or in a more lightly loaded typical system.[2]

The performance figures for the Nubus and Multibus II are almost identical because both use a synchronous protocol clocked at 10 MHz. The performance in the single transfer mode for Multibus II and Nubus includes some concurrency, which is possible between the address decode plus access time delays and the address/data multiplexing delays. The Nubus appears to have a faster arbitration time than Multibus II because its shorter backplane and fewer arbitration lines allow the logic to settle faster.

Reprinted from *IEEE Micro*, pp. 71–79, Dec. 1985.

A simple calculation shows that the average distance between any two communicating boards on a backplane is one third of the backplane length, so this figure is used in the calculation of the backplane delays for the asynchronous protocols. Synchronous buses have a fixed clock period, which must be long enough to cope with boards communicating from each extremity of the backplane. The performance of a synchronous bus is thus independent of whatever two boards happen to be communicating at any instant in time.

Identical fully loaded backplane delays were applied to the VME bus, Futurebus, and Fastbus, even though in the case of the Futurebus this would be an overestimation because Futurebus transceivers load the bus less. Fastbus and Futurebus use essentially the same protocol, and differences in bus bandwidth and arbitration performance are due primarily to the difference in the currently available technology that implements the two; i.e., advanced Schottky TTL for the Futurebus (the same as for the VME bus), and 10-K ECL for Fastbus.

A noteworthy result is shown in the figures for single transfer mode, where all of the buses have a very similar performance. This is due primarily to the fact that the VME bus, which is nonmultiplexed, does not suffer the delays of multiplexing the address and data on the same lines as do the other buses. In addition there are transactional overheads in the protocol for the Futurebus and Fastbus besides the multiplexing: the Futurebus incurs delays required to overcome the transmission line effect required called the wire-OR glitch[3] on the fully broadcast address transfers; the Fastbus has a 40-ns clean-up delay at the end of each transaction (to solve essentially the same problem).

Address pipelining, which is possible only on the VME bus because it is nonmultiplexed, is not taken into account in the calculations because of the complexity of the assumptions needed to justify the results.

The burst transfer mode, which is the usual "communications-oriented" assumption for transactions in a typical multiprocessor system, shows a wider difference in bus performance; but at longer access times performances start to equalize rapidly.

The lesson to be learned from this is that a high-performance bus alone is not sufficient to guarantee a high-performance system. Some architectural means are necessary to utilize fully the bus's available bandwidth. For example, a method is needed to reduce either the amount of bus traffic each board generates or to reduce the "effective" bus access time. (This may be done predominantly by using blocks to communicate across the bus and by using static column address or nibble-mode access RAMs on the memory boards.) Effective ways to reduce bus traffic are (1) cache memories between each processor and the bus and (2) local memories located on each board or accessible through some kind of local extension bus. A cache can be transparent to programs whereas local memories are generally not transparent. Effective ways to force the system to pass blocks over the bus rather than single transfers are using cache memories or restricting the system to a message-passing architecture. Cache memories and message passing are discussed later.

A high-performance bus alone is not sufficient to guarantee a high-performance system.

The highly artificial assumption of processor-, memory-, and bus-clock coherence is made in the figures for the performance of the synchronous buses. The clock-latency problem would effectively add a half-cycle (50-ns) penalty to every transfer on Multibus II and Nubus, lowering their performance in many real implementations.

The clock-latency problem can be viewed as follows. Because all bus-based multiprocessor systems would be limited by the bottleneck the bus would form if the processors accessed all instructions and data directly through the bus, it is necessary to find ways to keep as much as possible of the instructions and data local to each processor so it can reduce its bus-utilization requirements. Therefore, for a large percentage of the time (90 percent, say) processors are executing and manipulating data locally, and only a small percentage of the time (10 percent, say) do they need to use the bus. It therefore becomes pragmatic to optimize the processor to its local resources rather than to the bus; i.e., choose a processor clock speed and memory access as the best economically available at the time. The 12.5- and 16.7-MHz processors are typical this year, with 20- and 25-MHz processors expected in 1986. This means that each local processor clock will be different and mutually asynchronous to the bus clock. Consequently, in the one out of 10 times the processor needs access to the bus, its interface must synchronize the two somehow to pass the data. This synchronization causes two problems: the delay needed to wait for the first valid bus clock edge, and the metastable state problems intrinsic to the synchronizer circuits.

On each transfer the processor makes through the bus, after it presents its request to the interface, the interface must wait for the first valid clock edge. The request may arrive just before a bus-clock edge is due, so there would not be time to wait, or it may arrive just after a bus-clock edge has occurred, so the processor must wait an entire cycle before another clock edge is due. On average, the delay will be half a clock cycle. This is the clock-latency problem.

Multibus II recognizes this problem by providing a method of buffering the timing of the processor from that of the bus, called message passing. Provided the implementor is prepared to accept the constraints of such an architecture, clock latency can be mostly overcome by this technique. Nubus suffers from the clock-latency problem also, but does not explicitly offer a facility, such as message passing, to help overcome it.

Asynchronous buses do not suffer the same clock latency problem, because the bus adopts the timing of the master. On the other hand, it is often claimed that synchronous buses are easier to design, are more reliable, and have less noise problems than asynchronous buses. This is a highly subjective argument, which tends to generalize too much on categories of synchronous and asynchronous buses without taking into account the details of how carefully the individual buses are designed.

Arbitration. The information needed to estimate the arbitration overhead and average bus-acquisition latency is shown in algebraic form as well as numbers in the table, since this is very application specific. T_{arb} indicates the time it takes for the arbitration system to resolve multiple requests; it is equivalent to the time it takes a master to acquire the bus when it is not in use, assuming the bus was not previously owned by that master. All the buses have an effective "parking" mode, where there is essentially zero delay to acquire the bus, if there is no change in mastership. This is called Release On Request (ROR) in VME bus terminology. Release When Done (RWD) is not normally useful ex-

Table 1. Comparison of 32-bit buses.

This table is believed to be entirely accurate. However, it is the nature of these backblane buses that changes in their specifications, environment, and commercial support change with time. Consequently, this table will be updated periodically, and the latest version should always be obtained when the most accurate and up-to-date comparisons are sought.

General features

Aspect V / Bus->	VME bus	Futurebus	Multibus II	Nubus	Fastbus
Standardization status	IEEE P1014 Draft 1.2 IEC 821 draft	IEEE P896.1 Draft 7.2 due for release, 1Q 86	IEEE Pxxx Intel Rev. C	IEEE Pyyy Draft 1.0	ANSI/IEEE 960 Approved Standard IEC45 (Sec) 243
Primary sponsor	Motorola	IEEE P896 W.G.	Intel	Texas Instruments	US Nim Committee
Primary supporters	Signetics Mostek	Specification not yet released for commercial use		Lisp Machines Inc.	Kinetic Systems LeCroy Research Dr. B. Struck and others
Silicon support					
Now	Motorola, Signetics	National Semiconductor	Toshiba	None	Maruei Shoji Co. Several gate arrays
Expected	Hamilton Standard Digital Systems	Ferranti, Monolithic Memories, Signetics, Texas Instruments	Intel	Texas Instruments	Fujitsu, Valtronic Inc., Integrated Networks, Philips Elcoma (Zurich)
Performance	Continuously variable	Continuously variable	Quantized 100-ns wait states	Quantized 100-ns wait states	Continuously variable
Bus bandwidth (M bytes/s)					
Sponsor claims	20 to 57	117.6	40*	37.5*	160
Source	Motorola	*IEEE Micro,* Aug. 84 (boards adjacent)	Intel (assumes 10-MHz clock)	TI (16-cycle block and 10-MHz clock)	*IEEE Trans. Nuclear Science,* Feb. 85
Single transfer mode (average backplane delay = ⅓ backplane length) (M bytes/s)					
$T_{acc} = 0$ ns	25.0	37.0	20*	20*	37.0
$T_{acc} = 50$ ns	19.0	25.3	20*	20*	25.3
$T_{acc} = 100$ ns	15.4	19.2	13.3*	13.3*	19.2
$T_{acc} = 150$ ns	12.9	15.5	13.3*	13.3*	15.5
Burst transfer mode (handshaken, infinite-length block, average backplane delay = ⅓ backplane length) (M bytes/s)					
$T_{acc} = 0$ ns	27.9	95.2	40.0*	40.0*	173.9
$T_{acc} = 50$ ns	20.7	43.5	20.0*	20.0*	54.8
$T_{acc} = 100$ ns	16.5	28.2	20.0*	20.0*	32.5
$T_{acc} = 150$ ns	13.6	20.8	13.3*	13.3*	23.1
Pipelined mode (handshakes not waited for, infinite-length block) (M byte/s)	Not specified	Not specified	Not applicable	Not applicable	Limited only by skew
Ultimate future performance	~35	~280	40*	40*	~500
Message passing mode	Not defined	To be specified in P896.2	30M bytes/s	Not defined	Not defined
Fundamental limitations	Transition times, bus-driving problem, logic delays, skew, backplane prop delay, timing constraints built in spec.	Logic delays, skew, backplane prop delay	100 ns between signal sampling, due to fixed clock	100 ns between signal sampling, due to fixed clock	Logic delays, skew, segment prop delay

*Ignores clock latency

Table 1—continued

Arbitration					
Algorithms	RWD, ROR	Fair, priority	Fair, priority	Fair	Fair, priority
T_{arb} (typical ns)	200-500	250	300*	200*	150
T_{arb} (best ns)	150	100	300*	200*	90
T_m	$256.T_t$	Unconstrained	$32.T_t$	$16.T_t$	Unconstrained
T_{get} (priority)	$T_{arb}+2T_m$	$T_{arb}+T_m$	$T_{arb}+2T_m$	$T_{arb}+(N-1).T_m$	$T_{arb}+2T_m$
T_{get} (fairness)	$T_{arb}+(N-1).T_m$	$T_{arb}+(N-1).T_m$	$T_{arb}+(N-1).T_m$	$T_{arb}+(N-1).T_m$	$T_{arb}+(N-1).T_m$
Comparison with T_{arb} (typical), and T_m limited 16 transfers, in block transfer mode, 150-ns access time.					
T_{get} (best) μs	9.6	3.3	9.9	72.2	5.7
T_{get} (worst) μs	70.8	46.3	72.3	72.2	41.7

Protocol features

Aspect V / Bus->	VME bus	Futurebus	Multibus II	Nubus	Fastbus
Bus protocol	Asynchronous	Asynchronous technology-independent	Synchronous 10-MHz clock	Synchronous 10-MHz clock	Asynchronous with optional synchronous suboperations
Data path	Non-multiplexed	Multiplexed	Multiplexed	Multiplexed	Multiplexed
Primary	16 bit	32 bit	32 bit	32 bit	32 bit only
Secondary	32, 24, 16, 8 bit	32, 24, 16, 8 bit	32, 24, 16, 8 bit	32, 16, 8 bit	Not supported
Justification	16 bit justified	Nonjustified	16 bit justified	Nonjustified	Nonjustified
Nonaligned					
32/16-bit-operations	Rev. C only	Fully supported	Fully supported	Not supported	Not supported
Byte orientation	Big-endian	Not constrained	Little-endian	Little-endian	Not applicable
Address spaces					
Primary (bytes)	2^{24}	2^{32}	2^{32}	2^{32}	2^{32} (quadlets)
Secondary (bytes)	2^{32}	Expandable	None	None	Expandable
Interconnect	In I/O space	CSR space**	2^{14}	CSR space**	CSR space
I/O space (bytes)	2^{16}	CSR space**	2^{16}	CSR space**	Quadlet = 4 bytes
Broadcast (writes to multiple slaves)	Not supported	Broadcast on any write transaction	Message space only, not supported in memory or I/O space	Not supported	Broadcast on any write transaction; module subset and system subset selection facilities
Broadcall (Reads from multiple slaves)	Not supported	Broadcall on any read transaction	Not supported	Not supported	Broadcall on any read Sparse data scan through T-pin
Bus repeater					
Circuit switched	Not supported	Bus repeater deadlock prevention	Bus repeater deadlock prevention	Bus repeater deadlock prevention	Fully supported
Packet switched	Not specified	Extension beyond the backplane is considered as a store-and-forward (packet-switched) operation (896.2)	Fully specified message-passing mechanism can be used for 256 nodes	Not specified	Supported, but packet-switched operations are not specified in ANSI/IEEE 960
Provision for future expansion	1 reserved line, spare address modifier states	Extended command mode, built in protocol to ensure compatibility	2 reserved lines, 1 reserved state on SC lines	No comment	5 reserved lines; protocols designed to permit expansion by additional levels of multiplexing

Table 1—continued					
Locking					
Arbitration lock	Use BBSY* line and release when done	Release when done	Release when done when lock line is active	Continues request; relies on pure fairness mechanism	Release when done
Address lock	All transfers must be assumed locked	Fully supported (lock line)	Fully supported (lock line)	All transfers must be assumed locked	All transfers must be assumed locked
Single transaction lock	By AS* asserted through transaction	Fully supported (lock line)	Fully supported (lock line)	Not supported	By AS/AK lock
Multiple transaction lock	Not supported	Fully supported (unlocks on change of mastership)	Not supported	Not supported	GK lock supports multiple modules and bus segments
Bus diagnostic features					
Debugging	None	Fully handshaken broadcast mode, extender-board operation accounted for	None	None	Timeouts can be disabled; wait line can single-step transactions
Monitor/snoop	Non-handshaken address monitor timing specified	Fully asynchronous connection phase to allow inspection of address transfer; slave intervention capability	Clocked for easy logic analyzer inspection	Clocked for easy logic analyzer inspection	Wait line to slow handshake for inspection
Bus utilities available to the user	Spare address modifier codes, 64 pins free on P2 connector	All user-defined facilities are delegated to auxiliary connectors	Extra power buses +12V, −12V, +5V battery	Extra power buses +12V, −12V, −5.2V	Power buses: Standard +5, −5.2, −2.0; Optional +15, −15, +28. Daisy chain to right; daisy chain to left; eight terminated lines; two unterminated lines; four unbussed pins

**CSR space for these buses is incorporated within the main memory space.

"Not supported" means that no direct provision has been made in the bus specification for this facility. This does not mean that the feature cannot be implemented by some nonstandard means, or by future modification of the specification. However, since many of these features have significant architectural and protocol implications to the specification, the likelihood of being able to graft such features onto a specification adequately as an afterthought is remote.

Measures of cost and complexity					
Aspect V Bus->	**VME bus**	**Futurebus**	**Multibus II**	**Nubus**	**Fastbus**
Address spaces	64	1	4	1	2
Connectors	2	1	1	1	1
Pins	128	96	96	96	130
Number of active signal lines	107	67	67	46	60
Interrupt lines	7	0	0	0	1
Power rails	+5V, +5V SBY +12V, −12V	+5V only	+5V, +5V battery +12V, −12V	+5V, −5.2V +12V, −12V	Optional +5, −5.2, −2.0 Standard +15, −15, +28

Table 1—continued

Electrical/reliability issues

Aspect V / Bus->	VME bus	Futurebus	Multibus II	Nubus	Fastbus
Bus interface	TTL mixture 48 and 64 mA Tristate and open collector	BTL (50-mA backplane transceiver logic) (solves the bus-driving problem)	TTL mixture 48 and 64 mA Tristate and open collector	TTL mixture 48 and 64 mA Tristate and open collector	ECL 10K (darn near solves the bus-driving problem)
Parity	None	Optional	Mandatory	Optional	Optional
Inhibit control	None	Via CSR space	None	Enable line	Enable line
Parallel bus	None	1 bit per byte	1 bit per byte	1 bit for AD lines	1 bit for all
Control lines	None	1 bit	2 bits	None	None
Tag	None	1 bit	Not applicable	Not applicable	Not applicable
Arbitration	None	1 bit	None	None	None

Maintenance/configurability issues

Aspect V / Bus->	VME bus	Futurebus	Multibus II	Nubus	Fastbus
Live insertion	Not available	Fully supported with umbilical	Not available	Not available	Partially supported (halt line)
Extender card	Not allowed for	Fully supported	Not allowed for	Not allowed for	Partially supported
Geographical addressing	None	5-bit slot ID	LACHn pin (T-pin technique with power-up initialization	4-bit slot ID	5-bit ID
Autoconfiguration	Not supported	Fully supported at any time, including live insertion	Fully supported at power-up time only	Fully supported	Fully supported

Multiprocessor support

Aspect V / Bus->	VME bus	Futurebus	Multibus II	Nubus	Fastbus
Virtual interrupts (to specific processors)	Not specified	Supported, further specified in P896.2	Supported	Supported, further specified in separate document	Supported
Arbitration	4-level daisy chain	Fully distributed, asynchronous	Distributed, synchronous central clock	Distributed synchronous central clock	Distributed central timing element
Deterministic acquisition	Supported, 4-deep round-robin system	Fully supported (fairness)	Fully supported (fairness)	Fully supported (fairness) (16 levels)	Fully supported (assured access mode—fairness)

Table 1—continued					
Priority acquisition	Supported, 4 levels only, except in round-robin	Fully supported, 32 levels	Fully supported, 32 levels possible	Not supported	Fully supported (63 levels)
Message passing	Not supported	Format defined; fully specified in P896.2	Fully supported	Not supported	Not directly supported
Cache					
Write-through	Limited capability	Fully supported	Limited capability	Limited capability	Limited capability
Write-back	Not supported	Fully supported	Not supported	Not supported	Not supported
Tagged architectures (memory bits identify meaning of data)	Not directly supported; possible implementation with address modifiers	Fully supports tag bit with parity protection	Not directly supported	Not directly supported	Not directly supported

Physical features					
Aspect Bus-> V	VME bus	Futurebus	Multibus II	Nubus	Fastbus
Board sizes in mm (in.)					
Primary	233.35 × 160 (9.187 × 6.3)	366.7 × 280 (14.437 × 11.024)	233.35 × 220 (9.187 × 8.661)	366.7 × 280 (14.437 × 11.024)	366.7 × 400 (14.437 × 15.748)
Secondary	100 × 160 (3.937 × 6.3)	233.35 × 280 (9.187 × 11.024)	100 × 220 (3.937 × 8.661)	None	None
Board area in cm^2 ($in.^2$)					
Primary	373 (58)	1027 (159)	513 (80)	1027 (159)	1467 (227)
Secondary	160 (25)	653 (101)	220 (34)	None	None
Connectors					
Dedicated	2 IEC 603-2	1 IEC 603-2	1 IEC 603-2	1 IEC 603-2	Multisourced AMP 2-532956, or DuPont 66527-565 or SAE RTP 2525-1303
Number of pins	2 × 96	96	96	96	130
Undedicated	0 (64 pins spare) IEC 603-2	2 IEC 603-2	1 IEC 603-2	2 IEC 603-2	Multisourced e.g., AMP 2-532981-1
Number of pins	64 spare on second connector	2 × 96	96	96	195 maximum
Number of modules					
Logical modules (maximum)	Not logically constrained	32 per backplane 65,536 message nodes	32 per backplane 256 message nodes	16 per backplane	26 per backplane segment 16,777,216 × 255 in fully connected system
Physical slots					
Dedicated	1	0	1	0	0
Nondedicated	20	21 (19-in. rack)	19	16	26 (19-in. rack)

cept in master-slave multiprocessor architectures, an architecture particularly well suited to the VME bus.

T_m indicates the time for mastership; i.e., the time any one master is allowed to keep the bus under normal circumstances. This is not always specified clearly for some of the buses, and others deliberately do not specify it, claiming it is the privilege and responsibility of the system implementor to set this number. For the Nubus, this limit is built into the protocol by the way it does the block transfer. For the VME bus the limit is chosen arbitrarily to ease implementation difficulties and to solve the memory-boundary problem for block transfers. For Multibus II this is also an arbitrary limit related to the maximum useful size of a message in the message-passing mode. For the Futurebus and Fastbus, the system implementor is encouraged to program limits appropriate to his system. Typically, 16 or 32 quadlets (64 or 128 bytes) will be chosen as a maximum, and the boards will be programmed to split larger blocks into several smaller ones of this maximum size. However, it may make sense in some systems to set the maximum size at 1K bytes (256 transfers) or larger to pass an entire page of virtual memory from the disk controller to the main memory, for example.

The time for a master to acquire the bus in various T_{get} intervals is also shown in the table. This time interval calculation assumes 16-word-limited blocks, 150-ns slave-access times for the transactions, and 16 modules per system. The priority case T_{get} (best) assumes there is only one high-priority master in the system. The fairness case T_{get} (worst) assumes there are 16 modules operating in fairness mode.

T_{get}(best) is the maximum time after the instant a high-priority module requests the bus in a heavily loaded system until it receives bus control. Note that T_{get}(best) and T_{get}(worst) relate to the priority of the requesting module. T_{get}(best) may be of most importance in a system processing real-time data, or, in a system with a need to react to very fast events. This needs further explanation. Clearly, if the bus is in use, even if an arbitration has taken place, the winner cannot assume control until the previous master has finished. However, there is one more complication: a simple queueing model shows that on average there will be one board that is currently using the bus, and another that has arbitrated, won, and is waiting to use the bus (the master-elect). Thus, a new high-priority master requesting the bus must not only wait for the current master to finish, but for the master-elect to finish also, even though the master-elect may be of lower priority. This is reflected in the values for T_{get}(best) by the factor $2T_m$; i.e., the time for two masters to each use the bus for their maximum allotted time. The only buses that do not show this $2T_m$ behavior are the Futurebus and the Nubus.

Futurebus has an intrinsic facility called "preemption," which allows a high-priority master to displace a lower priority master-elect before the bus is handed over. The VME bus has a similar feature provided by the BCLR line, which informs the current master that a high-priority master is waiting to use the bus and which may be used to preempt the master-elect also. But this is not fully specified in the specification, and so it is not included in the comparison figures. The Nubus does not have a priority mechanism for arbitration, so T_{get}(best) and T_{get}(worst) are the same.

T_{get}(worst) is the maximum time after a standard priority module requests the bus in a heavily loaded system, until it receives bus control. This figure includes the fairness-arbitration algorithm, which ensures all requestors get a turn.

Cache. Cache-memory requirements for a bus are often misunderstood. All buses can implement some kind of cache system. The basic categories are instruction caches and data caches. With care, any bus can implement an instruction cache, since the instructions are unlikely to be modified. Data or combined instruction/data caches, are considerably more useful than pure instruction caches, but are more difficult to implement. If a system programmer can define which data is "private" and which data is "shared," he can, with help from a Memory Management Unit, cause the cache system to treat all shared data as "noncacheable." While this is a low-performance, messy, and nontransparent method, all buses can implement caches in this way.

Higher performance systems, which are required to be transparent and/or to cache shared data also, must have some basic facilities built into the bus to maintain consistency.[4] There are two basic consistency schemes possible: write-through, where all write data is written through the cache to the main memory via the bus; and write-back, where written data is simply stored in the cache until it is flushed at a later time. With the write-through system the transaction is visible on the bus and, provided the bus supports a fully handshaken broadcast mechanism for at least the address, other masters having a stale copy of this data can invalidate it (or copy the updated data off the bus as it becomes available).

With the highest performance write-back system, additional information must be stored along with each piece of data to define the ownership of the data. If the data is marked shared, the scheme reverts to write-through; if it is marked exclusive, the write transaction need not appear on the bus. Data becomes shared or exclusive, depending on the status lines on the bus when the data is first read. The data may become invalidated whenever another processor is seen writing the same location over the bus. If a piece of data exists in a cache and is marked exclusive, and if another board wishes to read the location in main memory containing that data, the cache must "intervene" in the read cycle to inhibit the stale data from the main memory and instead provide the master with most recent data from within itself.

Both the Futurebus and the Fastus support an adequate broadcast mechanism to support the write-through scheme fully, but only the Futurebus has the necessary bus status and protocol intervention facilities to support the high-performance write-back scheme.[5]

Measures of cost and complexity. This section of the table was included as an indication of the relative cost effectiveness of each bus. All of the buses are expensive at the moment, but proponents of each claim their bus is less expensive than their competitors. Multibus II may appear expensive to implement at the moment, but this is likely to change. Intel claims that in the near future a crossover point will be reached at which Multibus II will become less costly than, say, the VME bus, because the interface will become more fully integrated and the trend in the cost of silicon is always downward. This does tend to assume that semiconductor manufacturers supporting the VME bus will stand still and not become integrated also—which is hardly likely. However, in the long term, the number of active signal lines is indicative of the ultimate cost effectiveness of the bus interface, since silicon cost predominantly occurs in the interconnections.

A more important question to ask of each bus is how much of the facilities provided must be implemented to use or to gain the principal advantages of the bus. For the VME bus, clearly, cheaper implementations are possible which are wholly 16-bit data and 24-bit address, although this raises compatibility issues with 32-bit systems. The VME bus also presents a somewhat simple appearance because of its traditional design, and its duplication of the familiar 68000 component-level signals. For the Futurebus and Nubus one must always implement the full 32-bit-wide bus. This means that a minimum cost implementation is less cost-effective if only 16-bit processors are used, than say the VME bus, but it does overcome the compatibility problems and eliminates some complexity for 32-bit processors due to hybrid arrangements. However, the cache facilities, message-passing, broadcast facilities, and sophisticated CSR functions can be eliminated or considerably reduced in cost-conscious implementations of the Futurebus. In particular, boards can be readily constructed using slower but more highly integrated parts such as PALs and still ensure total compatibility because of the technology-independent asynchronous handshake. This makes a wide spectrum of cost and performance possible.

For Multibus II, message passing is necessary to gain any real advantage of the bus over, say, Multibus I because of the clock-latency problem. Message passing is expensive, in LSI, real-estate, and software redevelopment. However, Intel has an ingenious solution to this particular problem. The iSSB serial bus implements the same message-passing function as the parallel bus, so implementations that require low bandwidth and only one or two processors can use just the iSSB bus to become cost-effective.

The philosophy of Nubus is not to burden the user with unnecessary additional features. Nubus therefore has a refreshing sparcity of mechanism, which allows it to be priced considerably cheaper than Multibus II, by virtue of the absence of more sophisticated features. Fastbus tends to be used in very high performance systems, such as those involving the connection of large numbers of data-acquisition subsystems in a tree-structured network, typical of the requirements of the nuclear physics community.

Acknowledgments

I would like to thank Steve Cooper, Shlomo Pri-Tal, George White, and Dave Gustavson for their extensive comments on the first draft of this comparison table.

References

1. H. Kirrmann, "MicroStandards—Report on the Paris Multibus II Meeting," *IEEE Micro,* Vol. 5, No. 4, Aug. 1985, pp. 82-89.
2. R. V. Balakrishnan, "The Proposed IEEE 896 Futurebus—A Solution to the Bus Driving Problem," *IEEE Micro,* Vol. 4, No. 4, Aug. 1984, pp. 23-27.
3. D. B. Gustavson and J. Theus, "Wire-OR Logic on Transmission Lines," *IEEE Micro,* Vol. 3, No. 3, June 1983, pp. 51-55.
4. R. Katz et al., "Implementing a Cache Consistency Protocol," *Proc. 12th Ann. Computer Architecture Conf.,* pp. 276-283. Available from IEEE Computer Society Press.
5. P. Sweazey, "The Futurebus Cacheing System," *Proc. Midcon, Session on Advances in Backplane Bus Technology,* Sep. 1985. Available from Electronic Conventions Inc., 8110 Airport Blvd., Los Angeles, CA 90080.

Part IV
Software Issues

CONVENTIONAL computer systems have been built using von Neumann architecture with a single instruction stream and a single data stream (SISD). Instructions and data are fetched in alternate cycles.

With the use of multiple processors in a single system, it becomes necessary to funnel instructions and data to all the different resources. This implies that the single instruction stream and the single data stream must be decomposed into multiple streams (MIMD), each stream processed independently, and finally the partial results somehow integrated together. These are functions very different from what traditional operating systems have been designed for. Also, MIMD requires the design of new languages that enable parallel operations to be readily specified.

The above issues are delineated by Patton in the first paper of this part. She describes the concept of parallel control flow (PCF), originally developed at the Massachusetts Institute of Technology as a paradigm for multi-microprocessor architectures. Her paper also emphasizes the aspect of increasing overhead as the number of processors increases.

In the next paper, Fisher and Weatherly analyze the major issues in the design of a distributed operating system for Ada. The Ada computer is hosted on Apollo workstations and cross-compiles to a BBN Butterfly system. A Butterfly system typically contains between 16 and 256 processors, all belonging to the MC68000 family, connected together through a special switch.

In the third paper, van Tilborg and Wittie describe their operating systems for the Micronet Network Computer. This computer is a loosely coupled network of microcomputers with each node, consisting of three separate microcomputers, connected to two passive communication buses.

Next, Fathi and Krieger discuss the development of an executive for task-driven multimicrocomputer systems. They have used hierarchical control for task scheduling. Interlevel communication is via asynchronous handshake signals.

The fifth paper focuses on events and interrupts in tightly coupled multiprocessors. Kirrmann proposes the implementation of a special event receiver called a synapse and the utilization of several forms of acknowledge to store, queue, and acknowledge events in a decentralized environment.

Next, Boari *et al.* describe a new set of tools for multi-microprocessor programming. They describe a language and a computer for process and procedure definition, supplemented by facilities for hardware configuration description, resource allocation, run-time system construction, debugging, and execution control.

In the last paper of this part, Schell focuses on the security issue. He has developed a security kernel for a Z8000-based multiprocessor environment, which has been subsequently adopted for use with Intel 286 microprocessors.

In Part V, we will consider various methods for evaluating the performance of multi-microprocessor systems.

Software opens the way to true concurrency for multiprocessing

The intellectual leap beyond the von Neumann architecture is by no means recent. Early on, hardware designers envisioned the so-called myriaprocessor, which would link unlimited numbers of machines to achieve increases in speed directly proportional to the number of processing units. Such an achievement — the one-to-one correspondence between processor count and increased system speed—would represent truly concurrent processing.

But translating hypothetical advances into working equipment is a notoriously arduous task. So far, with the exception of special-purpose machines like signal processors, no commercial or experimental multiprocessing system has delivered the theoretical goods. That is, no multiprocessor can tackle general-purpose computing and come across with a linear boost in throughput.

The problem is with the software. From a hardware standpoint, multiprocessing became possible with the appearance of

Carole Patton

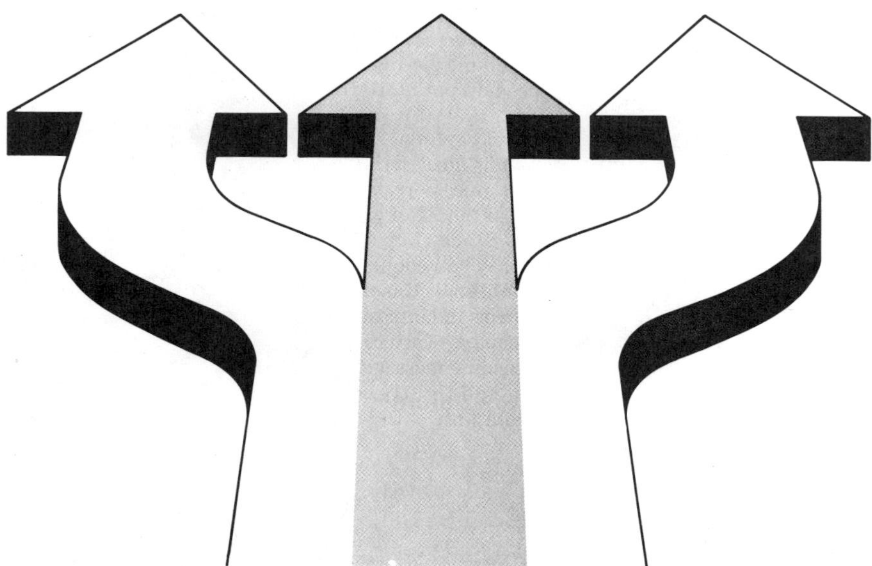

the microprocessor. Software designers, however, enjoyed no complementary breakthrough. In fact, all the tools of their trade, including all of the popular computer languages, are rooted in the von Neumann archetype.

Von Neumann machines are communicating sequential-process computers. But by definition, true concurrent processing is asynchronous. Each node in a system works on a particular task, or assignment, and when finished, it independently proceeds to the next chore. From a software point of view, that means breaking down, or unspooling, instructions and data into their component threads of code and regrouping them after processing. It also implies a control model for directing this flow of concurrent code. Both elements have eluded the computer-science community—at least until now.

The first steps toward concurrent programming are being taken. Programming languages like Multilisp are semantically geared to it. They allow researchers to split off parts of operations, employing instructions like Fork, and to reunite them later with instructions like Join. They also indicate when a value has not yet been computed and make allowances for inserting it later on.

In addition, a concept called parallel control flow (PCF) is beginning to emerge. Originally developed at the Massachusetts Institute of Technology (Cambridge), it is aimed at replacing the serial instruction flow, step-by-step mechanisms so deeply rooted in the von Neumann single-instruction, single-data stream (SISD) paradigm. Parallel control uses such built-in devices as values, which are pegged to an index, so that innumerable threads of code remain unsnarled. Moreover, each instruction specifies what statements are to be executed after it or completed before it.

In contrast, all of today's microprocessor-based systems—even those using multiple processors—are still programmed like von Neumann machines. Each node essentially acts like a stand-alone computer. One instruction partitions data into several processes, or subprocesses, to execute in parallel. But behind this orchestration is a single conductor, the system's program counter. Any microprocessor that finishes its task early must wait until its companions are done before it receives a new assignment.

Playing by a new set of rules

True multiprocessors (as opposed to parallel processors) cannot be programmed like SISD and single-instruction, multiple-data stream (SIMD) machines. Their multiple-instruction formats call for brand new language and control-flow concepts. The idea is that coupling a number of processors together requires a multiple-instruction, multiple-data path (MIMD) architecture.

The most common such configuration is a collection of independent processors, each with its own instruction and data streams. Since they are connected, they can cooperatively solve problems. Essentially, these systems fall into two types: loosely coupled, which communicate by sending messages over a network, and tightly coupled, which communicate through shared memory. Programs written for the latter typically share memory locations and employ some kind of semaphore (or blocking mechanism) to protect data. Communications with memory are generally via a bus.

Nearly all of the languages used for parallel programming (e.g., Ada, Concurrent Fortran, Modula2, CSP, Occam, and the like) have had some constructs added for parallel control, communication, as well as for synchronizing program data. But none of them can deal successfully with multiple instructions, which requires unspooling coded processes and dealing with threads of instruction code.

In fact, only a few concurrent computation models have emerged: GCF (general control flow), Mu Calculus, EBL (event-based language), tagged data flow, and the aforementioned program control flow. Mu Calculus, EBL and tagged data flow work with tokens or tags to join separate, concurrent execution paths and to synchronize events. They are best used in a value-oriented environment. GCF, on the other hand, does not use tokens, but is a low-level control-flow language that labels its statements with numbers. Although it breaks apart statements for concurrent execution, later reuniting them, it has no mechanism for distinguishing between more than two concurrent paths in a segment of code. At a fork, a particular segment of GCF code could be executed by any of the fork's prongs, so that a parallel Do operation can produce inaccurate results.

Parallel control flow's indexing feature, in contrast, makes the language much more promising. Currently, it is being refined by Harris Corp.'s Government Systems Division (Melbourne, Fla.) to run on a 32-node general-purpose multiprocessor called Concert (also designed at MIT). PCF is first written in simultaneous Pascal and then compiled into PCF statements. The language neither deals with single instructions nor demands that they be executed in lockstep, as the prevalent sequential control-flow model does. Rather, PCF is based on events with indexed names: Each statement has a trigger that determines when it will be executed. An event index tracks events and distinguishes between multiple, concurrent program invocations.

The right stuff

Unlike GCF, PCF can distinguish between concurrent tasks emanating from the same statement. Each has a different index value, and the set of index values is unique for every task in a specific statement. The language represents the first truly concurrent model suitable for general-purpose computing.

PCF programs are modular, but more than one procedure can exist simultaneously. A program is a list of procedures, and executing one of them is called an activation. Activations are organized dynamically in a tree structure, with the root of the tree being the first activation of

Parallel PCF programs

Suppose a segment of code is needed to compute the inner product of two vectors: the variables X and Y, of n elements each, to produce the scalar, R. As a purely sequential process written in Pascal, the program would read:

```
begin
    r:=0.0;
    for i:-1 to n do r:-r + x [i] * y[i]
end
```

After initializing the variable R to 0, Pascal starts an iterative process that adds the product pairs of all elements of the two vectors to R. But no parallelism is involved. One way to integrate parallelism in this algorithm is to express it in Simultaneous Pascal:

```
begin
    forall i:=1 to n do z[i] :=x[i] * y[i]
    r:=reduce(+ ,z)
end
```

Now the function has become two separate notations, with one computed after the other but each defined in parallel. The **forall** statement handles each of the passes (one for every possible value of the index variable i) simultaneously so that all multiples are done at the same time. The second statement derives R's value from **reduce**, a special construct in Simultaneous Pascal that applies a specific operator to all the elements of an array.

The same problem, solved in PCF, appears much more complex (see program below).

The first statement (second line of the program) calculates the product of X and Y element pairs, and puts the results in vector Z. A separate task is scheduled for each product, and tasks start when the event (start_here) is activated. As each product is completed, either an L or an R event (line 5) is activated, depending on their positions in a vector. (The decision to activate L or R events is made by the line starting with n cvtxi.

L and R are event names, used by the second statement to determine which of the two needed arguments for the pending task is furnished by completing the task.

The second statement carries out a binary reduction of the sum of the elements of Z. As Z pairs become available, they will be added together. That continues until there is only one element left (which is stored in R), and the event NEXT is activated.

```
( (( ) ((start_here)))
(((i 1 n)) (i cvtxi $i multi copyi copyi copyi x swappi addip fetchr swapri
          y swappi addip fetchr multr swapri z swappi addip storer
          n cvtxi copyi 2 divi swapi 2 modi addi lei brab) )
((( ) (L (i) (+ (/ n 2) (% n 2)))) (( )(R (+ (- n i) 1) (+ (/ n 2) (% n 2)))))
( ((j m) ((l. j m) (R j m)))
(( ) (j cvtxi $r multi x swapip addip copyp fetchr m cvtxi j cvtxi subi $r
    multi x swapip addip fetchr addr swappr storer m cvtxi copyi 2 eq
    brab copyi 2 divi swapi 2 modi addi j cvtxi lti brab) )
(((( ) (NEXT)) (( ) (NEXT))) ( (( ) (l. (j) (+ (/ m 2) (% m 2))))
               (( ) (R (- (+ m 1) j) (+ (/ m 2) (% m 2)))) ) ) )
```

the main procedure. It starts automatically when the program is booted up. Other activations are started by their parent, and may have one or more offspring activations. When the root activations of the main is completed, the program ends.

Since PCF is stack-oriented, every statement includes a trigger, a task template, and a terminator. The first defines the conditions to be met before a statement is executed. The task template specifies actions to be taken when a statement is executed, and the terminator determines the effect of a task's completion on the system's control state.

Complexity is the hallmark of a concurrent instruction set. Serial code for computing the inner product of two vectors might simply specify an iterative process. Its parallel equivalent might separate out the multiplications for simultaneous processing, but still require an equivalent amount of actual code. A concurrent instruction, in comparison, requires tasks to be separately scheduled to calculate each vector's products and needs specific mechanisms, like the concept of an event being activated, to begin and end each job (see "Parallel PCF Programs,'' p. 100). There must be a way of separating each small chore (like assigning an event name), of indicating when tasks are split into smaller ones (like a Branch or Fork commands), and of specifying the processing order (like Next).

Objectively speaking

In addition to the familiar arithmetic instructions, PCF contains logical commands like Pop (which moves all stack entries up one position), Grab (which pulls a value from the top of a stack), and JMP (which conditionally alters the path of task execution).

In a similar vein, Multilisp, an extension of Lisp, enables parallel execution to be specified. The language evolved in programming the Concert multiprocessor at MIT, and will be used to program other multiprocessors like the Butterfly machines from Bolt, Beranek and Newman Inc. (Cambridge).

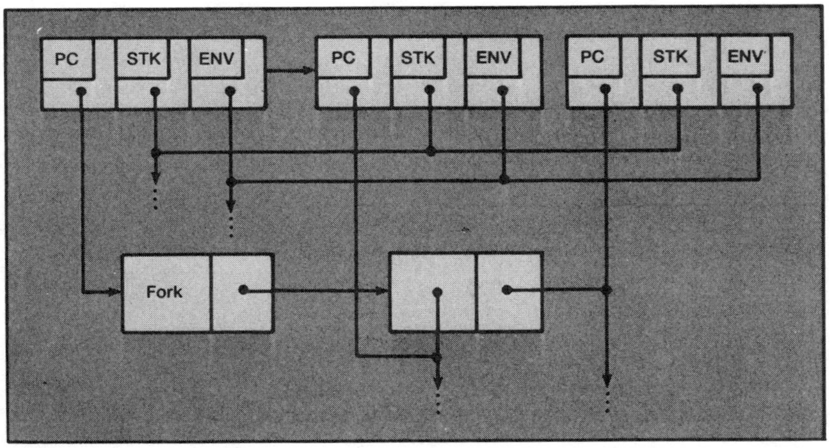

Like the parallel control flow model, Multilisp creates parallel threads of code. Its fundamental mechanism for achieving parallelism is the Future operator, which creates a task as well as an object to hold the value that the task will eventually compute.

Lisp itself is an object-oriented language, hence focused on objects and operations rather than values (see "Learning to Lisp," p. 103). It recognizes two kinds of objects, atoms and CONScells. An atom is any primitive (like an integer) and a CONScell is a means of representing data structures.

Multilisp establishes parallelism between two or more expressions, using a construct called pcall, instead of an explicit fork-join procedure like PCF. If an engineer wants more overlapping functions, the future construct is used. Tasks that attempt to examine future values are suspended until it has been computed. In Multilisp, future is the only primitive that activates tasks.

Every Multilisp task has a procedure associated with it that handles exceptions that arise during execution. Conditions like errors (say, divide by zero) or exceptions signaled by programs (like end-of-file on read) may necessitate a nonlocal exit from parallel blocks of code. In such cases, Multilisp uses two escape-value mechanisms. Catch/throw, as its name suggests, sets up a catcher whose tag is the value of the expression tag. Unwind/protect lets a program specify some type of mopping-up pro-

1. MIT's Lcode is an interpreter for dividing stack code into parallel jobs. Here, one Lcode task (using registers PC, STK, and ENV) is split in two using a Fork. Each job inherits the same STK and ENV register, but shares the PC register. STK and ENV will change as the tasks are executed, but PC—the list is being processed—will not.

cedure that will follow catch/throw.

Most implementations of Lisp view a program as a recursive data structure—a parse tree built from CONScells. An interpreter algorithm is used to manipulate data structures like stacks. But Lcode, another parallel implementation of Lisp (also from MIT), translates the Lisp interpreter into a stack structure that actually represents machine-level details.

Getting a Head

The language's op codes are the same atomic symbols used in Lisp proper (like CONS and Head). To execute a CONS operation, Lcode pops two object references off the machine's job stack and pushes a newly created CONScell in their place. The latter consist of the two references. Generally, a CONScell has op code in its head; its tail contains the remainder of the program to be executed after completing the operation.

Conceptually, the stack's interpreter code has three registers: PC, STK, and ENV. PC points to the current location of the program (which is stored as a list), and ENV is an extra list pointer for storing environmental data like the current value of variables. A stack is maintained as a Lisp list.

Lcode is made parallel by using many interpreters, each with its own PC, STK, and ENV register. In operation, the system resembles a large web of CONScells, with numerous interpreters moving about and continually reorganizing the web. Two Lcode tasks can be Forked. In so doing, however, they both inherit STK and ENV registers. One of the tasks, PC, becomes PC<—head [tail][PC]]; the other becomes PC<—tail [tail][PC]] (Fig. 1).

A critical feature to multiprocessing is the ability to synchronize concurrent activities after a program has been split into parallel parts. Currently, many different synchronization methods are being explored. Generally, they revolve around constraints placed between operations in different tasks, and the ability to exclude tasks that need to share resources.

One way to achieve synchronicity is to view program parts as modules. Researchers at Carnegie-Mellon University (Pittsburgh) do just that with the modular programming (MP) metalanguage. It divides programs into a sequence of serial and parallel modules. In MP, a sequence of serial operations is called a process, a parallel operation is called a task. A set of related tasks is known as a task group.

MP code does not explicitly specify locks to secure data from access by more than one processor at a time. Instead it uses the concept of a frame: a single, logical entity that includes an interprocess communications synchronization protocol. Frame operations are identified by the symbol $ (see the program, below).

Designating messages as either blocking or nonblocking is yet another approach to synchronization. This technique, put to work in a parallel language called Oil, is being used by the Fairchild Laboratory for Artificial Intelligence Research (Palo Alto,

Securing data within a frame

```
Process  Insert (x:item) =
Begin
         $MoveToRoot;
         Repeat
                 Switch  $Compare(x) Begin
                                 Case -1:   $MoveToRightChild;
                                 Case +1:   $MoveToLeftChild;
                                 Case  0:   Exit;
                         End;
         Until  $AddIfLeaf(x);
End
```

Communication primitives in Meglos

Primitive	Meaning
Write (cd, buf, n)	Write n bytes from buffer buf onto channel cd.
Multicast (cdlist, buf, n)	Write n bytes from buffer buf onto all channels specified in cdlist.
Read (cd, buf, n)	Read n bytes from channel cd into buffer buf.
Read (cdlist, buf, n, chn)	Multiplexed input: When a message arrives on any of the channels specified in cdlist, read n bytes into buffer buf. Return the descriptor of that channel in chn.
Readall (cdlist, buflist, n)	Read messages n bytes long from all channels in cdlist. For each channel in cdlist a message is placed into the corresponding buffer in buflist.

Calif.).

In an operation, when a nonblocking message is received, execution occurs. Receipt of a blocking message suspends activity at the sending node until a reply is received. Oil uses the T dialect of Lisp, which contains some parallel control and data structures.

On schedule

Similarly, subprocesses can be handled by a scheduler, with a resource manager allocating processes and communications channels. That is the tack taken with Meglos, from AT&T Bell Laboratories (Holmdel, N.J.) Meglos is unusual in that processes can establish communications channels between each other. (Each channel connects only two processes.) It contains a number of communications primitives that allow processes to read from, or write to, its channels (see the table, p. 102).

Although approaches to truly concurrent processing are garnering a great deal of attention in the laboratory, some partial solutions have appeared on the commercial scene. For example, engineers have hammered languages like Fortran into a rough semblance of parallelism in which one instruction can act on many data streams. That works fine for single-instruction, multiple-data path machines like pipelined processors and array processors. The former use multiple arithmetic units to simultaneously execute one instruction (like Add); the latter perform the same instruction on an array of data. Though a tremendous speedup in numeric computation is obtained, this improvement is limited strictly to special problems that lend themselves to parallelism.

Hardware designers running these parallel programs began to notice that their machines were behaving strangely: A program in which some process had been made parallel might run ten times faster on 12 processors, yet only twice as fast when 50 or more processors were employed. The crux of the problem is that message traffic between nodes increases as nodes are added, and contention between messages eventually produces enormous communication delays. This is why even the hottest commercial parallel processors, like the Balance 8000 from Sequent Computer System Inc. (Portland, Ore.) and the Flex/32 from Flexible Computer Corp. (Dallas, Texas), limit themselves to a configuration containing 12 to 16 microprocessors.

Sometimes a program that exhibits a large number of vectors runs more slowly on an array of machines than on a single CPU. The solution to that particular problem lies in special-purpose machines that optimally implement algorithms of a limited class. One of these machines is Dado. A highly parallel, special-purpose SIMD processor, from

Learning to Lisp

Lisp is a logic programming language that manipulates both symbolic concepts and numbers. Data is entered into the computer through an S-expression, which can be an atom or a dotted pair. The first is the smallest possible expression, one that cannot be broken down further. In most of the language's dialects, an atom is either an ordinary number (say, 37 or 635) or a single English word like bird or elephant. Dotted pairs consist of two atoms surrounded by parentheses and separated by a period like (BIRD.ELEPHANT).

The process of joining atoms or dotted pairs is called CONSing. The result is known as a CONS. When groups or dotted pairs are combined, as in (BIRD.ELEPHANT) . (WALK.FLY), the period following the first group of dotted pairs represents the main CONS. Any number of dotted pairs can be strung together.

The first part of a dotted pair, called the CAR, begins with the leftmost letter and continues until the main period. Everything that follows, everything to the right of the first parentheses, is identified as the CDR. Lisp programs contain so-called recognizers whose job it is to determine whether an expression is an atom or a dotted pair.

CDR, CAR, and CONS are not just a means of separating information into blocks, they are actual commands. Given the command CAR, for example, the language will find the first atom or dotted pair. The command CDR will find everything following CAR.

Lisp also has another way of representing expressions, through List. List is similar to predicate logic in its notation. In fact, in a List expression, most versions of Lisp eliminate the awkward periods and let the programmer use more familiar commas and parentheses. However, in List notation, the function comes first so that 2 + 2 is written (PLUS 2 2). Variables are assigned using the command SETQ. For example (SETQ × 2) assigns the value 2 to X. Expressions can be tested in List to determine whether they are true or false.

Columbia University (New York City), it is targeted at "if... then" rule-based systems, also known as productions. Its hardware has been designed to implement associative algorithms like the redundant tree algorithm, or RETE, which compares a production rule against facts in working memory to make matches. Dado consists of 15 processing elements connected in a binary tree, and runs off a host coprocessor. Essentially, it can be viewed as a peripheral device.

Speed, without a doubt, has been the main criterion in all these special designs. Some, like systolic arrays, can hit fantastic rates. One of them, Carnegie Mellon's Warp, is so heavily microcoded that each of its ten cells (Fig. 2) can rip through 10 million floating-point operations every second. That performance is impressive enough to pique the interest of Digital Equipment Corp. True to form, however, Warp maintains its dazzling speed only when solving the kinds of problems it was designed for—computations for signal, image, and vision processing.

Over the past few years, researchers have focused on "extracting" parallelism by separating out program chunks, or processes. In that way, they could be assigned to individual CPUs and thus executed in parallel. Most, like the Bulldog compiler from Yale University (New Haven, Conn.) and the Paraphrase, a compiler from the University of Illinois (Urbana) merely search existing languages for vectors for parallel execution. Poker, a research effort underway at the University of Washington (Seattle) is also specialized in that it constructs programs used for mapping an application into a configurable, parallel architecture. None of these projects attempt to redesign existing computer languages or support concurrent software for a general class of multicomputer structures.

In fact, all of the parallel machines racking up fantastic speeds are special-purpose peripherals, not general-purpose computers. Their programs are oriented toward numerical values, and the programmer's job is to funnel numbers into multiple arithmetic units. But all numeric programs (whether they involve matchmaking in a production system or solving an FFT) are data-independent. That is, the same sequence of calculations is run through no matter what the operand value. Programs and processes like these cannot generate data-dependent addresses for their data and control memories.

Symbolic programs, on the other hand, are meant to recognize data so that relevant information can be extracted. Algorithms that sort, compile or manage a data base are data-dependent and must maintain their ties to programming variables.

For the most part, writing a parallel program has not been viewed as different than writing one for multitasking or for servicing multiusers. That helps explain why the Unix operating system has been drafted into use in commercial and experimental parallel computers. Unix began life as a development environment for users of large VAX machines and has a multitasking facility called Pipes. On mainframe computers, Pipes partitions a CPU into segments so that separate processes can run simultaneously. In parallel systems, a user can ask that multiple programs be concurrently executed and the output of one is piped through as the input to another. Essentially, each program or process executes on one processor, but at this level there is little difference, between multitasking and multiprocessing. □

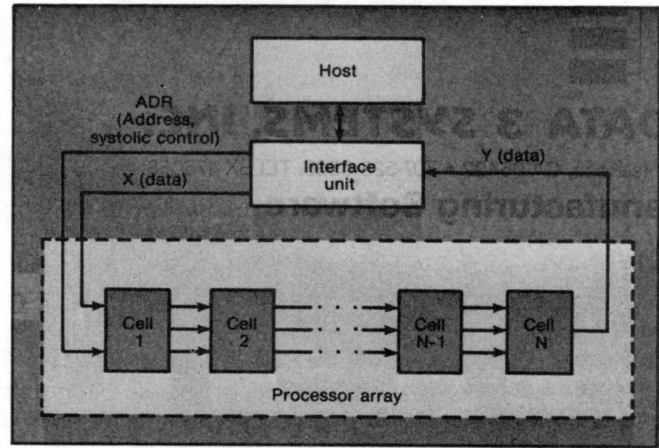

2. The Warp processor is a one-dimensional systolic array whose cells are all replicas of a single processor, the Warp cell. Like a von Neumann machine, the entire array of cells is synchronized by a single clock in the interface unit.

Issues in the Design of a Distributed Operating System for Ada

David A. Fisher and Richard M. Weatherly
Incremental Systems Corporation

This experimental run-time package combines the capabilities of Ada with the flexibility of loosely coupled networks to gain advantages in throughput, reconfigurability, and error recovery.

The Distributed Ada Run-time Package, or DARP, is a key component of a broader project to produce a high-quality Ada language system for programming a loosely coupled, distributed network of computers. The goal of the overall project is to provide a practical Ada system targeted to an instrumented, user-controllable, reconfigurable, distributed operating system running on a large number of processors (see Figure 1). Intended as a tool for conducting research in distributed systems, the language system demonstrates that Ada can be correctly and efficiently implemented on loosely coupled systems.

By *loosely coupled, distributed system* we mean any configuration of processors, memories, and links in which each processor has a designated local memory that it can access in significantly less time than it can access either shared memory or the local memory of other processors. Typically, such systems have a high bandwidth communication link between processors but little or no shared memory. The key to efficient use of these systems is to exploit low-cost intraprocessor communication and to avoid higher cost interprocessor communication.

Loosely coupled systems offer several potential advantages over shared-memory systems: greater throughput, easier scaling to larger configurations, and error recovery capabilities. Greater throughput is possible because independent tasks are not competing for access to shared memory and because the number of processors that can be accommodated in a system is not bounded. Similarly, with the appropriate software, loosely coupled systems should be scalable to any number of processors. If the number of processors can be dynamically altered, then it is possible to increase throughput by taking advantage of added processors. Error recovery is possible if the operating system and the application program together can detect and isolate failed components and then reconfigure the system for the most effective use of the remaining components.

Development of both application and operating system software is more difficult on loosely coupled systems than on conventional systems. The absence (or high overhead) of shared memory means that the traditional methods for multiprogramming and multitasking in uniprocessors and in shared-memory multiprocessor systems are not applicable. Thus, the issues of allocation of tasks and shared data, of intertask communication, and of distributed versus central control take on new influence in overall system performance. The desire to exploit the inherent scalability and recon-

Reprinted from *IEEE Computer*, pp. 38–47, May 1986.

figurability of loosely coupled hardware systems generates additional requirements for reconfigurable, scalable, distributed control and for fail-soft and fail-safe software.

Most of these added requirements fall on the target operating system. Optimal solutions to these problems are outside the scope of our effort in developing DARP. Instead, we have designed DARP as a reconfigurable, distributed-target system with sufficient "handles" to enable users (in this case, distributed-processing researchers) to interrogate, tune, and adjust it. DARP gives the user access to the dynamic state of the system, permits the user to control the allocation of tasks and data to processors, and generalizes certain Ada tasking features that would otherwise restrict the scope of distributed-processing research. The system will not be fail-soft or fail-safe, but it will provide sufficient information and control that fail-soft and fail-safe applications can be built.

The Ada compiler is hosted on Apollo workstations and cross-compiles to a BBN Butterfly system.[1] A Butterfly system typically has from 16 to 256 processors, each consisting of an MC68000 processor chip and from 256K bytes to 4M bytes of local memory. The processors are connected through a special switch mechanism, which simulates an N × N crosspoint network using only N × *ln*(N) components.

The Butterfly system is capable of mapping any processor's memory into the address of a given processor, providing the appearance of a shared-memory system to the user and making interprocessor communication convenient in software development. Efficient use of the system, however, requires that the illusion of shared memory not obscure the actual performance characteristics of a loosely coupled system.

The Ada language system includes the complete compiler front end, a distributed-target code generator, an instrumentation package, and the Ada run-time package. The front end supports all required Ada features plus the generalizations needed for distributed-processing research. The instrumentation package allows the user to interrogate and record the dynamic state of the target system. The run-time package takes the form of a distributed operating system for any Butterfly configuration, running on each node in the network.

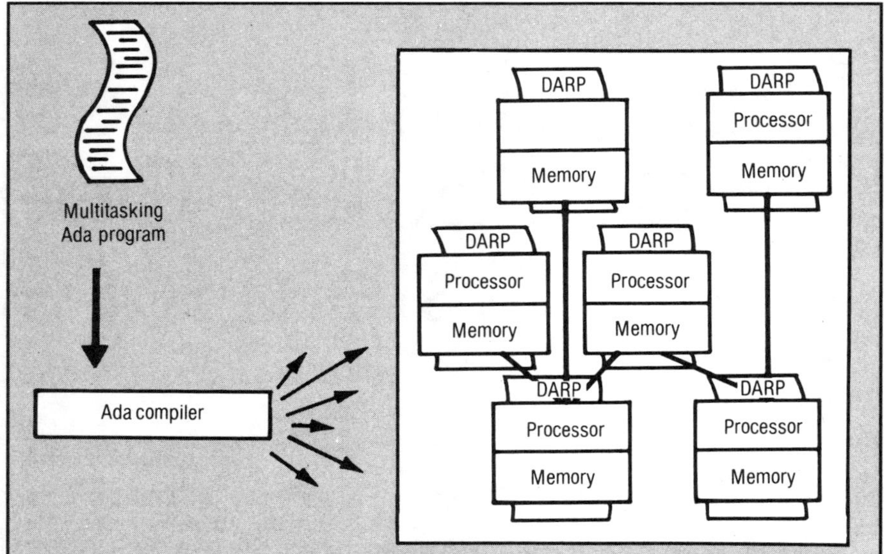

Figure 1. Ada system targeted to distributed operating system (DARP) for a loosely coupled network.

DARP must deal with a variety of unique issues. Each issue introduces problems in the design and implementation of correct and efficient features in the run-time system. In addition, certain language design issues arise from the need for the user to be able to specify and control the dynamic behavior of the system. For that reason we are fortunate to be using Ada, which has a number of useful features for specifying and controlling task activities.

Task synchronization

Ada provides both task synchronization and intertask data communication in the form of the rendezvous mechanism. *Rendezvous* is the intersection of the control paths of two tasks that were previously executing in parallel. The time at which the two paths become one is called a *critical region*. The point of intersection is called an *entry*. To rendezvous, one task must *call* an entry and the other must *accept* that same entry. Entries have arguments that act as actual parameters to the calling task and as formal parameters to the accepting task. (Terminology used here is that of the Ada reference manual.[2])

Once a rendezvous is attempted, the task remains suspended until rendezvous begins or a *timeout* occurs. Rendezvous begins when the calling task is accepted. Timeout occurs when a specified maximum time before the beginning of rendezvous is exceeded. The length of time the task wishes to wait for a rendezvous is specified by the task when it attempts to accept or call an entry.

Ada allows a task to attempt to accept more than one entry at a time. These simultaneous acccept attempts are grouped in "select" statements. A select statement may attempt to accept any subset of the entries declared by the task containing the select. The first entry called is allowed to rendezvous. If more than one entry is called before the select statement is reached, any one of them may be accepted. If no entry is called prior to the select, rendezvous will be with the first entry called. In Ada a task may call only one entry at a time.

Because DARP is intended for distributed-processing research, some of the synchronization restrictions imposed by the Ada language have been removed. Most important of these is the lack of symmetry in the Ada rendezvous. This restriction precludes multiple providers of the same service; that is, Ada does not allow two tasks to accept the same entry. The asymmetry arises from three Ada restrictions: multiple entry calls are not permited in the same select statement; an entry call cannot

Table 1. Task synchronization messages.

Name	Source	Destination	Parameter
Rendezvous request	Requesting task	Entry manager	Call/accept vector
Accept enable	Entry manager	Accepting task	Entry name, calling task
Call enable	Accepting task	Calling task	Entry name
Call acknowledge	Calling task	Accepting task	In parameters
Resume caller	Accepting task	Calling task	Out parameters
Timeout request	Requesting task	Entry manager	(Implicit)
Timeout accepted	Entry manager	Requesting task	Yes or no
Tasking exception	Calling or accepting task	Accepting or calling task	(Implicit)
Delete from queue	Requesting task	Entry manager	(Implicit)

appear in the same select as an accept; and entries can be accepted only by the task that declares them.

To overcome these restrictions, we have generalized the rendezvous mechanism to be symmetric, allowing a given task to call, and simultaneously accept, any subset of the entries visible to it. All transactions required during rendezvous are described in terms of a fixed set of messages and actions to be performed upon receipt of each message. The same messages are used whether the rendezvous is between processors or within a particular processor. To allow maximum control of load placement and observability of the system, the responsibility for rendezvous management is distributed rather than assigned to the processor hosting the accepting task or concentrated in a central system scheduler. Finally, unnecessary sharing of operating system functions is kept to a minimum. Just as it is reasonable in a system having several parallel processors to have a scheduler for each processor, the tasking activities of the system should be partitioned into as many independent management groups as possible so that the effort can be distributed and the parallelism exploited. These management groups, called *entry equivalence classes*, vary in number and composition from program to program.

Entry equivalence classes. Like all objects in Ada, entry visibility is arranged hierarchically, starting with the scope in which it is declared and spreading downward to all subordinate scopes. Unlike other objects in Ada, however, there are additional restrictions on where entries may be declared. An entry may be declared only in a task and only in the task allowed to accept that entry. This inconsistency is the root of the asymmetry of Ada rendezvous; removing it also removes most of the asymmetry. With the elimination of the close coupling between the entry and a particular accepting task, a new and more general structure is revealed.

Each entry can have its own independent rendezvous manager, provided that it does not appear in the same select statement with another entry. That is, we can define an equivalence relation among entries, making two entries equivalent, if there is a task waiting for both entries in the same select statement. With the Ada restrictions, entries of two different tasks can never appear in the same select and need not be in the same equivalence class. Thus, a separate manager can be associated with each task, as in the STC-Ada System.[3]

Without the Ada restriction, an equivalence class can grow arbitrarily large if there is a wide variety of entry combinations in multi-way select statements. On the other hand, an entry that is called and accepted by every task in the system can have its own class if it is never called or accepted in combination with other entries. Every entry equivalence class is assigned to a particular processor and administered by a unique task within that processor. This task, the *entry equivalence class manager*, receives request messages from tasks asking to call or accept some subset of the entries of its class. It coordinates the establishment of rendezvous but does not serve as an intermediary for other message traffic (parameter passing, for example).

Entry equivalence class manager. At the highest level the entry equivalence class manager receives rendezvous request messages from tasks that are calling or accepting entries in its equivalence class. It initiates rendezvous at the appropriate time by sending messages back to the requesting tasks. There are three parts to this scheme: the purpose and content of the messages, the state information and data structures contained within the manager, and the action associated with the transmission and reception of these messages.

Only nine types of messages (see Table 1) are required to implement rendezvous on a distributed system.[4] Each message type has a name and a destination as well as a number of parameters, which can be as simple as the name of the task that sent the message or as involved as the list of parameters supplied to the critical region of an accept statement. The requesting task may be calling, accepting, or some combination of these. The principle data structure of rendezvous is the call/accept vector.

Call/accept vector. With the Ada restrictions a task can simultaneously attempt to accept any subset of the entries of an equivalence class. With the symmetric rendezvous it can also simultaneously attempt to call any subset of the entries. The only constraint imposed on this generality is the requirement that the intersection of the calling and accepting entries of a given select statement be disjoint. That is, a task is not permitted to rendezvous with itself. The call/accept vector is an encoding of the subset of entries that a given task is attempting to call or accept.[5] The following type declaration gives a simple representation of the call/accept vector:

```
type c_a_vector(number_of_entries:integer)is
  record
    calling    :array(1..number_of_entries)
                  of boolean;
    accepting  :array(1..number_of_entries)
                  of boolean;
  end record;
```

Assuming a mapping has been established between the entries in an entry equivalence class and the integers *1 to number_of_entries*, a task T would build a call/accept vector V as follows: *V.calling*(i) will be true if and only if T is at-

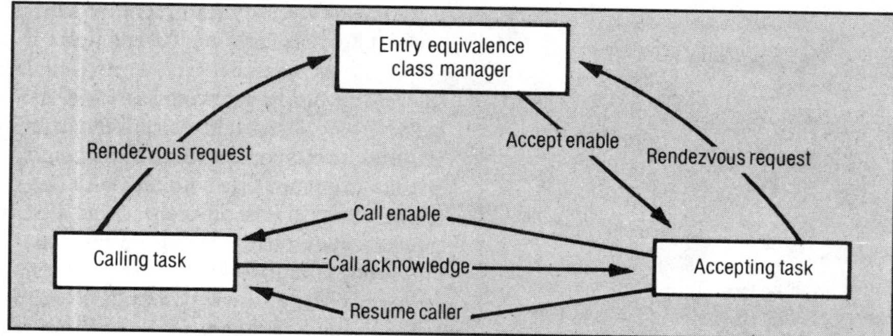

Figure 2. Message exchange during normal rendezvous.

tempting to call E_i, and *V.accepting*(i) will be true if and only if T is attempting to accept E_i. A tasking exception will be raised in T if for any i both *V.calling*(i) and *V.accepting*(i) are true. The vector, together with the task name T, would then be sent to the manager of the entry equivalence class as the parameters of a rendezvous request message.

When an entry equivalence class manager receives a rendezvous request message, two things can happen: the request will be honored immediately with the initialization of a rendezvous, or the request will be placed at the end of a list of existing requests. To make this decision, the manager compares the newly arrived call/accept vector to all those it has already received. This comparison proceeds sequentially, starting with the oldest existing request and working toward the newest. Searching the call/accept vectors of an equivalence in chronological order of arrival satisfies the Ada requirement for first-in-first-out queueing of requests at a given entry. Similarly, the oldest request that can be satisfied, will be. This ensures fairness by precluding permanent blocking, which is allowed by Ada. The ordered queue of outstanding rendezvous requests for a given entry class is represented by an array:

```
request_q:array(1..queue_size)of
  record
    c_a       : c_a_vector(class_size);
    requestor :task_name:
  end record;
```

The manager compares *request_q*(i)*.c_a.calling* with *V.accepting* and *request_q*(i)*.c_a.accepting* with *V.calling* in chronological order for each i from 1 to *queue_size*. A *true* in corresponding positions of either pair of vectors indicates that a rendezvous is possible between T, the task that sent the rendezvous request message, and the task *request_q*(i)*.requestor*. Should no match be found, the incoming request will be added to the end of *request_q*. This process is illustrated in the following program fragment:

```
--Receive a Rendezvous Request message
--with c_a_vector V from task T.
for i in 1..queue_size loop
  for j in 1..class_size loop
    if request_q(i).c_a.calling(j)
    and V.accepting(j) then
      --Send Accept Enable message to
      --task T along with name of entry be-
      --ing accepted, Ej, and name of call-
      --ing task, request_q(i).requestor.
      --Remove request_q(i) from request
      --queue.
      --Exit entry equivalence class
      --manager.
    end if:
    if request_q(i).c_a.accepting(j)
    and V.calling(j) then
      --Send Accept Enable message to
      --task request_q(i).requestor along
      --with name of entry being accepted,
      --Ej, and name of calling task, T.
      --Remove request_q(i) from request
      --queue.
      --Exit entry equivalence class
      --manager.
    end if;
  end loop;
end loop
queue_size: = queue_size + 1;
request_q(queue_size).c_a: = V;
request_q(queue_size).requestor: = T;
--Exit entry equivalence class manager.
```

In practice, the comparison often can be done with a single-integer-operation per *request_q* element. If the *class_size* is no more than half the number of bits in the integer of the target machine, then the entire call/accept vector can be encoded in a single integer. For purposes of the comparison, the accepting and calling portions of the arriving vector are interchanged. The comparison is accomplished by forming the bit-for-bit conjunction (inclusive *or*) of the interchanged arriving vector and an element of the *request_q* and then testing the resulting integer for nonzero.

The two scenarios below demonstrate the rendezvous process and illustrate how little the entry equivalence class manager is involved. The manager acts only as a broker to bring the two requesting tasks together; the actual rendezvous is executed without the manager's involvement. In the first scenario both tasks wait until rendezvous is possible; in the second scenario one of the rendezvous partners will timeout (give up) before rendezvous is possible.

Scenario 1: Normal rendezvous. For rendezvous to take place (see Figure 2), complementary rendezvous request messages must arrive at the manager, indicating the desire of one task to call a particular entry and of the other task to accept that entry. The manager initiates the rendezvous by sending an accept enable message to the accepting task. The accept enable message includes the name of the calling task as well as the name of the accepted entry. No further intervention by the manager is required. The accepting task sends a call enable message to the calling task, telling it which task and entry to rendezvous with. The calling task responds by sending the input parameters to the critical region in a call acknowledge message and then suspending its own execution. When the accepting task receives the call acknowledge message, it begins execution of the critical region of the rendezvous, and then it returns any output parameters to the calling task in a resume caller message. When the calling task receives the resume caller message, it continues its normal execution and the rendezvous is complete.

Scenario 2: Timeout. For a variety of reasons, we take the position that timeouts must be the responsibility of the individual calling and accepting tasks (more precisely, a timing task within their local processor). If timeouts were processed by a central controller, by the entry equiva-

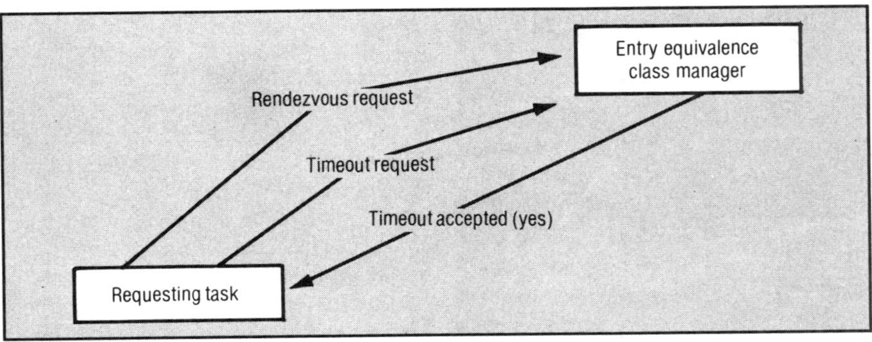

Figure 3. Message exchange for an expired rendezvous attempt.

lence class manager, or by any other foreign (i.e., in another processor) task, there would be a significant increase in the number and size of interprocessor control messages. Furthermore, in a distributed system there is no guarantee that clocks in different processors will agree on the time or even on the rate at which time passes. Finally, if there were a failure in the foreign processor to which the timeout function was delegated, the timeout would never be reported.

If timeouts are determined locally but the rendezvous manager is in a foreign processor, conflicting decisions and race conditions might arise. The DARP design avoids such situations by requiring that any timeout be confirmed by the entry manager prior to being reported to the requesting task. If the entry manager has already initiated the rendezvous by sending the accept enable to the accepting task, then the timeout request will be ignored and a negative timeout accepted sent to the requestor. Otherwise, the requesting task's call/accept vector will be removed from the *request_q* and the timeout accepted. The entry class manager is able to determine that it has already initiated the rendezvous only by the absence of a vector from the requesting task in its *request_q*. The message interactions for timeout are illustrated in Figure 3.

Exceptions and termination. Another issue to be considered is the possibility that while engaging in a rendezvous, a task or its rendezvous partner may become abnormal. It is also possible, through the *terminate select alternative,* that a rendezvous attempt could cause a task to end its own execution. The existence of the terminate select alternative in Ada greatly complicates the entry equivalence class manager and the rendezvous mechanism. The control of an abnormal task engaging in rendezvous, on the other hand, is relatively simple and requires only one additional message type.

Should a task become abnormal after transmitting a rendezvous request message, it can receive either an accept enable message from the manager (indicating the task is the acceptor of an entry call) or a call enable message from a rendezvous partner (indicating the task is the caller of some entry). In either case the task must send a tasking exception message to the task named in the parameter of the accept enable or call enable message. If a task becomes abnormal after receiving the call acknowledge (during the critical region of the accept), it sends a tasking exception message, rather than the normal resume caller message, to its partner. Having propagated the tasking exception, it is free to end its execution as dictated by the Ada rules for task completion and exception handling.

The terminate select alternative of Ada has little, if any, utility but imposes a great price in implementation complexity.[6] Five additional messages are required to accommodate it. Several entry equivalence class manager and task dynamic control functions must be combined. Briefly, to select a terminate alternative, a task must inform the manager of its intent to terminate, using the rendezvous request message. The manager must communicate with the task's master scope to determine whether termination is possible (i.e., whether all of the task's siblings are terminated or waiting at terminate alternatives). If the master scope indicates termination is possible, the manager must check to see if a rendezvous began between the arrival of the rendezvous request message and the master scope's reply. If so, the manager informs the task master scope of the task's change in status from waiting at a terminate alternative to activated. Otherwise, the manager informs the task that it is terminated and removes its call/accept vector from *request_q*.

Task dynamics

Task dynamics involves the creation of a task, the synchronization of its elaboration, the management of its local storage, and its orderly removal from the system when its mission is complete. The programmer is seldom aware of a task's dynamics because most of the operations are called implicitly and often occur in the declarative portions rather than the statement portions of programs.

A simple diagram of state transition in the life of a task is shown in Figure 4. In the "created" state a task's visible parts can be seen, but the elaboration of its declarative parts has not begun. In Ada this means the task's entries are callable. Once created, a task begins executing its declarations during create time or during the elaboration of the declaration of its creating scope, whichever occurs later. After the creating task signals the end of its declarative part, the task is considered active and can proceed with the parallel execution of its statements. Our discussion here assumes the Ada semantics for task dynamics (see Table 2).

The completion of the body of each dependent task and of the body of the master scope marks a common synchronization point between the master scope and all its dependents. Because the master scope cannot deallocate the storage for its siblings and terminate itself until its dependents terminate, a dependent terminated message is sent to inform the master as each dependent completes execution. When all its siblings are also terminated (or waiting at terminate select alternatives), the master sends deallocate task messages, permitting all the dependent tasks to delete their visible parts and surrender their storage.

To create a task, the creating processor need know only the task executing the create, the new task's master scope, and the location of the code for the new task. The new task will be allocated, but will not necessarily be visible, in the scope of its master. Once the new task is created, the creating processor gives the creating task access to the new task by sending it a pointer to the new task in a create acknowledge message. The creating processor also sends an add dependent message to the master scope so it can know which tasks to include in its list of dependents.

The resume task message signals the completion of the creating task's declarative part. After the creating task has elaborated its declarations, the dependents are free to begin execution of their declarative parts and bodies.

When a task finishes execution of its body, it uses the dependent terminated message to inform its master scope of its termination. The master scope then removes the dependent named in the dependent terminated message from its list of active dependents. When the list is empty, the master scope sends deallocate task messages to all its dependents.

The abort task message is sent to all tasks named in an abort statement. Ada semantics require that the aborting task not proceed until the specified tasks are aborted. Thus, an acknowledgment is required and takes the form of the abort acknowledge message.

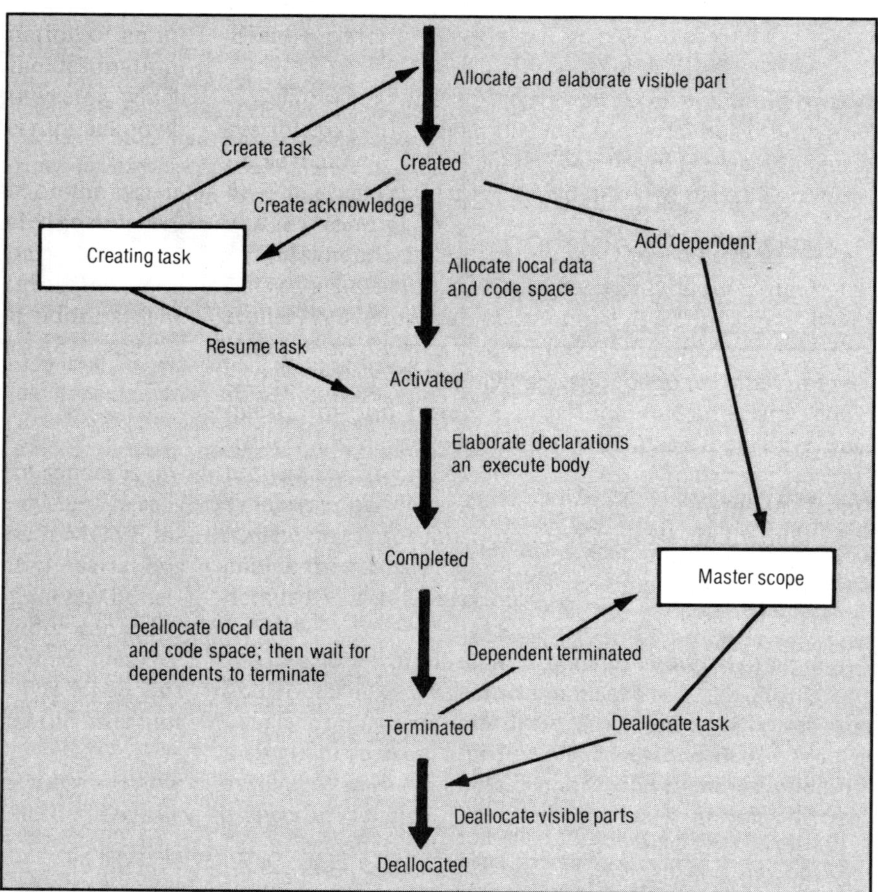

Figure 4. State transition in the life of a task.

Table 2. Task dynamics messages.

Name	Source	Destination	Parameters
Create task	Creating task	Creating processor	Master scope, code (task type)
Create acknowledge	Creating processor	Creating task	Task pointer
Add dependent	Creating processor	Master scope	Dependent task
Resume task	Creating task	Suspended task	(Implicit)
Dependent terminated	Completed task	Master scope	(Implicit)
Deallocate task	Master scope	Completed task	(Implicit)
Abort task	Aborting task	Abort victim	(Implicit)
Abort acknowledge	Abort victim	Aborting task	(Implicit)

Shared variables

A shared variable is any variable used by more than one task. Without global analysis of programs, it must be assumed that a variable is used by all tasks to which it is visible. Thus, in many systems, all variables visible to multiple tasks must be treated as shared variables. This is particularly expensive when programs are written in languages that couple the allocation and visibility of variables. In many programming languages *own* variables must be declared globally; consequently, they become visible to all tasks and thus appear to be shared variables. Ada eliminates much of this problem by providing global allocation of variables within the body of packages and tasks without their being visible outside the package.

For safe and correct use of shared variables, there must be synchronization between the using tasks. Typically, within each task there is a sequence of operations, called a critical region, during which the shared-variable value cannot change. If another task alters the value of the shared variable during a critical region, the computation may be erroneous. A simple example occurs when two tasks both attempt to increment a shared variable. Each accesses the variable, adds 1, and stores the result back in the variable. If both tasks access the variable before either stores the incremented result, the variable will be incremented only once rather than twice as intended.

Even uniprocessor and multiprocessor implementations with shared memory

For a loosely coupled, distributed system to be efficiently reconfigurable, resource allocation decisions must be localized to individual processors.

must have a mechanism for mutual exclusion of access within the critical regions associated with shared variables. The least restrictive (to the user) use of critical regions requires that if any task is in the critical region to update the shared variable, then no other task may be there. On the other hand, any number of tasks may enter the critical regions simultaneously, provided that all are reading and none are updating the shared variable. The Ada language imposes an equivalent restriction: if a task reads a shared variable between two synchronization points, then the variable is not updated by any other task. Likewise, if a task updates a shared variable, then the variable is not updated or read by any other task.

These Ada restrictions guarantee that local copies of shared variables can be maintained between synchronization points and that the master copy can be updated only at synchronization points terminating critical regions that update the shared variable.[7] This ability to maintain local copies becomes essential for efficient implementation of shared variables in the absence of shared memory.

Another view of shared variables in a distributed system without shared memory is that a task can update shared variables if, and only if, the task and the variables are in the same processor. Thus, in general, during the critical region of an update, either the variable must be moved to the processor of the task or the task must be moved to the processor of the variable. The latter can be accomplished by creating, within the processor of the shared variable, a surrogate task to execute the updating critical region on behalf of the real task. This mechanism is not provided in the DARP system as a primitive, but the user can construct it by declaring the surrogate task explicitly and rendezvousing with it. This method, however, is applicable only in situations in which all shared variables of a given critical region are in the same processor.

In the absence of shared memory, it must be possible to copy shared variables from processor to processor. The Ada shared-variable restrictions allow a copying technique with minimum overhead: Upon entry into a critical region, a shared variable is copied to the processor of the reading or updating task. Just prior to exit from a critical region updating it, the shared variable is copied back to its original processor. No additional management or analysis is required except the critical region synchronization itself. There is a trade-off between the cost of copying large data objects and the synchronization overhead on independent partitions of that data. The judicious partitioning of shared variables reduces both contention and copying time.

Resource allocation and reconfiguration

Resource allocation is the management and control of the association between the physical and logical components of the system. Most important are memory management and task allocation. A key goal in the design of DARP is that it be reconfigurable—that is, that we can dynamically alter the assocation between physical and logical devices.

There are three primary motivations for reconfiguration: dynamic load sharing, fail-safe execution, and fail-soft capability. Dynamic load sharing, a possibility in any multiple-processor system, is the ability to redistribute work loads (i.e., tasks and data) among processors to increase overall system throughput. Fail-safe execution—recovery from system component failures without loss of information—requires detection and isolation of faulty components, as well as the ability to reconfigure the system to use the remaining components. Fail-soft capability combines dynamic load sharing with fail-safe execution to give priority to the most important tasks when the remaining resources are inadequate to provide the full functionality of the system. In DARP we do not provide these capabilities. Instead, we provide facilities for user-controlled dynamic reconfiguration of the system, which, in combination with other system features, can be used to develop the higher level, dynamic load-sharing, fail-safe, and fail-soft capabilities in user programs.

For a loosely coupled, distributed system to be efficiently reconfigurable, resource allocation decisions must be localized to individual processors of the network. Thus, DARP provides system management without centralized decision making, scheduling, or record keeping. Instead, each processor manages its own resources, both physical and logical. Scheduling is done independently within each processor, and each processor allocates its own memory without coordination with other processors. Each physical device attached to a specific processor has a managing task within that processor. The managing task, called an *input-output responder*, acts as an interface between the device and any using task. Communication is through the normal rendezvous mechanism.

The binding of tasks to processors is specified by an implementation-defined pragma. The allocation pragma has two arguments; the first designates the task, and the second, the processor to which the task is allocated:

pragma allocate (task, processor);

The task parameter may be a task, an access task, a task type, or an access task type. In the first two cases, the pragma applies to the individual task, and in the latter two cases, to the entire task type. The pragma must appear between the declaration of its first argument and the activation of the task whose allocation it specifies. If multiple allocate pragmas are issued for the same task, individual specifications take precedence over task type specifications; otherwise the most recent specifications take precedence.

The processor specification in an allocation pragma can be either a processor number or the name of any visible task or variable. In the latter case, the designated processor is that in which the specified task or variable is located. If no allocation pragma is given for a task, it will be allocated in the processor of its master. Static binding of tasks to processors is achieved when the processor specification is a static expression. Dynamic binding occurs when the processor number can be computed only at run time.

The binding of tasks to processors is implemented by a single run-time primitive, which creates the task and allocates it within the designated processor. Calls on this function are emitted implicitly by the compiler at the point where each task is allocated. A similar allocation pragma is used to specify the allocation of shared variables.

In some systems, it also may be desirable to allow migration of tasks between processors once the task has been partially executed. The feasibility of such migrations is being investigated. There are several hardware (i.e., instruction set) architectural features that may preclude migration. Tasks cannot be moved if their associated execution stacks, including subprogram return marks, contain absolute memory addresses unrecognizable by the operating system. It appears likely that migration will be possible on the MC68000, but it may be too expensive to be worthwhile.

When migration is not feasible, an alternative is to restart the computation associated with the given task at some earlier known synchronization point. For such methods to work, tasks and subprograms must be guaranteed to act as pure functions—functions whose side effects occur at well-defined points in the computation. The DARP system accomplishes this by implementing all formal parameters with copy semantics. That is, all *in-out* and *out* parameters are copied into the called subprogram or task at the point of the subprogram or entry call and are copied out only when the subprogram or rendezvous has been completed without error. If any error or exception occurs during the execution of the subprogram or critical region, the update of the *in-out* and *out* parameters will not have occurred and, therefore, the erroneous computation will affect only the state of its local variables. Recovery can be made from the point of call.

Ada requires that "if two tasks with different priorities are both eligible for execution and could sensibly be executed using the same physical processors and the same other processing resources, then it cannot be the case that the task with the lower priority is executing while the task with the higher priority is not."[8] We agree with this Ada restriction and interpret it to mean that strict priority scheduling is required within an individual processor, may be required among multiprocessors of a shared-memory system depending on the costs involved, and is not required between processors of a loosely coupled, distributed system. The DARP design provides priority scheduling within each processor but not between processors. Any requirement for interprocessor-imposed priorities would have to be implemented by explicitly specified task synchronization. As anticipated in the Ada requirements, priorities cannot be used to achieve mutual exclusion.

Instrumentation

The DARP design includes an instrumentation package that provides a collection of functions for accessing the dynamic state of the system. Existing timeshared systems often collect a variety of information on the amount of processor time, input/output time, and other system resource allocation associated with a given task or program. Although such information may be appropriate for accounting and cost allocation, it may not be adequate for research in distributed systems. Researchers need more detailed data describing discrete events and system actions unrelated to cost apportioning.

One way to provide such data would be to record a complete history, showing each system event and the time of its occurrence. To be adequate for general research purposes, an event-recording system must collect a set of fine-grained events, including all events related to scheduling, resource allocation and deallocation, access to shared variables, task synchronization, and error propagation. Such a system would be very expressive, but it would produce far too much unneeded data. It also would fail to record events within the application program that may be important to the analysis of the experimental results but are unknown to the operating system.

Instead, DARP's instrumentation package provides an event-recording system that is fine-grained but controlled by the user. Events may be defined by the user or by the system. The subset of events to be recorded is specified by the user. Each recorded event includes its time, the processor on which it occurred, the task initiating it, its name, and any event parameters.

To minimize the overhead of event recording, each event is recorded locally within the processor generating it.

To minimize the overhead of event recording, each event is recorded locally within the processor generating it. Because each processor has its own record of events, the executing processor is implicit in the list of events and need not be recorded explicitly with each event. Each recorded event, however, is assigned a sequential integer indicating its chronological order among the recorded events of its executing processor. This integer can be used to index events and is recorded with certain interprocessor events to be discussed below.

Each user-defined event has a name and may be associated with any subprogram. A pragma is used to specify the association between the event name and the subprogram, and to turn the recording of the event on or off:

```
pragma event(event_name, subprogram_
  name, on_off);
```

When the event recording is on, the event, time, executing task, and all actual parameter values of the subprogram are recorded within the executing processor each time the subprogram is called.

All other events that can be recorded are defined by the system. System-defined events include all intertask and task-to-DARP messages and the scheduling of tasks within the run queue of each processor. For system-defined events, the event name is the message name. A pragma is used to turn recording of the event on and off and to determine which events for that message are to be recorded:

```
pragma event(message_name(parameter_
  association_list), on_off);
```

The parameter assocation list is a list of expressions of the form *id*= >*exp*, where *id* is a formal parameter name of the message or the identifier, *source_task*. The pragma refers only to that subset of events for the specified message, in which the named parameter (or the *source_task*) equals the value of the associated expression, *exp*. If no value is specified for a formal parameter, then all values match. Message-recording events include not only tasking messages but also memory and device allocation and deallocation, shared-variable copy-in and copy-out, input/output waiting, and delay.

Scheduling within a processor is treated as a single event type with the message name *schedule*:

pragma event(schedule(task_list), on_off);

The parameter association list of the pragma may be used to limit the effects of the pragma to the tasks listed. Both scheduling and unscheduling of a task are recorded when its scheduling event is on.

Correlating interprocessor events. The event-recording scheme assumes that each processor has its own clock. There is no guarantee that clocks in different processors are synchronized or even that they run at the same rate. An additional mechanism is required to correlate independently reported interprocessor events. This is a special case of the general problem of correlating interprocessor events in distributed systems with asynchronous clocks.

In the DARP design, the general synchronization problem is solved by a conventional, sequence-numbering, communication protocol scheme. For each pair of processors that have ever communicated, there is a counter in the sending processor. Before any message is sent, the counter in the sending processor is incremented and the value attached to the message. The receiving processor keeps a record of the message numbers received from each sending processor. Arriving message numbers are compared with expected numbers to detect lost or out-of-sequence messages.

These message numbers also provide a means to synchronize and correlate the times recorded for interprocessor events. Whenever an interprocessor event is recorded in any processor, DARP also records an interprocessor communication event consisting of the source and destination processor, the communications sequence number, and the local time. If the same event is recorded in the other processor, the combined records show the unique sequence number and the corresponding local times within both processors.

Future directions

DARP is experimental and ignores many important issues. Nevertheless, it provides a variety of instrumental control and error-reporting mechanisms, which should allow others to investigate distributed systems with greater ease. The system should provide a sound and efficient substrate for demonstrating distributed applications on loosely coupled networks with large numbers of processors.

The development of the distributed-target operating system as an Ada run-time package has had several advantages. It provided a well-defined, high-level framework for tasking and exception handling, thus limiting the scope of possible designs and allowing us to concentrate on an efficient implementation of the Ada model. For the application developer or the distributed-processing researcher, it means that development and experimentation can be done in the context of a modern, high-level language, designed specifically for large, multitasking, real-time applications. Ada provides a common syntactic and semantic framework for interpreting experimental results.

Retargetability. The DARP system, as currently defined, is not retargetable but should be relatively easy to port to other distributed targets. With the exception of the low-level functions of the input/output driver, interprocessor communications, and task synchronization, the design is independent of the BBN Butterfly and depends only on the general characteristics of loosely coupled systems.

Operating system retargetability depends on a target-independent design and on implementation in a machine-independent, high-level language, such as Ada. It is possible to automate the retargeting of DARP by replacing the code generator on the host machine of the Ada compiler. Ada encourages machine-independent design by providing high-level features for tasking, error handling, representation specification, and real-time control, eliminating the traditional need for assembly language in such applications. Ada also provides a conditional compilation facility that can be used in conjunction with the package called System, a formal description of the target machine configuration, to adapt applications to other configurations by recompilation. When Ada tasking, exception, and real-time features are used in applications, Ada does not provide explicit operating system calls, instead requiring the compiler to implicitly generate calls on the appropriate functions of the target operating system; thus, Ada programs also are operating-system independent.

Ada greatly simplifies retargeting applications at the expense of compiler complexity; Ada's operating-system independence raises DARP to the status of any other application program by transferring many machine dependencies from the application program to the compiler. In the context of several applications for multiple-target environments, this transfer reduces effort to implement n applications on m machines from $O(n \times m)$ to $O(n+m)$.

We expect the Distributed Ada Run-time Package to facilitate our own and others' distributed-system research, and we intend to exploit our experience with DARP to build Ada systems for commercial and industrial applications. □

Acknowledgment

This work was sponsored in part by the Department of Defense Advanced Research Projects Agency, Order No. 5057, monitored by the Department of the Navy, Naval Electronic Systems Command, under contract N00039-85-C-0126.

References

1. R. Rettberg et al., "Development of a Voice Funnel System," quarterly tech. report, nos. 1-9, Bolt Baranek and Newman, June 1981.
2. *Reference Manual for the Ada Programming Language,* ANSI/MIL-STD 1815A, US Dept. of Defense, 1983.
3. D. A. Fisher, D. A. Mundie et al., "Design of the STC-Ada System," Western Digital Corporation, 1982.
4. R. M. Weatherly, "Design of a Distributed Operating System for Ada," PhD dissertation, Clemson Univ., Aug. 1984.
5. J. F. Leathrum, "Design of an Ada Run-Time System," *Proc. 1984 Conf. Ada Applications and Environments,* IEEE Computer Society, pp. 4-13.

6. G. A. Riccardi and T. P. Baker, "An Applications Programmer Guide to Ada Tasking," *Proc. 1984 Conf. Ada Applications and Environments*, IEEE Computer Society, pp. 14-22.
7. D. A. Fisher, "Ada Can Be Efficiently Implemented on a Loosely Coupled Distributed System with Correct Error Recovery and Safe State Protection," presentation at panel on Distributed Systems and Ada at Fourth Intl. Conf. Distributed Computing Systems, San Francisco, May 14-18, 1984.
8. "Steelman, Department of Defense Requirements for High Order Computer Programming Languages," DoD report, June 1978, p. 22.

Operating Systems for the Micronet Network Computer

André M. van Tilborg
Calspan Advanced Technology Center

Larry D. Wittie
State University of New York at Stony Brook

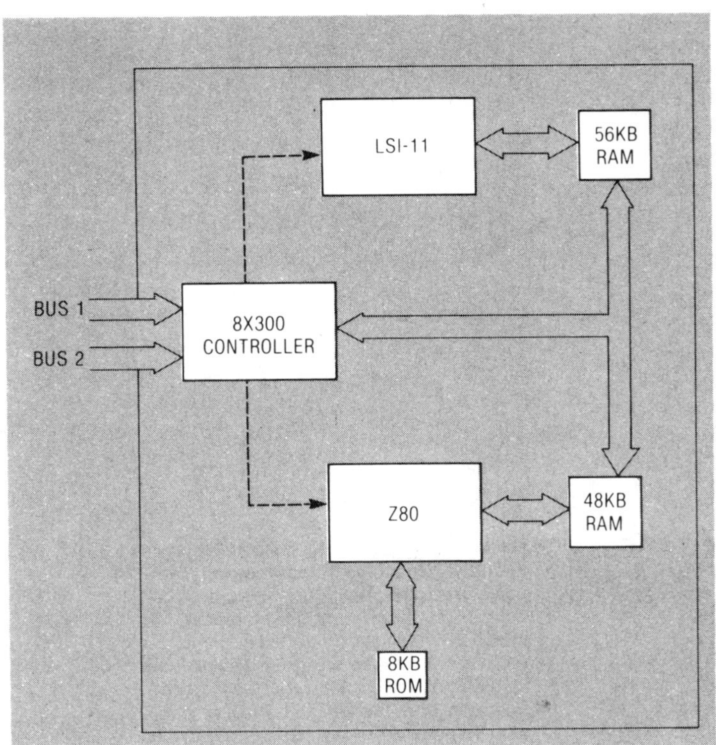

Figure 1. Schematic diagram of the main hardware components in each Micronet node.

In his classification of computer architectures, Flynn identifies multiple-instruction-stream multiple-data-stream (MIMD) computers as those in which different instruction sequences operate simultaneously on different sets of data.[1] A network computer is an MIMD computer built from a collection of independent, asynchronously executing, loosely coupled processing elements. Each processing element, called a node, consists of at least one central processing unit attached to a local random access memory that contains instructions and data. The memory of one node is not directly accessible by any other node. Moderately wideband connections, currently on the order of 1 to 10 megabits per second, link each node to a limited number of neighboring nodes, often forming the basis for a packet-switched communications subnetwork. Communication between nodes is accomplished through message passing. Peripheral devices are attached to a few nodes.

The Micronet network computer[2] is a loosely coupled, extensible, and reconfigurable network of microcomputer processing elements. Each node consists of three separate microcomputers and connects to exactly two passive communication buses. There may be many buses in a large network. The buses are passive in the sense that their control logic is distributed among the nodes that connect to a particular bus.

Figure 1 illustrates schematically the organization of a single node in the Micronet. A DEC LSI-11 microcom-

Reprinted from *IEEE Micro*, pp. 38–47, Apr. 1983.

puter functions as a task processor—it executes user- and operating-system tasks. Fifty-six kilobytes of random access memory are supplied to each LSI-11 as its private program and data memory. Attached to the task processor via a direct memory access channel is a front-end communications processor. This front end, built around a Zilog Z80 microcomputer, provides an interface between the task processor and each of the two buses that connect this node to other identical nodes. The details of managing both the DMA channel and the link-level bus protocol are assigned to a Signetics 8X300 microcontroller. Each node's hardware consists of a power supply and a single backplane that accepts all of the microcomputer circuit boards, including any interface cards for terminals and storage devices.

The Micronet is intended to be a vehicle for experimentation with interconnection structures and distributed control. Its architecture is fixed only at the node level. The nodes can be interconnected in countless ways by manually changing their bus connections. However, because each bus is electrically limited to supporting about seventeen nodes, large networks will tend to be built up out of the same repeated structure; i.e., they will consist of many small groups of nodes communicating over a local bus, with the other bus port of some of the nodes being used to link up ever larger clusters of groups. Several such cluster topologies, including the hypercube[3] and X-Tree,[4] have been generalized by Wu and Liu.[5] Figure 2 shows one possible configuration of 16 nodes in the Micronet, with each node sharing one horizontal and one vertical bus.

Network computers should be able to support fault-tolerant parallel computation and provide machine extensibility. However, achieving these goals depends not so much on the construction of the network computer hardware as on the availability of adequate operating systems.[6] But difficult questions about such operating systems remain unanswered. They concern decomposition, distribution, and synchronization of tasks; parallel applications languages; internodal communications facilities; task scheduling by global versus local procedures; static and dynamic deadlocks; and software recovery from hardware failures. Techniques for dealing with these questions should be general enough to work

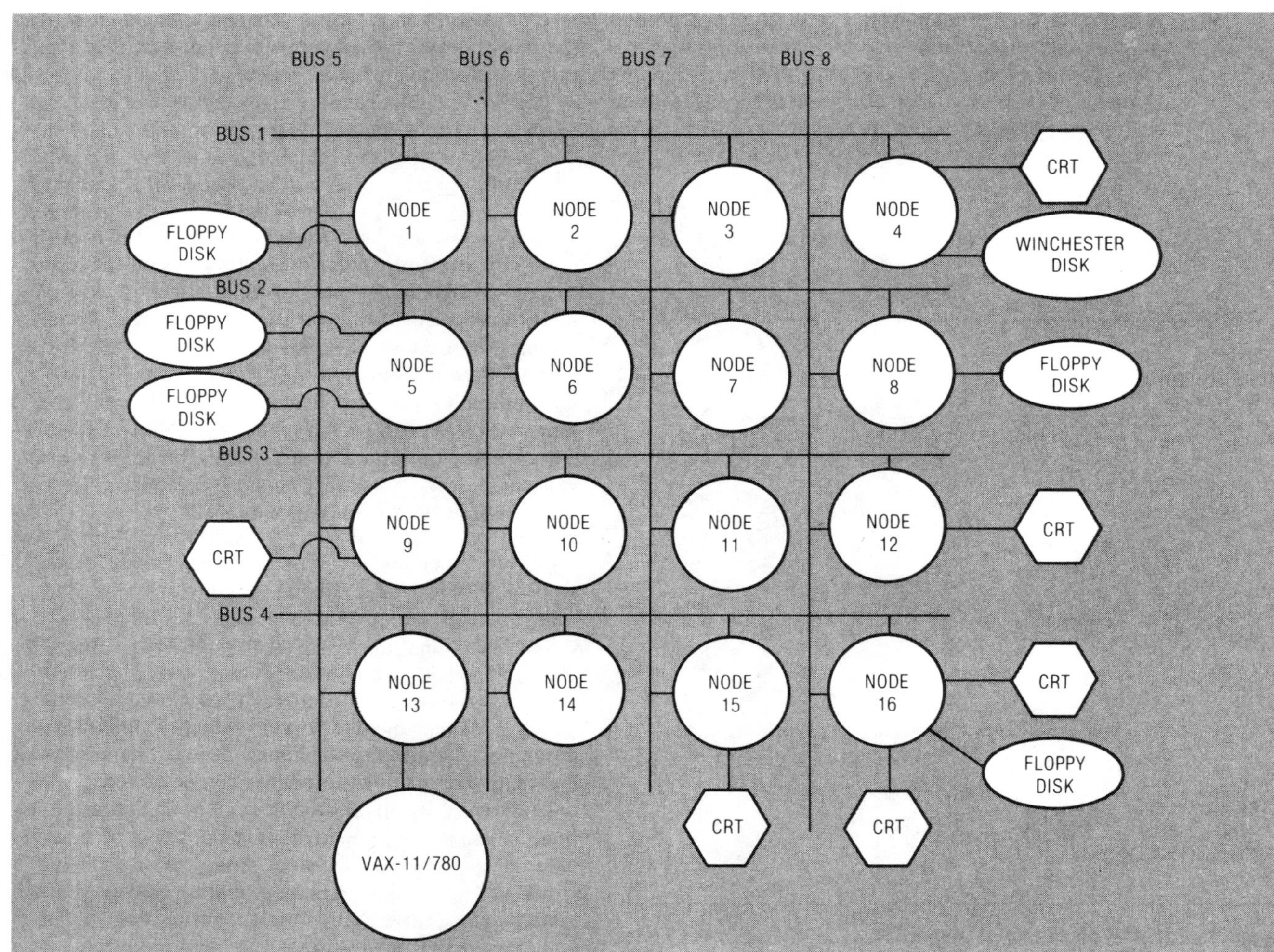

Figure 2. A configuration of eight buses connecting 16 microcomputer nodes in Micronet. Each node always connects to two buses. Here, each bus is shared by four nodes. Terminals and minicomputers are attached via serial interfaces.

on almost any network computer topology, just as conventional techniques are general enough to work on all sorts of uniprocessors. As a step in this direction, we will outline a strategy for structuring networks, one that we can exploit to build operating systems for general-purpose network computers.

Hierarchical control

Here, we present a schema from which network computer operating systems can be built. This schema is a compromise between central control and distributed control: Although it provides for many control sites, it specifies a hierarchy of responsibility. It is not an attempt to develop a complete high-level operating system for a network computer, but rather serves as a superstructure around which it should be possible to build operating systems for a variety of network topologies.

The control-structure schema we propose is illustrated in Figure 3, in which each circle represents a network node. The arcs indicate control links; they do not necessarily represent direct physical connections between nodes. The nodes at level zero (workers) are available for user tasks. Those at higher levels (managers) are responsible for maintaining the integrity of the communications subnetwork and for performing resource allocation in a local region. Although the exact number of managers will vary, each can probably manage about ten to twenty subnodes. A hierarchical control schema does not imply that the *physical* connections in the network form a hierarchy.

A hierarchy, the division of labor and responsibility into levels, is characteristic of complex social systems.[7]

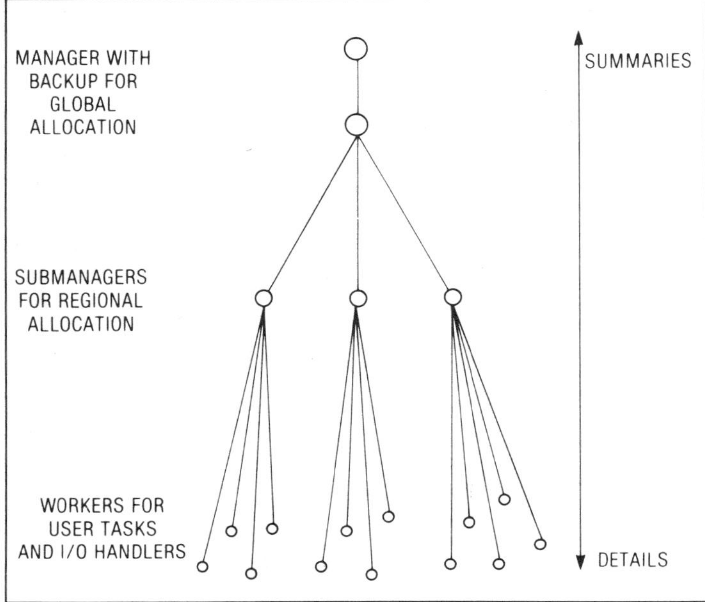

Figure 3. A logical hierarchy of global resource management nodes for Micros. Arcs between nodes may involve more than one hardware link. Nodes and arcs are chosen for efficient message passing within each subtree.

The advantages of hierarchical control are the same for complex computer systems as for complex social organizations—such control is resistant to failures of individual elements and prevents overloading of individual elements by enabling summarized information to be passed upward through the levels of the hierarchy. When there are many managers at many levels, the danger of total collapse is greatly reduced. When a manager is disabled for whatever reason, a higher-level manager can allocate the disabled manager's functions to other managers (or, in the case of a network computer, to other nodes). Redundant managers at the top of the hierarchy, and latent connections between managers at the same level, help recovery from individual manager/node failures.

To avoid communication and processing overloads, each node in the hierarchy normally exchanges control and status information only one level upward (with its manager) and one level downward (with its subnodes). Status information passed between hierarchy nodes includes measures of message traffic intensity and of resource utilization. Depending on the actual topology of the network, a node can have physical links to many other nodes at various levels. Intertask messages can be relayed along any physical link, regardless of the structure of logical control in the hierarchy. In other words, the communications subnetwork is not aware of functional distinctions between nodes.

The highest management level consists of a global-master root node backed up by an observer node that can swiftly replace the root if it should fail. To avoid overloads, a manager in each higher level of management keeps only summaries of the resource information known to its subnodes. The higher a manager is in the hierarchy, the more global is its information; the lower, the more detailed is that information. For example, level-*l* managers know which user task nodes are idle, but their managers know only the number of idle nodes each of them controls.

Establishing a control hierarchy in a network computer may seem to be a difficult task. However, there is a known computational technique that produces nearly optimal clusters in arbitrary network computers. Details can be found in a recent paper by us.[8]

Nodal operating system

The superstructure provided by a hierarchy like that described above is not an operating system; it is a foundation for many possible operating systems. A hierarchy forms a stable structure around which techniques for doing such things as scheduling, external resource allocation, and deadlock avoidance can be designed without reference to physical topology. Just as important as these considerations, though, is the problem of how to organize the operating system structure of each individual network node. Because operating systems do not logically and mechanically follow from axioms, trial and error experimentation is needed to identify useful ideas. A few experimental network computer operating systems have recently been reported.[4,9-17] This article discusses the design of the Micros operating system for the Micronet network computer, as implemented in Concurrent Pascal. It also describes a successor to Micros that is being written in Modula-2.

There are two main portions of each Micronet node's operating system—the Z80 front end's communication kernel and the task processor's control software. The packet switching communications subsystem has been described in a separate paper by us.[18] Here, we will concentrate on the task processor software.

Access graphs and Concurrent Pascal. Each Micronet task processor executes a version of the same operating system. This operating system is made up of processes that allow a task processor to talk to its front end, talk to interactive terminal devices, execute user task forces, manage local resources, and play a role in the control hierarchy. The processes are all written in Concurrent Pascal.[19] (Although it is not essential to be versed in Concurrent Pascal to read this article, a familiarity with the monitor concept, and with its use in designing hierarchical systems by means of access graphs, is helpful.) Before describing the task processor's operating system, we will take a short detour to explain the system components of Concurrent Pascal and to show how they are combined in access graphs.

Concurrent Pascal, or CP, is a variant of the language Pascal and is intended specifically for use in writing operating systems. It emphasizes structured and simple interprocess communication (data sharing) to an extent not found in most languages that have been used to build operating systems. Concurrent Pascal is an attempt to reduce significantly the complexity of designing and writing operating systems.

The most important thing CP adds to Pascal is a limited capability to define abstract data types. In particular, CP contains three new intrinsic data types: process, class, and monitor. These new types are known as abstract data types because they separate the specific representation of a data structure from the operations allowed on it. Routines that use a variable of an abstract type are constrained to do so only in ways defined by the creator of the type.

The process type in CP makes it possible to write programs made up of distinct tasks that execute concurrently at indeterminate relative rates. The process concept is fundamental in most modern operating systems but is usually not recognized explicitly by the languages used to write those systems. CP forces a designer to encapsulate each separate control thread as a process, glue all the processes together with monitors, and have a compiler check the consistency of interprocess references in much the same way as type checking is done in languages such as Pascal.

It is important to understand the monitor concept in CP. The use of monitors brings some order to the potential chaos of interprocess communications. A monitor is an abstract data type that ensures that processes sharing a data structure have mutually exclusive access to the data. If two or more processes try to execute procedures of a monitor simultaneously, they are allowed to proceed in first-come, first-served order. A new process is not permitted to execute within the monitor until its predecessor relinquishes control. A process relinquishes control by exiting from the monitor when it is finished or by suspending itself within the monitor until some local condition becomes true. It is the responsibility of the programmer to ensure that some other process will later enter the monitor to restart the suspended process.

Designing an operating system for implementation in CP consists of identifying the activities that are needed, partitioning those activities into processes, and interconnecting the processes into a hierarchical structure by means of monitors. Of course, the processes of a CP program do not actually execute simultaneously on a uniprocessor. They are time-sliced by a virtual machine kernel written in assembly language.

We will describe the structure of the Micros operating system in terms of the access graphs introduced by Brinch Hansen.[19] An access graph is a pictorial representation of the access rights of system components in a Concurrent Pascal program. An access right confers on a process or monitor the ability to call entry procedures in another system component. Access graphs reflect the structure of concurrent programs by showing how concurrent processes may communicate through monitors. Access graphs do not indicate the direction in which data flows.

As a simple example, consider the flow of data in Figure 4, which shows a system in which a card reader supplies card images to a card reader process. The card reader process passes the images to a printer process that writes them to a line printer. Communication between the card reader process and the printer process occurs in a buffer monitor. The flow of card images is in the direction of the arrows.

Now consider Figure 5, showing the same set of system components depicted as an access graph. The arrows indicate access rights. The card reader process has access to the card reader, the printer process has access to the line printer, and both processes have access to the buffer monitor.

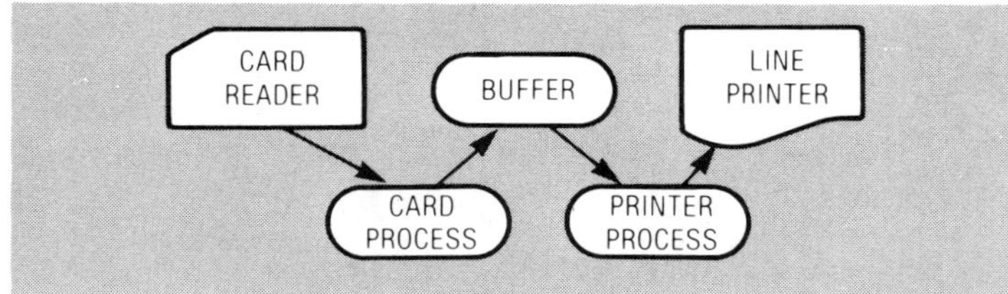

Figure 4. Flow of data in a simple input/output pipeline.

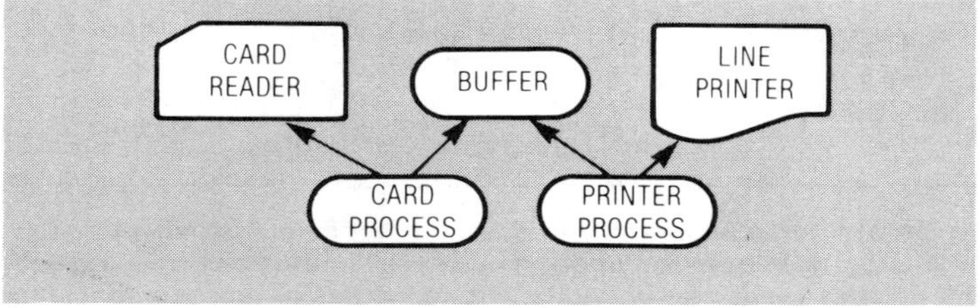

Figure 5. Access graph for the input/output pipeline of Figure 4.

Access graphs are useful design aids when they can be kept to less than a page in size. Micros was initially organized by means of access graphs. Although Micros is a simple operating system, the access graphs became unwieldy. The technique is not recommended for larger projects, unless a good way to partition graphs into subgraphs is devised.

Task processor control structure. Figure 6 illustrates a "clumped" access graph of the main components of the task processor operating system. Each of the boxes represents a group of related processes, classes, and monitors. The three boxes nearest to the bottom of the figure represent components that reside in all nodes. (These components are somewhat akin to Liskov's "primal guardians."[20]) The two boxes at the top contain a variable number of processes that may or may not be supplied to a node, depending on its peripheral connections. Not shown in Figure 6 is a monitor that manages the free memory left in the task processor after instruction code and data space have been allocated to the other system components of the operating system.

Figure 7 is a refinement of Figure 6. It shows almost all system components for the task processor, omitting a few classes that would further clutter the diagram. The free memory monitor, called BODY__SPACE, is shown without connections. All of the system components marked with an asterisk have access to BODY__SPACE. Also, MAIL__QUEUE is accessible to all processes marked with a plus sign. (Drawing arrows to show access rights to these two monitors would have been too confusing.)

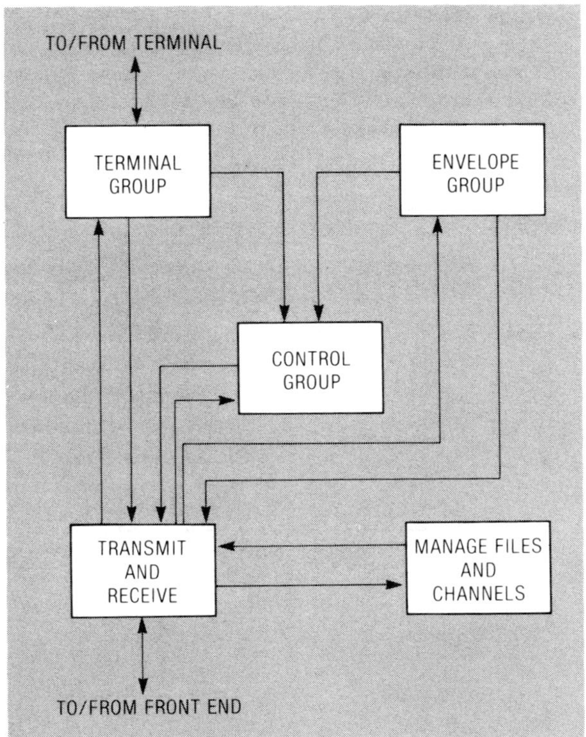

Figure 6. Clumped access graph of the main components in the Micros operating system.

The terminal group. Micronet is designed so that interactive user terminals attach directly to the LSI-11 task processors. In effect, each user terminal has a network node as its interface to the entire network. Large numbers of interactive terminals can be attached to Micronet. Because of their unique properties, interactive terminals are handled by a special set of system components known as a terminal group.

Each interactive terminal attached to a node is supported by a separate instantiation of the terminal group. Nodes with no interactive terminals do not initialize any terminal groups in their copies of the operating system. Since system components in Concurrent Pascal are implemented with re-entrant instruction code, nodes supporting more than one terminal share code and have separate spaces only for buffers. The CP version of Micros supports only a single type of terminal. The newer Modula-2 version of Micros (described later in this article) uses two layers of software modules to drive many types of terminals through a uniform virtual terminal interface.

The keyboard of a terminal device is always kept "live" by the KEYBOARD__HANDLER process. This process uses its TERMINAL class to build up complete input lines and echo them back to the terminal. KEYBOARD__HANDLER passes text lines through LINE__QUEUE to its own instantiation of the command language interpreter (CLI). If the line of text is a very simple command, it is acted on by the CLI itself. More complex commands are implemented by Sequential Pascal programs that normally are not resident in every node. A request to perform file-related operations or to execute a task force results in the CLI sending a "letter" of instructions to the NODE__CONTROLLER process in the control group. More than one such request can be active at any time. Output from ongoing activities initiated by a particular CLI is sent to the MAILBOX of that CLI. The CLI uses its SCREEN class to write the output to the terminal device. To avoid intermingling full-duplex-mode output from KEYBOARD__HANDLER with output from the CLI, a RESOURCE monitor is used to coordinate access to the output side of the terminal.

Because the TERMINAL and SCREEN classes exclude each other when they are writing characters, text from a different source always starts on a new line. User tasks that request input from the keyboard are automatically identified to the human operator by the CLI. The operator can direct input to any of his running tasks by prefacing text with the identifier of the intended task. By default, text lines continue to go to the last recipient explicitly identified by the operator. For example, text continues to go to the CLI until the operator specifies another destination. Returning to the CLI requires the typing of a special "escape" character.

The command language supported by Micros is similar to the one invented for Unix. In particular, it allows command pipes of filters. In addition to allowing sequentially executed pipes, Micros permits commands to specify parallel as well as sequential execution of pipe constituents. This mechanism makes it possible to start

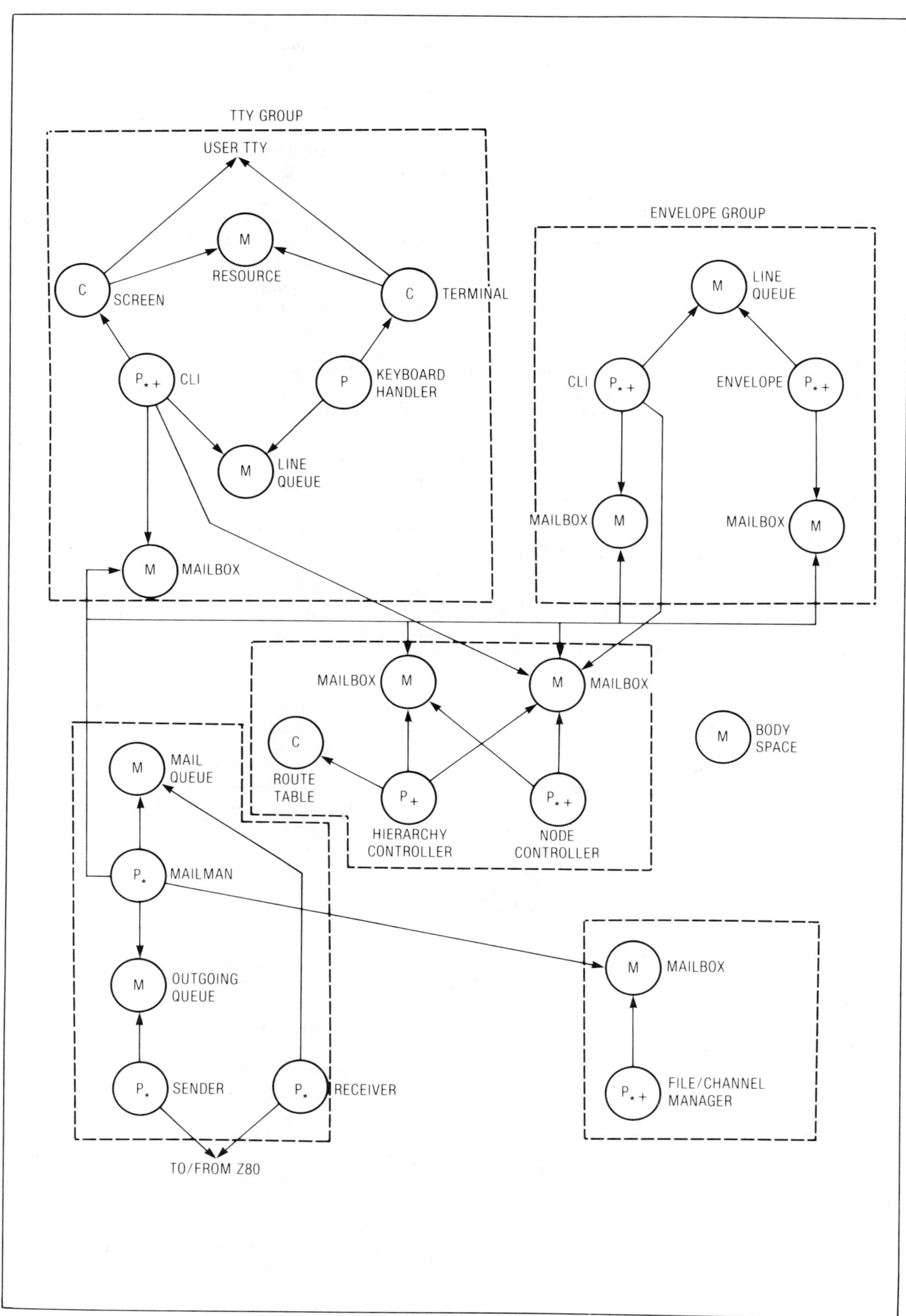

Figure 7. Detailed access graph of Micros.

execution of task forces, as will become evident in the next section.

The envelope group. The only user programming language that Micros supports is (Sequential) Pascal. The virtual machine kernel at the base of each node's operating system interprets Pascal p-code. Language processors for other languages would also have to generate p-code. Sequential Pascal programs execute in processes called ENVELOPEs. The processes and monitors that form the support environment for a Pascal program are called an envelope group.

An envelope group is similar to a terminal group, with the ENVELOPE process taking the place of KEYBOARD_HANDLER. A CLI command to run a program, coming from either a human operator or an already executing task, results in the selection of an envelope group to execute the program. The ENVELOPE may or may not reside at the same node as the requesting CLI. Each Micronet node has enough free memory to support three to five ENVELOPEs. However, because the ENVELOPEs share program memory space, a large program in one ENVELOPE may use all the available space in that node. Nodes with several attached terminals have few or no envelope groups.

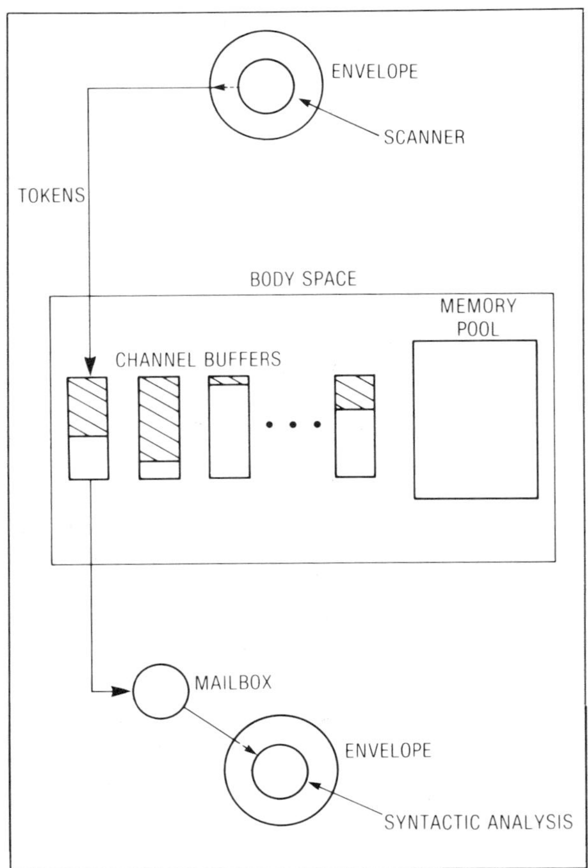

Figure 8. Two user processes communicating through a channel.

An ENVELOPE is a shell. Once it is created, it exists indefinitely. However, it performs no actions until it is supplied with a Sequential Pascal program. The shell consists of routines that allow the ENVELOPE to respond to requests to send messages to other tasks, open files, or return output to an interactive terminal. The ENVELOPE contains a "slot" into which a Sequential Pascal program can be loaded. The ENVELOPE reserves no memory space for any program in advance. Memory is supplied by means of a negotiation protocol between the CLI attached to each ENVELOPE and the NODE_CONTROLLER process resident in the same node. After a program is loaded into an ENVELOPE, it can issue commands to its CLI through a LINE_QUEUE exactly as a KEYBOARD_HANDLER does in a terminal group. The CLI in an envelope group is identical to one in a terminal group; both use the same reentrant instruction code.

Both the CLI and ENVELOPE in an envelope group have MAILBOXes that allow them to receive messages from other processes. For efficiency, MAILBOXes actually contain only pointers to message texts. The messages themselves are stored in BODY_SPACE. Space for message texts is carved from this area as needed. Repetitive, high-volume communications between a pair of tasks are supported by software "channels" in BODY_SPACE.

Figure 8 shows a channel for a typical one-way conversation between two processes in the same node. In the example, process SCANNER produces a continuous stream of tokens that SYNTACTIC_ANALYSIS uses. Since the association between the two processes will probably be prolonged, they have opened a channel between themselves. Opening a channel means that buffer space in BODY_SPACE is allocated to the pair of processes by the CHANNEL_MANAGER process. SCANNER sends a token to SYNTACTIC_ANALYSIS by calling its ENVELOPE to write the token into the proper channel buffer in BODY_SPACE. When a channel buffer becomes full, an entire 256-byte block of tokens is sent to SYNTACTIC_ANALYSIS by the CHANNEL_MANAGER. Message transmission overhead is much less than it would be if each token were sent individually. Channels in different nodes are also permitted, but require a buffer at each end and additional control transmissions.

The receive and transmit group. Messages enter and leave the task processor through the receive and transmit group. They are passed between processes in terminal and envelope groups in the same node via the MAILMAN process. Some processes in each node may never be initialized at run time. At compile time, all processes are given access rights only to the MAILBOXes of the fixed groups, i.e., the control group, the receive and transmit group, and the file/channel manager group. MAILMAN is given access rights to all of the MAILBOXes in a node. Any process can access another's MAILBOX without actually having direct access rights to it.

As explained above, message texts are stored in BODY_SPACE. Tasks that want to send messages do not need to know where the receiver resides. The message is placed in BODY_SPACE and a pointer to it is appended to MAIL_QUEUE. MAILMAN selects messages from MAIL_QUEUE and decides whether or not they should be transmitted out of the node. If not, they are deposited into the local receiving MAILBOX. Outbound messages are appended to the OUTGOING_QUEUE, from which the SENDER process chooses them for DMA transmission to the front end. Each message is sent when the LSI_TO_Z80 process finds room for it in the front end. Each complete message from the packet switching front end is captured by the RECEIVER process, which places the message text in BODY_SPACE and appends a pointer to MAIL_QUEUE. From there the message will be delivered by MAILMAN.

The control group. The control group is responsible for rationing local memory to ENVELOPEs, reserving local resources for tasks, enlisting the aid of other nodes to find paths to remotely located processes, and scheduling task forces. The NODE_CONTROLLER process performs the functions—such as local memory allocation—that do not require a knowledge of the hierarchical nature of the network control structure. The HIERARCHY_CONTROLLERs in worker nodes occasionally report node status to the HIERARCHY_CONTROLLER in their manager node. HIERARCHY_CONTROLLERs at higher levels are responsible for aggregating statistical information from below and passing it upward. The HIERARCHY_CONTROLLER is also responsible for trying to regroup clusters of nodes that become leaderless when a manager fails. HIERARCHY_CONTROLLERs at the lowest level are simple and self-sufficient. At higher levels, the intrinsic HIERARCHY_CONTROLLER may load more extensive control procedures into a local ENVELOPE.

The file/channel manager group. Obviously a network computer will be connected to many input and output devices other than interactive terminals. Many of these will be page-structured storage devices for saving data files. These devices all require specialized "driver" software. However, there is too little space for every node to have all possible drivers resident. A better technique is to load driver code into an ENVELOPE as needed. In this way each node becomes "customized" to its local environment while still executing the standard network operating system.

References to files occur with great frequency in all computer systems. To allow task ENVELOPEs to access files easily, and to supply nodes with appropriate peripheral device drivers, a file/channel manager group is included as part of the standard operating system at each node. As one of its functions, the file/channel manager group locates and installs the necessary device drivers. Its main function, though, is to allow processes to communicate with each other and with file-structured devices through channels.

The file/channel manager group hides the details of physical file structure from the users of files. It locates requested files and establishes a path between the file device and the requesting process. Communication between the two takes place through channels, with the group playing the active role for the passive file device.

Status of Micros

Most of the implementation of the LSI-11 portion of Micros in Concurrent Pascal was completed in 1979. This portion allows a user to compile and execute Sequential Pascal tasks on a single Micronet node. The user may concatenate tasks to form Unix-like pipes that run concurrently by means of time slicing. Packet switching communications code[18] was written in CP for the Z80 processor in every Micronet front end. The assembly language and microcode interfaces between processors within each node, and between nodes, were completed in 1981. The entire Micronet system can now be initialized from a single node. The CP code controlling each node is distributed, loaded, and started by means of commands sent over Micronet's external buses.

For a number of technical reasons, Micros is being rewritten in the newer concurrent programming language Modula-2.[21] One reason is run-time efficiency. The CP system compiler produces interpreted p-code instead of native LSI-11 instructions and executes only 9000 instructions, or 3000 Pascal lines, per second. A second reason is task loading. In the CP system, task loading is slowed by the access times of the floppy diskette drives used for file storage. A third reason involves message passing between processes. This passing is done (with mandatory mutual exclusion of messages) by means of entry-point calls to intermediate monitors. A fourth reason involves access rights. For the sake of simplicity in specifying access rights in the CP system, all messages in a node are passed by the central MAILMAN process, which can become a bottleneck. Thus, the original CP system is slow—it requires nearly 100 milliseconds to pass an 80-byte message.

The Modula-2, or M2, system is implemented on an LSI-11/23 twice as fast as that used in the CP system. A Winchester disk—much faster than the floppies used on the CP system—provides file storage. The M2 compiler produces native LSI-11/23 instructions that run about 30 times faster than CP p-code. Within a node, communications are handled by direct module-to-module calls. A remote procedure call mechanism is being developed that will map calls and replies between nodes onto system-generated messages, without the programmer being aware of the mapping. Mutual exclusion on entry-point calls to modules occurs only when required—that is, it does not occur in read-read situations as in CP.

The most important reason for the switch to Modula-2 is its extensive programming support environment. The M2 compiler and linker provide for separate compilation of modules but offer infallible type checking of parameters for calls between modules. An M2 Micros error can be corrected in three to eight minutes; more than 50 minutes would be needed to correct the same error in CP Micros, since the entire 5000-line operating system would have to be recompiled. In the CP system, even changes in the system entry points for separately compiled application tasks are not detected, let alone parameter incompatibilities. The M2 system has a powerful symbolic debugging package for interactive postmortem analysis of errors. Only a few keystrokes are needed to view the source code and variable values responsible for an error. The Concurrent Pascal system requires a different language, Sequential Pascal, for dynamically loaded application tasks, each of which must be a single sequential program. The Modula-2 system supports application programs written in the same Modula-2 language. However, the M2 system is being modified to restrict application programs so that they use only safe system entry points.

Because only a tiny amount of assembly language is needed to support M2 Micros, it is more portable and more easily maintained than CP Micros. I/O drivers for M2 Micros can be written in Modula-2; those for the CP system must be written in assembly language. The M2 system requires fewer than 1000 assembly language instructions for the entire support kernel. The CP system requires more than 9000 assembly instructions for kernel, interpreter, and a small selection of I/O drivers. The need to maintain CP I/O drivers in assembly language has been a significant problem, given the ever-changing mix of peripherals used in a research facility.

The M2 version of Micros is being coded with a much greater degree of layering than the CP version. There are hardware, physical, logical, and application layers for I/O services. Concurrent Pascal requires data types shared between modules to be declared globally, with all the details of the data types known and manipulable by all modules. Modula-2 allows data types shared between modules to be exported, but with the structural details of the data types hidden from all other modules. Other modules can hold access rights, or capabilities, to objects of hidden types, but these modules can manipulate the objects only indirectly by passing them as parameters to the module that defines the type. As a consequence, the M2 version of Micros emphasizes capabilities and object-oriented design. Such an emphasis enables nearly independent coding of modules and results in easier maintenance.

At present, M2 Micros allows neither communication between nodes, nor dynamic loading of user tasks, nor creation of task pipes. However, it already offers more extensive and efficient programming support facilities within a single node than does the CP system. It will take another three to six months to provide network capabilities within the new Micros. However, M2 Micros will be a more complete operating system, with editors, compilers, and debugging facilities. CP Micros has remained a demonstration system, with program support provided by other operating systems.

In summary, the Modula-2 system has proved to be three to thirty times faster than the Concurrent Pascal system for at least three tasks: production and debugging of code, compilation and maintenance of code, and execution of code.

Distributed parallel computation is not well understood. Experiments must be performed to find software control techniques and programming language features that are efficient in distributed systems. Micronet is a "laboratory" for such experiments, the first of which was the Concurrent Pascal version of the Micros distributed operating system.

We have argued that a network computer operating system consists of both a high-level control structure that binds the nodes together and a low-level operating system that executes on the nodes. We have proposed a hierarchical high-level control structure as a foundation on which network-wide resource management techniques can be built. We designed a low-level nodal operating system, Micros, that explicitly supports such a high-level control schema, and we implemented it in Concurrent Pascal. Micros allows task forces to execute on separate nodes by assigning them to ENVELOPE processes that can reside anywhere in the network. A Unix-like command language is used to construct distributed application experiments.

Experience with the first version of Micros indicates that it is too cumbersome to serve as a basis for extensive distributed systems research. Deficiencies in the programming support environment for Concurrent Pascal and restrictions in the language itself have made it more productive to write a new Micros in Modula-2 than to modify the existing software in Concurrent Pascal. The Modula-2 version of Micros is more modular, and much more efficient, than the CP version. It will serve as the foundation for distributed systems research on the Micronet network computer. Although the high-level control schema and some of the nodal operating system components of the original version of Micros are being included in the new version, substantial changes are being made to provide a more flexible and portable operating system. ■

Acknowledgments

A preliminary report on Micronet and Micros was presented at Compsac 80, the IEEE Computer Society's annual software and applications conference, in Chicago in October 1980. The authors would like to thank the dozens of students who have helped with Micronet/Micros, especially R. Spanbauer, P. Bechtel, D. Benua, P. Henderson, J. Kolkovich, H. Styliades, and S. Wilder, for engineering, and R. Curtis, A. Frank, W. Holmes, P. Lee, M. Palumbo, K. Tso, K. Wong, T. Bartkowski, A. Chin, G. Davidian, J. Day, W. Earl, S. Isaac, G. Masterson, D. Reif, P. Van Verth, and R. Wahl, for software development.

The work reported in this article was supported by the

following grants and contracts: National Science Foundation MCS78-03166, US Air Force RADC SCEEE/PDP81-38, NASA NAG-1-249, and US Army Research Office DAAG-29-82-K-0103. The construction of the Micronet network computer was funded under NSF equipment grants MCS77-09213 and MCS80-06925.

References

1. M. J. Flynn, "Some Computer Organizations and Their Effectiveness," *IEEE Trans. Computers*, Vol. C-21, No. 9, Sept. 1972, pp. 948-960.
2. L. D. Wittie, "Micronet: A Reconfigurable Network for Distributed System Research," *Simulation*, Nov. 1978, pp. 145-153.
3. L. D. Wittie, "Efficient Message Routing in Mega-microcomputer Networks," *Proc. 3rd Ann. Symp. Computer Architecture*, 1976, pp. 136-140.
4. A. M. Despain and D. A. Patterson, "X-Tree: A Tree-Structured Multiprocessor Computer Architecture," *Proc. 5th Ann. Symp. Computer Architecture*, 1978, pp. 144-151.
5. S. B. Wu and M. T. Liu, "A Generalized Cluster Structure for Large Multimicrocomputer Systems," *Proc. 1979 Int'l Conf. Parallel Processing*, pp. 74-75.
6. D. P. Siewiorek, "Process Coordination in Multi-microprocessor Systems," in *Microarchitecture of Computer Systems*, R. W. Hartenstein and R. Zaks, eds., North-Holland Publishing Co., New York, 1975, pp. 1-8.
7. H. Simon, *The Sciences of the Artificial*, 2nd ed., MIT Press, Cambridge, MA, 1981.
8. A. M. van Tilborg and L. D. Wittie, "High-Level Operating System Formation in Network Computers," *Proc. 1980 Int'l Conf. Parallel Processing*, pp. 131-132.
9. B. D. Fleish et al., "Amps: An Environment for Personal Computers," Tech. Report TR94, Computer Science Dept., University of Rochester, May 1981.
10. A. K. Jones et al., "StarOS, A Multiprocessor Operating System for the Support of Task Forces," *Proc. Seventh Symp. Operating Systems Principles*, 1979, pp. 117-127.
11. R. Kieburtz, "A Distributed Operating System for the Stony Brook Multicomputer," *Proc. 2nd Int'l Conf. Distributed Computing Systems*, 1981, pp. 67-79.
12. E. D. Lazowska et al., "The Architecture of the Eden System," *Proc. Eighth Symp. Operating Systems Principles*, 1981, pp. 148-159.
13. M. Maekawa et al., "Experimental Polyprocessor System (EPOS)—Operating System," *Proc. 6th Ann. Symp. Computer Architecture*, 1979, pp. 196-201.
14. J. K. Ousterhout et al., "Medusa: An Experiment in Distributed Operating System Structure," *Comm. ACM*, Vol. 23, No. 2, Feb. 1980, pp. 92-105.
15. G. Popek et al., "Locus, A Network-Transparent, High-Reliability Distributed System," *Proc. Eighth Symp. Operating Systems Principles*, 1981, pp. 169-177.
16. R. F. Rashid and G. G. Robertson, "Accent: A Communication-Oriented Network Operating System Kernel," *Proc. Eighth Symp. Operating Systems Principles*, 1981, pp. 64-75.
17. M. H. Solomon and R. A. Finkel, "The Roscoe Distributed Operating System," *Proc. Seventh Symp. Operating Systems Principles*, 1979, pp. 108-114.
18. A. M. van Tilborg and L. D. Wittie, "Packet Switching Using Concurrent Pascal in a Network Computer," *IEEE Trans. Communications*, Vol. COM-30, No. 6, June 1982, pp. 1426-1433.
19. P. Brinch Hansen, *The Architecture of Concurrent Programs*, Prentice-Hall, Englewood Cliffs, NJ, 1977.
20. B. Liskov, "Primitives for Distributed Computing," *Proc. Seventh Symp. Operating Systems Principles*, 1979, pp. 33-42.
21. N. Wirth, "Modula: A Language for Modular Multiprogramming," *Software—Practice & Experience*, Jan. 1977, pp. 3-35.

An Executive for Task-driven Multimicrocomputer Systems

Eli T. Fathi and Moshe Krieger
University of Ottawa

In the microcomputing literature, one can find a large number of papers relating to real-time executives for systems based on single microprocessors.[1-5] However, much less is reported about multimicrocomputer executives.[6] Brinch Hansen[7] proposed a new language concept for concurrent programming, called "distributed processes," which is suitable for real-time applications controlled by microcomputer networks with distributed storage.

Here, we describe an executive which is "tailor-made" to a specific multimicrocomputer architecture known as a task-driven system.[8] The basic ideas behind the executive are to use hierarchical control for task scheduling and to provide interlevel communication via asynchronous handshake signals. This approach results in a highly modular, easy-to-implement executive which can be easily adapted to other system architectures.[9]

System hardware

The main feature of a task-driven system is the hierarchical controller which supervises a number of heterogeneous processors, each having private program memory, read/write data memory, and some I/O capability. The system may also have global resources that include a global data memory used as a message center and as a place to store common variables. A simplified block diagram of a task-driven system is shown in Figure 1.

The various tasks available to the system are permanently stored in the local program memory of the individual processors. When a task is to be executed, it needs to be awakened by specifying its starting address rather than by being downloaded from central memory. Note that some tasks require parameters which have to be transmitted with the wake-up signal. In order to avoid excessive hardware duplication and restrict the size of the local program memory, not all tasks are duplicated in the program memories of all processors. However, for reliability reasons, and to maintain system performance at a specified level, each task is stored in two or more local program memories. In order to have complete identification, both the task and the processor must be specified.

The duplication of tasks in various program memories necessitates the establishment of a fairly long list associating the various tasks and processors. To simplify the list, each task is assigned the same apparent address in each processor which is capable of executing it. A

Reprinted from *IEEE Micro*, pp. 32–41, Oct. 1983.

typical processor organization and a profile of its program memory are shown in Figure 2.

The system executive

In general, a system can be partitioned into a number of units, each of which can be represented by a logical abstraction called a process. Each process consists of one or more tasks, where a task is considered to be the smallest logical entity in the system. This can be represented graphically, as shown in Figure 3.

Whenever one considers the execution of a number of processes/tasks, the possibility of data interdependency forces one to define a sequencing relation. Figure 4 indicates that some processes/tasks can be started at the same time (a), while others have to wait until another process/task is either partially executed (b) or completely executed (c). The simple notation shown in the figure can be used to represent the complete sequencing relation of any number of processes and/or tasks.

In a multimicrocomputer system, the executive has to maintain an orderly execution of tasks in the most concurrent fashion possible. The design philosophy behind such an executive is different from typical design approaches in that it emphasizes simplicity and flexibility rather than maximum utilization of resources. Because hardware is cheaper than software, one can afford to

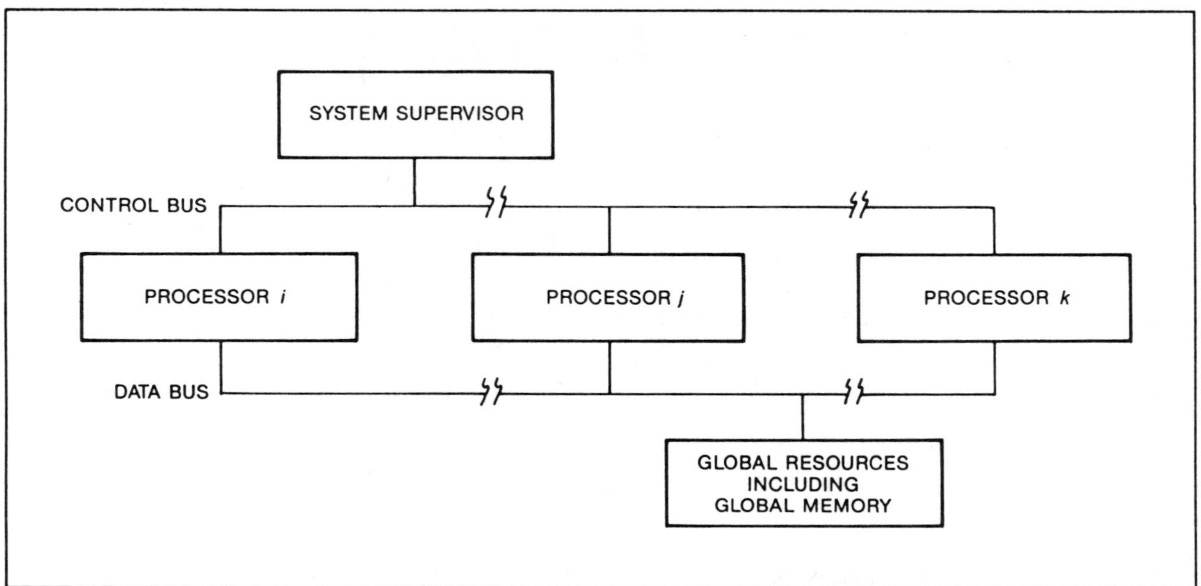

Figure 1. Simplified block diagram of a task-driven architecture.

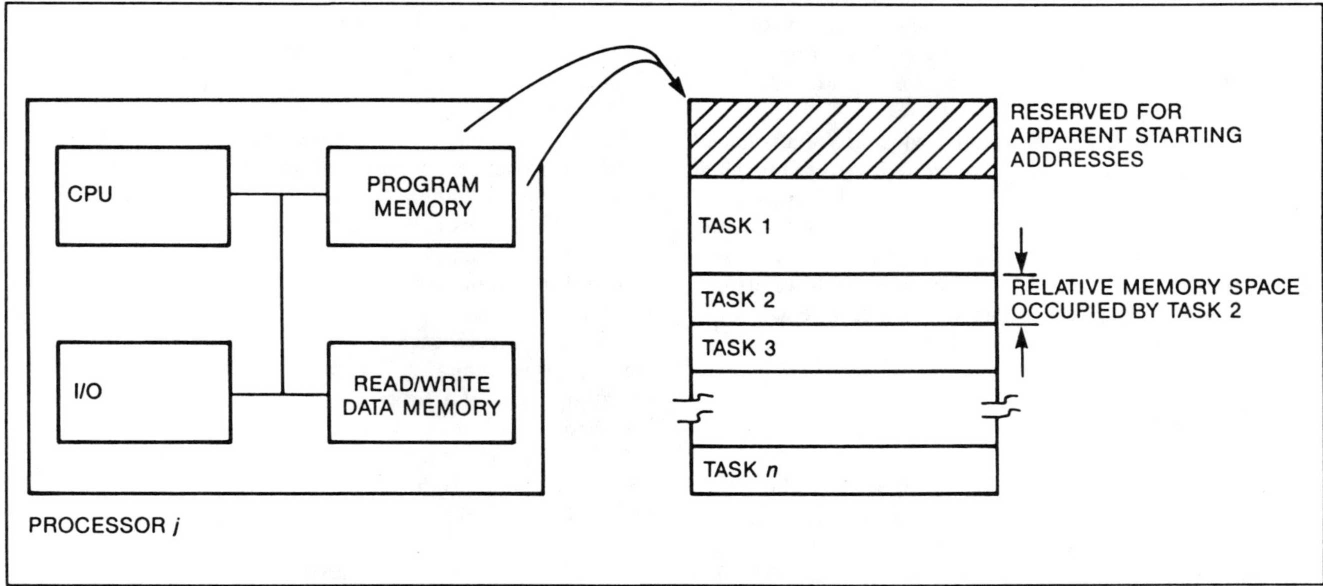

Figure 2. A typical processor organization and a profile of its program memory.

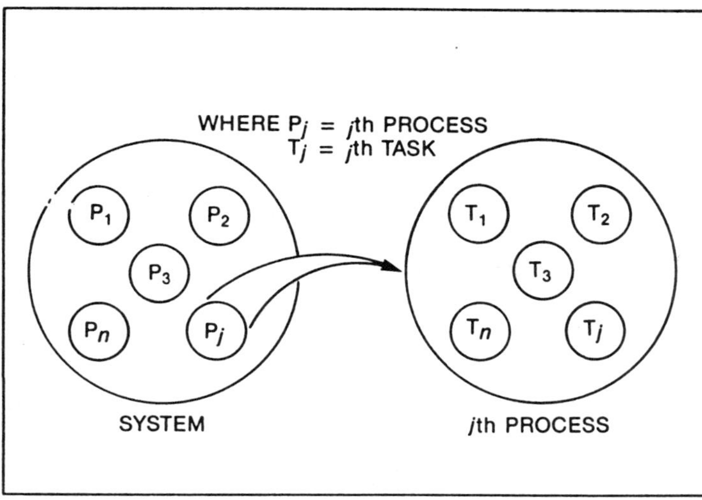

Figure 3. Graphical representation of systems in terms of processes and tasks.

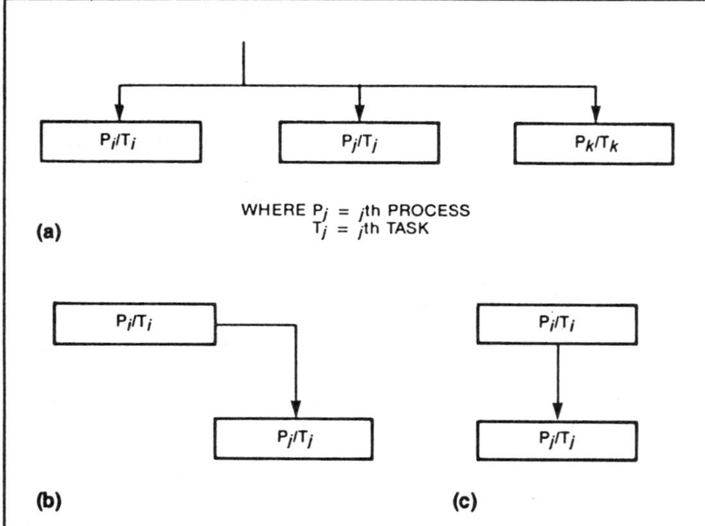

Figure 4. Graphical representation of process/task sequencing. Some processes/tasks can be started at the same time (a), while others have to wait until another process/task is either partially executed (b) or completely executed (c).

underutilize hardware resources in order to obtain the desired simplicity and flexibility. To reduce complexity, the following restrictions are introduced:

- Only a few types of tasks are allowed, each with specific interaction capabilities.
- All communications are done via well-defined logical interfaces.
- Processor allocation is done only by a centralized entity.

To provided maximum flexibility, the executive is designed according to the following principles:

- The executive has a multilevel hierarchical structure.
- Communication between levels and within each level is done via asynchronous handshake signals.
- The executive is defined and designed in a modular fashion to allow modifications and expansion.

The executive model consists of two levels: the process level, which contains all the relevant information about processes, relations, and system parameters; and the task level, which maintains information about task relations within each process. At the process level, the executive utilizes a process manager which, besides controlling the process sequencing, accepts requests for service from the various task managers operating at the task level and performs the actual task-to-processor assignment. It also controls all communication with the external world. At the task level, the executive has a number of active task managers, one for each currently running process. Each task manager controls the actual task sequencing for a given process by accepting information from the tasks it controls and using that information to initiate new requests to the process manager. The communication activities between levels and within each level are handled via asynchronous handshake signals. The two-level executive model is shown in Figure 5.

The process manager itself consists of a two-level hierarchical structure. The outer layer of the process manager and of the executive is the process sequencer, which communicates with the external world. It controls, at the process level, all the various activities not directly affecting the system hardware. It also transfers to the next layer of the process manager the proper information regarding the next process to be executed. The inner layer of the process manager contains the task allocator, which communicates with the system hardware and is responsible for the task allocation process. It awakens the various task managers, transmits the proper parameters unique to each process, and controls all subsequent task-to-processor assignments.

Since the actual problems involved in process sequencing and task sequencing are exactly the same, we will examine only one of the cases. We will consider the task sequencing problem, since tasks are the logical entities which have to be initiated on the system hardware. This will provide insight into various aspects of system implementation.

At the task level there are two distinct types of tasks: master tasks and service tasks. The master task is simply the task manager having the responsibility to coordinate the task sequencing within a given process with the communications activities associated with it. During system operation, the number of active task managers varies according to the number of currently running processes. Since the factors which distinguish one process from another are the sequencing and specifications of the tasks associated with each process, the master task can be a general-purpose program which receives from the task allocator the parameter specifications unique to each process. In addition to coordinating task sequencing relations, the task allocator provides for data passing by associating with each task manager "mailboxes" in a global memory. Thus, in order to transfer data between tasks, one needs only to pass pointers rather than move actual data. In order to enhance system responsiveness, the master-task program is included in each processor's local program memory; thus, each individual processor can act as a task manager.

Due to overhead associated with process suspension, a master task, once initiated, cannot be temporarily suspended. Thus, the processor assigned to it becomes dedicated to its execution. However, master task execution may be terminated voluntarily based on information received from one of its tasks or be aborted by the process manager as a result of external information. The master task controls several service tasks, which communicate with it via asynchronous handshake signals. Hence, it must be capable of requesting service tasks anytime during the course of its execution.

In contrast to the master task, service tasks are special-purpose programs and can be of two types. The majority of service tasks are regular tasks which cannot call any other tasks during their execution. When the processor on which a regular service task is running is required by a higher-priority task, the regular service task can be temporarily suspended (but only once) by the process manager and restarted when system conditions permit. The other service task type is the privileged service task, but in practice only a limited number of them exist. These tasks can call only regular service tasks, one at a time. To reduce overhead, neither the privileged task nor the service tasks which it calls can be temporarily suspended. By restricting tasks calls and suspensions in this fashion, one avoids nested loops of tasks and thus reduces the processing overhead associated with general multilevel suspension. Also, in this way one need not change task priority after suspension. However, one needs to associate a tag with the privileged tasks, with the regular service tasks called by the privileged tasks, and with the suspended regular service tasks indicating that they cannot be suspended.

One should note that in the event that a currently running task is displaced, control need not be returned to the displaced task after the execution of the higher-priority task. The next task to be executed is determined from a global priority list which varies depending on dynamic conditions within the sysm. This list is maintained by the process manager, which also assigns the appropriate task to an available processor.

Executive communication protocol. The handshake procedure used for the request, assignment, and execution of a given task can be described in terms of a communication protocol. Although a task manager may request the concurrent execution of a number of tasks, for illustrative purposes we will examine only the control signals associated with a single task. We assume that the *k*th task manager requests the execution of task *i*, and that the process manager assigns processor *j* to execute it. The communication protocol is as follows:

- At time t_1, task manager *k* initiates a request to the process manager, identifying itself and the requested task.
- The process manager, upon receiving the request and after a short processing time delay (Δt), acknowledges receiving the request. This is done in order to indicate to the task manager that its request is being looked after and to have some sort of check on the process manager. If the task manager does not receive an acknowledgment the first time, it repeats its request; if again it does not receive an acknowledgment, it sends an error message to the process sequencer, which is responsible for system diagnostics.
- After a search time t_s, the process manager assigns task *i* to processor *j* by identifying its apparent starting address and the task manager which requested it.
- The process manager notifies task manager *k* that it assigned task *i* to processor *j*. This is necessary so the task manager will know the processor with which it must communicate.
- Processor *j* sends a message to task manager *k* indicating that it was assigned to execute task *i*. If this signal is not received, the task manager signals the process manager to check the processor status.
- Task manager *k* specifies to processor *j* the mailbox pointers for data transactions.
- The task manager *k* or processor *j*, or both, signal the process manager that execution of task *i* has been started. The process manager may use this signal to start a down counter that indicates the remaining time for execution. This can be used as additional data when deciding which task to suspend and, in the event of processor failure, when to reinitiate task execution.
- Upon completion of the execution of task *i*, processor *j* notifies task manager *k* that it has completed execution.
- Task manager *k* signals the process manager that the execution of task *i* has been completed.

This communication protocol, along with the signals used, is shown in Figure 6.

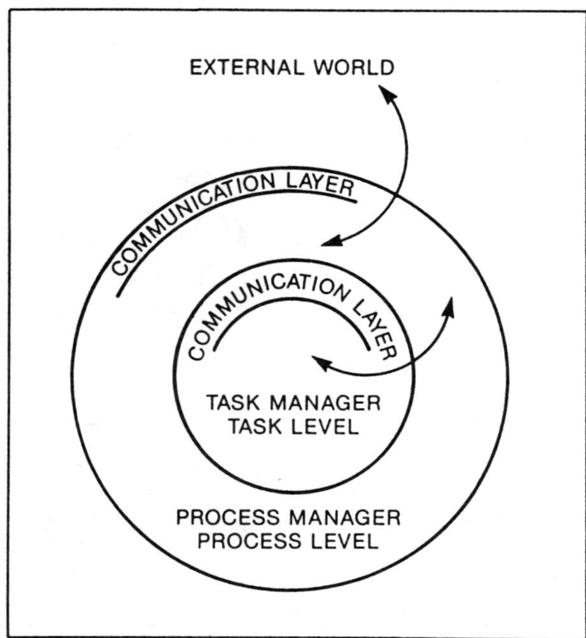

Figure 5. Graphical representation of a two-level executive model.

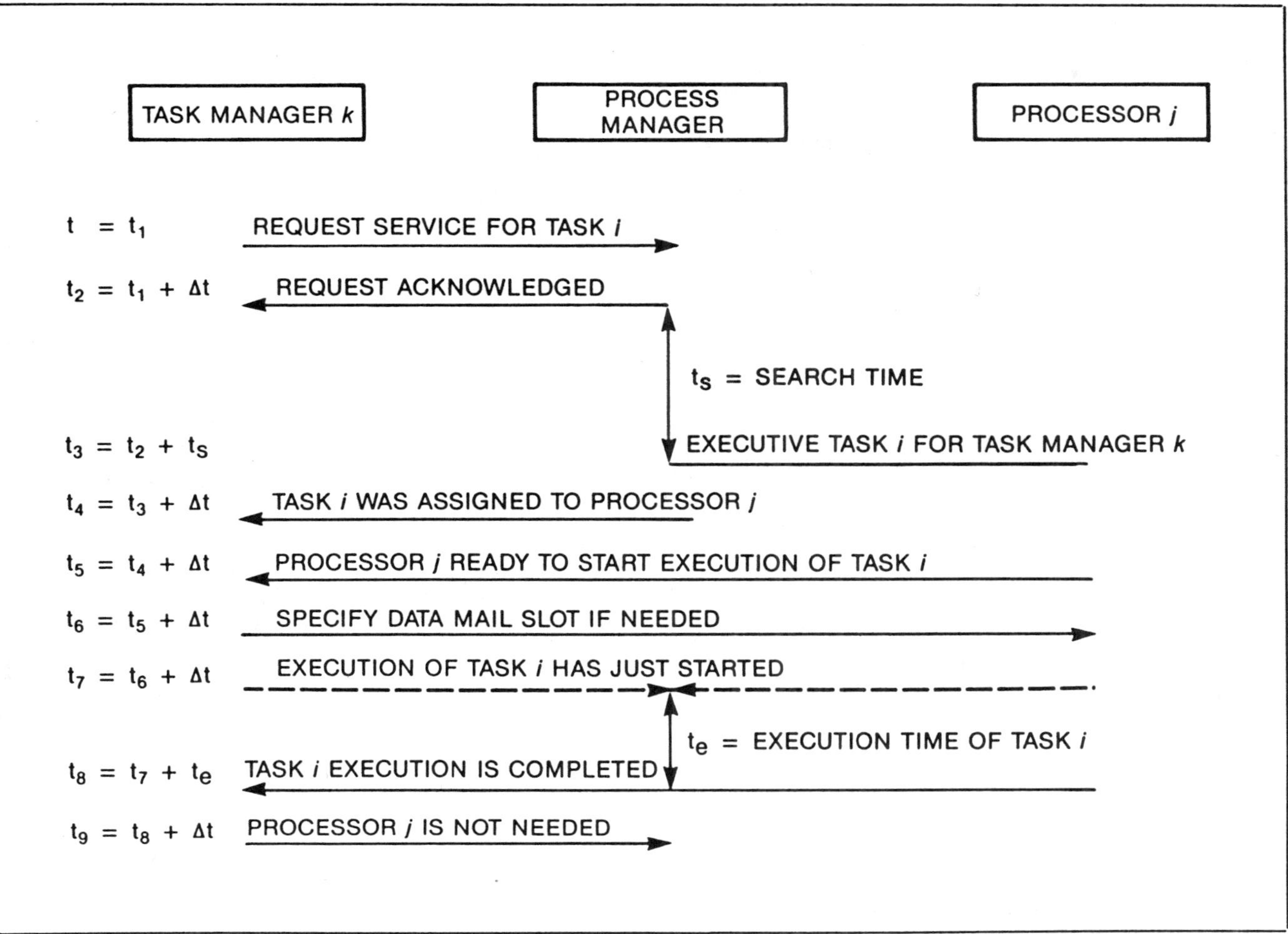

Figure 6. Communication protocol used during task call and execution.

Task interrelations

Tasks may be classified into two categories according to their interdependency and time relationship. The task interdependency aspect indicates whether tasks are independent or related. Independent tasks can be considered separate entities, as each is capable of operating alone and does not require the cooperation of other tasks. Related tasks, on the other hand, interact with each other through cooperation or competition. One should note that not all independent tasks can be executed in parallel, as their simultaneous execution may involve some sort of conflict. However, the order of their execution is irrelevant. Also, not all related tasks need be executed in completely sequential fashion. Ideally, in order to achieve maximum freedom, one would like to partition the process into a number of independent and parallel tasks which can be executed simultaneously. In practice, such partitioning is seldom feasible, although one can obtain a collection of tasks which permit some form of concurrent execution.

Using real-time constraints as a measure of urgency, one can classify the various tasks into urgent (time-critical) tasks and nonurgent tasks. Urgent tasks always take precedence and must be given the immediate attention of a processor, whereas nonurgent tasks need not be executed immediately. Furthermore, within each of these groups tasks are assigned various levels of priority based on their relative importance and are executed accordingly. This permits some tasks to displace a currently running nonurgent or lower-priority task, if necessary.

A state diagram can be used to provide a systematic presentation of task interrelations. In a state diagram, the states can represent task status, and the state transitions can be executed under the influence of the proper control primitives. All the concepts presented in this section apply equally to process interrelations and can be used to define actual process control.

At any time a task may exist in one of the following states: *inactive, ready, running, waiting,* or *suspended.*

- The inactive state is a basic state in the sense that all tasks must start and finish in it. The inactive state acts as a source for tasks which have not yet been scheduled for execution and as a sink for completed or aborted tasks.
- A task is in the ready state if it is able to run, but a higher-priority task is running and no other processor capable of executing its code is free.
- A task is in the running state if it has a processor

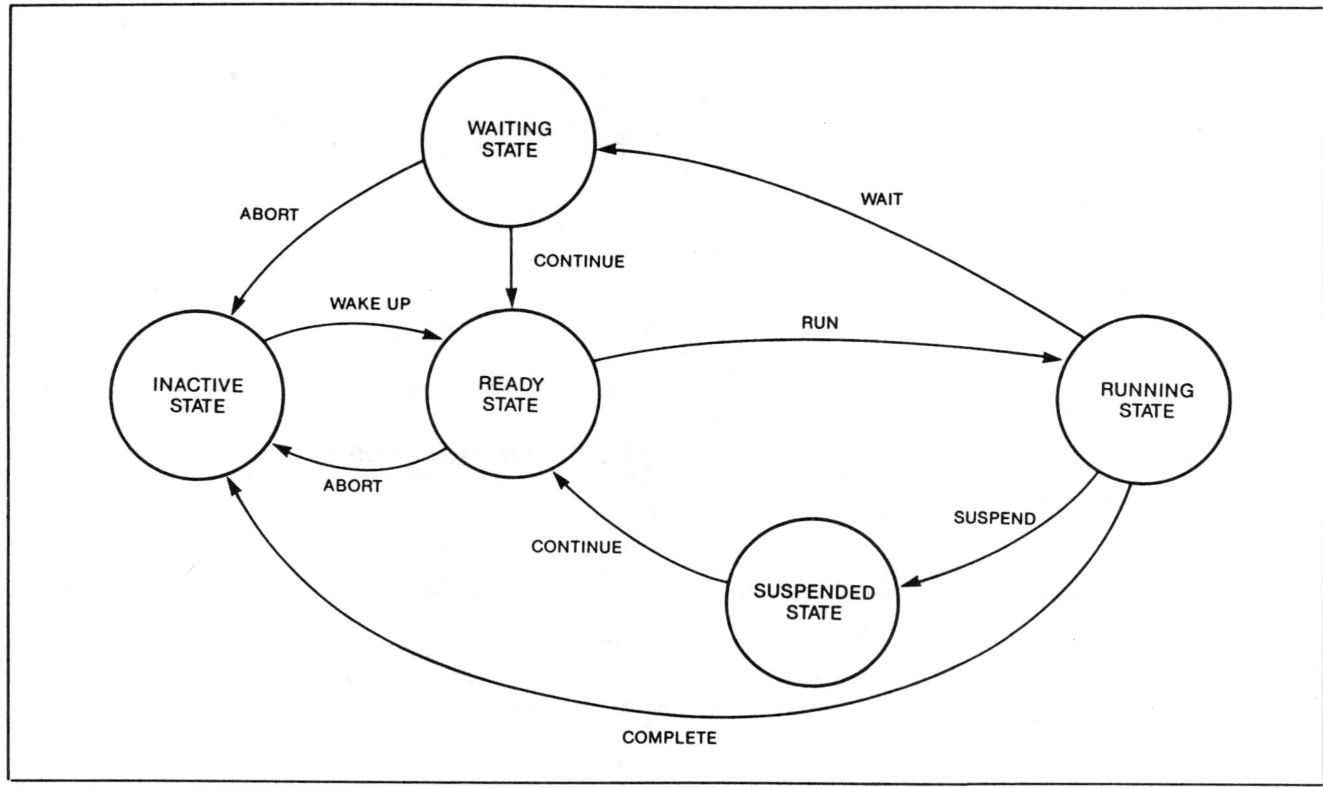

Figure 7. Complete state transition diagram for the system.

assigned to it and that processor is executing its code. In that sense, it is the only true active state in the task execution cycle.

- A task is in the waiting state during the time that it has to await the occurrence of a directly related and predefined event.
- A task is in the suspended state if its execution had to be discontinued as a result of system conditions unknown to it and not under its control.

The last two states correspond to temporarily inactive states, as no code of the tasks in these states is being executed. However, some activity takes place on behalf of a waiting task, but no activity is directly associated with a suspended task. Before a task can be transferred to either of these two states, relevant information concerning the task's status must be stored. This information can be stored either in local memory or in global memory. Storing the information in local memory implies that the task can be restarted only on a specific processor. This increases the contention for the specific processor and thus may cause unnecessary delay in the restart of waiting or suspended tasks. Storing the information in global memory eliminates this problem, since the task can be restarted on any appropriate processor, but it can increase the contention associated with global memory. However, in the implementation we suggest here the suspended state is only a transition state, since suspended tasks are automatically transferred to the ready state.

A complete state transition diagram, with all the control primitives associated with the system, is shown in Figure 7. The actions associated with the control primitives are listed below:

- WAKE UP—remove task from inactive state.
- RUN—start immediate execution of task.
- COMPLETE—task execution is completed.
- ABORT—return to inactive state.
- WAIT—relinquish control of processor and store relevant information.
- SUSPEND—relinquish control of processor and store relevant information.
- CONTINUE—return to ready state.

The difference between WAIT and SUSPEND primitives is in the type and amount of relevant information that must be stored.

Implementation aspects

The main role of the executive is to respond in an efficient manner to various asynchronous service requests by assigning the tasks for which the requests were made to the appropriate processors. In the design we suggest, the executive utilizes a number of look-up tables to control task assignment. It makes the actual decisions in a hierarchical fashion according to the contents of the various tables. These tables include relevant system information and are updated whenever a task changes its status. In this sense, one can consider these tables as a set of asynchronous task-driven lists. This design philosophy matches well the task-driven multimicrocomputer architecture mentioned earlier. The tables, besides facilitating control, can also be used to monitor task execution and to provide statistics about system utilization.

Aside from the simplicity of design, the main strength of the executive is the ease of obtaining system verification. Since all task control is based on interrelations among the various tables, the complete system operation can be simulated as chains of calls and verified prior to actual implementation. The simulation can be a generalized procedure, and for each system one needs only to provide its unique hardware and operational parameters—for example, the number of processors along with the tasks each one is capable of executing, the estimation of the time required to execute each task, and the proper sequencing relations at each level of the executive. The simulation procedure can be used to detect any bottleneck or sequencing problems. Having determined the problems, one can adjust and optimize system performance either by further partitioning critical tasks or by using processors with different characteristics.

Aside from simplicity of design, the main strength of the executive is the ease of obtaining system verification.

As outlined earlier, the executive is made up of the process manager and task managers. Each task manager is a simple general-purpose program whose functions were defined previously. The process manager, in turn, includes two parts, the process sequencer and the task allocator. Here, we shall concentrate on the exact definition of the task allocator since it is the most complex and critical element of the executive. Furthermore, in most of its aspects, the process sequencer can be regarded as a simplified version of the task allocator.

Task allocator. The task allocator subsystem is responsible for the various activities associated with task assignment. Considering the required activities, one can identify five programs.

Task ordering program. In a system, each task may assume various priority levels based on its relations to other tasks within the same process and on its process relation to other processes. Therefore, the task allocator must be able to determine the proper ordering of all tasks which have to be executed. The task ordering program utilizes static information about process relations and task priorities as well as currently available dynamic data about the system in order to generate the proper ordering of the tasks to be executed. The output of this program is a list of all tasks to be executed, starting from the highest-priority task. In addition, this list—called the ready list—also contains various parameters associated with the tasks. These parameters are used for control and decision purposes.

Task allocation/communication program. This program handles the various communications activities associated with the physical allocation of a task to a processor. It accepts hardware signals and software messages from the various task managers as well as from the processor assigned to execute the particular task. It responds with the proper control signals.

Task suspension program. In order to optimize performance, the decision to suspend a task is made on the basis of dynamic information. Whenever a time-critical task has to be executed and no appropriate processor is free, the task suspension program determines which processors can execute the time-critical task and then forms a list of tasks that are candidates for suspension. The program examines each candidate task's priority and the time needed to complete execution of each task, and determines the proper task to be suspended. The task allocation/communication program uses this information to initiate the task suspension procedure and perform the allocation of the urgent task to the freed processor.

List updating program. This program is used to maintain all lists used by the task allocator. It updates the appropriate entries in the relevant tables whenever there is a change in the system which affects any of the lists.

Global memory management program. The task allocator stores the relevant information associated with the various tasks in a global memory, the content of which continuously changes during system operation. The memory management program keeps track of this activity by maintaining a running file of all unused memory space. It assigns available memory to a task when the task allocation/communication program requests such memory. The latter program signals back to the memory management program whenever memory locations become available.

Lists of the executive. The executive utilizes two types of lists: static, which contain basic information which is fixed for a given system; and dynamic, which maintain running statistics about system operation. Dynamic lists can be classified into two categories. The first contains all lists which are needed for control purposes. This category encompasses the majority of the lists (some of which may be used for monitoring purposes). The second category includes all lists which are used *strictly for* monitoring purposes, i.e., which are used to get statistical information about the system. Lists in this category are not used for any control purpose and may be discarded without affecting system operation.

Static lists include the process master list, the task sequencing master list, and the task-processor master list.

Process master list. This list contains all process sequencing relations, including the relative priorities of the processes. It is used by the process manager to generate the proper ordering of the processes waiting to be executed.

Task sequencing master list. The proper task sequencing relation within each process is listed in this table. Whenever a task manager is awakened, the task sequencing relations of its process—as listed in this table—are transferred to it.

Task-processor master list. For each task in the system, this list includes all the processors that are capable of executing it. The apparent starting address, which is the same in each processor, is also recorded in this list. After finding the next task to be executed, the task allocator uses this list to find processors capable of executing that task. It also uses the list to locate the task's apparent starting address.

Dynamic lists include the process queue list, the active processes list, the task queue list, the ready list, the free processor list, the active processor list, the wait list, and the suspended list.

Process queue list. All new requests for process execution are placed momentarily in a queue and are subsequently transferred to the various task managers for execution.

Active processes list. This list contains data about currently active processes in the system. It is used strictly for monitoring purposes—it provides information about frequency of call for each process.

Task queue list. The process manager maintains a queue associated with the various task execution requests arriving from different task managers. The requested tasks are listed in their order of arrival along with their relative priority within the process and their requesting task managers. The task ordering program uses this information to place each requested task in the proper priority position in the ready list.

Ready list. As stated earlier, the ready list is generated by the task ordering program and lists in order of decreasing priority all the tasks waiting to be executed. Tasks of equal priority are listed in the order of their arrival. For each task, the task manager and the urgency level are listed. If a task is not time-critical, its "age" must also be listed—i.e., whether it is a new task or an old (suspended or waiting) one, so it can be restored properly. Note that if an old task's status information was stored in a local memory, that task's respective processor must also be listed, since it is the only processor capable of completing the task's execution.

Free processor list. All currently functional free processors are listed in sequential order. This list is updated every time a processor is assigned a task and every time a task is either completed or transferred to the waiting state. It is used by the task allocator to find a processor that is available to execute a specific task. This list may also be used to provide statistical information about processor underutilization.

Active processor list. Each currently active processor, along with the specific task it is executing, is listed. This list also contains information about whether the task can be suspended or not, and about the remaining time for execution if it can be suspended. This list is used by the task suspension program to determine the task that has to be suspended. It can also be used to provide data about the actual loading on each processor. This table is updated whenever there is a change in processor status; it is also periodically updated to indicate the change in remaining time for execution.

The wait list. For simplicity, the process manager maintains two waiting lists, one based on time delay and the other based on event occurrence. Each task's task manager and processor (if the task's status information is stored in a local memory) are listed. Tasks in the time-delay list are listed in ascending order according to wait time. For the first task in the list, the absolute delay time is listed; for each subsequent task, only the differential delay time from the previous task is listed. With this technique, only one time measurement counter is needed. It is reinitialized every time the task at the top of the list is transferred into the ready list. Note that because the wait list is an ordered list, each new task must be inserted into the proper position. Also, the time differential of each task that follows the newly inserted task must be readjusted.

Tasks in the event list are listed in the order of their arrival along with the codes of the events for which they are waiting. Event occurrence can be checked either periodically or on an interrupt basis. When an event is detected, the appropriate task can be transferred into the ready list.

The suspended list. This is a temporary list which contains in the order of their arrival all the suspended tasks not yet processed by the task ordering program. Each task's task manager and processor (if the task's status information is stored in a local memory) are listed.

Although designed for a task-driven multimicrocomputer, our modular executive can be easily adapted to other system architectures.

With respect to both waiting and suspended tasks, we should mention that in order to simplify control each processor has its own save and restore routines. Depending on the type and amount of data, different routines may be associated with suspended and waiting tasks. These routines have the same apparent starting address in all processors and are treated as regular service tasks. Each task manager holds pointers to either local or global memory and transfers them on request to the appropriate save or restore routines.

A flowchart of the task allocation process (Figure 8) indicates the usage of the various lists.

Although designed for a task-driven multimicrocomputer, our modular executive can be easily adapted to other system architectures. It consists of a two-level hierarchical structure comprising a process level and a task level. The process level is made up of the process sequencer and the task allocator. The processor sequencer is responsible for activities at the process level, such as deciding on the next process to be executed, and for communications with the external world. The task allocator is a general-purpose program consisting of five major routines; it controls the task allocation process and, by doing so, bridges the process level and the task level. At the task level there are a number of task managers running concurrently, with each responsible for one process. Because all task managers are identical and because there is a task manager on each processor, each processor can become a task manager. This reduces the possibility of a bottleneck associated with finding a free processor to act as a task manager. Note that the unique features of each process are kept at the process level and are passed to the appropriate task managers when they are awakened.

In our design static features unique to the system as well as dynamic system conditions are stored in tables. The executive utilizes these tables in an interactive fashion

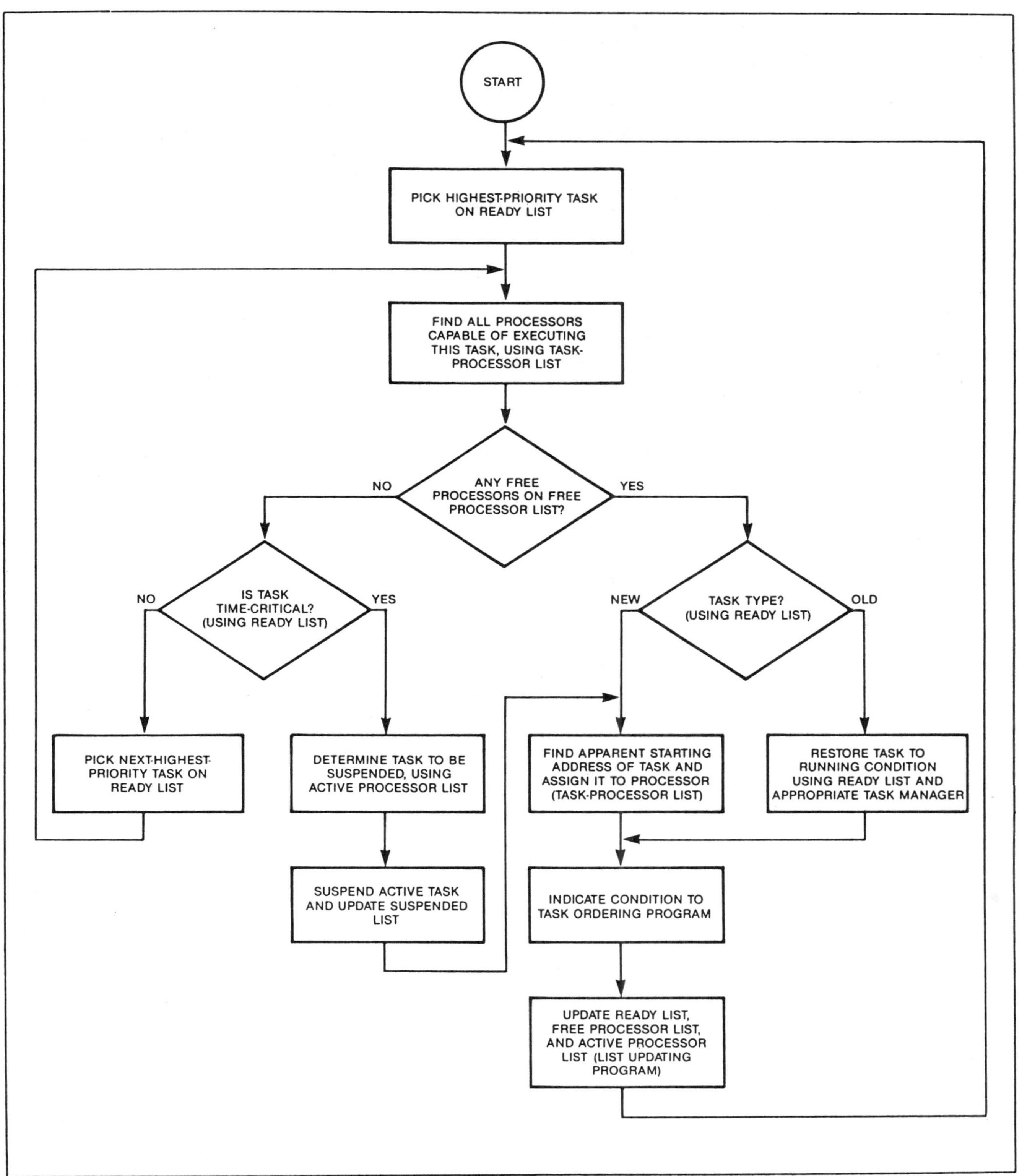

Figure 8. Detailed flowchart of the task allocation procedure.

to control the complete system operation. By changing the static tables, one can make the system execute new processes as long as they are based on tasks that are available in the system. For larger systems, one can use several of these executives, each controlling its own local system, which in turn are controlled by a central unit. Process information is prepared by the central unit and is then loaded into the proper executive for execution.

The problem of task segmentation was not considered here since it is a major topic in itself. However, in many systems one can start with a rough trial task segmentation and, by using a simulation procedure as outlined here, find system bottlenecks. Using the statistical information from the simulation, one can decide on a second task segmentation. These steps can be repeated until acceptable system characteristics are obtained. ■

References

1. K.C. Kahn, "A Small-Scale Operating System Foundation for Microprocessor Applications," *Proc. IEEE,* Vol. 66, No. 2, Feb. 1978, pp. 209-216.
2. D.A. Townen, "A Task Scheduling Executive Program for Microcomputer Systems," *Computer Design,* Vol. 16, No. 6, June 1977, pp. 194-202.
3. Y.P. Chien, "Multitasking Executive Simplifies Real-Time Microprocessor System Design," *Computer Design,* Vol. 19, No. 1, Jan. 1980, pp. 109-117.
4. F.V.D. Linden and I. Wilson, "Real-Time Executive for Microprocessors," *Microprocessors and Microsystems,* Vol. 4, No. 6, July/Aug. 1980, pp. 211-218.
5. C.J. Tavora, "A Basic Technique for Real-Time System Design," *Computer Design,* Vol. 19, No. 10, Oct. 1980, pp. 147-152.
6. B.A. Bowen and R.J.A. Buhr, *The Logical Design of Multiple-Microprocessor Systems,* Prentice-Hall, Englewood Cliffs, N.J., 1980.
7. P. Brinch Hansen, "Distributed Processes—A Concurrent Programming Concept," *Comm. ACM,* Vol. 21, No. 11, Nov. 1978, pp. 934-941.
8. M. Krieger, "Task-driven Multi-microprocessor System," *Proc. First Canadian Workshop on the Design and Development of Computer Systems,* May 1979, pp. 81-88.
9. M. Krieger and E.T. Fathi, "Design Aspects of a Simple Distributed Microprocessor System," *Proc. Int'l Conf. Communication, Circuits, and Systems,* Jadavpur University, Calcutta, Dec. 1981.

Events and Interrupts in Tightly Coupled Multiprocessors

Hubert Kirrmann

Brown, Boveri Research Center

All current multitasking operating systems try to give each task the illusion of having a processor and a memory space of its own, even if there is only one processor. This is termed *partitioning*. Communication between partitions takes place only on a well-defined basis—for instance, by "pipes" or by "mailboxes." The memory is partitioned at the lowest level by the memory management unit; the processor is partitioned at the lowest level by its interrupt system. The interrupt system is used to emulate a multiprocessor on a single processor. It multiplexes a processor among several tasks, either on a scheduled basis (clock interrupts) or on an event basis (I/O interrupts).

With a multiprocessor, one comes nearer to the ideal of having one processor and one memory for each task. The processors can be specialized—they can be I/O processors, disk controllers, arithmetic number crunchers, database managers, user servers, and so on. Processors of different kinds and technologies can be mixed, according to the application. But an individual processor may still need to run more than one task.

Identical processors can also work in parallel to increase processing power or availability. Identical processors which are interchangeable with respect to the tasks they can run form a *pool* of processors. For a task, a pool behaves roughly the same as a single processor: It does not matter on which processor of the pool the task is executed. An important requirement for pools is anonymity of the processors: The operating system and the task should be dependent neither on the number nor on the identity of the processors, although in practice this is not completely achievable. Such a concept is the basis of systems like the Intel iAPX 432 micromainframe.

Pools of different kinds can be built, from simple *static* pools in which tasks are bound to a specific processor for their lifetime, to *dynamic* pools in which tasks may change processors at every synchronization point, or even asynchronously after an interrupt. Since there is an upper limit to the number of processors, a pool will run more tasks than there are processors. There will be T tasks multiplexed upon P processors ($T, P \geqslant 1; T \geqslant P$). Again, it is necessary to interrupt a processor to achieve this.

Tightly coupled multiprocessors

Hardware structure. In a tightly coupled multiprocessor, the processors are connected by a high-speed

Reprinted from *IEEE Micro*, pp. 53–66, Feb. 1985.

parallel bus to a common memory. Some multiprocessors use an additional serial bus that is dedicated to the transmission of event messages. The hardware structure of a tightly coupled multiprocessor is shown in Figure 1.

Memory partitioning. The common memory contains all variables relevant to more than one processor. It can be concentrated or distributed:

- The common memory may be located at one dedicated place in the system. It is then called *global* memory.
- The common memory may be *replicated* on each board to reduce bus occupation.[1,2,11] All read accesses are then local and do not use the bus. All write accesses are done as broadcast write cycles on the bus to maintain the consistency of the copies.
- The common memory may be *partitioned*—a part of it may be installed on each processor board as a dual-port, *local* memory.

A local memory is especially interesting when its content is accessed frequently by the local processor and seldom by the others. A local memory can also be used to make a system modular (i.e., lacking centralized elements such as a global memory).[3]

Registers on a processor board that can be read or written from the outside belong to the *control and status registers* (CSRs) of that board. They form a kind of local memory used for system messages.

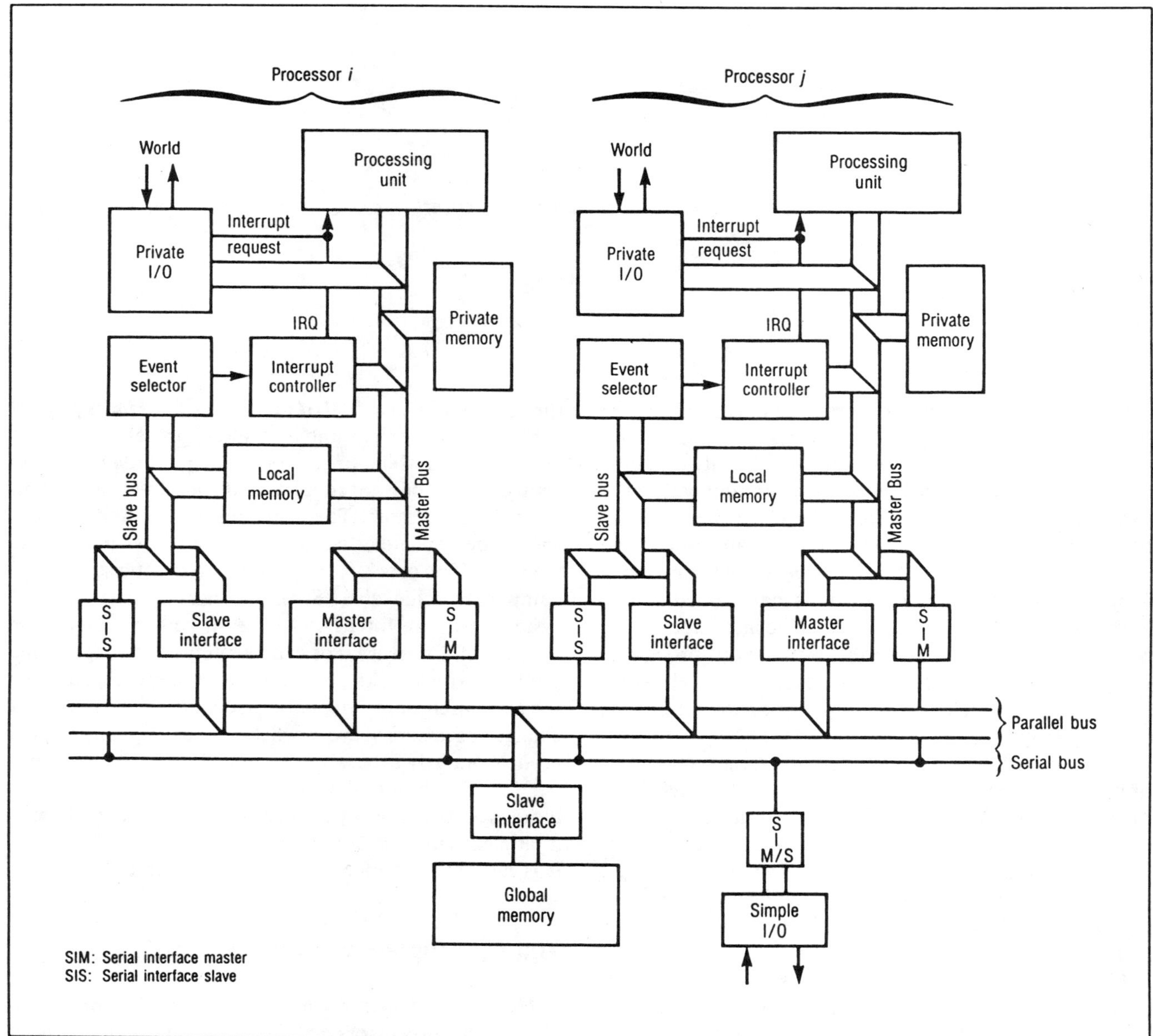

Figure 1. A tightly coupled multiprocessor.

Each processor also has a *private* memory area, which only that processor can access and which contains its program code (in ROM, for example) and local variables.

Interfacing. The differences among the various kinds of memory appear when one considers the functions of the bus interface.

A global memory needs only a *slave* function. It never asks for the parallel bus. A processor board which initiates a transfer on the parallel bus—to access the global memory or the local memory of another processor, for example—needs the *master* function (i.e., the arbiter and master logic). A processor board which has a local memory or CSR registers must have both the master and the slave function.*

The master and slave are difficult to integrate on a single chip, since the number of pins and the power dissipation rapidly become excessive. Each function requires its own buffers and takes a certain amount of board real estate that depends on the degree of integration. As a rule of thumb, each function, master or slave, costs about the equivalent of twelve 16-pin packages in a system with 24-bit addresses and 16-bit data.

A serial bus interface usually has both the master and the slave function on the same chip, which fits in a 48-pin DIP. As can be seen from Figure 1, it may be necessary to use two chips—one in the master mode and one in the slave mode—to access the master and the slave bus, respectively, if the processor bus is not operated in DMA.

Interrupt and control

Task management. In a multiprocessor, there are a large number of parallel tasks running in real or pseudoconcurrency. Task management is similar to that performed by a single processor with multitasking, the difference being that real parallelism is possible in a multiprocessor. A simplified model of the management of tasks, which is also valid for a single-processor multitasking executive, assumes that a task may be in one of three states: running, blocked, or ready (Figure 2).

A task is *running* when it is executing on a processor. In a single-processor system, there is at most one task running at one time.

A task goes from the running to the *blocked* state if it must wait for an event or for some information before proceeding. For instance, a task that manages a printer may exhaust its buffer and may have to wait for fresh data produced by another task. Or a device driver may have to wait for a DMA completion signal from a disk controller. A task asks for the event or the information it needs by calling a "consumer" kernel function such as WAIT or RECEIVE. If the event has not already taken place or the information is not yet available, the task releases the processor and is (conceptually) placed in a synchronization element such as a semaphore or a mailbox. Otherwise, the task proceeds immediately.

When the expected event occurs or the needed information is produced (e.g., by an interrupt or by a running task which executes a "producer" kernel function like SIGNAL or SEND), the task is pulled out of the synchronization element and set *ready*. It must wait, however, for its turn on a processor, so it is put into a *ready list,* which is a queue of tasks waiting for execution.

When a processor is free to execute a new task (e.g., because its running task has been blocked), it picks up a ready task from the ready list, sets it running, and executes it. Normally, a task's life cycle goes clockwise (see again Figure 2) through the states running, blocked, ready, running, and so on. The task's state changes from running to blocked when the task executes a "consumer" synchronization function like WAIT or RECEIVE; it changes from blocked to ready when another task executes a "producer" function like SIGNAL or SEND; and it changes from ready to running when there is a processor available to run it.

Preemption without interruption. Now, if one introduces priorities among the tasks, a task which produces an event or information may awake from the blocked state another task which has a higher priority than its own. In this case, the processor of the lower-priority task is *preempted,* with the consequence that the lower-priority

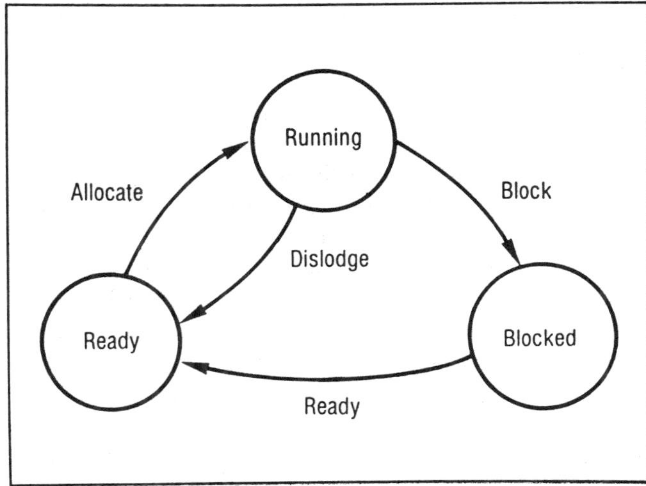

Figure 2. Task states and transitions.

*The local memory and the CSR registers are of the dual-port type, since a DMA access over the bus presents a deadlock problem—while a processor is waiting for the common bus, another device may want to access the local memory of that processor. Since a processor only accepts a DMA request when its instruction is completed, either some decoupling of the processor from its bus must be provided or the local memory must be dual-ported. Some recent processors can use a cancel-and-retry feature originally intended for virtual memory access to cancel the current cycle and break the deadlock.

The master and slave interfaces in Figure 1 are shown connected independently and directly to the system bus. This is done in some IEEE 796 (Multibus) cards, but the system bus capacitive load and the number of transceivers can be reduced if an intermediate bus is used to buffer the system bus.

running task is *dislodged* and set back to the ready state, while the task that has been awakened is set running on that processor.

Preemption corresponds to the counterclockwise transition "dislodge" in Figure 2. A direct transition from the blocked to the running state does not exist: A task always passes through the ready list, because this list may contain a task of a still higher priority.

Therefore, when preemption is allowed, a task may be blocked not only when executing a "consumer" kernel function like WAIT or RECEIVE, but also when executing a "producer" kernel function like SIGNAL or SEND that sets a task of a higher priority ready. Even if all priorities are equal, one often chooses to preempt at a "producer" function, in order to give the consumer task a chance to run.

Interruption. An external interrupt request is treated by the kernel like a foreign task (on another processor) that produces an event and requests the setting ready of a task.

So far, we have said that a task can be dislodged only while executing a "producer" kernel function. However, if the interrupt system is turned on and preemption is allowed, a task may be dislodged by an external interrupt request *at any place* (in principle, after a machine instruction), because a higher-priority task will have just been readied. This is called *asynchronous preemption,* as opposed to *synchronous preemption,* which occurs only at the well-defined places that are the kernel functions.

At each preemption, either synchronous (voluntary) or asynchronous (due to an external interrupt request), the tasks are redistributed among the processors. This operation is called a *redispatch.* In a multiprocessor, the redispatch does not necessarily affect the producer task: Even if the readied task has a lower priority than the running (producer) task, it may have a higher priority than another running task and will therefore asynchronously dislodge that task. For that to happen, the interrupt mechanism of the processor on which the low-priority task is running must be enabled and preemption allowed.

Systems without preemption. Of course, the kernel may be written in such a form that an interrupt request causes only a momentary disruption of the task, just long enough to store the interrupt request and possibly set the consumer task ready. The running task is then resumed in any case and it will not be dislodged, even if the readied task is of a higher priority. This corresponds to an intermediate task state that is not shown in Figure 2.

Some multiprocessor kernels do not allow asynchronous preemption; i.e., a task may not be interrupted between two synchronization primitives. This simplifies the kernel and reduces the overhead due to context switching, but it is feasible only when there is a large number of processors in a pool and as long as the outside world is patient and can wait for processing. When the external world cannot wait, either the synchronization functions must be placed close to each other (but this consumes processing power since it costs a kernel call each time) or preemption of a processor by interrupts must be allowed. An intermediate solution is to call at close intervals a redispatch kernel function, which checks regularly whether a redispatch is needed or not.

Time slicing in any case requires processor preemption. Therefore, a large number of processors cannot be viewed as a replacement for an interrupt system.

Centralized control. The control and dispatching of a multiprocessor can be centralized in a single processor, which then processes the events and schedules the tasks in the other processors. All system interrupt requests are directed to that processor, which redistributes the work by means of flagging or by interrupting the slave processors. This function is similar to that performed in a uniprocessor system.

Multiprocessor systems implemented on the IEEE 796 bus (the Multibus) are generally of the centralized kind. The interrupt requests are sent by dedicated lines and use the parallel bus to carry interrupt vectors which identify the requests.

Distributed control. In a general-purpose multiprocessor such as the one envisioned here, control is distributed. Every processor executes its own copy of the operating system's kernel. Overall management is obtained by having each processor stick to "the rules of the game" rather than by having it obey some sort of centralized control. Any processor can set a task ready and ask for its execution by another processor by sending a request to that processor.

The task state transition model (see again Figure 2) can be extended to show a *deactivated* state, in which a task is no longer present in memory. A task is deactivated by sending a *cancel* request from another task or a *retire* request from the same task. Both cancel and retire are, like the other synchronization functions, kernel calls. If the task to be deactivated is currently running, a *notify-to-cancel* must be sent to the corresponding processor. A processor can therefore request that a specific task be deactivated and, if it is already is execution, that it be canceled.

Since the interrupt request is issued by the processor which has readied or canceled the task, in principle any processor should be allowed to interrupt any other one. I/O devices are a special case, but one can assume that all I/O boards have a dedicated processor. An event signal from the outside world can be interpreted as a service request to a processor.

Events. A processor in a multiprocessor system can receive "local" interrupt requests from its attached peripherals and "system" interrupts from other processors. Both local and system interrupt requests signal a processor that an event has occurred. Local interrupt requests are signaled by static lines like the NMI line, which remain asserted until serviced. System interrupt requests, or *events*, are carried by event messages over the system buses. These event messages are more efficient than the dedicated lines used by local interrupts, but on the other hand they are volatile and must be stored accordingly. In the following, we will sometimes use the term *event* for *event message.*

The questions addressed in this article are how events are generated, how they are signaled, how they are stored at the receiver, and how they are acknowledged.

Events and interrupts

Single-processor interrupt system. In a single-processor system, there is only one processor to receive interrupt requests from I/O devices. The processor is usually located on one card and the peripheral devices on others. The cards are interconnected by a processor bus which carries the interrupt requests from the devices to the processor (Figure 3).

Asynchronous sharing of the processor among several tasks is the most common practice in single-processor systems. Task switching is performed in response to an external event like a clock tick or a completion signal from a peripheral device. The event is stored in the interrupt request flip-flop of the device and announced to the processor through the interrupt request line.

In a computer with a single master processor, all devices with interrupt capability hang onto the interrupt lines of the master processor. The processor services the interrupt during the interrupt acknowledge operation. The interrupting device identifies the request by issuing its interrupt vector. (When several devices ask for an interruption at the same time, an arbitration is performed to decide which device may generate the vector.) The device's interrupt request flip-flop is then reset by the processor with an explicit or implicit I/O operation. Only then is the interrupt request of that device retired.

The interrupt vector can be interpreted as the identifier of a service and, in general, as the identifier of a requester as well, since there is usually only one possible request per device. The vector depends on the specific memory map of the processor, i.e., on the location of the device driver in the processor's memory.

Multiprocessor events. The handling of *events* in a multiprocessor differs significantly from the handling of *interrupt requests* on a monoprocessor bus:

(1) In a monoprocessor, the interrupt request signal uses a static line (e.g., IRQ) to the processor; this line remains active until the interrupt is serviced. The interrupt acknowledge is also static.

In a multiprocessor, the communication path is shared among the processors, so a static line would block the other processors unless there were one line per processor. A general scheme for P processors would require 2P point-to-point lines for centralized control, whereas it would need P(P – 1) lines for decentralized control, since every device should be able to signal an event to every other device. One normally cannot afford such waste in bus lines. Therefore, in a multiprocessor events are carried by volatile messages. An event must be stored at the receiver, and it must be acknowledged by a defined mechanism. The event receiver is therefore more complicated than in a normal interrupt controller such as the VME bus's interrupt handler.[4]

(2) In a monoprocessor, an interrupt request goes only to the processor to which it is attached. In a multiprocessor, an event can be addressed to a processor or to a group of processors, i.e., a pool.

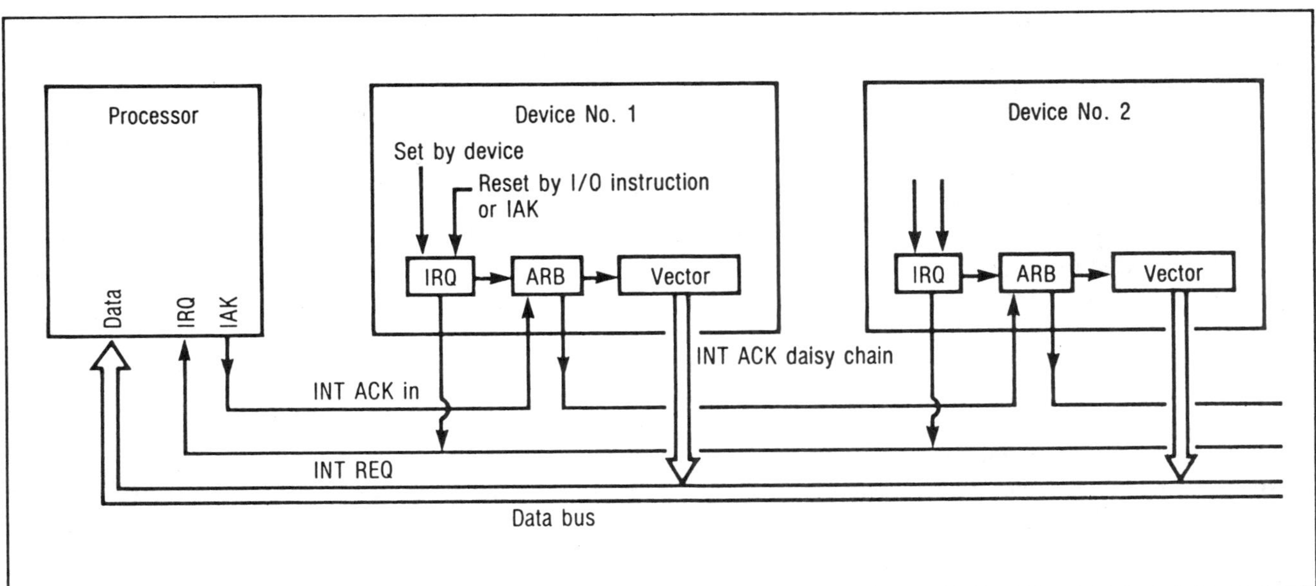

Figure 3. Interrupt scheme for a single-processor system.

(3) An interrupt request is, like an interrupt vector, specific to the hardware of a single processor. An event, however, is a system-wide message that must be understood by any type of processor.

An event is identified by an event number, which seems to correspond to an interrupt vector. But a service request like redispatch must be understood by several processors of different kinds. It causes the execution of a driver at an address dependent on the processor that is interrupted, since all processors do not necessarily have their routines at the same memory location. The event number is therefore dissassociated from the interrupt vector used by the receiving interrupt system, since the same event can be mapped onto different interrupt vectors by different processors. A mapping (event number→interrupt vector) must take place at the destination.

Events transmission mechanism

Event transmission on the parallel bus. A parallel system bus can be used for event transmission as well as for information. The mechanism used is the so-called memory-mapped interrupt. An event uses the same transmission medium and protocol on the parallel bus as a normal data (write) transfer. To a bus observer, an event on the bus is indistinguishable from a data write cycle, except for its destination address. It can be sent by a processor with a normal MOVE instruction. But instead of addressing a global memory location, the processor sends the data to a destination register in the message (local) address space of another processor. Each output line of that register is connected to a programmable interrupt controller (PIC), which generates a different interrupt vector for each line. (We shall generalize this structure in the next section by introducing the *synapse*.)

A mechanism like that described above is used in the Nubus,[5,6] in the Multibus II,[7] and in the IEEE P896 Futurebus.[8]

An interrupting device first gains control of the parallel bus by performing an arbitration. It then sends an address which accesses the local (CSR) space of the receiver and the data which specify the service that is being requested. Some part of the data can be used for additional selection. If the local address is replicated on several processors, a broadcast takes place.

The transmission of an event over the parallel bus requires the event sender to have the bus master logic. The receiver must have both the slave logic and the event receiver on board. Since the receiver board has a processor, it must also have a master interface so that it can communicate with the common memory. So, event transmission over the parallel bus requires that all devices have both the master and the slave interface on board.

Event transmission on the serial bus. Some multiprocessors use a dedicated serial bus—like the VMS,[9] iSSB,[7] or P896 serial bus[8]—for event transmission. The serial bus emerged as a necessity to implementing simple systems. To a large extent, the serial bus duplicates the functionality of the parallel bus, but at a slower speed.

The serial bus interface takes much less space than the parallel bus interface. On the other hand, the worst-case interrupt latency time is higher with the serial bus than with the parallel bus. The difference can be a factor of 10.

An event is transmitted over the serial bus according to the serial bus protocol. A typical serial bus message begins with the identity of the sender (which can be used for arbitration), followed by a selection field which begins with the identity of the receiver(s) and a data field which contains additional information:

source ID	destination selection	data

The selection field allows more sophisticated selection than that allowed by the parallel bus, as will be seen. The data field can be used for information transfer. The final destination of the serial bus message is, like that of an event on the parallel bus, a register in the local address space of another board connected to an interrupt controller.

Serial vs. parallel transmission. Given the availability of both serial and parallel bus capability, four kinds of boards can exist:

(1) Boards with both the master and slave function, on the parallel bus. These boards can use the parallel bus for memory-mapped events.

(2) Boards with only the master capability. The processor on these boards can interrupt another of the above class, but can only be interrupted over the serial bus.

(3) Boards with only the slave capability. These boards use the serial bus to request a service, and their data are read and written by the master over the parallel bus.

(4) Boards without access to the parallel bus. These boards must use the serial bus for both events and data transfer. Most process I/O boards can be used with the serial bus only.

A system which relies only on the memory-mapped interrupt over the parallel bus requires all participating boards to be of class 1, e.g., to have both the master and the slave interface on board. Use of the serial bus is justified when a system contains simple devices that need to have interruption capability without the overhead of master logic.

The transmission of an event over the serial bus requires both the sender and the receiver to have the serial bus interface on board. This interface can be integrated in a single IC and takes little room.

To ensure complete compatibility, one should be allowed to request a specific service by either the parallel or the serial event mechanism, or by both (Figure 4).

Event sender and receiver

Event addressing. The following considerations apply to both the parallel and the serial transmission of interrupts, since on the device side the function of both is the same.

In a multiprocessor system of the kind considered here, any board can have a processor, local memory, and local I/O on it. The processor bus is located on the board. Interrupts to a processor may have two sources: local peripherals or the system bus.

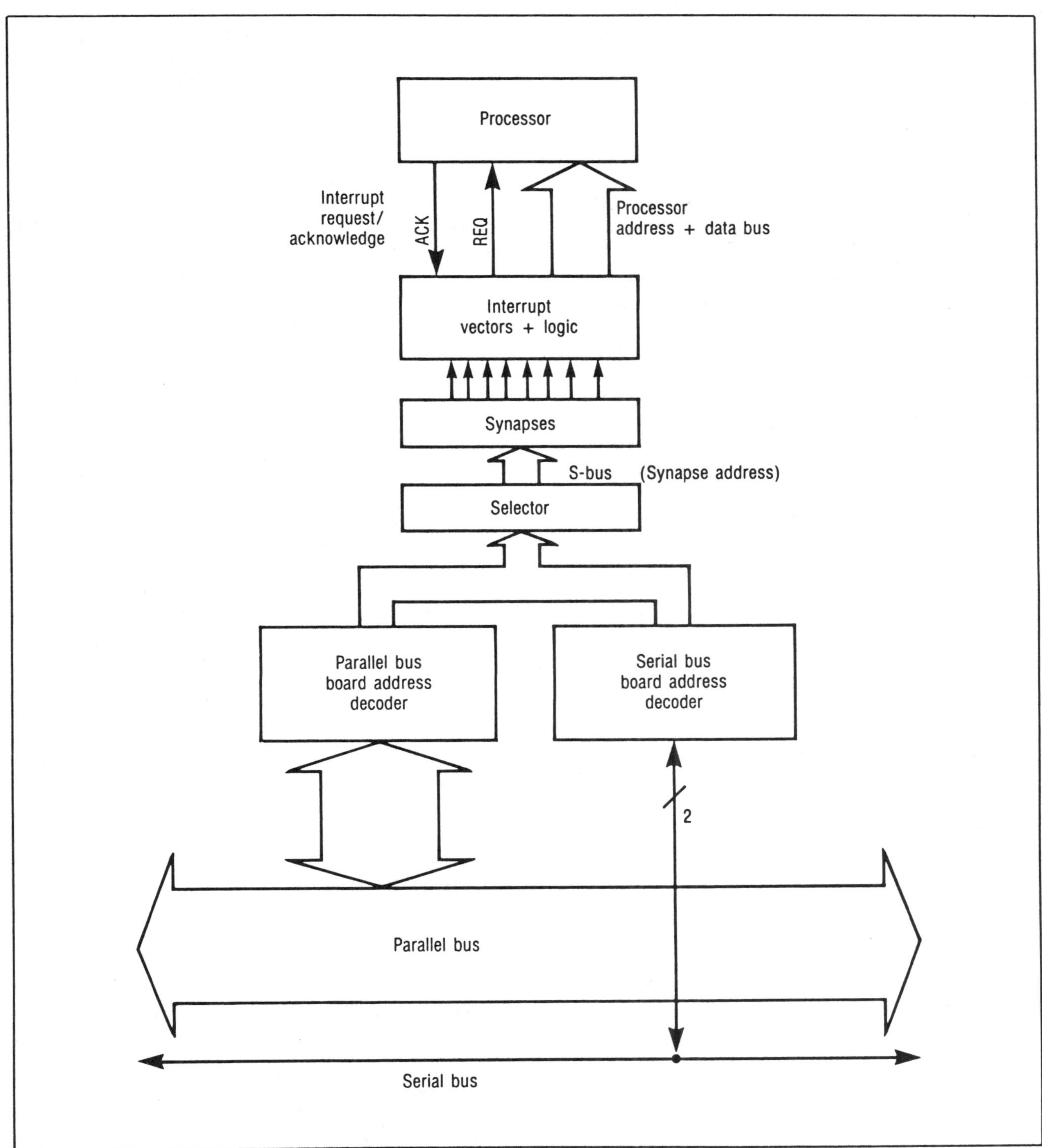

Figure 4. Parallel and serial event receiver.

In a single-processor system, the destination of an interrupt is always the processor. Within the destination, the service required is given by the interrupt vector, which is fetched by the processor during the interrupt acknowledge cycle on its bus.

In a multiprocessor, an interrupt request on the system bus may be issued by any board and directed to any processor board, including itself. Within a board, there may be several possible destinations. For that reason, the interrupt request must carry a destination address. The source identification is required only in a few cases.

Event sender

Operation. On the parallel bus, the event sender is implemented very simply by a normal write cycle. There is no need for special logic; a normal processor MOVE instruction is sufficient. The event sender on the serial bus is somewhat more complicated, since it involves the setting of registers. A default "hardware" mode can exist, which allows easy sending of a predefined message through the activation of just one pin. The VME bus defines a similar event sender device called the interrupt requester.

Source address. In some cases, it is necessary to know the source of an event. It is sometimes needed for the acknowledge, and it is a help in debugging. Hence, the source address should be regarded as an additional parameter, like data.

The source of an event is indicated on the P896 serial bus by the header field (which serves at the same time for the arbitration). The source address has a length of eight bits. The lower five bits of this address must be identical to the unique identity of the source board. The higher three bits can be used to define a priority level. On the P896 parallel bus, the source is indicated by the master identifier in the five-bit arbitration field.

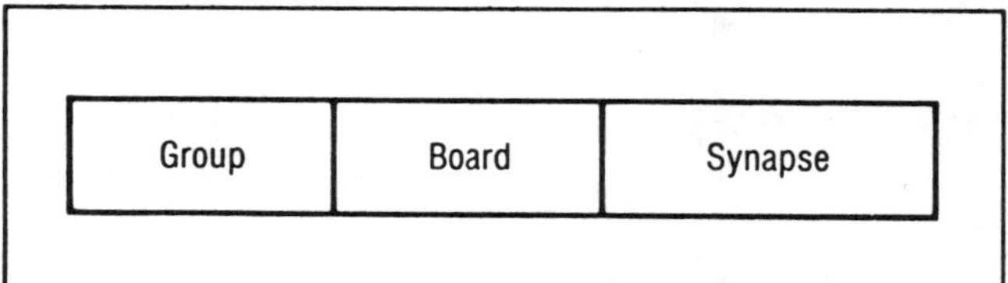

Figure 5. Event destination address (selection by board).

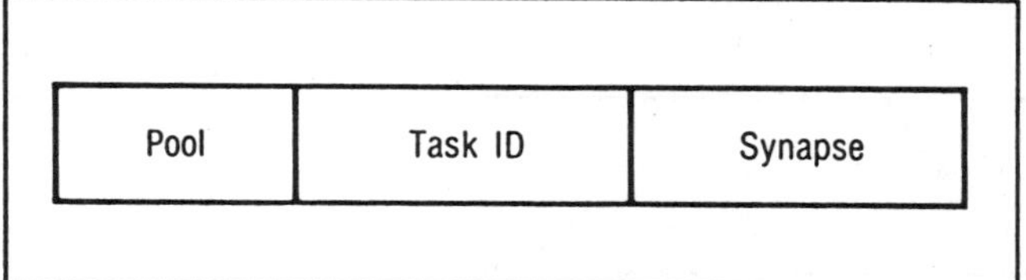

Figure 6. Selection by task name.

Event receiver

Synapse and selector. An event receiver should be accessible by both the parallel and the serial bus if both are implemented on the event receiver board (see again Figure 4). The event receiver is divided into two parts: a *synapse* and a *selector.*

The synapse is the element that stores the event. It consists of a storage element coupled with an interrupt controller. A synapse can be as simple as a flip-flop or have a more complicated structure with data queues. In most cases, a synapse roughly corresponds to an interrupt request flip-flop inside a programmable interrupt controller. A synapse, when fired, generates a local interrupt request for its processor. A processor may have several synapses, one for each service that may be requested from it. The processor must reset the synapses individually to enable them again. The function of the synapse will be detailed in a later section.

The selector decodes the destination address of an event and routes it to a specific synapse.

Selection by board address. An event may be sent to a single processor, a group of processors, or the whole system. Within a processor board, the event is routed to a specific synapse. Thus, the event destination address for selection by board comprises the three addresses shown in Figure 5. The synapse address can be interpreted as a request for a specific function or service to be provided by the destination board(s).

On the P896 serial bus, the group/board destination address has a length of eight bits. The lower seven bits address a specific board within the bus by its unique identifier. The lower five bits must be identical to that identifier. If the higher bit, bit 7, is set, the transmission is a group call. The group number is indicated by the remaining six bits. If the remaining bits are all zero, then the whole system is addressed (group 0 is broadcast). On the parallel bus, the format for the destination address is similar.

The synapse address has a length of eight bits on both the serial and the parallel bus. This allows the addressing of up to 256 synapses within a board. Additional synapses may be addressed on both the serial and the parallel bus through the use of the data field.

Selection by task name. In most cases, an event is sent to a particular processor with a specific resource statically assigned to it. In some cases, however, one wishes to send an event to a processor that holds a resource without knowing exactly which processor it is. Such an action is required to cancel a task in a multiprocessor pool, for example. A processor pool is a group of processors that are homogeneous and interchangeable with respect to the tasks they can run. When a pool is dynamic, a task can change processors during its lifetime.

To stop a task, an event called a *notify-to-cancel* must be sent to the processor running it. But one will not know which processor is running the task unless there is a table of running tasks and their processors. Such a table would, however, breach the concept of anonymous processors in a pool. Of course, one could send the notify-to-cancel message to all the processors in the pool and stop them all. A less disturbing solution would be to address the event to the entire pool of processors, but select specifically the processor which is running the task.

To accomplish this, the event carries as an additional selection the identifier of the task. The event receiver's selector responds only if the task identifier in the event matches the identifier of the running task. The structure of such a message is shown in Figure 6. This method is easily implemented on the serial or parallel bus.

Selection by task priority (highest/lowest). If the tasks in a pool are prioritized, a processor may be preempted to execute a task of higher priority if such a task has been readied. The activation of such a high-priority task involves a redispatch or redistribution of the tasks among the processors. The message that is sent to the processors of the pool informing them that a redispatch is required is called a *notify-to-redispatch.*

If this message were to interrupt all the processors in the pool, it could cause a major reconfiguration or even a time-consuming domino effect. In order to minimize task switching, only the processor which is currently running the lowest-priority task should be told to redispatch. There are two ways to achieve this:

(1) Maintain a table of processors and current task priorities in common memory (a running table). This structure must be locked for writes and reads. It introduces a bottleneck in the kernel, since all notified processors must access it one after the other. Even if it is not preempted, a processor must save its context, wait its turn, examine the list, and restore its context. The biggest drawback of this solution is that it breaches the concept of anonymous processors. One would prefer a solution which is completely independent of the number of processors.

(2) Have the notify-to-redispatch directed only to the processor running the lowest-priority task in the pool. If at the same time, the event announces the priority of the task that the processor should execute, then the event receiver can decide on its own whether to interrupt the processor or not. The event receiver should be intelligent enough to recognize this situation.

The second method can be quite easily implemented on the serial bus. It can also be implemented on the parallel bus if the parallel bus protocol allows broadcall (multiple reads).

To support this solution, the event message carries a field that indicates the priority of the task to be executed (Figure 7).

A kind of arbitration similar to the self-selection mechanism of the S-100 bus, P896 bus, and Multibus II is performed on the task priority field. This arbitration signals to one of the processors that it is the one in the pool with the lowest-priority task and that the new task has a higher priority than its own. The board identifier field is required to arbitrate between processors running tasks of equal priority.

This kind of arbitration scheme has been described by the author in an earlier paper.[10] It is called "lowest" or "highest" selection, depending on whether positive or negative logic is used. The synapse number may be implicit, since the notify-to-redispatch is practically the only service request which needs it.

Classes of events and types of synapses

Events can be of several classes: immediate functions, notifies, queued requests, and queued data. For some applications, the source of the event must be known; for others, it can be anonymous. For each event kind, there is an appropriate synapse receiver.

When the event selector has decoded an event for a synapse (e.g., according to the board identifier or to the task priority, as explained in the preceding section), it puts the synapse address on the S-bus (selector bus). The synapse address is part of the event message, or it is given implicitly by the selection mechanism. A synapse is addressed by its address on the S-bus.

Immediate function (I-type). An immediate function is an event which executes a function on a receiver board without the intervention of that board's processor. Typical applications are an order to disconnect a faulty interface, a nonconditional halt for debugging operations or fail-safe behavior, and a nonmaskable interrupt for a power fail or a system boot.

In the case of an immediate function, the synapse is not necessarily connected to the interrupt system of the processor and it does not need to generate a vector. The

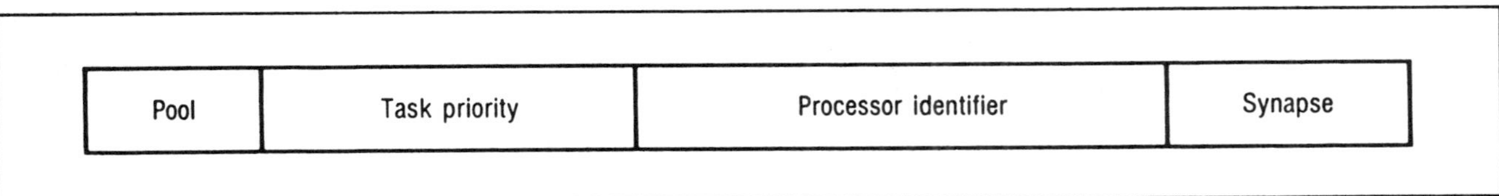

Figure 7. Selection by task priority.

synapse is a simple flip-flop whose output is directly connected to the line it steers. This flip-flop can be reset by another event or when the function has been executed (Figure 8). This kind of synapse is termed the I-type, and it can be implemented very simply with an address decoder and a register (Figure 9).

Resetting of an immediate function event may be done by a time-out, by another event, or by an action of the processor.

Notify (N-type). Notifies are forgettable events. Notifies are idempotent: When more than one notify is sent to a processor, it has the same meaning as only one. For instance, the message "new mail for you" may be repeated any number of times with the same meaning until the receiver handles it. We have already seen two kinds of notifies—the notify-to-cancel and the notify-to-redispatch.

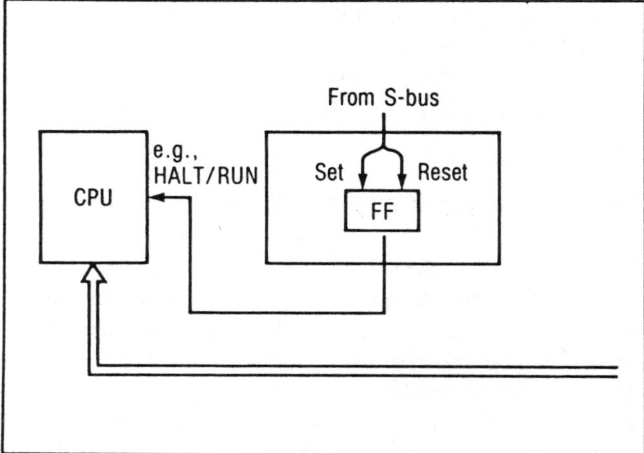

Figure 8. I-type synapse.

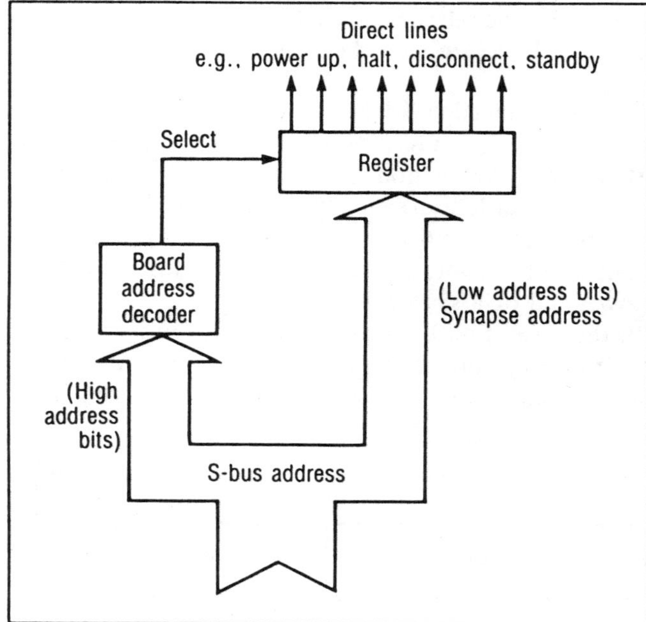

Figure 9. Implementation of an I-type synapse connected to a parallel bus.

The receiving processor must explicitly enable the reception of additional notifies. A synapse for the reception of notifies is termed the N-type and is represented in Figure 10.

Realization of an N-type synapse. An N-type synapse can be easily implemented with a PIC (programmable interrupt controller), which usually contains eight request latches with their associated vectors, corresponding to eight synapses (Figure 11). When an event occurs, the interrupt input of the PIC corresponding to the synapse address is asserted, the corresponding internal interrupt request flip-flop is set, and an interrupt request to the processor is generated. When the processor responds to the interrupt, it fetches the interrupt vector which was predefined for that interrupt request and starts executing the handler. The vector is meaningful only to the processor to which the interrupt controller is attached: It is possible that a synapse having the same meaning on two different boards will have two different vector addresses.

Masking and prioritizing of interrupts are relevant neither to the system bus nor to the sending device. They are private matters of the processor. A processor is free to ignore an event or to delay its handling.

To guarantee a consistent state of the executive, and contrary to what occurs in most monoprocessors, the resetting of an interrupt request should not occur implicitly by accessing a device or reading its vector. The processor terminates its interrupt handling by explicitly resetting the interrupt request flip-flop in the PIC. This allows a new notify to take place.

The notify-type synapse is sufficient for most applications. Indeed, all the synapse types discussed below can be realized with N-type synapses and by using the common memory. The usefulness of these other types is mostly a question of efficiency.

Queued request (Q-type). Queued requests are not forgettable events. Sending queued requests to a processor must result in operations to handle them. The Q-type synapse queues the requests. For example, in a factory application a queued request could mean "one brick has crossed the photodetector." Obviously, in order to maintain the brick count, the requests must be queued.

The request queue has, in practice, a limited length. If the queue length is one, the queued request is practically identical to a notify, with the difference that for a notify a queue overflow is not considered an error, while for a queued request it is.

If a queue overflows, two strategies are possible:

- The message can be ignored if the queue is already full.
- The last message can be overwritten by the new message.

If the loss of a message cannot be tolerated, the event sender must be informed of the queue overflow by a low-level acknowledge.

Figure 12 shows the Q-type synapse for the reception of queued requests.

Realization of a Q-type synapse. A Q-type synapse can be realized with a hardware FIFO in front of the programmable interrupt controller. The interrupt flip-flop remains asserted as long as the queue is not empty. Practical realization depends on the system designer's requirements. If prioritizing events is unimportant, then a single three-bit-wide FIFO can be used; this FIFO queues the three-bit synapse address needed to address an eight-bit PIC. (A nonprioritized Q-type synapse is shown in Figure 13.) If prioritizing of events is important, then each synapse must have its own one-bit-wide FIFO.

Events with data (D-type). To limit the number of synapses, one can distinguish only a few of them but permit the transmission of an additional parameter associated with each. This parameter must be queued by each synapse, since a parameter may not be forgotten. The length of the queue is application-dependent. In the simplest case, the length is one.

The general structure of a synapse with an additional parameter—called a D-type (for data) synapse—is shown in Figure 14.

The D-type synapse can be used for

- source identification,
- data transmission on the serial bus, and
- vectored interrupt requests.

Source identification. The requester's identity can be gained from the arbitration lines on the parallel bus, or from the header field on the serial bus, as mentioned above. In principle, it is not necessary to indicate the source of an event, since the synapse address specifies which service is required. The source identification is not meaningful for notifies: The work to be done in response to them depends on neither their number nor source. If the source of the event is identified, then the synapse must store the source identifier in a data queue.

Data transmission. The data queue can be used to store additional data related to the interruption. This is particularly interesting for the serial bus. On the serial bus, such data can be considered as the useful information the bus transmits, the event being that the data are ready.

Because of the high transmission speed, it may be necessary to queue a large number of messages. Flow control is then required, in the form of a low-level acknowledge. There is no restriction on the minimum length of the queue, however. The destination queue may be a single register.

Vectored interrupt requests. In a single-processor system, the interrupt system has direct access to the processor. To simplify scanning, the interrupting peripheral yields a vector that is a pointer to a dedicated memory location where the interrupt driver begins. This pointer

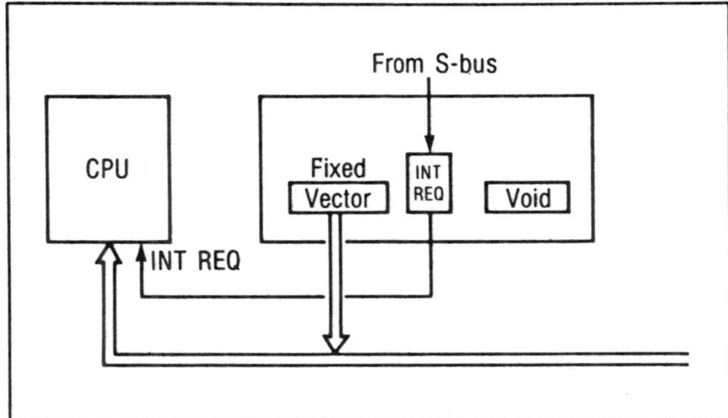

Figure 10. N-type synapse.

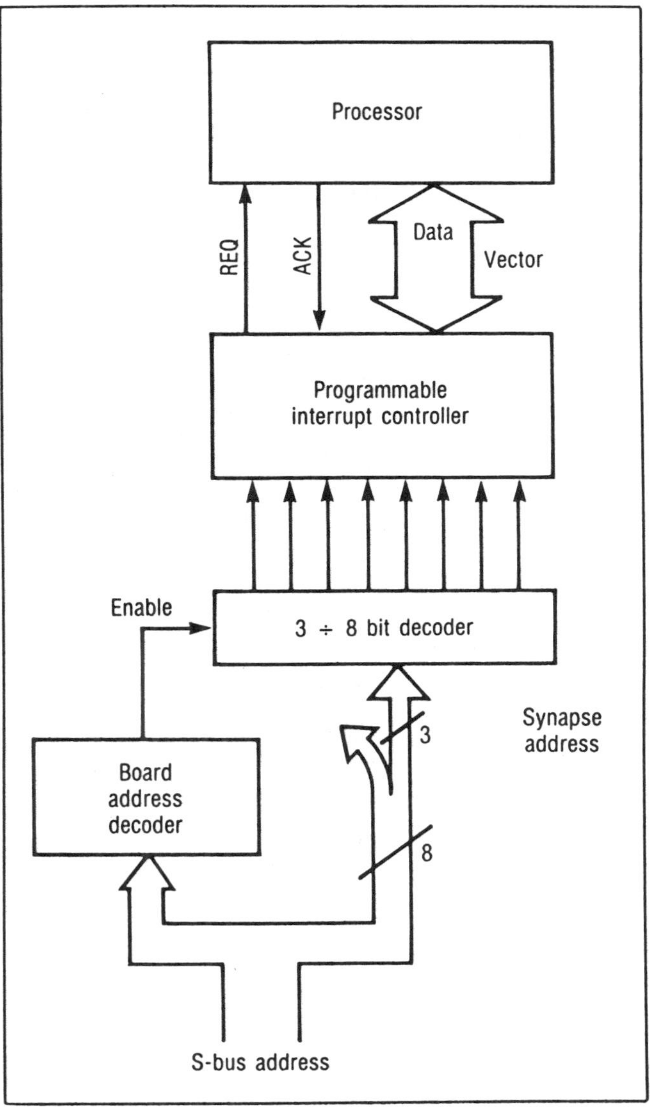

Figure 11. Implementation of an N-type synapse.

is meaningful only to the processor that manages the interrupt. In a multiprocessor system, such a pointer has no system-wide meaning; each processor has its own interrupt table and interrupt handling mode, which may not be known to the outside world. For this reason, events access only an interrupt controller and do not directly access the processor.

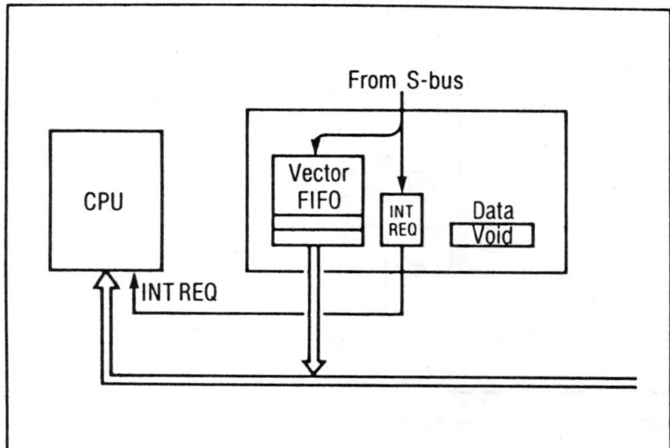

Figure 12. Q-type synapse.

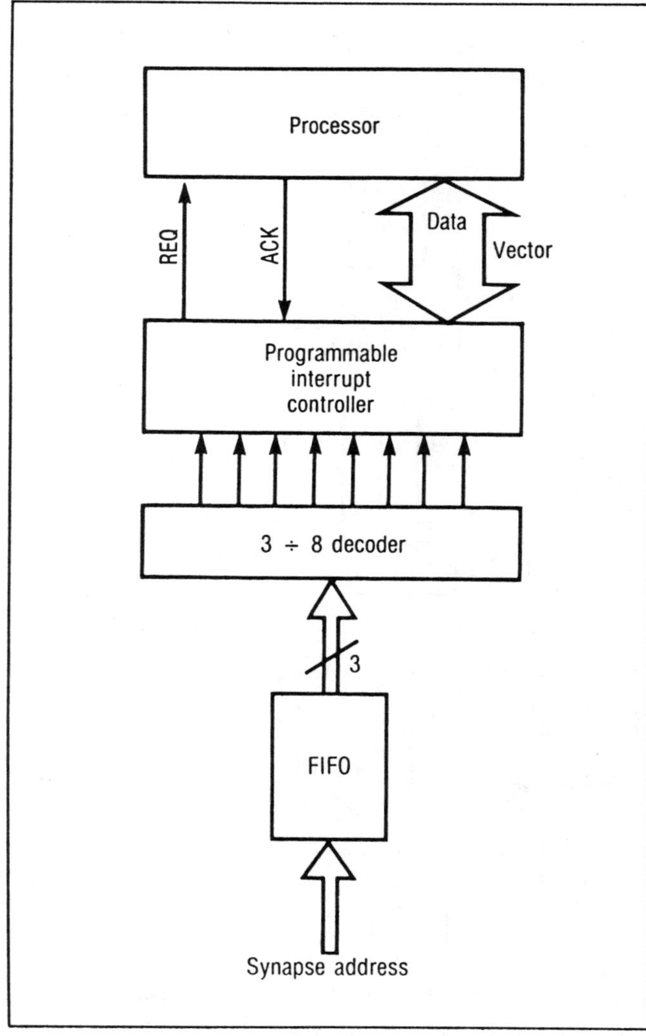

Figure 13. Nonprioritized Q-type synapse.

If few synapses are available, but the number of events is large, then a service number can be carried as additional information. It is read by the interrupt driver to enable a branch to a service handler.

General synapse (G-type). The most generalized structure of a synapse is shown in Figure 15. It contains two coupled queues, one for the event (the vector) and one for data. The interrupt request flip-flop remains set until both queues are empty. All synapse types can be deduced from this structure by removing elements.

Acknowledging an event

Types of acknowledge. An event is a request for a service at the destination. When a service is requested, some kind of acknowledgment is always required. The level of acknowledgment varies. There may be an acknowledge at every protocol level, such as in the ISO reference model. Here are some possible meanings of an acknowledge, beginning with a low-level acknowledge:

- I received your frame correctly (hardware acknowledge);
- I decoded and stored your message (queue not full);
- I interrupted my processor, and it has read the interrupt vector;
- I am ready to receive your next request; and
- the service you required has been successfully completed (high-level acknowledge).

A low-level acknowledge is often required when communication is not reliable, and for flow control when there is a buffer overrun. An acknowledge of a device driver is required to reset an interrupt receiver and to perform queueing in the memory.

All practical operating system communication primitives require a medium-level acknowledge. For instance, remote procedure calls or rendezvous cannot proceed until an acknowledge (or a time-out) has occurred. A high-level acknowledge is required for the user interface, especially when the delay between a service request and service execution is long.

Acknowledging a service in the computer is not always required. In most cases, a send-no-ack protocol is sufficient, e.g., when sending a file to the printer spool. In that case, the printed listing is the acknowledge to the user. A service which is never acknowledged may as well as never have been performed. At any level, the requester can choose not to wait (no-wait-send), to wait until completion (send-and-wait), or to wait until a negative acknowledge or a time-out comes (send-and-time-out).

Realization of the acknowledge. At the lowest level, the acknowledge is part of the baseline protocol. In a parallel bus, there is normally an acknowledge line that is asserted for each item of information successfully received during a bus cycle or transfer, whether it be in the form of a positive acknowledge signal, the removing of a wait signal, or a negative acknowledge signal.

In serial buses, the low-level acknowledge is used less, since such an acknowledge requires the READ capability. Parallel buses are short and they can read and write, but serial buses can be long and are often restricted to write operations because of the propagation delay. The VMS and P896 serial buses, however, can read back an acknowledge during the same bus transfer, since their length is limited to a few meters. These buses are therefore particularly well adapted to the scheme we have presented here.

Local-area networks like the Ethernet, on the other hand, lack the read function: All messages are write-only. An acknowledge can be done only by a return message. When the communication medium lacks the capability to read and write during the same transfer, the protocol becomes much more complicated. One must keep track of the message sequence and introduce time stamps and version numbers. The network people have found some good solutions to these problems, but they are not simple.

Fortunately, the existence of common memory in a multiprocessor allows for easy acknowledging. The acknowledge is done simply by setting a location in common memory. For this to be done, a common area for each service in global memory or in the auxiliary memory space must have been agreed upon. This is normally the case, since the servicing of an event requires additional parameters and data which must be available in common memory. For instance, if one processor requests a disk server processor to open a file, it supplies the file parameters in memory, sends an event, and expects a return status and the first file block in memory (assuming the file is a random access file). Since the disk server processor may be the same processor as the one which issued the request, the task which asked for the service must free the processor. A "completion" event will wake it up and set it running again.

If the source of the event is known, the completion signal can be sent directly to the requester of the service in the form of another event (send-and-ack). If the source is unknown, the acknowledge should be broadcasted. In this case, the name of the service is broadcasted along with a completion signal. The receiver must then be a data-type synapse.

The simple devices for which the serial bus is intended have no access to the common memory. If they did, they could also use the parallel bus to signal events. Therefore, to be consistent with the above scheme, the serial bus must be able to transport data to acknowledge a service.

Conclusion—the practical importance of the above structures

Interrupt requests are interchanged in a decentralized multiprocessor by event messages, either over the parallel bus or over the serial bus. A low-level acknowledge takes care of flow control. Acknowledging at a higher level can be done by using the common memory or by sending return event messages. The event mechanism in a multiprocessor system has some similarity to the network protocol in distributed systems. What makes it different is the possibility of synchronization on a common memory location.

The event message should carry a source identification, which is helpful in acknowledging and debugging. The event message carries a destination address which selects a particular processor board, a group of boards (a pool), or all processors.

Within a group of processors, the processor board which is running the lowest-priority task (the "highest" selection), or which is running a specific task, can be

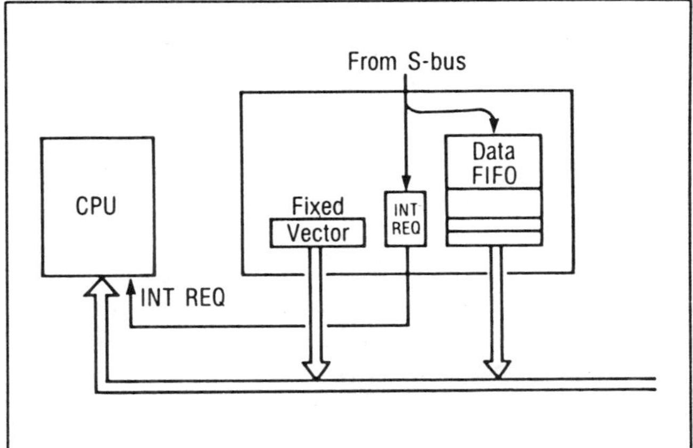

Figure 14. D-type synapse.

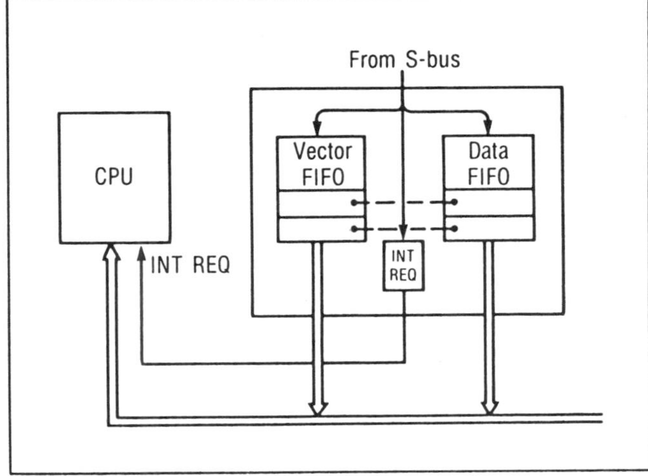

Figure 15. Generalized synapse (G-type).

selected. Within a board, the destination address specifies a particular synapse.

The synapse is a generalized structure which combines an input storage queue (prioritized or FIFO), an interrupt register (resettable by the processor), and a programmable interrupt controller. Several types of synapse exist, corresponding to immediate operations, forgettable events (notifies), queued events, and events with data.

The notify-to-redispatch function is requested by the combination of a "lowest" selection mode with a notify-type synapse. The only necessary event type is the notify. In a multiprocessor with a common memory, all other events can be reduced to a notify by executing the queueing in the common memory.

An implementation of queued requests in a Q-type synapse is justified where efficiency is of prime importance, such as in high-speed, real-time systems or when the devices do not have access to the parallel bus. The data synapse is most useful for data transmission on the serial bus, since devices connected to the serial bus may not have access to the parallel bus. The data synapse also allows the serial bus to duplicate the data transfer capability of the parallel bus, and thus opens it to use as a low-speed redundant path. A condition for this, however, is uniformity of address space on both the serial and the parallel bus. The general synapse should be considered a theoretical construct, unless a useful model of it can be cast in silicon. A typical system will probably have some I-type and N-type synapses and one D-type synapse for the serial bus; the latter will be able to queue from one up to four messages.

The acknowledge depends heavily on the structure of the operating system. Several levels of acknowledge which can make use of the common memory can be envisioned.

A practical implementation of these concepts has been achieved by the author at the Brown, Boveri Research Center. A multiprocessor based on a prototype described by Kirrmann and Kaufmann,[12] and using I- and N-type synapses, is being built. ■

References

1. S. Lillevik et al., "A Multiprocessor with a Replicated Shared Memory," *AFIPS Conf. Proc.*, Vol. 51, 1982 NCC.
2. L. Philipson et al., "A Communication Structure for a Multiprocessor Computer with Distributed Global Memory," *Proc. 10th Int'l Symp. on Computer Architecture*, June 1983, pp. 334-340.
3. P. Civera et al., "The μ* Project: An Experience with a Multimicroprocessor System," *IEEE Micro*, Vol. 2, No. 2, May 1982, pp. 38-50.
4. VME Bus Manufacturers Group, "VME Bus Specifications," Document No. M68KVMEB[D1]. (Available from Motorola, Philips, Signetics, or Mostek offices.)
5. S. Ward, "The Nu Personal Computer: Nubus Specifications," tech. report, Lab. for Artificial Intelligence, MIT, Boston, Nov. 1980.
6. Texas Instruments, "Nubus Specification," Feb. 1983. (Available from George P. White, Texas Instruments, 17891 Cartwright Rd., Irvine, CA 92714.)
7. Intel Corp., "Multibus II Bus Architecture Specification," Order No. 146077-B. (Available from Intel Corp., 3065 Bowers Ave., Santa Clara, CA 95051.)
8. IEEE Project 896—Futurebus, "Specifications for Advanced Microcomputer Backplane Buses, IEEE P896 D6.2," Nov. 1983. (Available from the IEEE Computer Society, PO Box 80452, Worldway Postal Center, Los Angeles, CA 90080.)
9. VME Bus Manufacturers Group, "VME Serial Bus (VMS) Specification Manual." (Available from Rick Main, Signetics Corp., PO Box 409, Sunnyvale, CA 94086.)
10. H. Kirrmann, "A Serial Interprocessor Link for Multiprocessor Management in the P896 Backplane Bus," *Proc. Euromicro Conf.*, Paris, Sept. 1981.
11. P. Borrill, "IEEE P896 Working Document," Apr. 1980. (Available from Paul Borrill, University College London, Mullard Space Science Laboratory, Holmbury St. Mary, Dorking, Surrey RH5 6NT England.)
12. H. Kirrmann and S. Kaufmann, "Poolpo—A Pool of Processors for Process Control Applications," *IEEE Trans. Computers*, Vol. C-33, No. 10, Oct. 1984.

Multiple-Microprocessor Programming Techniques: MML, a New Set of Tools

Maurelio Boari, Universitá di Bologna
Stefano Crespi-Reghizzi, Politecnico di Milano
Alberto Daprá, Techint Software e Telematica
Francesco Maderna, CISE
Antonio Natali, Universitá di Bologna

A growing number of embedded computer applications are better handled by a multiple-microprocessor system than by a single large computer. In such a system, microprocessors in a network cooperate in performing a predefined set of computing tasks. Although families of boards for such multi-micro systems are commercially available, a methodology and a set of tools for programming distributed interactive processes are needed.

The computing activity of the network includes interactions with the application environment and internal activities required for exchanging information between processors, monitoring the status of the net, and taking recovery action in failures or emergencies. For application systems made of well-identified subsystems, the structure of the application often demands a distributed solution whereby, ideally, each subsystem is controlled by a dedicated processor.

Our main objective is to provide a programming tool for a broad range of distributed microprocessor architectures and applications. The usual program development cycle consists of application analysis, hardware prototype design or selection, software development and testing on a host computer (the Micro Development System, or MDS), and program and prototype integration for overall real-time testing.

Hardware is frequently chosen before software design, so the designer can fully specify allocation of program modules to memory at compilation, linking, or loading time. However, software can be developed for a partial prototype, since an MDS can lend its resources, such as memory and CPU, to the prototype for emulation.

Similarly, our development system for multi-microprocessors—to be called the Multi-Micro Programming Line, or MML[1]—is based on the host-target approach, but the target can be any multi-micro configuration out of an open set of supported architectures. As a first requirement, MML can be retargeted to prototype systems of any reasonable architecture. Reorienting MML to a different architecture requires a fraction of the initial development cost. Within one architecture, configuration may differ considerably, ranging from a single processor to various forms of tightly or loosely coupled multiple microprocessors. Different processors may be present in the same configuration.

To take full advantage of multi-micro systems, the designer should not freeze the prototype configuration ahead of software design. He should be free to experiment with various configurations without having to rewrite his software or, even worse, to redesign the run-time support. Moreover, the allocation of hardware resources to functions should be the designer's responsibility. Thus, a second requirement for MML is that prototype configuration and allocation are design variables that should be exploited to meet such requirements as real-time response or system availability and to optimize the cost-effectiveness of resources.

These first two requirements clearly separate program description (data and algorithms) from hardware description (configuration). As a third requirement, MML provides specific tools for hardware description and resource allocation. MML includes a language and a compiler for process and procedure description, plus facilities for hardware configuration description, resource allocation, run-time system configuration, debugging, and execution control. MML allows software development without reliance on the final prototype. If the prototype does not exist, the host computer could be assigned to run all processes for software testing.

Reprinted from *IEEE Computer*, pp. 47–59, Jan. 1984.

Since microprocessors are generally used to control I/O equipment (sensors, actuators, and peripherals), effective tools for I/O programming and real-time response must be provided. Two paths toward a solution are possible:

- Assign I/O operations to assembly-language encoded modules that interface with higher level modules, as normally done with such sequential system languages for microprocessors as PL/M[2] and PLZ-SYS[3] or
- Express I/O operations in high-level language. The high-level stream-oriented I/O, such as in Pascal, however, is not adequate for embedded microprocessor applications.

The variety of peripheral chips and the need to be retargetable complicate the problem. Assigning I/O operations to modules coded in assembly language has the unpleasant effect of reducing machine independence, since the assembly languages of micros differ considerably. The economy of suppressing assembly-language programming made us opt to express I/O operations in high-level language. Consequently, MML's language offers elementary facilities for programming all sorts of I/O devices at a low level by allowing the addressing of peripherals and the control of interrupts.

To ensure real-time response to time-critical events, four techniques enacted at four levels can be joined:

- Hardware level: either increasing the actual parallelism of the target system by adding microprocessors to the net until eventually each process is executed on a dedicated processor or providing fast interprocessor communications where required. Broadband channels are achieved by tightly connecting micros via shared memories, a solution offered by most architectures, since configuration changes do not impact the source program.
- Allocation level: at system configuration time, assigning fixed pathways to intercommunicating processes having stringent time requirements. Other noncritical processes must contend for channels.
- Program level: ensuring top-priority to I/O interrupts on multitasked micros by introducing interrupt procedures automatically invoked when certain interrupt signals occur.
- Translation level: increasing the actual execution speed of object code. Processes can be translated to the faster machine code or interpreted.

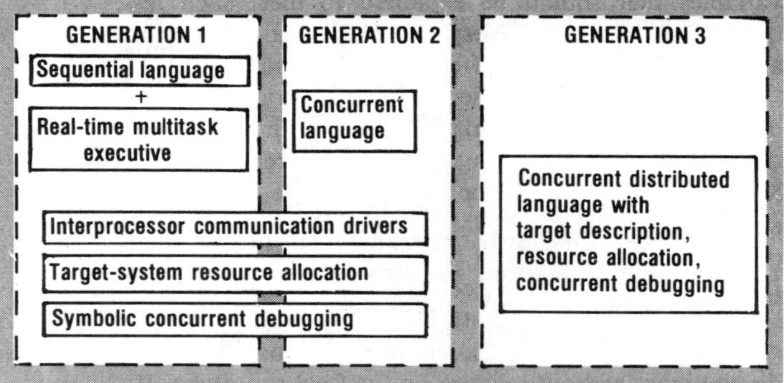

Figure 1: Three generations of tool sets at three levels of integration for multi-microprocessor systems.

Before discussing in detail the MML set of tools, we will survey other current proposals and available software tools for multiprocessors. Rather than exhaustively survey all proposed and established tools, we discuss several commercially available systems as well as some milestone proposals. We also cover some systems not originally conceived for microprocessors, since the frontier between traditional mainframes and microprocessors is steadily disappearing, leaving memory size and processor speed as discriminating parameters. Our discussion is organized by classifying software tools into generations.

Survey of software tools for multiprocessors

We have argued that a complete tool set for embedded multi-microprocessor products must support

(1) high-level sequential programming,
(2) parallel logical processing (that is, concurrency),
(3) distributed computation, and
(4) I/O treatment.

Therefore, existing or proposed tools can be classified into three generations based on the integration of (1), (2), and (3), as shown in Figure 1. Aspect (4) will be discussed separately, since it does not correlate with the generations.

First generation. The popular development systems for real-time microprocessor-based products exemplify this generation wherein no integration occurs. Separate tools provide (1), (2), and (3), as illustrated by the three typical systems in Table 1. These tools for high-level sequential programming, concurrent processing, and distributed computation can be interfaced by identifying for each microprocessor a set of sequential processes to be programmed in the high-level language and executed under control of the multitask executive (kernel). The sequential processes assigned to a microprocessor communicate and synchronize via facilities provided by the kernel, such as semaphores and mailboxes. However, since no such facilities are available for synchronization and communication between processes on different processors, the user must design his own communication drivers as concurrent processes to be synchronized with application processes.

Object code and data are downloaded onto the target using linking and loading directives. Symbolic debugging facilities for sequential programs are usually available and can be combined in some cases with commands that trace kernel events. On some development systems, multiple in-circuit emulation probes allow two processors to be observed simultaneously.

First-generation tool sets are similar, differing mainly in the sequential language used. Languages can be

Table 1.
Typical first-generation tool sets.

SYSTEM	HIGH-LEVEL SEQUENTIAL LANGUAGE	REAL-TIME MULTITASK EXECUTIVE	LOADERS, DRIVERS, AND MULTIPROCESSOR DEBUGGING	HOST SYSTEM	TARGET SYSTEM
Intel MDS (1973)	PL/M (1973)	RMX (1978)	Multi-ICE (1980) Generic-ICE (1983)	8085, 8086	All Intel micros
HP 64000 (1973)	Pascal (1970)	Not supplied by HP	Information not available	Dedicated machine	Most 8- and 16-bit micros
SPL Magic (1981)	RTL-2 (1981)	SMT-Plus	Optional	PDP-11	Most 8- and 16-bit micros

classified in four levels,[4] based on their distance from machine code:

(1) structured assemblers, such as ASZ and PLZ-ASM;
(2) high-level machine-dependent languages, such as Mistral and PL65;
(3) high-level machine-oriented languages, such as C, PL/M, and PLZ-SYS; and
(4) high-level languages, such as Pascal, RTL-2, and Fortran.

Excluding mass-produced computerized products or ultra-critical real-time systems in which assembly coding is mandatory, the best choice for most applications seems to be level (3) or (4) languages. For eight-bit microprocessors, however, level (4) languages are too resource-consuming for many applications.

Although first-generation tool sets differ in the sequential language used, their real-time operating system kernels provide similar functionalities, such as semaphores, mailboxes, and WAIT and SIGNAL primitives.

In our experience, carefully interfaced first-generation tools provide a low-profile, practical approach to multiple-microprocessor programming jobs of moderate complexity. The major weaknesses in the first generation include the lack of suitable control on overall correctness of parallel processes and the lack of tools for interprocessor communication, resource allocation, and system configuration. Advances in these directions characterize the second and third generations.

Second generation. Instead of sets of sequential tasks coordinated by multitask kernels, the second generation offers concurrent languages (see Table 2), clearly an improvement over the first generation. Many process synchronization primitives, from semaphores to monitors and rendezvous, have been proposed.

When semaphores were found to be too low-level for conveniently programming concurrent processes, the abstract model of concurrency known as a monitor[5] was introduced and implemented in Concurrent Pascal.[10] A monitor defines a collection of data structures and procedures used exclusively on the data. At most, one process at a time can be given access to a monitor procedure, since monitors implement mutual exclusion.

For more effective control of process scheduling within a monitor, operations on queues (similar to semaphores) can be used to delay a calling process or to resume a process already waiting in a queue. At run-time,

Table 2.
Some second-generation tool sets.

HIGH-LEVEL CONCURRENT LANGUAGE	SYNC/COMM CONSTRUCTS	DISTRIBUTED COMPUTING FACILITIES	HOST ENVIRONMENT	TARGET ENVIRONMENT
Concurrent Pascal[5] (1975)	Pascal extended with monitors	Same as in first generation	PDP-11	LSI-11, Intel 8080, and minis
Pearl[5] (1969-1976)	Similar to PL/1 extended with locks and rendezvous	Stations* division; allocation in load division	Same as target	8086, LSI-11, Z80, and minis
Micropower Pascal[7] (1981)	Pascal extended with semaphores	Same as in first generation	PDP-11	LSI-11/2, LSI-11/23, and SBC 11/21
Iliad[8] (1976)	PL/1 subset extended with locks and delay statements	Not mentioned	IBM 370	LSI-11, PDP 11, IBM Syst7, and 8080
ADA[9] (1980)	Larger Pascal-like language using rendezvous	Not specified	Large mini to host APSE	Most 16- and 32-bit micros

*in more recent descriptions for multicomputer configuration

concurrent processes are executed in quasi-parallelism under the control of an invisible kernel.

Most second-generation software instruments were designed for global memory environments, a fact reflected by the synchronization and communication primitives they provide. These primitives define a data structure shared by several processes, which can be accessed only in a controlled manner.

In a truly distributed situation—local networks, at the very extreme—this kind of interprocess exchange mechanism does not seem to fit the problem. Indeed, message-passing operations seem more natural to consider, which is why newer languages have adopted message-passing for process interaction.

The best known of the second-generation languages is Concurrent Pascal, despite its generally acknowledged inefficiency for real-time applications. Similar languages, proposed and implemented by academic and industrial groups, include

- *Modula*: a system programming tool for PDP-11's, designed in 1977 by Wirth, the father of Pascal.[11] Modula differs significantly from Concurrent Pascal, especially in improved modularity for data abstraction, delimitation of machine-dependent peripheral operations within device modules, and reduced run-time support due to more elementary process-switching criteria.
- *Portal*: a version of Modula designed in 1978 by Landis & Gyr, a Swiss automation company, for process-control applications using the PDP-11 and Motorola 68000.[12]
- *Micro-Concurrent Pascal*: a version of Concurrent Pascal for microprocessors.[13]
- *Pascal+*: an operating-system tool that blends the modularity of Modula with the monitor concept.[14]

Third generation. Second-generation systems do not provide facilities for assigning computation to processors and for handling interprocessor communication. These facilities plus a concurrent language create the third generation.

Concurrency, target configuration description, distribution of software modules onto target processors, and interprocessor communications are aspects of an integrated tool set. Specific debugging and execution control facilities for distributed systems are also important. Table 3 describes three representatives of third-generation tools.

I/O facilities. An essential feature of a microprocessor programming tool is the control of I/O operations. Languages and software tools adopt one of two approaches: kernel or packaged I/O.

Kernel I/O. I/O operations implemented by kernel routines are invoked in either low-level, machine-dependent procedure invocations or high-level, machine-independent I/O statements.

Kernel I/O is typical in traditional shop computer systems (Fortran, Basic, Pascal). Pascal provides high-level READ, WRITE, PUT, and GET statements implementing a sequential file abstraction. The "sequential file" virtual device of Pascal—intended for handling I/O from or to card readers, line printers, or file systems—is not particularly suited to plant I/O. Since such rarely required I/O operations increase the size of the kernel, they are omitted from real-time oriented versions of Pascal, such as HP 64000.

High-level kernel I/O operations provide a convenient virtual device, implemented by run-time routines; however, the variety of special I/O devices and interface controllers for microprocessors would require many different virtual devices with associated high-level syntactic notations and run-time routines. A few very generic high-level I/O statements could handle most devices, if one is ready to pay in terms of efficiency and memory size.

Table 3.
Examples of third-generation tools.

TOOLS	SEQUENTIAL FACILITIES	CONCURRENT FACILITIES	NETWORK ARCHITECTURE, CONFIG.	RESOURCE DISTRIB., ALLOCATION	RUN-TIME SUPPORT CONFIG.	HOST MACHINE	TARGET MACHINE	OPERATIONAL
Demos[15] (1979)	Same as Concurrent	Same as Concurrent Pascal*	Homogeneous network of 8086 processors	Under user control	Automatic†	VAX or 8086	8086-based multi-micros	Prototype
Edison[16] (1980)	Stripped down Pascal with improvements	Conditional critical region; dynamic process creation	Information not available	Process allocation by processor	Information not available	PDP-11/45	Mostek, PDP-11	Prototype
MML (1980)	Same as Zilog's PLZ-SYS	Remote procedure invocation with extended rendezvous	Interactive Configuration; processors in network may be heterogeneous	Under user control	Automatic†	PDP-11/34	Z80,8085, 8086, Z8001,...	Prototype

*for system engineer
†in accordance with specified resource allocation

Iliad[8] and Pearl[6] offer a considerable variety of virtual process-control-oriented I/O devices with associated high-level statements. In Iliad, there is no fixed set of I/O statements, but the language and the compiler are extensible. New "verbs" can be defined for devices such as optical scanners, A/D converters, modems, and a variety of sensors and actuators that connect to either a parallel or serial interface.

In Concurrent Pascal and Demos,[15] I/O is handled by standard procedure calls of the form: I/O (data, operation, device). As with most kernel I/O systems, the calling process is delayed until the operation is completed. Peripheral interrupts become irrelevant to the programmer, handled completely at the machine level within the kernel containing a separate piece of code for each kind of peripheral device. Consequently, industrial users must be prepared to extend the kernel when different devices are needed—quite a tricky job.

This approach is best suited to machine-independent, application-oriented languages for process control, such as Pearl and Iliad. It is not acceptable for specialized embedded systems, for which the level of description provided by packaged I/O seems necessary.

Packaged I/O. I/O operations are implemented by modules or packages written for specific peripheral devices in assembly language or the high-level language.

The use of assembly language, typical of first-generation systems such as PL/M and PLZ-SYS, requires trusting I/O operations to assembly-coded modules to be linked with application processes. However, it removes the benefits of high-level language programming from the sizable part of embedded computer applications dealing with I/O. In a practical compromise between low-level visibility of peripheral devices and high-level language syntax, Modula confines I/O to device modules allowing absolute addresses of I/O ports.

Edison[16] and MML follow Modula's approach. The PDP-11 version of Edison offers three standard procedures: *place* (deviceaddress), *obtain* (deviceaddress, value), and *sense* (deviceaddress, value). The last procedure checks the two operands for coincidence of bits. Interrupts are completely ignored, since the system is intended for inexpensive microprocessors. MML offers two standard operations similar to *place* and *obtain,* as well as the possibility of defining interrupt procedures. Concurrent languages have an innate facility for describing interaction between a peripheral device (viewed as a hardware process) and its driver.

The radical solution—relying on external packages possibly coded in another language to perform I/O operations—is used in RTL/2 and Ada,[9] which do not include any special statements for I/O operations. An extensive standard library of packages for frequently used I/O modes and devices is defined as an appendix to the Ada language. It would seem that most, if not all, I/O packages could be written in Ada using its features for controlling absolute addresses, interrupts, and physical representation of data.

The Multi-Micro Programming Line

MML is a portable software tool set for developing concurrent distributed programs for multiple microprocessors. As shown in Figure 2, it consists of a program development tool set called the Multi-Micro Development System, or MMDS, written in Pascal and currently hosted by a PDP-11/34 and a run-time system, or RTS.

MML includes a language and a compiler for process and procedure definition, plus facilities for hardware configuration description, resource allocation, run-time system construction, debugging, and execution control.

The language: sequential and concurrent features. An MML program consists of a fixed number of processes called *sequences,* which start simultaneously, exist forever, and cooperate to accomplish certain specific tasks.

The communication and synchronization mechanisms of MML were determined by the following two requirements:

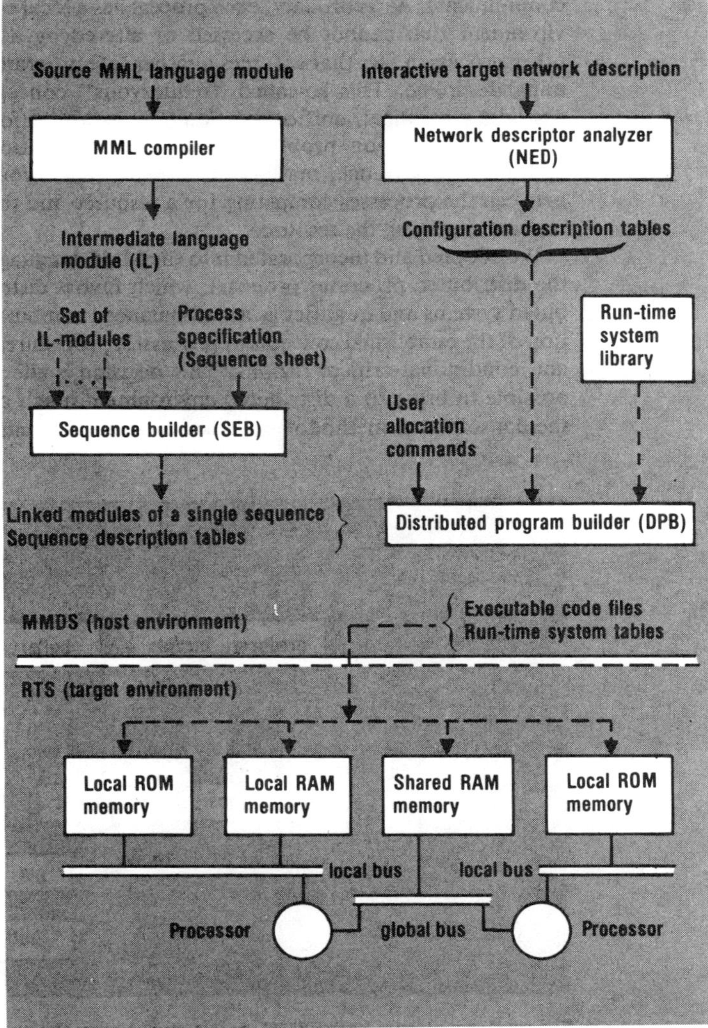

Figure 2. MML system overview.

- The design of the application software must be as independent as possible from the multiple-microprocessor architecture. The mapping of processes to processors, of data and algorithms to memories, and of logical to physical interprocessor channels is defined in the allocation phase following the design of application software. Therefore, the communication and synchronization mechanism must be efficiently implemented on a variety of architectures, ranging from multiple-microprocessor structures with shared memory to truly distributed systems.
- To simplify concurrent programming, one should choose either the global memory or the message-passing model of communication, but not both. We chose the latter in the "remote procedure call" form.

New proposals available at the time which seemed to satisfy the second requirement included communicating sequential processes,[17] distributed processes,[18] and Ada parallel tasking.[9] All three of them adopt a message-passing or remote procedure call model, with the fundamental property that synchronization and communication are considered two inseparable activities, that is, two processes need to be synchronized in order to communicate. As a corollary, each process has a local environment that cannot be accessed or altered by any other process, a fact that enforces a rather safe programming discipline. This so-called "rendezvous" concept provides a practical, unified solution to communication and synchronization problems. The mutual exclusion problem, for instance, may be solved by a rendezvous between the processes competing for a resource and the process managing the resource.

We adopted and incorporated into the MML language the distributed processes proposal, which favors distributed systems and qualifies as a well-balanced combination of the established concepts of processes, procedures, and conditional critical regions. This decision made it possible to bring to a distributed environment much of the consolidated methodology of global environments. Moreover, the notion of distributed processes is rather simple to graft onto an existing sequential language and does not require overwhelming run-time support. This decision, nevertheless, will be reconsidered after additional experimentation.

In Figure 3, sequences "producer" and "consumer" access a common data structure, managed in mutual exclusion by a sequence "buffer." Each sequence is made of one or more separately compilable modules, as described in a *sequence sheet*.

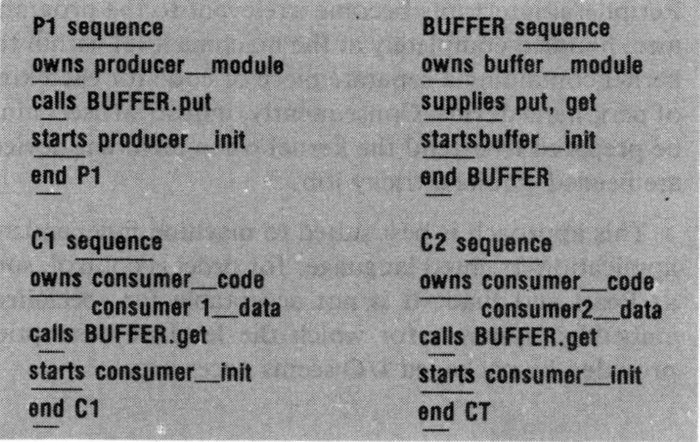

Figure 3. Sequence sheets defining four processes: one producer (P1), two consumers (C1, C2), and one communication buffer (BUFFER).

The sequence sheet also lists:

- the controlled procedures it supplies (these procedures can be invoked by other sequences);
- the controlled procedures belonging to other sequences that the sequence calls; and,
- optionally, the initial procedure that begins execution of the sequence at system start-up. If the indication is missing, the sequence remains idle until one of its controlled procedures is invoked by another sequence.

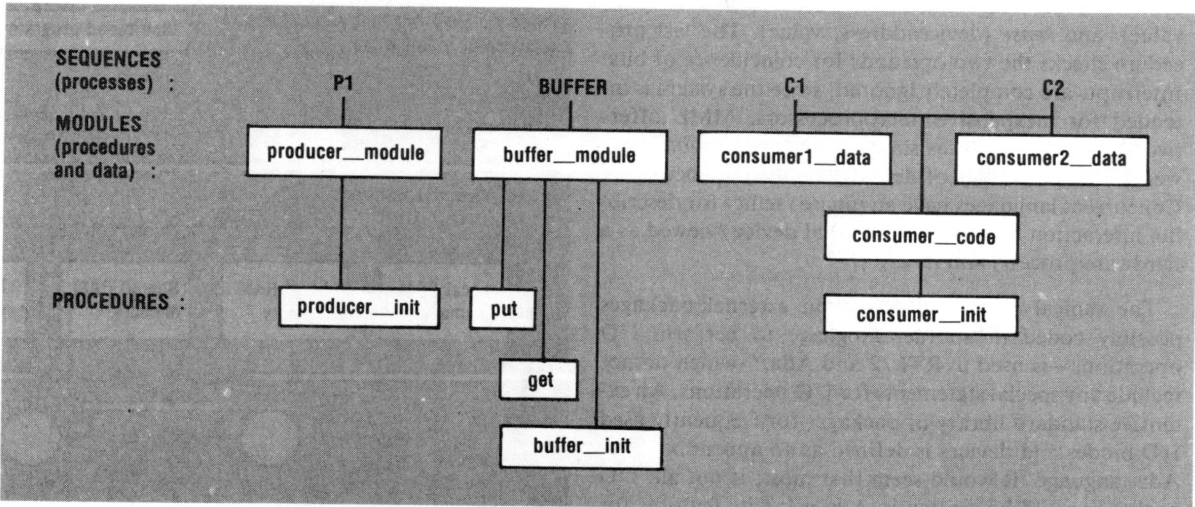

Figure 4. As shown in the MML program scheme above, the consumer_code module is replicated in two sequences. It can be shared, if it is a reentrant module with no global data and if it is allocated to a shared memory bank.

The essential aspects of the modules are illustrated in the box below. More instances of the same sequence type can be created by replicating the modules, as indicated in Figure 4. A *family* of almost identical processes can also be introduced as an array of sequences (e.g., producer(i) denotes a sequence in a family of producers).

Control of peripheral devices under interrupt is performed by special sequences called *drivers*. Communication between drivers and peripheral devices follows the same scheme used for communication between sequences; a peripheral device may be considered as a hardware "device sequence" whose controlled procedures, invoked by the corresponding driver, are the elementary I/O commands by which the device is operated.

I/O commands are the built-in procedures:

```
in (register-address : word) returns (datum : byte)
out (register-address : word, datum : byte)
```

Addresses passed to in and out are absolute, but their resolution can be deferred until after the target hardware is selected during the network description and DPB phase (see Figure 2).

A driver sequence usually supplies controlled procedures, to be called by other sequences in order to communicate with the driver, and one or more interrupt procedures. An *interrupt procedure* is "called" by the device sequence through a designated interrupt signal and performs the interrupt handling operations. As an example, see the input driver illustrated in the box on p. 156.

Our choice of a sequential language, for the reasons expressed earlier, was the machine-oriented system language PLZ-SYS,[3] a simplified and modularized Pascal. Because we did not rely heavily on any particular features of the selected language, the design philosophy of MML—if not the actual language translator—can easily accommodate a different language choice.

Procedure and data sheets in MML

```
producer__module module
internal item:byte
  . . .
global
 producer__init procedure
 entry. . .
      BUFFER.put (item)
      . . .
end
. . .
end producer__module

consumer__code module
external item:byte !from consumer__data!
  . . .
global
 consumer__init procedure
 entry. . .
      item: =BUFFER.get
      . . .
 end
 . . .
 end consumer__code

buffer__module module
constant N=10
type portion:byte
internal IN, OUT, COUNT : integer; B : array [N] portion
global
  put controlled procedure (C : portion)
  entry
     if COUNT <N then B [IN] :=C ; IN :=(IN +1)mod N
                        COUNT := COUNT + 1
     else
       retest ! wait for space available in the BUFFER!
       fi
  end put
global
  get controlled procedure returns (C : portion)
  entry
     if COUNT>0 then C :=B[OUT] ; OUT := (OUT + 1) mod N
                        COUNT := COUNT - 1
  else
        retest !wait for item available in the BUFFER!
     fi
  end get
global
  buffer__init procedure
  entry
       IN := OUT := COUNT :=0
  end buffer__init
end buffer__module
```

Sequence BUFFER controls the message exchange between sequences by supplying procedures "put" and "get" (defined in "buffer__module"). This sequence initiates by executing procedure "init__buffer" which completes its action and terminates. From then on, the sequence performs "put" and "get" operations as a result of external requests. Procedures such as "put" and "get" are called *controlled* procedures.

The producer P1 calls the procedure "put" to send a message to BUFFER, and it waits until BUFFER completes execution of this procedure. Execution of "put" can be completed if the condition COUNT<N is statisfied; otherwise, the operation is suspended by the retest statement. The operation will be resumed by the BUFFER when the condition becomes true as the result of the operation "get."

Sequences C1 and C2 (consumers) work similarly.

Note that BUFFER is similar to a monitor; it defines a shared data structure and the operations on it. These operations take place one at a time. After initialization, the sequence, as a monitor, is idle between external calls.

In view of our objectives, with the constraints of hardware available to us, PLZ-SYS was a reasonable choice. We readily recognized that PLZ could be easily extended to accommodate the requirements of interprocess communication and synchronization. In addition, the PLZ module is a natural unit for control of storage allocation.

Input driver in MML

```
KEYBOARD sequence
owns keyboard__module
supplies read
serves getchar ! interrupt procedure called by device !
starts init
end KEYBOARD

keyboard__module module
constant N=50; INTERRUPT-ADDR = ? !a deferred constant to be specified
                                  in the DPB phase !
         DATA__PORT__ADDR = ? !another deferred constant: the
                                 address of the device data port !
         CONTROL__PORT__ADDR = ? !the address of the device
                                 control port!
internal BUFFER : array [N] byte
         INPTR, OUTPTR, FULL : integer
global
         read controlled procedure returns (char : byte)
         entry
              if FULL50 then CHAR :=BUFFER [OUTPTR]; OUTPTR :=
              (OUTPTR + 1)mod NFULL := FULL - 1
              else retest ! wait for CHAR available !
              fi
         end read
         getchar interrupt (INTERRUPT__ADDR) procedure
         entry
              BUFFER [INPTR] := in (DATA__PORT__ADDR) ! reads a byte
              from  data port!
              INPTR : = (INPTR + 1) mod N
              FULL := FULL + 1
              if FULL= n then retest ! wait for space available!
              fi
         end getchar
         init procedure
         entry
              INPTR := OUTPTR: = FULL := 0
              startdevice
         end init
internal
         startdevice procedure
         entry
              ! initialize the device !
              end startdevice
end KEYBOARD
```

Controlled procedure "read" is called by other sequences to communicate with the driver. If the buffer is empty, the "read" operation is suspended on retest; otherwise, the operation is completed and a character is taken from the buffer. In any case, "read" and "getchar" are executed in mutual exclusion. Priority is given to the execution of interrupt procedure "getchar" over "read" procedure to handle interrupts as soon as possible.

Program development tools and run-time support. The MMDS integrated tool set shown in Figure 2 was designed with third-generation features. The MML compiler translates a source language module to an intermediate machine-independent language. The binding among intermediate language-coded modules belonging to a sequence—or, more generally to a "link-unit"—is performed by the sequence builder.

The allocation of sequences to processors, of modules to memory banks, and of logical interprocess channels to physical ones takes place under user direction during the distributed program building, or DPB, phase. Clearly, this phase requires knowledge of the architecture and configuration of the target, information previously entered during the network description phase.

First, an architecture is specified, such as Tomp[19] as shown in Figure 5. Then, in a conversation driven by architecture description tables, the user enters configuration details about processors, memories, interprocessor channels, and I/O devices, as shown in Figure 6. Finally, in the DPB phase, the user maps application programs onto target units (Figure 7). The output of DPB is a set of executable programs (either IL-coded or machine-coded) and some run-time tables to be used by the executive. Code can be downloaded or burned on EPROMs.

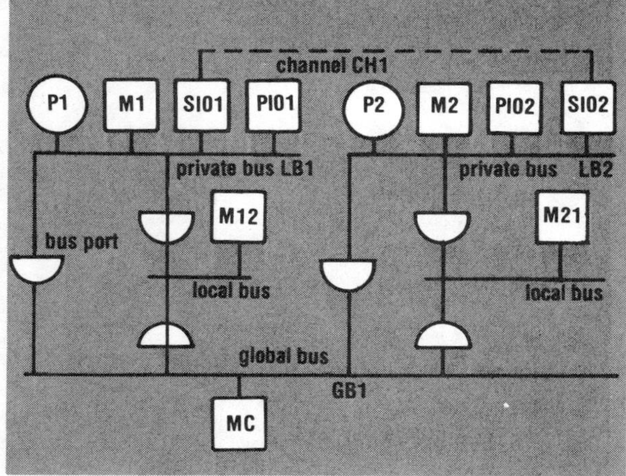

Figure 5. A two-processor prototype of Tomp architecture.

As indicated in Figure 7, intersequence communication is described at the logical level by channels. A channel can be handled by architecture-dependent (hardware + kernel) procedures and can be physically constituted by a shared memory bank, a serial line, or a local network. One such physical resource can be dedicated to a pair of sequences or shared by several such pairs. Mapping of logical channels to one or the other of the assumed communication facilities is decided by the application engineer or settled by default.

Another choice taking place during DPB is between code generation and interpretation of application programs. Since the same sequence occupies a different space when translated to IL or to machine-code, memory allocation is affected by the choice. To reduce the effort for producing generators for several machines, we are experimenting with the retargetable code-generation technique.[20]

The run-time system of each target processor includes a kernel, an IL interpreter or run-time library, debugging support, and execution control support. Their functions are:

- *Kernel*: first-level interrupt handler; sequence state transition; sequence scheduling; and intersequence and interprocessor message-passing.
- *IL interpreter*: execution of intermediate language or system routines generated by the code generator.
- *Debugging support*: breakpoints, tracers, enforcements of computational states, and interprocessor transfer of debugging commands and data.
- *Execution control support*: monitoring system operation and handling emergencies.

To achieve retargetability of the run-time system, we are redesigning it in MML with some parts—in particular, the IL interpreter and low-level mechanisms of

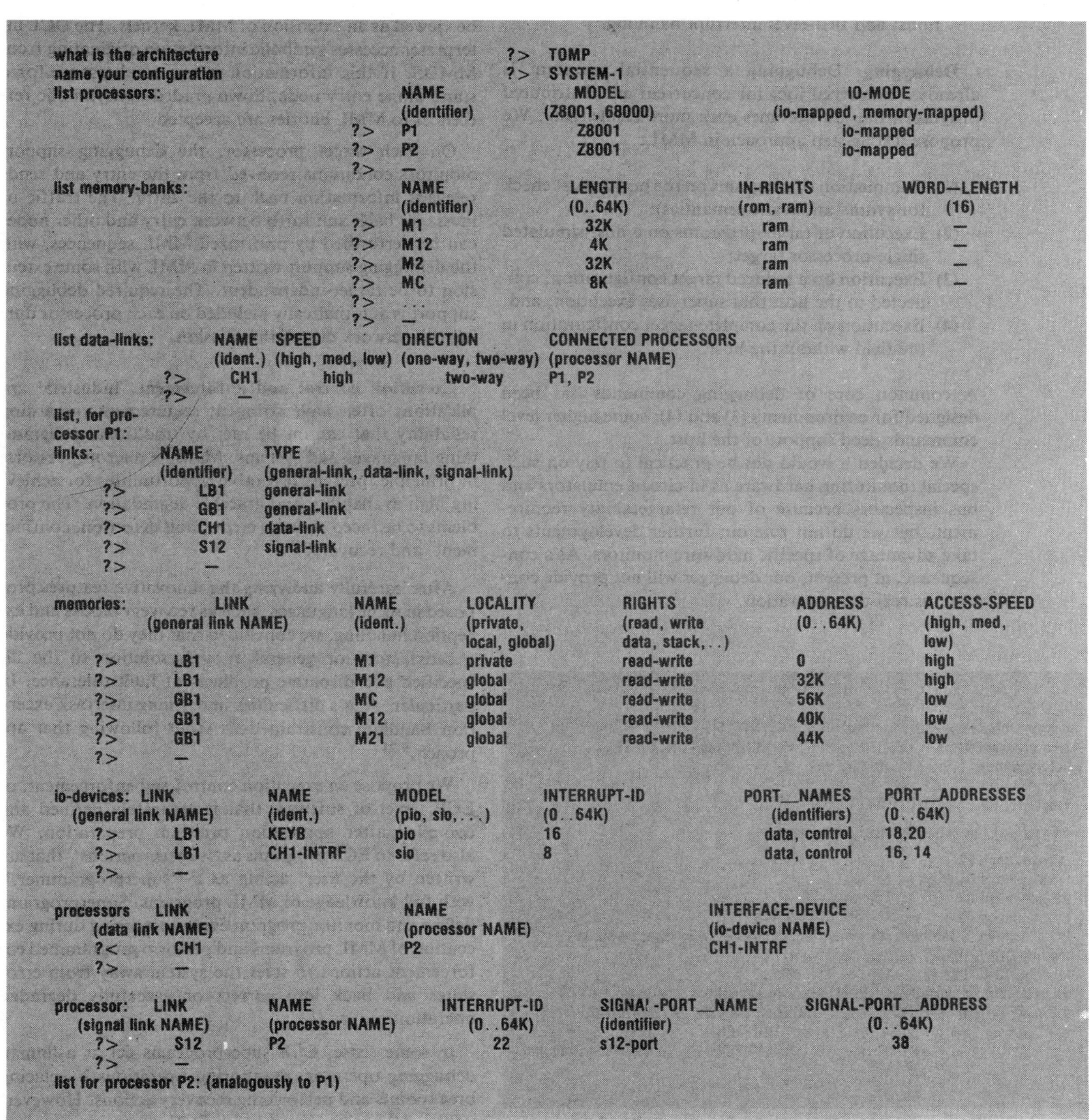

```
what is the architecture                      ?>  TOMP
name your configuration                       ?>  SYSTEM-1
list processors:           NAME                   MODEL               IO-MODE
                           (identifier)       (Z8001, 68000)      (io-mapped, memory-mapped)
                      ?>   P1                     Z8001               io-mapped
                      ?>   P2                     Z8001               io-mapped
                      ?>   —
list memory-banks:         NAME               LENGTH        IN-RIGHTS        WORD—LENGTH
                           (identifier)       (0..64K)      (rom, ram)       (16)
                      ?>   M1                 32K           ram              —
                      ?>   M12                4K            ram              —
                      ?>   M2                 32K           ram              —
                      ?>   MC                 8K            ram              —
                      ?>   . . .
                      ?>   —
list data-links:   NAME     SPEED                DIRECTION              CONNECTED PROCESSORS
                   (ident.) (high, med, low)    (one-way, two-way)     (processor NAME)
             ?>    CH1      high                     two-way            P1, P2
             ?>    —
list, for pro-
cessor P1:
links:       NAME           TYPE
             (identifier)   (general-link, data-link, signal-link)
      ?>     LB1            general-link
      ?>     GB1            general-link
      ?>     CH1            data-link
      ?>     S12            signal-link
      ?>     —

memories:        LINK              NAME      LOCALITY        RIGHTS             ADDRESS    ACCESS-SPEED
         (general link NAME)       (ident.)  (private,       (read, write       (0..64K)   (high, med,
                                             local, global)  data, stack,..)               low)
      ?>     LB1                   M1        private         read-write         0          high
      ?>     LB1                   M12       global          read-write         32K        high
      ?>     GB1                   MC        global          read-write         56K        low
      ?>     GB1                   M12       global          read-write         40K        low
      ?>     GB1                   M21       global          read-write         44K        low
      ?>     —

io-devices: LINK           NAME         MODEL          INTERRUPT-ID     PORT__NAMES     PORT__ADDRESSES
   (general link NAME)     (ident.)     (pio, sio,...)  (0..64K)        (identifiers)   (0..64K)
      ?>     LB1           KEYB         pio            16               data, control   18,20
      ?>     LB1           CH1-INTRF    sio            8                data, control   16, 14
      ?>     —

processors   LINK                  NAME                          INTERFACE-DEVICE
      (data link NAME)             (processor NAME)              (io-device NAME)
      ?<     CH1                   P2                            CH1-INTRF
      ?>     —

processor:   LINK          NAME               INTERRUPT-ID   SIGNA! -PORT__NAME   SIGNAL-PORT__ADDRESS
    (signal link NAME)     (processor NAME)   (0..64K)       (identifier)         (0..64K)
      ?>     S12           P2                 22             s12-port             38
      ?>     —
list for processor P2: (analogously to P1)
```

Figure 6. Network description session for the two-processor prototype in Figure 5.

the kernel—assembly-coded for efficiency. Kernels for different architectures will include only the modules required by the functions to be supported. The structure of the kernel is:

- *Level 4*: communication via routing of messages among processors (not implemented).
- *Level 3*: communication between sequences allocated to directly linked processors.
- *Level 2*: multisequence scheduling, debugging and execution control mechanisms, and communication between local sequences.
- *Level 1*: sequence concept and interleaving operations; and first-level interrupt handling.

Debugging. Debugging a sequential program is already a nontrivial job; for concurrent and distributed programs, the job becomes even more challenging. We propose a four-step approach in MML:

(1) Compilation of programs on the host (a first check for syntax and static semantics);
(2) Execution of target programs on a host-simulated single-processor target;
(3) Execution on a reduced target configuration, connected to the host that supervises execution; and
(4) Execution on the complete target configuration in the field without the host.

A common core of debugging commands has been designed for environments (3) and (4); some higher level commands need support of the host.

We decided it would not be practical to rely on such special monitoring hardware as in-circuit emulators and bus inspectors because of our retargetability requirement, but we do not rule out further developments to take advantage of specific hardware monitors. As a consequence, at present, our debugger will not provide continuous real-time operation.

```
give prototype configuration name : ?> SYSTEM-1
give program name                 : ?> PRODUCER-CONSUMER
list sequences to be executed by :
processor P1 ?> C1 , P1
processor P2 ?> C2 , BUFFER

do you want to choose memory allocation?

for sequence P1         ?> no
for sequence BUFFER     ?> no
for sequence C1         ?> no
for sequence C2         ?> yes
list allocation of the modules owned by sequence C2 to memory-banks:
module CONSUMER__CODE   to ?> M2
module CONSUMER2__DATA  to ?> M21
do you want to allocate private channels to sequences ?> yes
list        PRIVATE OWNER__1   PRIVATE OWNER__2   CHANNEL
     ?>           C1                 BUFFER        CH1
     ?>           P1                 BUFFER        on-memory channel
     ?>
```

Figure 7. A DPB session for the source program of Figure 3 and the target of Figure 5.

In a multi-microprocessor target, several parallel activities have to be monitored and reported to the debugger operator sitting at the host or at a specific processor of the target to be called the "entry" processor. Thus, we assume that the entry processor is directly linked via a channel to any other processor and to the host when the target is in the lab.

The main features of the debugging command language, a symbolic set of instruction for controlling execution (for inspecting and modifying variables, for tracing events, etc.), are listed in the box at right. The debugging system requires a DCL interpreter (host or entry resident) and run-time debugging support, which can be viewed as an extension of MML kernels. The DCL interpreter accesses symbolic information originating from MMDS. If this information is too cumbersome for a stand-alone entry node, down-graded nonsymbolic references to MML entities are accepted.

On each target processor, the debugging support monitors conditions received from the entry and sends relevant information back to the entry. The traffic of messages back and forth between entry and other nodes can be performed by prioritized MML sequences, with the debugging support written in MML with some extension to be target-independent. The required debugging support is automatically included on each processor during the network description session.

Execution control and enforcement. Industrial applications often have stringent requirements regarding reliability that cannot be met by traditional programming languages and systems. Multiple microprocessors, in principle, present favorable opportunities for achieving high availability and graceful degradation. The problems to be faced concern error/fault detection, confinement, and recovery.

After carefully analyzing the innovative features proposed in some languages, such as recovery blocks and exception handling, we concluded that they do not provide a satisfactory or general enough solution to the ill-specified and disparate problems of fault tolerance. In particular, Ada's difficulties in defining intertask exception handling constrained us from following that approach.[9,21]

We propose an execution control and enforcement, or ECE, level of software that is separately defined and compiled after application program preparation. We also refer to ECE programs as "superprograms" that are written by the user, acting as a "superprogrammer," with full knowledge of MML programs. Superprograms define and monitor program events occurring during execution of MML programs and perform programmed enforcement actions to steer the system away from error states and back into correct or gracefully degraded operation.

In some sense, ECE superprograms act as a human debugging operator, monitoring operations by placing breakpoints and performing recovery actions. However, unlike debugging commands, ECE superprograms are permanently present on the target.

ECE is still under design. It is an open-ended proposal for providing error detection and exceptions, checkpointing recovery, and mechanisms for implementing such known proposals as recovery blocks and triple-modulary redundancy.

Future plans. The first version of MML was completed at the end of 1981. The host environment is a PDP-11/34 under RSX. All tools are coded in OMSI Pascal.

This implementation produces executable programs for the Z80-based Mimp[22] architecture prototypes. Experimentation on the MML-programmed Mimp system is currently going on at the Politecnico di Milano. The same version also operates for Zeta boards,[23] an industrial set based on Intel 8085 processors.

A fuller version of MMDS and RTS, including debugging support, is in progress for 8- and 16-bit architectures, especially Tomp[19] and Modiac[24] boards, the latter a two-level bus architecture using Z8000 processors. Systems based on the LSI-11 are also being considered.

Like other industrial products, languages and programming tools can be examined with respect to their intended or actual markets, an issue clarified by considering the author or sponsoring organization.

The systems we have surveyed can be classified as

(1) technical proposals and demonstrative systems,
(2) proprietary systems distributed by manufacturers, or
(3) systems sponsored by industrial users or user associations.

The first group includes many innovative proposals, ranging from Concurrent Pascal to Modula. Some of them have been commercialized, but lack the support of manufacturers or large user organizations. None of these proposals are likely to have the incredible success of Pascal, a one-author language, because a complete multi-micro tool set requires much more than a language definition and a portable compiler.

The second group seems to be the more widespread, because customers tend to adopt software tools supplied by their hardware manufacturers. Intel's programming line for embedded microcomputer systems is a very well engineered example of a first-generation tool set based on high-level PL/M (or assembly) language and a RMX multitasking kernel, complete with practical resource-lending and debugging facilities. Quite naturally, systems in this second group are not portable. Quite frankly, it is not within the interest of their producers to encourage transportation to competing boards.

DEC's recently announced second-generation Micro Power Pascal also falls into this second category. Although it offers advanced facilities for prototype configuration control, the absence of specific tools for distributed computation does not qualify it for third-generation integration.

We are uncertain whether Edison, a third-generation system, should be considered as a proposal or as a manufacturer's supplied tool. As the latter, Edison would have a chance to conquer the lowest fringe of the market of multi-microprocessor systems due to its captivating simplicity.

Main MML debugging commands

Execution control commands:

- Step-by-step execution of an MML sequence (NEXT)
- Skip next statement of a sequence (SKIP)
- Suspend a sequence (SUSPEND)
- Resume the execution of a suspended sequence (RESUME)
- Restart a suspended sequence (RESTART)
- Remove a pending controlled procedure call (REMOVE)

Inspection and modification:

- Display the value of variables of a suspended sequence and assign new values to them (DISPLAY)
- Display the status of a sequence and the contents of kernel queues (STATE)
- Display the data collected during a TRACE command
- Display and delete debugging commands

Tracing:

Dynamic traces can be programmed to be displayed or stored on files or a local circular buffer.

Conditional commands:

Most DCL commands can be activated upon occurrence of specified conditions, which extend the lower level notion of breakpoint. Special care has been devoted to conditions related to concurrency.

Conditions in sequential operations:

(S1, S2 denote sequences; P denotes a controlled procedure; IP denotes an interrupt procedure.)

- S1 calls P of S2
- S1 receives return parameters from P of S2
- P of S2 starts executing for S1
- S1 enters a retest state
- S1 resumes from a retest state
- S2 starts serving IP
- S2 terminates serving IP

Conditions related with target hardware:

- Stack overflow
- Memory protect violation
- Parity error
- Transmission error
- Other conditions, depending on the target architecture

The third group includes new ambitious projects and some conservative products, such as RTL/2 and Pearl, based on earlier proposals. Pearl is being rejuvenated by the continuing support of the German community of process-control users. Its size qualifies it for the upper range of process-control applications.

Some of these third-group entries, initially designed for the private use of industrial firms, were taken over by software vendors all made available to third parties. Examples are Portal and RTL/2.

Ada is clearly the best-known entry in the third group. Its coverage of most software engineering concepts makes it a powerful and complex language. However, it is also clear that Ada was designed for one-processor systems or for homogeneous multiprocessors with shared memory. An EEC-sponsored study[25] is investigating the changes necessary to adapt Ada and APSEs to multi-microprocessors, as well as its suitability for industrial applications using 8-bit computers. Limitation on intertask communication must be enforced when Ada is targeted to distributed systems. In addition, APSE should be extended with target description and allocation facilities similar to those of MMDS. The latter, to our knowledge, is the only system providing complete independence of source programs from distributed target configuration and orientability toward different distributed architectures.

MML can be termed an evolutionary third-group product because of its experimental status and planned extensions. MML attempts to provide a reasonably practical tool set for programming distributed applications with as little departure as possible from today's practice. Simplicity of use and portability are its main concerns. It is expected to cover 8- and 16-bit multiple-microprocessor configurations, but it is not intended to be effective for larger machines.

Finally, we think that less ambitious tool sets—such as Edison, Demos, and MML—are likely to prove their continuing vitality for a few years, until low-cost computing resources and a widespread programming wisdom bring the wealth of Ada to every desk. ■

References

1. M. Boari et al. "MML: A Programming Line for Multiple-Microprocessor Systems," *Proc. Third Int'l Conf. Distributed Computing Systems,* 1982, pp. 680-688.
2. *PLM/80 Programming Manual,* Intel, 1977.
3. R. Conway et al., *Introduction to Microprocessor Programming Using PLZ,* Winthrop Publishers, Cambridge, Mass., 1979.
4. S. Crespi-Reghizzi et al., "A Survey of Micro-processor Languages," *Computer,* Vol. 13, No. 1, Jan. 1980, pp. 48-66.
5. C.A.R. Hoare, "Monitors: An Operating System Structuring Concept," *Comm. ACM,* Vol. 17, No. 10, Oct. 1974, pp. 549-557.
6. T. Martin, "Pearl at the Age of Five," *Proc. Fourth Software Engineering Conf.,* Sept. 1979 (Computer Society Order No. 249).
7. *Introduction to Micropower Pascal,* Digital Equipment Co., Preliminary Draft, Nov. 1981.
8. F. N. Krull, "Experience with Iliad: A High-Level Process Control Language," *Comm. ACM,* Vol. 24, No. 2, Feb. 1981, pp. 66-72.
9. *ADA Reference Manual,* proposed standard document, U.S. Department of Defense, July 1980.
10. P. Brinch Hansen, "The Programming Language Concurrent Pascal," *IEEE Trans. Software Eng.* Vol. 1, No. 2, 1975, pp. 199-207.
11. N. Wirth, "Modula: A Language for Modular Multiprogramming," *Software—Practice & Experience,* Vol. 7, No. 1, Jan.-Feb. 1977, pp. 3-35.
12. *Portal Reference Manual,* Landys & Gyr, 1979.
13. P. H. Droz and H. Jansson, "Micro-Concurrent Pascal Suits Real-Time Applications," *Electronic Designer,* 1981, pp. 117-122.
14. *Pascal+ Reference Manual,* Olivetti Advanced Technology Center, Cupertino, Calif., 1980.
15. B. Brinkman et al., *The Demos-86 Multiple Processor Computer,* Scicon Consultants Int'l, London, 1980.
16. P. Brinch Hansen, "Edison—A Multiprocessor Language," *Software—Practice & Experience,* Vol. 11, 1981, pp. 325-397.
17. C.A.R. Hoare, "Communicating Sequential Processes," *Comm. ACM,* Vol. 21, No. 8, Aug. 1978, pp. 666-677.
18. P. Brinch Hansen, "Distributed Processes: A Concurrent Programming Concept," *Comm ACM,* Vol. 21, No. 11, Nov. 1978, pp. 934-941.
19. G. Conte, D. Del Corso, and F. Gregoretti, "Tomp-80: A Multi-Processor Prototype," *Euromicro,* 1981.
20. R. S. Glanville and S. L. Graham, "A New Method for Compiler Code Generation," *Proc. Fifth ACM Symp. Principles of Programming Languages,* 1977.
21. I. C. Pyle, *The Ada Programming Language,* Prentice-Hall, Englewood Cliffs, N. J., 1981.
22. L. Mezzalira and F. Tisato, "An Approach to Modular Multicomputer Systems," *Euromicro,* 1979.
23. *Zeta Modules User Manual,* Zeltron automazione, 1982.
24. F. Bertora et al., "Sistema Modiac per l'automazione industriale: architettura del nodo di elaborazione," *Proc. Annual Congress AICA,* Italy, Oct. 1980.
25. *A Feasibility Study to Determine the Applicability of Ada and ASPE in a Multi-Microprocessor Distributed Environment,* initial report, TXT, CISE, and SPL, Milano, Italy, Oct. 1982.

A Security Kernel for a Multiprocessor Microcomputer

Roger R. Schell, DoD Computer Security Center

Security kernel technology can provide the technical foundation for a highly reliable method of protecting computerized information. However, to implement a kernel-based operating system for a microcomputer, we face two significant challenges: (1) providing adequate computational resources for applications tasks and (2) developing a clean, straightforward structure whose correctness can be easily reviewed. These were the challenges faced by the Computer Science and Electrical Engineering Departments of the Naval Postgraduate School in Monterey, California. As part of a three-year research project, our task was to explore realizations for microcomputer-based systems needing a high degree of security. The target implementation was the Intel iAPX 286 microprocessor, but running hardware was not available in time, and the Zilog Z8000 and Intel 8086 were chosen as interim implementations.

The systems envisioned emphasized shared file system controllers, signal processors, and a relatively static set of application programs, such as those for network processors. The wide range of required computational capacities led us to conclude that a system with multiple microcomputers must be provided. Our experience during this project, which began in late 1978, showed that the strictly hierarchical (loop-free) module structure provides a series of increasingly capable, separately usable operating system subsets. Performance issues evaluated include process switching, domain changing, and multiprocessor bus contention. Overall, the implementation demonstrated the ability of a modern microcomputer to effectively support the security kernel approach.

Project overview

Security kernel technology (discussed in detail earlier in this issue by Ames et al.[1]) was identified as the only viable approach for achieving the required security. However, the security kernel approach had previously been applied only to medium- or large-scale processors with supportive hardware features, which in some cases (such as the Scomp*) were specifically designed to support a security kernel. Furthermore, a multiprocessor kernel had never been designed and implemented. Thus, the challenge of this project was to identify a viable security kernel structure for a multiprocessor system using a commercially available microcomputer.

The effort began with the design of a rather general family of secure operating systems not tied to any specific microcomputer hardware. After reviewing available and anticipated processors, we determined that the planned Intel iAPX 286 was the best implementation choice.[3] In fact, its hardware directly supports the processor features identified earlier by Ames as important: explicit processes, memory protection, and execution domains. Unfortunately, as mentioned earlier, running hardware was not available in time for project implementation. Therefore, we chose two specific family members using a less supportive hardware base. The results discussed here are from these two implementations, with emphasis on the kernel rather than the particular application.

A secure archival storage system. The first effort has come to be known as the SASS, or Secure Archival Storage System, project.[4] We chose the Zilog Z8000 microprocessor[5] early in the project because of the protection afforded by its two processor states—the "Normal" and "System" modes—and the imminent hardware memory management unit. The Z8000 was primarily an interim choice to provide hardware support for kernel security experiments, pending the availability of the iAPX 286.

*The Honeywell Secure Communications Processor, or Scomp, is discussed earlier in the article by L. Fraim (this issue).[2]

Reprinted from *IEEE Computer*, pp. 47–53, July 1983.

However, at the outset no bus interface hardware was available to permit a multiprocessor Z8000 configuration.

The SASS was our principal testbed for exploring security, implementation, and single-processor performance issues. Although not fully implemented, the SASS supervisor was designed to provide a comprehensive multiuser, multilevel, secure file-storage system. As designed, the SASS has a Z8000-based single-board computer sharing a single bus with storage and I/O devices. The SASS is designed to interface via bidirectional lines to a number of host systems, as illustrated in Figure 1. The SASS provides each host with a hierarchical file system, which can be used to store and retrieve files and share files with other hosts. This design allows the SASS to serve as a central hub for a data-secure network of computers with diverse security authorization for sensitive information. The SASS provides archival, shared storage while ensuring that each interfaced host processor can access only the information appropriate to its security authorizations.

Real-time image processing. The second effort involved the use of a tightly coupled multiprocessor for processing digitized infrared images in real time.[6] We selected the commercial Intel 16-bit 8612 single-board computer, which is based on the Intel 8086 microprocessor, because its instruction set is directly upward compatible with the iAPX 286. In addition, multiprocessor bus hardware was available as part of the 8612 single-board computer. Although the Intel 8086 provides little hardware support for security, the strong compatibility with the iAPX 286 permits confidence in security, once the design is moved to the iAPX 286.

The image-processing applications run directly on the security kernel, with no additional supervisor support required, because the application programs are basically static. A version of this kernel was completed with fully functional image-processing algorithms using actual (prerecorded) digitized infrared sensor data. In exploring alternatives for parallel processing partitioning, more than 20 cooperating processes have been run in various parallel and pipeline combinations on up to six processors. This experimentation has provided the principal testbed for exploring multiprocessor performance issues.

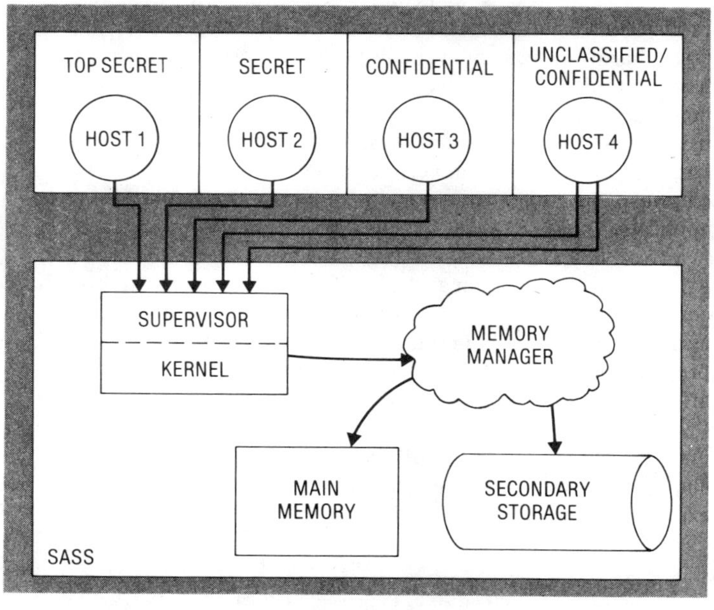

Figure 1. SASS system interfaces.

Design structure

Both the Z8000 and the 8086 implementations are but specific instances of the design for the same general family. For this family of operating systems the security kernel technology has been used not only to effect security but also to provide the underlying organizational framework for the operating system. The development experience has highlighted the importance of several features that are key to this family:

- the pervasive and systematizing impact of the security kernel methodology,
- the design simplicity accompanying a loop-free modularization that is highly compatible with the resource sharing and multiprogramming functions, and
- the significance of a high degree of configuration independence, particularly when using diverse microprocessors for testbed implementations.

Independent of security, this particular kernel structure is attractive as a canonical operating system interface. It appears adequate for a wide range of functionalities and capacities. Although specifically targeted for the iAPX 286, it shows a high degree of independence from hardware idiosyncrasies.

Kernel supervisor partitioning. Members of this operating system family are organized with three distinct extended machine layers (Figure 2): the security kernel, the supervisor, and the applications. The concept of a hierarchy of extended machines is, to be sure, not new; however, the security kernel significantly constrains the organization. In particular, for security reasons, all management of physical resources must be within the kernel itself. Furthermore, confidence is increased by keeping the kernel as small and simple as possible. Consequently, much of what is commonly thought of as the operating system is provided outside the kernel in the supervisor layer.

In the basic design for this family of operating systems, the kernel must provide extended virtual machines that specifically support both asynchronous processes and segmented address spaces. The kernel virtualizes processors, all levels of storage, and I/O, as well as creating virtualized objects—processes, segments, and devices. This "pure" virtual interface makes an attractive basis for canonical operating system features. The supervisor is in turn designed to be built on the kernel, using these virtualized objects to provide the usual functions of an operating system, such as a file system.

Both the kernel and the supervisor have certain responsibilities for system security. The kernel manages all physical resources, and the kernel is distributed (included) in the address space of every process. Isolation of the kernel—protection from users and the supervisor—must be provided by hardware-enforced domains. The design of the system is strictly hierarchical (that is, the kernel is more privileged than the supervisor), so the four hierarchical privilege levels provided by the iAPX 286 are an entirely satisfactory domain implementation. In the Z8000 version, the two CPU states are used to provide two domains. By exploiting the available hardware support, this kernel design avoids the need for any trusted processes.

The kernel is responsible for enforcing mandatory access limitations; that is, the kernel provides the mechanism for supporting nondiscretionary security policy. The kernel can support any policy that can be expressed by a lattice of access classes.[7] Every object—process, segment, or device—has a nonforgeable label that denotes its access class. This nondiscretionary security label has been assigned parameters such that exactly one module knows the interpretation of this label in terms of a specific policy. Thus, not only does the kernel support a broad range of security policies but only a single module has to be tailored to support a particular policy.

The design for the SASS supervisor provides the file structure and discretionary security (shared access within the bounds of the kernel's nondiscretionary policy) on the basis of individual user identification provided by the connected host. This discretionary security is completely outside the kernel, in contrast to the Scomp approach.

The SASS supervisor capabilities are achieved by associating two processes with each host link. These processes access the portion of the SASS file structure associated with that host. One of these processes provides I/O transmission and communication link management. The other, a file manager, is responsible for the file system structure for its associated host. Communication between these processes is achieved using shared segments as a mailbox (as is communication among all processes). Synchronization is provided because the kernel includes Reed's advance and await primitives.[8]

The complementary kernel/supervisor approach to security has several advantages for the SASS version. The size and the complexity of the kernel can be minimized, and if we have reliable authentication of the access class for the host, host weaknesses do not impact the reliable enforcement of the nondiscretionary security policy. Furthermore, with this approach, the same security kernel design can be used for the 8086 signal processing version, which needs neither a substantial supervisor nor discretionary security.

The security kernel approach constrains not only the interface but also the detailed design and implementation of internal state variables. One significant problem is preventing indirect information channels between processes with different access classes. This confinement problem can be addressed using essentially the approach detailed by Millen,[9] although without the rigor of a proof. Internal state variables, such as shared resource tables, are assigned an access class, and the design ensures that values will not be reflected to processes with an inconsistent access class. The most apparent result is that the success code (returned in response to the invocation of kernel primitives) reflects the state of the per-process virtual resources, not the shared physical resources. The same confinement problem requires a nonexclusionary approach to provide secure synchronization between processes of different access classes. The interprocess communication provided by Reed's event counts and sequencers[6] provides the solution to this "secure reader-writer problem."

Loop-free organization. A principal design property that has helped to keep the security kernel simple and understandable is the loop-free structure of the modules. The loop-free design supports the software engineering concept of "information hiding."[10] As a result, the SASS really does not have any global data structures. The kernel is internally organized into five distinct layers (Figure 3): (1) gate keeper, (2) segment and event managers, (3) traffic controller, (4) memory manager, and (5) inner traffic controller.

In practice we have been quite doctrinaire in enforcing the loop-free structure for the layers of this organization. While many operating systems claim to be modular or well-structured, our experience empirically validates this claim. The upper layers can be literally "peeled off" one at a time by removing the code and data. The remainder can then be loaded and run as a functionally intact, but obviously limited, operating system subset. Since the true substance of the system is in the lower layers, I will describe each layer from the bottom up.

Inner traffic controller. Processor multiplexing has two layers, similar to those proposed for Multics.[11] Each physical processor has a fixed number of "virtual processors" that are multiplexed onto it by the inner traffic controller. Two of these virtual processors are dedicated to system services: an idle process and a memory mana-

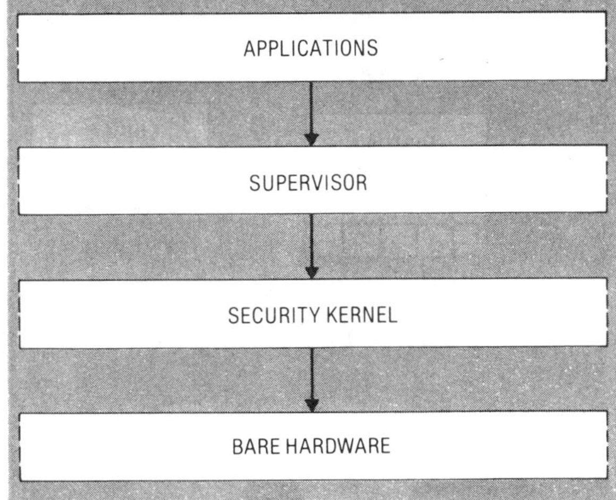

Figure 2: Extended machine layers. The security kernel significantly constrains organization, since for security reasons, all management of physical resources must be within the kernel itself.

ger process to manage the asynchronous access to secondary storage devices. The remaining virtual processors (currently two per physical processor) are available to the traffic controller (layer 3). The inner traffic controller provides primitives for synchronization between virtual processors. In terms of traditional jargon, we mean that the inner traffic controller provides multiprogramming by scheduling virtual processors to run on the CPU they are permanently associated with.

This structure implies that the security kernel is interruptible; that is, it is not a critical section. The inner traffic controller itself, however, is not interruptible. In addition, it provides all the multiprocessing interactions among individual physical processors, using a hardware "preempt" interrupt. An additional benefit of the strict layering is that the existence of multiple processors is visible only at this lowest level. Thus, the multiprocessing adds no difficulty to the design of the rest of the kernel.

Memory manager. This layer manages the multiplexing of the physical storage resources, such as the disk and core. It also manages the segment descriptors in the iAPX 286 description table for each process. (In the Z8000 design, the memory management unit provides the descriptors.) Most of the functions of this layer are executed by the per-CPU memory manager processes, with synchronization provided by inner traffic controller primitives. The single-board computers have per-processor, local memory that is addressable by only that one processor. Additional global memory is addressable by

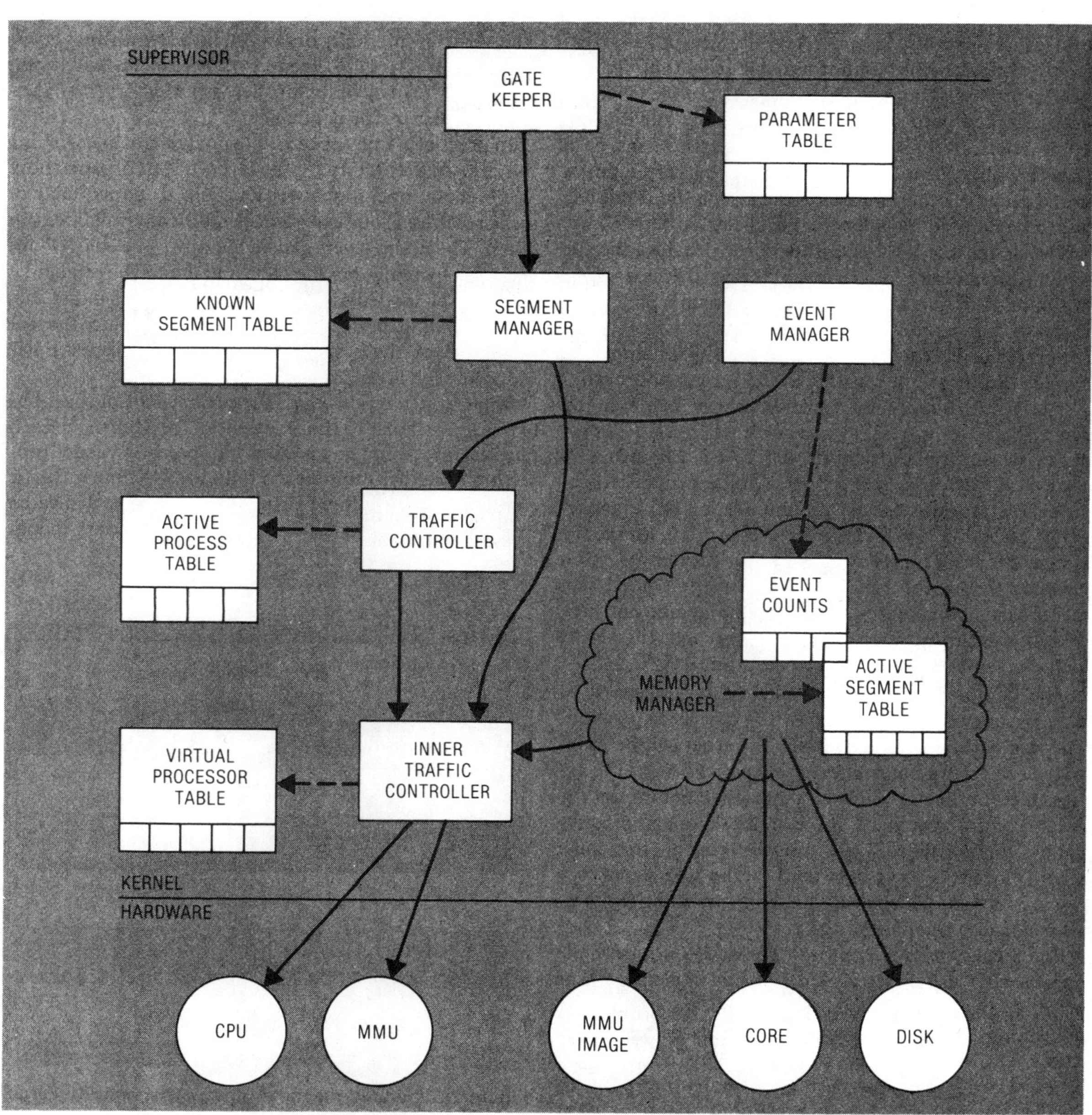

Figure 3. Internal kernel organization. The kernel has five distinct layers. From the top down are the gate keeper, the segment and event managers, the traffic controller, the memory manager, and the inner traffic controller.

all processes. The memory manager ensures that only shared segments (those needed by more than one processor) are in global memory. This policy can require some transfer between local and global memory, but this structure does minimize bus transfer requirements.

Traffic controller. The variable number of processes are multiplexed onto virtual processors defined by the inner traffic controller. Each process has an affinity to the physical processor whose local memory contains a portion of its address space at the time of the process scheduling decision. As indicated earlier, the traffic controller layer uses Reed's advance and await mechanism to provide secure interprocess communication.

Segment and event managers. All entries into the kernel pass through the segment/event manager layer. The explicit nondiscretionary security checks are made at this level by comparing the access class labels of subjects and objects. This layer uses a per-process segment table to convert process local names (segment number) for objects into systemwide names. In this kernel design, each segment has associated with it two event counts and a sequencer; thus, segment numbers also serve as the names used with the advance and await interprocess communication primitives. The segment manager provides for the creation and deletion of segments and their entry into and removal from a process address space.

Gate keeper. A process in the application or supervisor domain invokes a security kernel function using the traditional trap mechanism. A "system call" instruction causes a trap, and a gate keeper handles it. All parameters and return values are "passed by value" to simplify security validation. The instruction of the iAPX 286 for parameter verification provides further assistance in passing a parameter to the kernel. The gate keeper merely calls the particular procedure that corresponds to the requested function.

The implementation experience

The lessons learned up to now fall into three broad categories: the experimental testbed, programming (software engineering) experiences, and performance experiences.

Microprocessor testbed. One important aspect of this research was the actual implementation and testing of the concepts developed. Traditionally, the implementation of multiprocessor structures has been expensive. Today, however, sophisticated microprocessors such as the iAPX 286 are becoming available, which feature multiple domains, advanced segmentation addressing, support of multiprocessor configurations, and a standard bus configuration with peripheral support. With these developments, prototype implementation of advanced operating systems on a microprocessor base is economically feasible. As mentioned earlier, the Z8000 and 8086 processors were used in our testbed as an interim choice in anticipation of the iAPX 286.

In the 8086 kernel design, all the processors share the same bus; each processor is a commercial, single-board computer with on-board RAM. These processors also share a global memory and certain peripheral devices (Figure 4). This multiprocessor configuration was provided using the 8086 processors.

In general, security-kernel-based operating systems find three processor-supported execution domains (operating states) highly desirable—a separate domain for the kernel, supervisor, and applications layers. The Z8000 processor, however, provided only two domains (the "Normal" and "System" processor states).

The Z8000 hardware used for the SASS version was a single-board computer in a standard backplane. This configuration had a significant limitation in that it did not include the hardware memory management unit. Since we had to simulate in software the hardware segmentation, the kernel was not completely protected from the supervisor as the design specified. In spite of these limitations, we found the testbed quite effective as a research vehicle.

Programming experiences. This research effort was highly structured, emphasizing modularity at every opportunity. The software design is strictly "top-down," a matter of good design practice and necessity. Since most of the work was performed by a succession of graduate students, each of whom spent a brief six to nine months in research, the clear definition of distinct software modules has been vital to the success of the effort. We found that this high degree of modularity allowed the students to work on the project with a minimum of startup time, and a maximum of productive effort and learning.

The only access to the functions of the kernel is through the gate keeper. As mentioned before, the SASS supervisor has not been fully implemented. Consequently, the Z8000 kernel is a core-resident implementation that includes a simple external output primitive. To illustrate the nature of the kernel interface, all the kernel calls for the Z8000 kernel are shown in Table 1.

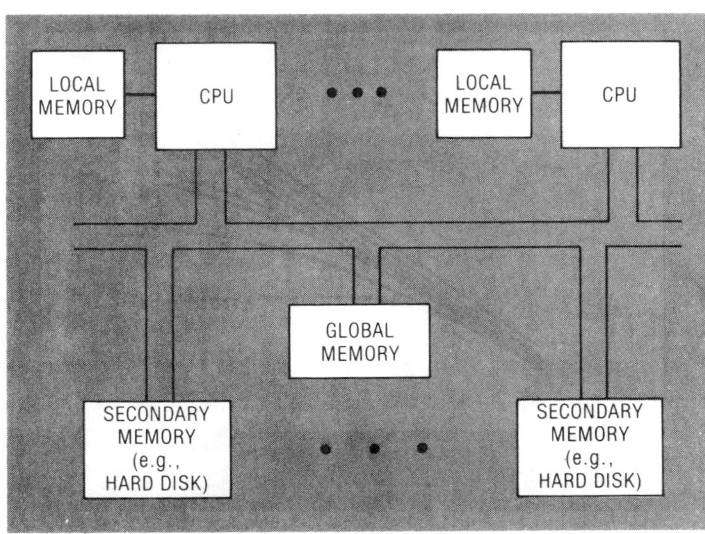

Figure 4. 8086 security kernel design. All processors share the same bus, a global memory, and certain peripheral devices.

The research goals of this project did not include verification methodology. However, we have thought about how the use of formal proof techniques could affect the design. In fact, as an experiment, we prepared a top-level specification of the kernel in a formal specification language, but without the aid of any supporting tools. This experience and the kernel's design to a formal nondiscretionary security model lead us to speculate that the kernel is indeed "verifiable." Verification would not immediately succeed, of course, but any problems discovered by verification would not require major changes to the design.

The actual implementation was essentially a bottom-up procedure, with test harnesses and stubs being written as necessary for testing. The modules were specified in a pseudolanguage resembling current high-level languages. The kernel for the 8086 multiprocessor was coded in PLM-86, a high-level language somewhat similar to PL/I. The high-level language had a definite positive impact on the time required for implementation.

For the Z8000, the modules were coded in PLZ-ASM, the Z8000 structured assembly language. We found that the pseudocode specifications of modules were adequate and that the translation from this code to the structured assembly language was straightforward. The structured assembly language of the Z8000 supported many of the constructs usually thought of as unique to high-level languages, including typed record structures, DO-loops, IF-THEN-ELSE, and CASE. In fact, our programmers thought of this assembly language as a high-level language. Approximately 40 percent of the statements in this implementation are directly equivalent to statements in modern programming languages.

Despite the qualities of the structured assembler, we selected it by default. When the decision was made, the prototype hardware boards were just becoming available and virtually no software support was available. In particular, no high-level language was available. The software environment was by modern standards very primitive, with no tools for operating system development—and it has grown slowly. Yet, this handicap was not significant. The Z8000 kernel was implemented as a core-resident kernel with no secondary storage devices needed to support segmentation. The size of the kernel significantly impacts the difficulty of verifying its correctness. For this implementation, the size of the kernel (Table 2) was considered small.

Table 1.
Z8000 kernel calls.

NAME	FUNCTION
Segment Manager	
Create _ seg	Create segment
Delete _ seg	Delete segment
Make _ known	Add segment to address space
Terminate	Remove from address space
Sm _ swap _ in	Make addressable in memory
Sm _ swap _ out	Make unaddressable
Event Manager	
Await	Process waits for an event
Advance	Signals occurrence of event
Read	Read value of an event count
Ticket	Obtain next sequencer value
Input/Output	
Sndmsg	Output message on serial link

Table 2.
Z8000 kernel size.

MODULE	SIZE (16-bit words) Code	Data
Inner Traffic Controller (includes initialization)	590	268
Memory Manager	742	1289
Traffic Controller	1384	243
Segment and Event Managers	804	---
Gate Keeper	114	---
Total	3634	1800

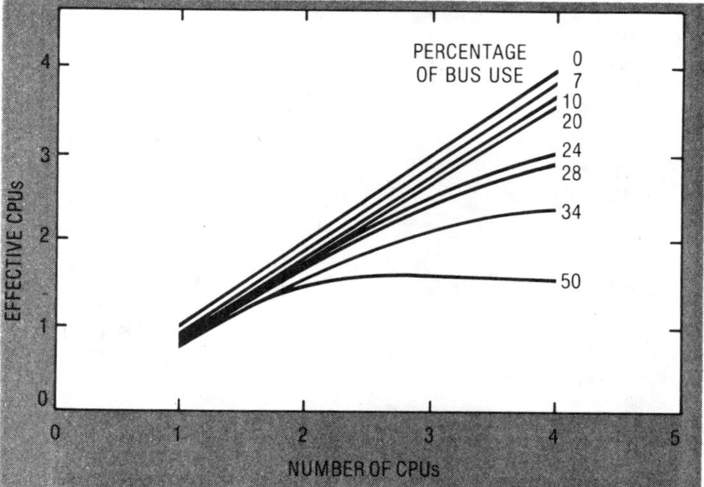

Figure 5. The performance of the multiprocessor system based on the 8086. If all code and data are located in shared global memory, even two processors would saturate the bus.

Performance issues. In programming the kernel, we generally treated performance as a secondary issue, in deference to more basic concerns such as security and modularity. However, we did address performance on a design level where it is strongly related to architectural choices.

Obviously, one basic design choice is the use of multiprocessing as a way to increase processing capacity. However, bus contention is a major performance concern in multiprocessor configurations, since all processors share a single bus. The actual performance for the signal-processing multiprocessor system based on the 8086 is shown in Figure 5 for various percentages of bus use. The figure shows, for example, that if all code and data are located in shared global memory, even two or three processors would saturate the bus. Fortunately, only shared, writable segments need to be in global memory. Our use of a purely virtual, segmented memory permits the kernel to determine exactly which segments are shared and writable. As noted before, the memory manager layer totally controls the allocation to local and global memory, and thus markedly controls bus contention by allocating segments to the processor-local memory whenever possible. Our experience with the signal processing applications is quite encouraging in that typically less than 10 percent of processor references are to global memory. Thus, a number of processors can be effectively used.

In the current implementation, we use the "Normal" and "System" modes of the Z8000 hardware, with the "System" mode dedicated to the security kernel. The domain change automatically generates a switch of the stack within the hardware. This automatic switching is particularly important to the efficiency with which we can switch domains while maintaining the integrity of the kernel. The iAPX 286 also provides this support for domain switching.

A process switch is achieved on the Z8000 and 8086 by switching the stack. The kernel saves the process history in the stack, so a process switch requires only the stack exchange. Preempt hardware interrupts between separate physical processors initiate scheduler changes and the associated virtual interrupts to the virtual processors. This sequence is relatively efficient given the hardware architecture. The iAPX 286 provides complete process switching in hardware for even greater efficiency.

The question of process-switching performance is more interesting in the context of processor multiplexing. The multiprogramming time is the interval from the time the inner traffic controller signal primitive is invoked in one virtual processor until a return from a (pending) wait invocation occurs in a different virtual processor. This interval includes both process switching and message passing operations.

For interprocess communication, the read and ticket calls from outside the kernel include a system call through the gate keeper to the kernel, the nondiscretionary security checks, and access to the event-count or sequencer value; however, no process switch is involved. The synchronization time includes the interval from the invocation of the system call for advance in one process until the return from a (blocking) await invocation in a different process. This interval includes the security checks and scheduling of both a virtual and a physical processor.

A set of measurements from the Z8000 implementation is summarized in Table 3. We made no effort to "tune" the system to improve performance, since these results are within our range of expectations for a single-chip microprocessor.

Table 3.
Z8000 performance measurements.

FUNCTION	TIME (milliseconds)
Multiprogramming signal/wait pair	0.5
Synchronization advance/wait pair	2.3
Read (Event count)	0.6
Ticket (Sequencer)	0.6

A modern operating system featuring kernel-based security, segmented memory, and multiple processors has been designed for the Intel iAPX 286 microprocessor. Initial testbed implementations on the Zilog Z8000 and Intel 8086 are finished, and preliminary data on the operating performance of such systems are encouraging. The focus on methodical design has paid off: The implementation of a carefully designed, simple structure using elementary software development tools has proceeded well.

Data gathered suggest that the security kernel is indeed an attractive structure for a modern operating system. A wide range of applications exist where sophisticated operating systems can be implemented on microprocessors, and performance levels are high, particularly when multiple processors are used. ■

Acknowledgments

I thank Lyle A. Cox for his most helpful participation in the project and his contributions and assistance in the preparation of this paper. The many long hours of creative and dedicated work by the students working on the project is also gratefully acknowledged.

References

1. S. Ames, M. Gasser, and R. Schell, "Security Kernel Design and Implementation: An Introduction," *Computer,* Vol. 16, No. 7, July 1983.
2. L. Fraim, "Scomp: A Solution to the Multilevel Security Problem," *Computer,* Vol. 16, No. 7, July 1983.
3. *Introduction to the iAPX 286,* tech. report 210308, Intel Corporation, Santa Clara, Calif., 1982.
4. R. R. Schell and L. A. Cox, "A Secure Archival Storage System," *Proc. Compcon Fall,* Sept. 1980, pp. 679-682.
5. B. L. Peuto, "Architecture of a New Microprocessor," *Computer,* Vol. 12, No. 2, Feb. 1979, pp. 10-20.
6. R. R. Schell et al., "Processing of Infrared Images by a Multiple Microcomputer System," *Proc. SPIE Symp.,* Vol. 241, 1980, pp. 267-278.
7. D. F. Denning, "A Lattice Model of Secure Information Flow," *Comm. ACM,* Vol. 19, No. 5, May 1976, pp. 236-242.
8. D. P. Reed and R. K. Kanodia, "Synchronization with Eventcounts and Sequencers," *Comm. ACM,* Vol. 22, No. 2, Feb. 1979, pp. 115-124.
9. J. K. Millen, "Security Kernel Validation in Practice," *Comm. ACM,* Vol. 19, No. 5, May 1976, pp. 243-250.
10. D. L. Parnas, "On the Criteria To Be Used in Decomposing Systems into Modules," *Comm. ACM,* Vol. 15, No. 12, Dec. 1972, pp. 1053-1058.
11. M. D. Schroeder, D. D. Clark, and J. H. Saltzer, "The Multics Kernel Design Project," *Proc. Sixth ACM Symp. Operating Systems Principles,* Nov. 1977, pp. 43-56.

Part V
Performance Evaluation

PERFORMANCE evaluation of a multi-microprocessor configuration involves two distinct components—evaluation of the microprocessor and evaluation of the interconnection network. We first consider the issue of microprocessor evaluation.

Until the advent of third-generation chips, microprocessor evaluation was easy. The instruction set was comprised of only about 50 instructions, and the timing figures provided by the vendors for common instructions (such as ADD and MULTIPLY) could be used to compare different chips. However, due to the growing sophistication in chip architectures and the fact that modern microprocessors are consciously designed to support and process multiple jobs concurrently, comparison of chips requires a comprehensive analysis of the computing environment and the jobs that can or will run in parallel.

This brings us to the issue of workload characterization. For the subset of chips that will be used in dedicated systems (e.g., on-line monitoring of processes), it may be feasible to accurately define input data rates. But the greater usage is in general-purpose systems—personal computers, word processors, desk-top computers—environments in which it is virtually impossible to define "typical" usage, especially since this parameter is heavily dependent on the speed and the flexibility of the system itself.

The above problem is further compounded in a multi-microprocessor configuration. Most multiprocessor models assume that all processors are identical, that the workload is equally distributed between all processors, and that there is no overhead involved in splitting up a job to make it run in parallel on an arbitrary number of processors. None of these assumptions is true, except in the case of a very small number of specialized applications.

On the basis of the above facts, the essential criterion should be the overall system productivity. If a user takes ten minutes to solve a problem using System X and an hour to solve the same problem using System Y, System X is six times as powerful as System Y, provided the particular problem represents a close approximation of the totality of the user's work function. Such broad productivity comparisons are rarely available.

To mitigate the above shortcoming, alternative measures are used in benchmarking exercises. The first paper of this part describes four different levels of evaluation and summarizes the performance characteristics of many popular microprocessors. An analytic model for evaluating multi-microprocessor systems is also developed in this paper.

In the second paper, Agrawal *et al.* discuss theoretical techniques for evaluating the performance of multicomputer configurations and the importance of different parameters of throughput and reliability.

Finally, Irani and Önyüksel discuss their development of a closed-form solution for a multiple-bus multiprocessor system. The graphs presented in this paper provide useful information for system designers.

After the analytic modeling stage, it is a general practice to develop simulation models before embarking upon the actual hardware integration effort.

Microcomputers in Industrial Control Applications

AMAR GUPTA AND HOO-MIN D. TOONG, MEMBER, IEEE

Abstract—**In their thirteen years of existence, microprocessor chips have evolved through four generations. Contemporary 16-bit and 32-bit microprocessors offer sophisticated architectures and powerful instruction sets. However, in many industrial applications, data rates are very high and the control structure has a decentralized configuration. In either case, multiple processors must be used. The major constraint in multiprocessor systems is usually the speed of the interconnection mechanism used for communication between the computing elements. This paper covers several of these issues. First, it compares and contrasts the performance of advanced microprocessors. Second, it discusses a split transaction protocol that mitigates the problem of overloading of the interconnection bus. Third, it describes an interactive tool to model multimicroprocessor systems. Overall this paper enumerates the steps involved in the design of efficient multimicroprocessor-based systems.**

I. INTRODUCTION

INDUSTRIAL ELECTRONICS applications involve data collection, data communications, and data analysis. In the early seventies, the advent of microcontrollers enabled these functions to be performed with fewer hardware components than before. As the sophistication of microcomputers improved tremendously over the past decade, their plummeting prices and increased flexibility have encouraged the use of microcomputers in virtually every conceivable application area, including areas requiring one or more of the following:

a) very high computational bandwidths and/or small response times;
b) high system resilience and fault tolerance capabilities;
c) ability to operate under adverse environmental conditions;
d) geographically distributed computing with an associated need for effective communication between centers;
e) storage and retrieval of large volumes of data within a pre-specified time period;
f) very close interaction between equipment and human beings.

This paper attempts to highlight the computing and communications aspects of contemporary microcomputers.

In general, any *computer,* irrespective of size, power, and capabilities, consists of a processing unit, some memory, and input/output circuitry. *Microprocessors* contain the central processing function (CPU) on a single silicon chip (sometimes several chips) holding thousands of transistors, resistors, and similar circuit elements [1]. *Microcomputers* contain the memory and peripheral control circuitry in addition to the CPU. If all these functions are implemented on a single chip, it is referred to as a *single-chip microcomputer.* Since a fraction of the chip area must be allocated for memory and peripheral support functions in single-chip microcomputers, these chips offer less processing power than single-chip microprocessors. In this world of increasing spectrum of 16-bit microprocessor chips, the task of selecting a particular chip involves evaluation of system performance at several levels as follows [8]:

era, to half a million today. The increase in the number of devices, accompanied by bigger and more powerful instruction repertoires, has enabled overall throughput provided by a single chip to increase by two to three orders of magnitude over the past twelve years [2].

Manuscript received June 20, 1983; revised December 15, 1983.

The authors are with the Sloan School of Management, Massachusetts Institute of Technology, Cambridge, MA 02139.

II. EVOLUTION OF MICROPROCESSORS

The microprocessor revolution represents a trend towards implementing all desired computer functionality on a decreasingly small number of chips [3], [4]. Single-chip microprocessors using 4-bit, 8-bit, 16-bit, and 32-bit word sizes were introduced in 1971, 1972, 1974, and 1981, respectively [5]. Availability of single-chip microcomputers of similar power lags by a couple of years. For example, the first 8-bit single-chip microcomputer, the Intel 8048, became available in 1976 four years after the first 8-bit microprocessor [6]. Similarly, the first 16-bit single-chip microcomputer, the Texas Instruments TMS9940, was introduced in 1981 [7], seven years after the first 16-bit microprocessor. To supplement the basic computing power, a whole spectrum of specialized chips ranging in function from memory management to direct memory access (DMA) control, have become available. The wide variety of chips and capabilities complicates the chip selection process.

Within a particular generation of chips, the performance and capabilities improve significantly with time. Table I summarizes these trends over the past seven years for 16-bit microprocessors. In this world of increasing spectrum of 16-bit microprocessor chips, the task of selecting a particular chip involves evaluation of system performance at several levels as follows [8]:

a) Instruction Level: Comparison of timings on an instruction by instruction basis as in Table II [2].
b) Routine Level: Comparison of timings and code sizes for sample user tasks. Two examples based on Booth's multiplication algorithm and a polynomial evaluation algorithm are summarized in Tables III and IV [8].
c) Support Task Level: Comparison at the level of sophistication of operating system support. Two examples based on the hash algorithm and stack manipulation are summarized in Tables V and VI [8], respectively.

Reprinted from *IEEE Trans. Ind. Electron.*, vol. IE-31, no. 2, pp. 109–119, May 1984.

TABLE I
SPECIFICATIONS OF 16-BIT MICROPROCESSORS NOT INCLUDING FUNCTIONS PROVIDED BY CO-PROCESSORS OR AUXILIARY CHIPS

	TI 9900	Intel 8086	Zilog-Z8000	Motorola 68000	NS 16032	Intel 80286
Year of Commercial Introduction	1976	1978	1979	1980	1982	1982
No. of Basic Instructions	69	95	110	61	82	121
No. of General-Purpose Registers	16	14	16	16	8	14
Pin Count	40	40	48/40	64	48	68
Direct Address Range (Bytes)	64K	1M	48M*	16M/64M	16M	16M
Number of Addressing Modes	8	24	6	14	9	24
System Structures						
Uniform Addressability	X	X	X	✓	✓	X
Module Map and Modules	X	X	X	X	✓	X
Virtual	X	X	X	X	✓	✓
Primitive Data Types						
Bits	✓	X	✓	✓	✓	X
Integer Byte or Word	✓	✓	✓	✓	✓	✓
Integer Double-Word	X	X	✓	✓	✓	X
Logical Byte or Word	✓	✓	✓	✓	✓	✓
Logical Double-Word	X	X	X	✓	✓	X
Character Strings (Byte, Word)	✓	✓	✓	X	✓	✓
Character Strings (Double-Word)	X	X	X	X	✓	X
BCD Byte	X	✓	✓	✓	✓	✓
BCD Word	X	X	X	X	✓	X
BCD Double-Word	X	X	X	X	✓	X
Floating-Point	X	X	X	X	X	X
Data Structures						
Stacks	✓	✓	✓	✓	✓	✓
Arrays	✓	X	X	X	✓	X
Packed Arrays	✓	X	X	X	✓	X
Records	✓	✓	✓	✓	✓	✓
Packed Records	X	X	X	X	✓	X
Strings	X	✓	✓	X	✓	✓
Primitive Control Operations						
Condition Code Primitives	✓	X	✓	✓	✓	X
Jump	✓	✓	✓	✓	✓	✓
Conditional Branch	✓	✓	✓	✓	✓	✓
Simple Iterative Loop Control	✓	✓	✓	✓	✓	✓
Subroutine Call	✓	✓	✓	✓	✓	✓
Multiway Branch	X	X	X	X	✓	X
Control Structure						
External Procedure Call	X	X	X	X	✓	X
Semaphores	X	✓	✓	✓	✓	✓
Traps	✓	✓	✓	✓	✓	✓
Interrupts	✓	✓	✓	✓	✓	✓
Supervisor Call	✓	X	✓	✓	✓	X
Others						
User Microcode	X	X	X	✓	X	X
Debug Mode	X	X	X	✓	X	X
Compatibility with other microprocessors	X	X	X	X	X	✓

*6 segments of 8M each
✓ indicates capability available, X indicates capability not available [2].

d) Application Level: Comparison of timings for entire applications. These comparisons, of course, are heavily application-dependent.

Useful comparisons of 16-bit microprocessors have been carried out, among others, by Toong and Gupta [8], [9], by Heering [11], by Grappel and Hemenway [12], [13], and by Rajalu and Rajaraman [14].

The growing availability of 32-bit microprocessors (Table VII) brings microprocessors into the performance bracket of mid-range systems like the VAX 11-780 (Table VIII). In fact, the architecture of these chips is specifically oriented towards real-time applications. These chips offer potential for both on-line data monitoring as well as for data manipulation.

III. MULTIPROCESSOR CONFIGURATIONS

In spite of their sophisticated architectures and powerful instruction sets, individual microprocessors do not offer enough throughput and resilience for all possible application environments. In several cases, multiple processors must be used to provide higher computational throughput, better system reliability, and enhanced system modularity. Many industrial environments are characterized by very high data rates and by a decentralized configuration of the process to

TABLE II
EXECUTION SPEEDS (IN MICROSECONDS) OF 16-BIT MICROPROCESSORS [2]

Operation	Data Type	Chips and Clock Frequency: TI 9900 at 3 MHz	Intel 8086 at 5 MHz	Zilog Z8000 at 5 MHz	Motorola MC68000 at 8 MHz	National NS16032 at 10 MHz	TI 99110 at 6 MHz
Register-To-Register Move	Byte/Word	4.60	0.40	0.75	0.50	0.30	0.50
	Double-Word	9.80	0.80	1.25	0.50	0.30	1.00
Memory-To-Register Move	Byte/Word	7.30	3.40	3.50	1.50	1.00	0.83/0.67
	Double-Word	14.60	6.80	4.25	2.00	1.50	1.33
Memory-To Memory Move	Byte/Word	9.90	7.00	7.00	2.50	1.70	1.00/0.83
	Double-Word	19.80	14.00	8.50	3.75	2.50	1.67
Add Memory To Register	Byte/Word	7.32	3.60	3.75	1.50	1.20	0.83
	Double-Word	21.30	7.20	5.25	2.25	1.60	2.00
Compare Memory To Memory	Byte/Word	9.90	7.00	7.25	3.00	1.70	1.00
	Double-Word	19.80	14.00	9.50	4.00	2.50	2.00
Multiply Memory-To Memory	Byte	21.90	13.00	20.25	N/A	3.50	4.17
	Word	21.90	23.00	16.00	8.75	5.10	4.17
	Double-Word	180.64	115.20	85.75	43.00	8.30	26.38
Conditional Branch	Branch Taken	3.60	1.60	1.50	1.25	1.60	0.50
	Branch Not Taken	2.90	0.80	1.50	1.00	0.80	0.50
Modify Index Branch If Zero	Branch Taken	7.60	2.20	2.75	1.25	1.30	1.00
Branch To Subroutine		7.90	3.80	3.75	2.25	2.00	1.00

Note that different chips use different clock frequencies.

TABLE III
MICROPROCESSOR BENCHMARK RESULTS—BOOTH'S ALGORITHMS [8]

S. No. Case	8086 Path length	8086 Time (clocks)	Z 8000 Path length	Z 8000 Time (clocks)	68000 Path length	68000 Time (clocks)
1 0×0	225	2112	182	1635	182	1869
2 −3×−5	534	2186	470	1673	470	1913
3 Worst case	214	2944	182	1827	182	1985
total (1)+(2)+(3)		7242		5135		5767
Performance relative to 8086		1.00		1.41		1.26

TABLE IV
MICROPROCESSOR BENCHMARK RESULTS—POLYNOMIAL EVALUATION [8]

Characteristic	8086	Z 8000	68000
Program size	33	27	17
Path length (instructions)	33	27	17
Time in 'clocks'	870	484	441
Performance relative to 8086	1.00	1.80	1.97

TABLE V
MICROPROCESSOR OPERATING SYSTEM SUPPORT BENCHMARKS—HASH ALGORITHMS [8]

Characteristic	8086	Z8000	68000
Program size (instructions)	24	26	18
Time in clocks	144 + 48*n	188 + 66*n	141 + 54*n

(where n is number of search through before an open slot is found)

TABLE VI
MICROPROCESSOR OPERATING SYSTEM SUPPORT BENCHMARKS—STACK EXERCISER [8]

S. No.	Table size	No. of tables	8086 Path length	8086 Time (clocks)	Z 8000 Path length	Z 8000 Time (clocks)	68000 Path length	68000 Time (clocks)
1	100	2	1838	18399	44	2220	436	5326
2	100	3	2751	27621	60	3332	648	7938
3	200	2	3638	36407	44	4236	836	10328
	Total (1)+(2)+(3)			82427		9788		23592
	Performance relative to 8086			1.00		8.42		3.49

TABLE VII
GENERAL CHARACTERISTICS OF 32-BIT MICROPROCESSORS [8]

	BELLMAC-32A	HP 32-BIT CPU	INTEL IAPX 432
YEAR OF COMMERCIAL INTRODUCTION	1982*	1982*	1981
TECHNOLOGY	2.5-μm DOMINO CMOS	1.5/1.0-μm NMOS	HMOS
NO. OF TRANSISTORS	146,000	450,000	219,000 ON 3 CHIPS
SIZE OF CHIP	160,000 MIL^2	48,400 MIL^2	100,000 MIL^2 EACH
POWER DISSIPATION	0.7 WATT AT 8 MHz	4 WATTS	2.5 WATTS/CHIP
PIN COUNT	63 ACTIVE 84 TOTAL	83	64 PER CHIP
BASIC CLOCK FREQUENCY	10 MHz	18 MHz	8 MHz
DIRECT ADDRESS RANGE (BYTES)	2^{32}	2^{29} REAL; 2^{41} VIRTUAL	2^{24} REAL; 2^{40} VIRTUAL
NO. OF GENERAL-PURPOSE REGISTERS	16 USER-VISIBLE	28 (NOT ALL GENERAL-PURPOSE)	NO REGISTERS VISIBLE TO USER
NO. OF BASIC INSTRUCTIONS	169	230	221
NO. OF ADDRESSING MODES	18	10	5

*Currently for internal use only.

TABLE VIII
EXECUTION TIMES [2], [16], [17]

MACHINE	LANGUAGE	WORD SIZE	TIME (MILLISECONDS) SEARCH	SIEVE	PUZZLE	ACKER
VAX-11/780	C	32	1.4	250	9400	4600
	PASCAL (UNIX)	32	1.6	220	11,900	7800
	PASCAL (VMS)	32	1.4	259	11,530	9850
68000 (8 MHz)	C	32	4.7	740	37,100	7800
	PASCAL	16	5.3	810	32,470	11,480
	PASCAL	32	5.8	960	32,520	12,320
68000 (16 MHz)	PASCAL	16	1.3	196	9180	2750
	PASCAL	32	1.5	246	9200	3080
8086 (5 MHz)	PASCAL	16	7.3	764	44,000	11,100
432/REL 3 (8 MHz)	ADA	16	4.4	978	45,700	47,800
80286 (8 MHz)	PASCAL	16	1.4	168	9138	2218
80286 (10 MHz)	PASCAL	16	1.1	135	7311	1774
HP 32-BIT CPU* (18 MHz)	PASCAL	32	NA	NA	7450	2590
NS 16032* (7 MHz)	PASCAL	32	NA	NA	24,000	9900

*Indicates experimental prototype.
**Indicates vendor-provided information.

be monitored. Consider, for example, the machine tool application shown in Fig. 1. There are several independent variables to be controlled and monitored as follows:

a) rotation speed of parts,
b) lateral movement of parts,
c) lateral position and angle of each of the cutting tools.

To increase productivity, it is essential that multiple tools must operate concurrently; also, at no instant should any tool interfere with another tool. Each of the independent variables can be monitored by a separate microprocessor, but the overall concurrency of tool operation will be determined by the ability to maintain noninterfering profiles. The latter aspect is dependent on the communication bandwidth between the computing elements. The overall performance of such multiprocessor configurations is affected by the number of processors, the communication mechanism among the computing resources, the characteristics of the computational workload, and the control program. Whereas the major constraint in single processor systems is the speed of the processor itself, the major constraint in multiprocessor systems is usually the speed of the interconnection mechanism used for communicating between the computing elements.

Fig. 2 shows an example of a multiple microprocessor-

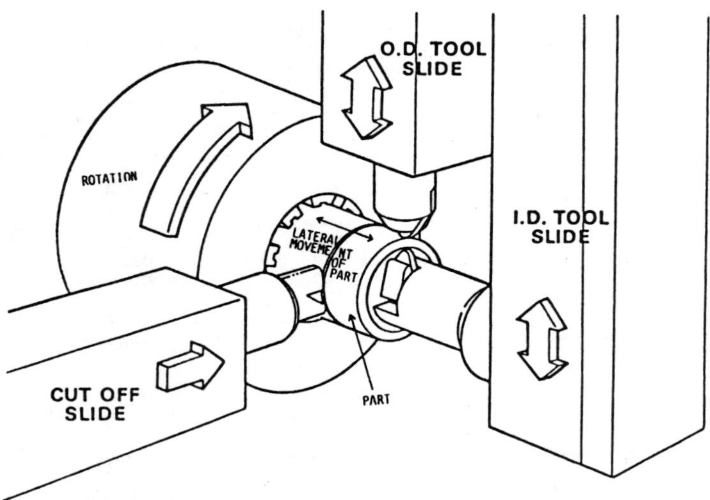

Fig. 1. A typical machine tool application with multiple tools.

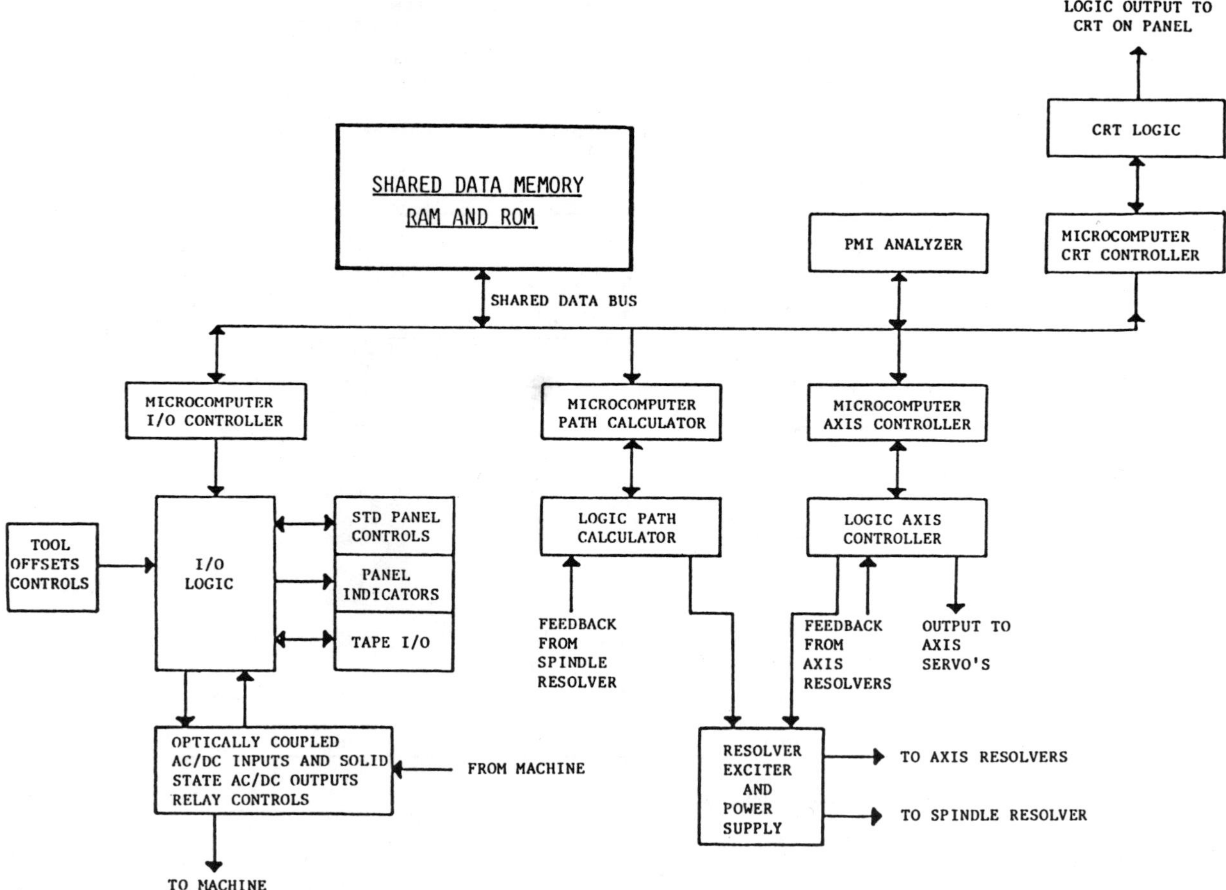

Fig. 2. Computer system configuration for machine tool application.

based multi-axis machine tool control that uses a shared common data bus. Machine tool throughput is limited not so much by the number of microprocessors attachable to the shared bus, but more by the utilization under load of the shared data bus and data memory. The memory utilization for two typical functions executed under the multi-axis machine tool control environment is summarized in Table IX. The total utilization figures have been broken up by principal microprocessor tasks. In each case, the program code resident in each microprocessor subsystem has been optimized to make minimum use of shared memory. For nonoptimized programs in which flags and status registers are maintained in shared memory, frequent accesses to shared memory are essential. This often has the undesirable result of driving up memory and bus utilizations to 70-90 percent. At this level, queuing contention will have a severe adverse impact upon system

TABLE IX
MEMORY UTILIZATION BY MICROCOMPUTER TASKS—MEASURED WITH A MULTICHANNEL LOGIC ANALYZER [32]

Tasks	Function 1: Drawing a Map	Function 2: Drawing a Circle
Axis control	0.064	0.073
Path calculations	0.061	0.061
Input-Output control	0.069	0.083
CRT control	0.009	0.011
Programmable machine interface	0.047	0.043
Total	0.25	0.271

throughput and response. In a programmed interrupt environment, when a microprocessor reads or writes information from or to shared memory, an interrupt is generated if the shared memory is being used by another microprocessor. This interrupt causes the microprocessor to cease normal instruction execution and to reference the shared memory again after some period of time. If the shared memory is utilized heavily, the microprocessor may receive repeated program interrupts. In such a case, the interconnection bus is handling a heavy load of repeated aborted memory references—this overhead is several times the bus usage for successful memory retrievals.

By convention, the interconnection mechanism in microprocessor systems is normally a bus structure which provides for transfer of instructions and/or data between the processing elements, the memory units, and the peripherals. Estimates of bus usage in several current systems are summarized in [15] and [31]. A single processor and a single memory causes bus utilization to be around 60 percent on the average. With more processors/memories, the bus becomes a performance bottleneck. Most designers opt for multiple-bus solutions. The resulting network is named on the basis of its geometry as a star [18], cube [19], hypercube [20], [21], hypertree [22], snowflake [23], cluster [24], and others [25]. In all of these cases, a few pairs of resources have direct links with each other, but other pairs must communicate via one or more intermediate nodes, thus introducing time delays and performance degradation. In the case of microprocessors, each additional bus mandates more pins on the chip (unless one resorts to multiplexing with its inherent performance limitation), and hence increased production costs. Often, additional buses will cause the number of pins needed by the microprocessor chip to exceed the limits of commercially feasible chip carriers. Thus, it is desirable to minimize the number of buses. A single central bus is the ideal solution provided it can handle the required communication load. In this paper, we develop a queueing model of such a bus, and use it to study an innovative protocol that offers high bandwidth and the ability to accommodate large numbers of concurrently executing microprocessors with minimal bus contention.

IV. DESCRIPTION OF MODEL

In a single processor system shown in Fig. 3, the number of message paths are ${}^3C_2 = 3!/2! = 3$. When several of such monoprocessor systems are connected together, any element of the system (CPU, Memory, or I/O) should be capable of communicating with any other element of the system (CPU, Memory, or I/O), and a typical two processor system, shown in Fig. 4, permits ${}^6C_2 = 15$ different message paths. It is obvious that, as the number of processors increases, the load on the interface increases sharply. If one provides a different bus for each path, the cost of such multiple-bus connections increases as the square of the number of processors. On the other hand, if only one bus is used, the contention problem between different messages may become critical.

In order to reduce the load on the bus, it is now becoming common for individual processors to have cache memories. On the other hand, the intelligence of I/O control units is increasing, and the dividing line between processor and I/O elements is becoming blurred. We categorize devices into two major groups.

a) Primary Processing Modules (PPM): These are elements with higher levels of intelligence; these elements *control* the operation of other elements. A traditional CPU is an example of a PPM. Another term for such modules is "masters."

b) Secondary Processing Modules (SPM): These are elements which control no other elements. A typical example is a memory. The operation of SPM is initiated and controlled by a PPM. Another term for such modules is "slaves."

In traditional single processor systems, there is one and only one PPM, and typically more than one SPM. In multimicroprocessor systems, there are several PPM's each "controlling" the functions of a number of other SPM's, in coordination with other PPM's. The term PM or Processing Module is used to represent an element which may be either a PPM or a SPM.

The term "message" is used in the literature to represent a wide spectrum of communication levels. In this paper, messages are considered to be of one of the following two main types.

a) "m-message" (short for macro-message): This type of message is initiated by any PPM, and includes the resulting supplementary processes and communications that are executed in response to this PPM's command. In general, an m-message will involve one or more PPM's, several SPM's, and a sequence of bus usages not necessarily immediately succeeding each other in the time domain.

b) "e-message" (short for elementary-message): Such messages require a single usage of the bus and involve only two PM's (both PPM's or both SPM's or one PPM and one SPM). An example of an e-message is a simple WRITE from a processor to a memory. Essentially, an e-message is the most elementary message communication between two processing modules.

In general, each m-message will result in one or more

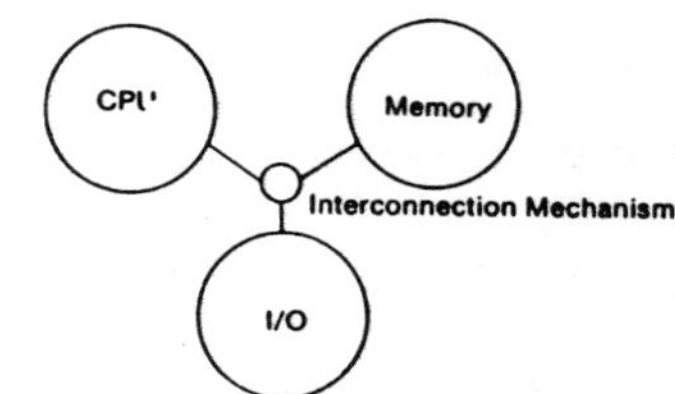

Fig. 3. Single processor system.

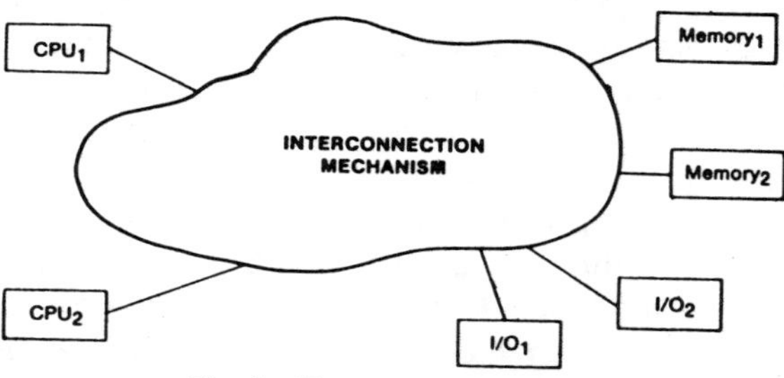

Fig. 4. Two processor system.

e-messages. A simple store instruction of type Register to Memory (direct addressing) will usually result in a single WRITE message that includes the value to be written. This is an example of an m-message resulting in a single e-message. On the other hand, a READ-MODIFY-WRITE sequence may be a single m-message, but would necessarily involve a sequence of e-messages.

The Interactive Multimicroprocessor Performance System, IMMPS, described in this section is an interactive analytic modeling tool that can be used to analyze any multimicroprocessor system with a central shared communication bus in terms of utilization factors, response times, queue lengths, and several other "customized" statistical parameters. Such networks with '*p*' primary processing modules and '*s*' secondary processing modules can be depicted as shown in Fig. 5.

An equivalent representation is depicted in Fig. 6. Here, an m-message is generated by a PPM and transmitted as an e-message on the bus to a pre-specified PM (PPM or SPM). After appropriate processing at this PM, another e-message may be transmitted to a specific PM via the bus. In general, this process is repeated several times, and a given PM may be accessed zero, one, or more times during the lifetime of a specific m-message. The m-message ends with either a reply to the initiating PPM (similar to an answer to a customer's query at an automated bank teller) or it just "dies" in the network after all the specified operations have been carried out. The total existence time of an m-message is analogous to the concept of system response time and will depend on the bus service time, on the PM service time (time taken for the processing), and on the wait time (waiting because the facility is busy) at both PM's and the bus. The model uses the following input data:

Messages:

- number of message types (either as e-messages or m-messages or any appropriate combination);
- the frequency (arrival rate) and priority of each message type.

System Configuration:

- the system configuration in terms of numbers of different PPM's and SPM's; details of similar PM's (e.g., memory units with same access time) have to be specified only once;
- the bus required to transmit a message (may be different for different messages);
- average processing time for each PM.

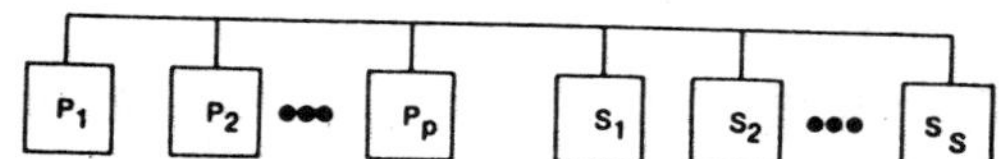

Fig. 5. Typical single bus multimicroprocessor configuration.

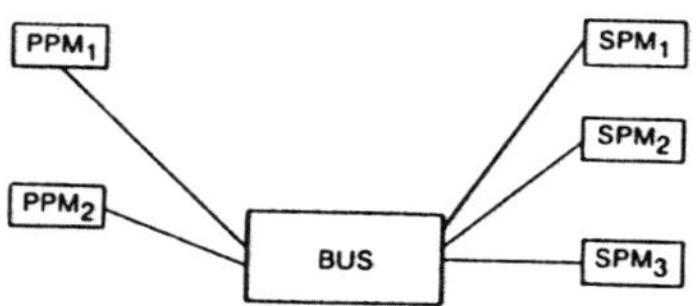

Fig. 6. Equivalent single bus multiprocessor configuration.

If the system is specified in terms of m-messages, the movement path of each type of message (number of requests to each PM) must be specified. For example, a credit query request may result in two accesses to a particular PPM and four accesses to a particular SPM.

The configurations indicated earlier in Figs. 5 and 6 can be represented by the open network incorporating a central model depicted in Fig. 7. This is a system with a single bus and multiple processing elements. The term "server" refers to any PM or to the bus. Each of the servers is represented by a circle, and the rectangle in front of each circle represents the queue of messages for that server. Different types of m-messages enter the system from terminals or conventional input devices and are then regarded as entitites which circulate through the network, making requests (e-messages) for processing from each server they encounter, and waiting in queues at times when they make a request to a busy server. Different messages may be assigned different priorities, or several messages may share the same priority. This affects their chances of getting the bus. An m-message may cause several e-messages involving various processing modules.

We analyze the performance of the multimicroprocessor system in a steady state. The bus service request from any PPM are independent of request of other PPM's, but may depend on a previous request from the same PPM. If the number of PM's is large, the total arrivals can be treated as Poisson distributed even though individual distributions are nonPoisson distributed [33]. As for service times, they are neither truly constant or exponentially distributed. In general, an e-message tends to have a constant service time and an m-message tends to have a variable service time which can be approximated as being exponentially distributed. Alternatively, an m-message can be analyzed as an aggregate of a group of e-messages with different service times.

On the above basis, the bus, under the m-message environment, can be considered to be an M/M/1 system where the first M(for Markovian) indicates that the inter-arrival times of the messages are exponentially distributed, the second M indicates that the service times required per message are also

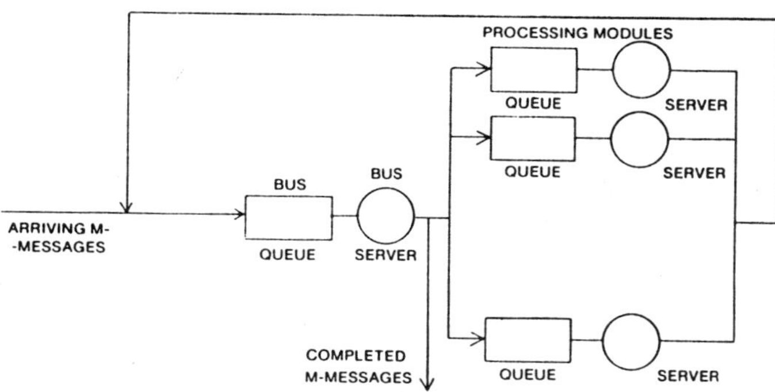

Fig. 7. The multimicroprocessor model.

exponentially distributed, and the 1 denotes the single (central) server. Even if the requirement for exponential distribution of timings is not satisfied, the following analysis still provides accurate results for systems in the steady state [34].

The following variables and indices are used:

- n — total number of processing modules in the system configuration,
- m — total number of message types,
- Index i — denotes a processing module ($1 \leqslant i \leqslant n$),
- Index j — denotes a message (m or e type) ($1 \leqslant j \leqslant m$),
- Index k — denotes a priority ($1 \leqslant k \leqslant l$) where 1 is the highest priority,
- a_{ij} — arrival rate of type 'j' messages at processing module 'i',
- a_i — total arrival rate of messages at processing module 'i',
- a_j — total arrival rate of type 'j' messages into the system,
- s_i — average service time of processing module 'i',
- I_{ij} — number of e-messages to processing module 'i' due to message type 'j' (if j represents an m-message, I_{ij} is a nonnegative integer; if j represents an e-message, the value of I_{ij} is either 0 or 1),
- $S_{\mathrm{BUS}j}$ — total bus service time for message j.

We consider the processing modules first. For an M/M/1 model, and a first-come-first-serve (FCFS) discipline, the following formulas are valid:

Utilization, $U_i = a_i \cdot s_i$ (1)

Expected Queue Length, $Q_i = U_i/(1 - U_i)$ (2)

Response time for an e-message, $R_i = S_i/(1 - U_i)$ (3)

Total module response time for an m-message of type 'j' due to module 'i' = (No. of e-message per m-message) × (Response time of the e-message) $= I_{ij} \cdot R_i$. (4)

Therefore, total response time for an m-message of type 'j' due to all 'n' modules is given by

$$R_{\mathrm{DEV}j} = \sum_{i=1}^{n} I_{ij} \cdot R_i. \tag{5}$$

The analysis for bus response time must include the impact of the priority assigned to different messages. The total number of discrete bus usages by m-message 'j' is

$$I_{\mathrm{BUS}j} = 1 + \sum_{i=1}^{n} I_{ij}. \tag{6}$$

(The term 1 is because an m-message commences with and ends with a bus usage—refer to Fig. 7.) The average duration of each bus usages by e-message 'j' is

$$s_{\mathrm{BUS}j} = \frac{S_{\mathrm{BUS}j}}{I_{\mathrm{BUS}j}}. \tag{7}$$

Note that $I_{\mathrm{BUS}j}$ is equal to 1 in the case of all e-messages. In order to evaluate the expected response time, the expected wait time must be calculated first. This wait is dependent on the priority of the 'j' message with respect to other messages in the system. We define

$$P_{jk} = \begin{cases} 1, & \text{when priority of '}j\text{' message equals '}k\text{'} \\ 0, & \text{otherwise.} \end{cases}$$

Then the total arrival rate of messages on the bus with a priority level of k is given by

$$A_{\mathrm{BUS}k} = \sum_{j=1}^{m} P_{jk} \cdot I_{\mathrm{BUS}j} \cdot a_j. \tag{8}$$

The bus utilization by messages of priority k is

$$U_{\mathrm{BUS}k} = \sum_{j=1}^{m} P_{jk} \cdot I_{\mathrm{BUS}j} \cdot a_j \cdot s_{\mathrm{BUS}j}$$

$$= \sum_{j=1}^{M} P_{jk} \cdot a_j \cdot S_{\mathrm{BUS}j}. \tag{9}$$

Hence, the average bus service time of these e-messages is

$$S_{\mathrm{BUS}k} \triangleq \frac{U_{\mathrm{BUS}k}}{A_{\mathrm{BUS}k}} = \frac{\sum_{j=1}^{m} P_{jk} \cdot a_j \cdot S_{\mathrm{BUS}j}}{\sum_{j=1}^{m} P_{jk} \cdot I_{\mathrm{BUS}j} \cdot a_j}. \tag{10}$$

Since we are considering the bus alone, we delete the word 'BUS' from the subscripts for the sake of simplicity. Let the probability of usage of bus by priority levels 1, 2, ⋯, l be given by $U_1, U_2, \cdots, U_l$. Thus, a message of priority 'k', $1 \leqslant k \leqslant l$, can contend for the bus during a fraction

$$\left(1 - \sum_{q=1}^{k-1} U_q\right)$$

of the total time period, and as such the response time will be proportional to the inverse of this fraction

$$\text{Bus Response Time } \alpha \ 1/\left(1 - \sum_{q=1}^{k-1} U_q\right). \tag{11}$$

Also, the priority 'k' request will have to compete with other priority 'k' messages. The wait time in an environment where all messages have the same priority for service is given by

$$w = \frac{a \cdot s^2}{1 - U}. \tag{12}$$

In case there are messages with different priorities and bus operation is on a pre-emptive basis, that is, service of a request is interrupted for servicing a newly arrived request with higher priority, the wait time for a message with priority 'k' is given by [35]

$$w_k = \frac{\sum_{j=1}^{m} \sum_{q=1}^{k} P_{jq} \cdot a_j \cdot s_j^2}{2\left(1 - \sum_{q=1}^{k-1} a_j \cdot s_j\right)\left(1 - \sum_{q=1}^{k} a_j \cdot s_j\right)}. \tag{13}$$

Adding the service time s_k to w_k gives the response time r_k for a message of any given priority.

The IMMPS model is a modified and expanded version of the central server queueing model developed in [26], [27]. It is an interactive tool that provides decision support in the design and implementation of multimicroprocessor systems. The formulas assume that there is no upper limit on the queue size, a fact never true in real systems. For M/M/l systems, the probability of the total number of messages in the system exceeding a given value is given by

$$p(N \geqslant \beta) = U^{\beta}. \tag{14}$$

The utilization of a service facility is generally designed to be 70 percent or less, as the response time degrades exponentially at higher utilization. Suppose $U = 2/3$. Then, if the maximum physical queue length is restricted to 10, the maximum value N can attain physically is 11 including the message being serviced. The probability of an error due to the infinite queue capacity is given by (14) with a β value of 12. This is

$$\text{Approximation Error} = \text{probability } (N \geqslant 12) = T^{\beta}$$

$$= (\tfrac{2}{3})^{12} < 0.78\%.$$

Hence, the error due to the infinite queue capacity assumption is very small in this case. If the queue length is set to 64 (not too difficult to realize), the probability of queue overflow becomes 2.4×10^{-12}, which is essentially zero. The result obtained with IMMPS matches very closely with results obtained using a companion simulation model for finite queue capacity analysis [28].

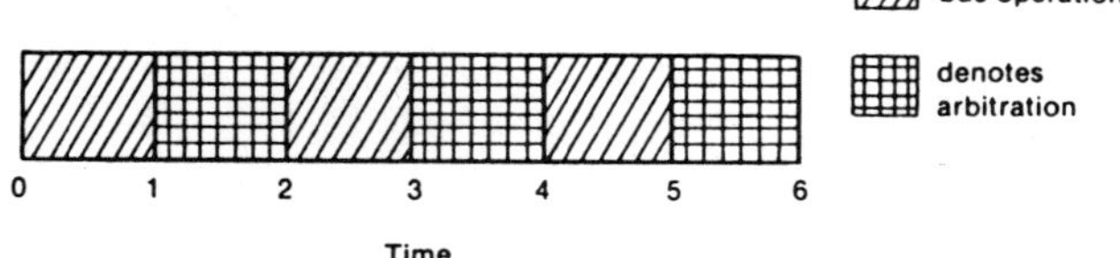

Fig. 8. Effect of arbitration cycle.

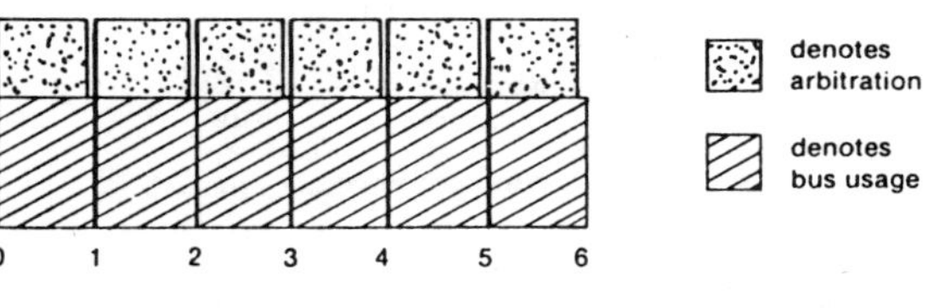

Fig. 9. Overlapped operation.

A. Arbitration Modes

In any real multimicroprocessor system, there will always be occasions when several PM's want to use the bus at the same time. In order to permit meaningful operation, there must be logic, either centralized or decentralized, to grant the bus to a particular PM. This process is called *arbitration*. Fig. 8 depicts a case where an arbitration cycle is carried out every time the bus becomes free. The arbitration cycle and the bus service time are each assumed to be one unit of time long. In this case, the bus is actually used for 3 units of time out of 6 units of time, i.e., for 50 percent of the cycles; during the remaining time, arbitration is in progress and the bus is forced to be idle.

One way to increase bus throughput would be to permit overlapping of bus operation and the arbitration cycle. Such a case is shown in Fig. 9. While the bus is being used, the arbitration unit decides the next PM to use the bus. As soon as the bus becomes available the PM starts using the bus, and the arbitration cycle starts afresh to decide the next candidate for using the bus.

In the case of fully overlapped operation, the bus is available for use at all times, and the throughput is not adversely affected by the arbitration overhead. In the case of nonoverlapped operation, the arbitration overhead is taken into account in the model by assuming the bus service time to be the sum of the actual bus service time plus the arbitration overhead.

B. Workload Characterization–An Idealized Case

Consider a multimicroprocessor configuration with 10 processors (PPM) and 10 memory units (SPM), all sharing a single bus. For this case, assume the memory service time (read/write) is 500 ns, and the bus service time is 100 ns. Assume that each processor makes 1.4 accesses to memory every microsecond, and all memory units are used equally on the average (i.e., a uniform distribution of processor requests to the 10 memories, as shown in Fig. 10).

In the specific case described above, there are 1.4 messages per processor per microsecond, or a total of (1.4 messages/processor/microsecond) $\times$ (10 processors) $\times$ 10^6 microsecond/second) = 14×10^6 messages per second. Using traditional

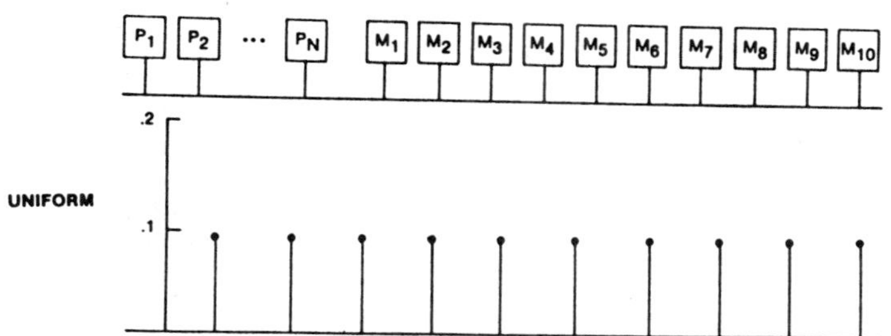

Fig. 10 Multiprocessor configuration with uniform workload.

TABLE X
SYSTEM IMPROVEMENT USING SPLIT TRANSACTION PROTOCOL

Number		Service Times		Memory Evaluation		Bus Evaluation		Response Time for a Memory Read Operation =(I)+2(II)
Processors	Memory Units	Bus	Memory	Utilization	Response Time (I)	Utilization	Response Time (II)	
5	5	0.05	0.5	0.2	0.63	0.2	0.06	0.75
10	5	0.05	0.5	0.4	0.83	0.4	0.08	0.99
20	5	0.05	0.5	0.8	2.5	0.8	0.25	3.0
24	5	0.05	0.5	0.96	12.50	0.96	1.25	15.0
20	10	0.05	0.5	0.4	0.83	0.8	0.25	1.33
10	5	0.1	0.5	0.6	0.83	0.8	0.50	1.83
60	10	0.02	0.1	0.24	0.13	0.96	0.50	1.13

The communication load is too large to be handled by a single bus, using traditional protocols, in all above cases. Each processor issues a memory request every 2.5 μs; all memories have equal probability of being assessed; all timings in microseconds.

methods of memory access, each message keeps the bus busy for (1 bus service time + 1 memory service time + 1 bus service time) = (100 ns + 500 ns + 100 ns) = 700 ns. Using these values of service time and message arrival rate, the IMMPS analysis indicates that the bus utilization exceeds 97 percent, causing an average wait time exceeding 12 μs, and the response time for each memory access is almost 13 μs.

C. Split Transaction Protocols

As the number of processing modules increases, the bus communication load also increases. In order to avoid the need for replicating single bus structures, several designers came up with innovative ideas. Haagens [29] and Toong *et al.* [30] proposed the "Pended" split transaction protocol that significantly increases the useful bandwidth of the bus structure. Unlike traditional methods of memory access where the bus is kept busy for the actual duration of bus usage and for the entire duration of memory service, the Pended protocol essentially keeps the bus busy for the actual duration of the bus usage only, and the bus is used by other processors during the memory service time. The memory units have high-speed input and output buffers and the bus is released after the memory request is latched from the bus into the input buffer of the memory unit. The data is transferred from the memory to its output buffer; the bus is then used to transfer the data to the requesting processor. The memory units must now contend with processors for control of the bus, and an additonal wait state is generated using an overlapped arbitration mode; the bus usage is fully optimized in terms of the useful bandwidth.

Consider our previous example of 10 processors and 10 memory units, but in the Pended environment (Fig. 10). In this case, the m-message consists of the following:

i) an e-message from processor to memory—bus service time of 100 ns;

ii) actual memory access—memory service time of 500 ns (bus is released during this entire period);

iii) an e-message from memory to processor—bus service time of 100 ns.

The IMMPS generated the following results:

i) response time for first e-message = 119.23 ns

ii) memory response time = 537.31 ns

iii) response time for replay e-message = $\frac{119.23 \text{ ns}}{775.77 \text{ ns}}$
total time for transaction
bus utilization = 119 + 119/775 = 27.78%.

It is seen that the Pended Transaction protocol drastically reduces the response time (from 13 μs to less than 1 μs) and the bus utilization from 97 to 28 percent. Analysis of other cases (Table X) shows similar benefits from using Pended protocol in other cases also.

A more formal mathematical treatment of split-transaction protocols is presented in [31]. Since bus speeds are typically ten times or more higher than memory speeds, such split transaction protocols, if designed and implemented properly, hold the potential of enhancing overall system performance by an order of magnitude.

V. CONCLUSION

Contemporary microprocessors offer tremendous computing power at minimal costs. The success of microprocessor-based system designs for industrial applications is dependent on several factors. First, the basic chip must be chosen very carefully. Second, for decentralized operations, the communications protocol must offer the required bandwidth. The symbiosis between high computing power and large communication bandwidth encourages use of contemporary microelectronics technology in many diverse application areas. This paper has demonstrated the use of elements of queueing theory to analyze alternative interconnection protocols.

REFERENCES

[1] H-M. D. Toong, "Microprocessors," *Scientific American*, pp. 66-77, Sept. 1977.

[2] A. Gupta and H-M. D. Toong, "Microprocessors—The first twelve years," *Proc. IEEE*, pp. 1236-1256, Nov. 1983.

[3] H. W. Lawson, Jr., "New directions for micro- and system architectures in the 1980's," in *Proc. Nat. Computer Conf.*, 1981, pp. 57-62.

[4] D. A. Patterson and C. Sequin, "Design considerations for single-chip computers of the future," *IEEE J. Solid-State Circuits*, vol. SC-15, pp. 44-52, 1980.

[5] A. Gupta and H-M. D. Toong, *Advanced Microprocessors.* New York: IEEE Press, June 1983, p. 1.

[6] R. N. Noyce and M. E. Hoff, Jr., "A history of microprocessor development at Intel," *IEEE Micro*, vol. 1, no. 1, pp. 8-21, Feb. 1981.

[7] J. Fattal, "Single-chip microcomputers—Cost effective solution to system problems," in *Proc. WESCON 1981*, session 17, paper 0, pp. 1-4.

[8] H-M. D. Toong and A. Gupta, "Evaluation kernels for microprocessor analyses," *Performance Evalution*, vol. 2, no. 1, pp. 1-8, May 1982.

[9] H-M. D. Toong and A. Gupta, "An architectural comparison of contemporary 16-bit microprocessors," *IEEE Micro*, vol. 1, no. 2, pp. 26-37, May 1981.

[10] A. Gupta and H-M. D. Toong, "An architectural comparison of 32-bit microprocessors," *IEEE Micro*, vol. 3, no. 1, pp. 9-22, Feb. 1983.

[11] J. Heering, "The Intel 8086, the Zilog Z8000 and the Motorola MC68000 Microprocessors," *EUROMICRO J.*, vol. 6, pp. 135-143, 1980.

[12] R. Grappel and J. Hemenway, "Evaluating the 16-bit chips," *Mini-Micro Systems*, pp. 152-162, Dec. 1980.

[13] R. Grappel and J. E. Hemenway, "A tale of four μP's: Benchmarks quantify performance," *EDN*, pp. 179-185, Apr. 1, 1981.

[14] R. G. Rajulu and V. Rajaraman, "Execution-time analysis of process control algorithms on microprocessors," *IEEE Trans. Ind. Electron.*, vol. IE-29, no. 4, pp. 312-319, Nov. 1982.

[15] I. Gerson, "Evaluation of microprocessor bus requirements for application to multiprocessor configurations," S. B. thesis, M.I.T., Cambridge, MA, May, 1976.

[16] P. M. Hansen *et al.*, "A performance evaluation of the Intel iAPX 432," *Comput. Arch. News*, vol. 10, no. 4, pp. 17-26, June 1982.

[17] David A. Patterson, "A performance evaluation of the Intel 80286," *Comput. Arch. News*, vol. 10, no. 5, pp. 16-18, Sept. 1982.

[18] H. D. Toong, "Micro-star—A microprocessor controlled distributed minicomputer network," in *IEEE COMPCON '77*, 1977, pp. 320-324.

[19] F. P. Preparata and J. Vuillemin, "The cube connected cycles: A versatile network for parallel computation," *Communicat. ACM*, vol. 24, no. 5, pp. 300-309, May 1981.

[20] L. D. Wittie, "Communication structures for large networks of microcomputers," *IEEE Trans. Comput.*, vol. C-30, no. 4, pp. 264-273, Apr. 1981.

[21] L. D. Wittie, "Efficient message routing in mega-microcomputer networks," in *Proc. 3rd Symp. Comput. Arch.*, Jan. 1976, pp. 136-140.

[22] J. R. Goodman and C. H. Sequin, "Hypertree: A multiprocessor interconnection topology," *IEEE Trans. Comput.*, vol. C-30, pp. 923-933, Dec. 1981.

[23] R. A. Finkel and M. H. Solomon, "Processor interconnection strategies," *IEEE Trans. Comput.*, vol. C-29, pp. 360-371, May 1980.

[24] S. B. Wu and M. T. Liu, "A cluster structure as an interconnection network for large multimicrocomputer systems," *IEEE Trans. Comput.*, vol. C-30, pp. 254-264, Apr. 1981.

[25] K. J. Thurber and B. M. Masson, *Distributed-Processor Communication Architecture* Lexington, MA: Lexington Book, 1979.

[26] S. E. Madnick, "BEST/S write-up," unpublished document, M.I.T., Cambridge, MA, 1981.

[27] J. P. Buzen, "Computational algorithms for closed queueing networks with exponential servers," *Communicat. ACM*, vol. 16, no. 9, pp. 527-532, Sept. 1973.

[28] A. Gupta, T. Abdel-Hamid, and H. D. Toong, "Comparison of results using analytic and simulation models," C.I.S.R. Tech. Rep. M.I.T., Cambridge, MA, 1980.

[29] R. B. Haagens, "A bus structure for multi-microprocessing," S.M. thesis, M.I.T., Cambridge, MA, 1978.

[30] H-M. D. Toong, S. O. Strommen and E. R. Goodrich II, "A general multi-microprocessor interconnection mechanism for non-numeric processing," in *Proc. Fifth Workshop Comput. Arch. for Non-Numeric Processing*, 1980, pp. 115-123.

[31] A. Gupta and H-M. D. Toong, "Increased concurrency in *m-n* multiprocessor systems," in *Proc. 3rd Int. Conf. Distributed Computing Systems*, (Miami/Ft. Lauderdale), Oct. 18-22, 1982, pp. 146-151.

[32] H-M. D. Toong and L. Evenchik, "Multimicroprocessors in industrial control," *Joint MIT-General Motors Reserach Study*, unpublished report, Apr. 1979.

[33] J. R. Jackson, "Networks of waiting lines," *Oper. Res.*, vol. 5, pp. 518-521, 1957.

[34] P. J. Denning and J. P. Buzen, "The operational analysis of queueing network models," *Computing Surveys*, vol. 10, no. 3, pp. 225-261, Sept. 1978.

[35] L. Kleinrock, *Queueing Systems*, vol. 2. New York: Wiley-Interscience, 1976.

Evaluating the Performance of Multicomputer Configurations

Dharma P. Agrawal and Virendra K. Janakiram,
North Carolina State University
Girish C. Pathak, Texas Instruments Inc.

Interconnections for multicomputers can be evaluated using such parameters as distance between nodes, number of communication links, degree of fault tolerance, and machine expansion capability.

As ever more powerful computers were developed, so did the demands made upon them (which is, of course, just an instance of Parkinson's law in action). However, there is a limit to the maximum speed obtainable from a computer based on a single processor. The closer we approach this limit, the more rapidly does the cost of such a computer rise. An alternative and radically different solution is to move from this uniprocessor architecture to a newer architecture employing the time-tested device of parallelism, i.e., using a number of cooperating processors. The concept underlying parallel architectures is not new. Nature is full of instances where seemingly powerless creatures, such as ants and bees, achieve incredible feats by collective endeavor. All modern technology is the result of joint human effort. In fact, this approach has another point in its favor: because of advances made in VLSI technology, it has become possible to fabricate cheaply many processors on a single chip. Undoubtedly, there are many problems to be overcome, some of which seem almost insurmountable. We will discuss here some of the most fundamental of these, and show the various ways in which these are being overcome.

A crucial decision that must be made in the design of such Multi-Computer Systems, or MCS, is the level of parallelism, or, in other words, the size of the subtasks that the original task is split into. Different design philosophies have favored different sizes.[1] Each has its own strengths and weaknesses. At one end of the spectrum is the Data Flow Machine, or DFM, where each subtask is a single operation. The DFM has a problem in the amount of the communication overhead involved as each processor sends or receives data from another. On the other hand, using large subtasks, while reducing this burden, involves another (nontrivial) problem of properly partitioning the given algorithm into reasonably sized chunks, and then mapping these resulting subtasks on the available architecture in the most efficient manner.

There have been many approaches to these new architectures that employ parallelism. In one of the simpler implementations, numerous relatively simple processors work on different sets of the data, performing the same set of instructions on each set. These processors will need to interact often in order to synchronize themselves. Alternatively, we can have processors working independently, interacting

Reprinted from *IEEE Computer*, pp. 23–37, May 1986.

only briefly and not very often. These processors can be geographically distant from one another.

The approach we discuss here takes a middle road. This architecture consists of medium-power processors (such as those used in single-board computers), which are physically close together so that they may communicate easily, via dedicated links or communication paths, but which at the same time work relatively independently of one another.

Flynn[2] categorized the various classes of computers based on the way they operate and handle data. These categories are: SISD (Single Instruction Stream, Single Data Stream), SIMD (Single Instruction Stream, Multiple Data Stream), MISD (Multiple Instruction Stream, Single Data Stream), and MIMD (Multiple Instruction Stream, Multiple Data Stream). The classification is fairly logical and self-explanatory. In this article we are concerned with MIMD schemes, where different processors work on different or multiple data schemes, with each possibly executing different instructions. It would be extremely useful to have a reasonable methodology to evaluate the performance of various MIMD schemes, and thereby provide a possible design tool for use in such systems. Thus far, new architecture designs have been done mainly on an ad hoc basis. There is a need to replace such intuitive techniques with some systematic methodology. Although the MCS can conceptually provide a linear speedup over a uniprocessor system, practical systems fall far short of this because of problems with mismatch between the algorithm and architecture, overheads associated with data management and communications, etc.[3]

What can be done to optimize the performance of an MCS? From a commonsense point of view, three factors that could have a bearing on performance come to mind: (1) the interconnection scheme that ties all the processors together, (2) the scheduling and mapping of the algorithm on the architecture, and (3) the mechanism for detecting parallelism and partitioning the algorithm into modules, or subtasks, which, when run on an MCS, will achieve a computational speedup. The last of these issues is quite involved, and space will not permit a summary that would do it justice.

Interconnection scheme issues

When several processors are required to work cooperatively on a single task, one expects frequent exchange of data among the several subtasks that comprise the main task. The amount of data, the frequency with which they are transmitted, the speed of their transmission, and the route that they take are all significant in affecting this intercommunication. The first two factors depend on the algorithm itself and how well it has been partitioned. The speed of transmission is a function of the hardware used and is not the point of the discussion here. In this section, we concern ourselves with the last factor.

Ideally, if one processor wants to communicate with another, then it should do so over a channel that directly connects the two. A channel between every pair of processors would yield a system that is most versatile. Given a sufficient number of processors, there would be little or no problems with scheduling. Such a system is undoubtedly the most desirable. It would also be prohibitively expensive. A channel between every pair of processors would require $\mathbf{O}(n^2)$ channels for n processors. For any significant n the total cost of these channels would swamp all other costs. We must, therefore, trade cost for speed and versatility. The compromise that is made involves routing data from one processor to another via intermediate processors, in cases where there is no direct link between the two processors. This has several repercussions. First, there is now an extra delay added in data transmission because of possible intermediate stages. Second, and perhaps more important, is the added capability that must be built into each processor that would allow it to perform this routing intelligently. The processor must know whether a block of data it has received is for itself or is en route to another processor, in which case it must forward this block to the appropriate processor, which could be the destination processor or another intermediate processor. And conversely, when a processor wishes to acquire data from another, it must know how and when to access this data. In other words, the processors must be aware of some routing and synchronization rules, and these should be, preferably, both simple and efficient. The interconnection scheme must take into account all these factors.

There have been many approaches that try to address this problem, viz., given these n processors, how to connect them in the most cost-effective manner.

Broadly speaking, a viable interconnection strategy (or topology) must have a small number of channels, and relatively easy routing rules. There are also such other considerations as fault tolerance: how to reroute data and recover gracefully in case a processor fails. Each of the schemes has been proposed with a certain class of applications in mind. Therefore, it would not be possible to directly compare these schemes as there is, in general, no "best" scheme. Instead, what we have is a number of schemes, each of which has its particular area of usefulness. With the range of possible applications in mind, the designer must choose the most cost-effective one for his purposes. Any evaluation of the performance of these schemes must be, to a certain extent, qualitative. However, once a few candidate networks have been tentatively selected, detailed (and expensive) evaluation including simulation can be carried out and the "best" one selected for the proposed application.

It is instructive to examine, at least qualitatively, some of the important characteristics of these interconnection schemes. We will first describe and define these characteristics and then evaluate various interconnection schemes vis-a-vis these characteristics. In what follows a distinction is made between two classes of interconnection schemes. *Link*-oriented structures or schemes comprise those interconnection schemes in which there is a dedicated link or channel available for data transfer between two computers that are to be connected. *Bus*-oriented structures consist of multiple buses. Each bus is shared by a group of computers; communication takes place in a series of hops, from computer to computer, via these buses.

Network characteristics. We now look at some of the considerations in the evaluation of interconnection networks. In all these networks, it should be emphasized that improving one parameter might adversely affect some other parameters: what is sought is an optimization of the network.

Average distance. One of the more important evaluative measures of an interconnection network is the *average distance.* This is the distance messages must travel, on an average, in the network. It is advantageous to make this as short as possible. The average distance (in terms of the number of links) is defined as:[4]

$$\text{AvgDist} = \frac{\sum_{d=1}^{r} d N_d}{N-1}$$

where N_d is the number of computers at a distance d links away, r is the diameter (maximum of the minimum distance between any two pairs of nodes), and N is the total number of computers.

For regular networks, i.e., those in which each computer is connected to the same number of other computers, the AvgDist is a constant. For irregular networks, the formula will yield different results, depending on the node from which d is measured. A network that has a low average distance may require an unreasonable number of communication ports for each computer. In order to distinguish these cases, a *normalized average distance* is defined[4] for link-based structures:

$$\text{NormAvgDist (link)} = \text{AvgDist} \times \text{Ports/comp} \quad (2)$$

where Ports/comp is the number of communication ports required of each computer.

In the case of bus structures, the distance d is the number of buses a message has to cross on the way to its destination. Also, the number of computers tied to a bus is of importance as several computers on a single bus may create bottlenecks due to bus contentions. To account for this, we define the normalized average distance for bus structures as the average distance weighted by the number of computers that may have access to a single bus.

$$\text{NormAvgDist (bus)} = \text{AvgDist} \times \text{Ports/bus} \quad (3)$$

Communication links. The total number of communication links in a network of given size is another useful measure. Clearly, among two networks, the one that has fewer connecting links is the more desirable, assuming (naively) all else is equal.

Routing algorithm. When a message is to be routed from one computer to another, the route it must take is obtained from the *routing algorithm.* It is desirable that the routing algorithm be simple and not require a complete knowledge of the entire network. In particular, it would be convenient if, by merely having the destination address, it is possible to obtain the exact—and preferably the shortest—sequence of computers the message must traverse.

Fault tolerance. If one of the computers along this route were to be faulty, then a breakdown in communication would result, and this could make any further computation pointless. To preclude such a possibility, networks must be fault tolerant. Fault-tolerant networks have at least one redundant path between any two computers; and these redundant paths are used in the case of a fault in a connecting channel. Another fault that is potentially more dangerous is the failure of a computer. Should such a fault arise, it is desirable that the system bypasses this faulty computer in all future computations and remain functional although possibly impaired. This "graceful degradation" feature is desirable in certain critical areas, such as space and military applications.

Expansion capability. Any large system must be capable of expansion in such a way that it causes a minimum of disruption of the existing setup. Clearly, a network that requires a complete rebuilding, with fresh demands on the number of communication ports of individual computers, every time extra computers are added is less preferable to one that can be extended in a natural way, without major upheaval of the entire system.

Link-oriented structures

In this section we analyze some link-oriented structures. The issues mentioned in the previous section are dealt with in seriatim.

The ring network. The ring structure is one of the simplest networks. The routing is simple and the structure has been well analyzed, mainly because, along with the star and tree networks, it is among the most popular of the topologies used in Local Area Networks, or LANs. The topology has also been used in a Dataflow machine architecture.[5,6] It consists of a number of computers connected in the form of a ring, i.e., each connected to its two neighbors. Although most LAN topologies use a unidirectional ring (i.e., one in which data flows in one direction only around the ring), because of its obvious problem of poor fault tolerance, we will assume a bidirectional ring.

> The routing algorithm of link-oriented structures is relatively straightforward, because of the simplicity of the network.

Average distance. The average distance is easily found to be $(N+1)/4$, for a ring of N computers, where N is odd. The case for N even is also easy to deal with, but the relations are not so neat. The normalized average distance is, of course, $(N+1)/2$, as there are two ports on each computer. This linear relationship means that the distance may become unacceptably large for large N.

Communication links. The total number of communication links is N.

Routing algorithm. The routing algorithm is relatively straightforward, because of the simplicity of the network. It is simplest for unidirectional rings and only slightly more involved for bidirectional rings.

Fault tolerance. The fault tolerance of the ring structure is questionable. If any node in a unidirectional ring fails, it may render the entire system nonfunctional. In a bidirectional ring the failure of two nodes will cause the same result. In order to alleviate this problem, several variants

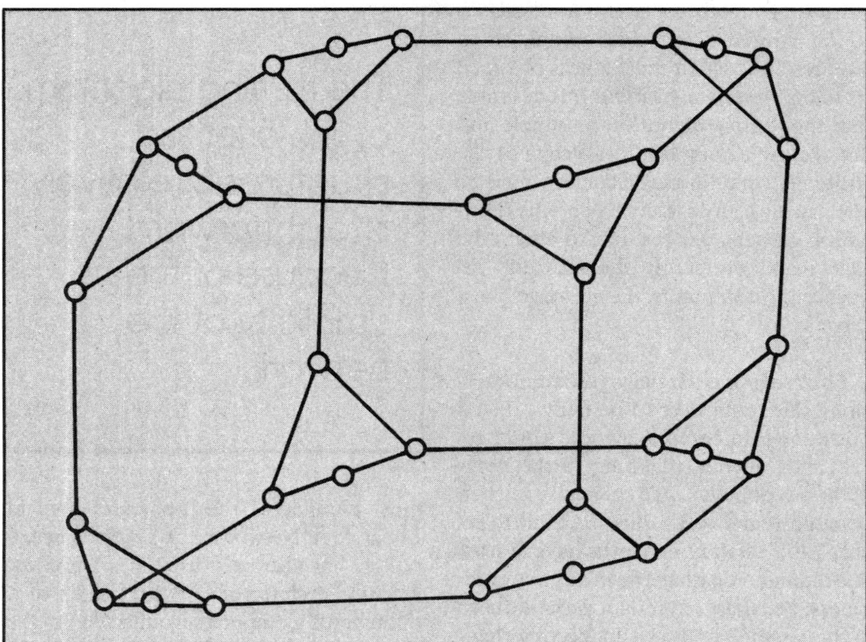

Figure 1. A 32-node cube connected cycles network (k = 5).

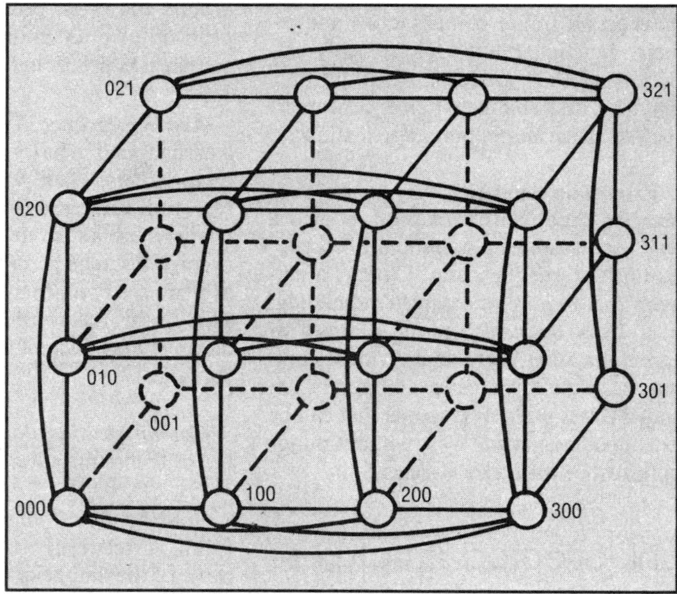

Figure 2. A $4 \times 3 \times 2$ alpha network.

have been considered by different researchers.

Expansion capability. The ring network is obviously one of the simplest to expand.

The cube connected cycles network. This network, proposed by Preparata,[7] connects 2^k computers (k is an integer) in such a way that groups of 2^r (r is the smallest integer such that $r + 2^r \geq k$) are interconnected so as to form a $(k-r)$-dimension cube. Each computer has a k-bit address that is expressed as a pair (l,p) of integers, l having $(k-r)$ bits, and p having r bits. There are three ports, called F, B, and L (for Forward, Backward, and Lateral) provided on each computer, and the interconnection rule is:

$F(l,p)$ is connected to $B(l, (p+1) \bmod 2^r)$;
$B(l,p)$ is connected to $F(l, (p-1) \bmod 2^r)$;
$L(l,p)$ is connected to $L(l + \epsilon^p)$;

where $\epsilon = 1 - 2 \times (p^{th}$ bit of $l)$. An example of such a structure for $k = 5$ is shown in Figure 1.

Average distance. The average distance for the CCC is obtained as the product of the average distance of the subgroup of 2^r processors (which form a ring) and the main $(k-r)$ cube network. The number of ports in each computer is three, so the normalized distance is simply the average distance times three.

Communication links. The total number of communication links is at most $(3/2)N$, where N is the total number of nodes in the network.[7]

Routing algorithm and fault tolerance. Wittie[8] gives a simple algorithm to route messages between computers. Even when a node is faulty, an alternative path may be found with ease.

Expansion capability. Because of the cube structure employed, expansion is not easy. Not only must the expansion be in powers of two, but the system must be completely restructured.

The alpha network. This is a generalized hypercube structure.[4] Unlike the hypercube, which needs the number of nodes to be of the form $N = W^D$, the alpha network is valid for all nonprime values of N. The alpha network is constructed in the following manner: Let $m_1, m_2, \ldots, m_D$ be chosen such that m_i is integer and

$$\prod_{i=1}^{d} m_i = N$$

Then each node can be expressed in a mixed radix form as a D-tuple $(x_D, x_{D-1}, \ldots, x_1)$, which forms the address of the node. Connections are made from each node to every node whose address differs by 1 in any one coordinate. An example of an alpha network is shown in Figure 2.

Average distance. The average distance in a network is given by

$$\text{AvgDist(alpha)} = \frac{D(W-1)\,W^{N-1}}{N-1} \quad (4)$$

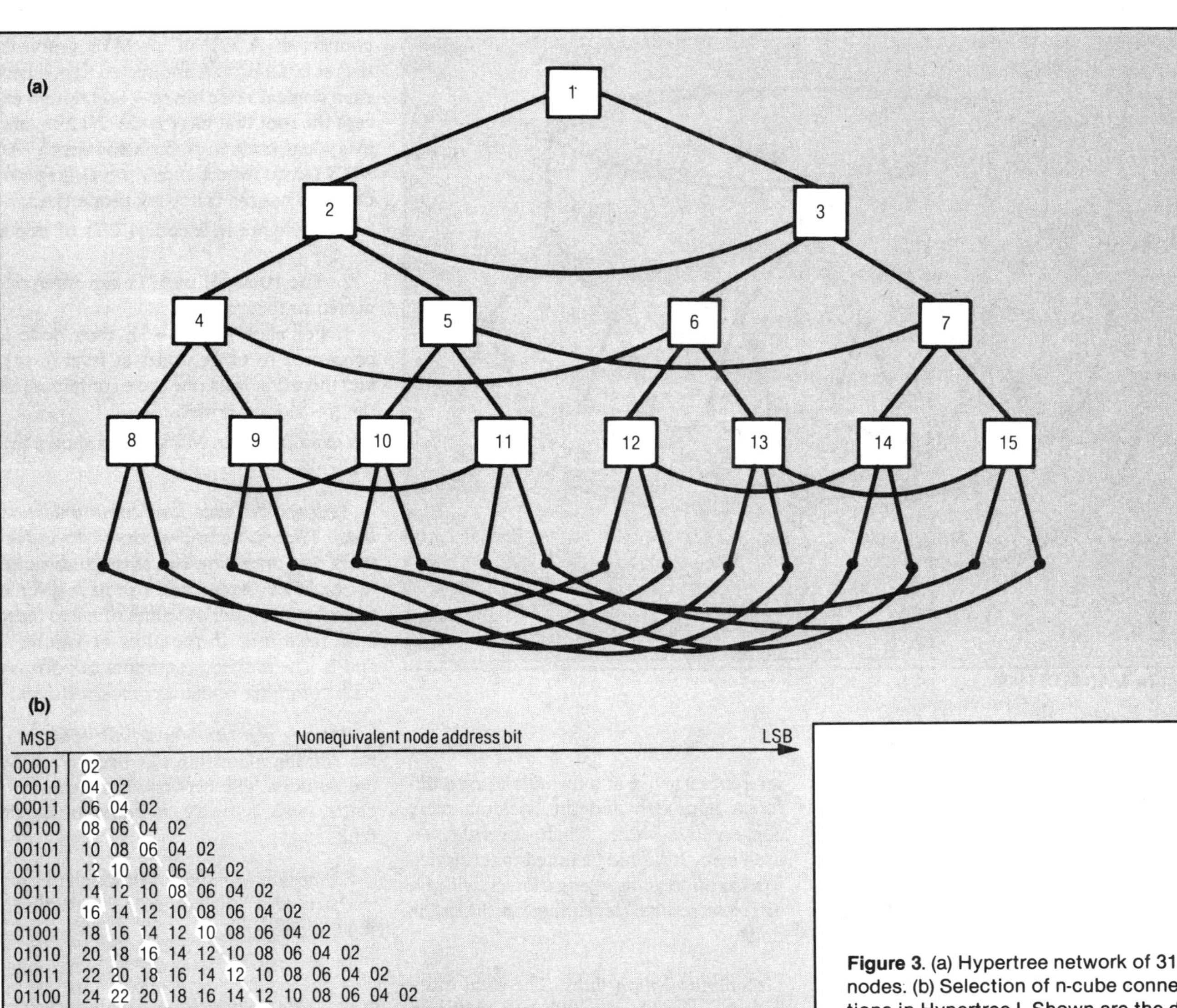

MSB	Nonequivalent node address bit → LSB																			
00001	02																			
00010	04	02																		
00011	06	04	02																	
00100	08	06	04	02																
00101	10	08	06	04	02															
00110	12	10	08	06	04	02														
00111	14	12	10	08	06	04	02													
01000	16	14	12	10	08	06	04	02												
01001	18	16	14	12	10	08	06	04	02											
01010	20	18	16	14	12	10	08	06	04	02										
01011	22	20	18	16	14	12	10	08	06	04	02									
01100	24	22	20	18	16	14	12	10	08	06	04	02								
01101	26	24	22	20	18	16	14	12	10	08	06	04	02							
01110	28	26	24	22	20	18	16	14	12	10	08	06	04	02						
01111	30	28	26	24	22	20	18	16	14	12	10	08	06	04	02					
10000	32	30	28	26	24	22	20	18	16	14	12	10	08	06	04	02				
10001	34	32	30	28	26	24	22	20	18	16	14	12	10	08	06	04	02			
10010	36	34	32	30	28	26	24	22	20	18	16	14	12	10	08	06	04	02		
10011	38	36	34	32	30	28	26	24	22	20	18	16	14	12	10	08	06	04	02	
10100	40	38	36	34	32	30	28	26	24	22	20	18	16	14	12	10	08	06	04	02

Figure 3. (a) Hypertree network of 31 nodes. (b) Selection of n-cube connections in Hypertree I. Shown are the distances between nodes on the same level which differ only by one bit in their addresses for the ordinary binary tree. Each circle represents a set of n-cube connections, chosen in such a manner that the longest distance between a pair of nodes with Hamming distance 1 at the level gets returned to one.

The number of ports on each processor is given by

$$\text{Ports (alpha)} = D(W-1) \qquad (5)$$

Communication links. The total number of links is

$$\text{Links (alpha)} = N \times \text{Ports}/2 \qquad (6)$$

Routing algorithm and fault tolerance. A simple routing algorithm is given in reference 4. Because of the several redundant paths that exist, this network is highly fault tolerant.

Expansion capability. Since this network is a generalized cube network, expansion is not easy as the number of ports is dependent on network size. Unlike cube networks, however, any nonprime value of N can be accommodated.

The hypertree network. The hypertree[9] is basically a binary tree network, which by the judicious addition of extra edges connecting sibling nodes, has been made to have a smaller average distance, and a measure of fault tolerance. These new edges are chosen to be n-cube connections; i.e., they link nodes that have (binary) addresses that differ in only one bit. Each processor has four ports—one from the

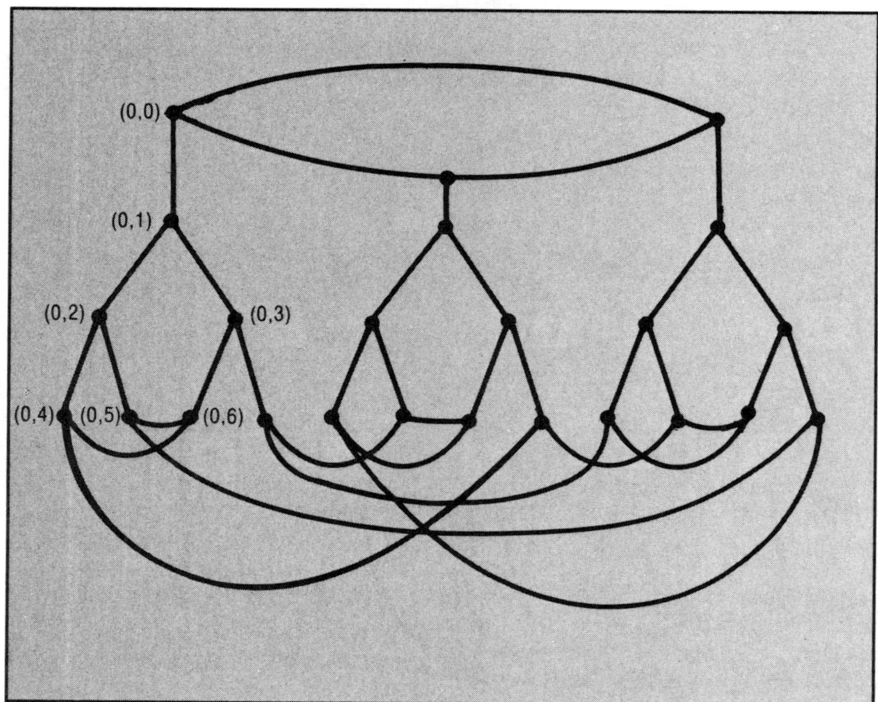

Figure 4. An MTS (4:3).

parent, two to the children, and one to the sibling.

As mentioned above, the linking of nodes is done with a view to decrease the distance between them. For example, in Figure 3(a), which shows an instantiation of a 15-node hypertree, the distance between nodes 8 and 15 is six (ignoring sibling links for the moment). So the sibling links are chosen to reduce this distance. Figure 3(b) is a table given by Goodman and Sequin[9] showing these distances. An entry in the ith row and j^{th} column of the table gives the distance between those siblings in the $(i+1)^{th}$ row whose addresses differ in the jth bit position. A circled entry represents the maximum for that row. Entries just below a circled entry are not considered because they are effectually reduced to three by the sibling links in the previous level. Entries two rows below a circled entry are reduced to five, and so on. With this table, the sibling links may be chosen in a fairly straightforward manner. For every level i, links are given by the value of the circled entry of the table.

Average distance. The average distance of the hypertree is tedious to calculate using equation (1). The authors of reference 9 arrive at a formula using a different approach and this yields a more conservative value. Their formula was used here. It should be noted that this network is not regular so equation (1) will give different results, depending on the origin node.

Communication links. The total number of communication links can be shown to be

$$N + 2(2^{[\log_2 N] - 1} - 1)$$

Routing algorithm and fault tolerance. The routing algorithm is given in reference 9. Under fault conditions, the algorithmic procedure becomes rather more complex.

Expansion capability. In common with tree structures, the network is easily extensible, and expansion requires a minimum disruption of the rest of the system.

The multitree structure. The multitree structure[10] is another tree type structure that uses connections to sibling nodes to reduce the distance between them. An MTS $(m{:}t)$ consists of m identical Component Trees, or CTs, each of t levels, which have their roots and their leaves circularly connected. A CT of an MTS graph of degree d is a rooted undirected tree, where each nonleaf node has $(d-1)$ children, except the root that has $(d-2)$ children, and every leaf node is of the same depth. An MTS $(m{:}t)$, (where $m \geq 3$, $t \geq 1$) graph of degree d has the following properties:

1. There are m identical CTs of depth $(t-1)$.
2. The roots of m CTs are interconnected to form a ring.
3. For each level $(t-1)$, each node is connected to other nodes at level $(t-1)$, and there is at least one cycle containing all the $(t-1)$-level nodes.

An example of an MTS(4:3) is shown in Figure 4.

Average distance and communication links. There is no known closed-form formula for obtaining the average distance for an MTS. Arden and Lee have given a table for a number of values of n and these have been used in the plots of Figures 7 and 8. The maximum number of ports on each computer remains constant (four).

Routing algorithm and fault tolerance. No routing algorithm has been given by the authors. The network has redundant paths, and is hence tolerant of single faults.

Expansion capability. Although this is a tree structure, it is not easily extensible in small increments.

Bus-oriented structures

We now analyze two representative bus structures with regard to the criteria described earlier.

The spanning bus hypercube. The spanning bus hypercube connection is similar to the mesh connection.[8] There are N computers connected on several buses. Each computer is connected to D buses that span each of the D dimensions of the hypercube space. Nodes that have all their coordinates—except the ith—the same are connected to the ith bus. Figure 5 shows a 3^3 spanning bus hypercube structure.

Average distance. The average distance for the spanning bus hypercube is given by equation (4), the alpha structure formula, because of the similarity of the addressing

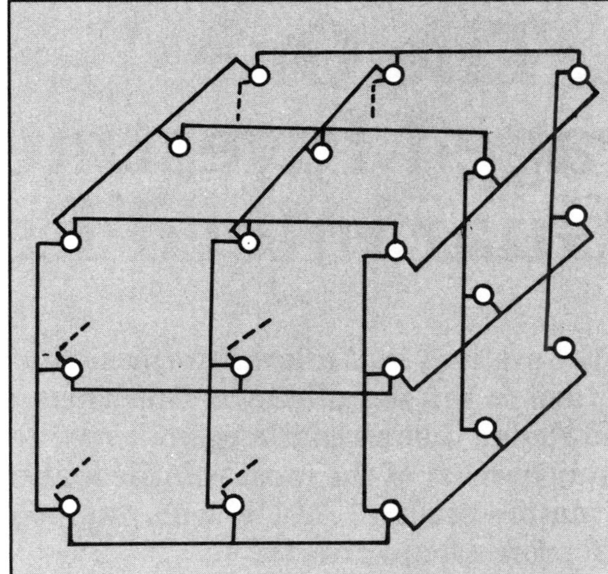
Figure 5. A 3^3 spanning bus hypercube.

Figure 6. A 2×3 beta network.

schemes between these networks.

The number of buses used is[8] DW^{D-1}.

Routing algorithm and fault tolerance. Wittie[8] gives the routing algorithm for this network. A single fault in a bus can be tolerated by such networks.

Expansion capability. Spanning bus hypercube structures may be expanded by increasing D or W. Increasing W has the advantage of not requiring fresh ports in each computer.

Beta networks. The beta structure[4] is of the same topology as the alpha structure. However, a link in the alpha structure is substituted for a node (computer) in the beta. The node of an alpha network is a bus in a beta structure. Figure 6 is an example of a beta network.

Average distance. There exists no known closed-form relation for directly computing the average distance of such a network. The plots of Figures 7 and 8 were obtained by numerical methods.

Communication links. The number of buses is given by W^D. The number of nodes is given by

$$N = \frac{W^D(W-1)}{2} \qquad (7)$$

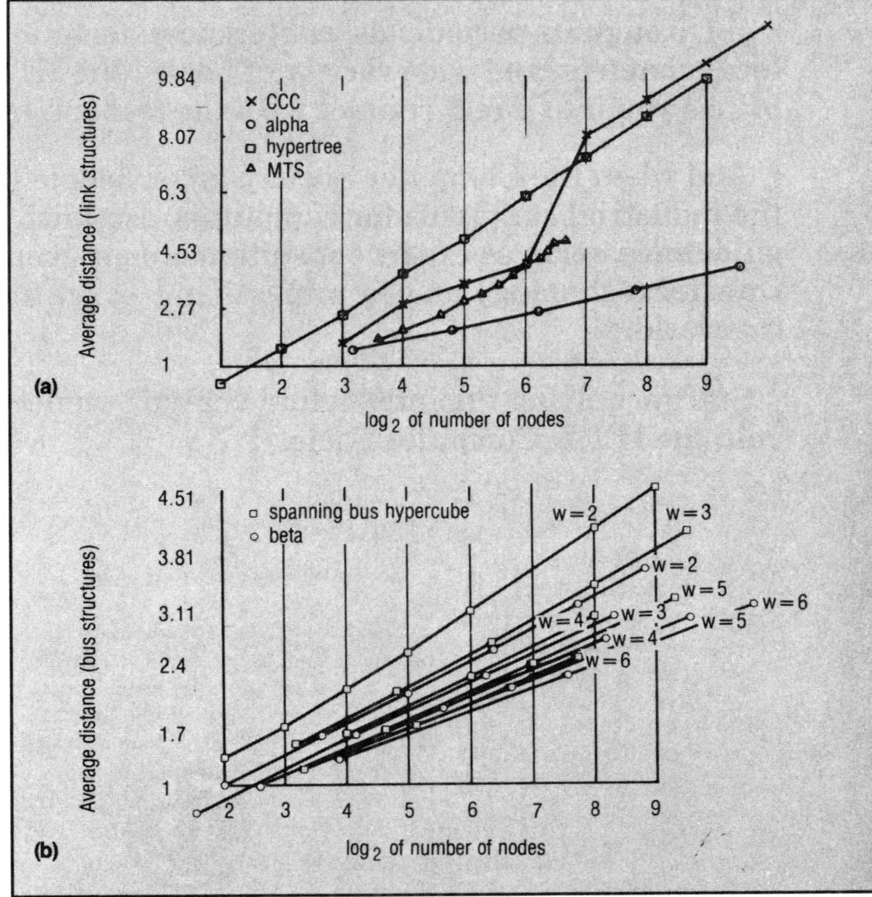

Figure 7. (a) Average distance (link structures) versus number of nodes. (b) Average distance (bus structures) versus number of nodes.

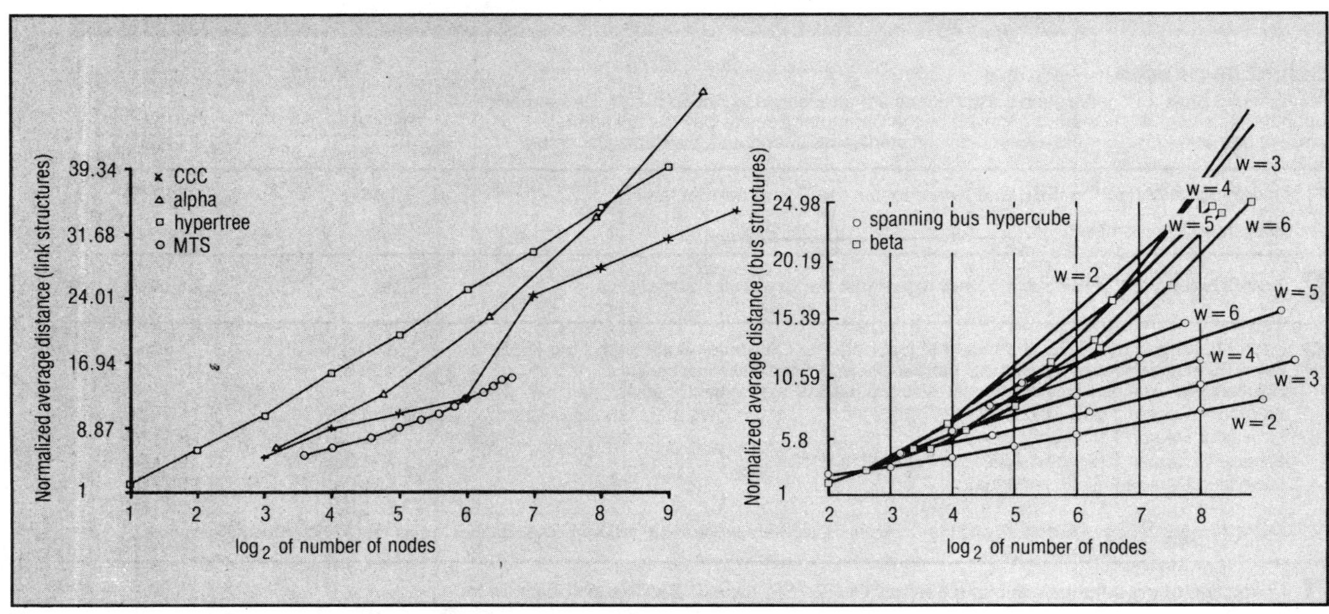

Figure 8. (a) Normalized average distance (link structures) versus number of nodes. (b) Normalized average distance (bus structures) versus number of nodes.

Routing algorithm and fault tolerance. The routing procedure is simple and similar to that of the spanning bus hypercube. Beta networks are also fault tolerant.

Expansion capability. An expansion of the beta network does require rerouting of the network, but the number of ports demanded of each computer remains fixed at two.

Figures 7 and 8 show plots of the average distance and normalized average distance vs. the number of computers for these networks. Among link structures, alpha networks have the smallest average distance. The next best structure is the MTS, followed by the CCC structure. The MTS has the best normalized average distance. However, the routing poses a significant hurdle to its performance. The CCC is the next best and, together with its simple routing algorithm and its fault tolerance, looks attractive indeed.

In the case of bus structures, the beta network possesses smaller average distance, but its normalized average distance is larger and also increases at a faster rate than the spanning bus hypercube.

Table 1 summarizes the important properties of these interconnection schemes. Note that the formulae given therein for the average distances are empirical and approximate, and to be used for comparison only. The term *message density* is defined as

$$\text{Mess. Dens.} = \frac{\text{Avg. Dist.} \times \text{no. of nodes}}{\text{Total no. of links}}$$

As was mentioned earlier, no concrete conclusion can be drawn at this stage as to the relative merit of any scheme based on these figures alone. For example, the CCC seems to be a reasonable choice from a consideration of only the average distance, but from an application viewpoint the alpha structure is the most versatile, as is shown later in a simulation study.

Mapping and scheduling issues

Suppose we have at hand a computational task and, to perform it, we are also given a suitable algorithm to be used. In addition, assume this algorithm has been divided into some number of subtasks in a way that some of these subtasks may be run concurrently. As these subtasks run (on the different processors), they may need to exchange data amongst themselves, and it may not be possible to start the execution of one subtask before the completion of some other subtasks. If we can estimate the extent of this data exchange, i.e., communication between subtasks (see, for example, reference 5), and their data dependencies, then we can estimate the general behavior of the algorithm on the system. The scheduling problem is: How does one find an optimum allotment of these subtasks among the processors so that the maximum possible speedup (or, equivalently, some other performance parameter) may be achieved? For example, if two subtasks exchange data frequently, they should be allotted to two processors that are adjacent, i.e., directly connected to one another.

So, on one hand we have the several subtasks and their interrelationships with respect to data dependency; and on the other, we have the many (not necessarily identical) processors, with their interrelationships, i.e., interconnection scheme. We now need to "map" one on the other. In a most general purpose computer, no information will be available beforehand on the nature of the tasks to be performed on it, so the mapping described above must be done at runtime, dynamically, as subtasks are created. The time spent on this mapping will contribute to the total time that it takes to complete the task. This mapping time is not negligible, and may significantly detract from the performance of the system, especially in real-time applications, where time is of the greatest im-

Table 1. Properties of interconnection schemes.

	Average distance	Ports/node (link structures) or ports on a bus (bus structures) (P)	Normalized average distance (L)	Message density	Number of links (buses)	Fault tolerance (link failures)
Fully connected network	1	$N-1$	N	N	(N^2-N)	$N-1$
Ring (bidirectional)	$(N+1)/4$	2	$(N+1)/2$	$(N+1)/4$	N	2
Cube connected cycles	$\approx 0.8 \log_2 N - 2.4$	3	$\approx 2.4 \log_2 N - 7.2$	$5D/4$	$\frac{3N}{2}$	2
Alpha	$\approx k \log_2 N + 0.2$, $k \approx 0.3$ to 0.5	$D(W-1)$	$D(W-1)L$	$\frac{2L}{D(W-1)}$	$\frac{ND}{2}$	$D(W-1)-1$
Hypertree	$\approx 1.1 \log_2 N - 0.7$	4	$\approx 4.4 \log_2 N - 2.8$	$\frac{L}{2}$	$\approx 2(N-1)$	3
MTS	$\approx \log_2 N - 2$	3	$\approx 3 \log_2 N - 6$	$2 \log_2 N - 4$	–	2
Single global bus	1	N	N	N	1	$N-1$
Spanning bus hypercube	$\approx k \log_2 N + 0.2$, $k \approx 0.3$ to 0.5	W	$\approx W\log_2 N + 0.2W$, $k \approx 0.3$ to 0.5	W	DW^{D-1}	$W-1$
Beta	$\approx k \log_2 N + 0.25$, $k \approx 0.30$ to 0.37	$D(W-1)$	$D(W-1)L$	L	W^D	$D(W-1)-1$

portance. The performance parameter to be optimized could be just the total execution time, or a weighted combination of execution and communication times, or channel and processor utilization. Numerous authors have considered the problem of allocating noninteracting tasks in a distributed environment. They have not considered the effects of data dependency or communication amongst these tasks. But in a multiprocessor environment, interprocessor communication overheads play an important part in determining the performance of the system.

An optimal assignment of subtasks, or modules, to a two-processor system has been considered by Stone,[11] in which the cost of interprocessor communication has been taken into account, in addition to the communication and other collective costs. The basic idea used by Stone is to apply a maximal-flow algorithm to the graph model of a modular program, i.e., one in which each module is represented by a node and the weight on the edge connecting two nodes represents the cost of an intermodule reference when the two nodes (or modules) are assigned to different computers. Each cutset of this graph partitions the graph into two disjoint subsets, and each subset could be assigned to each processor such that the weights of the edges comprising the cutset (which account for all costs) could be minimized. This, in turn, will minimize the total runtime. Stone also provides a way of extending this technique for systems with more than two processors.

A more complete solution to this issue for an arbitrary number of processors was provided by Bokhari.[12] His method assumes that the intermodule communication requirements (which form a precedence relationship) could be represented by a tree-like structure. The method then uses a dynamic programming approach, and minimizes the sum of execution and interprocessor communication costs for an arbitrarily connected distributed system.

Tilborg and Wittie[13] introduced another method called *wave scheduling*, which is applicable to a large homogeneous multicomputer system. The method assumes that there is a hierarchical level of control in the form of a tree (although the computers themselves need not necessarily be connected in a tree-like form). It also assumes that any task can be executed on any one of the processors, and that all cooperating tasks form a *task force*, and that these are known a priori. A task force needing a specific number of nodes is entered in a queue at any node, and the hierarchical control at the root of the subtree schedules the enqueued task forces that are no larger than the number of nodes in the subtree. Tilborg and Wittie have observed that decentralized wave scheduling works well with at low to moderate levels of work load and its efficiency is comparable to that of centralized scheduling.

There are several other scheduling and load balancing strategies advocated by various researchers. But these efforts are limited to scheduling of noninteractive and independent tasks on multiprocessors of distributed systems, where the major concern has been optimization of execution times, and the appropriate placement of distributed databases. As applied to the

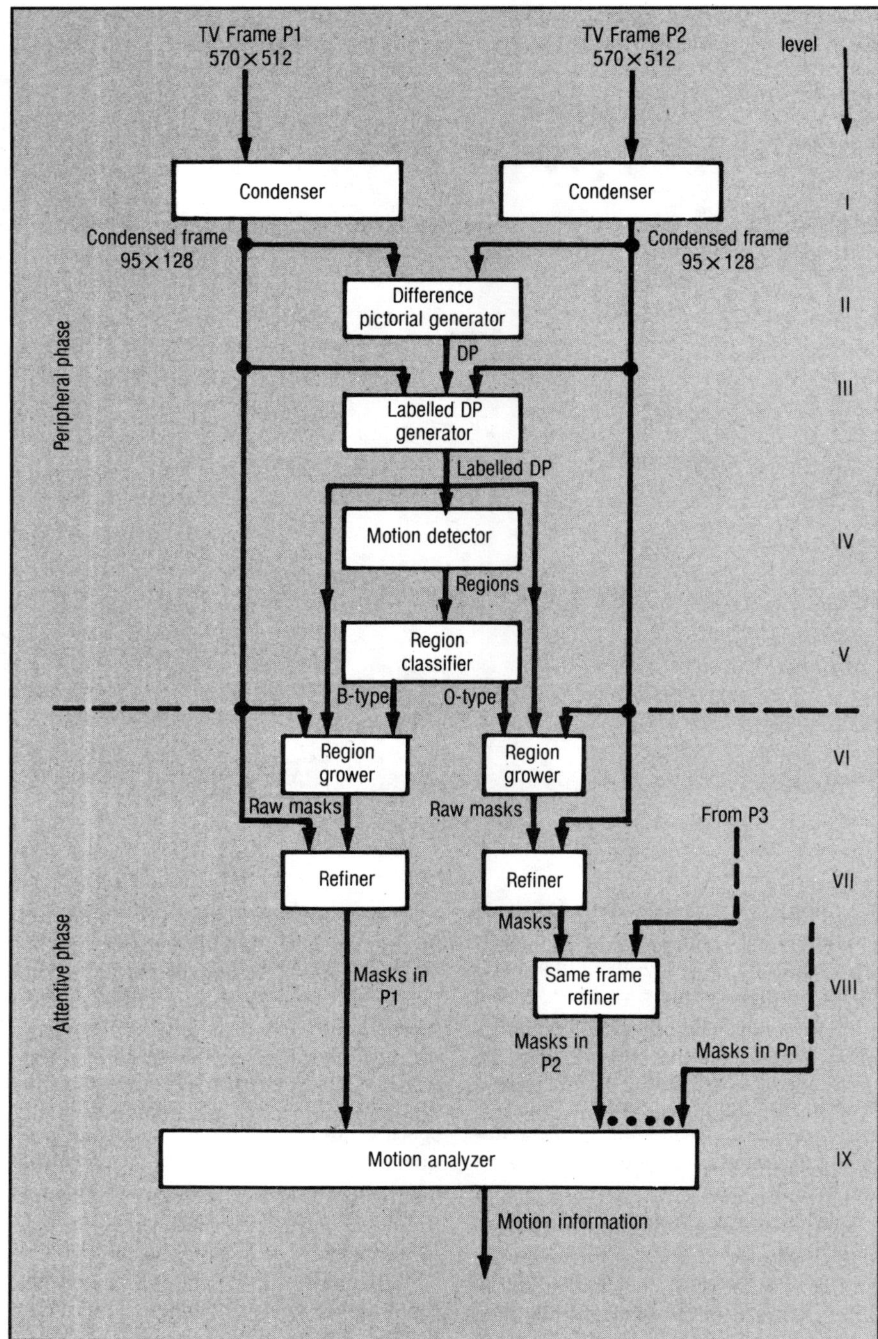

Figure 9. Flowchart of the dynamic-scene-analysis (DSA) algorithm.

architecture we are discussing, the crucial issues of data dependency between subtasks and the interprocessor communication overhead has been neglected.

Bokhari[12] showed that when assigning tasks to the processors, pairs of tasks, or modules, that need to communicate with each other should be placed, if possible, on processors that are directly connected. The property that characterizes such an assignment is known in graph theory as the *cardinality* of the mapping. Cardinality refers to the number of data transfers of the communicating subtasks falling upon physically or directly connected processors. In other words, it gives a number indicating how well the algorithm has mapped on the architecture in a physical sense. It has been shown[12,14] that the mapping problem falls into a class of intractable problems, called *NP-Complete*. In order to solve the allocation problem with the expenditure of reasonable effort, some approximations have to made and some heuristics employed. Furthermore, if some of the typical algorithms that will be used are known previously, then the various attributes of the subtasks can be estimated and this mapping can be done before the actual runtime of the algorithm. This is called *static allocation*. Many real-time applications can be easily served by using static allocation, and, as we will see later, pipelining.

The heuristic employed by Bokhari allows pairwise interchange of mapped nodes. The exchange that leads to the maximum increase in cardinality of the mapping is selected. The rationale behind the optimization of cardinality is to reduce the communication overhead in incompletely connected systems of multicomputers.

Bokhari's work, though important, has some shortcomings. It assumes the processors are identical and that the channel bandwidths are the same for all the channels. No consideration is given to the amount of computation to be done at each node, and the amount of data to be transferred along each connecting edge.

Some of these issues have been addressed by Pathak.[14] The heuristic he employs is the one known as the *greedy* heuristic. For each node, the algorithm looks at the node's immediate surroundings and obtains the optimal mapping, in an attempt to eventually achieve a global optimization. The algorithm makes use of two graph theoretic constructs called the *Computation Flow Graph* and the *Computation Resource Graph*. It is common practice to model the software for parallel machines in the form of directed graphs with directed edges representing the data dependencies, and other parameters being associated with each node and the connecting edges. In the same way the processors and their resources could be modeled by graphs. The CFG is a directed graph that shows the data dependency or the interrelationships with respect to data ex-

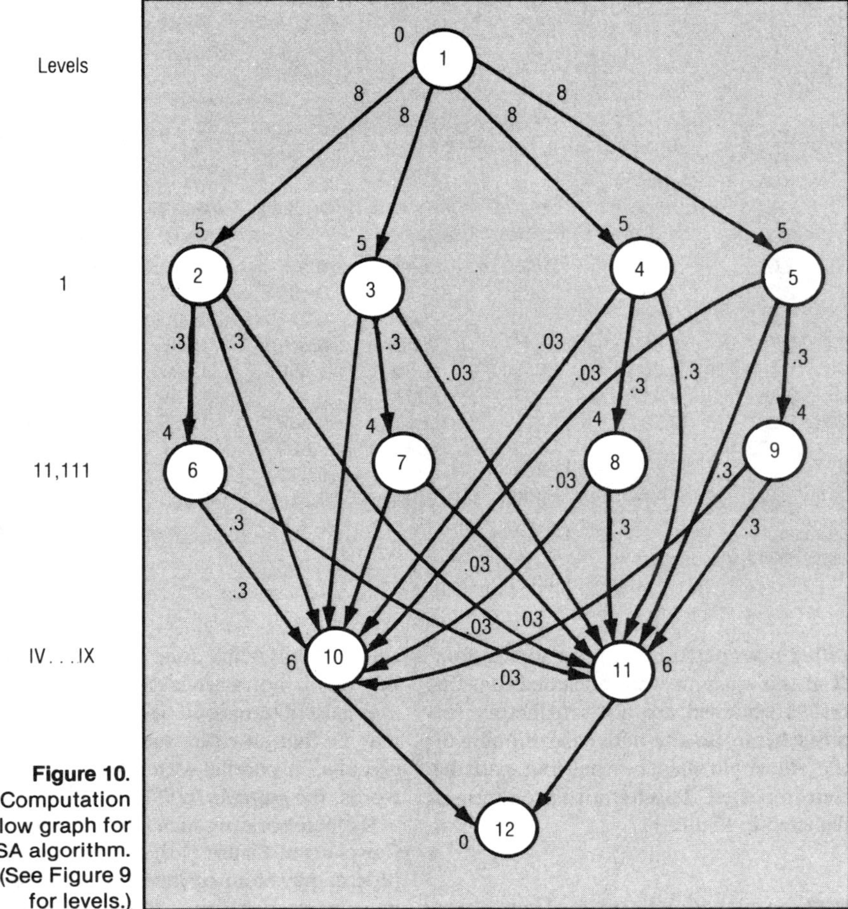

Figure 10. Computation flow graph for DSA algorithm. (See Figure 9 for levels.)

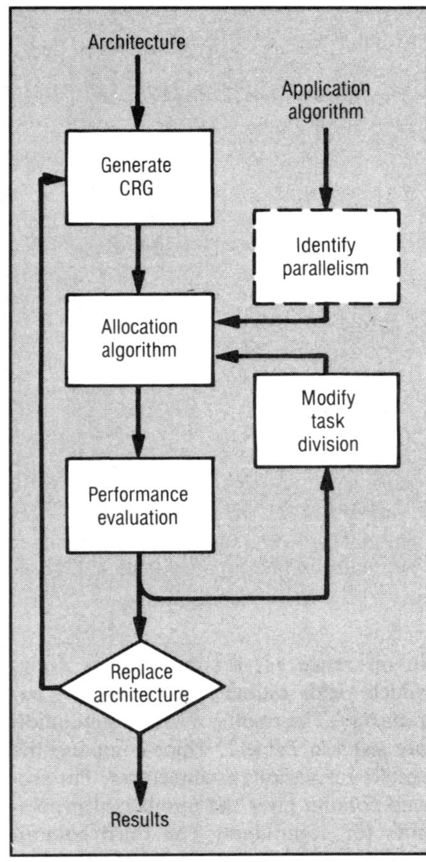

Figure 11. Flowchart for suboptimal mapping.

change between the various subtasks. Each node of this graph represents a subtask and each edge in it has a value equal to the amount of data that will need to be transferred. The CFG is defined to be acyclic.

The CRG is an undirected graph in which the nodes are the processors and the edges denote the channel between the two adjacent processors. The mapping algorithm accepts these two graphs as input, and produces as output the mapping of the CFG on the CRG. Each node of the CFG can be associated with a level. A node has level 1 if it is a source node; i.e., it does not need any input data from any other node. Nodes that need data from level 1 nodes are at level 2, and so on. The algorithm works as follows: Allocation starts from level 1 nodes. For each level l, a node of the CFG of level l is chosen per a criterion that selects nodes with the maximum computation and data communication. A match for this node is searched for in the CRG. A node of the CRG that would minimize the total communication and computation time is selected. Once all the nodes at level l have been matched, scheduling is continued for level $l+1$, and so on, until all the nodes of the CFG have been mapped. The algorithm assumes that the number of processors are at least equal to the number of nodes of the CFG.

Once the mapping is done, a simulation program is run that will give an estimate of some important parameters that can be used to judge the effectiveness of the architecture/algorithm combination that has been employed. If the results are not encouraging, another combination may be tried.

A simple example would serve to illustrate the procedure.

An application example

The Dynamic Scene Analysis algorithm[15] provides a method for extracting images of moving objects. The algorithm works in several stages and thus can be pipelined. Recall that the CFG was stipulated to be acyclic. Also, since each subtask of the algorithm maps on a unique processor, when a processor is done with a subtask, it will not be used again in this instance of the algorithm. These two conditions allow for pipelining. Figure 9 shows the various stages of the algorithm. The algorithm yields a CFG that is shown in Figure 10. For a more complete description, see reference 13. It is required to find a suitable architecture on which the algorithm could be mapped so as to achieve a respectable speedup.

The next stage in the evaluation process is to consider possible architectures, and by studying the results of the evaluation, pick the most suitable one. From Figure 7(a), which gives a plot of the average distance, the alpha structure, the CCC, and the MTS seem to be reasonable choices. Now with each of these schemes, the mapping algorithm is run and an allocation is made. Next, using the software described

Table 2. Simulation results for various architectures.

	Number of processors	Degree	Cardinality	Average communicating distance	Average mapping distance	Channel utilization*	Resource utilization*	Speed up*	Turnaround time*
Alpha	24	6	10	2.000	1.833	1.193	1.035	0.955	1.064
B-Cube	16	4	8	2.133	1.792	1.025	0.772	0.603	1.383
B-Tree	13	3	3	3.282	3.000	1.679	0.837	0.371	1.935
CCC	24	3	4	3.217	3.458	1.641	0.810	0.359	1.985
Full	13	12	24	1.000	1.000	1.000	1.000	1.000	1.000
H-Tree	13	4	5	2.269	2.417	1.497	0.807	0.407	1.754
Mesh	16	4	6	2.667	2.583	1.276	0.864	0.639	1.286
EAMesh	16	4	6	2.133	1.958	1.229	0.847	0.639	1.317
Ring	13	2	2	3.500	3.292	1.494	0.833	0.491	1.552
Star	13	12	3	1.846	1.875	1.839	0.780	0.214	2.990

*Normalized with respect to fully connected scheme.
Normalizing factors are 0.0143, 0.7248, 6.034 and 1.514, respectively.

in reference 13, a simulation is done, which yields estimates of important parameters. The results of such a simulation are given in Table 2, which compares the results for various architectures. The second column gives the number of processors (or computers) The third column gives the degree, or the number of processors connected directly to a given processor. Column 4 gives the cardinality of mapping. The fifth column gives the average communicating distance between two processors (in number of hops). The next column gives the average mapping distance, which is the average data communication distance of subtasks on the particular architecture. Column 7 gives the channel utilization, and column 8 the resource utilization. By utilization we mean the proportion of time the item is kept busy. The next column (9) gives the speedup over a conventional uniprocessor. The last column gives the turnaround time, which is the total time for execution. Note that the last four columns have been normalized so that the fully connected scheme has value 1 for these parameters. The computing power and the data transfer rates are assumed to be 1 MIPS and 0.5M bytes/s, respectively.

An examination of the table shows that the alpha and mesh structures perform close to the fully connected, ideal scheme. The cube connected cycles scheme that, after a study of Figure 7(a), seemed to be a reasonable network to use turns out to be a rather poor performer in this application. If at this stage, it was concluded that the results obtained are not satisfactory for any scheme, an alternative partitioning of the algorithm may be tried out and the steps repeated. This iterative procedure is depicted in Figure 11.

The methodology outlined here serves two purposes. One, it provides a way of choosing the appropriate architecture for a class of applications and, two, gives a method of determining how good this choice was by actually doing the mapping of the algorithm on the architecture and performing a simulation of the execution.

We have tacitly assumed so far that the algorithms that will be used have somehow been already partitioned into their respective subtasks. At present this partitioning must be done by the programmer. On the one hand, this has the advantage that it forces the programmer to think in a "concurrent" way; future algorithms may benefit from this way of thinking. On the other hand, there is a vast body of programs that has already been written, and which may be speeded up by exploiting any inherent parallelism each may possess. It would be tedious to rewrite all these programs. Instead, it would be extremely helpful to have an intelligent compiler that could extract parallelism from a program written for a sequential machine. Already some work is being done in this direction. But this is not a trivial task. Parallelism may exist in terms of a single do loop, or it may be that an entire subroutine may be executed in parallel with others. In other words, the *granularity*[16] is variable.

By incorporating such a compiler in the flowchart of Figure 11 the whole mapping process may be automated to yield an optimum or near-optimum allocation after a few iterations. The (appropriately named) B-HIVE project is a nascent multicomputer project at North Carolina State University.[17] Here the ideas contained in this article have been incorporated in a 24-computer network, using the alpha interconnection scheme. Each node (or computer) consists of two processors: an Application processor that actually executes the application program, and a Communication processor that takes care of the details of sending and receiving data, routing, etc. This hierarchical construction of each node serves to keep separate the two logically different functions. The philosophy behind the B-HIVE project is to build a functional MCS using a "no-frills" approach. It is hoped that the hands-on experience we gain from such a working system will prove invaluable in future designs. □

Acknowledgments

This work is part of the B-HIVE multicomputer project currently being implemented at North Carolina State University. It has been partially supported by NASA Ames Research Center contract no. NAG 2-337, and a summer grant from the Center for Communication and Signal Processing and the Electrical and Computer Engineering Department, North Carolina State University.

References

1. P. C. Treleaven, D. R. Brownbridge, and R. P. Hopkins, "Data-driven and Demand-driven Computer Architecture," *ACM Computing Surveys,* Vol. 14, No. 1, pp. 93-143, March 1982.
2. M. J. Flynn, "Some Computer Organizations and Their Effectiveness," *IEEE Trans. Computers,* Vol. C-21, No. 9, pp. 948-960, Sept. 1972.
3. B. Lint and T. Agerwala, "Communication Issues in the Design and Analysis of Parallel Algorithms," *IEEE Trans. Software Engineering,* Vol. SE-7, pp. 174-188, March 1981.
4. L. N. Bhuyan and D. P. Agrawal, "A General Class of Processor Interconnection Strategies," *Proc. 9th. Ann. Symp. Computer Architecture,* Austin, Texas, pp. 90-98, April 26-29, 1982.
5. W. W. Chu et al., "Task Allocation in Distributed Data Processing," *Computer,* Vol. 13, No. 11, pp. 57-69, Nov. 1980.
6. K. P. Gostelow and R. E. Thomas, "Performance of a Simulated Data-flow Computer," *IEEE Trans. Computers,* Vol. C-29, No. 10, pp. 905-919, Oct. 1980.
7. F. P. Preparata and J. V. Vullemin, "The Cube Connected Cycles: A Versatile Network for Parallel Computers," *CACM,* Vol. 24, pp. 300-309, May 1981.
8. L. D. Wittie, "Communication Structures for Large Networks of Microcomputers," *IEEE Trans. Computers,* Vol. C-30, No. 4, pp. 284-273, April 1981.
9. J. R. Goodman and C. H. Sequin, "Hypertree: A Multiprocessor Interconnection Topology," *IEEE Trans. Computers,* Vol. C-30, No. 12, pp. 923-933, Dec. 1981.
10. B. W. Arden and H. Lee, "A Regular Network for Multicomputer Systems," *IEEE Trans. Computers,* Vol. C-30, pp. 60-69, Jan. 1982.
11. H. S. Stone, "Multiprocessor Scheduling with the Aid of Network Flow Algorithms," *IEEE Trans. Software Engineering,* Vol. SE-3, pp. 85-94, Jan. 1977.
12. S. H. Bokhari, "On the Mapping Problem," *IEEE Trans. Computers,* Vol. C-30, No. 3, pp. 207-214, March 1981.
13. A. M. van Tilborg and L. D. Wittie, "Wave Scheduling—Decentralized Scheduling of Task Forces in Multicomputers," *IEEE Trans. Computers,* Vol. C-33, No. 9, pp. 835-844, Sept. 1984.
14. G. C. Pathak, "Towards Automated Design of Multicomputer System for Real-time Applications," PhD. dissertation, N.C. State Univ., Raleigh, July 1984.
15. D. P. Agrawal and R. Jain, "A Pipelined Pseudoparallel System Architecture for Real Time Dynamic Scene Analysis," *IEEE Trans. Computers,* Vol. C-31, No. 10, pp. 952-962, Oct. 1982.
16. R. G. Babb II, "Parallel Processing with Large-Grain Data Flow Technique," *Computer,* Vol. 17, No. 7, pp. 55-61, July 1984.
17. D. P. Agrawal and W. E. Alexander, "B-HIVE: A Heterogeneous, Interconnected, Versatile and Expandable Multicomputer System," *ACM Computer Architecture News,* Vol. 12, No. 2, pp. 7-13, June 1984.

A Closed-Form Solution for the Performance Analysis of Multiple-Bus Multiprocessor Systems

KEKI B. IRANI, SENIOR MEMBER, IEEE, AND IBRAHIM H. ÖNYÜKSEL, STUDENT MEMBER, IEEE

Abstract — **A closed-form solution for the performance analysis of multiple-bus multiprocessor systems is presented. A Markovian queueing network model has been developed to investigate the effects of memory and bus contentions on the system performance. The symmetrical structure of the Markov chains of the queueing model makes it possible to demonstrate that the local balance is satisfied. Consequently, the probabilities of the states of Markov chains can be expressed by simple formulas. Processing efficiency is used as a performance measure. However, this method is easily extendable to other performance measures. To investigate the effects of the system design parameters on the multiprocessor system performance, comparative results have been obtained for a large family of multiprocessor configurations from unibus to bus-sufficient systems.**

Index Terms — **Bus contention, Markov chains, Markovian queueing networks, memory contention, multiple buses, multiprocessor systems, performance analysis, processing efficiency.**

I. Introduction

ONE intuitively expects that more computing power can be obtained by increasing the number of processors in a computer system. However, the entire system may perform less satisfactorily since more processors can cause more conflicts for the common resources. Therefore, before designing and implementing a real system, one should estimate the performance of the proposed system by applying analytic or simulation techniques.

Our primary concern is to develop analytical tools for the performance evaluation of multiple-bus multiprocessor systems. A typical bus-oriented system is illustrated in Fig. 1 where each processor has its private memory, and processors can share information only through a common memory which consists of several modules. A processor can access common memory via one of the time-shared buses if the referenced module is free and a bus is available. We assume that all modules of the common memory are single-port memories, so that at most one processor can access a module at a given time. The configuration of this type of system is usually denoted by a 3-tuple $(p \times m \times b)$ where p, m, b are the number of processors, number of memory modules, and number of buses, respectively.

Since the memory modules and buses are shared, conflicts can occur between the processors. To analyze the performance of a multiprocessor system under conflicts, one can model the behavior of the system by a closed queueing network [1]–[4]. Fig. 2 illustrates such a queueing model for multiple-bus multiprocessor systems where a buffer is attached to each memory module for queueing the processors. We note that this is not a conventional queueing model because a processor cannot access the server if a bus is not available for access. This constraint creates some nonempty queues with empty servers. For a given scheduling policy, the allocation of memory modules and buses is managed by a controller unit.

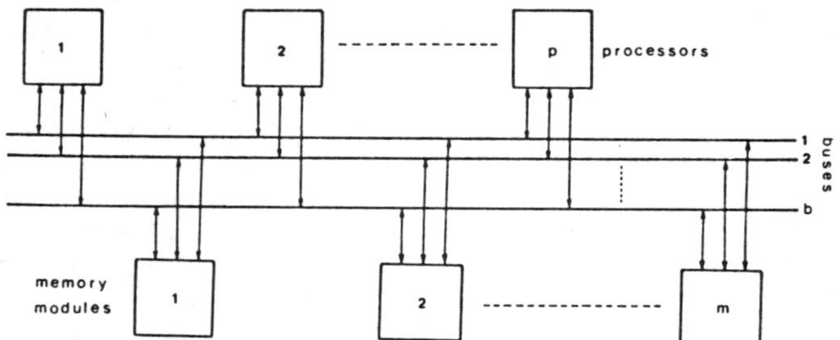

Fig. 1. A typical bus-oriented multiprocessor system.

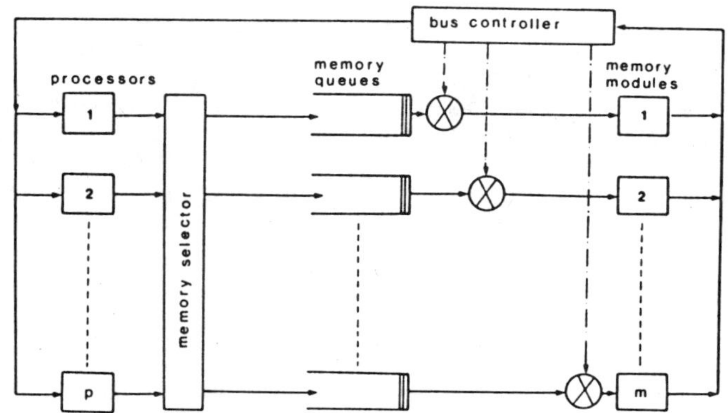

Fig. 2. A queueing model for multiple-bus multiprocessor systems.

If $b \geq \min(p, m)$, then the system will be called a *bus-sufficient* (BS) system; otherwise, it will be called a *bus-deficient* (BD) system. It is clear that no bus conflict exists in a BS system. When $b = \min(p, m)$, the interconnection network (IN) between processors and the common memory behaves as a crossbar, but its reliability and its cost are higher than those of a crossbar.

The performance of a crossbar multiprocessor system has been widely analyzed in recent years [5]–[10]. However, considering the current low cost of microprocessors and memories, a crossbar IN would probably cost more than the rest of the system because the cost of an $N \times N$ crossbar is proportional to N^2. It is also known that a crossbar provides

Manuscript received February 29, 1984; revised July 13, 1984.

The authors are with the Computing Research Laboratory, Department of Electrical Engineering and Computer Science, University of Michigan, Ann Arbor, MI 48109.

Reprinted from *IEEE Trans. Comput.*, vol. C-33, no. 11, pp. 1004–1012, Nov. 1984.

a bandwidth much higher than is required. Therefore, it is very difficult to justify the use of a crossbar for large-scale systems. A more attractive alternative would be a bus-oriented IN.

To overcome the computational complexity of the exact queueing model for the performance analysis of multiple-bus multiprocessor systems, several approximate and algorithmic methods have been introduced for synchronous [11]–[13] and asynchronous [14]–[17] systems.

Marsan and Gerla [15] used Markovian models to solve the problem. Since the number of states for their model increases very rapidly with the system size, they reduced the size of the Markov chains (MC's) by a lumping technique on the assumption that the lumping process still satisfies Markov property. Marsan [16] also derived lower and upper bounds for the system performance. Jacobson and Lazowska [14] used another approximate method. They partitioned the queueing delay for the overlapped possession of the common resources, and then they iterated between the two models, each one of which accounts for the delay at one of the simultaneously held resources.

In this paper, we present a closed-form solution for the performance analysis of the Markovian queueing model for multiple-bus multiprocessor systems. Because the size of the MC for the queueing model grows exponentially, our previous algorithmic approach [17] can be used only for moderate sized systems. However, now we have the analytic results which are easily applicable to a system of any size.

In Section II, we state the assumptions of the queueing model and define some performance measures for this model. The analysis of the model in Section III leads Section IV to determine the probabilities of the levels of the MC, and hence, to the simple expressions for the defined performance measures. In Section V, we discuss the effects of the input parameters on the system performance.

II. Model Assumptions and Performance Measures

We make the following assumptions for the queueing model for multiple-bus multiprocessor systems.

1) When a processor accesses the common memory, a connection is immediately established between the processor and the referenced module, provided the referenced module is not being accessed by another processor and a bus is available for connection.

2) A processor cannot have another memory request if its present request has not been granted.

3) The duration between the completion of a request and the generation of the next request to the common memory is an independent exponentially distributed random variable with the same mean value $1/\lambda$ for all the processors.

4) The duration of an access by a processor to the common memory is an independent exponentially distributed random variable with the same mean value $1/\mu$ for all the memory modules.

5) The probability of a request for access from a processor to a common memory module is independent of the module and is equal to $1/m$.

If a queueing model satisfies the assumption 5), then it is called a *uniform reference model* (URM). Although this assumption considerably simplifies the analysis, in general, it may not be satisfied for some systems for the following reasons.

1) Programs generally exhibit the property of locality of references. If the kth request of a processor is for the memory module i, then its $(k + 1)$st request will be for the same module with probability $\alpha > 1/m$ and for a module $j (j \neq i)$ with probability $1 - \alpha$. This is called a *local reference model* [18].

2) Suppose the local memory of a processing element is also accessible by the other processors. If λ^0 is the rate of a request of a processor for its local memory and λ^1 is the rate of a request for any other memory module, then usually $\lambda^0 >> \lambda^1$.

Several researchers [18]–[20] have attempted to solve the problem with nonuniform access probabilities. Unfortunately, their methods are applicable to small-scale systems only.

We use traditional *Markovian queueing network theory* [21] to analyze multiprocessor systems with the assumptions stated above. We are mainly interested in determining the steady-state probabilities of the states of the MC.

The goal of the analysis of the queueing model is to determine the value of a performance measure for a given set of input parameters. For example, *processing efficiency* (PE), which is equal to the expected value of the percentage of active processors, can be used as a performance measure. A processor is called active if it is neither accessing nor waiting to get access to the common memory. The relative processing efficiency η_p is defined as follows:

$$\eta_p = \mathrm{PE}/\mathrm{PE}^0$$

where PE^0 is the processing efficiency of the same system but without conflicts for the common resources. Obviously, $\mathrm{PE} \leq \mathrm{PE}^0$ and $\eta_p \leq 1$.

Instead of considering the number of active processors, we may consider the number of busy memory modules, and the expected value of the percentage of this number can be used as another performance measure. In this paper, we consider utilization of processors only. Deriving expressions for memory utilization is a dual problem and can be solved by using the same technique which is presented in the next section.

III. Model Analysis

By using the assumptions stated in Section II, we can construct a continuous-time MC to model the behavior of multiple-bus multiprocessor systems. If we use both positive and negative numbers, then a state of the MC is defined by an m-tuple of integers $(k_1, \cdots, k_m)$ where for $j = 1, \cdots, m$, $|k_j|$ indicates the total number of processors queued for memory module j, including the one being served. If $k_j > 0$ then jth module is busy, but if $k_j < 0$ then a bus is not available to access this module. We use $\bar{k}_j$ to denote $-k_j$.

Let $\delta(x)$ be a binary variable where $\delta(x) = 1$ for $x \neq 0$ and

$\delta(x) = 0$ for $x = 0$. If $\sum_{j=1}^{m} \delta(k_j) \leq b$ for a state, then that is a type-0 state; otherwise, it is a type-1 state. It is clear that a BS system has only type-0 states.

If the total number of nonactive processors is n for a state, then that state is said to be a level n state. Formally, if Φ_n is the set of states at level n of the MC, then

$$\Phi_n = \left\{(k_1, \cdots, k_m) : \sum_{j=1}^{m} |k_j| = n\right\} \qquad \text{for } n = 0, \cdots, p.$$

If $b \geq \min(n, m)$ for level n of the MC, then n is called a BS level since all the elements of Φ_n are type-0 states; otherwise, n is called a BD level. Indeed, if $b = \min(\hat{n}, m)$ then the levels $n = 0, \cdots, \hat{n}$ are BS levels and $n = \hat{n} + 1, \cdots, p$ are BD levels. For any level n of the MC there exists at least one type-0 state, namely $(n, 0, \cdots, 0)$.

The one-step transitions between the states of the MC can be categorized into two groups: λ-transitions and μ-transitions. Let $Q = (k_1, \cdots, k_m) \in \Phi_n$ be the present state and $R = (l_1, \cdots, l_m)$ be the next state of a transition.

i) If a processor requests access to memory module i, then $R \in \Phi_{n+1}$, and the transition is a λ-transition. If $k_i \neq 0$, then $|l_i| = |k_i| + 1$ and $\text{sign}(l_i) = \text{sign}(k_i)$. If $k_i = 0$ and $\sum_{j=1}^{m} \delta(k_j) < b$ then $l_i = 1$; otherwise, $l_i = \bar{1}$. Since the total number of active processors is $p - n$ for the state Q, the transition rate is $\lambda_n = (p - n)\lambda/m$.

ii) If a memory access is terminated at memory module i, then $R \in \Phi_{n-1}$, and the transition is a μ-transition. This transition requires that $k_i > 0$. If Q is a type-0 state, then $l_i = k_i - 1$, and the transition rate is μ. If Q is a type-1 state, then let Q' be an intermediate state for this transition such that $Q' = (k'_1, \cdots, k'_m)$ with $k'_i = -(k_i - 1)$ and $k'_j = k_j$ for all $j \neq i$. Let $J(Q')$ be the index set of the negative elements of Q'. For a given bus scheduling policy, the controller will assign the released bus to a memory module s where $s \in J(Q')$. This implies that $l_s = -k'_s > 0$ and $l_j = k'_j$ for all $j \neq s$. The transition rate is $r_s\mu$ where r_s is the probability that a processor queueing for memory module s gets the released bus. By definition, $\sum_s r_s = 1$ with $s \in J(Q')$.

As an example, the MC for a $3 \times 3 \times 2$ system is illustrated in Fig. 3. For simplicity, μ transitions between type-0 states are deleted from the figure. As seen from the figure, the MC consists of 4 levels, namely $n = 0, \cdots, 3$. Levels 0, 1, 2 are BS levels and level 3 is a BD level. Thus, all the states of the MC are type-0 states except the states $(1, 1, \bar{1})$, $(1, \bar{1}, 1)$, and $(\bar{1}, 1, 1)$ at level 3.

Since the transition rate from a type-1 state at level n to a type-1 state at level $n - 1$ depends on the bus scheduling policy, we define macro states to eliminate this dependency. A macro state $\hat{Q}$ is a collection of states (micro states) of the MC and it is defined by

$$\begin{aligned}\hat{Q} &= \{(k_1, \cdots, k_m) : k_{j_1}, \cdots, k_{j_t} < 0 \quad \text{and} \quad k_{i_1}, \cdots, k_{i_{m-t}} \geq 0 \\ &\qquad \text{for } \{j_1, \cdots, j_t\} \cup \{i_1, \cdots, i_{m-t}\} = \{1, \cdots, m\}\} \\ &= \langle l_1, \cdots, l_m; t\rangle \quad \text{with} \quad l_j = |k_j| \qquad \text{for } j = 1, \cdots, m.\end{aligned}$$

This definition implies that $\hat{Q}$ is a collection of $\binom{b+t}{t}$ micro states where t $(0 \leq t \leq m - b)$ indicates the total number of negative elements in a micro state. For type-0 states, a macro state consists of a single state, so that every type-0 state is identified with a distinct macro state. For a $3 \times 3 \times 2$ system, $\langle 1, 1, 1; 1\rangle = \{(1, 1, \bar{1}), (1, \bar{1}, 1), (\bar{1}, 1, 1)\}$ is the only type-1 macro state.

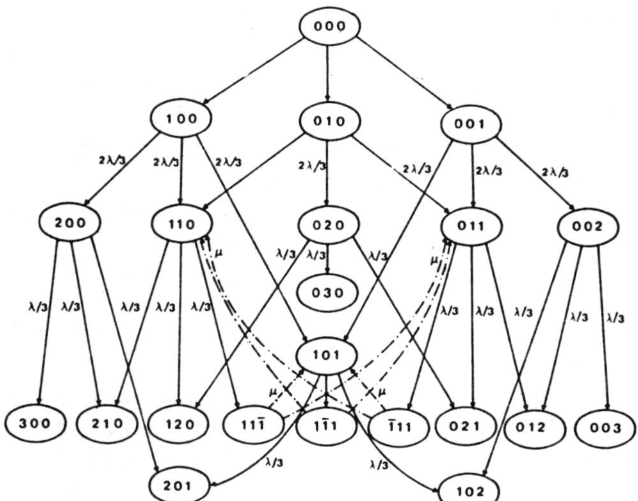

Fig. 3. The MC for a 3 × 3 × 2 multiprocessor system.

For URM, the local balance exists between the macro states of two consecutive levels of the MC. The proof is outlined in the Appendix (Theorem A).

Theorem 1: For URM, the probabilities of all type-0 states at the same level of the MC are equal and given recursively by the equation $\mu L(n) = \lambda_{n-1} L(n - 1)$ where $L(n)$ is the probability of a type-0 state at level n.

Proof: We prove this theorem by induction. For $n = 0$ the result is trivial because there is only one state at level 0. Suppose our claim is true for level $n - 1$. Using the local balance property, we have the following equation for a macro state $\hat{Q}$ at level n:

$$\alpha\mu P[\hat{Q}] = \lambda_{n-1} P[\Phi_{n-1}(\hat{Q})] \tag{1}$$

where $\alpha \leq b$ is the number of busy memory modules for $\hat{Q}$, and hence the number of nonzero components of $\hat{Q}$. Furthermore, $\Phi_{n-1}(\hat{Q})$ is the set of level $n - 1$ macro states which have one-step transitions to $\hat{Q}$, and $P[X]$ denotes the probability of the set X. If $\hat{Q}$ is a type-0 state, then it is clear that $\Phi_{n-1}(\hat{Q})$ contains only type-0 states.

By assumption, the probabilities of all type-0 states at level $n - 1$ are equal. If β is the total number of states in $\Phi_{n-1}(\hat{Q})$, then we get the following equation for a type-0 state:

$$\alpha\mu P[\hat{Q}] = \beta\lambda_{n-1} L(n - 1).$$

However, $\beta = \alpha$ because the number of states at level $n - 1$ which have one-step transitions to the state $\hat{Q}$ must be equal to the number of nonzero components of $\hat{Q}$. This yields the following recurrence relation between the probabilities of type-0 states at two consecutive levels of the MC:

$$\mu L(n) = \lambda_{n-1} L(n - 1) \qquad \text{for } n = 1, \cdots, p. \tag{2}$$

Q.E.D.

Let us now define $\rho_n = \lambda_n/\mu$ and $R_n = \rho_{n-1} \cdots \rho_0$ with

$R_0 = 1$. Then the above recurrence relation yields

$$L(n) = R_n L(0). \quad (3)$$

To distinguish the probabilities of states at the same level of the MC, we attach weight factors to the states. The weight of a type-0 state is defined to be 1, and the weight of a type-1 state is defined by the following recurrence relation:

$$bW[Q] = W[\Phi_{n-1}(Q)] \quad (4)$$

where $W[Q]$ denotes the weight of a type-1 state at level n, and $W[\Phi_{n-1}(Q)]$ is the total weight of states at level $n - 1$ which have one-step transitions to Q. By this definition, the weight of a macro state is simply the sum of the weights of its micro states. For example, by applying (4) to the type-1 macro state $\langle 1, 1, 1; 1\rangle$ of the MC for a $3 \times 3 \times 2$ system, we get

$$W[\langle 1, 1, 1; 1\rangle] = 3W[(1, 1, \bar{1})] = \frac{3}{2} W[(1, 1, 0)] = \frac{3}{2}.$$

Theorem 2: The probability of a macro state $\hat{Q}$ at level n of the MC is given by the following relation:

$$P[\hat{Q}] = W[\hat{Q}]L(n).$$

Proof: If $\hat{Q}$ is a type-0 state, then the proof is trivial because the weight of a type-0 state is equal to 1. Now we give the proof of the theorem by induction. We know that the level 0 of the MC has only a type-0 state, and since the theorem is true for a type-0 state, we have established the basis for induction.

Now suppose the equation of the theorem holds for a macro state at level $n - 1$. Since $\alpha = b$ for a type-1 state, we can rewrite the local balance equation (1) for a type-1 macro state $\hat{Q}$ at level n as

$$\begin{aligned} b\mu P[\hat{Q}] &= \lambda_{n-1} P[\Phi_{n-1}(\hat{Q})] \\ &= \lambda_{n-1} W[\Phi_{n-1}(\hat{Q})] L(n - 1). \end{aligned}$$

Combining this result with (2), we obtain

$$bP[\hat{Q}] = W[\Phi_{n-1}(\hat{Q})]L(n).$$

This completes the proof because $W[\Phi_{n-1}(\hat{Q})] = bW[\hat{Q}]$ by definition. Q.E.D.

Let $\hat{L}(n)$ and $\kappa(n)$ be the probability and the total weight of level n states of the MC, respectively. For example, for a $3 \times 3 \times 2$ system, $\kappa(0) = 1$, $\kappa(1) = 3$, $\kappa(2) = 6$, and $\kappa(3) = 9 + 3/2 = 21/2$ since there are 1, 3, 6, and 9 type-0 states at levels 0, 1, 2, and 3 of the MC, respectively. By definition and by the result of Theorem 2, we have

$$\hat{L}(n) = P[\Phi_n] = \kappa(n)L(n). \quad (5)$$

Combining (2) and (5), we get the following recurrence relation:

$$\mu\hat{L}(n) = [\kappa(n)/\kappa(n - 1)]\lambda_{n-1}\hat{L}(n - 1) \qquad \text{for } n = 1, \cdots, p.$$

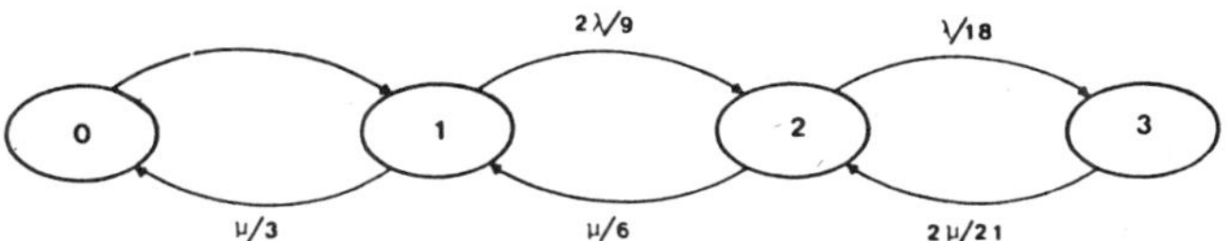

Fig. 4. The birth–death process for a $3 \times 3 \times 2$ multiprocessor system.

Let us define $\hat{\lambda}_n = \lambda_n/\kappa(n)$ and $\hat{\mu}_n = \mu/\kappa(n)$. Then the above equation yields

$$\hat{\mu}_n \hat{L}(n) = \hat{\lambda}_{n-1}\hat{L}(n - 1) \qquad \text{for } n = 1, \cdots, p.$$

This recurrence relation suggests that we can replace the original MC by a simple birth–death process if we are only interested in determining the probabilities of the levels of the MC and not the probabilities of individual states at a given level. Each state of the birth–death process corresponds to a level of the original MC: $\hat{\lambda}_n$ and $\hat{\mu}_n$ are the birth and death rates, respectively. For the example of the MC for a $3 \times 3 \times 2$ system (Fig. 3), the corresponding birth–death process is depicted in Fig. 4.

Theorem 3: There exists a recurrence relation between the weights of two consecutive levels of the MC such that the weight of level n can be obtained from the weight of level $n - 1$ for $n = 1, \cdots, p$ with $\kappa(0) = 1$.

Proof: Let $\kappa(n) = \kappa_0(n) + \kappa_1(n)$ where $\kappa_0(n)$ and $\kappa_1(n)$ denote total weights of type-0 and type-1 states at level n, respectively, and let $T_0^k(n)$ be the number of type-0 states at level n with exactly k $(0 \leq k \leq b)$ nonzero elements.

The transition diagram from level $n - 1$ states to level n states is depicted in Fig. 5 where type-0 and type-1 states are grouped separately.

We define $\gamma_{ij}(n - 1, n)$ to be the total number of one-step transitions from type-i states at level $n - 1$ to type-j states at level n. It is obvious that a type-1 state cannot have a one-step λ-transition to a type-0 state, so that $\gamma_{10}(n - 1, n) = 0$.

We have shown that the number of λ-transitions to a type-0 state is the same as the number of μ-transitions out of this state, and this number is equal to the number of nonzero elements of the state. Thus,

$$\gamma_{00}(n - 1, n) = \sum_{k=1}^{b} kT_0^k(n). \quad (6)$$

Every state has exactly m λ-transitions to the states of the next level. Combining this fact with (4) and (6), we obtain the following equation:

$$b\kappa_1(n) = m\kappa(n - 1) - \sum_{k=1}^{b} kT_0^k(n). \quad (7)$$

To get the number of type-0 states at level n with k nonzero elements, first we choose k memory modules out of m and then we distribute n processors among these k modules. Hence, we get

$$T_0^k(n) = \binom{m}{k}\binom{n - 1}{k - 1} \qquad \text{for } n = 1, \cdots, p \quad \text{and} \quad k = 1, \cdots, b.$$

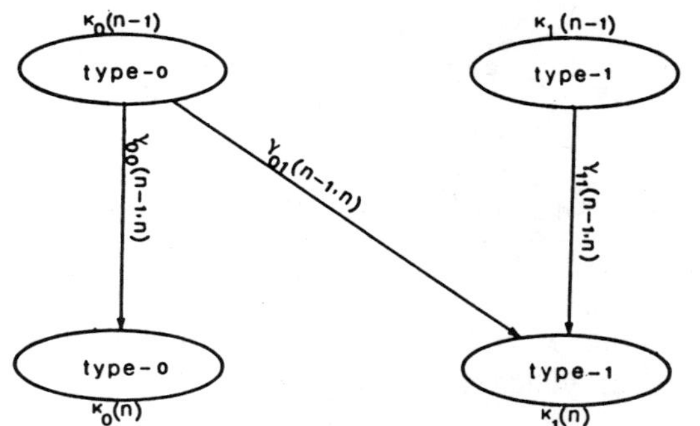

Fig. 5. The transition diagram from level $n - 1$ states to level n states of the MC.

Furthermore, $\kappa_0(n) = \sum_{k=1}^{b} T_0^k(n)$. Thus, (7) yields the following recurrence relation for the weights of the levels of the MC:

$$\kappa(n) = \frac{m}{b}\kappa(n-1) + \sum_{k=1}^{b-1}\left(1 - \frac{k}{b}\right)\binom{m}{k}\binom{n-1}{k-1} \quad \text{with } \kappa(0) = 1 \,. \tag{8}$$

Q.E.D.

From (8) we obtain the following simple relations for unibus and two-bus systems:

$$b = 1: \quad \kappa(n) = m^n \tag{8a}$$

$$b = 2: \quad \kappa(n) = \frac{m}{2}(\kappa(n-1) + 1) \quad \text{with } \kappa(0) = 1 \,. \tag{8b}$$

For example, the weights of levels of the MC for a $3 \times 3 \times 2$ system can be easily computed by (8b) without knowing the internal structure of the MC. As found before, the weights are $\kappa(0) = 1$, $\kappa(1) = 3$, $\kappa(2) = 6$, and $\kappa(3) = 21/2$.

IV. Processing Efficiency

In this section, we obtain a simple polynomial expression for PE by using the results of the previous section.

If Φ is the set of all states of the MC, then

$$P[\Phi] = \sum_{n=0}^{p} P[\Phi_n] = \sum_{n=0}^{p} \hat{L}(n) = 1 \,.$$

Further, using (3), we obtain

$$L(0) = \left(\sum_{n=0}^{p} \kappa(n) R_n\right)^{-1} \tag{9}$$

We know that there are $p - n$ active processors for a state at level n of the MC. By definition,

$$\text{PE} = \frac{1}{p}\left(\sum_{n=0}^{p-1} (p-n)\hat{L}(n)\right).$$

Further, using (3) and (5), we get

$$\text{PE} = \frac{1}{p}\left(\sum_{n=0}^{p-1} (p-n)\kappa(n) R_n\right) L(0) \,. \tag{10}$$

As defined previously, $\lambda_n = (p - n)\lambda/m$ for $n = 0, \cdots, p - 1$. Then we have

$$R_n = \prod_{i=0}^{n-1} \rho_i = \prod_{i=0}^{n-1} (p - i)\rho/m = (p)_n(\rho/m)^n$$

where $\rho = \lambda/\mu$ and $(p)_n = p(p-1)\cdots(p-n+1)$ with $(p)_0 = 1$. Using the above equation for R_n and (9), we obtain from (10)

$$\text{PE} = \left(\sum_{n=0}^{p-1} \kappa(n)(p-1)_n(\rho/m)^n\right)\left(\sum_{n=0}^{p} \kappa(n)(p)_n(\rho/m)^n\right)^{-1}. \tag{11}$$

We observe that PE is a ratio of two polynomials of ρ/m with the degree of numerator one less than the degree of denominator. For example, for a $3 \times 3 \times 2$ system, (11) yields

$$\text{PE} = \frac{4\rho^2 + 6\rho + 3}{7\rho^3 + 12\rho^2 + 9\rho + 3}$$

For a given multiprocessor configuration, we have

$$\lim_{\rho \to 0} \text{PE} = 1 \quad \text{and} \quad \lim_{\rho \to \infty} \text{PE} = 0 \,.$$

For BS systems, the states of the MC are all type-0 states; therefore, $\kappa(n)$ is equal to the number of states at level n and is the same as the number of ways n processors can be distributed among m memory modules. This number is given by $\kappa(n) = \binom{n+m-1}{m-1}$. We can convert (11) to a more suitable form for a BS system by using the following equalities:

$$\kappa(n)(p)_n(\rho/m)^n = \pi(n, m)\binom{p}{n}\rho^n$$

where

$$\pi(n, m) = (n + m - 1)_n \div m^n = \prod_{k=1}^{n-1}\left(1 + \frac{k}{m}\right) \quad \text{with } \pi(0, m) = \pi(1, m) = 1 \,.$$

Thus, for a BS system, we obtain

$$\text{PE} = \left(\sum_{n=0}^{p-1} \pi(n, m)\binom{p-1}{n}\rho^n\right)\left(\sum_{n=0}^{p} \pi(n, m)\binom{p}{n}\rho^n\right)^{-1}.$$

Indeed, a closed-form formula for BS systems was first obtained by McCredie [22] using Jackson's theorem [23].

If $m \to \infty$ then $\pi(n, m) \to 1$. In that case, the above equation yields the following result for a BS system:

$$\lim_{m \to \infty} \text{PE} = (1 + \rho)^{-1}.$$

For $m \to \infty$ a BD system can be represented by a $M/M/b//p$ queueing model because the number of buses is the only limiting factor for the system performance. This model is known as the machine repair model, and its analysis can be found in [24]. Furthermore, for $b \geq p$ the machine repair model corresponds to a multiprocessor system with no conflicts for the common resources. Thus, we have

$$\text{PE}^\circ = \lim_{m \to \infty} \text{PE}(b = p) = \text{PE}(p = 1) = (1 + \rho)^{-1}$$

so that

$$\eta_p = (1 + \rho)\text{PE} \,.$$

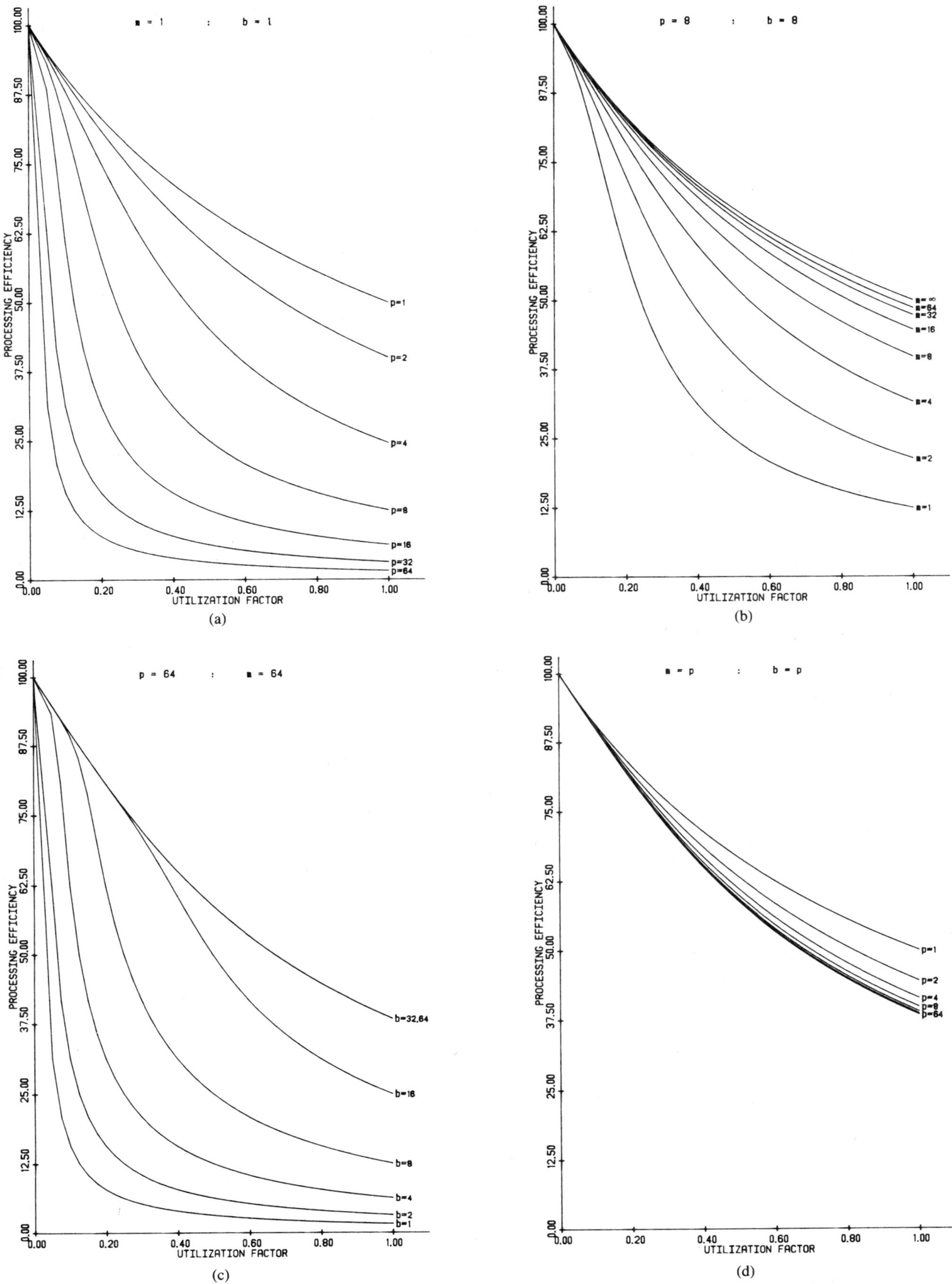

Fig. 6. (a) Effects of the number of processors on a single memory system. (b) Effects of the number of memory modules on a BS system with $p = 8$. (c) Effects of the number of buses on a $64 \times 64 \times b$ multiprocessor system. (d) Effects of the number of processors on a BS system with $p = m$.

V. Numerical Results

To investigate the variations of PE as a function of system input parameters and to determine its general characteristics, we evaluated (11) and (8) for $p, m, b = 2^n$ with $n = 0, \cdots, 6$ and for $\rho = [0, 1]$.

Fig. 6(a) illustrates the effects of the number of processors and the utilization factor on a single memory system ($m = 1$). We see that PE decreases rapidly as p and/or ρ increases. This is an obvious result because more processors and a higher utilization factor can cause more conflicts for the common memory. For example, if $\rho = 0.5$ then PE = 2/3 for a uniprocessor system, whereas PE = 1/32 for a 64-processor system.

Let us define F_k to be the percentage of increase in the active processors if the total number of processors is changed from p to kp. For a single memory system, the values of F_2 with $\rho = 0.5$ are tabulated in Table I(a). We see that the performance is not affected significantly by more than 8 processors.

Addition of more processors to a multiprocessor system can be justified if a given minimum value for PE is realized. Let MPE denote a specified minimum value for PE. If MPE = c then PE $\geq c$ implies $\rho \leq \hat{\rho}(c)$ where $\hat{\rho}(c)$ is the utilization factor for PE = c. As an example, $\hat{\rho}(1/2)$ values are tabulated in Table I(b) for a single memory system. These values indicate that we can have a large number of processors for small utilization factors only. Otherwise, we cannot improve the system performance by adding more processors.

Fig. 6(b) illustrates the effects of the number of memory modules and the utilization factor on a BS system with $p = 8$. Since an increase in the number of memory modules decreases the probability of contention for the same memory module, PE increases with m.

Let PE be the processing efficiency of a given system, and let PE_1^m and PE_2^m be the processing efficiencies of two other systems which have the same parameters as the original system, but the former is a single memory system and the latter is an infinite memory system. It is clear that $PE_1^m \leq PE \leq PE_2^m$. Indeed, PE_1^m and PE_2^m are the lower and upper bounds of the processing efficiencies of a family of multiprocessor systems for which the number of memory modules is the only design parameter.

The memory effect factor ξ_m is defined as follows:

$$\xi_m = PE/PE_2^m.$$

By definition, $\xi_m \leq 1$. Since ξ_m is a performance measure relative to an ideal system, it is a direct representation of the memory contention.

For a BS system with $p = 8$, the values of ξ_m for $\rho = 0.5$ are tabulated in Table II. We see that increasing the number of memory modules by more than 8 in a 8-processor BS system does not significantly increase the system performance.

For a $p = m = 64$ system, the effects of the number of buses on PE can be observed in Fig. 6(c). Let PE_1^b and PE_2^b denote the lower and upper bounds of PE if the number of buses in the IN is the only design parameter for the system.

TABLE I
(a) Values of PE and F_2 for a Single Memory System with $\rho = 0.5$.
(b) Values of Utilization Factor for PE = 50 Percent.

$\rho = 0.5$	$p = 1$	$p = 2$	$p = 4$	$p = 8$	$p = 16$	$p = 32$	$p = 64$
PE (%)	66.667	60.000	45.238	24.979	12.500	6.250	3.125
F_2 (%)	—	80.000	50.793	10.434	0.084	0.000	0.000

(a)

$m = 1$	$p = 1$	$p = 2$	$p = 4$	$p = 8$	$p = 16$	$p = 32$	$p = 64$
$\hat{\rho}$ (1/2)	1.000	0.707	0.437	0.241	0.124	0.062	0.031

(b)

TABLE II
Values of PE and Memory Effect Factor for an 8-Processor BS System with $\rho = 0.5$

$\rho = 0.5$	$m = 1$	$m = 2$	$m = 4$	$m = 8$	$m = 16$	$m = 32$	$m = 64$	$m = \infty$
PE (%)	24.98	40.24	52.77	59.84	63.32	65.02	65.85	66.67
ξ_m (%)	37.47	60.36	79.16	89.76	94.99	97.53	98.78	—

By definition, $PE_1^b \leq PE \leq PE_2^b$. Indeed, PE_1^b and PE_2^b are the processing efficiencies of two other systems which have the same parameters as the original system, but the former is a unibus system and the latter is a BS system.

The bus effect factor ξ_b is defined as follows:

$$\xi_b = PE/PE_2^b.$$

By definition, $\xi_b \leq 1$. Since ξ_b is a performance measure relative to a BS system, it is a direct representation of the bus contention.

For a $64 \times 64 \times b$ system, the values of ξ_b for $\rho = 0.5$ are tabulated in Table III(a). We see that reducing the number of buses required for a BS system to half of its original value does not significantly affect the system performance. Table III(b) shows the values of ξ_b for several systems with $p = m$ and $b = p/2$. These values show that increasing the number of buses by more than $p/2$ does not make a significant improvement in the system performance.

To get the benefit of the increase of the number of processors to the system performance, we need to divide the common memory into several modules in such a way that the number of memory modules increases with the number of processors. Fig. 6(d) illustrates this fact for the case $p = m$.

VI. Conclusions

We have presented a closed-form solution for the performance analysis of multiple-bus multiprocessor systems. In this paper, processing efficiency is used as a performance measure. However, our results can easily be modified for other performance measures.

To investigate the effects of memory and bus contentions on the system performance, a Markovian queueing network model has been developed under the assumptions outlined in Section II. Of course, these assumptions make the MC's highly symmetrical, and therefore they yield simple relations for the steady-state probabilities of the states of the MC's.

TABLE III

(a) VALUES OF PE AND BUS EFFECT FACTOR FOR A $64 \times 64 \times b$ SYSTEM WITH $\rho = 0.5$. (b) VALUES OF BUS EFFECT FACTOR FOR $p \times p \times p/2$ SYSTEMS WITH $\rho = 0.5$.

$\rho = 0.5$	$b = 1$	$b = 2$	$b = 4$	$b = 8$	$b = 16$	$b = 32$	$b = 64$
PE (%)	3.125	6.250	12.500	25.000	49.822	58.740	58.740
ξ_b (%)	5.32	10.64	21.28	42.56	84.82	100.00	—

(a)

$\rho = 0.5$	$p = 2$	$p = 4$	$p = 8$	$p = 16$	$p = 32$	$p = 64$
ξ_b (%)	95.00	98.04	99.51	99.94	99.99	100.00

(b)

However, if a multiprocessor system does not satisfy these assumptions, then the results in this paper can give only an approximate estimation for a defined performance measure. Exploring the symmetrical structure of the MC for the queueing model, we have observed and proved the local balance for the states of the MC, which has enabled us to extend the results to bus-deficient systems as well as to bus-sufficient systems.

For a large family of $p \times m \times b$ multiprocessor configurations, we have determined the probabilities of the states for each MC, and then we have evaluated a simple polynomial expression for PE to get comparative results from unibus to BS systems. Our results indicate that if we reduce the number of buses in a BS system to half its original value, the performance degradation becomes very negligible.

APPENDIX
LOCAL BALANCE

Lemma 1:

$$\sum_{j=1}^{b} W[(k_1, \cdots, \bar{k}_j, \cdots, k_b, 1, 0, \cdots, 0)] = 1 \qquad \text{for } k_1, \cdots, k_b > 0 .$$

Proof: See [25]. Q.E.D.

Lemma 2: If $\hat{Q}$ is a type-1 macro state at level n of the MC and if $\Phi_{n+1}(\hat{Q})$ is a set of macro states at level $n + 1$ which has one-step transitions to $\hat{Q}$, then the weight of $\hat{Q}$ can be obtained from the weights of macro states in $\Phi_{n+1}(\hat{Q})$ by the following equation:

$$W[\hat{Q}] = \frac{1}{m} W[\Phi_{n+1}(\hat{Q})] \qquad \text{for } n = 0, \cdots, p - 1 .$$

Proof: See [25]. Q.E.D.

Theorem A: The unique probabilities of macro states, obtained under the assumption of local balance, satisfy the global balance equations.

Proof: Let $\hat{Q} = \langle k_1, \cdots, k_m; t \rangle$ be a level n macro state, then we have the following global balance equation for $\hat{Q}$:

$$(\bar{b}\mu + m\lambda_n)P[\hat{Q}] = \lambda_{n-1}P[\Phi_{n-1}(\hat{Q})] + \mu P[\Phi_{n+1}(\hat{Q})]$$

where $\bar{b}$ is the number of positive elements in $\hat{Q}$ such that

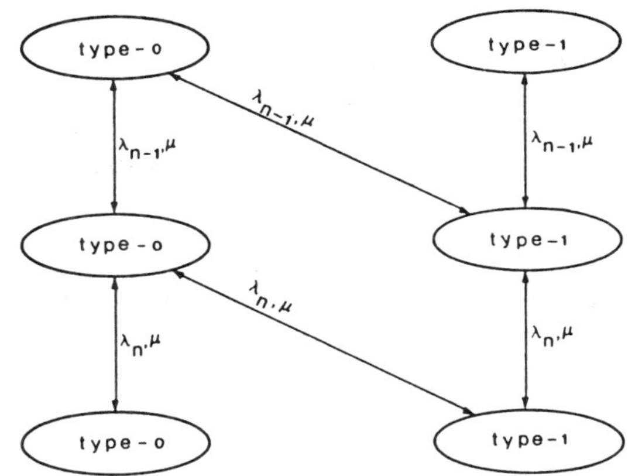

Fig. 7. The transitions between level $n - 1$, level n, and level $n + 1$ states of the MC.

$0 \le \bar{b} \le b$. The transitions between level $n - 1$, level n, and level $n + 1$ states are illustrated in Fig. 7 where type-0 and type-1 states at each level are grouped separately.

Case 1: $\hat{Q}$ is a type-0 state.

In this case, $\Phi_{n-1}(\hat{Q})$ consists of only type-0 states but $\Phi_{n+1}(\hat{Q})$ may consist of type-1 states as well as type-0 states. We may write

$$\Phi_{n-1}(\hat{Q}) = \dot{\Phi}_{n-1}(\hat{Q}) \quad \text{and} \quad \Phi_{n+1}(\hat{Q}) = \dot{\Phi}_{n+1}(\hat{Q}) \cup \ddot{\Phi}_{n+1}(\hat{Q})$$

where $\dot{\Phi}$ and $\ddot{\Phi}$ are used to indicate type-0 and type-1 states, respectively. This yields

$$(\bar{b}\mu + m\lambda_n)P[\hat{Q}] = \lambda_{n-1}P[\dot{\Phi}_{n-1}(\hat{Q})] + \mu(P[\dot{\Phi}_{n+1}(\hat{Q})] + P[\ddot{\Phi}_{n+1}(\hat{Q})]) .$$

Using Theorem 1, the above equation yields the following result:

$$(\bar{b}\mu + m\lambda_n)L(n) = \bar{b}\lambda_{n-1}L(n - 1) + \mu(\tilde{m}L(n + 1) + P[\ddot{\Phi}_{n+1}(\hat{Q})])$$

where $\tilde{m} = m$ for $\bar{b} < b$ and $\tilde{m} = b$ for $\bar{b} = b$.

i) $\bar{b} < b$: It is clear that $\ddot{\Phi}_{n+1}(\hat{Q}) = \emptyset \rightarrow P[\ddot{\Phi}_{n+1}(\hat{Q})] = 0$. Then, we have

$$(\bar{b}\mu + m\lambda_n)L(n) = \bar{b}\lambda_{n-1}L(n - 1) + m\mu L(n + 1) .$$

By using recurrence relation (2) for levels n and $n + 1$, the above global balance equation is satisfied.

ii) $\bar{b} = b$: Let $J = \{j_1, \cdots, j_b\}$ and $I = \{i_1, \cdots, i_{m-b}\}$ be the index sets for nonzero and zero elements of $\hat{Q}$, respectively. Then by Lemma 1, we have

$$\begin{aligned} W[\ddot{\Phi}_{n+1}(\hat{Q})] &= \sum_{j \in J}\sum_{i \in I} W[(k_{j_1}, \cdots, \bar{k}_j, \cdots, k_{j_b}, 0_{i_1}, \cdots, 1_i, \cdots, 0_{i_{m-b}})] \\ &= (m - b)\sum_{j \in J} W[(k_{j_1}, \cdots, \bar{k}_j, \cdots, k_{j_b}, 1_{i_1}, 0_{i_2}, \cdots, 0_{i_{m-b}})] \\ &= m - b . \end{aligned}$$

By Theorem 3, we get

$$P[\ddot{\Phi}_{n+1}(\hat{Q})] = W[\ddot{\Phi}_{n+1}(\hat{Q})]L(n + 1) = (m - b)L(n + 1) .$$

Substituting this value in the global balance equation, we obtain the same result as in case i).

Case 2: $\hat{Q}$ is a type-1 state.

In this case, the global balance equation is

$$(b\mu + m\lambda_n)P[\hat{Q}] = \lambda_{n-1}P[\Phi_{n-1}(\hat{Q})] + \mu P[\Phi_{n+1}(\hat{Q})].$$

By Theorems 1 and 3, the above equation yields

$$(b\mu + m\lambda_n)W[\hat{Q}]L(n) = \lambda_{n-1}W[\Phi_{n-1}(\hat{Q})]L(n-1) + \mu W[\Phi_{n+1}(\hat{Q})]L(n+1).$$

Since the recurrence relation $\mu L(n) = \lambda_{n-1}L(n-1)$ holds for $n = 1, \cdots, p$, we obtain

$$(b\mu + m\lambda_n)W[\hat{Q}] = \mu W[\Phi_{n-1}(\hat{Q})] + \lambda_n W[\Phi_{n+1}(\hat{Q})].$$

By definition of weight and by Lemma 2, we have

$$W[\Phi_{n-1}(\hat{Q})] = bW[\hat{Q}] \quad \text{and} \quad W[\Phi_{n+1}(\hat{Q})] = mW[\hat{Q}].$$

After substituting these values, we see that the global balance equation is satisfied.

Since we have obtained the steady-state probabilities of the states of the MC under the assumption of local balance and these unique probabilities satisfy the global balance equations, the local balance must exist. Q.E.D.

References

[1] W. J. Gordon and G. F. Newell, "Closed queueing systems with exponential servers," *Oper. Res.*, vol. 15, pp. 254–265, 1967.

[2] F. S. Baskett, K. M. Chandy, R. R. Muntz, and F. G. Palacious, "Open, closed, and mixed networks of queues with different classes of customers," *J. Ass. Comput. Mach.*, vol. 22, pp. 248–260, Apr. 1975.

[3] P. J. Denning and J. P. Buzen, "The operational analysis of queueing network models," *ACM Surveys*, vol. 10, pp. 225–261, Sept. 1978.

[4] S. S. Lam, "Dynamic scaling and growth behavior of queueing network normalization constants," *J. Ass. Comput. Mach.*, vol. 29, pp. 492–513, Apr. 1982.

[5] D. P. Bhandarkar, "Analysis of memory interference in multiprocessors," *IEEE Trans. Comput.*, vol. C-24, pp. 897–908, Sept. 1975.

[6] F. S. Baskett and A. J. Smith, "Interference in multiprocessor computer systems with interleaved memory," *Commun. Ass. Comput. Mach.*, vol. 19, pp. 327–334, June 1976.

[7] C. H. Hoogendoorn, "A general model for memory interference in multiprocessors," *IEEE Trans. Comput.*, vol. C-26, pp. 998–1005, Oct. 1977.

[8] B. R. Rau, "Interleaved memory bandwidth in a model of multiprocessor computer systems," *IEEE Trans. Comput.*, vol. C-28, pp. 678–681, Sept. 1979.

[9] T. N. Mudge and B. A. Makrucki, "Probabilistic analysis of a crossbar switch," in *Proc. 9th Int. Symp. on Comput. Arch.*, Apr. 1982, pp. 311–320.

[10] K. O. Siomalas and B. A. Bowen, "Performance of crossbar multiprocessor systems," *IEEE Trans. Comput.*, vol. C-32, pp. 689–695, July 1983.

[11] D. W. Yen, J. H. Patel, and E. S. Davidson, "Memory interference in synchronous multiprocessor systems," *IEEE Trans. Comput.*, vol. C-31, pp. 1116–1121, Nov. 1982.

[12] T. Lang, M. Valero, and I. Alegre, "Bandwidth of crossbar and multiple-bus connections for multiprocessors," *IEEE Trans. Comput.*, vol. C-31, pp. 1227–1234, Dec. 1982.

[13] M. Valero, J. M. Llaberia, J. Labarta, E. Sanvicente, and T. Lang, "A performance evaluation of the multiple-bus network for multiprocessor systems," in *Proc. 1983 ACM Sigmetrics Conf. on Meas. and Mod. Comput. Syst.*, Aug. 1983, pp. 200–206.

[14] P. A. Jacobson and E. D. Lazowska, "Analyzing queueing networks with simultaneous resource possession," *Commun. Ass. Comput. Mach.*, vol. 25, pp. 142–151, Feb. 1982.

[15] M. A. Marsan and M. Gerla, "Markov models for multiple-bus multiprocessor systems," *IEEE Trans. Comput.*, vol. C-31, pp. 239–248, Mar. 1982.

[16] M. A. Marsan, "Bounds on bus and memory interference in a class of multiple-bus multiprocessor systems," in *Proc. 3rd Int. Conf. Distrib. Comput. Syst.*, Oct. 1982, pp. 792–798.

[17] I. H. Önyüksel and K. B. Irani, "A Markovian queueing network model for performance evaluation of bus-deficient multiprocessor systems," in *Proc. 1983 Int. Conf. on Parallel Processing*, Aug. 1983, pp. 437–439.

[18] A. S. Sethi and N. Deo, "Interference in multiprocessor systems with localized memory access probabilities," *IEEE Trans. Comput.*, vol. C-28, pp. 157–163, Feb. 1979.

[19] H. C. Du and J. L. Baer, "On the performance of interleaved memories with non-uniform access probabilities," in *Proc. 1983 Int. Conf. on Parallel Processing*, Aug. 1983, pp. 429–436.

[20] D. Towsley, "An approximate analysis of multiprocessor systems," in *Proc. 1983 ACM Sigmetrics Conf. on Meas. and Mod. Comput. Syst.*, Aug. 1983, pp. 207–213.

[21] L. Kleinrock, *Queueing Systems I*. New York: Wiley, 1975.

[22] J. W. McCredie, "Analytic models as aids in multiprocessor design," in *Proc. 7th Princeton Conf. Inform. Sci. and Syst.*, Mar. 1973, pp. 186–191.

[23] J. R. Jackson, "Jobshop-like queueing systems," *Manag. Sci.*, vol. 10, pp. 131–142, Oct. 1963.

[24] A. O. Allen, *Probability, Statistics, and Queueing Theory with Applications*. New York: Academic, 1978.

[25] I. H. Önyüksel, "Markovian queueing network models for performance evaluation of multiple-bus multiprocessor systems," Ph.D. dissertation, Univ. Michigan, Ann Arbor, MI, in preparation.

Part VI
System Examples

TWO strong motivations for using multiple microprocessors are increased fault tolerance and enhanced overall throughput. The first two papers in this part focus on the fault-tolerance aspect while the remaining papers deal with enhancing system performance.

In the first paper, Serlin describes a number of commercially available fault-tolerant systems that use multiple microprocessors. In addition to highlighting the main features of each system, the author provides a tabular summary of most major makes of fault-tolerant systems.

Next, Emmerson and McGowan present examples of the use of Intel 432 microprocessor chips to implement fault-tolerant systems. They distinguish between different levels of fault tolerance, and suggest various strategies for attaining the desired level of system resilience.

In the third paper, Neri and Cinotti describe a prototype system built with Intel 286 microprocessors. They have preferred to use a lesser known bus called M3 (Multiplexed Multimicroprocessor Bus), which possesses some features similar to those of the P896.

The next paper describes a highly programmable multi-microprocessor architecture that attempts to merge contemporary chip sets and a sophisticated, functional programming approach to solve computationally intensive algorithms at speeds offered so far by mainframe computers only. Gaudiot *et al.* use the Inmos Transputer (see *Advanced Microprocessors, II*) as the basic building block.

Finally, Hayes *et al.* describe a microprocessor-based hypercube supercomputer. Their system is built with custom-designed 32-bit processors. Their largest model, NCUBE/ten, contains 1024 such processors organized as a 10-dimensional hypercube. The paper contains performance results which seem to indicate that the NCUBE node processor offers throughput roughly equivalent to that of a DEC VAX-11/780 equipped with a floating point accelerator.

The above examples illustrate the various approaches adopted to design high-performance systems. Today's multi-microprocessor systems offer performance levels comparable to those of mid-range mainframe systems, at a fraction of the cost of the latter. Just as microprocessor-based systems are gradually replacing minicomputers, similarly multi-microprocessor-based systems will increasingly be used in markets previously served exclusively by mainframe computers.

Fault-Tolerant Systems in Commercial Applications

Omri Serlin, ITOM International Company

Although fault-tolerant techniques were employed in some of the earliest digital computers, the advent of solid-state devices—first the transistor, and later integrated circuits—greatly improved the overall reliability of computer systems. One notable exception to this trend, however, is the popular dynamic MOS RAM: memory systems based on such ICs are actually less reliable than the magnetic cores they replaced. In fact, the reliability of solid-state memory systems has been made to equal that of the older, magnetic-core systems only through the use of error correcting codes; however, parity and ECC schemes are applicable only to subsystems that do not perform any data transformations, but perform only pure data transport (such as computer buses and I/O channels) or offer pure storage (such as main memory and disks).

As a result of the improvement in basic component reliability on the one hand and the development of error-correcting codes on the other, the initial interest that computer scientists had in developing fault-tolerant techniques soon faded. During the 1960's and early 1970's, interest in such techniques remained limited to a number of specific applications areas, including computer-controlled telephone switching systems, military and commercial real-time monitoring and control systems, commercial time-sharing systems, and airline reservations systems.

Early dual-processor systems

Computer-controlled, electronic switching systems began to appear in central offices of the public telephone network in the US and in France around 1965. Because of the nature of the services they render, the computers incorporated in such switching complexes must provide very high availability. A typical requirement is that there be no more than two hours of system outage (downtime) in 40 years.

To achieve the goal of high availability, various techniques have been devised by AT&T Bell Laboratories for use in its family of ESS computers, of which the latest is the 3B20D processor used in the No. 5 ESS and recently released as a commercial product (see Figure 1). Details differ in each ESS implementation, but the general scheme is to duplicate all critical components (such as the control unit and memory system). The running system utilizes one set of subsystems, while a duplicate set is either in a "hot backup" mode or is executing synchronously with the on-line set. The system detects errors either by matching the results produced by both sets (as in the No. 1A ESS) or by constructing each set from self-checking modules, which are themselves duplicates that match one another's results (as in the No. 3A ESS and 3B20D).

In real-time monitoring and control applications, a computer system is integrated into its environment through various sensors that permit it to monitor the state of physical devices and processes. If the computer is also entrusted with the task of controlling some devices or processes with a variety of actuators, it becomes a "closed-loop" system. Applications include industrial process control, both continuous and discrete; power plant monitoring, both conventional (fossil fuel) and nuclear; aerospace telemetry and on-board control systems; air traffic control systems; and military command and control systems.

To address the high-availability issues inherent in these applications, dual-processor configurations similar to the

Reprinted from *IEEE Computer*, pp. 19–30, Aug. 1984.

one shown in Figure 2 were (and in many cases, still are) employed. The particular system depicted in the figure closely resembles the SEL 88 system, manufactured between 1970 and 1974 by Systems Engineering Laboratories.

In the SEL 88 system, four-port memory modules allowed access from two pairs of CPUs and direct memory access I/O processors. Modules connected in this way created a shared memory region, which mapped into the high end of each processor's address space. This shared memory was typically used to hold "global common" areas (the main programming language was Fortran), which allowed programs running in the two separate processors to share data. In addition, the operating system copy in each processor, which occupied the low end of the address space, could use the shared, high-address locations to communicate with each other at high speeds.

To coordinate the use of shared memory, the system supported a *test bit and set* instruction, which was used to manage semaphores. This instruction read the word containing the addressed bit, set the bit to "one" and the condition code to reflect the status of the bit prior to setting, then rewrote the word into the shared memory—all in one uninterruptible sequence. In this way, a program running in one processor could both test a flag and, upon finding it clear, set the flag to indicate that it was about to modify a certain region of memory; the other CPU was then expected to refrain from modifying (or even reading) the same region.

A special "peripheral switch" permitted I/O controllers to be accessed by either one (but not both) of the I/O processors. Each controller attached to the switch (up to 14 could be accommodated) was actually controlled by a single-pole, double-throw switch, with the peripheral controller at the center position and the I/O processors at the two "throws." This was simplified, since the I/O processor normally communicated with the controllers over coaxial cables in bit-serial fashion, but parallel interfaces could also be similarly switched. Both manual and computer-controlled switching were supported. Typically, the "process I/O" interfaces (such as analog-digital converters and discrete I/O lines) and one or more disk controllers were attached to the peripheral switch.

In addition to the usual parity checking and various error traps, each CPU in this system was equipped with a "watchdog timer" designed to detect "stalls." This timer (actually a downtime counter) could be loaded with an initial count by the CPU; it then counted down at a fixed, clock-controlled rate. The operating system or the applications programs running in each CPU were expected to reload periodically the initial value into their timers. An interrupt signal was sent *to the other CPU* if the program failed to do so before the watchdog timer counted down to zero.

Assuming that no branch of either the system or user programs took longer to execute than the countdown time, such a situation could only come about either because of a complete CPU failure or because of a program bug or hardware error leading to an "infinite loop." In any event, the receipt of the watchdog timer interrupt at a given processor signaled that the other CPU was probably "stalled."

Dual- or multiple-processor systems, similar to the one just described, whether with or without the shared-memory feature, were available from a number of suppliers, including DEC, Data General, and Perkin Elmer's Interdata Division. The five-computer complex that supported the NASA Manned Space Flight Center was of this type, as were the IBM 9020 systems installed in the en-route air

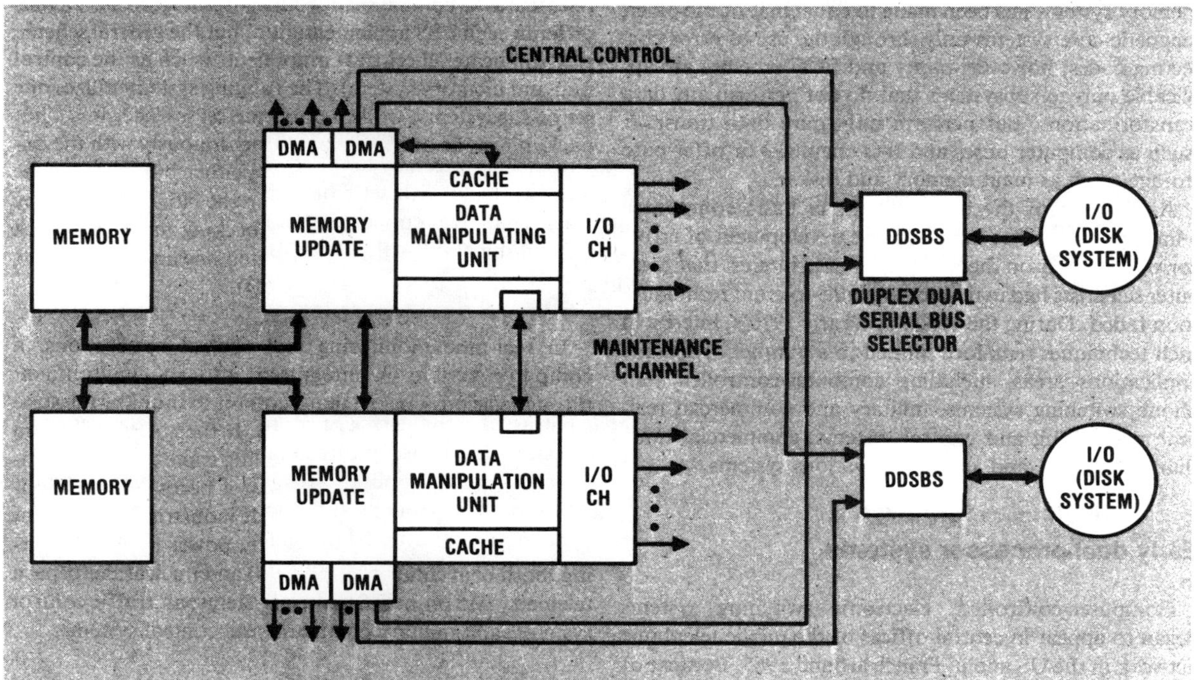

Figure 1. General block diagram of the 3B20D system.

traffic control centers. Variants of this arrangement are still available from several manufacturers, including Hewlett-Packard and, in the UK, Computer Technology, Ltd.

However, these systems provide only the illusion of fault tolerance. For example, they incorporate a number of "critical points," the failure of any of which can bring the entire system down. Examples of such critical points include the shared memory, the peripheral switch, and the shared controllers and devices attached to the switch. Such deficiencies are part of the reason that computer-based "closed-loop" control systems are not permitted in certain critical applications in the US (for example, nuclear power plant control).

Equally serious is the fact that failed components can neither be removed nor be returned to service without powering down one or both processor systems. Furthermore, few of these systems can accept additional processors to accommodate growing workloads.

The most notable limitation of such systems is that they include practically no software support. It is generally left to the end user to supply even the most basic mechanisms for interprocessor communications and control of shared memory and shared peripherals; recovery procedures are entirely within the user's own responsibility.

The main reason for these and other deficiencies is that the elements employed in these multiprocessor systems were never designed for fault-tolerant operation. Indeed, even SEL's four-port memories and bit-serial peripheral controllers were—and still are—highly unusual. By and large, these systems were (and are) "force-fitted" into the fault-tolerant application by incorporating only superficial hardware and software modifications into products that were originally meant to function in a stand-alone, single-processor environment.

Variations of this architecture have been employed in commercial time-sharing systems and in airline reservations systems. Both environments are particularly sensitive to downtime, not only because of the actual monetary losses resulting from such disruptions, but also because of the large number of users affected, both internal employees and outside customers.

On-line transaction processing

Airline reservations systems, initially based on Univac and IBM computers, were quite unlike other real-time systems in several important respects—not least of which was that the hardware manufacturers actually undertook to develop the specialized operating systems, terminal communications protocols, and applications interfaces. This task proved so onerous for Univac, especially at United Airlines, that the company could never recover its original momentum. Only a handful of airlines now use Univac's USAS reservation system.

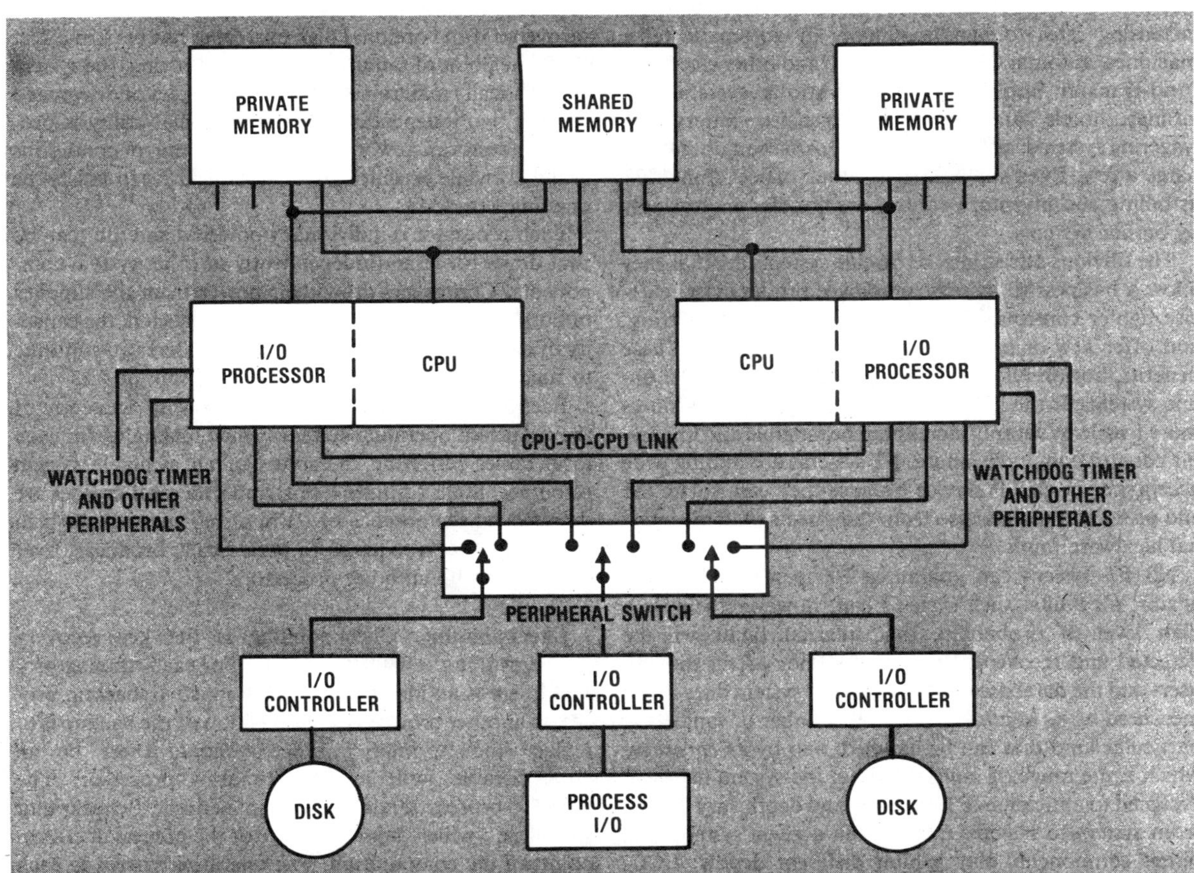

Figure 2. SEL 88-type dual processor (ca.1970).

IBM hardware and the IBM PARS and IPARS software systems became de facto airline industry standards in the US and abroad. The underlying software, the Airline Control Program, is now fully interfaced to SNA, IBM's "grand design" in computer networking. Under SNA's multisystems networking facility, user terminals can access application programs throughout a network of mainframes, even when the application is physically located in a processor to which the terminal has no direct connection. ACP has been so successful that it is now offered by IBM as a more or less standard product for such applications as on-line banking and credit verification.

Unlike real-time monitoring and control systems, which make little use of disk-resident data because disk accesses are too lengthy relative to the required response time, airline reservations systems are created expressly for the manipulation of disk-resident databases. The issues of shared access from a large number of terminals, database consistency and integrity, and system recovery are therefore of prime importance. ACP, for example, includes facilities for periodic dumping of critical data items, called "keypoints" and "globals," to different disk modules. The concepts of checkpointing, audit trails, record locking and disk mirroring or shadowing, also supported by ACP, originated largely from the requirements of on-line transaction processing, or OLTP, of which airline reservations systems were early examples.

The explosive growth in on-line applications is responsible to a large extent for the recent increased interest in FT systems. On-line systems are being installed at ever-increasing rates to handle support of automatic teller machines, automatic gasoline pumps, and other electronic fund-transfer applications; reservations systems for airlines, hotels, and auto-rental agencies; lottery and wagering systems; and videotex or information utilities, to name a few. Even such classical "back office" functions as billing and inventory control are handled increasingly by on-line systems.

The obvious attractions of on-line systems are that they allow a business to increase employee productivity, exercise tighter controls through more up-to-date reporting, and offer new or improved services to customers. These benefits, however, are accompanied by a serious risk: on-line systems at the heart of a business make the business more fragile by sharply increasing the tangible and intangible costs of computer failure. FT systems are finding wide acceptance in OLTP service because they can isolate the end user and the database from the effects of some internal hardware faults.

No FT system can guarantee 100 percent immunity against all faults; such systems can, however, achieve a high level of probability that internal faults will be detected and recovered from before they affect the end users and the database. How well an FT system does this is measured by its *depth,* which is the number of faults of a particular kind that can be handled; and by its *coverage,* which is the range of fault types that the system has been designed to anticipate. FT coverage and depth vary greatly from system to system. Even within a given system, different components may exhibit different depths: ECC-equipped memory systems, for instance, can withstand several successive faults; processors and I/O controllers typically have zero depth in conventional systems and a depth of one or more in FT systems.

The Tandem approach

In 1975, Tandem took a new and more systematic approach to fault tolerance. The Tandem multiprocessor architecture eliminated single points of failure by, among other things, eliminating "master/slave" relations among processors and providing dual paths to all subsystems. Moreover, for the first time in a commercial system, it provided for on-line repair, i.e., the ability to remove defective components (for example, printed circuit boards) and return repaired ones to service without impacting running applications programs. The key architectural features of the Tandem system that underlie these capabilities are processor replication, dual-access I/O controllers, a redundant power system, and a message-based operating system.

A Tandem Nonstop system (Figure 3) includes from two to 16 processors, each with its own memory and I/O channel. These minicomputer-type processors communicate over a high-speed, duplexed, 16-bit parallel bus system called Dynabus. All I/O controllers are dual ported; each is accessible from two I/O channels, typically of two different processors. Disk drives are, in addition, dual-ported; each is attachable to two controllers. Disk data therefore remains accessible even when both a processor and a disk controller have failed.

Should a disk drive fail, the database can still be recovered if the optional disk mirroring has been in effect up to the point of failure. With disk mirroring, the system automatically maintains two identical copies of designated files on two independent drives. A special utility is provided to restore a newly repaired drive to mirror conditions gradually while permitting the surviving drive to satisfy the ongoing workload.

Each processor is individually powered and thus can be shut down for repair independently of other system components. Controllers draw their power from the supplies of both processors to which they are connected; the capacity of each supply is such that the controllers can continue to function even when one processor is shut down.

Each processor in the system contains its own copy of the Guardian operating system, which maintains for each local tables reflecting the status of all available system resources. Stalls (infinite loops) and processor crashes are detected by the absence of "I'm alive" messages, which each processor is required to periodically broadcast over the Dynabus to all other processors.

Checkpointing. Checkpointing is the key recovery mechanism in the Tandem system. For each running process, there is an identical, but semi-inactive, backup process in another processor. The function of the backup is to replace the "primary" process should there be an unrecoverable fault in the primary's processor. The primary process sends its backup periodic "checkpoint messages," which define the state of the process at critical points in the computation. The operating system in each processor "wakes up" the relevant backup process upon discovering that its corresponding primary has failed. The backup can then resume the task from the state defined in the last checkpoint.

Checkpointing is conceptually simple, but its efficient application requires a high degree of programming skill and understanding of system details. Checkpointing is still employed internally by Tandem-supplied system components. One such component is the transaction monitoring facility, or TMF, which maintains database consistency by undoing the effects of aborted or incomplete transactions and supports database recovery. Another checkpointing-based Tandem product, Pathway, is responsible for handling communications with the user terminals. User applications can now be implemented through higher level abstractions called *requesters* and *servers,* which are interjected between the TMF-enhanced DBMS and Pathway. These requesters and servers can be coded as conventional high-level language programs; their loss entails no more than a manual restart of an interrupted transaction.

Message system. Isolation of user processes from configuration details is accomplished by forcing all interprocess communications to be carried out via the *message system.* For example, a user process needing some disk data formulates a "message" addressed to the logical disk controller process. By consulting its resource tables, the local operating system copy determines the actual location of the destination process. The user process therefore does not need to know which two processors are currently connected to the disk in question or which of the two processes is currently the primary.

The isolation of user tasks from configuration details is essential for on-line repair. Furthermore, such isolation facilitates "graceful growth," or the ability to increase the transaction-processing capacity of the system by merely plugging in additional processors. Although this capability is not entirely "seamless," it is, nevertheless, one of the key advantages Tandem has over conventional systems, in which growth involves painful "upgrades." In addition, a

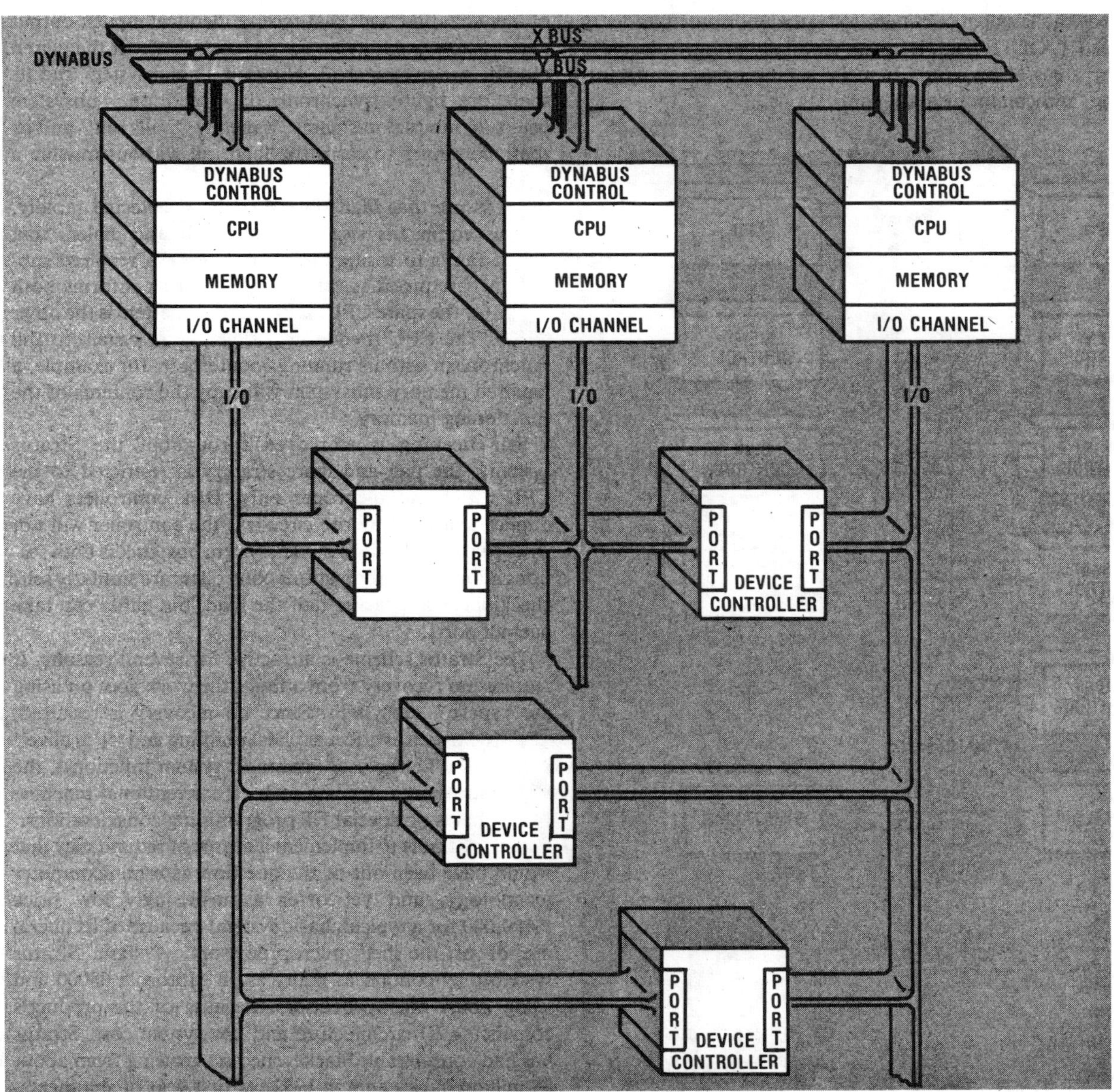

Figure 3. Tandem Nonstop architecture.

network of geographically remote Tandem systems can be created. A relatively minor enhancement to the basic message-based Tandem software is needed to support this important capability.

The Tandem system has undergone a number of notable improvements. Along with enhanced performance, the Nonstop II, introduced in 1981, added "extended addressing" to allow data access beyond the 64K-word limitation of the original product. The Nonstop TXP,[1] introduced in November 1983, achieved a substantially higher performance level through an additional 64K-byte cache and other refinements; the model is expected to receive an enhancement later this year to allow execution of programs larger than 64K-word.

By combining minicomputer technology with architectural innovation, Tandem brought to market an attractive FT system with a substantial price-performance edge over mainframe-based, redundant backup systems. As a result, it enjoyed five years of vigorous growth in revenues and earnings. Despite some recent moderation in its rate of growth, Tandem continues to be the undisputed leader in the FT/OLTP field. It has an especially strong presence in the areas of banking, financial institutions, manufacturing, and communication applications.

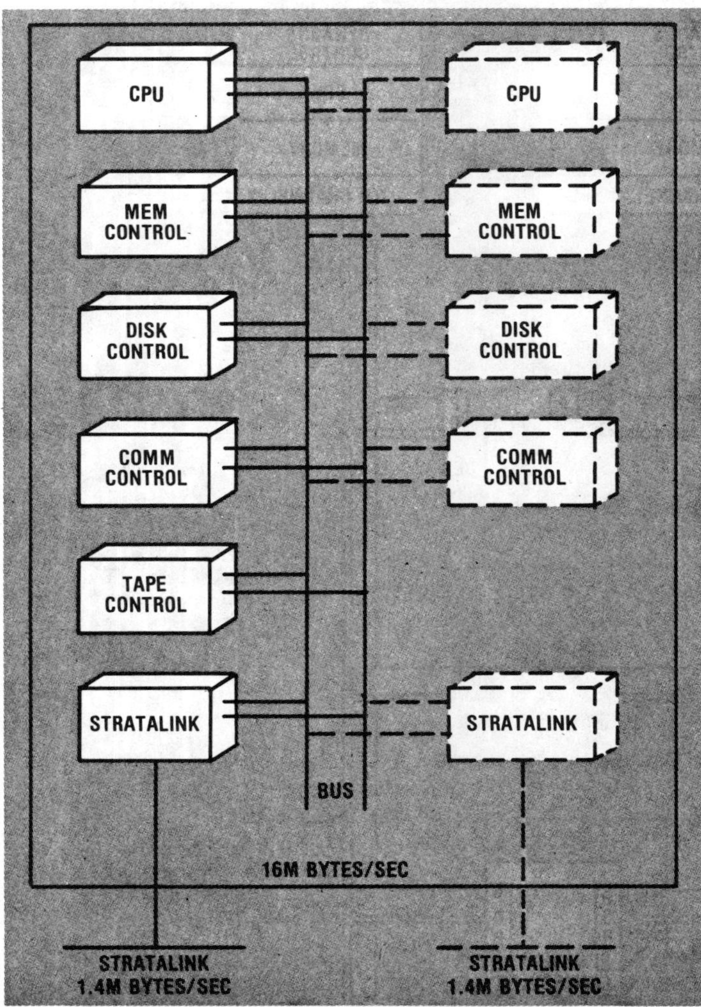

Figure 4. Stratus "pair and spare" architecture.

Over the last several years, a number of new FT/OLTP suppliers have emerged. They are using powerful, low-cost, 16/32 MPUs to create innovative FT designs that were not economically feasible only a few years ago. Most are targeting the OLTP applications that are being addressed by Tandem.[2-5]

Pair and spare

One particularly interesting strategy, dubbed *self-checking*, is employed by Stratus Computer of Natick, Massachusetts, and, to some extent, by the Intel 432 MPU family and the AT&T 3B20D processor. Stratus, a 1980 start-up which went public in August 1983, developed an architecture (Figure 4), informally known as "pair and spare," in which major functions are replicated four times. First, each subsystem (a printed circuit board) has an identical counterpart, its "spare." Both are self-checking: each consists of a "pair" of identical functions that receive identical inputs; output comparators generate an error signal whenever the paired outputs are mismatched. Normally, a subsystem and its spare are tightly synchronized; should one subsystem detect an internal mismatch, it merely "pulls out" and its spare continues to carry the load, all without missing a beat.

To assure that faulty subsystems are detected rapidly, Stratus equips its systems with automatic dialers that report faults to a support center. When a repaired subsystem is returned to service, an interrupt informs both CPUs (or the spare CPU, if the repaired system is the other CPU). The CPU then brings the repaired system to full synchronism with its running counterpart; for example, a repaired memory subsystem will copy the contents of the functioning memory.

Self-checking is employed throughout the Stratus system;[6] the pair-and-spare strategy is restricted to the CPU and memory proper only. Disk controllers have duplicate read and write circuitry; the controller will not write to the disk, or the duplex system bus, unless both sections agree. Communications controllers are similarly self-checking: each handles half the load, but either can take over all ports.

The Stratus scheme is attractive for several reasons. It requires no recovery from a fault: the work goes on using the "spare" subsystem. Since no recovery is required, neither are such artifices as checkpointing and "I'm alive" broadcasts. To the user (and most system functions), the Stratus computer appears to be a conventional machine that requires no special FT programming considerations.

Stratus is able to implement a degree of redundancy that would have been out of the question with minicomputer technology, and yet offer a surprisingly low price ($180,000 for a typical, basic system) because of its liberal use of off-the-shelf microprocessors. A basic Stratus system may contain as many as 18 Motorola 68000 and Zilog Z80A microprocessors. Because of the product's convincing FT architecture and low system cost, Stratus has had considerable market success, growing from about $5 million in revenues in 1982, its first year of shipments, to $20 million in 1983. A significant number of independent software vendors have adopted vertical market applications, especially in banking and finance, to the Stratus system.

Members of the Intel 432 microprocessor family feature functional redundancy checking, which facilitates the construction of pair-and-spare and/or self-checking systems. The comparators needed to implement self-checking are built into each chip and can be activated with an external signal. Thus, a self-checking module can be created by connecting all corresponding input and output pins of a pair of identical chips. As noted earlier, the AT&T 3B20D processor also employs self-checking and mirror-image memories, although it differs in implementation details from the Stratus approach and cannot be expanded beyond the basic, two-CPU configuration.[7]

Tightly coupled systems

A disadvantage of the pair-and-spare strategy is that when growth becomes necessary, the basic unit must be "cloned" in its entirety. Stratus can accommodate up to 32 processing modules, interconnected over a duplexed, ring-type local area network. However, the PMs are, in effect, stand-alone computers that are not normally able to share resources with other PMs.

Synapse Computer, a well-funded, 1980 start-up in Milpitas, California, has developed an architecture (Figure 5) that avoids this limitation. In this scheme, multiple 68000-based processors are "tightly coupled" through a duplexed, high-speed, 32-bit parallel bus to a common, shared-memory system, which holds the only copy of the operating system. The processors, some of which are specialized for I/O while others concentrate on running the transaction-processing applications, act as a pool from which resources are drawn as required to service the load. The processors are self-dispatching: when idle, they look up work queues in main memory and assign themselves to the next task that needs doing. A somewhat similar architecture is employed in the System 9000 from GEAC Computers International (Markham, Ontario, Canada); variations have been used in the BTI 8000 and the Elxsi systems as well.

Synapse calls its architecture N + 1: by configuring just one more processor than the *N* required to service some workload, essentially the same FT depth can be achieved as in a 2*N* scheme, in which each processor or process is backed by a duplicate counterpart.

Applications and I/O processors schedule work for each other by making entries in various dispatching queues in main memory. I/O processors have substantial local buffers, while each application processor is equipped with a 16K-byte, high-speed cache that minimizes memory bus utilization.

The caches are managed under a "non-write-through" policy,[2] which leaves updated data in the cache as long as possible. This technique improves the hit rate but creates a problem when shared data structures or I/O buffers are involved. Synapse evolved an elegant "ownership" scheme to allow the multiple processors to hold shared data in their caches. It handles read-only accesses, such as instructions, simply by giving each requester a copy of the requested item; shared memory continues to "own" such items.

When a processor issues a write request against a shared data item, ownership of the item, along with the item itself, is transferred from main memory to the requesting processor. Should another processor need access to that item, the owner will either furnish a copy (for read-only access) or generate a "busy" response. All caches monitor bus traffic for requests for the data items they hold. IOPs have special privileges that allow them to write data to shared memory without previously reading it; all caches note such writes and invalidate any corresponding entries.

A high degree of graceful growth is possible with this approach. Additional processors can be added to handle independent growth either in applications (transaction) load or in I/O load.

Processor failures are handled through a semi-transparent checkpointing system. Users need not code explicit checkpoint calls; they must instead build their applications from small "program units" by following a set of design rules. The system then undertakes to insert checkpoints automatically between such program units; this activity can be suppressed. A relational database

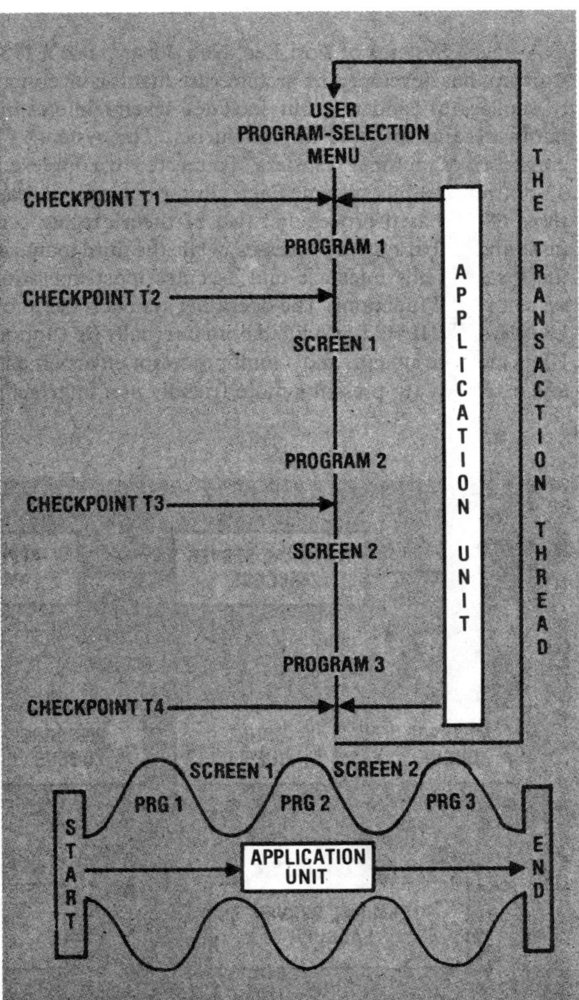

Figure 5. Synapse checkpoint model.

system, integrated with (rather than grafted onto) the operating system facilitates a "Commit" strategy which assures transaction atomicity (that is, the transaction either completes successfully or its effects are removed). A "write-ahead log" technique is used.

The shared-memory system is a single point of failure. A memory failure is the most severe problem that can occur, since it can wipe out work queues, the disk buffers, or parts of the operating system. The memory controller detecting the fault deals with this problem by interrupting all running processors. The mass-storage controller in the highest-priority I/O slot then reloads the operating system, taking care to bypass the failed memory module. Should it fail to do so within a given time period, the next-highest priority I/O controller will try. After a successful reboot, the database recovery process examines the mirrored log file and proceeds to implement all pending committed transactions while undoing the effects of uncommitted (incomplete) transactions. End users should suffer no more than the loss of the screen data they were manipulating at the time of the crash. This recovery process may take up to a few minutes.

Other approaches

Auragen Systems of Fort Lee, New Jersey, also a 1980 start-up, has developed an architecture that is conceptually similar to Tandem's but includes several interesting hardware and software improvements. The system[8] is composed of multiple "clusters" connected to a duplexed, 32-bit, parallel-bus system. Each cluster contains at least three 68010-based processors: two of them execute user tasks and global system processes, while the third manages the system's bus interface and executes most operating system kernel functions. The operating system is based on Unix System III but is modified both internally (to support FT, a message system, and a multiprocessor environment) and externally (to present a more friendly user interface).

For fault recovery, Auragen employs "synchronization" (Figure 6), an interesting variation of the checkpointing idea. After a primary process and its backup have been brought to identical states (synchronized), the backup receives and saves all messages sent to its primary; it also keeps track of the number of messages issued by its primary since the last synchronization. Should the primary fail, the backup would reprocess the saved input messages, suppressing output messages already issued by the primary while it was still functioning.

Synchronization occurs under system control and requires no insertion of checkpoints in the applications code. Moreover, synchronization can occur at a lower frequency than conventional checkpointing and involves less data. The penalty is that more processing steps are involved during recovery, since the backup goes through the motions of some of the actions already completed by the primary. The suggested justification is that the reduction in overhead during normal operation is well worth the longer recovery from rare (one hopes) faults.

Tolerant Systems (San Jose, California), founded in 1982, also employs a synchronization scheme but within the context of a distributed architecture. The basic system building blocks, each based on a pair of National Semiconductor Corporation's NS16000 microprocessors, are interconnected over a duplexed Ethernet local area network.[9]

Computer Consoles, Inc., (Rochester, New York), is developing a multiple processor architecture based on its successful Directory Assistance System. The CCI FT system, dubbed Power 5/55, provides full point-to-point connections among as many as eight 68000-based processors and eight disk controllers. These connections enable the system to implement an interesting generalization of the disk-mirroring scheme: multiple copies of the database are automatically maintained by the system to reduce greatly the response time for inquiry-only transactions, which generally constitute 70 to 90 percent of the transaction load. A local area network connects all pro-

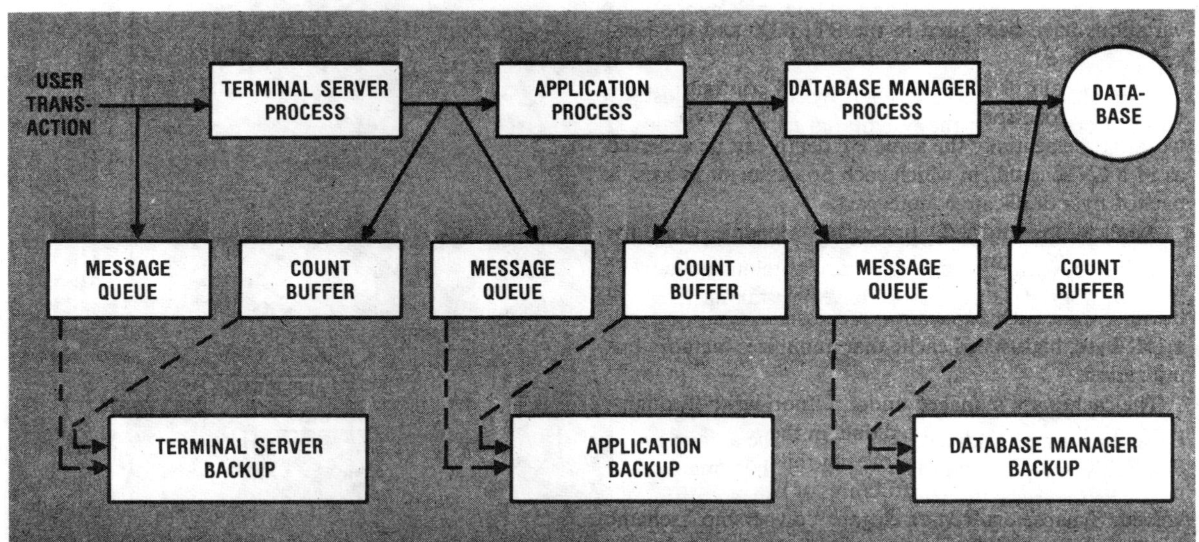

Figure 6. Auragen synchronization scheme (simplified).

cessors to all front-end communications and terminal controllers.

Sequoia Systems (Marlboro, Massachusetts), founded in 1981, is preparing to introduce an FT/OLTP system that combines self-checking processors within a tightly coupled, shared-memory architecture.[10] Encore Computer is also believed to be developing a transaction-processing system along similar lines. Interestingly, Stratus has recently introduced new, "extended architecture" models in which four or six self-checking processors share the duplexed memory system within a Processing Module.

A few firms are addressing FT systems to the special needs of the process control and industrial automation environments. August Systems (Tigard, Oregon) has a system that employs TMR in its front end (analog/ digital interfaces) while the triple-processor main engine runs an interesting variation of TMR called SIFT (software-implemented fault tolerance). The three 8086-based processors perform identical computations and periodically "vote" on the results by reading each other's memory (the links are strictly read-only to prevent one processor from corrupting another's memory). The repetitive nature of the computation involved in process applications makes this approach viable. Voting occurs just prior to launching the next iteration of the algorithm.[11]

Autech (Pompano Beach, Florida) has a system in which duplexed basic units, designed and packaged for harsh-environment service, can be interconnected over a duplexed local area network to a supervisory computer. Hewlett-Packard offers a conventional, hot backup, dual-processor system—dubbed Systemsafe 1000—for supervisory control applications.

The comparison table on pp. 214–215 summarizes the salient features and intended applications of several FT systems now being offered commercially by US manufacturers.

Some open issues

Moves by the established suppliers. Most of the established mainframe and minicomputer manufacturers are known to be considering FT systems. The problem they face is that offering convincing FT architectures may well cause them to lose a great part of their large investments in existing software. This loss clearly would be unacceptable to both vendors and users. Consequently, the established manufacturers can be expected to introduce a variety of solutions involving slightly modified existing products. Examples of this approach are the Vax Cluster from DEC, the NCR V8500/V8600 cluster, the IBM Series/1 ring, and the Perkin Elmer Series 3200 Resilient System, to name a few.

The absence of the established manufacturers from the FT/OLTP scene is both a boon and an obstacle for the existing FT suppliers. Lack of competition from the established vendors helps the newcomers sell their solutions. However, the proprietary nature of the new architectures is limiting their appeal to new applications only: the effort involved in converting existing applications may be too large. This has been a problem for Tandem and is likely to continue to be the principal factor limiting the acceptance of the new FT systems.

Long-range prospects. As more functions are compressed onto fewer and fewer chips, the reliability of a system providing constant functionality and performance can be expected to improve. The suggestion has been made that this will eventually lead to a loss of interest in FT techniques.

A much more likely scenario is that very simple machines, equivalent to today's desktop microcomputers, will indeed become so reliable as to obviate the necessity of equipping them with special FT features. Even today it can be argued plausibly that the correct FT strategy for desktop systems is to stock spare machines and simply replace a malfunctioning unit.

However, the spread of such desktop computing resources is likely to create demand for "file servers" at several levels of the corporate hierarchy. Such file servers, or "group computers," will be used mainly as custodians of shared data (database managers) and as electronic mail hubs, rather than as shared computing (time-sharing) resources.

These computers are likely to continue to be fairly complex. Furthermore, as more workers begin to depend on file servers for the performance of their daily duties, the demand for FT features in such systems will intensify.

Reliable power. As fewer electronic parts are required to implement computing systems, the role of factors other than electronics in system availability will become more pronounced. Several firms (Arete, No Halt, Parallel Computers) are beginning to offer built-in battery-backup systems to counteract the effects of power failures, already a major source of system downtime. Due to the reduced power requirements of today's smaller disks and progress in small-battery technology, such systems can often maintain the complete computer configuration for up to several hours.

Transaction throughput. Almost without exception, today's FT architectures are based on multiplicities of relatively low-powered processors. While these architectures are justified by the nature of transaction processing, which is characterized by relatively limited CPU requirements and fairly heavy I/O loads, they are inherently less efficient than ones in which a relatively small number of very powerful processors can take advantage of economies of scale. It is likely that both approaches will eventually find market acceptance. Meanwhile, FT suppliers are answering the need for higher throughput by adding performance-enhancing features within the context of their basic architectures. The Tandem TXP and the Stratus XA models are examples of such moves.

Software fault tolerance. As the hardware becomes more reliable, software faults—already recognized as being more of a problem than hardware faults in many situations—will become even more visible. High hopes raised by a variety of panaceas ("structured programming," "correctness proofs," "reusable software," "recovery blocks," etc.) have proven premature.

COMMERCIAL FAULT-TOLERANT SYSTEMS

COMPANY/SYSTEM	ADDRESS & PHONE	TARGET MARKETS	CPU TECHNOLOGY	OPERATING SYSTEM NAME & TYPE
August Systems, Inc./ Can't Fail 300	18277 SW Boones Ferry Rd. Tigard, OR 97223 (503) 684-5330	Industrial automation and process monitoring/ control.	Three Intel Corp. 8086-based processors run identical code when in FT mode.	RTTS (real-time task scheduler), one copy per CPU.
Auragen Systems Corp./ System 4000	2 Executive Dr. Ft. Lee, NJ 07024 (201) 461-3400	On-line transaction processing (OLTP); medium to large applications.	Up to 32 clusters of three Motorola 68010 each; clusters interconnect over a high-speed, duplex 32-bit bus.	AT&T Bell Laboratories' Unix with internal modifications; one copy per cluster.
Autech Corp./ DAC-6000	Data Systems Division 1301 W. Copens Rd., Pompano Beach, FL 33064 (305) 979-2700	Industrial automation and process monitoring/ control.	Dual 68000-based Displaymaster and Decmaster. Zilog, Inc., Z80A-based process I/O modules.	Aide process control development system plus read-only memory routines in Decmaster's controller and process I/O modules.
Computer Consoles, Inc./ Power 55/5	97 Humboldt St. Rochester, NY 14609 (716) 482-5000	OLTP, medium to large applications.	Up to eight 68000-based CPUs with 68000-based disk and terminal controllers.	Perpos (perpetual processing OS), Unix-based, one copy per CPU plus special control in inter-computer controllers, (ICC).
Hewlett-Packard Co./ Systemsafe/1000	Data Systems Division 11000 Wolfe Rd. Cupertino, CA 95014 (408) 257-7000	Industrial automation and process monitoring/ control.	Two HP1000 Models 60 or 65 working in "hot backup" mode (16-bit, microprogrammed).	RTE-6/VM, real-time, multitasking, virtual memory, one copy per CPU.
Parallel Computers, Inc./ Parallel 300	3004 Mission St. Santa Cruz, CA 95060 (408) 429-1338	OLTP, very small to small applications.	Two 68010's on a multi-bus.	Berkeley Unix; kernel in both CPUs; one does I/O.
Sequoia Systems/ No Name Yet	3 Metropolitan Corp. Center Marlboro, MA 01752 (617) 480-0800	OLTP, medium to large applications.	Up to 64 CPUs and 96 IOPs, all 68010-based and self-checking.	UNIX-based with new kernel, one copy in shared memory.
Stratus Computer, Inc./ FT200, XA400, XA600	17 Strathmore Rd. Natick, MA 01760 (617) 653-1466	OLTP, small to large applications.	Self-checking CPUs based on Motorola 68000s. Each Processing Module can have duplexed CPU, memory and controllers. Maximum 32 Processing Modules on a ring-type local area network.	VOS (Virtual OS), one copy per CPU (FT200) or four CPUs (XA400) or six CPUs (XA600).
Synapse Computer Corp./ Synapse N+1	801 Buckeye Ct. Milpitas, CA 95035 (408) 946-3191	OLTP, medium to large applications.	Up to 28 68000-based CPUs and IOPs (I/O processors) working with a shared memory via a duplexed, high-speed 32-bit parallel bus.	Synthesis, one copy in shared memory.
Tandem Computers, Inc./ NonStop I, II, TXP	19333 Vallco Pkwy. Cupertino, CA 95014 (408) 725-6000	OLTP, medium to large applications.	Up to 16 CPUs on a duplexed, high-speed, 16-bit parallel bus. CPU is 16-bit microprogrammed.	Guardian, one copy per CPU.
Tolerant Transaction Systems/Eternity	81 E. Daggett Dr. San Jose, CA 95134 (408) 946-5567	OLTP, small to medium applications. Also real time.	Two National Semiconductor Corp. 16000's in each system building block.	Transaction executive, transaction operator interface elements may be replicated in same or multiple system building blocks.

MEMORY SYSTEM	PERFORMANCE/CPU (MIPS and TPS)	FT STRATEGY	CPU FAULT DETECTION*	RECOVERY SCHEME
32K bytes per CPU on-board; up to 1M byte per CPU on Multibus.	Approximately 0.4 MIPS—up to 256 A/D points. TPS not relevant.	CPUs: SIFT; analog front end: TMR	At start of each iteration, three CPUs check state data and vote out odd processor.	Repaired processor reads programs from read-only link or from disk; synchronized at next voting point.
Up to 8M bytes per cluster (1M byte/board).	0.85 MIPS/cluster (company figure). Nominally 27 MIPS/ system at full expansion. 1.5 TPS/CPU (estimate).	Queue and count	Self-detect via idle diagnostics and absence of "I'm alive" messages.	Backup process reprocesses input messages since last sync, discarding outputs already effected.
64K bytes to 256K bytes per CPU, with parity; battery backup on board; CMOS static.	Decmaster supports up to 256 process points. TPS: not relevant.	Hot backup	Timeouts, cross diagnostics.	Auto switchover to backup Decmaster on stall (timeout).
512K bytes to 4M bytes per CPU, error checking and correction, battery backup. Each of two ICCs has 512K bytes.	Nominally 5.6 MIPs (0.7 per 68000). Two TPS/ CPU (ITOM estimate) due to multicopy database.	Checkpointing	ICC timeout transactions; bad ICCs detected by CPU voting scheme.	Next available CPU completes stalled transaction.
256K bytes to 2M bytes per CPU; 1 parity bit/16 bits of data.	1 MIPS (200K floating-point operation/sec mod 65); TPS not relevant.	Hot backup	Watchdog timer times out.	Peripheral switch flips over, hot backup CPU informed via interrupt.
Maximum 4M bytes/processor.	0.7 MIPS.	Hot backup	Hardware and software synchronization between CPUs.	Manual replace and restart.
2M bytes to 64M bytes with ECC (seven bits per 32-bit word).	Sequoia claims up to 40 MIPS at full expansion.	Automatic reassignment	Self-checking subsystem electrically disconnects.	Next available CPU picks up stalled transaction.
FT200: 8M bytes logical XA400: (16M bytes physical) XA600: 16M bytes logical (32M bytes physical).	0.7, 2.0, 3.0 MIPS; 2, 4, 6 TPS; for FT200, XA400, and XA600, respectively.	Pair and spare	Self-checking subsystem pulls out and generates red-light interrupt to operating system.	Re-education procedures synchronize repaired module with one that's running.
16M bytes/system (1M byte boards), error checking and correction.	0.7 MIPS/CPU; system MIPS depend on how many CPUs configured. 2 TPS/CPU (ITOM estimate) if supported by enough I/O processors.	Checkpointing	Timeout mechanisms.	Next available processor picks up stalled transaction that's been checkpointed into shared memory.
8M bytes/CPU (2M bytes/board), error checking and correction.	0.7, 0.8, 2 MIPS; 1, 1.5, 5 to 6 TPS for Nonstop I, II, and TXP, respectively.	Checkpointing	Absence of "I'm alive" message; each CPU must broadcast over Dynabus each second.	Backup process in another CPU picks up transaction from last good checkpoint sent by primary.
1M byte to 4M bytes per system building block.	1.5 MIPS/system building block (Tolerant estimate).	Checkpointing	Timeouts and "I'm alive" message.	Backup system building block takes over.

*Beyond conventional parity and error traps.

An intriguing idea is that software creation might be brought up to a fault-free level comparable to that of hardware design if software designers had available the equivalent of computer chips—small, well-tested, widely used off-the-shelf packages. With the increasing popularity of rehostable-kernel operating systems, such as Unix, universally applicable packages could become a reality within the foreseeable future. Still, the design of reliable software is very much an intractable problem today. Whoever solves it will gain a well-deserved place of honor in the history of computing. *

References

1. R. Horst and S. Metz, "New System Manages Hundreds of Transactions/Second," *Electronics,* Apr. 19, 1984, pp. 147-151.
2. O. Serlin, "New Microprocessor-Based Computer Architectures," *AFIPS Conf. Proc.*, Vol. 54, 1984 NCC, AFIPS Press, Reston, Va.
3. O. Serlin, "Fault Tolerance," *Computerworld Buying Guide,* Aug. 1983.
4. O. Serlin, *Fault-Tolerant Transaction Systems*, Datamation (OEM edition), Jan. 1983.
5. O. Serlin, *Fault-Tolerant Systems,* ITOM International Co., Aug. 1982.
6. R. Freiburghouse, "Making Processing Fail-Safe," *Mini-Micro Systems,* May 1982.
7. W. N. Toy and L. E. Gallaher, "Overview and Architecture of the 3B20D Processor," *Bell System Technical J.,* Jan. 1983, part 2.
8. A. Borg, J. Baumbach, and S. Glazer, "A Message System Supporting Fault Tolerance," *Proc. Ninth ACM Symp. Operating Systems Principles,* Oct. 1983.
9. "Computer System Isolates Faults," *Computer Design,* Nov. 1983.
10. "Sequoia Unveils Self-Checking, Shared-Memory FT System," *FT Systems Newsletter,* ITOM International Co., May 1984, pp. 2-7.
11. J. H. Wensley, "Industrial Control System" *Electronics,* Jan. 27, 1983, pp. 98-102.

Fault Tolerance Achieved in VLSI

Richard Emmerson
Intel Corporation

Michael J. McGowan
High Integrity Systems Ltd.

Fault-tolerant computer systems are typically required for applications involving revenue or some form of safety measure. In general terms, there are two areas where fault tolerance is currently of interest. The first of these, and probably the best known, encompasses transaction processing and/or database management systems that use fault tolerance to guarantee uptime or data preservation. This type of fault-tolerant system has achieved widespread fame, principally through Tandem's Non-Stop computer family. The second major area where fault tolerance has long been important is that of embedded real-time computers. A wide variety of installed systems use fault tolerance to satisfy the specific requirements of an application environment, such as a chemical plant or a communications switch. Within these systems, the requirements imposed and the solutions adopted differ greatly.

In both of these sectors, there is considerable scope for improvement. Typical fault-tolerant systems carry a high price penalty compared with non-FT systems of otherwise similar facilities. Particularly in the embedded sector, FT systems tend to be ad hoc and often contribute little to the projects that follow. Not only do these difficulties raise costs unnecessarily in current application scenarios, but they impede the market development for FT systems. For example, new market sectors could be opened up by systems that can satisfy still higher demands, such as those used to save lives, and by low-cost, standardized FT machines that could become competitive in many large-volume sectors such as financial terminals and word processors.

There is great interest in providing fault tolerance with a significantly higher capability-to-price ratio, and important business opportunities exist for suppliers who can make progress in this direction. The introduction of microprocessors may help, but it should be noted that long-heralded price reductions have yet to appear in any significant sense. For example, recently introduced systems based on the Motorola 68000 microprocessor demonstrate marginal, rather than massive, price reductions over minicomputer-based solutions.

The Intel 432 offers two powerful strategies for achieving fault tolerance in both the delivered configuration and development projects:

- The VLSI implementation provides fault-handling mechanisms in a highly efficient and compact manner, at chip level. This arrangement reduces overhead and complexity in the installed system.

Reprinted from *IEEE Micro*, pp. 34–43, Dec. 1984.

- The 432 architecture has the unique attribute of hardware/software independence. In development projects aimed at an FT computer system, this separation allows a better structured and more clearly partitioned organization of effort.

System requirements and design tradeoffs

Mechanisms designed to achieve fault tolerance are usually incorporated in systems to improve their quality and the continuity of performance. The requirements at issue typically include the following: integrity (greater probability of correct operation and the preservation of stored data) and availability (a larger proportion of uptime).

Traditionally, features that support fault tolerance are incorporated in all levels of the system design and require tradeoffs during the design process. As a result, system costs may be higher, typically because of the replication of equipment. Failure rates (and thus maintenance attention), may also increase due to the compounded effects of hardware unreliability through replication, and as a result of design faults attributable to excessive complexity or inadequate testing.

Successful fault-tolerant systems have been produced through the careful analysis of tradeoffs. To date, FT systems are most widely deployed in "up-market" applications where high system prices can be justified against the potential costs of failure or of other (for example, manually supervised) solutions. In opening up new market sectors, the pressure on tradeoffs will continue to increase.

Traditional approaches

Presently, fault-tolerant systems take one of two architectural directions: loosely coupled systems rely primarily on software to ensure reliable operation, while tightly coupled systems (also called n-modular redundant systems) provide a hardware solution. In a loosely coupled fault-tolerant system, communication channels join two identical computer systems. Periodically, normal processing is suspended while each system compares its state with the state of its companion to determine if an error has occurred since the last checkpoint. If no error is detected, each system saves its current state and processing resumes. If an error is detected, each system is "rolled back" to the last recorded state (the last error-free state) and processing resumes from that point. If the same failure is detected at the next checkpoint, the error is diagnosed as a permanent failure.

Three aspects of loosely coupled systems hinder their general acceptance. First, since software must periodically perform all consistency checks, errors frequently propagate to error-free portions of the system. This can result in the corruption of valid files or the occurrence of incorrect I/O operations. Furthermore, during the error recovery process, significant portions of error-free work can be lost by restoring the system to the last recorded state. A second, related problem is that the system is not capable of responding to external events during consistency checks. This interruption in system response can seriously disrupt real-time applications. Finally, most loosely coupled systems provide no fault tolerance after a single permanent failure occurs. Thus, users must either suspend normal processing until repairs are made or continue to operate in a non-fault-tolerant environment.

N-modular redundancy

N-modular redundant systems use several identical modules (such as CPUs or memory) to perform the same operation in lock step synchronism. During each clock cycle, special-purpose hardware compares the outputs of each module and gates the majority's data to subsequent units.

Since n-modular redundancy validates system operation during normal processing, errors cannot propagate to other portions of the system. The refined error confinement areas obviate roll-back and prevent the loss of valid work. By eliminating software checkpoints, n-modular redundant systems also maintain real-time responses. These benefits occur without any software intervention. The operation system is informed of an error for logging and operator notification purposes only. Tri-modular redundancy and quad-modular redundancy are two n-modular redundant architectures currently being marketed.

In tri-modular redundant systems, a single logical module consists of three identical physical modules and a hardware unit called a voter. The voter unit compares the outputs of the three physical modules cycle by cycle and forwards the data on which at least two of the three physical modules agree.

Figure 1 illustrates a basic TMR unit. Although this method offers the benefits of n-modular redundancy, it also has a few drawbacks. For example, a performance penalty occurs when data passes through the voter. Fortunately, most of the voter's processing time is masked by the high degree of parallelism in today's computer architectures. Thus, a physical module in a TMR unit can perform the next operation while the voter is finishing the previous one.

A more serious drawback to simple tri-modular redundancy is that the voter components are unprotected and expose the system to single-point failures. One solution, shown in Figure 2, is to triplicate each voter so that the system is protected from both processor failures and voter failures, albeit at a much higher cost.

A logical quad-modular redundant module consists of four physically identical modules organized as primary and shadow pairs of master and checker modules (see Figure 3). Although all four modules receive and process the same input data, only the primary's master module is capable of transmitting data. When the primary's master module is driving data, its checker module is comparing external data and that presented to its disabled output drivers. This technique is called functional redundancy checking and is shown in Figure 4. If the primary's checker module detects an error, it initiates a procedure that disables the primary pair and allows the shadow pair to take over the primary role.

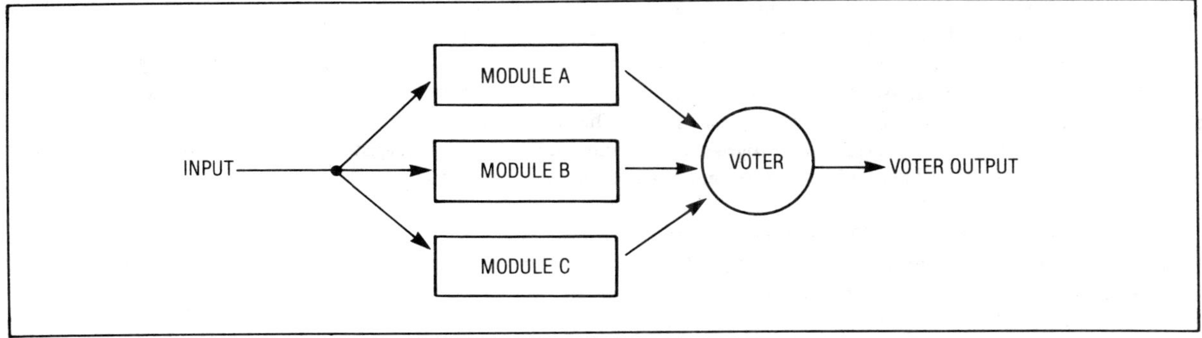

Figure 1. Basic tri-modular redundancy configuration.

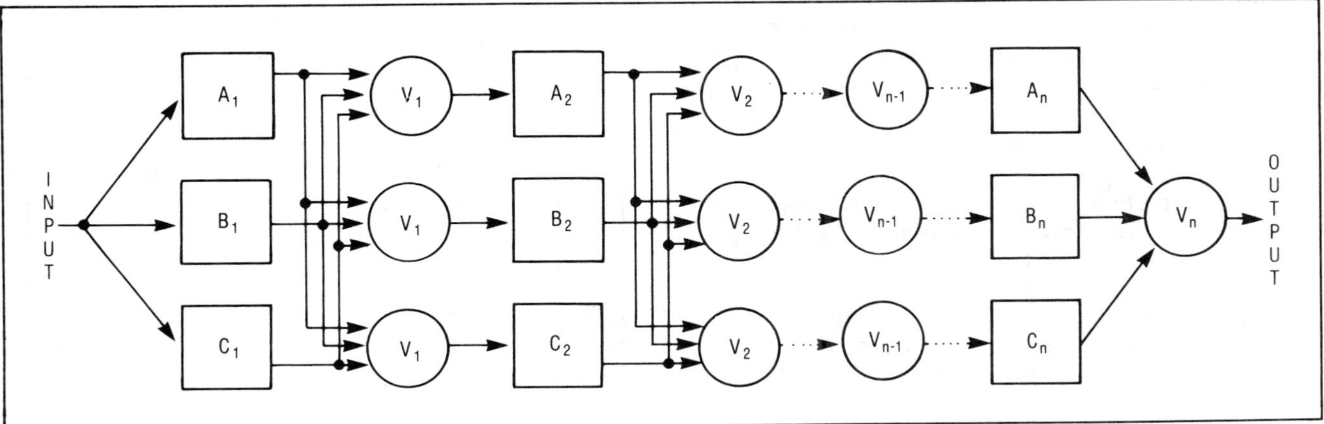

Figure 2. The use of TMR voters to remove single points of failure from a network.

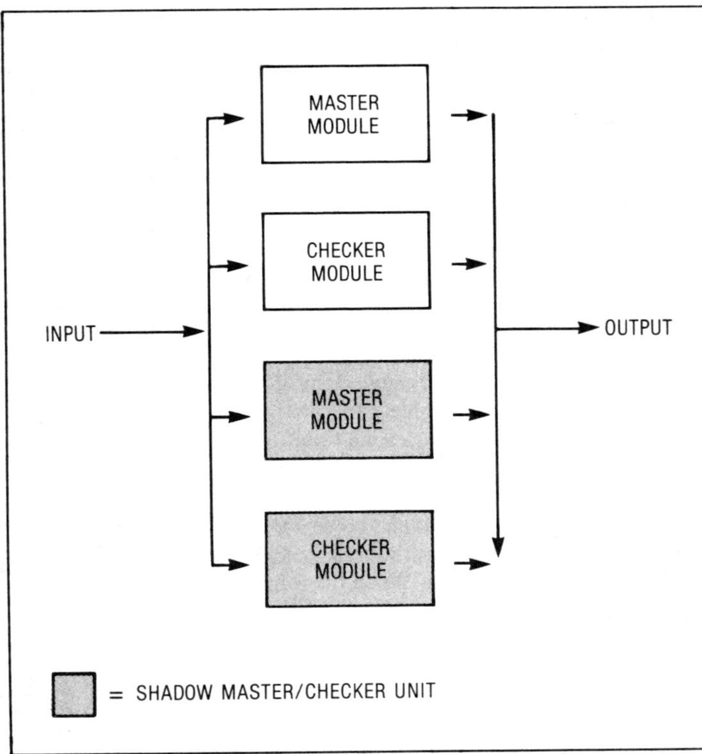

Figure 3. Basic quad-modular redundancy configuration.

Although quad-modular redundancy eliminates the problems associated with tri-modular redundancy's voter circuitry, the replication of each module can become prohibitively expensive. For this reason, Intel builds QMR-based systems by integrating functional redundancy checking and other fault-tolerant support features directly into the silicon interconnect components of the iAPX 432 processor family.

FT support in silicon

The iAPX 432 is based on quad-modular redundancy. The components provide comprehensive detection facilities for processor operations, as well as for the operation of buses and memories. Recovery is possible from both permanent and transient errors. Detection and recovery are performed totally in the VLSI components; there is no need for additional TTL logic or diagnostic software.

In an iAPX 432 based-system, there are three distinct steps in responding to an error. First, the error is detected and localized to a confinement area. Next, the error is reported to all the modules in the system, which prevents the incorrect data from propagating into another confinement area and provides all of the modules with the information required to perform recovery. Finally, the faulty confinement area is isolated from the system. Recovery occurs using redundant resources available in the system.

The purpose of a confinement area is to limit damage from error propagation and to localize the faulty area for recovery and repair. A confinement area is defined as a unit (module or memory bus) of the system having a limited number of tightly controlled interfaces. Detection mechanisms are placed at every interface to ensure that no inconsistent data can leave the area and corrupt other confinement areas.

All communication in an iAPX 432-based system is carried out over buses; there are no point-to-point signals or daisy-chained signals. This approach makes on-line repair possible, since no signal definition is dependent on the number of resources in the system. The presence or absence of a given module cannot prevent communication between any other modules. In addition, the memory bus defined by the BIU and MCU provides a uniform and regularly structured communications path that supports the modular expansion of both fault-tolerant and standard system capabilities.

Error confinement

Figure 5 shows the four types of confinement areas in an iAPX 432-based system. There is a confinement area for each module and memory bus in the system. When an error is detected, it is confined to one of these system building blocks, and recovery and repair strategies are built around the block's replacement. When a module or bus has its confinement mechanisms activated, it can be viewed as a self-checking unit. Detection mechanisms reside at every interface, and all data are checked as they flow across the interface between confinement areas.

An example of processor memory operation may help to clarify the function of the confinement areas (see Figure 6). Assume that a general data processor makes a read request from a memory location. That request will be mapped through the bus interface unit on the addressed memory bus. As the information flows onto the memory bus, it will be checked by the BIU. If there is any failure in the GDP confinement area, it will be detected at this time. The information then flows across the memory bus and into the addressed memory module. Before the information is accepted by the module, the memory controller unit

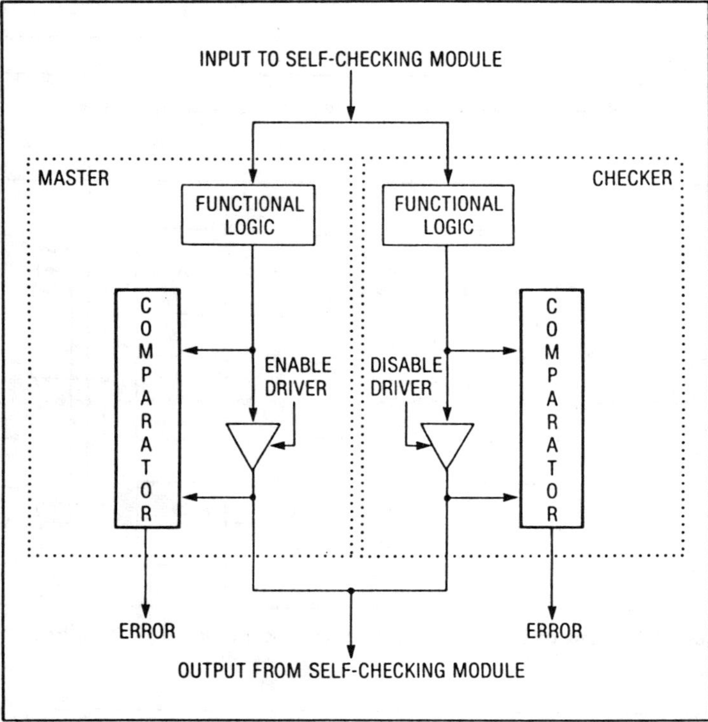

Figure 4. Functional redundancy checking.

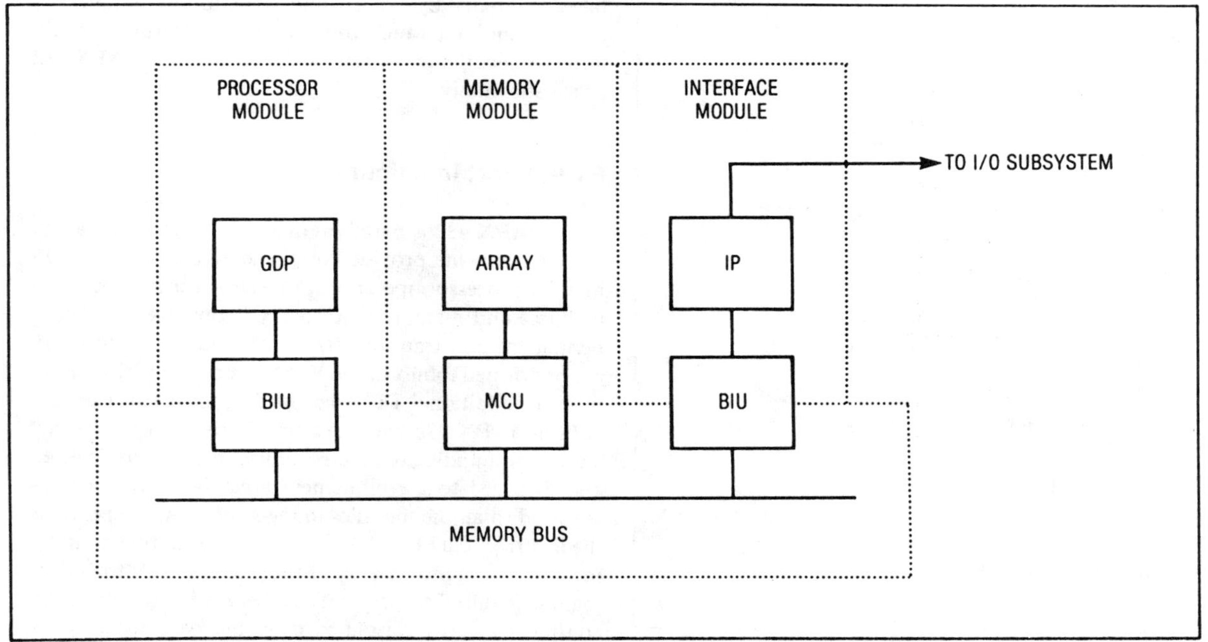

Figure 5. iAPX 432 confinement areas.

checks it for correctness. If a failure is detected, it is confined to the memory bus because the information was valid when it left the GDP confinement area. The MCU performs the memory operation and returns data to the memory bus. As data flows onto the bus, it is checked for correctness by the MCU, and again by the BIU before being used by the GDP module.

The confinement area interfaces provide tight error control and isolate failures to one of the system building blocks. These confinement areas were formed by applying five different detection mechanisms: duplication, parity, Hamming error-correction codes, timeouts, and loop back checks (used to detect errors in the TTL bus drivers). Some of the detection mechanisms themselves are self-checking (the detection circuits are checked as part of normal operation); others can be exercised during normal system operation to expose any latent faults.

Error reporting

Upon detecting an error, a message is broadcast to all the nodes in the system. This error-reporting message identifies the faulty confinement area, the type of error that occured, and whether the error is permanent or transient. There are two reasons for sending such a report. First, it informs the rest of the system that an error has occurred, which prevents other confinement areas from using the inconsistent data. Second, it provides the necessary information for system recovery. After recovery, the error message is recorded in a log register in every node in the system. The log is available to software and is useful in monitoring the health of the system.

Error messages are broadcast over a set of serial buses that are totally independent from the buses used during normal operation. This error-reporting network is fully

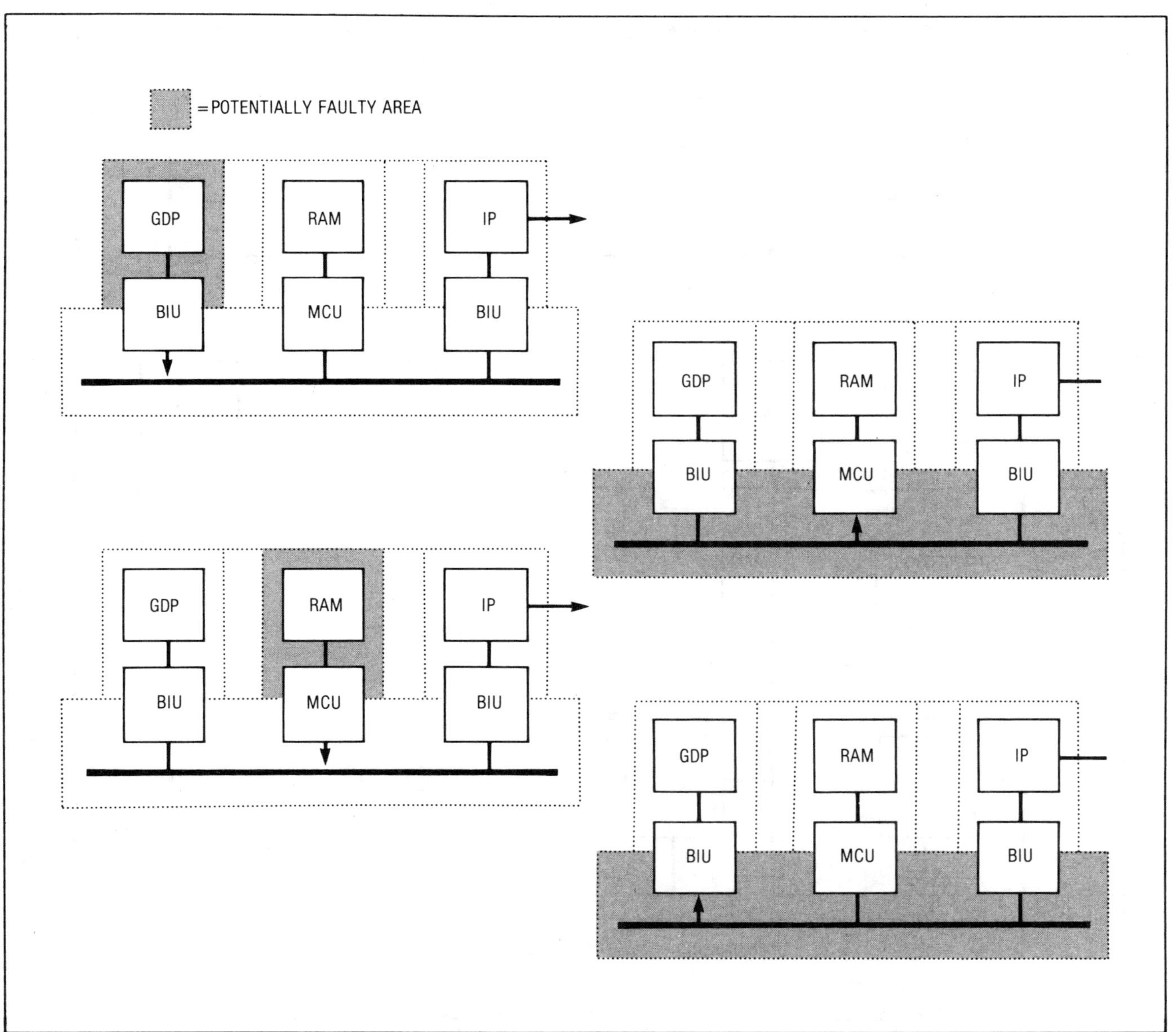

Figure 6. iAPX 432 confinement area operation.

fault tolerant; that is, no single failure in the error-reporting network can prevent the correct and timely reporting of an error in the system. This network of serial buses follows exactly the same topology as the buses used for normal operation. A failure on one of these buses is limited to one of the confinement areas. It will not com-

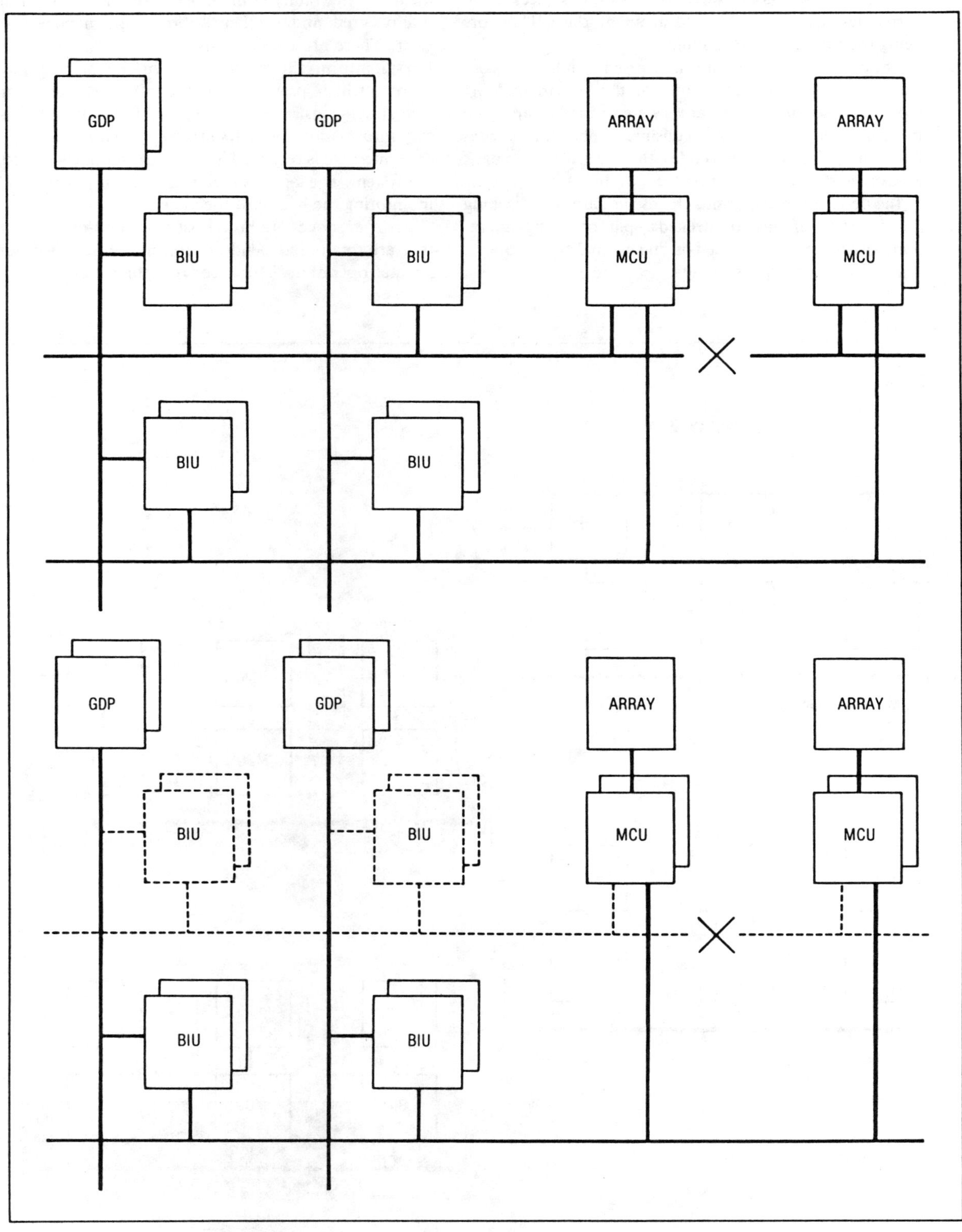

Figure 7. iAPX 432 bus reconfiguration. When a permanent error is detected on a bus, further data transmission is suspended. The BIUs on the faulty bus automatically close down, while the MCUs switch to their backup buses. Following fault recovery, memory requests that would have originally been transmitted over the faulty bus are rerouted over the backup bus.

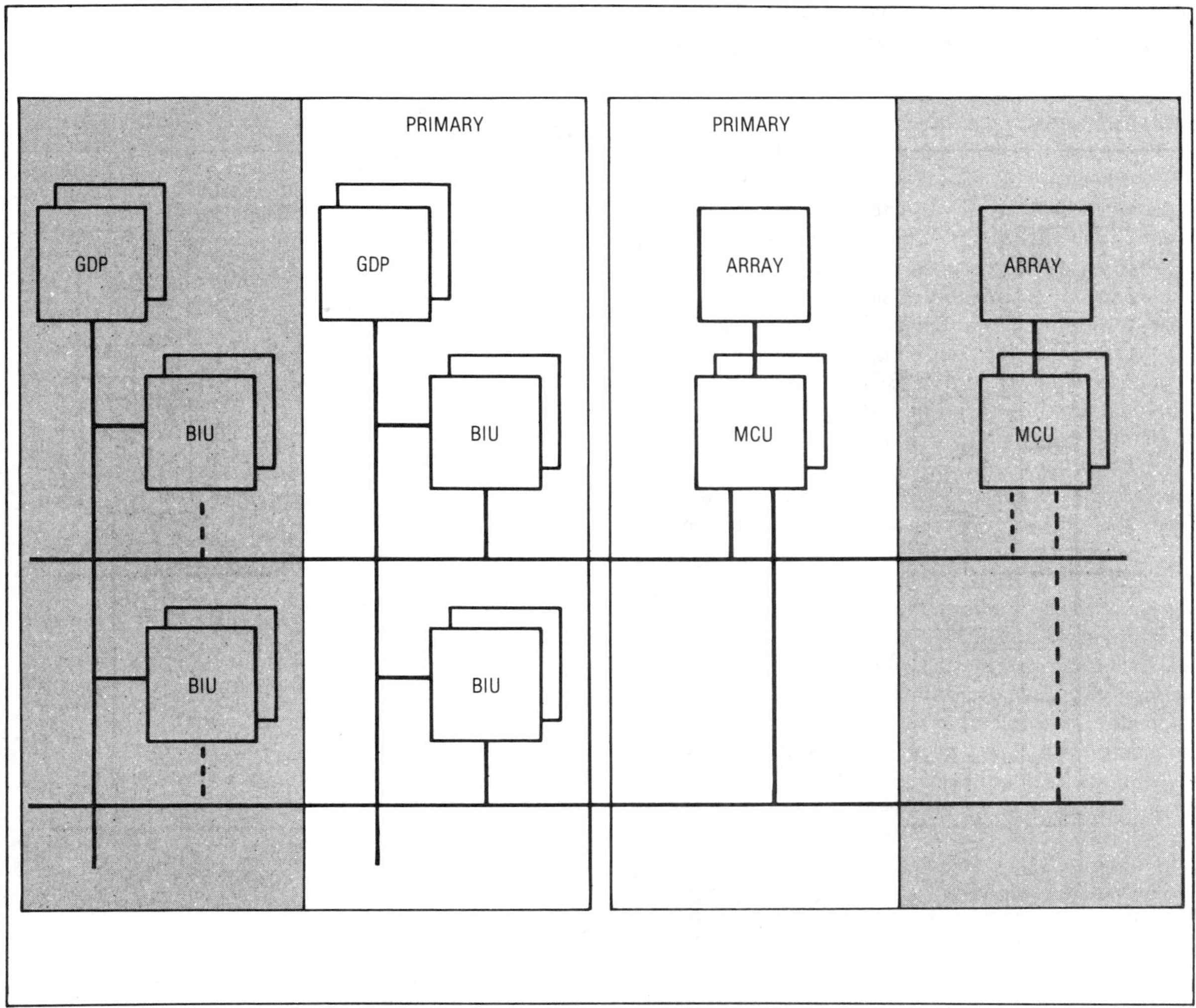

Figure 8. iAPX 432 module reconfiguration. Faults have been detected in both shadow processor and shadow memory modules. The primary modules continue operation while the shadows are disconnected automatically from the system.

promise the fault-tolerant capabilities of the system, because other error-reporting buses (in the other confinement areas) take over its reporting responsibilities. The error-reporting circuitry may be tested during normal operation to uncover any latent faults.

Error recovery

The recovery process begins after an error-report message has been broadcast throughout the system. Recovery is a distributed operation on iAPX 432-based systems. That is, each node in the system reads the error-report message and decides what recovery action needs to be taken.

There are five redundancy mechanisms in iAPX 432-based systems. Retry and single-bit correcting error correction codes are used for recovery from transient errors, while shadowed modules, backup buses, and spare memory bits are used in cases of permanent errors. These redundant resources cover the entire system, allow recovery from any detected error, and have no impact on system performance.

Each BIU maintains an internal buffer that allows outstanding processor requests to be retried if a transient error occurs. A single-bit correcting ECC code is also applied to each word in the memory arrays. Although this arrangement provides redundancy for both permanent and transient errors, its primary purpose is to correct soft errors that occur in dynamic RAMs.

For permanent errors, every self-checking module in the system may be paired with another self-checking module of the same type. This pair of modules operates in lock step and provides a complete and current backup for all state information in the module. This mechanism is known as module shadowing because the shadow is ready for immediate recovery should the primary fail, or vice versa. A fault-tolerant module is also called a quad-modular redundant module because the iAPX 432 VLSI components are replicated four times (two self-checking modules, with a master and checker in each).

Each memory bus in the system may be paired with another memory bus. During normal operation, the buses run independently; both contribute to the total bandwidth available in the system. However, if one bus fails, the other is capable of handling the requests that would normally be handled by the failed bus. Similarly, if one bit in the array fails, the spare memory bit can be switched in to replace the failed bit.

For transient errors, all of the outstanding accesses are retried. If there are any single-bit errors in the memory arrays, the MCUs return corrected data. For permanent errors, the redundant resource is switched in to replace the failed unit. This switch is done on a node-by-node basis; there is no centralized element that controls the switch. Each node knows which module or memory bus it is backing up (shadowing). If the error report identifies its partner as the faulty unit, then the node becomes active and takes over operation. After the resource switch is complete, all of the outstanding memory accesses are automatically retried, allowing operation to resume at a point before the failure could corrupt any data.

These reconfiguration and recovery actions are performed by the hardware without any software intervention. After recovery is complete, the hardware informs the system software of the error and subsequent recovery actions. System software then makes policy decisions regarding the optimum system configuration given the resources remaining. The software may choose to maintain the full capabilities of the system and switch in a spare resource, or it may maintain fault tolerance and degrade performance by switching out the unit that no longer has a shadow. It could also maintain performance and run with an increased probability of failure by keeping the shadow unit in operation without bringing a spare on line. All of these configuration options are under software control and require no manual intervention or hardware changes. These policy decisions are carried out while normal system operation continues. Figures 7 and 8 show two recovery operations.

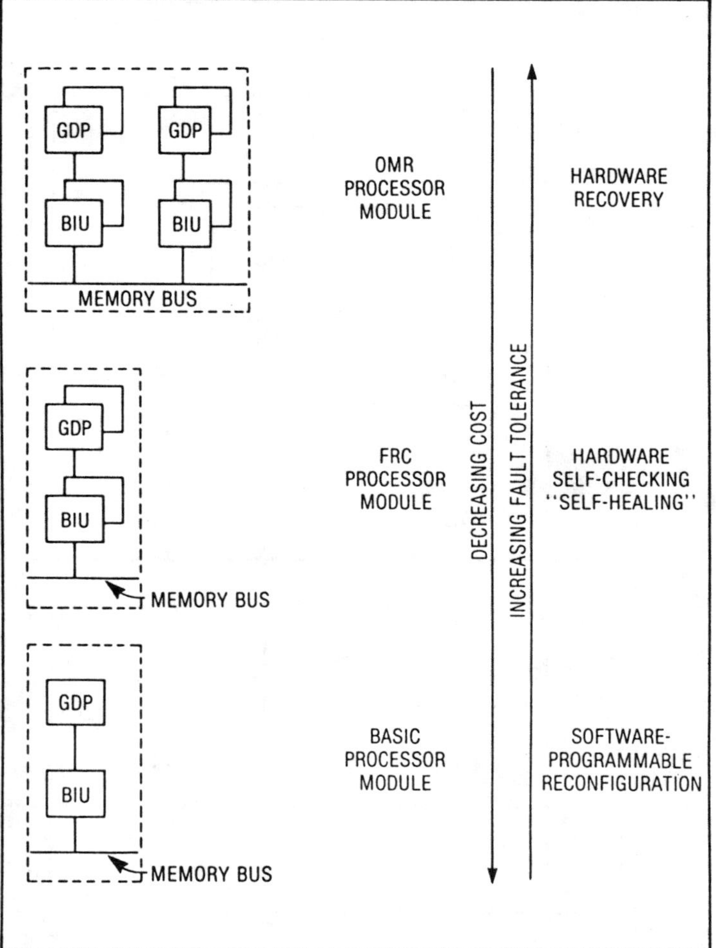

Figure 9. Fault-tolerant alternatives.

Levels of fault tolerance

Not all applications require the extensive protection of quad-modular redundancy. While immediate recovery is essential for real-time systems, transaction processing systems, for example, may be able to tolerate a small delay between the time a fault is detected and the system's recovery. The same set of iAPX 432 components can be used to build systems with more modest fault-tolerant capabilities at comparable savings in system cost.

The least expensive alternative is to eliminate all functional redundancy and rely on the system's basic fault detection mechanisms such as bus parity, error-correcting codes across memory arrays, and access retry. In this base-level design, the downtime after a system crash is limited by the time needed to reinitialize the system, run a diagnostic program to locate the error, and reconfigure the system to disconnect the faulty module. Since any 432 system is likely to use multiple processors, it is likely that several functioning processors will be left even if one of them fails. The processing power after system recovery will be lower than before, but the system will be able to function with a lighter load until a replacement is available for the faulty module. This arrangement is suitable for systems that are principally required to achieve a large portion of uptime but that can tolerate occasional periods of interruption for reloads and restarts. The most significant drawback of the basic system is that the database can be corrupted unless the operating system employs the checkpointed techniques common in loosely coupled fault-tolerant systems.

The most cost-effective alternative for a transaction processing system may be what is sometimes called a "self-healing" system. Fault detection is done by hardware and fault isolation is automatic, but recovery requires software intervention. The primary objective of the system is to protect the database rather than to eliminate downtime.

In a self-healing system, functional redundancy checking is used to guarantee that all hardware faults are caught as they occur and that no error is allowed to propagate beyond the confinement area in which it occurs. The difference between a self-healing system and a system using quad-modular redundancy is that once a fault is detected, the normal program flow must be interrupted. The faulty module shuts itself down and the operating system is requested to intervene. The 432 will then rely on the remaining fuctional modules and the operating system to reconfigure the system and restart the programs. The recovery time might be as long as several seconds. Figure 9 illustrates the range of fault-tolerant capabilities using the

432, and Figures 10-14 show typical system configurations for each alternative.

With the opportunities provided by the 432 VLSI, system builders can devote their attention to higher-level configurational issues and derive benefits from guaranteed low-level support. In practical 432-based fault-tolerant systems, the user remains responsible for making I/O channels and controllers suitably secure, and for providing clock and power supplies that do not erode the basis of the fault-handling principles by introducing significant unreliability. Nevertheless, these responsibilities are minor

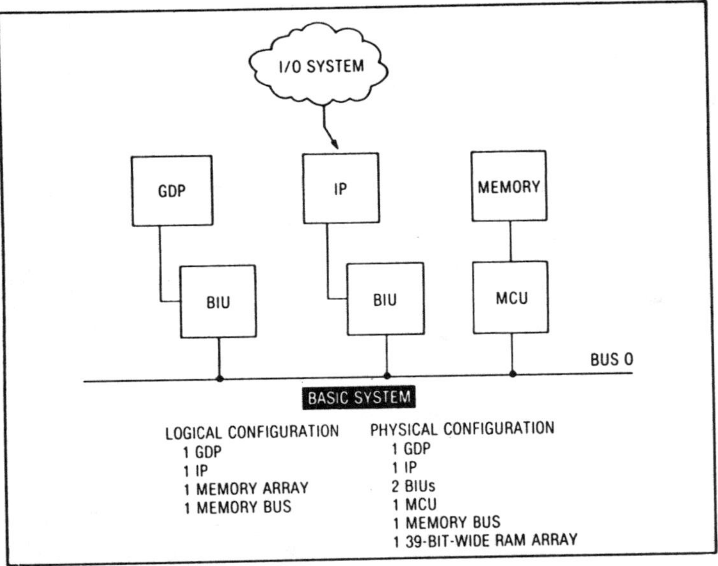

Figure 10. The most basic system that can be constructed using the iAPX 432 family of components. The only detection mechanisms are parity and retry. If any of the resources should fail, the system will be out of service until the module is repaired.

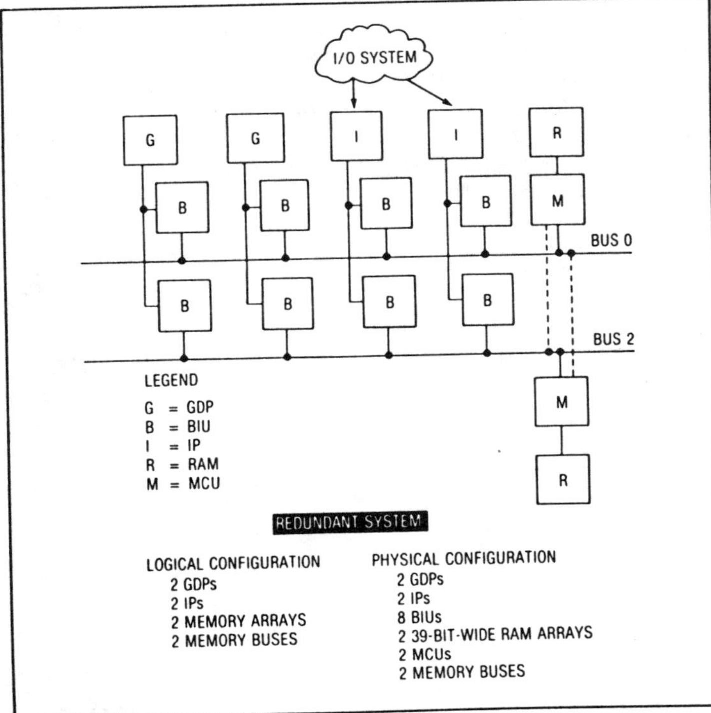

Figure 11. A more flexible system, with two of each type of resource. If any of the resources should fail, software could reconfigure the system, which would be back on-line as soon as the diagnostics had isolated the faulty resource.

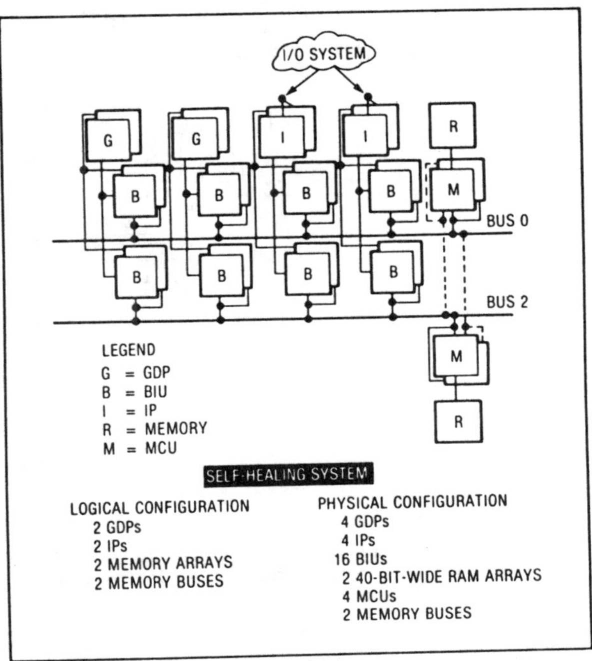

Figure 12. This system is capable of a comprehensive deferred maintenance strategy. The system uses all of the detection mechanisms of the 432 BIU and MCU and has more than one of every resource in the system. When an error occurs, it will be detected immediately and isolated from the system. Software can then rapidly reconfigure the system around the faulty module and return to operation within seconds.

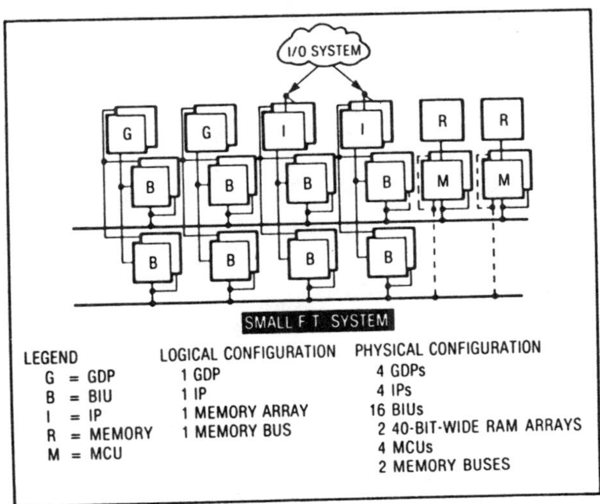

Figure 13. The smallest possible 432 system offering complete fault tolerance. Each self-checking module has a backup. All faults are isolated by the hardware, and recovery is immediate. No software intervention is required.

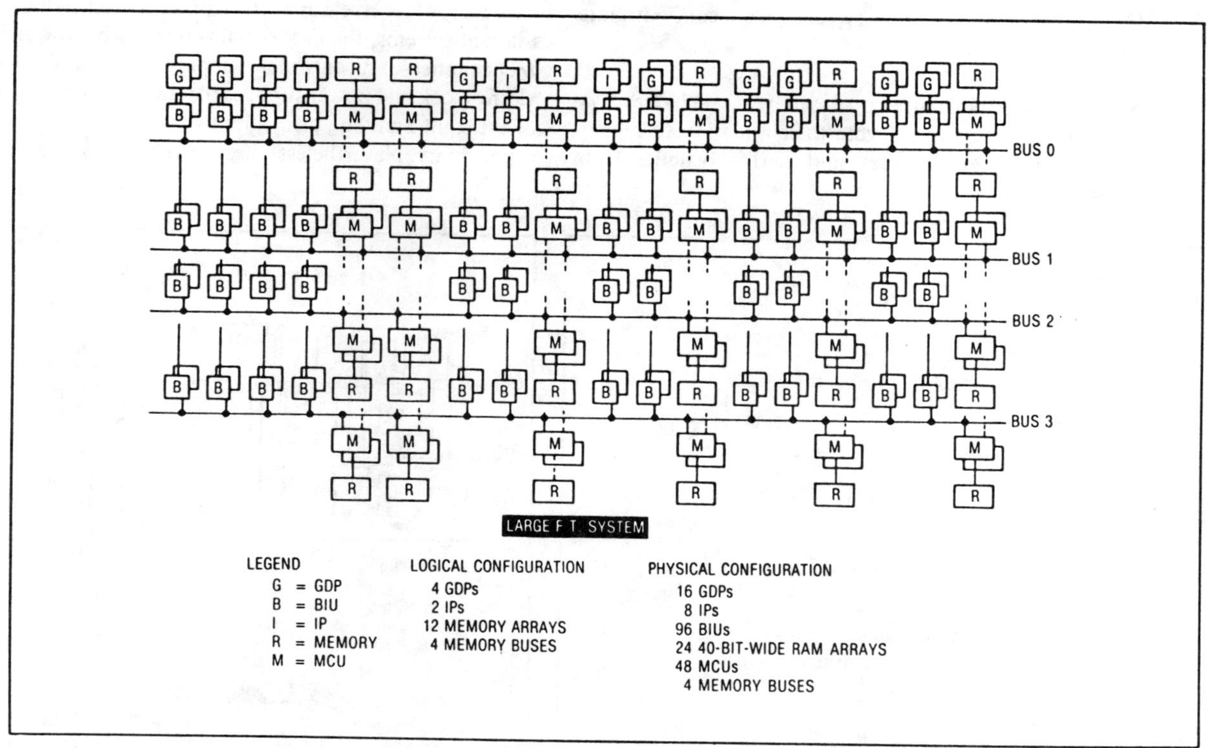

Figure 14. A large fault-tolerant computer such as that used in a process control system. Four memory buses are used to provide high bandwidth for the four logical processors.

compared with those arising from designs based on conventional system components that neither directly support fault tolerance nor offer hardware/software independence. In these cases, the user must usually develop a special-purpose operating system, and both the hardware and software will acquire a major project-specific component, providing little or no contribution to future developments. By contrast, the modular nature of the 432 forms a widely usable system foundation. ■

Additional reading

1. *Intel 432 System Summary: Manager's Perspective,* Intel Corp., Santa Clara, Calif., 1982.
2. *iAPX 432 General Data Processor Architecture Reference Manual,* Intel Corp., Santa Clara, Calif., 1982.
3. D. Siewiorek and R. Schwartz, *The Theory and Practice of Reliable System Design,* Digital Press, Bedford, Mass., 1982.
4. *iAPX 432 Interconnect Architecture Reference Manual,* Intel Corp., Santa Clara, Calif., 1983.

The Modiac Multiprocessor—A 286-based Design

Giovanni Neri and Tullio Salmon Cinotti
University of Bologna

Modiac is a multiprocessor system for control applications based on an advanced bus structure called M3. The Modiac CPU board, which we developed under a grant from the Italian National Research Council, is based on a high-performance microprocessor, the Intel 80286. The board is double-Eurocard in size and features dual bus control, 64K bytes of dual-ported RAM, 128K bytes of EPROM, an 80287 mathematics coprocessor, a RS-232 serial line, a RS-422 serial line, software-programmable registers for card customization, and optional system protection at both the memory and I/O level. M3 is a high-speed, multiplexed bus that uses a serial line for module interconnection and a parallel arbitration scheme.

Here, we discuss how we designed the Modiac CPU board to work on the M3 bus. We describe the characteristics and behavior of M3, and the implementation of the board. We conclude with several observations about the performance of 80286-based processors on a multiplexed bus.

Background

In 1979, the Italian National Research Council launched the Progetto Finalizzato Informatica (Special Program for Computer Science) to expand the automation of Italian industry through a joint research effort by universities and industry. Among the various projects, special attention has been paid to the development of an advanced process control system called Modiac—the Modular Integrated System for Automation and Process Control.[1] Modiac is based on a set of computing nodes linked through a local-area network using either a token-passing or a CSMA/CD bus arbitration scheme.[2,3] The design targets of Modiac are modularity, cost-effectiveness, high reliability, and sophisticated node-to-process interfacing. In the most complex Modiac configuration, each node is implemented as a cluster of processors tightly linked through a shared, or "system," bus. Each processor in turn exploits a private, or "local," bus whose characteristics are the same as those of the system bus. Boards use the extended, "double-Eurocard" format. A distributed multiprocessor operating system kernel called Modosk[4]—Modular Distributed Operating System Kernel—has been implemented for Modiac; it supports the entire Olivetti MOS operating system,[5] which has been made available to the Italian National Research Council through a cooperative agreement.

Modosk implements a virtual machine in which processes running on different processors are executed in parallel and processes running on the same processor are executed in a multitasking environment. A process belongs to a particular processor when it resides in that processor's private memory; shared memory is used only for processes interactions. Each processor has its own copy of the kernel in its memory. Because the kernel has been designed as a set of modules, it can be configured to the needs of each processor—in other words, Modosk can be thought of as a family of kernels.

Modosk is implemented around the classic scheme of process state transitions and synchronization primitives; its behavior is completely transparent to users. Interactions among processes are handled without concern for the processes' physical allocations—if a process invokes the kernel, the relative primitive checks where any other interacting process is located and takes the appropriate actions. To avoid system bus overhead, a programmer can distinguish among local and global semaphores. From a user point of

Reprinted from *IEEE Micro*, pp. 7–15, Feb. 1986.

view, Modosk can be regarded as an extension of a standard sequential Pascal virtual machine. Synchronization primitives are invoked as Pascal procedures and do not require any compile-time controls. Modosk has been written mostly in Pascal to allow easy porting among different processors.

The M3 bus

In 1979 the most widely used processor-independent buses were the Multibus, now standardized as IEEE 796,[6] and the S-100, now standardized as IEEE 696.[7] Although very important from a historical point of view, these two buses suffer from several drawbacks:

- They have a rather unsophisticated interrupt system. They do not have specific interprocessor interrupts, which are vital in multiprocessor systems.
- Their mechanical standards are supported by few manufacturers. (There are virtually no suppliers of Multibus and S-100 mechanicals Europe.)
- They provide few or no status lines for identifying the operation currently being carried out.
- They make no provision for bus debugging and monitoring.
- They have poor bus arbitration schemes (especially the Multibus).
- They provide no local bus expansion—that is, they make no provision for expanding the private on-board bus to accommodate local system enhancements. Intel has recently at least partially dealt with this problem for the Multibus by introducing the SBX and LBX expansions; however, the use of the P2 connector with different signals (for the LBX) has created havoc among Multibus users.

To eliminate these flaws and add new features, an IEEE standards group, P896,[8] was established to define a manufacturer-, technology-, and processor-independent bus. The proposals of the P896 group are an appealing reference point for bus developers. The bus adopted for Modiac, M3 (Multiplexed Multimicroprocessor Bus),[9] has many features in common with P896, although some modifications—like strong protection against failures—have been made to meet the specific needs of process control computers.

M3-based systems rely on the Eurocard mechanical structure, which is used around the world and has been chosen by the designers of both the P896 bus and the VMEbus.[10]

M3 is a fully multiplexed bus—its data, address, interrupt, arbitration priority, and status lines are time-multiplexed to save power and space. M3 uses the 96-pin DIN 41612 connector; Table 1 shows M3's pin assignment. Signal lines in Column B are not used in simple systems. This allows the use of 64 pins only and provides all the benefits arising from the use of single-layer boards.

Table 1.
M3 pin assignment.

	A	B	C
1	GND	GND	GND
2	+5V	+5V	+5V
3	INF 0	Reserved	INF 1
4	INF 2	Reserved	INF 3
5	INF 4	Reserved	NF 5
6	INF 6	Reserved	INF 7
7	INF 8	Reserved	INF 9
8	INF 10	Reserved	NF 11
9	INF 12	Reserved	INF 13
10	INF 14	Reserved	INF 15
11	INF 16	Reserved	INF 17
12	INF 18	Reserved	INF 19
13	INF 20	Reserved	INF 21
14	INF 22	Reserved	INF 23
15	INF 24	Reserved	INF 25
16	INF 26	Reserved	INF 27
17	INF 28	Reserved	INF 29
18	PAREN*	Reserved	DAER*
19	WRITE*	GND	CYCLE*
20	LODAVAL*	GND	HIDAVAL*
21	ADDREN*	GND	TRACK*
22	PAR 0	Reserved	BRACK
23	PAR 1	RES	PAR 3
24	PAR 2	Reserved	SERCK*
25	SUPON*	Reserved	INHIB*
26	RES	GND	BUSBUSY*
27	PWFAIL*	GND	SERDAT*
28	NMI*	GND	RESET*
29	PROCDW*	ABORT*	−15V
30	+15V	PROCINT*	SYSCK
31	+5V	+5V	+5V
32	GND	GND	GND

A timing diagram illustrating M3 behavior is presented in Figure 1. The nature of the information carried by lines INF 0-29 depends on the value of signal CYCLE, which times the multiplexing. In the first half of the cycle, lines INF 0-23 carry the address of the requested data (with the 24 lines permitting a system address space of 16M bytes) and lines INF 24-29 carry the status signals. The latter information indicates which types of operation is currently being carried out—e.g., memory accessing, stack management, interrupt acknowledging, or peripheral addressing. The status lines can be fruitfully exploited—in bus-level memory protection, for example, line INF 29 can be used locking dual-port memories during critical regions of software execution.

Addresses are strobed by the ADDREN* signal during normal data transfers. (The asterisk indicates negative-true signals.) Data transfer direction is signaled by means of the WRITE* signal. The two signals LODAVAL* and HIDAVAL* enable transfers on lines INF 0-7 and INF 8-15, respectively, in both read and write operations. Asynchronous transfers between modules having different speeds are achieved through signals TRACK* and BRACK. The M3 bus in fact relies on the concept that an addressed module is not ready until it explicitly informs the sender. In a module-to-module transfer TRACK* is used to do this; it is activated by a slave module only when the slave is ready. In a broadcast transfer BRACK, which is positive-true and driven by open-collector devices, is used to inform the sender that all modules are ready. Transfers are therefore synchronized to the slowest of the bus modules involved.

In the second half of the cycle, lines INF 0-15 carry the actual data to be transferred, and lines INF 16-23 carry the pending interrupt signals. Lines INF 24-27 are used for the next system bus cycle arbitration, if there is one.

In addition to the usual write and read cycles, M3 supports indivisible read-modify-write cycles (for operating system support), indivisible read-after-write cycles (for system reliability), and block transfers.

In a process control environment such as Modiac's, particular attention must be paid to the safety of data transfers. To this end, M3 has been provided with four parity lines (PAR0, PAR1, PAR2, and PAR3), one for each byte of information, including the status signals. The signal DAER*, when inactive, indicates that the addressing and data transfer phases have ended without transmission errors. DAER* is activated in the data transfer phase only when data are being transferred to a slave module. If data are not being transferred to a slave module, the slave does not activate the ready signal and force the master to time out. To allow the coexistence of parity-equipped modules with modules not so equipped, an additional signal, PAREN*, is provided; it is activated when parity signals are meaningful.

Arbitration in M3 is carried out through the same mechanism as that used in the Fastbus,[11] the S-100 (IEEE 696) bus, and the proposed IEEE 896 bus and involves lines BUSBUSY* and SYSCLK. When BUSBUSY* is high, all processors competing for the bus try to assert their own priority on the bus priority lines (INF 24-27) via open-collector devices. Each processor compares its asserted priority with the priority it reads from the bus lines and turns off its driver if its own priority is lower. Eventually only one processor, the bus winner, has its drivers still on. The entire arbitration process must take place within a period of SYSCLK, and therefore the complexity of the combinatorial circuits must be kept to a minimum.

In M3, interrupts by peripherals demanding service are handled as follows: Upon reception of interrupt signals (on lines INF 16-23 when ADDREN* is high), the CPU detects the highest-priority interrupt and transfers on data lines INF 0-7 an acknowledgment vector which is decoded by the peripheral controllers. All peripherals detecting a match with their own preselected internal code turn on their open-collector drivers and try to assert their own priority codes on lines INF 8-15. Arbitration among priorities occurs in the same way as during bus competition—thus, up to 255 interrupts can be pending on the same line. In a typical application, however, a simpler approach is usually taken: Each peripheral activates only one line during arbitration, leading to much more simple combinatorial logic but allowing only eight interrupts to be pending on the same line.

The interrupt scheme previously described is customarily used in M3 local buses or in monoprocessor applications,

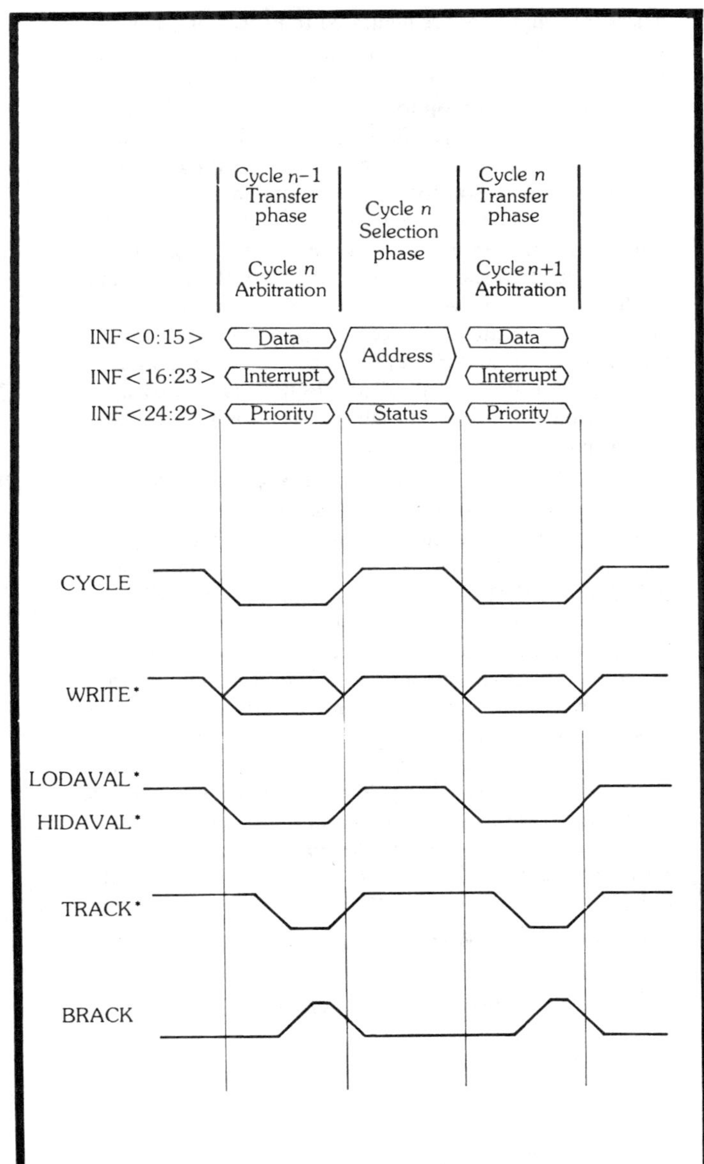

Figure 1. M3 bus timing.

where interrupt lines are dedicated to processors. In general, multipoint interrupts (i.e., interprocessor interrupts) are used when M3 is employed for system buses. Two implementation options are available. The simplest one is to transfer to specific locations of the destination processor the relevant information, such as the name of sender and the reason for the interrupt. The locations involved can be in either memory or I/O address space. The other implementation is to send the relevant information over the bus to a special register on each CPU board, and to clock each board with signal PROCINT*. Each processor, upon an internal interrupt signal, examines the register contents and makes the appropriate decision. A special interrupt signal called ABORT* is used to stop an operation and is provided mainly for use by paged or virtual memory systems as a fault trap.

A trend in contemporary bus design is to provide systems with a serial bus in addition to a parallel one. A serial bus consists of two lines: one carrying data and one carrying the synchronizing clock. A serial bus has been implemented in M3; line SERDAT* carries the data, and line SERCK* carries the clock. In any serial bus, information is exchanged through a software protocol that requires one module to act as the "sender" and all other modules to act as "receivers." Obviously, contention between two or more modules can arise if they want to get hold of the serial line at the same time. However, in M3 the line is open-drain-driven, and as a result an arbitration scheme like that used in M3 parallel bus arbitration is employed. The particular scheme used is the one embedded in the Philips MAB 8400 microprocessor,[12] which is essentially a modified version of the 8048 microcomputer.

The serial bus in Modiac can be used in the following cases, among others:

- as an alternative approach to interprocessor interrupt implementation,
- for emergency calls in case of partial or total failures of the parallel bus, and
- for cross-module checks for system consistency in redundant configurations.

The M3 bus offers another important option to system designers: the supervisor function. By using lines SUPON* and INHIBIT*, which delay the address cycle and inhibit the drivers, respectively, a bus monitoring module (the supervisor) can substitute its own addresses and data on the bus for on-the-fly data and/or addresses generated by system modules. Moreover, by monitoring bus arbitration and by having information about the access rights of processes running on each CPU, the supervisor can provide a sophisticated memory protection scheme that makes Modiac a capability-based system.[13] This feature, in fact, allows chased or unwanted transfers to be trapped and the appropriate response to be taken. A possible use of it is in the implementation of a bus-level real-time emulator.

When the supervisor is not present in the system, memory protection is normally achieved through the use of MMU-like devices like the processor on-chip protection mechanism of the Intel 80286. To enforce system protection, M3 offers an additional option—line INF 28, when carrying status information, states whether data transfer takes place under SYSTEM* or USER mode.

M3 provides the usual "system trouble" lines: PWFAIL* (power failure), PROCDW* (processor down), and NMI* (nonmaskable interrupt). While the function of each of these lines is obvious, the policy for each line's use is determined by system designers. M3 also provides a RESET* line, and it reserves other lines for future use.

Modiac node implementation

So far little has been said about the way the M3 bus is used in Modiac or about the implementation of Modiac nodes (i.e., the implementation of Modiac modules on M3). In the following discussion, we will use the customary symbols for controlling and slave modules—a circle with an "out" arrow will represent a module able to get control of the bus, and a circle with an "in" arrow will represent a module that is a slave. For an interface module, however, we will use our own representation—an AND symbol. An interface module allows interbus data exchange and is driven by a device connected to an AND input; its outputs are connected to slaves only.

There are several possible Modiac architectures:

- Monoprocessor (Figure 2a): There is only one (local) bus with one master and several slaves.
- Multimaster (Figure 2b): There is only a local bus with a "primary master" (a CPU) and several "secondary masters" (DMA controllers).
- Multiprocessor (Figure 2c): Two or more monoprocessor (local) buses and one multimaster (system) bus are provided.

As shown in Figure 2, modules can be connected to the local bus, to the system bus, or to both. Modules connected to the system bus can exchange data through dual-port memories accessible both from the system bus and from one local bus. (This solution obviously lowers system bus occupation.) Mechanically, modules are double-Eurocards connected in the manner shown in Figure 3, where the top bus is the system bus and the bottom buses are the local ones.

The serial bus is physically connected to all local and system buses.

Modules such as parallel and serial interfaces, disk controllers, token-passing and Ethernet controllers, RAM boards, and bubble memory boards are available for Modiac. There are Z8001- and Z8002-based CPU boards—the first for high-level (multiprocessor) applications and the second for low-cost (monoprocessor) systems; a J11 board is also available. Process control interfaces have been designed which utilize local intelligence and onboard interchangeable adapters to offload central processors. These boards are based on the Z8002 micro-

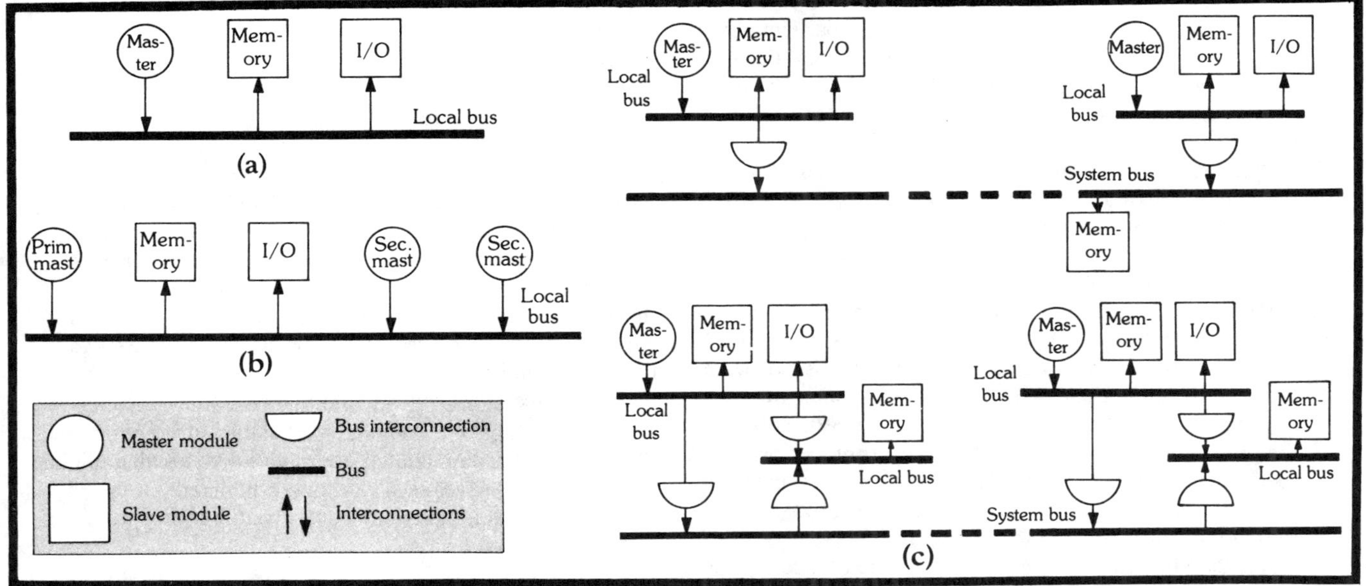

Figure 2. Modiac architectures—monoprocessor (a), multimaster (b), and multiprocessor (c).

processor and are provided with three sockets for adapters that are primarily used for signal conditioning or very low level data handling. In many respects these adapters can be considered equivalent to SBX boards.

M3-286 CPU board characteristics

Modiac evolution and development during the period 1980-83 showed that in very complex distributed applications some nodes require very high computing power. This is especially true for supervising nodes which handle man-process interactions through graphic displays and which process all information coming from peripheral nodes.

To satisfy this need, we decided to design a new high-end Modiac CPU board. At the time (1982), several new microprocessors had been announced. We chose the Intel 80286[14] because

- it offers very high computing power,
- it provides memory management on the chip, which saves board space, and
- it supports virtual memory operations through restartable instructions.

Another important reason why we chose the 80286 was the massive amount of software already available for the 8086 family. The 80286 has two modes of operation—compatibility mode, in which it behaves exactly as a 8086 with an enhanced instruction set, and noncompatibility mode, which is protected. In compatibility mode, 8086 software can be readily used. One more reason why we chose the Intel chip involved the availability of languages. Of the six compilers running on VAX systems—ASM, PLM, Pascal, Fortran, Basic, and Jovial—four are available on at least two Intel development systems, the MDS Series III and IV and the 86/330. With these systems, programs can be built using different languages and linked without problems.

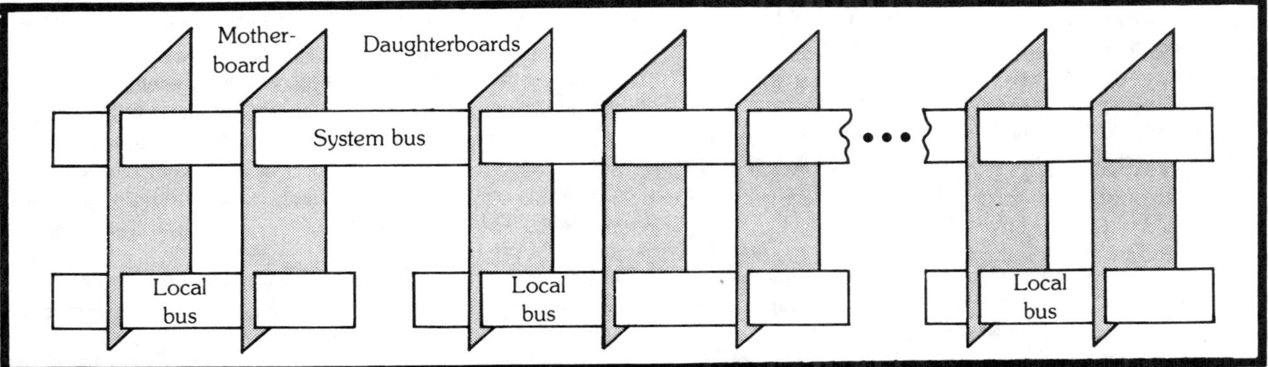

Figure 3. Connection of double-Eurocard modules in M3.

Two real-time operating systems, RMX86 and RMX88, are also available and ready to use. They are particularly attractive for use in process control environments. Furthermore, a new, powerful real-time operating system for the protected mode of operation, RMX286, made the 80286 even more attractive.

Another decisive factor in our choice of the 80286 was the availability of a mathematical coprocessor, the 80287. In a process control environment, in which complex control algorithms have to be implemented, a fast numerical processor is an invaluable asset.

Once we chose the microprocessor, we had to consider what other features the board needed. To guarantee compatibility with Intel's new 80286 software (that is, software designed to run in non-8086-compatibility mode), we designed the board as a superset of the Intel SBC 286/10,[15] the first Multibus board with a 80286 microprocessor. By specifying the same devices at the same addresses under the same modes of operation, we maximized the probability of instant compatibility. And by adding features not provided by the 286/10 (see below), we enhanced the ultimate system effectiveness.

M3-286 CPU board implementation

The M3-286 CPU board includes

- on-board EPROM of up to 128K bytes (four sockets with 27256 devices), located at high addresses for system bootstrapping (as required by the 80286 architecture),
- 64K bytes of dual-port dynamic memory, expandable to 256K bytes with 256K devices,
- an 80287 mathematics coprocessor,
- two 8259 interrupt controllers,
- an 8254 programmable timer,
- a multifunction 8274 USART, and
- an MAB 8400 serial line controller.

The system bus is accessed when a memory data transfer takes places at addresses 400000-5FFFFF in protected mode (16M bytes available) or at addresses 40000-5FFFF in compatibility mode (1M byte available) and when an I/O operation is performed at addresses E000-FFFF. All other accesses are either on the local bus or on the on-board bus. We handled accesses in this way in order to provide maximum compatibility with the other CPU boards already available for Modiac. We must emphasize that when memory address space FD0000-FDFFFF is addressed in protected mode, I/O status signals instead of memory signals are generated on the M3 bus by the M3-286 board, allowing the protection mechanism available for memory to be extended to the I/O environment.

We encountered several problems in using the 80286 on the M3 bus. A significant one was that status signals generated by the 80286 are insufficient for detecting all the information required by the M3 status lines. Given such a limitation, we could implement only a subset of the possible functions:

- instruction fetching,
- I/O operations,
- memory operations,
- interrupt acknowledging,
- fault trapping, and
- idling.

However, this restriction has an impact only in systems having a supervisor module, since in simpler systems decisions can be based on less detailed status information.

Another important decision we made involved parity. As we pointed out previously, the parity protection system in the M3 bus is extremely powerful. However, it is also *very* cumbersome and requires a lot of board space. So we had to face a complex decision—either to drastically reduce the number of features provided on the board or to give up parity checking. We eventually chose the latter option, since we can always add an external parity-checking module to the bus whenever such checking is required. (It must be remembered that parity can be disabled in M3 by the PAREN* signal.)

System bus arbiter implementation and sequencing. A detailed schematic of the M3 bus arbiter implemented on the M3-286 board is presented in Figure 4. To understand the arbiter's behavior, let us first suppose that the LOCK* signal is inactive and that therefore LATCHLOCK is inactive. When a system bus address is decoded (by means of ON-BOARD IGBUSREQ) and either of the data-enable signals (ON-BOARD ILODAVAL* or IHIDAVAL*) is asserted, the D1 flip-flop is set, which activates the board priority network. Arbitration takes place continuously while BUSBUSY* is at a low level, reflecting the various requests on the bus from boards. At the same time, flip-flop D2 is blocked as long as ON-BOARD GRANT* is inactive.

BUSBUSY* goes high when no processor is using the bus anymore. When it goes high, flip-flop D2 is allowed to sample a new value, and a new bus winner is chosen. In the board that wins the bus (WIN = 1), the GRANT* signal is asserted, blocking further requests from flip-flop D1. Once the bus has been won, signal GRANT is kept asserted (as is signal BUSBUSY*) as long as the data-enable signals HIDAVAL* and LODAVAL* are asserted on the bus. At the same time, signal LATCHLOCK has the same value as GRANT and therefore does not play any significant role. When HIDAVAL* and LODAVAL* both become inactive, a new bus winner is allowed to gain the control of the bus. Note that with this scheme the bus cannot be won again by the same processor, since a new addressing phase must first take place before a processor can be allowed to get control of the bus again. However, if a processor asserts LOCK* once it has gained control of the bus, it does not release the bus (it keeps BUSBUSY* active) for as long as it keeps signal LATCHLOCK asserted.

The scheme of the arbiter actually implemented in the M3-286 board is slightly more complex than the above since it includes WATCHDOG signals. The entire arbiter has been implemented with two PALs (a 16L8A for the priority network and a 16R4 for the sequential arbitration logic).

Once a master has gained control of the bus, a system bus signal generator—whose time diagram is shown in Figure 5—is activated. It should be noted that in the synchronous timing of the bus control signals shown in the figure, the Tw period must be present if bus contention is to be eliminated when the INF lines switch from addresses to data signals. Again, the actual M3-286 sequencer is more complex, since it also generates several on-board signals for buffer enabling. This sequencer is implemented with a PAL 16R4.

Dual-port memory. The M3-286 board's dual-port dynamic memory exploits 16K × 4 devices. This results in a chip count of only four to implement the dynamic RAM, instead of the 16 that would be required if 64K × 1 devices were used. Moreover, the M3-286 uses 18-pin stacked dip sockets, leading to a 64K-byte memory in one fourth the usual space.

The dynamic RAM controller is the Intel 8207, which can control a variety of devices and can be directly interfaced to the 80286. Moreover, it provides dual-port access and an on-chip arbiter. It is interesting to note that more than one half of the relative space of the entire memory system is used by latches and three-state buffers. From the system bus side, addresses must be latched on board; data and addresses, then, must be enabled onto the RAM pins only when the arbitration has been won. RAM addresses are 0 to 64K when accessed from the 80286 and can be set with 256K granularity for accesses from the system bus.

Interprocessor interrupts are generated whenever a location is written in a 32-byte area located at RAM base address plus 4K. This arrangement reserves the first 4K for use by operating systems—like Intel RMX—that require it.

The RAM system also supports local and system LOCK* signals. This allows indivisible operations on a memory area to be carried out. But it must be noted that if the memory area is split among many dual-port memories located on different boards, it cannot be guaranteed that no on-board accesses will be made, since LOCK* is active only for the area currently being accessed. There is no problem with possible unwanted system bus accesses, however, since the bus can be locked out by blocking BUSBUSY* active.

Software-programmable registers. Two 8255 devices have been provided on the M3-286 board for special purposes. The first device uses its first two registers as temporary buffers for data transfer from and to the MAB 8400 serial line controller. In its third register, two bits act as buffer enable lines for MAB 8400 transfers, one bit activates the RS-422 loop-back test mode, and one bit enables RS-422 drivers.

The second 8255 device uses one of its registers to support the interrupt mechanism of the local M3 bus. When an interrupt is serviced, the first of the two INTA* signals generated by 8259 is ignored. When the second INTA* is asserted, the vector generated by the interrupt controller is sent on the local bus on lines INF 0-7. The leading edge of the second INTA* then causes the priority vector generated by the peripheral boards as a result of the arbitration de-

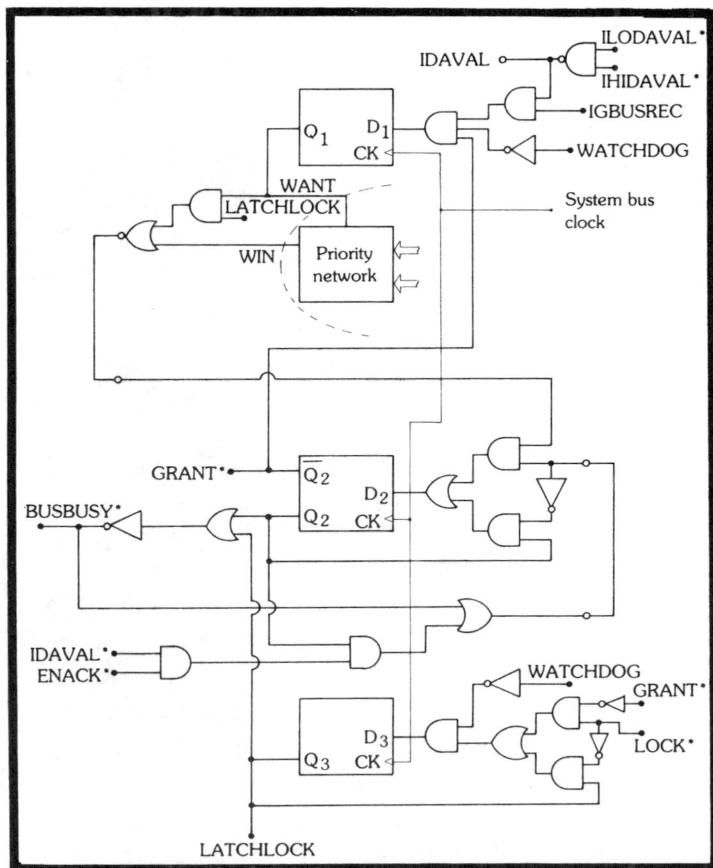

Figure 4. The M3 bus arbiter implemented on the M3-286 board.

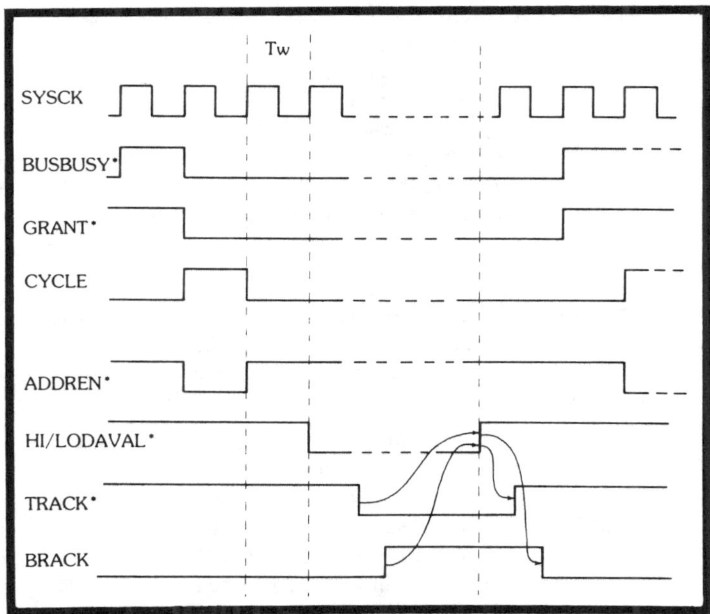

Figure 5. M3 bus control timing provided by the M3-286 board.

Figure 6. The M3-286 CPU board. Card format is double-Eurocard, with DIN 41612 connectors. The board features dual bus control, 64K bytes of dual-ported RAM, 128K bytes of EPROM, and an 80287 math coprocessor.

scribed earlier to be stored in one of the 8255's registers, which can be read by the microprocessor. The other registers of the device are used to set the mode of operation to either 8086 compatibility or protected mode (thus enabling, on the bus, the highest nibble of the addresses otherwise zeroed), to retrigger the watchdog one-shot that is used to ensure that the microprocessor is performing meaningful operations, and to set the system bus priority value.

A photograph of the M3-286 CPU board is shown in Figure 6.

Today's integrated circuits and multilayer boards allow a designer to implement an extremely powerful computer on a single board. We have drawn several conclusions from our M3-286 design experience:

- Although fully multiplexed buses are very attractive for what they do to power consumption and motherboard complexity, they require very cumbersome interfaces at the board level. This problem obviously becomes worse when *non*-multiplexed microprocessors are used. In the case of the M3-286 CPU board, in fact, about one third of the entire board space is wasted on three-state buffers needed to synchronize data flow on the buses. Although M3 timing specifications allow up to two transfers per microsecond to be executed (without wait states), present Modiac implementations, including the M3-286, achieve a much lower speed. This is mainly due to the fact that in order to keep the PAL-based bus controller simple (and to avoid further board space wastage), M3's behavior is synchronized by SYSCLK, the system bus clock, which has a maximum frequency of 4 MHz. Tw is therefore 250 ns, and a minimum of five periods are needed on the M3-286 to complete a system bus transfer when no wait states are required. Efficient use of M3 (and, in general, of multiplexed buses) can be achieved only through silicon-implemented dedicated devices (as provided for by Intel on the Multibus II, for example[16]).

- A great benefit can be derived from the extensive use of PALs in complex boards. There are four reasons for this: First, the input/output delay is constant, even for very complex combinatorial functions, since the internal structure of PALs is always two-level. Any change within the same device does not affect system timing. Second, at the prototype level, possible combinatorial design faults can be often dealt with *without modifications to the PCB,* provided the missed or unwanted signals are already used in the same PAL. In our experience this is very likely. Third, with PALs the structure of the PCB becomes very regular. And fourth, the use of PALs greatly reduces the number of different parts that need to be stocked for manufacturing. In the M3-286 board, there are only six different random-logic devices (excluding buffers). ▪

Acknowledgments

We are very much indebted to M. Di Manzo, G. Menga, S. Rivoira, A. Serra, and R. Zoppoli, who gave so much time, skill, and enthusiasm to the design and implementation of Modiac.

References

1. M. Di Manzo et al., "Modiac: A Modular Integrated Microprocessor System for Industrial Automation and Process Control," *Proc. 6th IFAC Workshop on Distributed Computer Control Systems,* May 20-22, 1985, Monterey, Calif.
2. *IEEE Project 802—Local Network Standards Committee, Draft B,* IEEE Computer Society, Oct. 1981.
3. J. F. Schoch et al., "Evolution of the Ethernet Local Computer Network," *Computer,* Vol. 15, No. 8, Aug. 1982, pp. 10-27.
4. W. Ansaldi et al., "Modosk: il nucleo di sistema operativo distribuito di un nodo della rete Modiac," *Automazione e Strumentazione,* May 1982, pp. 61-66.
5. *Introduction to MOS,* Olivetti tech. manual (code no. 4002130G), Sept. 1982.
6. *IEEE Standard 796-1983, Microcomputer System Bus,* IEEE order no. CN928. (This is the Multibus standard.)
7. *IEEE Standard 696-1983, Interface Devices,* IEEE order no. CN927. (This is the S-100 bus standard.)
8. A. A. Allison, "Status Report on the P896 Backplane Bus," *IEEE Micro,* Vol. 1, No. 1, Feb. 1981, pp. 67-82.
9. D. del Corso et al., *M3 Bus Systems and TOMP Architectures,* Sottoprogetto P1, Progetto Finalizzato Informatica, Consiglio Nazionale delle Ricerche, Obiettivo MUMICRO, Sept. 1983.
10. *VMEbus Specification manual,* Pub. no. M68KVBS (D4), Motorola, Inc., Phoenix, Ariz., Oct. 1981.
11. R. A. Downing, "Fastbus—Details of Addressing and Bus Mastership," *IEEE Trans. Nuclear Science,* Vol. NS-26, No. 4, 1979, pp. 4525-4530.
12. "Single-Chip 8-bit Microcomputer," *Philips Handbook,* Pub. no. IC3-09-82, Part 3, Sept. 1982.
13. R. Fabry, "Capability-based Addressing," *Comm. ACM,* Vol. 17, No. 7, July 1974, pp. 403-412.
14. *iAPX 286 Hardware Reference Manual,* Pub. no. 210760-001, Intel Corp., Santa Clara, Calif., Mar. 1983.
15. *SBC 286/10ES Single-Board Computer Design Guide,* Rev. 2, Pub. no. 145439-001, Intel Corp., Santa Clara, Calif., Sept. 1982.
16. *Multibus II Bus Architecture, Specification Handbook,* Rev. B, Manual no. 146077, Intel Corp., Santa Clara, Calif., Nov. 1983.

The TX16: A Highly Programmable Multi-microprocessor Architecture

Jean-Luc Gaudiot, Michel Dubois,
Liang-Teh Lee, and Nadim G. Tohme
University of Southern California

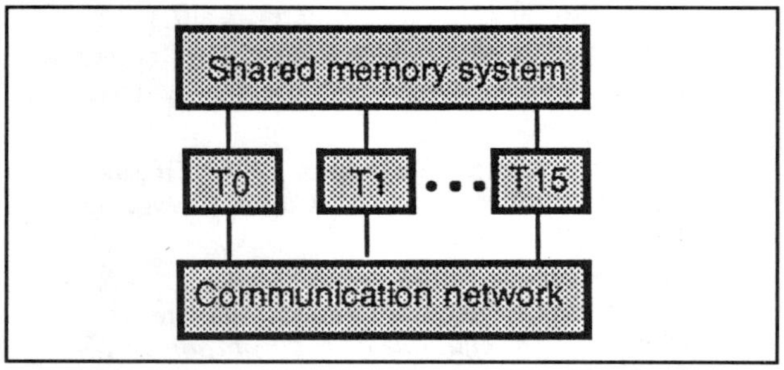

Figure 1. Overall architecture of the TX16.

After years of research and experimentation in universities, multiprocessing technology is reaching the marketplace. Multiprocessing is a cost-effective solution to the increasing need for more throughput and faster speeds. Low-cost microprocessor boards can be connected in multiprocessor configurations for general- and special-purpose computing. The bus interconnection—a very economical and effective way to connect processors—works particularly well when a cache or a local memory is connected to each processor.

With a high-bandwidth bus, computing powers equivalent to tens of MIPS can be attained easily,[1] and throughputs of 100 MIPS or more are possible. This is a higher computing power than available with today's general-purpose mainframes, at a small fraction of the cost.

This trend toward multiprocessing is also spurred by the development of very powerful 32-bit microprocessors with large address spaces, support for virtual memory, and hardwired primitives to support asynchronous concurrency. Moreover, several high-bandwidth bus protocols have begun to meet general acceptance as industrial standards: the Multibus and the VMEbus (Motorola)[2] and the Futurebus (IEEE).[3] All provide facilities for multiple processors. Bus-oriented multiprocessors, with the possibility of connecting multiple buses in parallel, will be viable and even dominant architecture styles well into the next decade.

Early commercial multiprocessors were throughput oriented. In these multiprocessors, typified by the IBM308X series, the parallelism is not exploited to reduce the execution time of a given application but to increase the number of individual jobs that can be run per time unit. However, more recently, manufacturers are turning to multitasking[4] to speed up time-critical tasks.[5] Multitasking projects include supercomputer applications such as weather forecasting, CAD/CAM/CAT, real-time processing, and complex AI problems. In a multitasked system the application is structured as a set of cooperating processes running concurrently on different CPUs and working toward the completion of a given global task.

While computer architecture brings us this new revolution in computing, software tools to take advantage of multitasking are slowly forthcoming. Three software approaches seem to be emerging. The first relies on sophisticated compiling technologies to partition a global application written in a sequential language such as Fortran. The advantage of this approach is that the complexity of program development is no worse than it is for traditional uniprocessors: If the compiler has been carefully debugged, program decomposition is correct by construction.

The disadvantage is the complexity of the compilation task, which makes the approach unsuitable for most programs that are run only a few times. Also this method has only been proven for rather simple numerical computations; for more sophisticated applications such as nonnumerical algorithms, operating system design, and control of embedded systems, there are doubts that this method will succeed.

Reprinted from *IEEE Micro*, pp. 18–31, Oct. 1986.

The second approach lets the programmer manage the concurrency of the application by coding directly in a concurrent language such as Ada or CSP.[6] These languages have specific statements for task initiation, synchronization, and message passing. They allow the efficient coding of sophisticated applications. The problem of debugging concurrent programs is much more complex than it is for uniprocessor programs, due to the problems related to concurrency. An error in a concurrent program is much more difficult to track than an error in a uniprocessor program because of the sharing of data and of the intermittent nature of errors.

At USC we are studying a third concept in the programming of multitasked systems. Advocated by Backus[7] and Dennis,[8] it is based on the functional language model. Indeed, it has been found that the conventional methods of programming multiprocessor systems could rapidly become unworkable as it is impossible for a programmer to keep "juggling" the large number of tasks that should remain active in a large-scale multiprocessor. Instead, an implicit approach to multiprocessor programming is needed.

The conventional programming methods imply reliance on a central program counter to schedule instructions. In the functional approach, instructions are scheduled directly by the availability of their operands. This is a very natural sequencing mechanism that can be applied successfully to distributed architectures.

We present here a very simple multiprocessor structure similar to the Cm*, an early experimental multiprocessor developed at Carnegie Mellon University.[9] It is a bus-oriented multiprocessor in which the memory is distributed among the processors. This architecture has been called a distributed global memory system because each microprocessor can access the memory of any other microprocessor board. A schematic of the architecture appears in Figure 1.

While the architecture is very simple to design, taking advantage of the parallelism to speed up a computation is a difficult problem. Issues of task partitioning and memory allocation must be addressed. In our design, programs are written in a functional language; they are then compiled in a dataflow graph, which is partitioned to define processes and to allocate processors and memory. In this methodology the actual structure of the multiprocessor itself remains transparent to the programmer.

We consider the development of a small (16 processors) cluster to demonstrate the programming methodology. This cluster is called the TX16 and is built around the Inmos Transputer. It is foreseen that multiple TX16's can be connected by bus hierarchies to create large multiprocessor configurations. We see the TX16 as a dedicated, attached processor accessed by one user at a time through a front-end minicomputer, for solving computationally intensive algorithms in the same way that a Cray machine would be used. The algorithms targeted for the machine belong to numerical and symbolic applications.

The particularities of the architecture are:

- a flexible interconnection pattern that allows data to be communicated among processors either by a shared memory system or by message passing;
- the utilization of off-the-shelf components such as the Inmos Transputer and bus controllers such as Futurebus or Multibus modules;
- a modular design that allows expandability (no central controller); and
- an integrated programming methodology that allows the user to program problems without explicit regard to the actual structure of the multiprocessor system. This transparency is afforded by the application of functional principles of execution and the use of a high-level dataflow language (SISAL).

Overall, we attempt to describe an integrated methodology that makes the programming of large parallel systems more reliable and even feasible. Existing chip sets allow an easy hardware integration, while a sophisticated functional approach to programming offers easy schedulability of the processes in the target machine.

Dataflow multiprocessors

The design of multiprocessor systems involves issues at the architectural level and at the software level. Both of these aspects have been studied in the recent past in several research projects. The following are the most representative projects.

Model of execution. With the advent of VLSI and the declining cost of hardware, large multiprocessors are made possible. Corresponding increases in speeds should be obtained, provided synchronization between the processors can be achieved efficiently.

Dataflow languages have been introduced in an attempt to easily sequence the operations in fully distributed systems and afford easy programmability in multiprocessor systems. Instead of a central controller (that is, the program counter) as would exist in a von Neumann-style machine, control is distributed. This fact explains why in a dataflow environment data carries with it its own control in the form of a pointer, which contains the address of the instruction that will operate on the attached value. In contrast to the sequential organization in which the program counter decides on the moment when a given instruction should be executed, scheduling in a dataflow multiprocessor is entirely asynchronous.

The dataflow principles can be summarized as follows. A dataflow actor (instruction) can fire (execute) when there are data tokens on all its input arcs. The execution has two effects: The operands disappear from the input set, and data tokens corresponding to the result of the operation are sent on the output arcs.

Figure 2 shows the execution of an actor. In the first diagram the input arcs of the actor carry tokens that bear data values. After execution, only the output arcs carry data tokens. These data tokens are sent only to those instructions

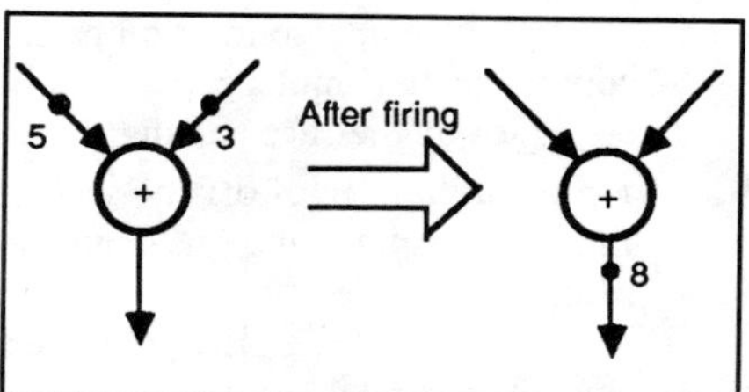

Figure 2. The execution of a dataflow actor.

in the program that need them. In other words, the execution of instructions is based on the flow of data. As an example, Figure 3 shows the solution of a quadratic equation in a dataflow program format.

All operations are, as the name implies, data driven. In fact, two main computational models exist, data driven and demand driven. In the data-driven mode an instruction can be executed as soon as its operands are available (themselves the results of another instruction); this is the mode of operation usually chosen for dataflow machines. In the demand-driven approach, an instruction is executed only when its results are required (or demanded) by another instruction; reduction machines [10] and the Rediflow architecture [11] belong to this class.

The Hughes Data-flow Machine. Several dataflow architectures have been proposed in the literature and have been implemented to one degree or another. We describe here a typical dataflow architecture. Like most current proposals, it makes use of custom-designed circuitry to implement the dataflow principles of execution. We demonstrate later how these principles of execution can instead be efficiently implemented at the software level by using the architecture of the Inmos Transputer.

The Hughes Data-Flow Multiprocessor (HDFM) as described by Gaudiot et al. [12] is designed to be used as an on-board processor for signal- and data-processing applications. The HDFM is programmed in the Hughes Data-Flow Language (HDFL), which is a functional high-level language based on VAL. [13] The company developed a compiler that translates from HDFL to a parallel dataflow graph form. This graph is then distributed to the processing elements (PE) of the multiprocessor by a software tool called the Allocator.

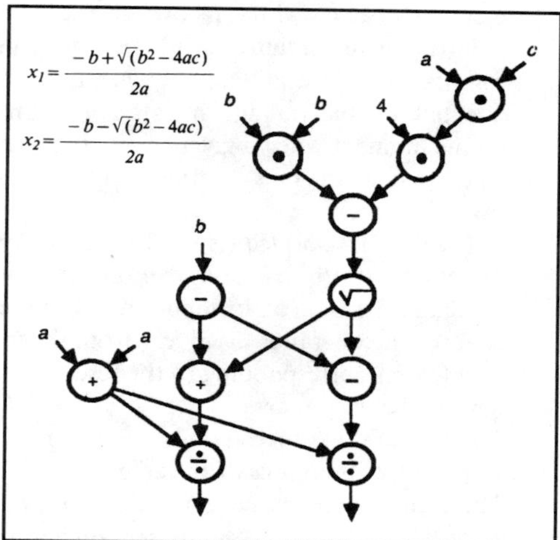

Figure 3. A sample dataflow graph.

The Allocator employs static graph analysis to produce a compile-time assignment of program graphs to hardware. It attempts to maximize the number of operations that can proceed in parallel while minimizing the interprocessing element communication.

At the architectural level, several requirements of processors for embedded applications introduced several constraints in the design. For standardization and minimization of the part count, each PE is limited to two VLSI custom-designed chips, in addition to some external memory chips.

The HDFM consists of one to hundreds of identical PEs connected by a global packet-switching network. This network is a three-dimensional, bused cube network as shown in Figure 4. Packet transmission proceeds via a store-and-forward protocol, which allows any PE to transfer data to any other PE. Each PE can execute the instruction set and perform the dataflow sequencing and addressing. Each PE has its own local memory for both program and data storage; there is no global memory.

The program, which consists of dataflow actors (templates), is allocated to the local memories of the PEs at compilation time. The PEs are targeted for VLSI implementation, resulting in a simplified design to reduce I/O pins and minimize the number of different types of VLSI chips.

The communication network is integrated with each PE to allow growth of both processing power and extension of the communication network with the addition of a single modular unit. Each PE consists of a communication chip (Com), a processing chip (Proc), and memory as shown in Figure 5.

The Com receives packets from the routing network and either forwards them on to other PEs or sends them to its attached Proc. When the Proc receives a packet, it checks to see whether this packet (token) has enabled a template to fire. If it has, the operands and opcode for this template are sent to the ALU. The ALU performs the indicated operation and sends the result to be matched with its destination address and sent either back to this same PE or out into the routing network.

Performance evaluation of the machine has been pursued by an extensive simulation of the machine; it has demonstrated the validity of the approach and of the choices made.

Hardware description of the TX16

The architecture of the TX16 is based on the Inmos Transputer. This new microprocessor allows not only interconnection with a memory system but also communication with other processors of the same kind via four serial communication links. Instead of relying only on the message-passing capabilities of the Transputer, we have also provided a shared memory system for bulk data transfer.

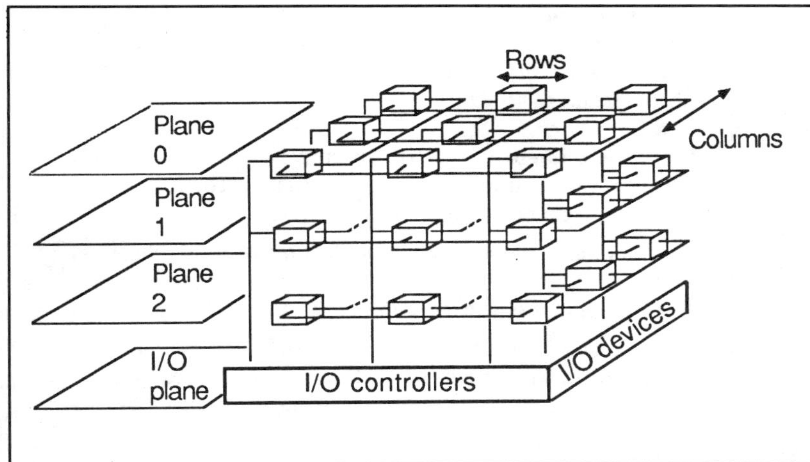

Figure 4. The Hughes Data-Flow Machine.

Internal description of the Inmos Transputer. While conventional microprocessors are interfaced with the external world through a single memory bus (address, data, and control), the Transputer possesses a memory bus plus the four serial communication links. Each of these communication links allows point-to-point transmissions between two Transputers. As we show later, this architecture is reflected at the language level. The arrival of data on one of these links will trigger the execution of processes inside the receiving Transputer. This data-driven function as well as the ease of interconnection dictated our choice of processing element.

The internal structure of a Transputer is shown in Figure 6. It clearly displays how the communication function on the serial links can be performed independently of the processing, for the links have direct access to the on-chip memory. The processor, based on RISC design principles, provides throughputs of up to 20 MIPS. It supports the parallel language, Occam, and allows fast procedure calls, fast context switching, and low interrupt latency. The internal 2048-byte, 50-ns, multiport static RAM allows a maximum memory bandwidth of 80 Mbytes/s. More memory space can be attached to the external memory bus. External memory transfers are, however, slowed down to the rate of 25 Mbytes/s.

In addition, the four 10M-bit/s, full-duplex serial links allow direct asynchronous message passing between two Transputers. We intend to connect the Transputers in a mesh topology similar to the Illiac IV. Though more complex multiplexing may allow better connectivity, it diminishes the bandwidth available on any single link.[14]

At the execution level the Transputer reflects the structure of the Occam language. It allows the presence of several different processes though only one can be active at a time. Message transmission with other processes is based on the synchronous principles of CSP as described by Hoare.[6] This means that when the active process must communicate an intermediary result with another process (possibly located in another processor), the active process is held until the other process has been found to be ready for the transmission (see Figure 7). While the process is held, it is stacked in the inactive process queue. Another ready process is then activated until it either terminates or is itself suspended because of a required transmission. This low-level context-change mechanism compares favorably to the busy-wait model found in conventional multiprocessor systems. Instead of idling a processor while waiting for an intermediary operand to arrive, the system allows the context to be switched to another ready process until the operand is available.

Overall architecture. The system consists of 16 interconnected Transputers. The four links of each Transputer are used for scalar data communications and for interprocess

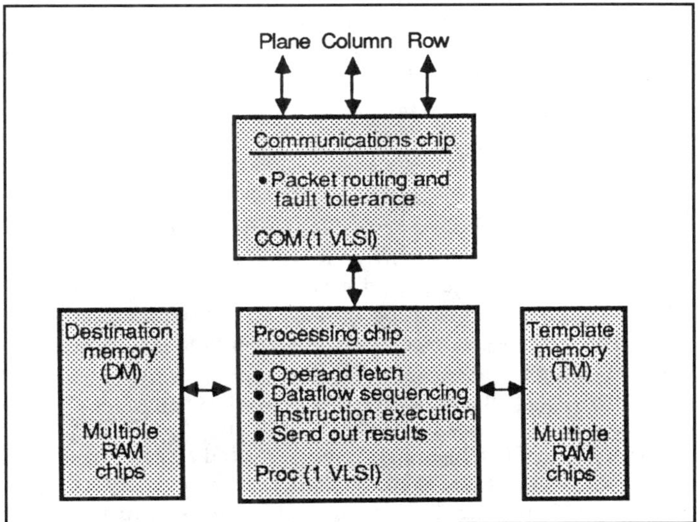

Figure 5. A processing element in the HDFM.

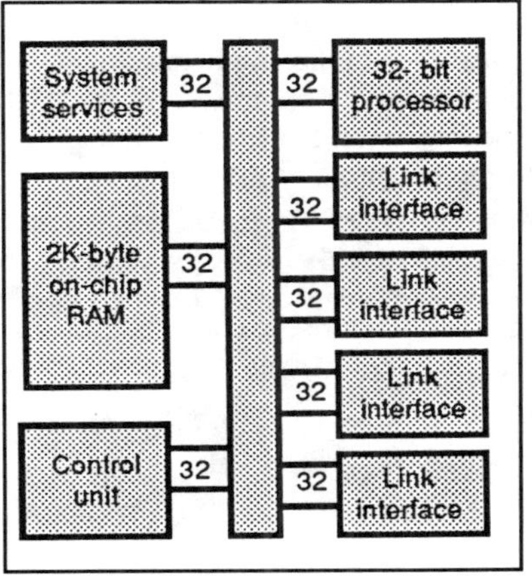

Figure 6. The internal structure of the Inmos Transputer.

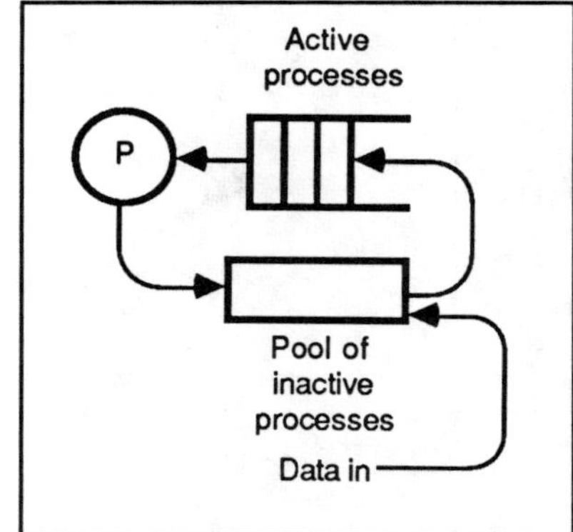

Figure 7. An active process in the Transputer.

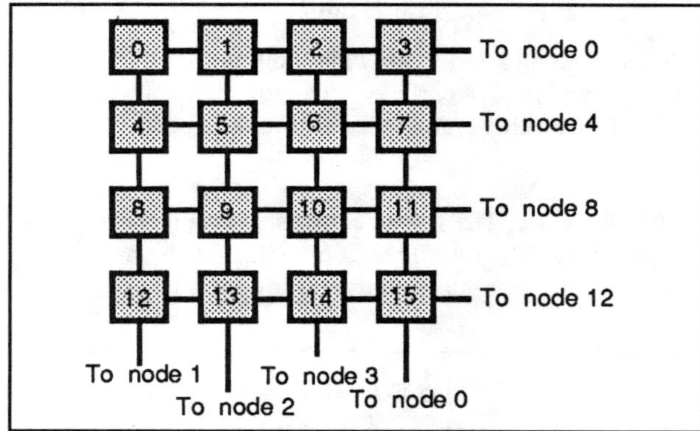

Figure 8. Mesh topology.

synchronization messages. Several topologies for a "passive" network can be envisioned (dual rings, four nearest-neighbor connections, fourth-order or binary X-trees, four cubes, quadruple bus, and so on). We have retained an Illiac IV-like topology (wrapped-around mesh), as seen in Figure 8.

The shared memory system is distributed throughout the machine. Each processing element owns a single bank of the memory system (see Figure 9). A processor can access its own memory bank directly through the external memory bus of the Transputer. This action would correspond to a local access.

A remote access can be made into the bank owned by another processor. In this case the bus controller formats the request from the PE into a packet and takes control of the bus. The request is then forwarded to the destination PE. When the request is a read request, a response is sent back in the same fashion to the originator. Note that in both cases the memory access is formatted into a packet. This method increases the complexity of the controller but also increases the throughput on the inter-PE bus.

For these reasons we chose the Multibus II as the memory bus. It allows fast transfer and, furthermore, several off-the-shelf chips are available for direct interfacing.

The communication networks. Two forms of communication capabilities exist in the Transputer through the hardware links and through remote memory accesses in the shared memory system.

The hardware links. Each Transputer is connected through four hardware links to its neighbors. The communication channels have a dual purpose:

- they allow communication of data between two chips, and
- they permit synchronization of the processes.

The synchronization function is the most important characteristic of the Transputer, for it allows several processes to coexist while some are awaiting data prior to proceeding.

The memory system. Each processor shown in Figure 9 is physically located on a board together with one megabyte of dynamic memory and an interface to a 32-bit, multiplexed bus system with an address/data backplane. Each processor board owns a bank of the shared memory. The physical location of a memory cell will be reflected in the access time. However, it will be transparent to the microprocessors themselves. The Transputers can access the local memory bank through the memory controller and any other bank over the global memory bus. A similar implementation is presented in detail by Philipson et al.[15] We required that the bus selected in our design perform message passing. Every node of the TX16 should be able to send data to the address space of any other module.

To transfer messages, the Transputer sends the local starting address, size, and destination address(es) of the packet to be transmitted to its local bus controller, which performs bus arbitration. Once the bus is reserved and the destination(s) bus controller(s) is(are) ready to receive data, the packet can be transferred.

After transmission, the sender releases control of the bus and is ready to accept new inputs in its buffer before contending again for bus access. When the whole message has been transferred, the bus controllers on each side acknowledge the local Transputers for termination of the job.

The Multibus II system chosen for this purpose can pass 32-byte data blocks (which contain four bytes of address data) in 900 ns, giving an effective rate of 35.5M bytes/s. This is faster than a microprocessor transfer rate or a DMA controller. Intel has designed a single chip for the Multibus II that handles the distributed bus arbitration and control and passes messages. This chip moves data faster than any CPU and DMA. However the bus throughput is also affected by the amount of traffic on the bus. Later, we take this disadvantage into account in our simulation and analytical performance evaluation.

Communication synchronization. Context change operations are required by the Occam model of computation, which imposes synchronous communications: proper handshaking must be established before data can be exchanged between any two processes. No process should send any message before the receiver is ready to accept it. An exchange of data between process A and process B will occur only when A has executed an output instruction and B has performed the corresponding input operation. Occam communication channels implement processes internally (through the on-chip memory) and externally (through one of the four hardware Transputer links).

In an internal communication a memory word represents the Occam communication channel. Communicating processes can determine each other's status by interrogating this flag, the location of which is known to both processes. Note that this cell experiences no access conflicts since the two processes are located in the same processor and therefore must be executed sequentially. The first process to request a transmission finds that the status of the channel is "empty;" it then leaves a pointer to the information pertaining to the desired transfer. The second channel finds the channel "ready to communicate." When both processes are in such a communicating stage, data can be transferred, using parameters present in the workspaces of the processes. Note that the transfer simply consists of a memory copy operation followed by a resetting of the communication channel word to empty. Figure 10 illustrates this process.

In the case of an external connection, requests for transmission on one of the four links generate pointers to the data to be sent. The pointers are stored in the link hardware, the requesting process is deactivated, and its state is saved. The next process on the active list resumes execution where it left off, while the link initiates the transfer of the message. When the transfer has been completed, the link mechanism reactivates the initiating process by placing it back on the active process list.

The arrival of a message in a processor is handled similarly. The data is stored directly into the memory by the receiving process. Since each physical link is a full-duplex connection, a total of four Occam channels can be mapped onto the four inter-Transputer connections.

For these reasons it is not possible to consider the direct folding of several (that is, more than one in each direction) Occam channels onto one physical link. Instead, one must imagine the notion of multiplexer MUX and demultiplexer DMUX processes (Figure 11). While "logical" connections (dotted lines) are used for transferring data between actual processes, these must be folded onto one physical link (and therefore one single Occam channel). The core of the MUX process is an **ALT** construct, which authorizes the OR on the inputs and enables the activation of MUX when an input from any of the processes (P_1, P_2, etc.) is present. The input value is then transmitted transparently to the output channel mapped onto the inter-Transputer physical link.

In the receiving Transputer, the DMUX process accepts the Occam messages and dispatches them to the proper receiving process (Q_1, Q_2, etc.). This dispatching is based on information contained in the message itself. Note that the DMUX process actually accomplishes a switching function based on received data. The MUX process, on the other hand, performs no visible function except that of a merge operator. It is not possible to merge the data paths

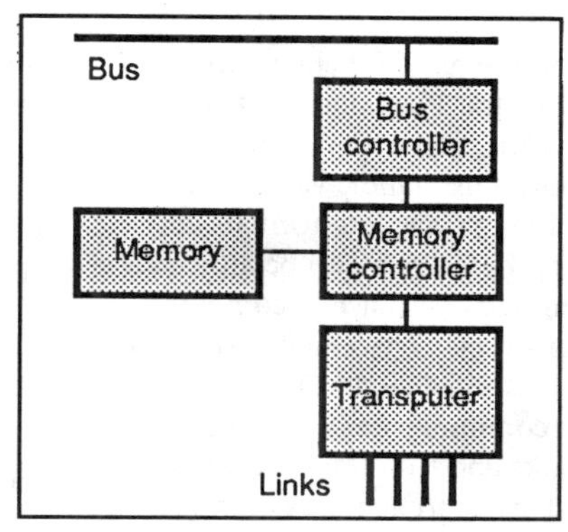

Figure 9. A processor of the TX16.

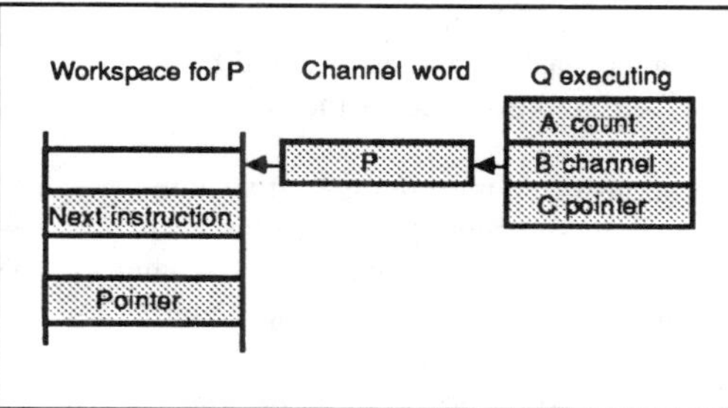

Figure 10. Internal communication.

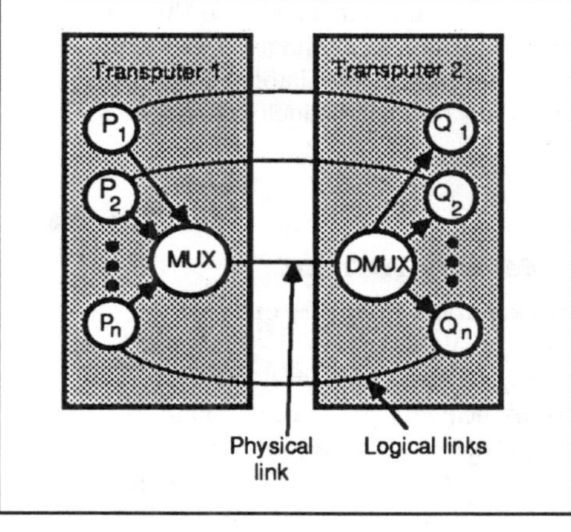

Figure 11. Multiplexer and demultiplexer.

directly into a single Occam channel due to hardware restrictions in the current implementation of the Transputer. There is no provision to arbitrate conflicts between two processes attempting to take over the link at the same time.

As a possible improvement for a future version of the Transputer, we propose to directly implement in hardware the functions associated with the MUX and DMUX software processes. This would relieve the processor itself from the burden of communication interfacing. Instead the "intelligent" links would act as Occam processes (MUX and DMUX described above). The restriction of one Occam channel per physical, unidirectional link originates from the register limitation in each hardware link mechanism. In the new scheme no such constraint is imposed, for the link can behave as an Occam process and communicate with the desired processes via internal communications through the virtually unlimited memory. The drawbacks are in the complexity associated with the new communication protocols and the difficulty in standardizing for a variety of users.

Coprocessing. In addition to the basic functions provided by the reduced instruction set of the Transputer, other operations may be required by the application. For instance, numerical computations must handle various data formats. In applications rich in multiple data formats and floating-point instructions, coprocessors are to be attached to the basic processing element for assistance in computationally intensive program constructs. This can be arranged very easily through the use of a special circuit (the Inmos C0001 Link Adaptor), which communicates with the Transputer over one of the links and translates the serial data for a parallel interface. This approach, however, has the disadvantage of reducing the communication capabilities of each node of the machine. In addition, communication over the Transputer links is serial and therefore slower. Alternatively, we consider that a coprocessor could be attached to the memory bus and accessed by memory mapping.

Symbolic manipulations often require associative comparisons. These can include searching for a specific key in a character string (word-processing application) or retrieving a complex piece of information in a large database. In addition, the logic programming model relies heavily on content access for its unification mechanisms. For these reasons it is important to include the capability for associative retrieval by an appropriate memory unit attached to each processing element. Special-purpose VLSI implementation of this function is planned to support the corresponding software constructs. Also, special-purpose circuits available now provide "string-matching" functions and will be included in the near future.

The software environment

In addition to these dataflow principles of execution, high-level languages such as VAL,[13] Id,[16] LAU,[17] and HDFM[12] have been proposed as a high-level interface.

To demonstrate the applicability of the functional mode of execution to such a problem, we have chosen the high-level functional language SISAL developed at the Lawrence Livermore National Laboratory by McGraw and Skedzielewski.[18] This language has also been selected for high-level language programming of the University of Manchester dataflow machine.[19]

In describing the high-level language (SISAL) and the Transputer low-level language (Occam), we give particular attention to the first step of the translation: the compilation of SISAL into an Intermediate Dataflow Graph IF1.

Occam. Occam[20, 21] is directly related to CSP (Communicating Sequential Processes) as introduced by Hoare.[6] It is an efficient paradigm for the specification of parallel modules and their communications. The basic construct in Occam is the process. Communication is allowed between processes over communication links between processes. This model is evidently based on communication by message passing. It allows the execution of a process when arguments have been received. This corresponds to executability by data availability.

An Occam program can be represented as a graph depicting processes as nodes interconnected by links. Figure 12 represents a simple Occam program as well as its corresponding graphical representation.

Three basic commands can be invoked in Occam:

- The *assignment statement*—variable := expression, where the variable is set to the value of the expression.
- The *input command*, which can be stated as channel ? variable, means that a value is sought from the channel named "channel" and will be stored in the variable "variable."
- The *output command*, which can be stated as channel ! expression, where the value of the expression named "expression" is output to the channel.

The synchronization between Occam processes is accomplished by the transmission and reception of data to and from the channels. When an output command is encountered in a process, the process is halted until another process has executed the corresponding input command. In other words, communication can occur between two processes only when they are both ready to perform the I/O transfer.

In addition to the simple constructs described above, some keywords must be introduced:

- The **VAR** keyword serves to declare the variables inside the process;
- An **indentation** indicates that the corresponding statements are part of the same process;
- The **SEQ** declaration signifies that the statements inside the process are to be executed sequentially;
- The **PAR** keyword indicates that the following processes are to be executed independently from each other; processes 1 and 2 can be initiated in parallel:

```
PAR
  { process 1}
  { process 2}
```

- the **ALT** construct is employed in cases where a subset of the input channels may be used to initiate computations within a process:

```
ALT
  inputchannel1 ? x
    outputchannel ! x
  inputchannel2 ? x
    outputchannel ! x
```

The process described in the above example would output on outputchannel either of the values present on inputchannel1 or inputchannel2. This process simply effects a merge function of two Occam channels into a single one.

It should be noted that the dataflow principles of execution can be mapped directly into Occam. The converse is not true, however, since it is possible to design unsafe Occam programs that would have no corresponding part in the dataflow world. This mapping is made possible by the fact

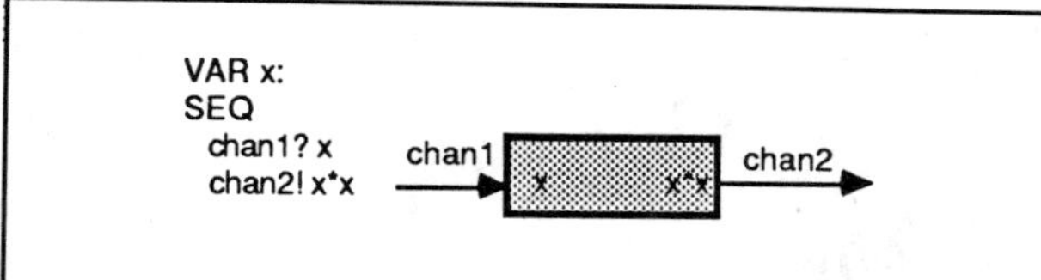

Figure 12. An Occam program and its geographical representation.

that both programming approaches rely on the principles of scheduling upon data availability.

SISAL. SISAL (Streams and Iterations in a Single Assignment Language) is a dataflow language. The compiler has been ported on a VAX 11/750 under Unix Berkeley 4.2 bsd. It accepts SISAL as its input and produces a complex dataflow graph called IF1 (Intermediary Form 1).

There are six basic scalar types of SISAL: Boolean, integer, real, double real, null, and character. The data structure of SISAL consists of records, unions, arrays, and streams. Each data type has its associated set of operations, while record, union, array, and stream types are treated as mathematical sets of values just as are the basic scalar types. Under the **forall** construct, these types can be used to support identification of concurrency for execution on a highly parallel processor.

Since SISAL is a single-assignment language, it greatly facilitates the detection of parallelism in a program. A SISAL program comprises a set of functions. The input and output of the program are passed through a main program, which is one of these functions. Figure 13 shows a SISAL function, which performs the multiplication of two matrices.

It is used as an example of a translation into Occam.

Intermediate Form 1 (IF1). The IF1 graph produced by the SISAL compiler is a direct reflection of the original SISAL input. IF1 corresponds to a combined graph of PSG (program structure graph) and DFG (dataflow graph). In IF1 there are compound and simple nodes. A compound node can be considered as a control point that affects a sequence of actors in its controlled range. The simple node is the elementary processing actor; it consists of the information of its input and output arcs.

The tree-structured PSG describes the relationships among the compound and simple nodes, according to the original user's program. The root and internal nodes of the tree are compound nodes, while leaves are all simple nodes. In addition to the compound and simple nodes in IF1, we define a third kind of node and call it a block node. It is an internal node of the PSG. The block node is a dummy node created for the convenience of partitioning only.

In the system the iteration is controlled by the **forall** node. To process a multidimensional array, we can use multilevel **forall** nodes to control all successors. Figure 14 shows a combined graph of PSG and DFG. It corresponds to an IF1 description and describes the multiplication of two matrices. The corresponding SISAL program was shown in Figure 13. The solid lines in the graph represent the edges of the PSG, and the dashed lines link the leaves to form a DFG.

```
type OneDim = array[ integer ];
type TwoDim = array[ OneDim ];

function MatMult( A, B: TwoDim ; M,N,L : integer
returns          TwoDim)

for i in 1,M Cross j in 1,L
  S :=
    for K in 1,N
      R := A[ I,K ] * B[ K, J ]
    returns value of sum R
    end for
returns array of S
end for
end function % MatMult
```

Figure 13. Multiplication of two matrices in SISAL.

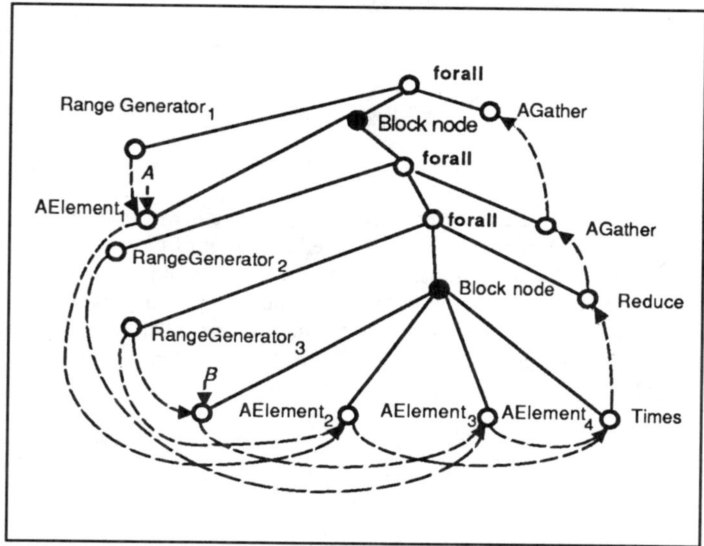

Figure 14. An IF1 representation of matrix multiplication.

In the graph the actors RangeGenerator1 and RangeGenerator3 broadcast index values *i* and *k* to the actors AElement1 (Array Element select) and AElement2. Once AElement1 and AElement2 have received the index values, they forward the pointers $A[i,*]$ and $B[k,*]$ to AElement3 and AElement4. AElement3 and AElement4 are also waiting for the index values *k* and *j*, which are sent from RangeGenerator3 and RangeGenerator2 to generate the elements $A[i,k]$ and $B[k,j]$. The actor Times receives the two elements $A[i,k]$ and $B[k,j]$ and sends the product to the actor Reduce, which accumulates the received data and forwards the result to actors AGather1 as well as AGather2 to form a two-dimensional array.

The basic mapping mechanism. From the previous section, we know that a leaf of the PSG is an actor and that its input and output arcs correspond to channels in Occam. If two arguments *x* and *y* are passed through two input arcs of a Plus actor to be the operands of this Plus operation, this part of the graph could be translated as:

C0001 ? *x*
C0002 ? *y*

In this discussion the Plus actor receives data *x* and *y* from the channels C0001 and C0002. After the actual operation has been completed, the sum of x and y is passed through the output of the process to the next process. This could be channel C0003. This action is translated into the following Occam code:

```
C0003 ! x + y
```

If this result is to be sent to several actors, more than one channel should be created, and data will be sent out in parallel through all the channels that have been so declared.

In summary, a simple add actor, if allowed its own Occam process, is translated by:

```
SEQ
  PAR
    C0001 ? x
    C0002 ? y
  SEQ
    C0003 ! x+y
```

Furthermore, if several actors are set together to form a group, this group could be mapped into a set of Occam code, and some channels between the actors could be eliminated. For example, assume that we need to perform the function $(a+b) * (c+d)$ in an Occam process. (The corresponding graph is shown in Figure 15.) The corresponding Occam program is the process described by:

```
SEQ
  PAR
    C0001 ? a
    C0002 ? b
    C0003 ? c
    C0004 ? d
  SEQ
    C0005 ! (a+b)*(c+d)
```

The translator environment. Our translator can logically be divided into five phases: SISAL compilation, graph generation, basic partitioning, optimization, and Occam code generation. Figure 16 is an overview of a flowchart of the translator, depicting its passes instead of viewing the translator in terms of its five logical phases:

- **Pass 1** corresponds to the SISAL compilation phase. It translates the user SISAL program into IF1.
- **Pass 2** corresponds to the graph generation phase. It scans the IF1 descriptions and generates a graph, which consists of two subgraphs, the PSG (Program Structure Graph) and the DFG (Dataflow Graph).
- **Pass 3** corresponds to the basic partitioning phase. Based on the PSG and DFG, it generates a partitioned dataflow graph (PDFG), a channel table, and a communication cost matrix. Passes 2 and 3 could be combined by treating graph generation as part of the partitioning routine that scans IF1 and generates PSG and PDFG directly.
- **Passes 4 through *N*-1** correspond to the optimization phase. Each separate type of optimization may require several passes of repartitioning. It also needs a resource table (the number of PEs provided) to facilitate the work. A complete study of optimization would be beyond the scope of this work and will not be described further.

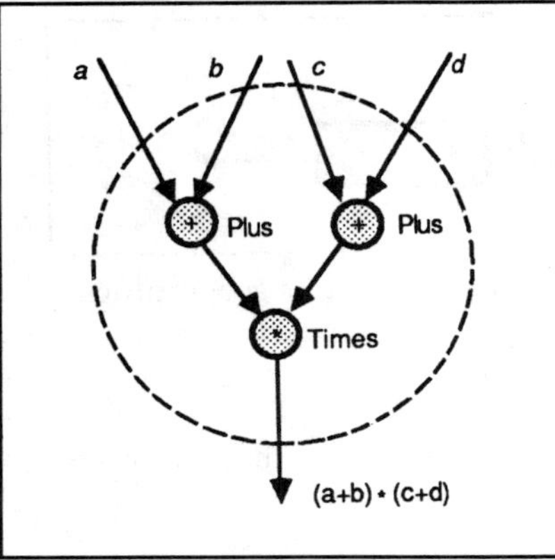

Figure 15.
A macro-actor.

- **Pass *N*** corresponds to the Occam code generation phase. It traverses the PSG, DFG, and PDFG and considers each partitioned group, combines the separated processes, eliminates the unnecessary channels, and generates the Occam object code.

Example: matrix multiplication

Because of the flexibility of the TX16, multiple implementations of an algorithm are possible. We present different ways to decompose and execute the matrix multiplication algorithm on our machine. Several allocation methods have been used and contrasted by simulation and analytical models. Each of the allocation strategies presented can then be inserted in step N of the software environment described in the previous section.

Algorithm. The matrix multiplication algorithm used here is the standard method. The multiplication of an $l \times n$ matrix by an $n \times m$ matrix produces an $l \times m$ result matrix by applying the following equation:

$$c_{ij} = \sum_{k=1}^{n} a_{ik} \cdot b_{kj} \quad [i \epsilon [1,l] \text{ and } j \epsilon [1,m]] \qquad (1)$$

In all the schemes derived, the initial state is that of two matrices **A** and **B** loaded into the private memories of each processor. Each element of the matrices **A** and **B** is present in one processor only and is not duplicated prior to runtime. In addition, results are left in the local memories in the same way.

Partitioning strategies. We have identified several allocation and partitioning strategies for the matrix multiplication algorithm. For introduction purposes we limit our analysis to two strategies only: the iteration-pipelining scheme and the block-partitioning method. Each are studied in turn, and their performance is contrasted by an analytical approach.

Iteration pipelining. Notice first from the algorithm described above that only the inner loop index k contains data dependencies, while the two outer loops, indexes i and j, are strict vector operations. Therefore, parallelism can readily be extracted with regard to the i and j indexes. For a given i and j this first strategy considers the successive accumulation of the partial product as a pipeline with n segments. Each block of the pipeline corresponds to one value of k of the inner loop. For all values of i and j, it

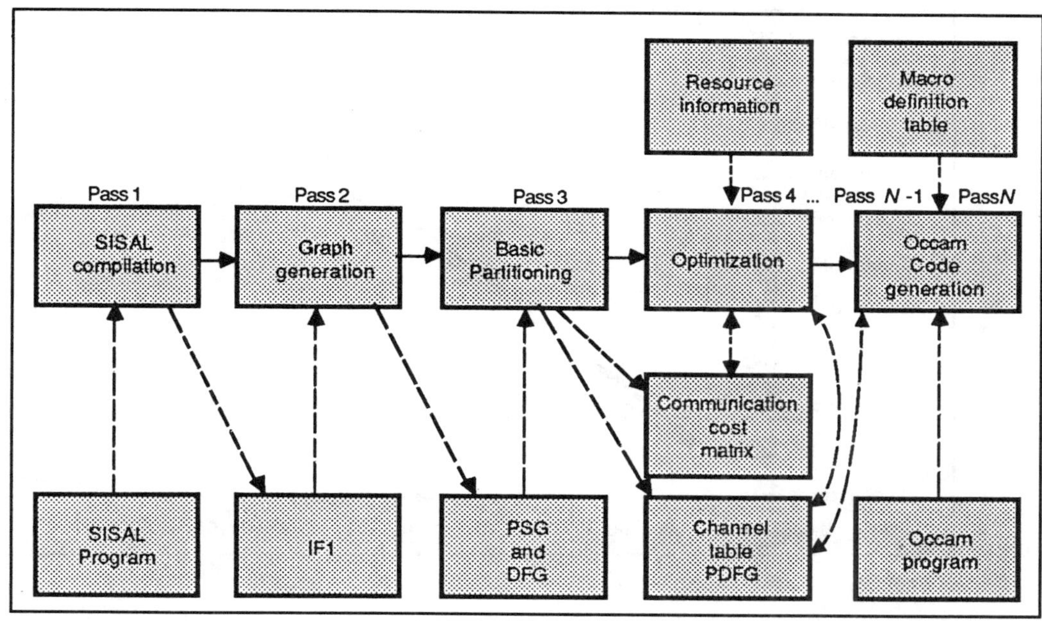

Figure 16. The programming environment.

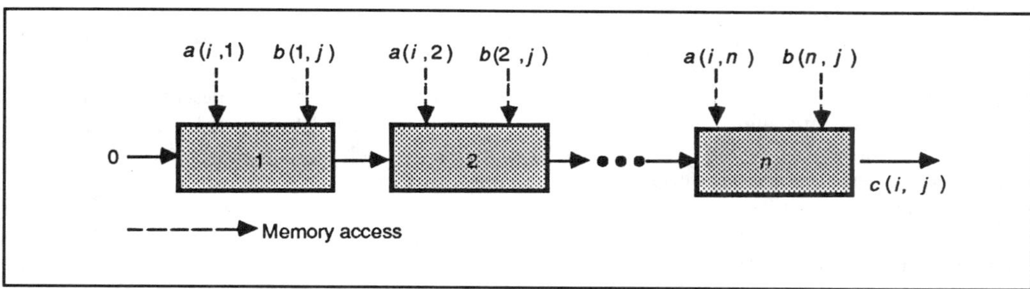

Figure 17. An example of iteration pipelining.

fetches a_{ik} and b_{kj}, multiplies them, and accumulates the result with the input to the block (Figure 17). The result is then sent to the next block. The various iterations on i and j are initiated one at a time, in successive order, through the pipe to produce one c_{ij} at every iteration of the pipe. When n^5P (the number of iterations is greater than the number of available processors), the computation shown in Figure 17 must be *folded* so that several boxes now belong to one processor. For P processors each processor accumulates n/P products before sending the partial product on the link.

Allocation. Three allocation schemes are described in the case of iteration pipelining (note that n, the number of stages, is always assumed to be a multiple of P, the number of processors). F_{alloc} is a function of process and data allocations, and its value corresponds to the number of bus accesses per accumulation.

- *Worst-case allocation.* All memory accesses are remote. An access may correspond, for example, to the case of a previous computation that has produced the input matrices **A** and **B**, regardless of the optimal allocation needed by the "consumer" algorithm. In this case all the accesses a_{ik} and b_{kj} are remote. $F_{alloc} = 2$, because each accumulation requires two remote bus accesses.
- *Random allocation.* In this case assume that the data is randomly allocated in the memory; that is, when a processor makes a memory reference, there is a probability $1/P$ that the data is in its own memory module and a probability $(P-1)/P$ that a bus access to a remote module is required. In this case

$$F_{alloc} = 2 \cdot \frac{P-1}{P} \tag{2}$$

- *Best-case allocation.* This is the ideal memory allocation where all memory accesses are local. There is no access to the intracluster memory bus. Instead, memory accesses are all made to the local bank of the shared memory system. $F_{alloc} = 0$.

Throughput evaluation. Since the matrix multiplication requires a total of $(2n-1) \cdot lm$ floating-point operations, the throughput in FLOPS of the multiprocessor for matrix multiply is bounded by[21]

$$Th(P) \leq \frac{(2n-1) \cdot lm}{[(P-1)+lm]} \cdot MIN\left[\frac{1}{n \cdot T_{pipe}(P)}, \frac{BW}{n \cdot F_{alloc}}\right] \tag{3}$$

where

$$T_{pipe}(P) = \frac{n}{P} \cdot (T_{ACC} + F_{alloc} \times T_{BUS}) + T_{NET} \tag{4}$$

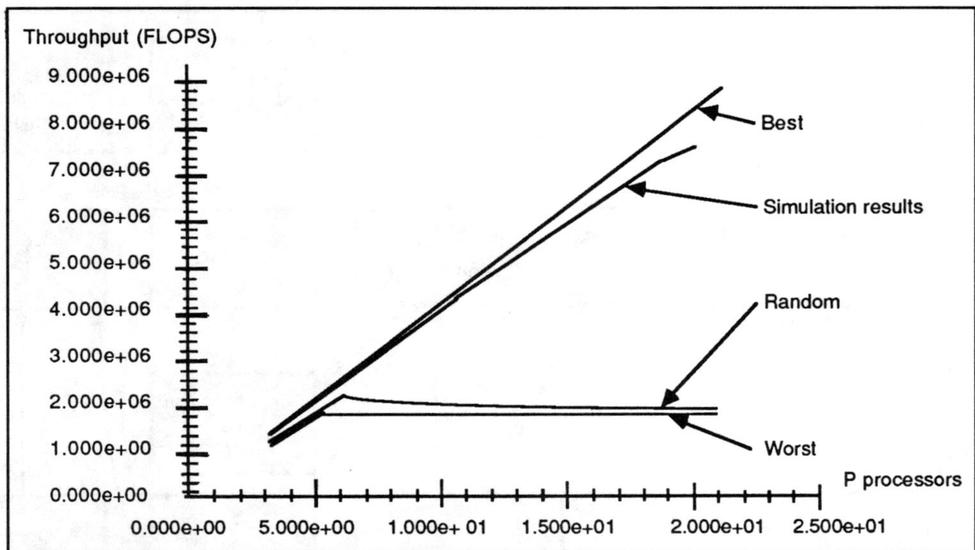

Figure 18. Performance results of iteration pipelining.

In this expression T_{ACC} is the execution time of one accumulation if operands are in local memory (two local fetches, one scalar multiplication, and one addition). T_{NET} is the communication overhead needed for data transmission between two segments of the pipeline and T_{BUS} is the bus overhead for a remote memory fetch.

The results are plotted in Figure 18 for three allocations (worst, best, and random).

The best allocation has very good performance. However, the graph shows that the partitioning based on iteration pipelining is very sensitive to allocation. Indeed, since the best allocation allows no remote access, the observed throughput can grow almost linearly with the number of processors—which is the ideal performance speedup of a multiprocessor. When more remote accesses are involved, the performance is observed to fall drastically.

One significant drawback of the iteration-pipelining technique is that all of matrix **C** ends up in the last memory module. This may seriously affect the performance of the next step in a complex application, or it may be totally impossible if **C** cannot be held in a single memory module. If **C** is redistributed in the *P* processors of the machine as its elements are produced, the performance of the iteration pipelining will be affected. This is especially true of the best allocation scheme.

Block partitioning. Instead of passing the partial sum for each c_{ij} from one processor to the next, an alternative partitioning of the matrix multiplication problem separates the **C** matrix in *P* blocks and assigns the computation of $[(lm)/P]c_{ij}$'s to each PE (assume *l* or *m* is a multiple of *P*). This means that while the **C** matrix was always produced by the same PE in the previous case, the various elements of the **C** matrix will be found in different PEs for this case. This mode of operation is illustrated in Figure 19.

There are two partitioning schemes in this case depending on whether *l* or *m* is a multiple of *P*. In the first case a row grouping of the **C** matrix would be performed. Otherwise, a column grouping would take place. The same allocation analysis applies to the two partitioning schemes described above. In the following section, C_{ij} is a single element of matrix **C**. C_{*i} corresponds to the *i*th-row vector and C_{*j} to the *j*th-column vector.

Note that for a *P* processor system each processor will therefore accumulate $[lm/P]n$ products.

Allocation. We describe three allocation schemes in the case of block partitioning. F_{alloc} is defined as previously to be the number of remote memory requests per accumulation.

- *Worst-case allocation*. This case is similar to the one described above in which $F_{alloc} = 2$, because each accumulation requires two accesses.
- *Random allocation*. This case has also been described previously. In this case

$$F_{alloc} = 2 \cdot \frac{P-1}{P} \tag{5}$$

- *Best-case allocation*. Here the vector $\mathbf{A}_{i*}$, or alternatively the vector $\mathbf{B}_{*j}$, is locally accessed. This means that only one remote memory request is required per accumulation: $F_{alloc} = 1$.

Throughput evaluation. It can be shown[22] that the throughput of the multiprocessor for matrix multiply is thus bounded by:

$$Th(P) \le \frac{2n-1}{n} \cdot MIN\left[\frac{P}{T_{ACC} + F_{alloc} \cdot T_{BUS}};\ \frac{BW}{F_{alloc}}\right] \tag{6}$$

The results are plotted in Figure 20 for the three allocations (worst, random, and best).

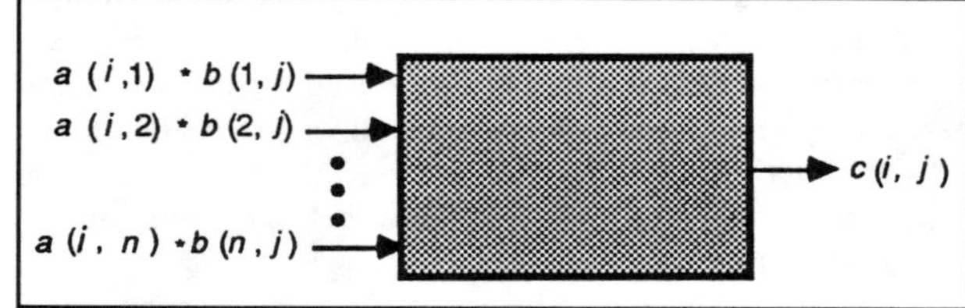

Figure 19. An example of block partitioning.

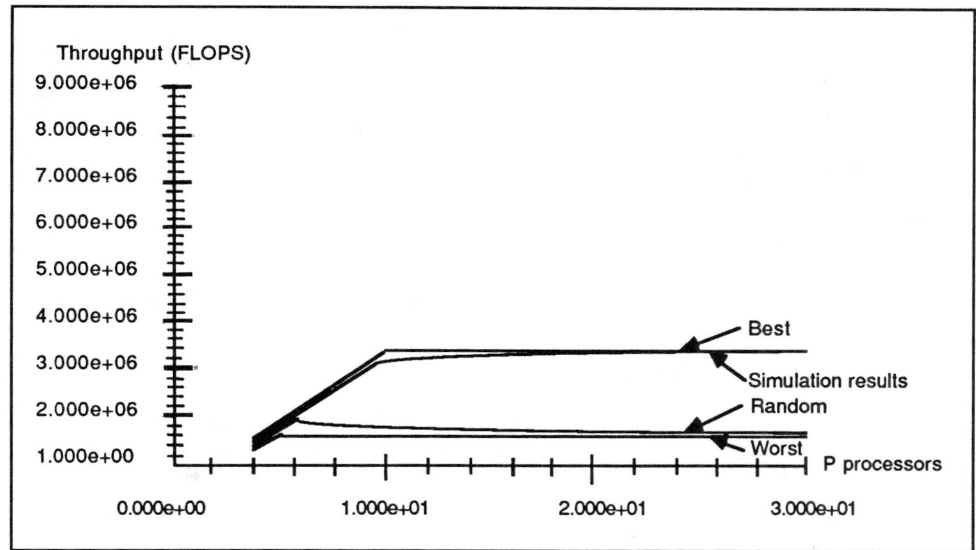

Figure 20. Performance results of block partitioning.

The best allocation in this case does not give as good a performance as experienced in the iteration-pipelining case. However, the newly produced matrix **C** is more evenly distributed across the system memories so that overall performance can be improved.

Note that many other methods are available. These include systolization, matrix broadcast, and rotation.[5] However, we feel that these approaches to program partitioning and allocation are too specific and do not represent the realistic capabilities of an automatic approach to program partitioning.

Simulation results. To verify the validity of the analytical models for the performance of the TX16, we simulated the execution of the different partitioning schemes of matrix multiplication with the SMPL event-driven simulation package.[23]

We also simulated the two different partitioning schemes for matrix multiplication to determine their respective best cases. The simulation curves proved our theoretical results and are displayed in Figures 18 and 20.

Matrix multiplication using iteration pipelining was simulated in the case having no remote memory fetches ($F_{alloc} = 0$) for 32, 64, and $1k$ square matrices. The simulation results confirm our theoretical results. The maximum processing speed of every node is the main bottleneck in this computation.

In simulating block partitioning, the matrix size does not affect the simulation results. The system was simulated in the case of $F_{alloc} = 1$. The throughput in this case is limited by the traffic on the bus as is expected from the theoretical results.

We have investigated the implementation of a powerful multi-microprocessor in which the basic building blocks of the system were deliberately selected as off-the-shelf components to demonstrate the immediate low-cost feasibility of the architecture. Such systems have traditionally suffered from a notoriously low programmability.

One of our major contributions demonstrates that the choice of the programming environment could provide the user with a transparent approach to the programming of multiprocessors. We have shown that the Transputer chip was particularly suited to this approach. The dataflow principles of execution also are very suitable to such a problem and can be integrated in a high-level language environment. Synchronization mechanisms automatically ensure the safe execution of user programs. Since the structure of the machine is hidden from the programmer, it is the task of the compiler to partition the applications and to allocate resources.

We have also shown several partitioning and allocation strategies in the context of a matrix algorithm. These strategies can be expanded and applied to many other problems. We are currently investigating these strategies for more complex applications and have plans to integrate them into the programming environment.

We developed a simple analytical model based on throughput analysis. A simulation was also undertaken to validate the throughput models. The results of the simulation have been quite encouraging. The simplicity of the analytical model enables it to be integrated easily within the programming environment; this provides automatic and fast analysis of various decomposition strategies. The models can therefore be used to efficiently compile functional programs into object codes for multiprocessor systems.

The predicted performance of the machine shows the execution of matrix algorithms at speeds competitive with those of a first-generation Cray for a fraction of the cost. The current performance of our configuration is limited by the arithmetic capabilities of the nodes. In the future as powerful floating-point coprocessors become available for the Transputer, we expect to witness a dramatic improvement in the performance of this machine. However, it has also been shown that the current design is limited by such parameters as the bandwidth of the intermemory bus.

Future improvements over the current architecture of this multiprocessor would use the TX16 as the basic building block of a larger system. A hierarchy of TX16 clusters could demonstrate a high potential for scalability and will be studied in future research.

Acknowledgments

We gratefully acknowledge the assistance of the Computer Research Group at the Lawrence Livermore National Laboratory and particularly James McGraw and Steve Skedzielewski for supplying us with assistance on using their SISAL compilers.

This material is based on work supported in part by the National Science Foundation under grant ECS-8404345 and by the USC Faculty Research and Innovation Fund.

References

1. M. Dubois, "Cache-Based Multiprocessors with High Efficiency," *IEEE Trans. Computers*, Vol. C-34, No. 10, Oct. 1985, pp. 968-972.
2. K. Marrin, "New Silicon Intensifies Debate Over VMEbus/Multibus II Multiprocessor Support," *Computer Design,* Vol. 25, No. 2, Jan. 15, 1986, beginning pg. 31.
3. P. Borrill and J. Theus, "An Advanced Communication Protocol for the Proposed IEEE 896 Futurebus," *IEEE Micro*, Vol. 4, No. 4, Aug. 1984, pp. 42-56.
4. A. K. Jones, "Experience Using Multiprocessor Systems—A Status Report," *ACM Computing Surveys*, Vol. 12, No. 2, June 1980.
5. G. C. Fox, "Are Concurrent Processors General-Purpose Computers?," *IEEE Trans. Nuclear Science*, Vol. NS-32, No. 1, Feb. 1985.
6. C. A. R. Hoare, "Communicating Sequential Processes," *Comm. ACM*, Vol. 21, No. 8, Aug. 1978.
7. J. Backus, "Can Programming Be Liberated from the von Neumann Style? A Functional Style and Its Algebra of Programs," *Comm. ACM*, Vol. 8, No. 8, Aug. 1978, pp. 613-641.
8. J. B. Dennis, "Data-Flow Supercomputers," *Computer*, Vol. 13, No. 11, Nov. 1980, pp. 48-56.
9. E. F. Gehringer et al., "The Cm* Testbed," *Computer*, Vol. 15, No. 10, Oct. 1982, pp. 40-53.
10. G. A. Mago, "A Cellular Computer Architecture for Functional Programming," *Proc. Compcon Spring 80*, Feb. 1980, pp. 179-187.
11. R. M. Keller and F. C. H. Lin, "Simulated Performance of a Reduction-Based Multiprocessor," *Computer*, Vol. 17, No. 7, July 1984, pp. 70-82.
12. J. L. Gaudiot, R. W. Vedder, G. K. Tucker, D. Finn, and M. L. Campbell, "A Distributed VLSI Architecture for Efficient Signal and Data Processing," *IEEE Trans. Computers*, Special Issue on Distributed Computing Systems, Vol. C-34, No. 12, Dec. 1985, pp. 1072-1087.
13. J. R. McGraw, "Data-Flow Computing: The VAL Language," *ACM Trans. Programming Languages and Systems 4*, 1982, pp. 44-82.
14. J. L. Gustafson, S. Hawkinson, and K. Scott, "The Architecture of a Homogeneous Vector Supercomputer," *Proc. 1986 Int'l Conf. Parallel Processing,* Aug. 1986, pp. 649-660.
15. L. Philipson et al., "A Communication Structure for a Multiprocessor Computer with Distributed Global Memory," *Proc. 10th Int'l Symp. Computer Architecture,* Stockholm, June 1983.
16. Arvind, K.P. Gostelow, and W. Plouffe, "An Asynchronous Programming Language and Computing Machine," TR 114a, Dept. of Information and Computer Science, University of Californai, Irvine, Dec. 1978.
17. J. C. Syre, D. Comte, and N. Hifdi, "Pipelining, Parallelism and Asynchronism in the LAU System," *Proc. 1977 Int'l. Conf. Parallel Processing*, Aug. 1977, pp. 87-92.
18. J. R. McGraw, and S. K. Skedzielewski,"SISAL: Streams and Iterations in a Single-Assignment Language, Language Reference Manual," tech. report M-146, Lawrence Livermore National Laboratory, July 1983.
19. J. R. Gurd, C. C. Kirkham, and I. Watson, "The Manchester Data-Flow Computer," *Comm. ACM.*, Vol. 28, No. 1, Jan. 1985, pp. 34-52.
20. "Occam Programming System: Reference Manual," Inmos, Ltd., Colorado Springs, Colorado, 1984.
21. D. May, "Occam," informal tech. notes at Inmos, Colorado Springs, Colo., 1983.
22. M. Dubois, J. L. Gaudiot, and N. Tohme, "Analysis of Partitioning and Allocation Techniques in a Cluster-Based Machine," tech. report CRI-85-39, USC Computer Research Institute, Los Angeles, Calif., Nov. 1985.
23. M. H. MacDougall, "SMPL—A Simple Portable Simulation Language," tech. report, Amdahl Corp., Apr. 1, 1980.

Bibliography

Andrews, G. R., et al., "Concepts and Notations for Concurrent Programming," *Computing Surveys*, Vol. 15, No. 1, Mar. 1983.

Arvind and Iannucci, R. A., "Two Fundamental Issues in Multiprocessors: the Data-flow Solutions," tech. report MIT/LCS/TM-241, MIT Laboratory for Computer Science, Cambridge, Mass., Sept. 1983.

Ercegovac, M. D., Chan, P. K., and Ravi, T. M., "A Data Flow Multimicroprocessor Architecture for High-Speed Simulation of Continuous Systems, " *Proc. Int'l Workshop on High Level Computer Architecture 84*, May 1984, pp. 2.9-2.17.

Ercegovac, M. D., and Karplus, W. J., "On a Dataflow Approach in High-Speed Simulation of Continuous Systems," *Proc. Int'l Workshop on High-Level Computer Architecture 84*, May 1984, pp. 2.1-2.8.

Ercegovac, M. D., and Lu, S-L, "A Functional Language Approach in High-Speed Digital Simulation," *Proc. Summer Computer Simulation Conf.*, 1983.

Ercegovac, M. D., Patel, D. R., and Lang, T., "Functional Languages and Data-Flow Architectures," *Proc. Summer Computer Simulation Conf.*, 1983.

Gajski, D. D., Padua, D. A., Kuck, D. J., and Kuhn, R. H., "A Second Opinion on Data-Flow Machines and Languages," *Computer*, Vol. 15, No. 2, Feb. 1982, pp. 58-69.

Gaudiot, J. L., "Structure Handling in Data-Flow Systems," *IEEE Trans. Computers*, Vol. C-35, No. 6, June 1986, pp. 489-502.

Gaudiot, J. L., and Dubois, M. D., "An Integrated Solution to Large-Scale Computing Problems," *Proc. Internal Symp. New Directions in Computing*, Trondheim, Norway, Aug. 1985.

Gostelow, K. P., and Thomas, R. E., "Performance of a Simulated Data-Flow Computer," *IEEE Trans. Computers*, Vol. C-29, No. 10, Oct. 1980, pp. 905-919.

Hwang, K., and Briggs, F. A., *Computer Architecture and Parallel Processing*, McGraw-Hill, New York, 1984.

Wu, S. B., and Liu, M. T., "A Cluster Structure as an Interconnection Network for Large Multimicrocomputer Systems," *IEEE Trans. Computers*, Vol. C-30, No. 4, Apr. 1981, pp. 254-264.

A Microprocessor-based Hypercube Supercomputer

John P. Hayes, Trevor Mudge, and Quentin F. Stout
University of Michigan

Stephen Colley and John Palmer
NCUBE Corporation

Each node in the NCUBE/ten parallel processor is organized around a custom, VAX-like, 32-bit CPU chip. With 1024 nodes, the NCUBE/ten provides a throughput of 500 MFLOPS.

The most straightforward and least expensive way to build a supercomputer capable of hundreds of millions of instructions per second is to interconnect a large number of microprocessors. Supercomputers built by corporations such as Cray Research and Control Data do not use this approach, but rely on very fast components and pipelined operations. However, such machines are quite expensive, and each performance improvement of them is increasingly difficult to achieve. In contrast, the performance of machines consisting of interconnected microprocessors can be significantly improved simply by adding more microprocessors, faster microprocessors, and better interconnections among them.

An important consideration for systems made up of interconnected microprocessors is the question of local versus global memory and its effect on the interconnection scheme. In a global memory system, memory is shared by all the processors. Since two or more processors may try to use the same memory location at the same time, a global memory scheme requires the use of hardware or software protocols for arbitrating among processors. Further, since memory references are a very large fraction of any program's execution, the time required to access memory must be kept small. These two requirements make severe demands on the interconnection system between processors and the global memory, and thus they limit the number of processors that can be economically used.

In a distributed memory system each processor has its own memory, and information is exchanged as messages between processors. If each processor has most of the data it will need, the number of messages between processors can be kept relatively small, and the numbers of processors in the system can be larger. This is particularly true in interconnection systems using processor-to-processor connections instead of bus connections. In a processor-to-processor connection scheme, each processor is directly connected to a subset of the other processors (its "neighbors"). Messages between processors not directly connected must be passed through intermediate processors. Because a processor can pass messages more quickly to its neighbors than to processors not directly connected to it, tasks that need extensive intercommunication should be placed on neighboring processors. An interconnection scheme that makes it easier to achieve such placement is the hypercube.

An n-dimensional hypercube computer, also known as a binary n-cube computer, is a multiprocessor characterized by the presence of $N = 2^n$ processors interconnected as an

Reprinted from *IEEE Micro*, pp. 6–17, Oct. 1986.

n-dimensional binary cube. Each processor P forms a node, or vertex, of the cube and has its own CPU and local main memory. P has direct communication paths to n other processors (its neighbors); these paths correspond to the edges of the cube. There are 2^n distinct n-bit binary addresses or labels that may be assigned to the processors. Thus, each processor's address differs from that of each of its n neighbors in exactly one bit position. Figure 1 illustrates the hypercube topology for $n \leq 4$; note that a zero-dimensional hypercube is a conventional single processor. The usual method for constructing a hypercube and assigning binary addresses to its nodes employs the following recursive procedure: Start with a one-dimensional cube (two nodes) and label one of its nodes with a 0 and the other with a 1. In general, an n-dimensional cube is constructed from two $(n-1)$-dimensional cubes. The labels in one of the cubes are prefixed with a 0 (the zero-cube) and those in the other with a 1 (the one-cube); then each node in the zero-cube is connected to its counterpart in the one-cube, i.e., to the node that has the identical address except for the prefix. Thus, node P_{0x} is connected to P_{1x} (subscripts are the binary addresses). All hypercubes of higher dimension and their node addresses can be generated from this procedure. Each dimension of a hypercube has an associated axis that is defined as follows: Node P_{x0y} is connected to P_{x1y} by an edge that is in the direction of the ith axis if there are $i-1$ bits in y.

It has been known for some time that the hypercube structure has a number of features that make it useful for parallel computation. For example, meshes of all dimensions and trees can be embedded in a hypercube so that neighboring nodes are mapped to neighbors in the hypercube. Figure 2 shows how a 3×4 mesh can be embedded in a 4-cube. The communication structures used in the fast Fourier transform and bitonic sort algorithm can be embedded similarly in the hypercube. Since a great many scientific applications use mesh, tree, FFT, or sorting interconnection structures, the hypercube is a good candidate for a general-purpose parallel architecture. Even for problems with less regular communication patterns, the hypercube's maximum internode distance (graph diameter) of $n = \log_2 N$ means any two nodes can communicate fairly rapidly. This diameter is larger than the unit diameter of a complete graph K_N, but is achieved with nodes having only a degree or fanout of $\log_2 N$, as opposed to the $N-1$ degree of nodes in K_N. Other standard architectures with small degree, such as meshes, trees, or bus systems, have either a large diameter (N for a two-dimensional mesh) or a resource that becomes a bottleneck in many applications because too much communication must pass through it (as occurs at the apex of a tree, or at a shared bus). Thus, from general topological arguments we can conclude that hypercube architectures balance node connectivity, communication diameter, algorithm embeddability, and programming ease. This balance makes them suitable for an unusually broad class of computational problems.

Proposals to build large hypercube computers have been made for more than 20 years. In 1962, Squire and Palais at the University of Michigan carried out a detailed paper design of a hypercube computer.[1,2] They estimated that a 4096-node (12-dimensional) version of their machine would require about 20 times as many components as the IBM Stretch, one of the largest and most complex computers

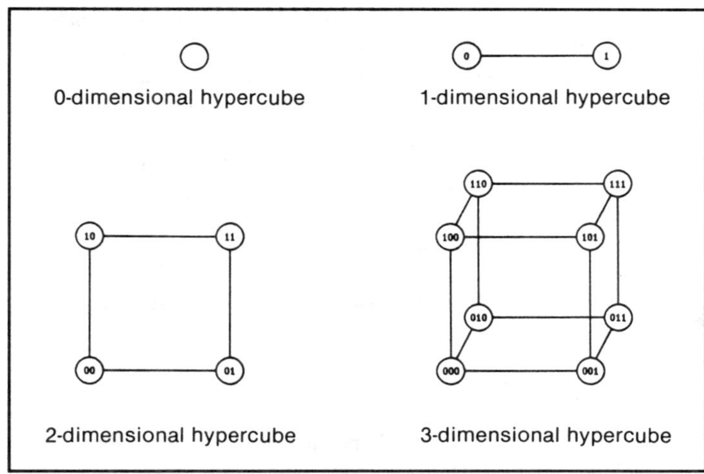

Figure 1. Hypercubes for $n = 0, 1, 2$, and 3.

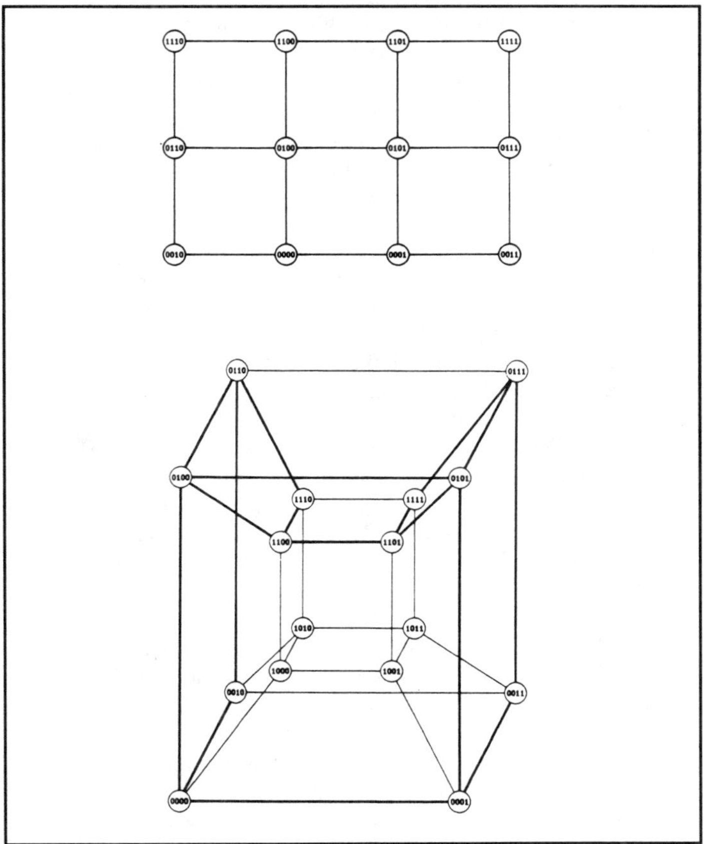

Figure 2. Embedding a 3×4 mesh in a 4-cube.

built up to that time. Around 1975 IMS Associates, an early manufacturer of personal computers, announced a 256-node commercial hypercube based on the Intel 8080 microprocessor, but they neither published details of its design nor produced a machine. In 1977, Sullivan and his colleagues at Columbia University presented a proposal for a large hypercube called the Columbia Homogeneous Parallel Processor, or CHOPP, which would have contained up to a million processors.[3,4] In the same year, Pease published a study of the "indirect" binary n-cube architecture, for which he suggested a multistage interconnection network of the omega type for implementing the hypercube topology.[5] Several other interesting architectures closely related to the hypercube have been proposed—for example, the cube-connected-cycles structure.[6]

It is clear that the early hypercube designs were impractical because of the large number of logic and memory elements they would have required, given the then-available circuit technologies. The situation began to change rapidly in the early 1980's as advances in VLSI technology allowed powerful 16/32-bit microprocessors to be implemented on a single IC chip, and as RAM densities moved into the 100,000- to 1,000,000-bit-per-chip range. The first working hypercube computer—the 64-node Cosmic Cube at Caltech[7]—was demonstrated in 1983. For the hypercube node processor, it uses a single-board microcomputer containing an Intel 8086 microprocessor and an Intel 8087 floating-point coprocessor. Since then, Caltech researchers have built several similar hypercubes and successfully applied them to numerous scientific applications, often obtaining impressive performance improvements over conventional machines of comparable cost.[8]

Influenced primarily by the Caltech work, several companies have developed commercial hypercubes since 1983. In July 1985, Intel delivered the first production hypercube, the Intel Personal Supercomputer, or iPSC, which has a 16-bit 80286/287 CPU as its node processor and up to 128 nodes. If we assume a peak performance of 0.1 MFLOPS per node, the 128-node iPSC has a potential throughput of about 12 MFLOPS, far below that of a traditional vector supercomputer such as the Cray-1, which has a peak throughput of 160 MFLOPS. Other commercial hypercubes introduced in 1985 include Ametek's System/14 and NCUBE Corporation's NCUBE/ten. The System/14 hypercube can have up to 256 nodes, each employing an 80286/287-based CPU similar to that of the iPSC and an 80186 processor for communication management. The NCUBE/ten can accommodate up to 1024 nodes, each based on a VAX-like 32-bit custom processor with a peak performance of 0.5 MFLOPS. Thus, a fully configured NCUBE system has a potential throughput of around 500 MFLOPS. This high performance level is supported by extremely fast communication rates (both input/output and node-to-node), making the NCUBE/ten a true supercomputer. NCUBE machines have been installed at several beta-test sites, including the University of Michigan, since early 1985, and have been in general production since December 1985. Other recently introduced hypercube-style machines with supercomputing potential include the Caltech/JPL Mark III,[9] the Connection Machine,[10] the Intel iPSC-VX, and the Floating Point Systems T Series. The last two machines include a pipelined vector processor at each node. Much faster successors to the current commercial hypercubes can be expected to appear over the next few years. Because of the effort being devoted to the development of hardware and software for these machines, and because of their relatively low cost, hypercube supercomputers seem likely to provide an increasingly attractive alternative to conventional pipelined supercomputers for many applications.

Here, we discuss the architectural and technological issues influencing the design of microprocessor-based supercomputing hypercubes, employing the NCUBE/ten as an example. We pay particular attention to the influence of component packaging, reliability, communication speed, and the operating system environment on the system implementation.

General design issues

To provide supercomputer-level performance, the designer must build a machine with extremely high integer and floating-point execution rates as well as extremely high I/O throughput. He must also provide very large primary (RAM) and secondary (disk) memory spaces. For the principal supercomputer user base of scientific programmers, he must develop a programming environment that includes Fortran and a powerful operating system such as Unix. To achieve low cost and high reliability, he must minimize the component count at all levels, particularly the number of chips and boards. He should also provide some degree of fault tolerance. Since a very large amount of RAM storage is needed, he should consider employing an error-correcting code, or ECC, to detect and correct memory faults, despite the fact that it increases the chip count. To increase reliability and decrease operating cost, the designer should use an air-cooled configuration suitable for a standard office environment. (An examination of existing computer systems shows that air cooling limits machine complexity to 50,000 chips.) The designer should use off-the-shelf parts, since they are cheaper and usually more reliable than custom chips. If he does need custom parts, and if his company relies on outside suppliers, he should use conservative design rules that will be accepted by several silicon foundries. Because large error accumulation can occur in large-scale numerical calculations, he should make individual calculations as accurate as possible. He can do so by adhering to the IEEE 754 floating-point standard and by providing double-precision, floating-point operations.

A key decision in the design of a parallel computer is the choice of interconnection network. Multistage interconnection networks simplify the programming process by providing a global shared memory, but they cannot be built with current technology without significantly delaying the information being passed over them. Since the speed of information passing over the network strongly affects performance, direct connection networks, with local memory at every node, provide the most desirable means of achieving supercomputer performance. Many direct interconnection schemes have been analyzed and implemented but, as noted previously, the hypercube structure has a number of inherent advantages. The ease with which efficient application programs were developed for the hypercubes at Caltech has also shown the hypercube to be superior to alternative architectures such as meshes or trees. The neighbor-to-neighbor links of the hypercube provide almost the same communication capabilities as a complete graph while using nodes with only a logarithmic degree. The achievable degree is constrained by a variety of packaging considerations, but with current technology one can build hypercubes with thousands of nodes. In contrast, a complete graph connection of a few tens of nodes may not be possible.

There are additional features of the hypercube that are useful in designing a supercomputer, but that have not been exploited prior to the development of the NCUBE/ten. For example, the hypercube is homogeneous in that all nodes look the same, so an I/O channel can be attached to each node. This provides the potential of extremely high system I/O rates. Also, since there are numerous ways to divide a hypercube into subcubes, the designer, by giving each user a dedicated subcube, should find it easy to support multiprocessing. These dedicated subcubes can be allocated so that all processor-to-processor and I/O communications occur within them and do not use processors or communications lines in other subcubes. Further, the designer can allow the user to define the size of the subcube in the programs he writes; in this way, the user can develop programs in small subcubes and then do production runs in larger ones. This partitionability makes it easier for the system to tolerate faults, since the operating system can allocate subcubes that avoid faulty processors or faulty communication lines.

As we noted previously, technological developments have made it possible to build a reliable hypercube computer with a large number of processors. A fine-grained hypercube architecture, i.e., one with a large number (tens of thousands) of very simple processors, has a high ratio of communication to computation. Thus, the suitability of such an architecture—the Connection Machine is an example—to general scientific computation is uncertain. A very coarse-grained architecture with, say, tens of large and fast processors requires that the nodes achieve extremely high performance. For example, to achieve 10^9 instructions per second with 10 processors, such an architecture requires those processors to be capable of 10^8 instructions per second. The Caltech/JPL Mark III is an example of a coarse-grained hypercube. The designers of the NCUBE machine felt that achieving 10^9 instructions per second was best done with a medium-grained approach—1000 processors running at 10^6 instructions per second.

The Caltech machines and their commercial successors are MIMD (multiple-instruction- and multiple-data-stream) machines, meaning that each processor has its own program as well as its own data. These machines are customarily used in an SCMD (single-code, multiple-data) fashion, in which all processors have a copy of a single program, though they may be executing different branches at a given time.

Experience with the Caltech machines has demonstrated that a medium-grained MIMD hypercube architecture can attain high efficiency on a variety of scientific problems without demanding an intolerable amount of revision of serial code and algorithms from its users.[8] This is in contrast to the much greater amount of program and algorithm redesign required of users of fine-grained SIMD (single-instruction- and multiple-data-stream) machines such as the MPP[11] and Connection Machine. In SIMD machines, a controller broadcasts instructions that all processors receive and perform on their own data. The node processors in MIMD machines are more complex than those in SIMD machines since they must fetch instructions rather than just receive broadcasted ones. Further, distributed-memory MIMD machines need additional memory to store the program at each node. In general, one can build more SIMD processors than MIMD processors on a given amount of silicon and have a greater potential system throughput; however, the gain in programming simplicity provided by MIMD machines more than compensates for this, except for a narrow range of applications in which almost any penalty can be tolerated if it yields the required speed. Furthermore, MIMD machines can accommodate multiple independent users, while SIMD machines cannot.

Since there may be hundreds or thousands of nodes in a hypercube supercomputer, their chip count is the most significant component of the total system chip count. Using the densest memory chips available is the most effective way the designer can decrease the total number of chips. The NCUBE/ten, for example, uses 256K DRAM chips to implement the local memories of the hypercube nodes. The next most effective way the designer can reduce the chip count is by putting all node functions onto a single chip. This implies that the processor chip must perform all communication, memory management, and floating-point operations as well as other data processing functions. At present there is no widespread market pressure to produce standard processor chips of this type; consequently, they are not available off the shelf. In 1983, when design of the NCUBE/ten started, the only way to achieve supercomputer performance with a single-chip node processor was to undertake the risky step of custom designing such a chip. INMOS made a similar decision with the Transputer processor chip, with the important difference that the initial version of the Transputer did not provide floating-point operations and has four rather than eleven I/O channels.[12] The performance and functionality demands on the NCUBE processor chip were quite severe, and numerous trade-offs were made to enable it to be built.

System architecture

The overall goal of the NCUBE's designers was to use massive parallelism to build a range of inexpensive and

Figure 3. Six-dimensional hypercube with 64 nodes and 8M bytes of memory fits on one 16 × 22-inch board.

reliable software-compatible machines achieving supercomputer performance at the high end of that range. The NCUBE/ten is the largest model in the series; it is a 10-dimensional hypercube containing 1024 custom-designed 32-bit processors, each with a 128K-byte local memory. It uses up to eight front-end host processors to manage I/O operations, with those processors under control of a multiuser Unix-based operating system. It achieves a level of system integration high enough to allow a six-dimensional hypercube with 64 nodes and 8M bytes of memory to be placed on a single 16 × 22-inch board (Figure 3). Its backplane connections are rather formidable—640 connections just for communication channels—since each processor node has off-board bidirectional channels to four more processors of the hypercube plus one bidirectional channel to an I/O board. A maximum-sized NCUBE/ten system is composed of 16 processor boards and eight I/O boards and is housed in a small air-cooled enclosure.

The NCUBE/ten's I/O boards provide the connections between the hypercube and the external world. At least one of the I/O boards must be a host board, and there can be as many as eight. The host board uses an Intel 80286 to run the operating system and has 4M bytes of RAM that is used as a shared memory by the various processors on it. It supports a variety of peripherals, including eight ASCII-standard terminals, four SMD disk drives (which can be as large as 500M bytes), and three Intel iSBX connectors that can accept daughterboards for functions such as graphics control or networking. The host board incorporates a real-time clock and temperature sensors for automatic shutdown on overheating. Besides the host board, other I/O boards available with the NCUBE/ten include a graphics board with a 2K × 1K × 8-bit frame buffer, an intersystem board that connects two NCUBE systems, and an open system board that has about 75 percent of its space left open for custom design.

A distinguishing feature of the I/O boards is that each has 128 bidirectional channels directly connected to a subcube of the hypercube (Figure 4). This permits extremely high I/O data transfer rates into the hypercube. To accomplish this, each I/O board contains 16 NCUBE processor chips, each of which serves as an I/O processor and is connected to eight nodes in the main hypercube. Like the hypercube node processors, an I/O processor has a 128K-byte RAM that occupies a fixed slot in the 80286 host's 4M-byte memory space. An I/O processor performs an input operation from the outside world—a disk read, for example—by first transferring the input data to the host's 4M-byte memory. It then transfers the data through its DMA channel directly to the target hypercube nodes. It handles output operations in a similar fashion. In a maximally configured NCUBE/ten system with 16 processor and eight I/O boards, the hypercube nodes do not have to redistribute I/O data to other nodes. This is not always the case with smaller NCUBE systems; it depends on the number and configuration of the I/O and processor boards.

All the I/O and processor boards of a fully configured system, along with their fans and power supplies, fit into a single enclosure that is less than three feet on a side. A maximally configured system dissipates about 8 kW and can be placed in a normal air-conditioned office or lab. An NCUBE/ten peripheral enclosure is about 3 × 2 × 3 feet and contains a 65M-byte cartridge tape drive and up to four disk drives. A minimal stand-alone NCUBE system consists of one host board and one processor board containing a six-dimensional hypercube, and can handle up to eight user terminals. By adding a second processor board, one obtains a seven-dimensional hypercube. Since the operating system can allocate subcubes of arbitrary size, one can have a number of processor boards that do not form a complete hypercube. For example, three boards provide a seven-dimensional and a six-dimensional hypercube, which could also be allocated as three six-dimensional hypercubes or as numerous smaller hypercubes. A maximally configured system (Figure 4) contains a 10-dimensional hypercube. The 1024 processors of such a system have a potential instruction execution rate of about two billion instructions per second, or about 500 MFLOPS, with a 10-MHz clock. The total amount of memory in the nodes is 128M bytes. If all of the I/O boards are host boards, it is possible to support 64 terminals and provide as many as 16 billion bytes of storage. A host board can provide input or output at up to 12M bytes per second, giving a system input or output rate of about 90M bytes per second. In the case in which a single data set is to be broadcast to all nodes, input rates can exceed 90M bytes per second per host board—that is, they can approach 720M bytes per second per system.

The node processor

The NCUBE node processor provides, on a single VLSI chip, the functions of a 32-bit supermini-class CPU, in-

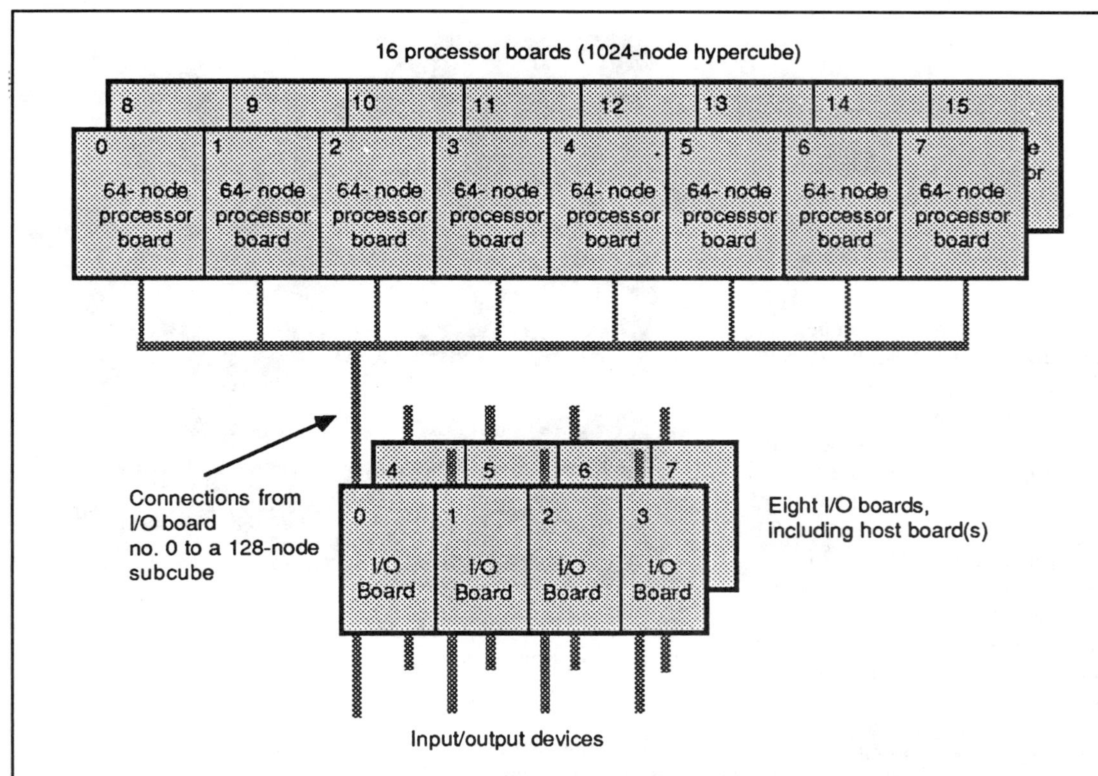

Figure 4. Complete NCUBE/ten system.

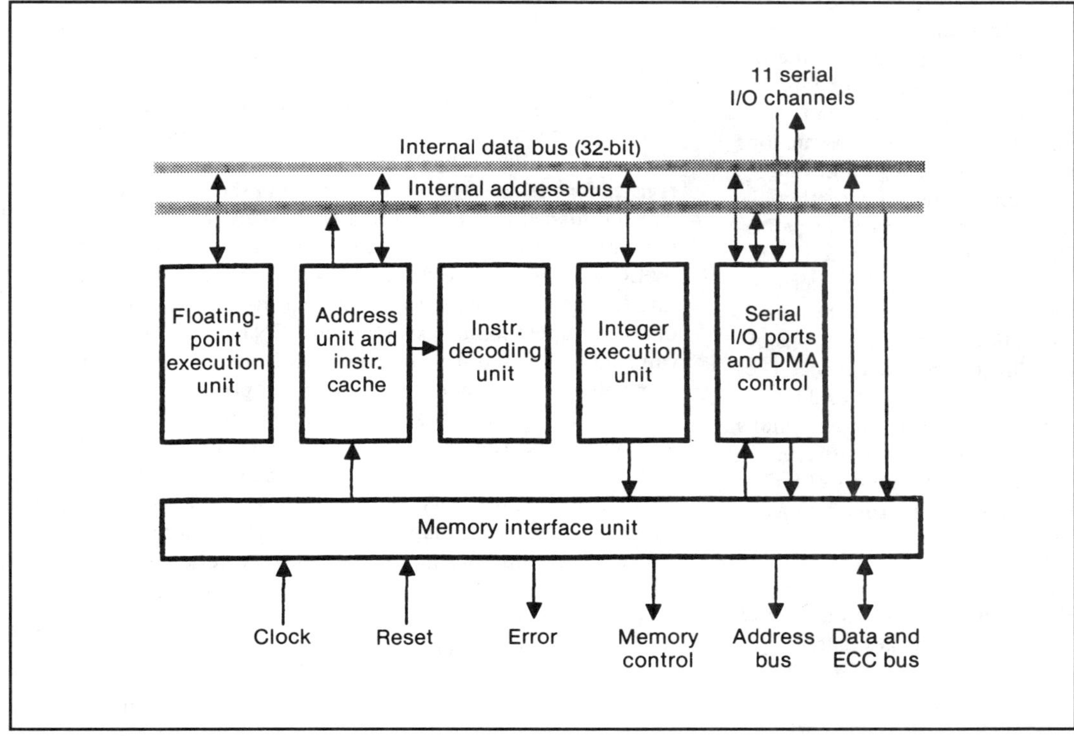

Figure 5. Organization of the NCUBE processor chip.

cluding a full floating-point instruction set and all the logic needed for memory management and interprocessor communication. Figure 5 shows the major functional blocks of the chip, and Figure 6 is a photograph of the chip in its package. NCUBE began design of the node processor chip in 1983, constraining itself to 2-μm NMOS design rules that were acceptable to several silicon foundries. The chip contains about 160,000 transistors and is housed in a pin-grid-array package having 68 pins. Including six 256K-bit DRAM chips (each organized as 64K $\times$ 4 bits), an entire NCUBE/ten node requires only seven chips. This unusual compactness has prompted the introduction of a four-node (two-cube) IBM AT board. Four such boards can be combined to provide a 16-node (four-dimensional) hypercube.

The NCUBE/ten has a conventional two-address instruction set with addressing modes similar to those found in the VAX instruction set.[13] There are three main classes of information: addresses (unsigned integers), integers, and floating-point numbers (reals). Addresses are 32 bits long, but the current node implementation only supports a 17-bit physical address space. Integers can be 8, 16, or 32 bits long. Floating-point numbers can contain either 32 or 64 bits and conform to the IEEE 754 floating-point standard. There are 16 general-purpose registers of 32 bits each. A variety of addressing modes are available, including literal (immediate), register direct, autodecrement/increment, autostride, offset, direct, indirect, and push/pop. The instruction set contains a full complement of logical, shift, jump, and arithmetic operations (including square root). Several instructions have been included to facilitate internode communications. For example, the "find first one" instruction, or FFO, which finds the bit position of the first 1 in a word by means of a right-to-left scan, can be used in internode routing. Other examples include the "load pointer" (LPTR) and "load counter" (LCNT) instructions, which are used for transmitting and receiving data. In a system with a 10-MHz clock, nonarithmetic instructions can be executed at about 2 MIPS, single-precision floating-point operations at 0.5 MFLOPS, and double-precision floating-point operations at 0.3 MFLOPS. (These performance figures assume that register-to-register operations predominate.) A 32-byte instruction cache allows loops of up to 16 bytes to be executed directly from the cache. The node processor has a vectored interrupt facility, and it generates various interrupts to indicate program exceptions such as numerical overflow or address faults, software debugging commands such as breakpoint and trace, I/O signals such as input ready, and hardware errors such as correctable or uncorrectable memory errors.

Pin and silicon space limitations forced a number of design compromises in the selection of the width of various system data paths. The node memory supplies data in 16-bit halfwords and adds an extra byte containing ECC check bits. The processor performs single-error correction and double-error detection (SECDED) on all memory words, generating an interrupt in the case of an error. This use of SECDED is an example of a situation in which the pin limitations affect performance, for it requires two memory fetches to obtain a full 32-bit word. It also increases the number of memory chips required, since the SECDED code used for 32-bit data could be supplied by five RAM chips organized as 32K × 8 bits, if such chips were available.

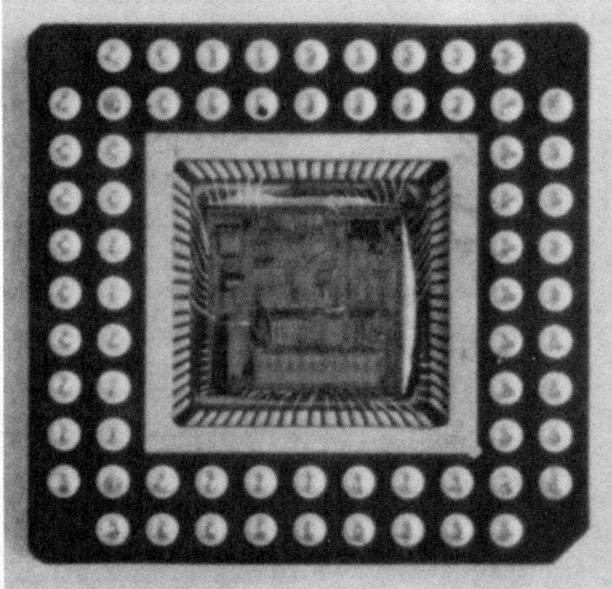

Figure 6. The NCUBE processor chip in its pin-grid-array package.

The node processor communicates with other nodes by means of asynchronous DMA operations over 22 bit-serial I/O lines. These I/O lines are paired into 11 bidirectional channels which permit the formation of a 10-dimensional hypercube and allow one connection to an I/O board. Each node-to-node channel operates at 10 MHz with parity check, yielding a data transfer rate of about 1M bytes per second per channel in each direction. A channel has two 32-bit write-only registers associated with it: an address register for the message buffer location in the node RAM, which is loaded by LPTR; and a count register indicating the number of bytes left to send or receive, which is loaded by LCNT. There is also a ready flag and an interrupt enable flag for each channel. Once a processor has initiated a send or receive operation by executing an LCNT instruction, it can continue with other operations while the DMA channel completes the internode communication operation. Interrupts can be used to signal when a channel is ready for a new operation. Alternatively, the interrupts can be disabled and the ready flag polled to check for channel readiness. An interrupt is also generated if there is a channel overrun, which can occur on an input operation only if more than nine channels are transmitting data into the node. To reduce DMA activity, a broadcasting feature is supported that transmits the same data word along an arbitrary set of output channels in a single DMA operation.

Table 1 summarizes the results of some performance experiments, designed by Donald Winsor at the University of Michigan, that compared the NCUBE node processor to two other CPUs with floating-point hardware: the Intel 80286/80287 (the NCUBE host processor served for this) and the Digital Equipment Corporation's VAX-11/780 with a floating-point accelerator. The measurements were made with the NCUBE node and host processors running at 8 MHz. Extrapolated figures for the 10-MHz version of the NCUBE node processor now nearing production are also given; they assume no wait states. Two widely used syn-

Table 1.
Performance figures.

Processor	Fortran Dhrystones/s	Fortran Whetstones/s*
NCUBE node processor at 8 MHz	999	381,000
NCUBE node processor at 10 MHz (est.)	1249	476,000
Intel 80286 (NCUBE host) at 8 MHz with 80287 floating-point coprocessor	510	101,000
DEC VAX-11/780 with floating-point accelerator	741	426,000

*Double precision.

thetic benchmark programs were employed in this study: the Dhrystone and the Whetstone codes.[14,15] The Dhrystone benchmark is intended to represent typical system programming applications and contains no floating-point or vectorizable code. The original Dhrystone Ada code[15] was translated into a Fortran 77 version with 32-bit integer arithmetic that attempted to preserve as much of the original program structure as possible. This entailed simulating Ada records with Fortran arrays, and simulating access variables for those records with the array index variables. This "Fortran Dhrystone" produced a substantial performance degradation compared to Dhrystone benchmarks in Ada, Pascal, and C, all of which have pointer or access variables. For example, the C Dhrystone ran two to three times faster on a VAX-11/780 than the Fortran Dhrystone. However, in the study presented here the degradation appears to apply uniformly to all processors considered, since all were given the same Fortran source code and used very similar Fortran compilers. The Whetstone benchmark, which aims to represent scientific programs with many floating-point operations, was used in a double-precision Fortran 77 version that closely resembled the original Algol code.[14] The Dhrystone results in Table 1 are reported in "Dhrystones per second," each of which corresponds roughly to one hundred Fortran statements executed per second. The Whetstone figures represent the number of hypothetical Whetstone instructions executed per second. We can conclude from the data in Table 1 that the NCUBE node processor is quite fast and fully meets its performance targets.

System software

The emergence of several commercial hypercube computers has demonstrated the feasibility of constructing low-cost massively parallel machines. The focus of research can now be expected to shift to the issue of how these machines can be programmed effectively. Indeed, the recent report on the Supercomputing Research Center concludes that the absence of appropriate parallel programming languages and software tools is the single biggest impediment to the successful use of parallel machines.[16] The operating system is also a major design issue, since memory management and interprocessor communication are critical to the functioning of the programming languages. Three software issues need to be considered. The first is the operating system that is used for developing application programs for the hypercube. The second is the operating system that provides run-time support for application programs running on the hypercube nodes. The third is the set of application languages to be used.

An operating system for application program development that provides the kind of environment associated with a "programmer's workbench" is Unix. Unfortunately, there are two versions of Unix, System V and bsd 4.3, and many lesser-known variants. This leaves the system designer with a dilemma: he can work in a proven, widely known development environment, but he can't exploit the benefits of standardization, since no Unix standard has emerged. The solution chosen by NCUBE was to develop a Unix-like operating system, Axis,[13] that embodies the features common to the major Unix dialects. Changes or additions can be readily made to Axis when a true Unix standard is agreed upon. There are two features of Axis that greatly facilitate program development for a very large hypercube. The first is its ability to share files, and the second is the way it manages the main cube array.

Axis runs on the 80286 host processor that acts as the CPU for each I/O board. (Recall that up to eight I/O subsystems can be accommodated in a 1024-processor NCUBE/ten.) It provides the large number of utilities for editing, debugging, and file management that one has come to expect in a Unix-like operating system. Axis' file system is its most prominent feature, and almost all system resources are treated as files. This is consistent with the Unix philosophy. Massively parallel systems require high I/O bandwidth if they are to be useful for applications that are not simply computation-intensive. The problem of managing high I/O was not foreseen in the earlier generation of massively parallel machines and has proven to be a great limitation.[11] The ability to incorporate up to eight

I/O subsystems in the NCUBE/ten is intended to avoid this problem. However, it introduces the potential for eight separate file systems. To avoid this, Axis provides the capability to organize the eight file systems as one distributed file system; Axis further allows complete systems to be networked through iSBX connections so as to provide a single multisystem file system.

Axis manages a hypercube of node processors as a device, which is simply one type of file. A device can be opened, closed, written to, and read from as if it were a normal file. Axis permits users to allocate subcubes that have the appropriate size for their application. Thus, one or two users with large problems or several users with small problems can share the hypercube. This flexibility greatly increases the system's efficiency and gives a hypercube supercomputer a significant advantage over conventional supercomputers. Partitioning the main hypercube into subcubes is simplified by the fact that each subcube is protected from access by any other subcube.

Vertex, the operating system for the NCUBE/ten node processors, is a small nucleus (less than 4K bytes) resident in each of those nodes. Its primary function is to provide communication between the nodes. It achieves this through, among other facilities, send and receive functions that transfer messages between any two nodes in the hypercube, and through a **whoami** function that allows a program to determine the logical node on which it is executing and the I/O processor to which it is connected. The internode send and receive functions are implemented as subroutine calls **nwrite** and **nread**, respectively; the whoami function is implemented as a subroutine call **whoami**. The messages transferred by **nwrite** and **nread** are arrays of bytes having four attributes: source, destination, length, and type. The first two attributes are numbers in the range 0 to 1023 and indicate the logical nodes being used for the source and destination. The length attribute is the number of bytes in the message; messages as long as 64K bytes are supported. The type attribute can be used to distinguish messages and so permit their selective reception at a destination node.

The subroutine **nwrite** passes the following parameters: **length**, **message**, **dest**, **type**, **status**, and **error**. They are passed in the general-purpose registers. **Length** is the length of the outgoing message in bytes; **message** is the name of the buffer from which the message is to be taken; **dest** is the logical number of the node in the hypercube that is to receive the message; **type** is the type number of the message; **status** indicates when the message leaves the buffer, i.e., when the buffer is reusable; and **error** is an error code. Message transmission breaks the message into packets of 512 bytes (or some other user-defined size) and sends them to the destination node using the following routing algorithm. Assume that in an n-dimensional cube, the logical number of the source node is $s_n s_{n-1} \ldots s_2 s_1$ and the logical number of the destination is $d_n d_{n-1} \ldots d_2 d_1$. The bit-wise exclusive-OR $x_n x_{n-1} \ldots x_2 x_1$ of the two numbers is formed as follows: $x_i = s_i \oplus d_i$ for $i = 1, \ldots, n$. The values of the x_i's are used to control the routing process. Those values of i for which $x_i = 1$ indicate the dimensions that must be traversed to transfer a message from source to destination. The FFO instruction mentioned previously can be used to determine the values of i. Since it works by scanning right to left, it will route messages along the lower dimensions first. The routing algorithm was chosen for its simplicity; however, as noted by Valiant,[17] it creates the potential for congestion in some situations. He defines an alternative routing algorithm that avoids congestion by routing each message to a randomly chosen node; from there the message is forwarded to its originally intended destination. The randomization assures that message congestion at nodes will be dispersed. Unfortunately, Valiant's router does not perform as well as the straightforward algorithm in many routine parallel processing tasks, and its more complex implementation requirements discouraged use of it in the initial NCUBE/ten design. Future insights into the behavior of parallel algorithms may change this, however.

In addition to determining the routing path, Vertex must perform the store-and-forward function at each node along the path. At the destination node, it places the message in a queue that is allocated from a heap of 20K bytes. The receive function, **nread**, passes the following parameters: **length**, **message**, **source**, **type**, **status**, and **error**. It looks for the first message from **source** of type **type** in the input queue, and copies it to buffer **message**. Don't-care conditions are indicated for **type** or **source** by setting these parameters to -1. This allows the next message from a particular source to be received regardless of type, the next message of a particular type to be received from any source, and the next message of any type from any source to be received. Messages with negative types other than -1 are system messages for Vertex and are used for process control at a node, e.g., for node program debugging. In summary, the calls **nwrite** and **nread** provide a fast internode message communication mechanism. The main contributors to this speed are the machine instructions provided explicitly for internode communication and the fact that messages enter nodes through DMA channels.

The current NCUBE/ten application languages, apart from the node and host assembly languages, are Fortran 77 and C. Fortran 77 and C were chosen because the computer is targeted for a user community interested primarily in scientific problems; this group has traditionally programmed in Fortran. Compilers for other languages, including Occam, are presently being developed. The programming model adopted for the initial set of languages, Fortran and C, is a simple extension of the conventional uniprocessor model. Each node is treated as a separate processor. No symbols are shared between nodes—the naming scope is contained within a node. Values of variables are shared by means of calls to the Vertex subroutines **nwrite** and **nread**.

We noted earlier that the hypercube array can be shared by several users if it is partitioned into suitably sized subcubes. When a d-dimensional subcube is allocated to a user, its nodes are given a logical number from 0 to $2^d - 1$. Vertex records the correspondence between the logical numbers of the nodes and their physical address in the main hypercube array. Along with the **whoami** function, logical numbering makes it possible to write programs that run on subcubes of arbitrary location and size.

The **whoami** function returns four identification parameters: **node, process, host,** and **dim**, where **node** is the logical node number of the calling process, **process** is the process number of the calling process, **host** is the id number for the host communication, and **dim** is the allocated subcube dimension.

We conclude this section with a sample Fortran program for the NCUBE/ten that calculates the sum of squares of the elements of a vector V. The Fortran uses the extensions NWRITE, NREAD, and WHOAMI, which are based on the Vertex functions discussed above. Figure 7 shows the program. We assume that a copy of this program has been loaded into each of the nodes in the subcube allocated for the job. The idea behind the program is to distribute equal numbers of the elements of V among the nodes, form local partial sums of squares, and then accumulate these partial sums along successive dimensions of the hypercube. The internode accumulation collapses the active part of the computation into smaller and smaller cubes. The example computes

$$\mathrm{S} = \sum_{i=1}^{K} \mathrm{V}(i)^2 ,$$

where $K = N \cdot 2^M$.

Calling WHOAMI on line 008 of the program establishes the caller's logical node number (PN), the node on the host board for I/O communications (HOST), and the order of the allocated subcube (M). Line 012 reads in an N-element slice of V from the host. The parameters of interest in this example have the following meaning: SR is a completion code, V is the address of the message buffer for the vector, N is the length of the vector in single-precision words of four bytes each, and HOST is the node on the host for cube communications. The loop on lines 017 to 018 (loop 1) forms the sum of squares of the slice, putting the result in S. This is done in parallel in each node. For this phase of the computation, all 2^M nodes are doing useful work and the utilization of the allocated cube approaches 100 percent. The loop from lines 020 to 042 (loop 2) accumulates the partial sums. Starting with 2^M partial sums in each of the nodes, it forms 2^{M-1} partial sums by adding pairs of partial results in nodes that are immediate neighbors on the Mth axis. The new partial sums are now confined to an $(M-1)$-dimensional hypercube—the original cube is collapsed to half its initial size. This process of collapsing the cube by half and accumulating the partial sums is repeated until the final sum is accumulated in logical node 0. The internode accumulation procedure is simulating an addition tree. Figure 8 illustrates this for a 3-cube. This phase of the computation is less efficient than the first phase. For an M-dimensional cube, the total processor utilization is given by

$$\mathrm{U} = \frac{100}{M}\left(\frac{1}{2} + \frac{1}{4} + \ldots + \frac{1}{2^M}\right) \approx \frac{100}{M}\%.$$

Loop 2 counts down through the axes. Line 024 selects the nodes (PNs) in the part of the hypercube that remains active after the collapsing along the (I + 1)th axis. The neighboring nodes (NPNs) of the PNs are those that differ in the Ith position. Their numbers are calculated in line 030 by an exclusive-OR between the PN and $2^{(\mathrm{I}-1)}$. The operator .NEQV. (not equivalent) performs this—it is an extension to Fortran 77. Line 031 partitions the active nodes into two sets: those that are to receive partial sums (line 038) and those that send them (line 036). Those nodes that send will not be active in the next iteration of loop 2. Line 047 transmits the result from node 0 to the host.

```
001 *          NODE PROGRAM TO CALCULATE:      SUM ( V(I) * *2 )
002
003 *PN      :   caller's logical processor number in subcube
004 *PROC    :   process number in node
005 *HOST    :   node on Host for cube communication
006 *M       :   dimension of allocated cube
007
008          CALL WHOAMI  (PN,PROC,HOST,M)
009
010 *receive vector V of length N (4N bytes) from Host
011
012          SR = NREAD  (V,N*4,HOST,TYPEH,FLAG1)
013
014 *compute sum of subset of V that is in this node;
015
016          S = O
017          DO 1  I = 1,N
018 1               S = S + V(I)* *2
019
020          DO 2  I = M,1,-1
021
022 *execute once for each axis of the hypercube;
023
024                IF (PN  .LT.  2* *I) THEN
025
026 *if this node is in the active part of the collapsed cube,
027 *do the computation below, otherwise the node is done
028 * NPN is neighbor of PN on the I-th axis
029
030                   NPN = PN  .NEQV.  (2* *(I-1))
031                   IF (NPN  .LT.  PN) THEN
032
033 *if neighbor's number is less, send the current accumulation;
034 *otherwise, receive it and update its value
035
036                            SW = NWRITE (S,4,NPN,TYPEN,FLAG2)
037                      ELSE
038                            SR = NREAD (A,4,NPN,TYPEN,FLAG3)
039                            S = S + A
040                   ENDIF
041                ENDIF
042 2        CONTINUE
043
044 *send final result back to host
045
046          IF (PN  .EQ.  O) THEN
047                SW = NWRITE (S,4,HOST,TYPEH,FLAG4)
048          ENDIF
```

Figure 7. Fortran sum-of-squares program for the NCUBE/ten.

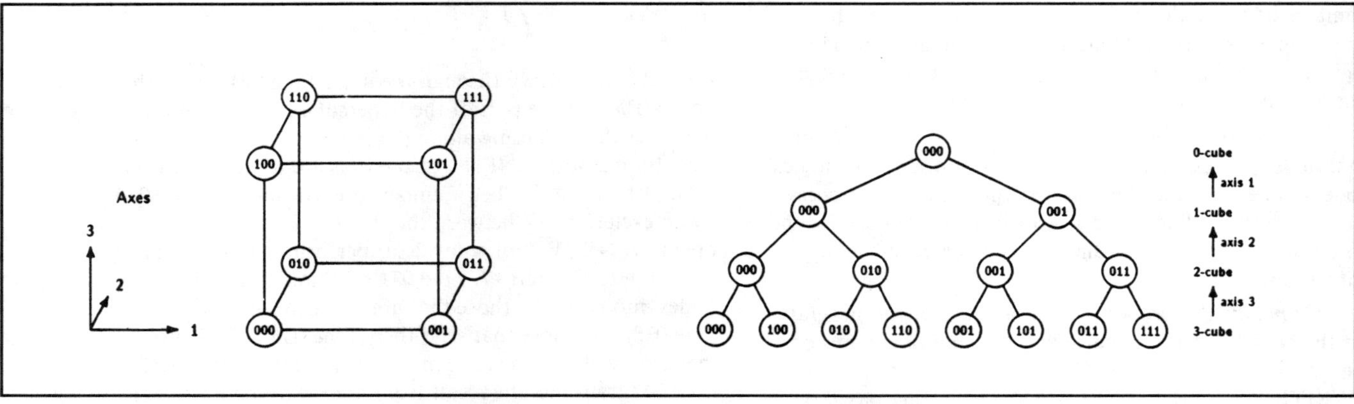

Figure 8. Addition tree for partial sums.

Hypercube architectures are well suited to implementing microprocessor-based massively parallel supercomputers, given the constraints imposed by current technology. They offer an unusually good combination of high node connectivity, software flexibility, and system reliability. The NCUBE/ten is an example of a new generation of low-cost and compact hypercube machines capable of supercomputer performance. Unlike earlier machines, it exploits the inherent homogeneity of the hypercube to provide a Unix-like multiuser programming environment, along with support for extremely high I/O data transmission rates.

Acknowledgments

The portion of the work reported here that was performed at the University of Michigan was supported in part by the Office of Naval Research under contract N00014 85 K 0531, by the National Science Foundation under contract DCR-8507851, and by the Army Research Office under contract DAAG29-84-K-0070.

References

1. J. S. Squire and S. M. Palais, "Physical and Logical Design of a Highly Parallel Computer," tech. note, Dept. of Electrical Engineering, University of Michigan, Oct. 1962.
2. J. S. Squire and S. M. Palais, "Programming and Design Considerations for a Highly Parallel Computer," *AFIPS Conf. Proc.*, Vol. 23, 1963 SJCC, pp. 395-400.
3. H. Sullivan and T. R. Bashkow, "A Large Scale, Homogeneous, Fully Distributed Parallel Machine, I," *Proc. 4th Ann. Symp. on Computer Architecture*, 1977, pp. 105-117.
4. H. Sullivan, T. R. Bashkow, and D. Klappholz, "A Large Scale, Homogeneous, Fully Distributed Parallel Machine, II," *Proc. 4th Ann. Symp. on Computer Architecture*, 1977, pp. 118-124.
5. M. C. Pease, "The Indirect Binary *n*-cube Microprocessor Array," *IEEE Trans. Computers*, Vol. C-26, No. 5, May 1977, pp. 458-473.
6. F. P. Preparata and J. Vuillemin, "The Cube-connected Cycles: A Versatile Network for Parallel Computation," *Comm. ACM*, Vol. 24, No. 5, May 1981, pp. 300-309.
7. C. L. Seitz, "The Cosmic Cube," *Comm. ACM*, Vol. 28, No. 1, Jan. 1985, pp. 22-33.
8. G. Fox, "The Performance of the Caltech Hypercube in Scientific Calculations," Report CALT-68-1298, California Institute of Technology, Pasadena, Calif., Apr. 1985.
9. J. C. Peterson et al., "The Mark III Hypercube-Ensemble Concurrent Processor," *Proc. Int'l Conf. on Parallel Processing*, Aug. 1985, pp. 71-73.
10. W. D. Hillis, *The Connection Machine*, MIT Press, Cambridge, Mass., 1985.
11. J. P. Potter, ed., *The Massively Parallel Processor*, MIT Press, Cambridge, Mass., 1985.
12. *Transputer Reference Manual*, INMOS Corp., Colorado Springs, Colo., 1985.
13. *NCUBE Handbook*, Version 1.0, NCUBE Corp., Beaverton, Ore., Apr. 1986.
14. H. J. Curnow and B. A. Weichman, "A Synthetic Benchmark," *Computer J.*, Vol. 19, Feb. 1976, pp. 43-49.
15. R. P. Weicker, "Dhrystone: A Synthetic Systems Programming Benchmark," *Comm. ACM*, Vol. 27, No. 10, Oct. 1984, pp. 1013-1030.
16. *Report of the Summer Workshop on Parallel Algorithms and Architectures for the Supercomputing Research Center*, Aug. 1985.
17. L. G. Valiant, "A Scheme for Parallel Communication," *SIAM J. Computing*, Vol. 11, May 1982, pp. 350-361.

Author Index

A

Agrawal, D. P., 181

B

Boari, M., 149
Borrill, P. L., 88

C

Cinotti, T. S., 227
Colley, S., 250
Crespi-Reghizzi, S., 149

D

Daprá, A., 149
Dubois, M., 236

E

Emmerson, R., 217

F

Fathi, E. T., 4, 125
Feng, T-Y., 24
Fisher, D. A., 105

G

Gaudiot, J-L., 236
Gupta, A., 62, 170
Gustavson, D. B., 72

H

Hayes, J. P., 250

I

Irani, K. B., 194

J

Janakiram, V. K., 181

K

Kirrmann, H., 135
Krieger, M., 4, 125
Kuhl, J. G., 50

L

Lee, L-T., 236

M

Maderna, F., 149
McGowan, M. J., 217
Mudge, T., 250

N

Natali, A., 149
Neri, G., 227

O

Önyüksel, I. H., 194

P

Palmer, J., 250
Pathak, G. C., 181
Patton, C., 98

R

Reddy, S. M., 50

S

Schell, R. R., 161
Serlin, O., 205
Stout, Q. F., 250

T

Tohme, N. G., 236
Toong, H-M. D., 62, 170

V

van Tilborg, A. M., 115

W

Weatherly, R. M., 105
Wittie, L. D., 40, 115

Z

Zorpette, G., 14

Subject Index

A

Ada language
  distributed operating system, 97, 105
Allocation, 236
  of tasks, 125
Arbitration, 170
  bus, 72, 88, 227
Architectures
  alternative bus, 62
  microcomputers, 40, 97
  microprocessors, 4
  Tomp, 149
  von Neumann, 97

B

Benchmarking, 169
  microprocessors, 170
Block transfers, 72
Busing and buses
  computers, 72, 170
  global, 62
  high performance, 88
  multiple, 194
  M3, 227
  practices, 71
  protocols, vii, 72
  signal transmission, 72
  split-transaction, 62
  standards, 1, 71, 72
  32-bit, 71, 88
Butterfly system, 97
Byzantine agreement problem, 50

C

Cache memories
  bus, 88
Checkpointing
  Tandem system, 205
Communication networks, 181
  cost effectiveness, 24
Computer languages
  Ada, 97, 105
  Lisp, 98
  Pascal, 115
Computer networks
  Micronet, 115
Computers
  buses, 72
  distributed, 40, 50, 97, 105
Concurrent processing, 24, 98
Control
  hierarchical, 115
  industrial, 170
CPU board
  Modiac, 227
Cube-connected cycles, 40, 181

D

Data-flow machines
  Hughes, 236
Data manipulators
  versatile, 24
Debugging
  of programs, 149
Distributed operating systems
  design, 105
Dual-bus hypercubes, 40
Dynamic scene analysis (DSA)
  algorithm, 181

E

Error confinement
  iAPX 432-based system, 217
Error recovery, 217
Error reporting, 217
Events
  in multiprocessors, 135
  recording, 105
  sender and receiver, 135
Executives
  for task-driven multimicrocomputer, 125
  system, 125

F

Fault tolerance
  bus operation, 72
  computers, 4, 14, 23
  in commercial applications, 205
  in VLSI, 217
  multiple processors, 50
  software, 205
  tandem approach, 205

H

Handshake lines
  asynchronous, 125
Hierarchical structure
  two-level, 125
Hypercubes
  connections, 40
  dual bus, 40
  spanning bus, 181
  supercomputers, 203, 250

I

Image processing
  real-time, 161
Industrial control
  use of microcomputers, 170
Intel 286, 203
Intel 432
  error confinement, 217
  fault tolerance, 14, 203
Interconnections
  alternatives, vii, 23
  bus, 170
  issues, 1
  multiple microprocessors, 4, 50, 181
  networks, 24, 40
Interpreters, 98

Interrupts
in multiprocessors, 135

J

Jetliners
landing, 14
Job mix
impact, 62

K

Kernel
security, 161

L

Large multiple processors
fault tolerance, 50
Links
communication, 181

M

Machine tools, 170
Mapping
networks, 181
Markov chains, 194
Masking
for fault tolerance, 50
Matrix multiplication, 236
Memories
cache, 88
dual-port, 227
global, 62, 161
local, 62
partitioning, 135
Message system, 205
Microcomputers
in industrial control, 170
interconnection, 23, 40
large networks, 40
single chip, 40
see also Computers, Intel 286, Intel 432, Modiac multiprocessor, Supercomputers
Micronet
operating systems, 115
Microprocessors
characteristics, vii
distributed, 4
evaluation, 169
hypercube supercomputers, 250
technology, 1
vendors, 71
see also Computers, Intel 286, Intel 432, Microcomputers, Supercomputers
Modiac multiprocessor
286-based design, 227
Multi-microprocessors
architecture, 97, 203, 236
buses, 71, 170, 194
coupling, 14, 97, 105, 135, 205
design, 170
distributed, 50, 105
fault tolerance, 4, 14, 23, 50, 181, 203
interconnection, 4, 23
logical structure, 4
modes, 4
organization, 1
performance, 169, 181, 194
programming, 97, 149, 161
reliability, 4, 14
resource sharing, 4
security, vii, 161
serviceability, 4
tasks, 97, 105, 125
TX16, 236
workloads, 170
Multiple microprocessors *see* Multi-microprocessors
Multiprocessing and multiprocessors
concepts, 1
concurrency, 98
coupling, 97, 105, 135, 205
data flow, 236
events, 135
hardware, vii, 14, 236
interrupts, 135
Modiac, 227
multiple bus, 169, 194
software, vii, 1, 14, 98, 149
support, vii, 88
throughput increase, 62
Z8000, 97, 161
Myriaprocessors, 98

N

NCUBE/ten parallel processor, 250
Networks
alpha, 181
beta, 181
hypertree, 181
large, 40
Markovian, 194
Micronet, 115
ring, 181
topology, 24, 40
Node processors
NCUBE, 250

O

Operating systems
distributed, 105
for Micronet, 115
nodal, 115

P

Parallel control flow, 97
programs, 98
Partitioning
block, 236
PCF *see* Parallel control flow
Permutations, 24
Pipelining
impact, 62
iteration, 236
Productivity, 169
Programming
multiple-microprocessors, 149
Protocols
bus, vii, 72, 88
communication, 24, 125
split transaction, 170

Q

Queueing networks
Markovian, 194

R

Reconfigurability, 105
Redundancy
  N-modular, 217
Replications
  for fault tolerance, 50
Resource allocation, 105
Retargetability, 105

S

Security kernel
  multiprocessor microcomputer, 161
Shared variables, 105
Signal allocation
  bus, 72
Signal transmission
  bus, 71, 72
Single chips
  microcomputers, 40
Single-processor systems, 1
Skew delay, 72
Software
  buses, 72
  fault tolerance, 205
  multiprocessors, 149
  NCUBE, 250
Spacecraft
  fault tolerance, 14
  Voyager probes, 14
Supercomputers
  hypercube, 203, 250
Synapses, 97, 135
Systolic arrays
  warp processors, 98

T

Tandem system
  checkpointing, 205
Tasks
  dynamics, 105
  interrelations, 125
  multi-microcomputers, 125
  processor control, 115
  synchronization, 105
Throughput
  multiprocessors, 62
  NCUBE/ten, 250
  transaction, 205
Topology
  networks, 24, 40
Transaction processing
  on-line, 205
Transputers, 203
  Inmos, 236
TX16
  architecture, 236
  hardware, 236

V

VLSI
  fault tolerance, 217
  single, 250

Editor's Biography

Amar Gupta (SM'85) is Principal Research Associate at the Sloan School of Management, Massachusetts Institute of Technology, Cambridge. He holds a bachelors degree in electrical engineering from the Indian Institute of Technology, Kanpur, a masters degree in management from the Massachusetts Institute of Technology, and a doctorate in computer technology from the Indian Institute of Technology, New Delhi. He conducted the research for his doctorate dissertation at three prestigious universities in India, England, and the United States.

Dr. Gupta has been involved in research, management, and publishing activities since 1974. Since joining M.I.T. in 1979, he has been active in the areas of multiprocessor architectures, performance measurement, distributed homogeneous and heterogeneous data bases, expert systems, personal computers, and transfer of information technology. He serves as a consultant to a number of corporations, government agencies, and international bodies on various aspects of computer technology, and is an active technical advisor to several international organizations and committees.

Dr. Gupta is the Chairman of the Technical Committee for Microprocessor Applications of the IEEE Industrial Electronics Society, and Assistant Chairman for several annual IECON conferences. He was also involved with the Very Large Data Base Conference (VLDB '87), held in England in 1987. He received the Rotary Fellowship for International Understanding in 1979 and the Brooks Prize (Honorable Mention) in 1980.

He has written more than 30 technical articles and papers, and produced seven books, including two on expert systems to be released by IEEE PRESS.

Dr. Gupta is a permanent resident of the United States.